PHILIP'S

MODERN SCHOOL ·ATLAS·

In association with Heinemann Educational

George Philip Limited
59 Grosvenor Street
London W1X 9DA

Heinemann Educational
Halley Court, Jordan Hill
Oxford OX2 8EJ

CONTENTS

Published by George Philip Limited
59 Grosvenor Street, London W1X 9DA

Eighty-ninth Edition © 1992 George Philip Limited

BRITISH ISLES MAPS

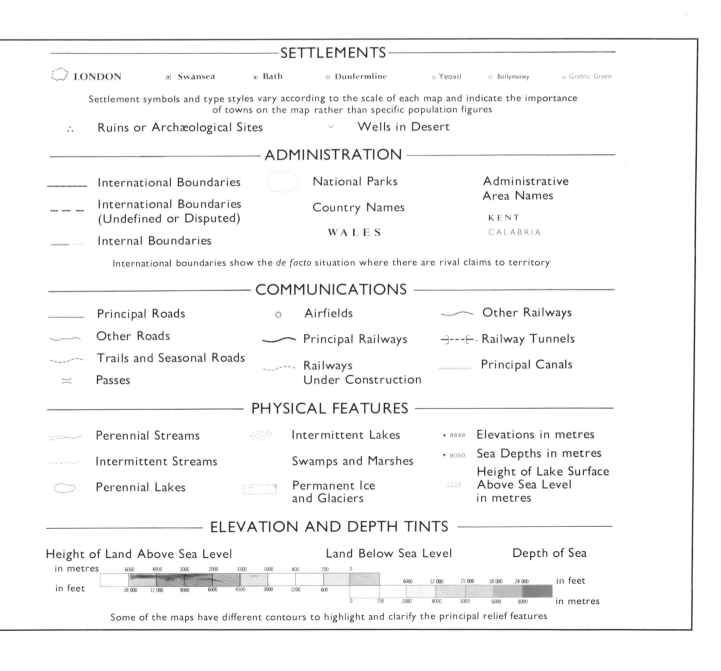

SETTLEMENTS

⬡ LONDON   ▣ Swansea   ◉ Bath   ◎ Dunfermline   ○ Yeovil   ○ Ballymoney   ○ Gretna Green

Settlement symbols and type styles vary according to the scale of each map and indicate the importance
of towns on the map rather than specific population figures

∴   Ruins or Archæological Sites   ᵕ   Wells in Desert

ADMINISTRATION

International Boundaries

International Boundaries
(Undefined or Disputed)

Internal Boundaries

National Parks

Country Names

WALES

Administrative
Area Names

KENT

CALABRIA

International boundaries show the *de facto* situation where there are rival claims to territory

COMMUNICATIONS

Principal Roads

Other Roads

Trails and Seasonal Roads

Passes

☼   Airfields

Principal Railways

Railways
Under Construction

Other Railways

Railway Tunnels

Principal Canals

PHYSICAL FEATURES

Perennial Streams

Intermittent Streams

Perennial Lakes

Intermittent Lakes

Swamps and Marshes

Permanent Ice
and Glaciers

▲ 8848   Elevations in metres

▼ 8050   Sea Depths in metres

Height of Lake Surface
Above Sea Level
in metres

ELEVATION AND DEPTH TINTS

Height of Land Above Sea Level

in metres   6000   4000   3000   2000   1500   1000   400   200   0

in feet   18 000   12 000   9000   6000   4500   3000   1200   600

Land Below Sea Level

6000   12 000   15 000   18 000   24 000   in feet

0   200   2000   4000   5000   6000   8000   in metres

Depth of Sea

Some of the maps have different contours to highlight and clarify the principal relief features

Projection: Conical with two standard parallels

1:1 000 000

ISLE OF WIGHT

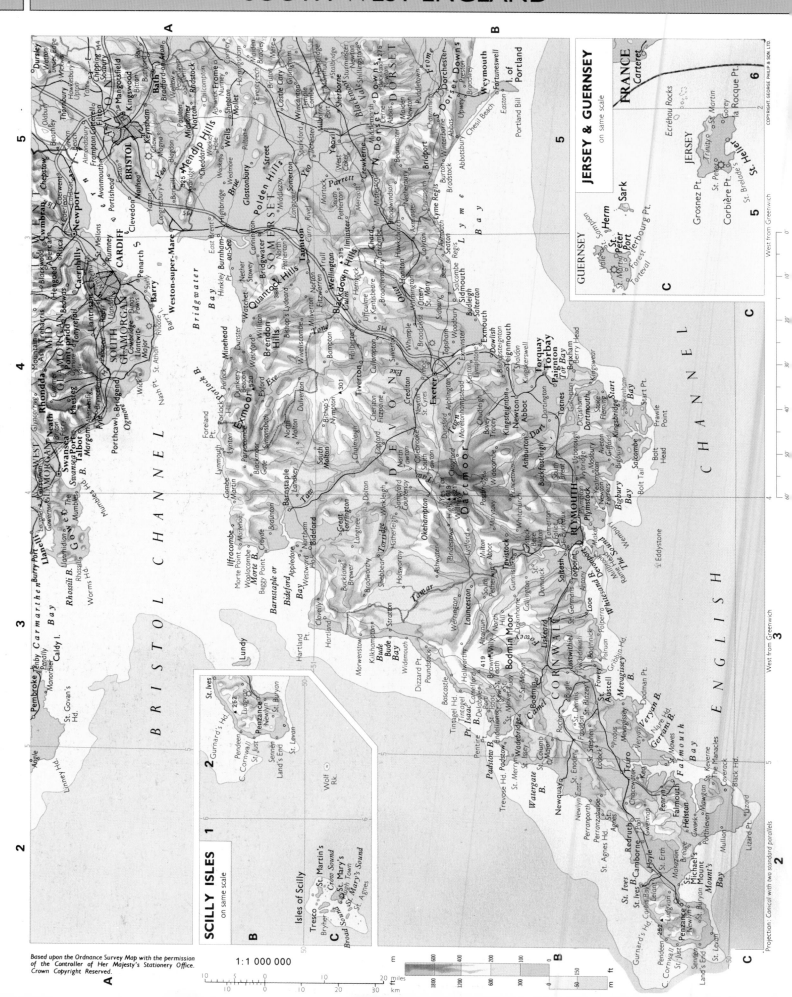

JERSEY & GUERNSEY on same scale

FRANCE on same scale

SCILLY ISLES on same scale

1:1 000 000

COPYRIGHT GEORGE PHILIP & SON LTD.

Projection : Conical with two standard parallels

West from Greenwich

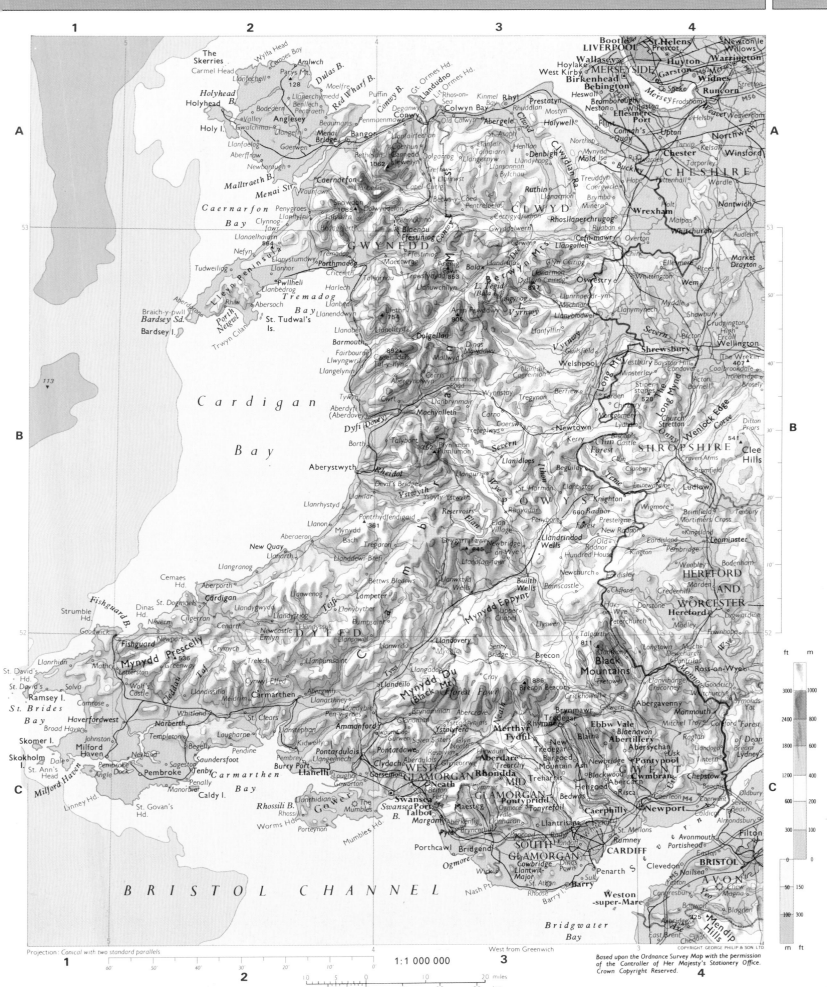

Projection: Conical with two standard parallels

1:1 000 000

West from Greenwich

NORTH SEA

Continuation
Northwards
on same scale

1:1 000 000

West from Greenwich

East from Greenwich

COPYRIGHT GEORGE PHILIP & SON LTD.
Based upon the Ordnance Survey Map with the permission
of the Controller of Her Majesty's Stationery Office.
Crown Copyright Reserved.

Projection: Conical with two standard parallels

West from Greenwich

1:1 000 000

10 10 20 miles

10 0 10 20 30 km

ORKNEY ISLANDS
on same scale

Based upon the Ordnance Survey Map with the permission of the Controller of Her Majesty's Stationery Office. Crown Copyright Reserved.

COPYRIGHT. GEORGE PHILIP & SON. LTD.

1:1 000 000

10   0   10   20 miles
10   0   10   20   30 km

West from Greenwich

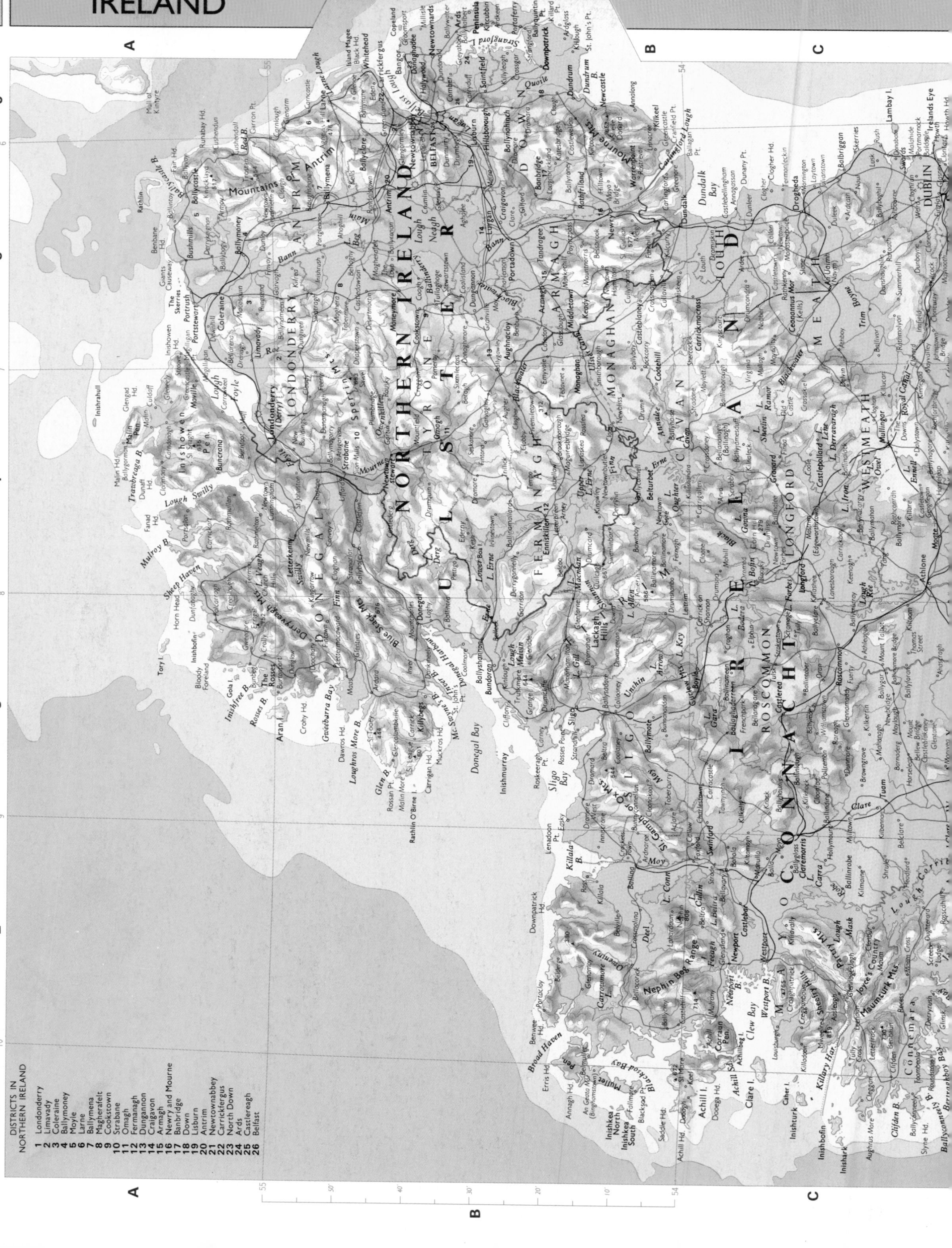

DISTRICTS IN
NORTHERN IRELAND

1 Londonderry
2 Limavady
3 Coleraine
4 Ballymoney
5 Moyle
6 Larne
7 Ballymena
8 Magherafelt
9 Cookstown
10 Strabane
11 Omagh
12 Fermanagh
13 Dungannon
14 Craigavon
15 Armagh
16 Newry and Mourne
17 Banbridge
18 Down
19 Lisburn
20 Antrim
21 Newtownabbey
22 Carrickfergus
23 North Down
24 Ards
25 Castlereagh
26 Belfast

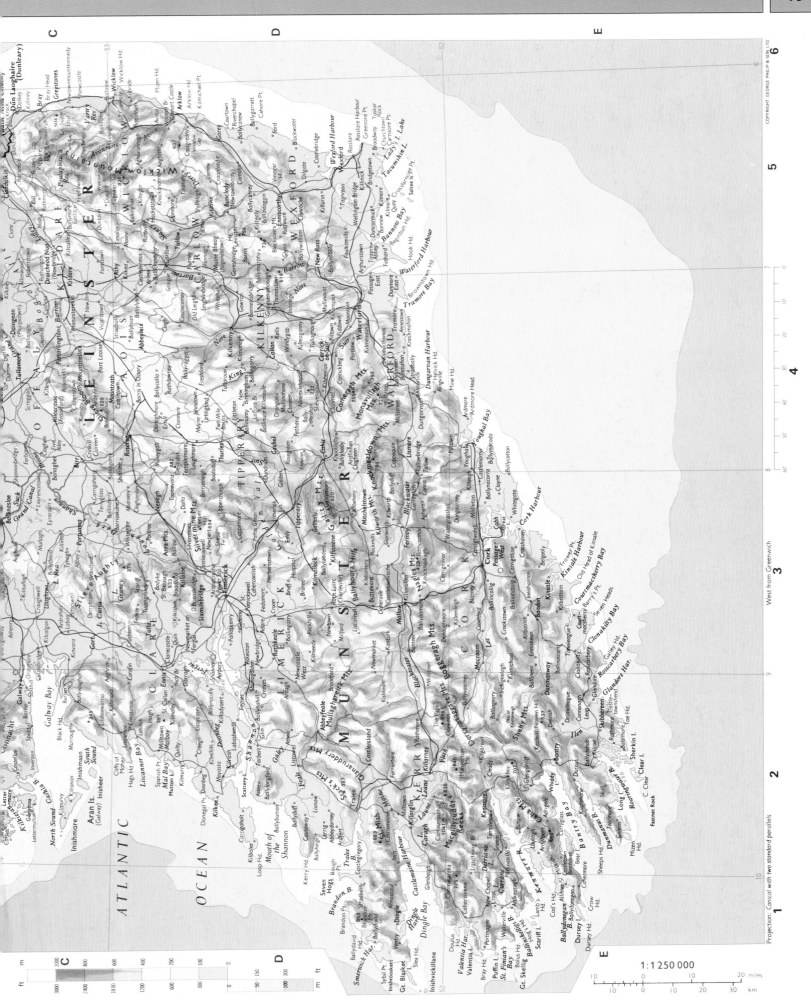

ATLANTIC OCEAN

C — LEINSTER

CONNACHT

MUNSTER

WATERFORD

CORK

KERRY

CLARE

LIMERICK

TIPPERARY

KILKENNY

WEXFORD

WICKLOW

KILDARE

OFFALY

LAOIS

Galway Bay

Din Laoghaire (Dunleary)

Waterford Harbour

Wexford Harbour

Bantry Bay

Dingle Bay

Kenmare R.

COPYRIGHT GEORGE PHILIP & SON, LTD.

West from Greenwich

Projection: Conical with two standard parallels

1:1 250 000

20 miles

30 km

m ft
1000 3000
800 2400
600 1800
400 1200
200 600
100 300
0
150
100
50
0
m ft

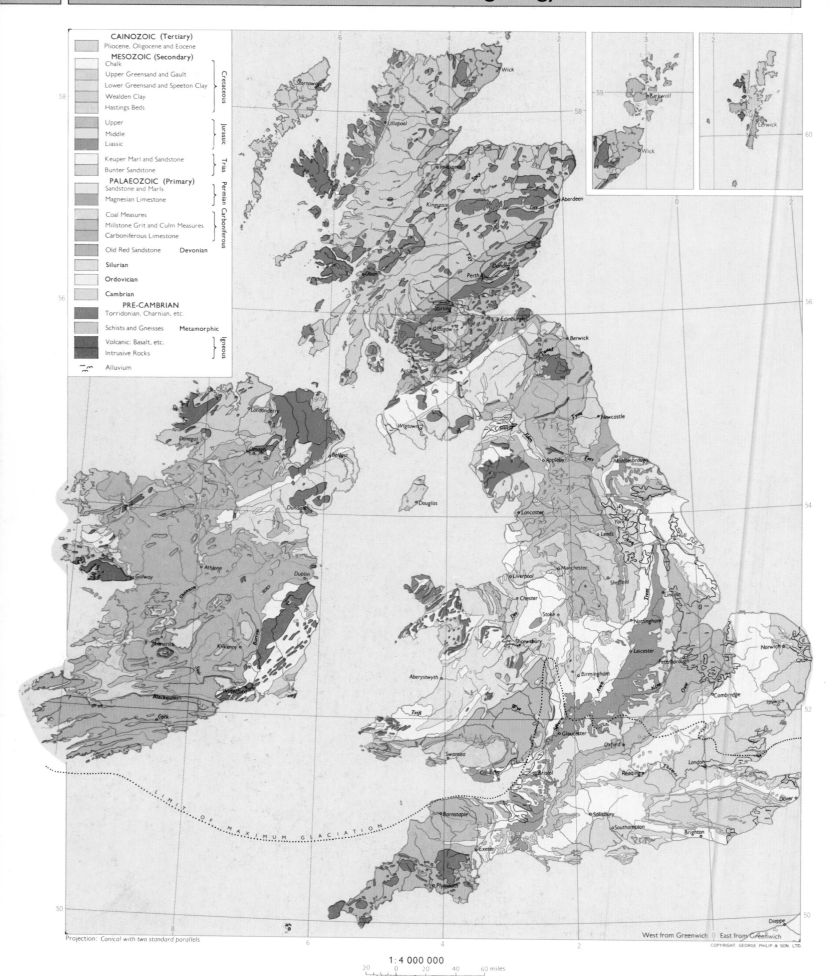

CAINOZOIC (Tertiary)
 Pliocene, Oligocene and Eocene

MESOZOIC (Secondary)
 Chalk
 Upper Greensand and Gault
 Lower Greensand and Speeton Clay
 Wealden Clay
 Hastings Beds

 Upper
 Middle
 Liassic

 Keuper Marl and Sandstone
 Bunter Sandstone

Cretaceous / Jurassic / Trias

PALAEOZOIC (Primary)
 Sandstone and Marls
 Magnesian Limestone
 Coal Measures
 Millstone Grit and Culm Measures
 Carboniferous Limestone
 Old Red Sandstone   Devonian
 Silurian
 Ordovician
 Cambrian

Permian / Carboniferous

PRE-CAMBRIAN
 Torridonian, Charnian, etc.
 Schists and Gneisses   Metamorphic
 Volcanic: Basalt, etc.
 Intrusive Rocks

Igneous

 Alluvium

Projection: *Conical with two standard parallels*

West from Greenwich   0   East from Greenwich

1 : 4 000 000

20   0   20   40   60 miles
20 0 20 40 60 80 km

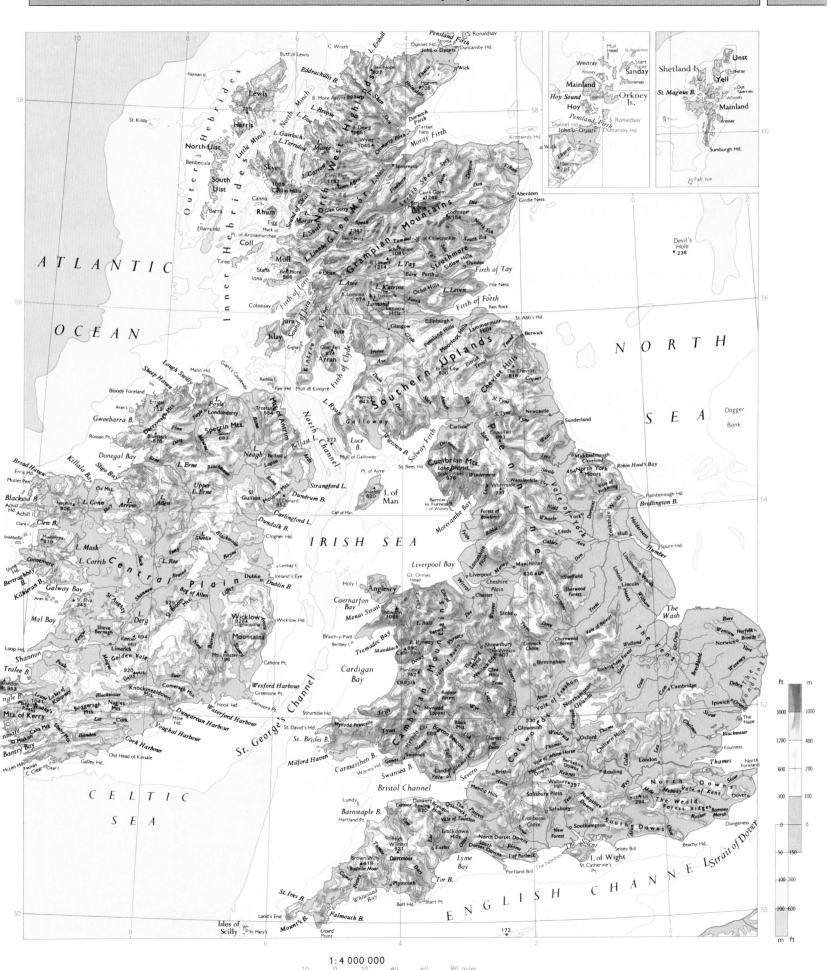

1 : 4 000 000

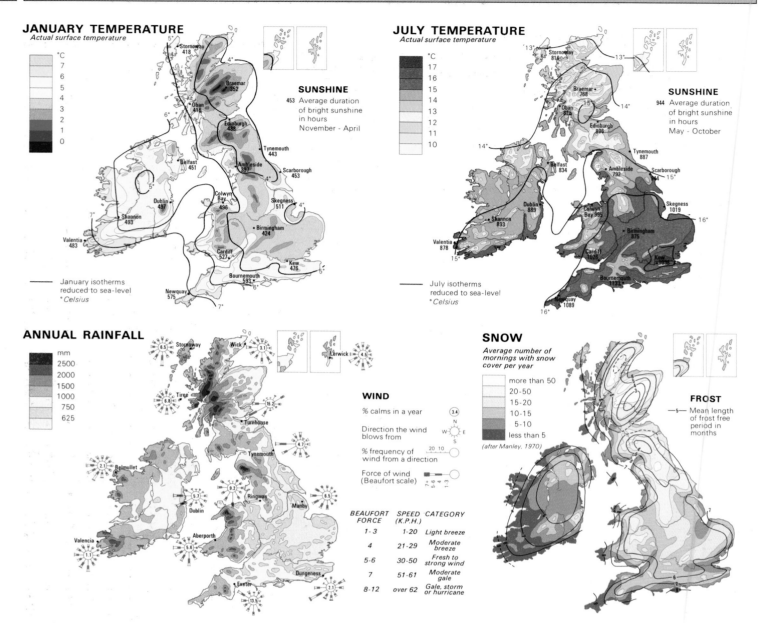

JANUARY TEMPERATURE
Actual surface temperature

°C
7
6
5
4
3
2
1
0

SUNSHINE
453 Average duration of bright sunshine in hours
November - April

Stornoway 418
Braemar 352
Oban 418
Edinburgh 488
Tynemouth 443
Belfast 451
Ambleside 397
Scarborough 453
Colwyn Bay 496
Dublin 457
Skegness 511
Shannon 493
Birmingham 424
Valentia 483
Cardiff 527
Kew 476
Bournemouth 593
Newquay 575

—— January isotherms reduced to sea-level
°Celsius

JULY TEMPERATURE
Actual surface temperature

°C
17
16
15
14
13
12
11
10

SUNSHINE
944 Average duration of bright sunshine in hours
May - October

Stornoway 818
Braemar 768
Oban 825
Edinburgh 806
Tynemouth 887
Belfast 834
Ambleside 792
Scarborough 944
Colwyn Bay 995
Dublin 889
Skegness 1019
Shannon 893
Birmingham 875
Valentia 878
Cardiff 1076
Kew 1036
Bournemouth 1133
Newquay 1089

—— July isotherms reduced to sea-level
°Celsius

ANNUAL RAINFALL

mm
2500
2000
1500
1000
750
625

Stornoway 6.5
Wick 3.1
Lerwick 4.5
Tiree 6.8
15.2
Turnhouse
Tynemouth
Belmullet 2.1
9.2
Ringway 5.7
Manby 8.5
Dublin
Valencia 5.6
Aberporth
Dungeness 2.1
Exeter 13.5
1.1

WIND
% calms in a year   3.4

Direction the wind blows from

% frequency of wind from a direction   20 10

Force of wind (Beaufort scale)   7+ 6 5 4 1-3

BEAUFORT FORCE	SPEED (K.P.H.)	CATEGORY
1 - 3	1-20	Light breeze
4	21-29	Moderate breeze
5-6	30-50	Fresh to strong wind
7	51-61	Moderate gale
8-12	over 62	Gale, storm or hurricane

SNOW
Average number of mornings with snow cover per year

more than 50
20-50
15-20
10-15
5-10
less than 5

(after Manley, 1970)

FROST
—5— Mean length of frost free period in months

VARIABILITY OF RAIN

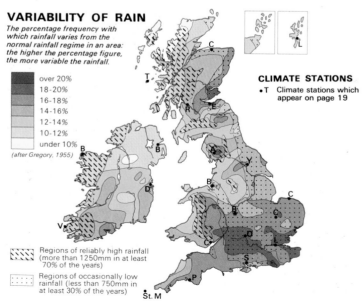

The percentage frequency with which rainfall varies from the normal rainfall regime in an area: the higher the percentage figure, the more variable the rainfall.

over 20%
18-20%
16-18%
14-16%
12-14%
10-12%
under 10%

(after Gregory, 1955)

CLIMATE STATIONS
• T   Climate stations which appear on page 19

▨ Regions of reliably high rainfall (more than 1250mm in at least 70% of the years)

▨ Regions of occasionally low rainfall (less than 750mm in at least 30% of the years)

SYNOPTIC CHART FOR A TYPICAL WINTER DEPRESSION
21st January 1971

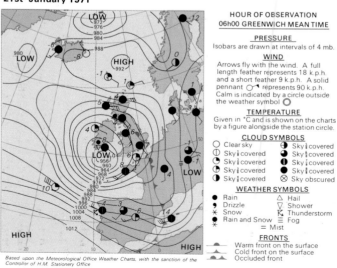

HOUR OF OBSERVATION
06h00 GREENWICH MEAN TIME

PRESSURE
Isobars are drawn at intervals of 4 mb.

WIND
Arrows fly with the wind. A full length feather represents 18 k.p.h. and a short feather 9 k.p.h. A solid pennant represents 90 k.p.h. Calm is indicated by a circle outside the weather symbol ○

TEMPERATURE
Given in °C and is shown on the charts by a figure alongside the station circle.

CLOUD SYMBOLS
○ Clear sky	◑ Sky ½ covered
◔ Sky ¼ covered	◕ Sky ¾ covered
◒ Sky ⅜ covered	◐ Sky ⅞ covered
◑ Sky ½ covered	● Sky ⅞ covered
◓ Sky ½ covered	⊗ Sky obscured

WEATHER SYMBOLS
● Rain	△ Hail
9 Drizzle	▽ Shower
✳ Snow	R Thunderstorm
⊛ Rain and Snow	≡ Fog
	= Mist

FRONTS
Warm front on the surface
Cold front on the surface
Occluded front

Based upon the Meteorological Office Weather Charts, with the sanction of the Controller of H.M. Stationery Office

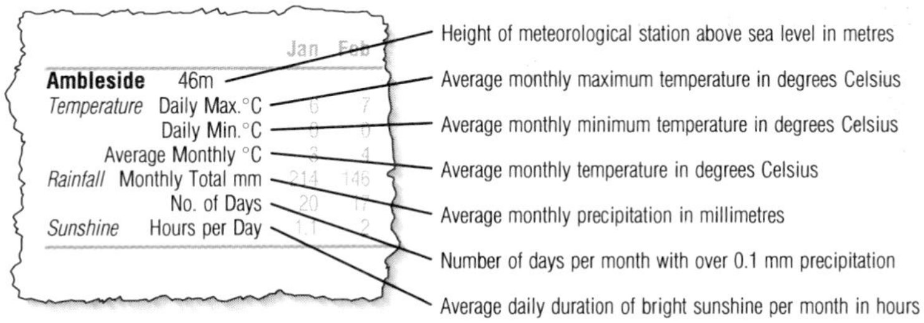

Ambleside 46m
Temperature Daily Max.°C
Daily Min.°C
Average Monthly °C
Rainfall Monthly Total mm
No. of Days
Sunshine Hours per Day
Height of meteorological station above sea level in metres
Average monthly maximum temperature in degrees Celsius
Average monthly minimum temperature in degrees Celsius
Average monthly temperature in degrees Celsius
Average monthly precipitation in millimetres
Number of days per month with over 0.1 mm precipitation
Average daily duration of bright sunshine per month in hours

	Jan	Feb	Mar	Apr	May	June	July	Aug	Sep	Oct	Nov	Dec	Year
Ambleside 46m													
Temperature Daily Max.°C	6	7	9	12	16	19	20	19	17	13	9	7	13
Daily Min.°C	0	0	2	4	6	9	11	11	9	6	3	1	5
Average Monthly °C	3	4	6	8	11	14	15	15	13	10	6	4	9
Rainfall Monthly Total mm	214	146	112	101	90	111	134	139	184	196	209	215	1851
No. of Days	20	17	15	15	14	15	18	17	18	19	19	21	208
Sunshine Hours per Day	1.1	2	3.2	4.5	6	5.7	4.5	4.2	3.3	2.2	1.4	1	3.3
Belfast 4m													
Temperature Daily Max.°C	6	7	9	12	15	18	18	18	16	13	9	7	12
Daily Min.°C	2	2	3	4	6	9	11	11	9	7	4	3	6
Average Monthly °C	4	4	6	8	11	13	15	15	13	10	7	5	9
Rainfall Monthly Total mm	80	52	50	48	52	68	94	77	80	83	72	90	845
No. of Days	20	17	16	16	15	16	19	17	18	19	19	21	213
Sunshine Hours per Day	1.5	2.3	3.4	5	6.3	6	4.4	4.4	3.6	2.6	1.8	1.1	3.5
Belmullet 9m													
Temperature Daily Max.°C	8	9	10	12	14	16	17	17	16	14	10	9	12
Daily Min.°C	3	4	4	6	8	10	11	11	10	8	5	4	7
Average Monthly °C	5	6	7	9	11	13	14	14	13	11	8	6	10
Rainfall Monthly Total mm	108	64	82	70	75	80	76	95	108	116	127	131	1132
No. of Days	18	13	16	15	14	12	14	17	16	18	20	22	195
Sunshine Hours per Day	1.9	2.5	3.4	5.2	7	6	4.6	5.1	3.9	2.9	1.9	1.3	3.8
Birkenhead 60m													
Temperature Daily Max.°C	6	6	9	11	15	17	19	19	16	13	9	7	12
Daily Min.°C	2	2	3	5	8	11	13	13	11	8	5	3	7
Average Monthly °C	4	4	6	8	11	14	16	16	14	10	7	5	10
Rainfall Monthly Total mm	64	46	40	41	55	55	67	80	66	71	76	65	726
No. of Days	18	13	13	13	13	13	15	15	15	17	17	19	181
Sunshine Hours per Day	1.6	2.4	3.5	5.3	6.3	6.7	5.7	5.4	4.2	2.9	1.8	1.3	3.9
Birmingham 163m													
Temperature Daily Max.°C	5	6	9	12	16	19	20	20	17	13	9	6	13
Daily Min.°C	2	2	3	5	7	10	12	12	10	7	5	3	7
Average Monthly °C	3	4	6	8	11	15	16	16	14	10	7	5	10
Rainfall Monthly Total mm	74	54	50	53	64	50	69	69	61	69	84	67	764
No. of Days	17	15	13	13	14	13	15	14	14	15	17	18	178
Sunshine Hours per Day	1.4	2.1	3.2	4.6	5.4	6	5.4	5.1	3.9	2.8	1.6	1.2	3.6
Cambridge 12m													
Temperature Daily Max.°C	6	7	11	14	17	21	22	22	19	15	10	7	14
Daily Min.°C	1	1	2	4	7	10	12	12	10	6	4	2	6
Average Monthly °C	3	4	6	9	12	15	17	17	14	10	7	5	10
Rainfall Monthly Total mm	49	35	36	37	45	45	58	55	51	51	54	41	558
No. of Days	15	13	10	11	11	11	12	12	11	13	14	14	147
Sunshine Hours per Day	1.7	2.5	3.8	5.1	6.2	6.7	6	5.7	4.6	3.4	1.9	1.4	4.1
Cardiff 62m													
Temperature Daily Max.°C	7	7	10	13	16	19	20	21	18	14	10	8	14
Daily Min.°C	2	2	3	5	8	11	12	13	11	8	5	3	7
Average Monthly °C	4	5	7	9	12	15	16	17	14	11	8	6	10
Rainfall Monthly Total mm	108	72	63	65	76	63	89	97	99	109	116	108	1065
No. of Days	18	14	13	13	13	13	14	15	16	16	17	18	180
Sunshine Hours per Day	1.7	2.7	4	5.6	6.4	6.9	6.2	6	4.7	3.4	1.9	1.5	4.3
Craibstone 91m													
Temperature Daily Max.°C	5	6	8	10	13	16	18	17	15	12	8	6	11
Daily Min.°C	0	0	2	3	5	8	10	10	8	6	3	1	5
Average Monthly °C	3	3	5	7	9	12	14	13	12	9	6	4	8
Rainfall Monthly Total mm	78	55	53	51	63	54	95	75	67	92	93	80	856
No. of Days	19	16	15	15	14	14	18	15	16	18	19	18	197
Sunshine Hours per Day	1.8	2.9	3.5	4.9	5.9	6.1	5.1	4.8	4.3	3.1	2	1.5	3.8
Cromer 54m													
Temperature Daily Max.°C	6	7	9	12	15	18	21	20	18	14	10	8	13
Daily Min.°C	1	1	3	5	7	10	12	13	11	8	5	3	7
Average Monthly °C	4	4	6	8	11	14	16	16	15	11	7	5	10
Rainfall Monthly Total mm	58	46	37	39	48	39	63	56	54	61	64	53	618
No. of Days	18	16	13	13	11	11	13	12	14	16	18	18	173
Sunshine Hours per Day	1.8	2.6	4	5.4	6.4	6.8	6.3	5.8	5	3.6	2	1.9	4.3
Dublin 47m													
Temperature Daily Max.°C	8	8	10	13	15	18	20	19	17	14	10	8	14
Daily Min.°C	1	2	3	4	6	9	11	11	9	6	4	3	6
Average Monthly °C	4	5	7	8	11	14	15	15	13	10	7	6	10
Rainfall Monthly Total mm	67	55	51	45	60	57	70	74	72	70	67	74	762
No. of Days	13	10	10	11	10	11	13	12	12	11	12	14	139
Sunshine Hours per Day	1.9	2.5	3.4	5	6.2	6	4.8	4.9	3.9	3.2	2.1	1.6	3.8
Durham 102m													
Temperature Daily Max.°C	6	6	9	12	15	18	20	19	17	13	9	7	13
Daily Min.°C	0	0	1	3	6	9	11	10	9	6	3	2	5
Average Monthly °C	3	3	5	7	10	13	15	15	13	9	6	4	9
Rainfall Monthly Total mm	59	51	38	38	51	49	61	67	60	63	66	55	658
No. of Days	17	15	14	13	13	14	15	14	14	16	17	17	179
Sunshine Hours per Day	1.7	2.5	3.3	4.6	5.4	6	5.1	4.8	4.1	3	1.9	1.4	3.6
Lerwick 82m													
Temperature Daily Max.°C	5	5	6	8	11	13	14	14	13	10	8	6	9
Daily Min.°C	1	1	2	3	5	7	10	10	8	6	4	3	5
Average Monthly °C	3	3	4	5	8	10	12	12	11	8	6	4	7
Rainfall Monthly Total mm	109	87	69	68	52	55	72	71	87	104	111	118	1003
No. of Days	25	22	20	21	15	15	17	17	19	23	24	25	243
Sunshine Hours per Day	0.8	1.8	2.9	4.4	5.3	5.3	4	3.8	3.5	2.2	2.2	0.5	3
London (Kew)													
Temperature Daily Max.°C	6	7	10	13	17	20	22	21	19	14	10	7	14
Daily Min.°C	2	2	3	6	8	12	14	13	11	8	5	4	7
Average Monthly °C	4	5	7	9	12	16	18	17	15	11	8	5	11
Rainfall Monthly Total mm	54	40	37	37	46	45	57	59	49	57	64	48	593
No. of Days	15	13	11	12	12	11	12	11	13	13	15	15	153
Sunshine Hours per Day	1.5	2.3	3.6	5.3	6.4	7.1	6.4	6.1	4.7	3.2	1.8	1.3	4.1
Oxford 63m													
Temperature Daily Max.°C	7	7	11	14	17	20	22	22	19	14	10	8	14
Daily Min.°C	1	1	2	5	7	10	12	12	10	7	4	2	6
Average Monthly °C	4	4	7	9	12	15	17	17	14	11	7	5	10
Rainfall Monthly Total mm	61	44	43	41	55	52	55	60	59	64	69	57	660
No. of Days	13	10	9	9	10	9	10	10	10	11	12	13	126
Sunshine Hours per Day	1.7	2.6	3.9	5.3	6.1	6.6	5.9	5.7	4.4	3.2	2.1	1.6	4.1
Plymouth 27m													
Temperature Daily Max.°C	8	8	10	12	15	18	19	19	18	15	11	9	14
Daily Min.°C	4	4	5	6	8	11	13	13	12	9	7	5	8
Average Monthly °C	6	6	7	9	12	15	16	16	15	12	9	7	11
Rainfall Monthly Total mm	99	74	69	53	63	53	70	77	78	91	113	110	950
No. of Days	19	15	14	12	12	12	14	14	15	16	17	18	178
Sunshine Hours per Day	1.9	2.9	4.3	6.1	7.1	7.4	6.4	6.4	5.1	3.7	2.2	1.7	4.6
Renfrew 6m													
Temperature Daily Max.°C	5	7	9	12	15	18	19	19	16	13	9	7	12
Daily Min.°C	1	1	2	4	6	9	11	11	9	6	4	2	6
Average Monthly °C	3	4	6	8	11	14	15	15	13	9	7	4	9
Rainfall Monthly Total mm	111	85	69	67	63	70	97	93	102	119	106	127	1109
No. of Days	19	16	15	15	14	15	17	17	17	18	18	20	201
Sunshine Hours per Day	1.1	2.1	2.9	4.7	6	6.1	5.1	4.4	3.7	2.3	1.4	0.8	3.4
St Helier 9m													
Temperature Daily Max.°C	9	8	11	13	16	19	21	21	19	16	12	10	15
Daily Min.°C	5	4	6	7	10	13	15	15	14	11	8	6	9
Average Monthly °C	7	6	8	10	13	16	18	18	17	13	10	8	12
Rainfall Monthly Total mm	89	68	57	43	44	39	48	67	69	77	101	99	801
No. of Days	19	15	13	12	11	10	11	12	15	15	17	19	169
Sunshine Hours per Day	2.3	3.1	5	6.7	7.8	8.5	7.8	7.6	5.6	4.1	2.5	1.8	5.3
St Mary's 50m													
Temperature Daily Max.°C	9	9	11	12	14	17	19	19	18	15	12	10	14
Daily Min.°C	6	6	7	7	9	12	13	14	13	11	9	7	9
Average Monthly °C	8	7	9	10	12	14	16	16	15	13	10	9	12
Rainfall Monthly Total mm	91	71	69	46	56	49	61	64	67	80	96	94	844
No. of Days	22	17	16	13	14	14	16	15	16	17	19	21	200
Sunshine Hours per Day	2	2.9	4.2	6.4	7.6	7.6	6.7	6.7	5.2	3.9	2.5	1.8	4.8
Southampton 20m													
Temperature Daily Max.°C	7	8	11	14	17	20	22	22	19	15	11	8	15
Daily Min.°C	2	2	3	5	8	11	13	13	11	7	5	3	7
Average Monthly °C	5	5	7	10	13	16	17	17	15	11	8	6	11
Rainfall Monthly Total mm	83	56	52	45	56	49	60	69	70	86	94	84	804
No. of Days	17	13	13	12	12	12	13	13	14	14	16	17	166
Sunshine Hours per Day	1.8	2.6	4	5.7	6.7	7.2	6.5	6.4	4.9	3.6	2.2	1.6	4.5
Tiree 9m													
Temperature Daily Max.°C	7	7	9	10	13	15	16	16	15	12	10	8	12
Daily Min.°C	4	3	4	5	7	10	11	11	10	8	6	5	7
Average Monthly °C	5	5	6	8	10	12	14	14	13	10	8	6	9
Rainfall Monthly Total mm	117	77	67	64	55	70	91	90	118	129	122	128	1128
No. of Days	23	19	17	17	15	16	20	18	20	23	22	24	234
Sunshine Hours per Day	1.3	2.6	3.7	5.7	7.5	6.8	5.2	5.3	4.2	2.6	1.6	0.9	4
Valentia 9m													
Temperature Daily Max.°C	9	9	11	13	15	17	18	18	17	14	12	10	14
Daily Min.°C	5	4	5	6	8	11	12	13	11	9	7	6	8
Average Monthly °C	7	7	8	9	11	0	15	15	14	12	9	8	11
Rainfall Monthly Total mm	165	107	103	75	86	81	107	95	122	140	151	168	1400
No. of Days	20	15	14	13	13	13	15	15	16	17	18	21	190
Sunshine Hours per Day	1.6	2.5	3.5	5.2	6.5	5.9	4.7	4.9	3.8	2.8	2	1.3	3.7
York 17m													
Temperature Daily Max.°C	6	7	10	13	16	19	21	21	18	14	10	7	13
Daily Min.°C	1	1	2	4	7	10	12	12	10	7	4	2	6
Average Monthly °C	3	4	6	9	12	15	17	16	14	10	7	5	10
Rainfall Monthly Total mm	59	46	37	41	50	50	62	68	55	56	65	50	639
No. of Days	17	15	13	13	13	14	15	14	14	15	17	17	177
Sunshine Hours per Day	1.3	2.1	3.2	4.7	6.1	6.4	5.6	5.1	4.1	2.8	1.6	1.1	3.7

WATER SUPPLY

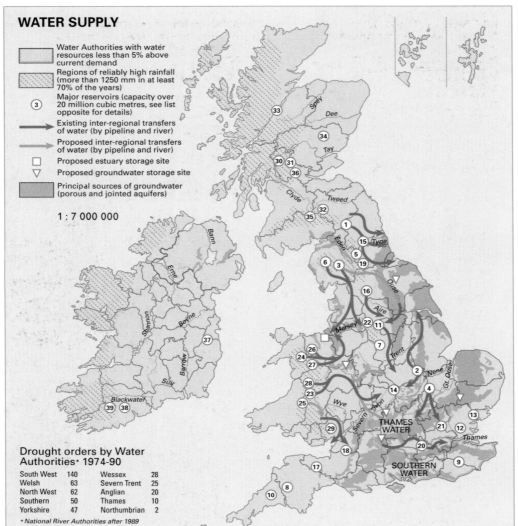

	Water Authorities with water resources less than 5% above current demand
	Regions of reliably high rainfall (more than 1250 mm in at least 70% of the years)
③	Major reservoirs (capacity over 20 million cubic metres, see list opposite for details)
→	Existing inter-regional transfers of water (by pipeline and river)
→	Proposed inter-regional transfers of water (by pipeline and river)
☐	Proposed estuary storage site
▽	Proposed groundwater storage site
	Principal sources of groundwater (porous and jointed aquifers)

1 : 7 000 000

Drought orders by Water Authorities* 1974-90

South West	140	Wessex	28
Welsh	63	Severn Trent	25
North West	62	Anglian	20
Southern	50	Thames	10
Yorkshire	47	Northumbrian	2

National River Authorities after 1989

Major reservoirs (with capacity in million m³)

England

1	Kielder Res.	198
2	Rutland Water	123
3	Haweswater	85
4	Grafham Water	59
5	Cow Green Res.	41
6	Thirlmere	41
7	Carsington Res.	36
8	Roadford Res.	35
9	Bewl Water Res.	31
10	Colliford Lake	29
11	Ladybower Res.	28
12	Hanningfield Res.	27
13	Abberton Res.	25
14	Draycote Water	23
15	Derwent Res.	22
16	Grimwith Res.	22
17	Wimbleball Lake	21
18	Chew Valley Lake	20
19	Balderhead Res.	20
20	Thames Valley (linked reservoirs)	
21	Lea Valley (linked reservoirs)	
22	Longendale (linked reservoirs)	

Wales

23	Elan Valley	99
24	Llyn Celyn	74
25	Llyn Brianne	62
26	Llyn Breinig	60
27	Llyn Vyrnwy	60
28	Llyn Clywedog	48
29	Llandegfedd Res.	22

Scotland

30	Loch Lomond	86
31	Loch Katrine	64
32	Megget Res.	64
33	Loch Ness	26
34	Blackwater Res.	25
35	Daer Res.	23
36	Carron Valley Res.	21

Ireland

37	Pollaphuca Res.	168
38	Inishcarra Res.	57
39	Carrigadrohid Res.	33

Average daily domestic water use in England and Wales (1990)

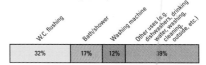

W.C. flushing	Bath/shower	Washing machine	Other uses (e.g. dishwashers, drinking water, washing, cleaning, outside, etc.)
32%	17%	12%	39%

Water abstractions in England and Wales (1990) 35 249 megalitres per day* of which:

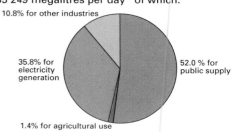

10.8% for other industries

35.8% for electricity generation

52.0 % for public supply

1.4% for agricultural use

average daily domestic consumption per head 136 litres.

WATER ABSTRACTIONS   1 : 12 000 000

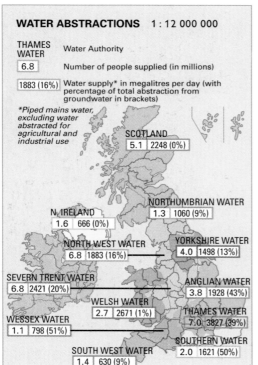

THAMES WATER — Water Authority

6.8 — Number of people supplied (in millions)

1883 (16%) — Water supply* in megalitres per day (with percentage of total abstraction from groundwater in brackets)

Piped mains water, excluding water abstracted for agricultural and industrial use

SCOTLAND	5.1	2248 (0%)
N. IRELAND	1.6	666 (0%)
NORTHUMBRIAN WATER	1.3	1060 (9%)
NORTH WEST WATER	6.8	1883 (16%)
YORKSHIRE WATER	4.0	1498 (13%)
SEVERN TRENT WATER	6.8	2421 (20%)
ANGLIAN WATER	3.8	1928 (43%)
WELSH WATER	2.7	2671 (1%)
THAMES WATER	7.0	3827 (39%)
WESSEX WATER	1.1	798 (51%)
SOUTHERN WATER	2.0	1621 (50%)
SOUTH WEST WATER	1.4	630 (9%)

WATER QUALITY   1 : 12 000 000

The percentage of all rivers and canals of poor or bad quality within each water authority 1990

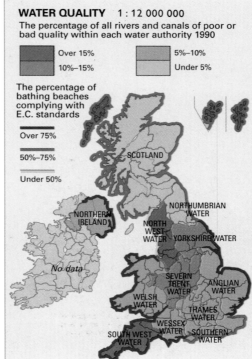

■	Over 15%	■	5%–10%
■	10%–15%	■	Under 5%

The percentage of bathing beaches complying with E.C. standards

Over 75%

50%–75%

Under 50%

No data

SOILS   1 : 12 000 000

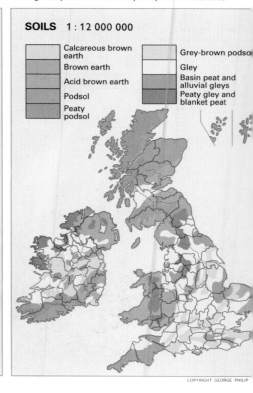

Calcareous brown earth	Grey-brown podsol
Brown earth	Gley
Acid brown earth	Basin peat and alluvial gleys
Podsol	Peaty gley and blanket peat
Peaty podsol	

AIR QUALITY : Emissions in thousand tonnes

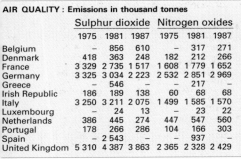

	Sulphur dioxide			Nitrogen oxides		
	1975	1981	1987	1975	1981	1987
Belgium	–	856	610	–	317	271
Denmark	418	363	248	182	212	266
France	3 329	2 735	1 517	1 608	1 779	1 652
Germany	3 325	3 034	2 223	2 532	2 851	2 969
Greece	–	546	–	–	217	–
Irish Republic	186	189	138	60	68	68
Italy	3 250	3 211	2 075	1 499	1 585	1 570
Luxembourg	–	24	13	–	23	22
Netherlands	386	445	274	447	547	560
Portugal	178	266	286	104	166	303
Spain	–	2 543	–	–	937	–
United Kingdom	5 310	4 387	3 863	2 365	2 328	2 429

FORESTRY   1 : 12 000 000

The percentage of the total area covered by woodland and forest

- Over 20%
- 15%-20%
- 10%-15%
- 5%-10%
- Under 5%

△ 50%-80% coniferous
△ Over 80% coniferous

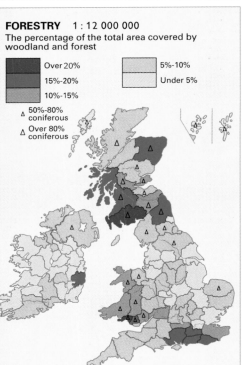

NATURAL VEGETATION   1 : 12 000 000

The plant cover associated with a particular environment if it is unaffected by human activity

- Oak
- Beech and Oak
- Ash and Oak
- Birch and Oakwood
- Scots Pine
- Heath, moorland, water meadows, fen, bog and marsh

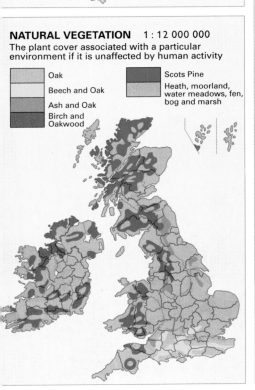

ACID RAIN   1 : 12 000 000

Average acidity of precipitation in the U.K. (pH scale)

- 4.29 and under (most acidic)
- 4.30-4.39
- 4.40-4.49
- 4.50-4.59
- 4.60-4.69
- 4.70-4.79
- 4.80 and over (least acidic)

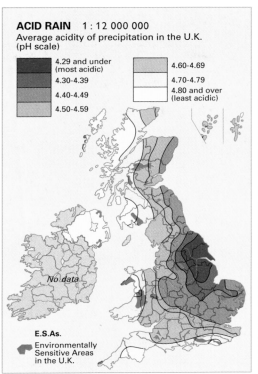

No data

E.S.As.
Environmentally Sensitive Areas in the U.K.

AIR QUALITY   1 : 12 000 000

Hourly average of tropospheric ozone (O$_3$) exceeding 100 parts per billion (summer 1990)*

- Over 45
- 30-45
- 15-30
- Under 15

Ground-level concentrations of smoke in the U.K., by region
U.K. average: 12 micrograms per m^3

- Less than the U.K. average
- More than the U.K. average
- Over 3x the U.K. average

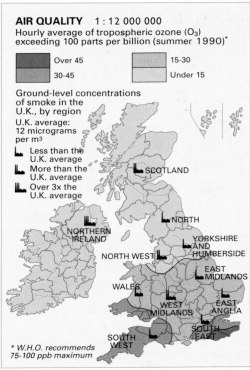

SCOTLAND
NORTHERN IRELAND
NORTH WEST
NORTH
YORKSHIRE AND HUMBERSIDE
EAST MIDLANDS
WALES
WEST MIDLANDS
EAST ANGLIA
SOUTH EAST
SOUTH WEST

* W.H.O. recommends 75-100 ppb maximum

CONSERVATION

- National Parks
- Areas of Outstanding Natural Beauty
- National Scenic Areas
- Forest Parks and Special Protected Areas
- Green Belts (and the urban areas they surround)
- Heritage Coast (England and Wales)/Coastal Conservation Zones (Scotland)
- * World Heritage Sites in the U.K.

1 : 7 000 000

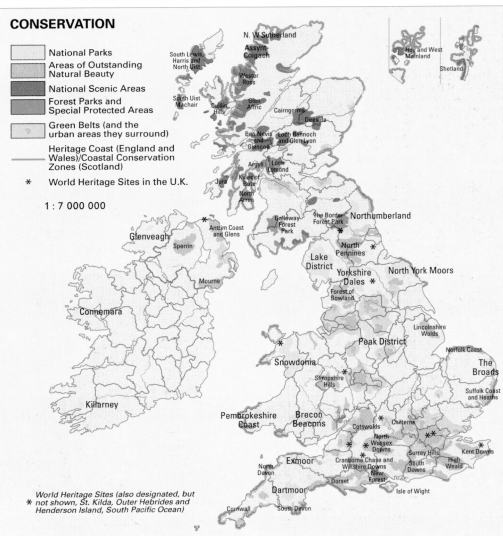

N. W. Sutherland
South Lewis, Harris and North Uist
Assynt-Coigach
Wester Ross
South Uist Machair
Cuillin Hills
Glen Affric
Cairngorms
Deeside
Ben Nevis and Glencoe
Loch Rannoch and Glen Lyon
Argyll
Loch Lomond
Jura
Kyles of Bute
North Arran
Hoy and West Mainland
Shetland
Glenveagh
Antrim Coast and Glens
Sperrin
Galloway Forest Park
The Border Forest Park
Northumberland
North Pennines
Lake District
Mourne
Yorkshire Dales
North York Moors
Connemara
Forest of Bowland
Lincolnshire Wolds
Peak District
Norfolk Coast
Snowdonia
Shropshire Hills
The Broads
Killarney
Suffolk Coast and Heaths
Pembrokeshire Coast
Brecon Beacons
Cotswolds
Chilterns
North Wessex Downs
Surrey Hills
Kent Downs
North Devon
Exmoor
Cranborne Chase and Wiltshire Downs
New Forest
South Downs
High Weald
Dartmoor
Dorset
South Devon
Isle of Wight
Cornwall

World Heritage Sites (also designated, but not shown, St. Kilda, Outer Hebrides and Henderson Island, South Pacific Ocean)

TYPES OF FARM

- Dairy cattle
- Beef cattle
- Sheep
- ● Pigs and/or Poultry
- Mixed farming
- Market gardening (fruit and vegetables)
- Cereals
- Other crops (mainly potatoes, sugar beet)
- ⌒ Northern limit of 9 month growing season
- Forests
- Built-up areas

1 : 7 000 000

Areas with over 1000mm rainfall per year

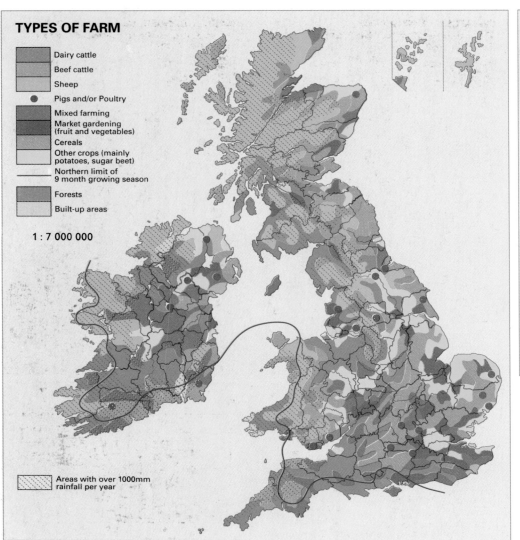

LAND UNDER AGRICULTURE   1 : 12 000 000

The percentage of the total land area used for farming

- Over 80%
- 60%-80%
- 40%-60%
- 20%-40%
- 0-20%

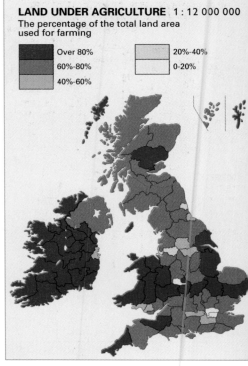

AGRICULTURAL LAND USE 1990 (U.K. only)

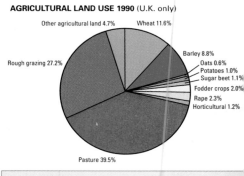

- Other agricultural land 4.7%
- Wheat 11.6%
- Rough grazing 27.2%
- Barley 8.8%
- Oats 0.6%
- Potatoes 1.0%
- Sugar beet 1.1%
- Fodder crops 2.0%
- Rape 2.3%
- Horticultural 1.2%
- Pasture 39.5%

WHEAT   1 : 12 000 000

The percentage of the total farmland used for growing wheat

- Over 40%
- 30%-40%
- 20%-30%
- 10%-20%
- 0-10%

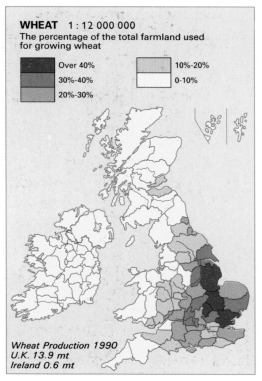

Wheat Production 1990
U.K. 13.9 mt
Ireland 0.6 mt

BARLEY   1 : 12 000 000

The percentage of the total farmland used for growing barley

- Over 20%
- 10%-20%
- 0-10%

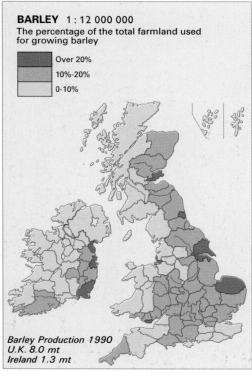

Barley Production 1990
U.K. 8.0 mt
Ireland 1.3 mt

PASTURE   1 : 12 000 000

The percentage of the total farmland used for grazing livestock

- 80%-100%
- 60%-80%
- 40%-60%
- 20%-40%
- 0-20%

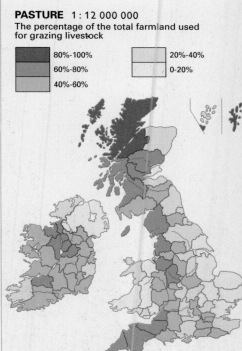

NUMBER AND SIZE OF AGRICULTURAL HOLDINGS IN THE U.K.

Average size of holdings (hectares)

	1940	1980	1989
England & Wales	33.8	60.2	57.9
Scotland	81.8	96.2	195.9
Northern Ireland	13.7	24.2	25.2

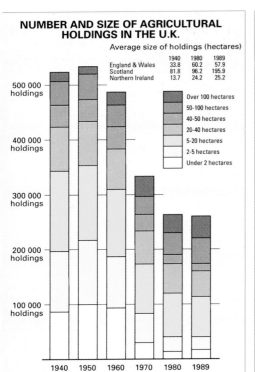

- Over 100 hectares
- 50-100 hectares
- 40-50 hectares
- 20-40 hectares
- 5-20 hectares
- 2-5 hectares
- Under 2 hectares

POTATOES 1 : 12 000 000
The percentage of the total farmland used for growing potatoes

- Over 3%
- 2%-3%
- 1%-2%
- Under 1%

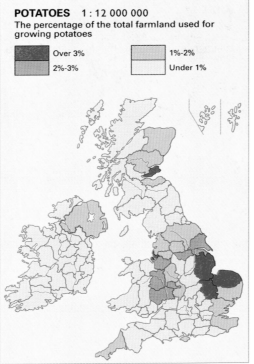

MARKET GARDENING 1 : 12 000 000
The percentage of the total farmland used for market gardening

- Over 5%
- 2.5%-5%
- 1.0%-2.5%
- Under 1%

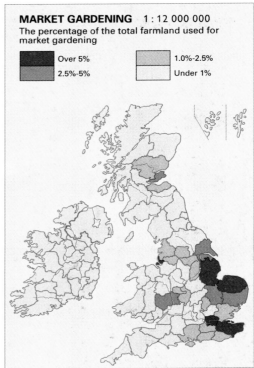

FISHING
Quantities of fish landed at major ports (port districts in Scotland) in 1989

Type of fish landed
- Demersal (Deep Sea Fish)
- Pelagic (Shallow Water Fish)
- Shellfish

Fishing Regions
- IV North Sea
- VIa West Scotland
- VIIa Irish Sea
- VIIb South & West Ireland
- VIId English Channel
- VIIf Bristol Channel

Fish landed according to region of capture (1989)
- Demersal
- Pelagic

1 fish represents 10 000 caught

Region boundary

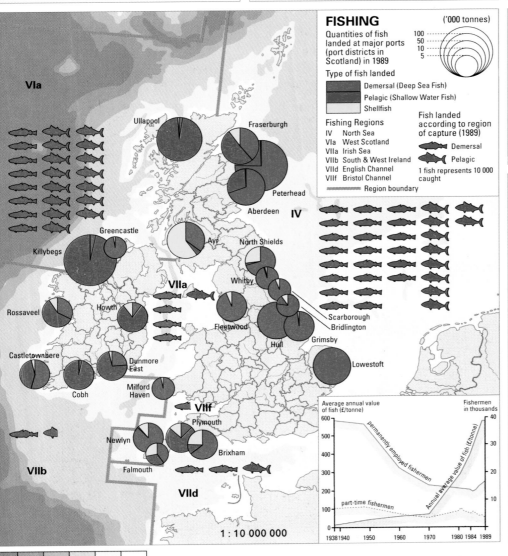

Average annual value of fish (£/tonne) / Fishermen in thousands
permanently employed fishermen
part-time fishermen
Annual average value of fish (£/tonne)

1 : 10 000 000

1000 500 200 100 50 m

VALUE OF AGRICULTURAL OUTPUT (U.K. only)

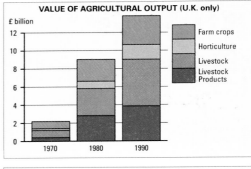

£ billion
- Farm crops
- Horticulture
- Livestock
- Livestock Products

AGRICULTURAL LAND & LIVESTOCK, 1970-90 (U.K. only)

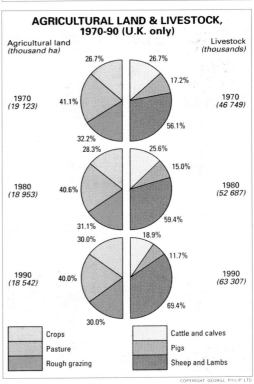

Agricultural land (thousand ha) / Livestock (thousands)

1970 (19 123) / 1970 (46 749)
1980 (18 953) / 1980 (52 687)
1990 (18 542) / 1990 (63 307)

- Crops
- Pasture
- Rough grazing
- Cattle and calves
- Pigs
- Sheep and Lambs

COPYRIGHT GEORGE PHILIP LTD.

EMPLOYMENT IN MANUFACTURING
The percentage of the workforce employed in manufacturing in 1989

- Over 30%
- 25%-30%
- 20%-25%
- 15%-20%
- 12.5%-15%
- Under 12.5%

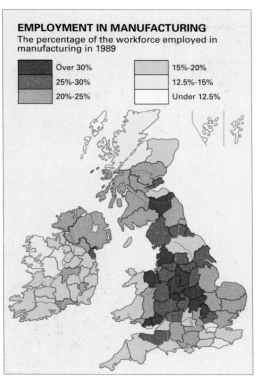

CHANGE IN MANUFACTURING EMPLOYMENT
The percentage change in the number of people employed in manufacturing 1980-89*

- Over 10% gain
- 0-10% gain
- 0-10% loss
- 10%-20% loss
- 20%-30% loss
- Over 30% loss

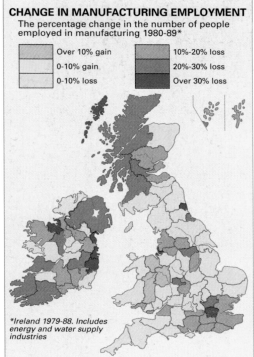

*Ireland 1979-88. Includes energy and water supply industries

LOCATION OF MANUFACTURING INDUSTRY

Heavy Industry
- ▲ Chemicals
- ■ Iron and Steel
- ● Motor vehicles

Light Industry
- ◆ Electrical Engineering

Grangemouth
Sunderland
Teesside
Sheffield
Halewood
Leyland
Ellesmere Port
Scunthorpe
Killingholme
Dublin
Solihull
Birmingham
Coventry
Longbridge
Luton
Llandarcy
Cowley
Port Talbot
Llanwern
Swindon
Avonmouth
Fawley
Dagenham

EMPLOYMENT IN AGRICULTURE
The percentage of the workforce employed in agriculture in 1989

- Over 25%
- 10%-25%
- 2.5%-10%
- 1%-2.5%
- 0-1%

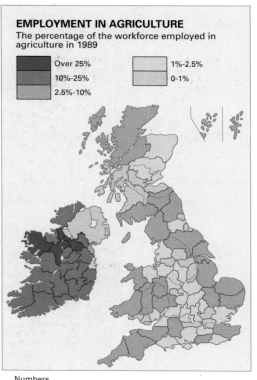

EMPLOYMENT IN SERVICES
The percentage of the workforce employed in the service industry in 1989

- Over 80%
- 70%-80%
- 60%-70%
- 50%-60%
- Less than 50%

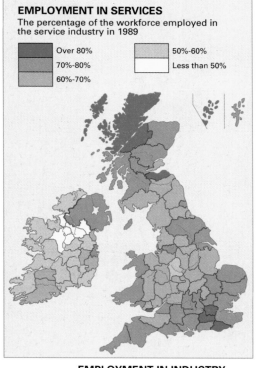

ASSISTED AREAS
These are areas in which extra financial support is focused to encourage economic growth

- Development areas in the U.K.
- Intermediate areas in the U.K.

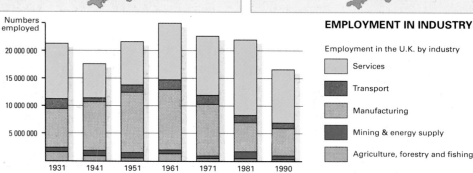

*Separate legislation applies to the whole of N.Ireland

1 Arbroath	22 Liverpool
2 Dundee	23 Wigan & St Helens
3 Dumbarton	24 Widnes & Runcorn
4 Greenock	25 Wirral & Chester
5 Irvine	26 Flint & Rhyl
6 Glasgow	27 Wrexham
7 Kilmarnock	28 Holyhead
8 Bathgate	29 Corby
9 Lanarkshire	30 Lampeter & Aberaeron
10 Cumnock & Sanquhar	31 Cardigan
11 Workington	32 South Pembrokeshire
12 Newcastle-upon-Tyne	33 Neath & Port Talbot
13 South Tyneside	34 Aberdare
14 Sunderland	35 Pontypridd & Rhondda
15 Hartlepool	36 Merthyr & Rhymney
16 Stockton-on-Tees	37 Ebbw Vale & Abergavenny
17 Bishop Auckland	38 Newquay
18 Middlesbrough	39 Redruth & Camborne
19 Whitby	40 Penzance & St. Ives
20 Scunthorpe	41 Helston
21 Rotherham & Mexborough	42 Falmouth

EMPLOYMENT IN INDUSTRY

Employment in the U.K. by industry

- Services
- Transport
- Manufacturing
- Mining & energy supply
- Agriculture, forestry and fishing

Numbers employed

20 000 000
15 000 000
10 000 000
5 000 000

1931   1941   1951   1961   1971   1981   1990

1 : 12 000 000

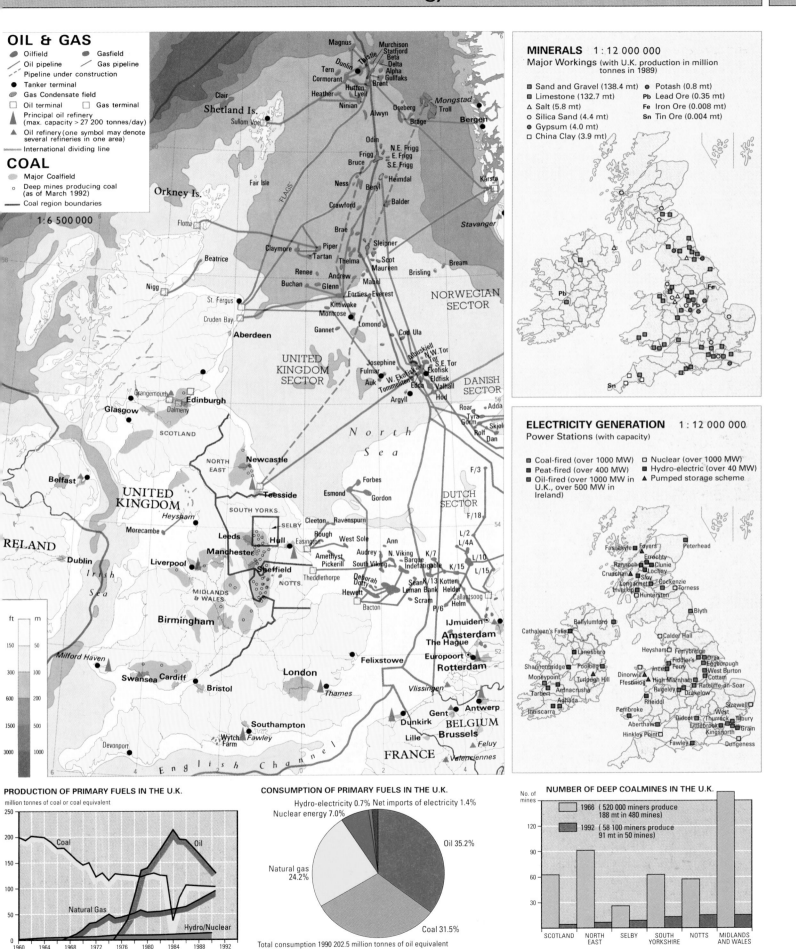

OIL & GAS

- Oilfield
- Gasfield
- Oil pipeline
- Gas pipeline
- Pipeline under construction
- ● Tanker terminal
- Gas Condensate field
- □ Oil terminal   □ Gas terminal
- ▲ Principal oil refinery (max. capacity > 27 200 tonnes/day)
- ▲ Oil refinery (one symbol may denote several refineries in one area)
- International dividing line

COAL

- Major Coalfield
- ○ Deep mines producing coal (as of March 1992)
- Coal region boundaries

1:6 500 000

MINERALS 1:12 000 000

Major Workings (with U.K. production in million tonnes in 1989)

- ■ Sand and Gravel (138.4 mt)
- ■ Limestone (132.7 mt)
- △ Salt (5.8 mt)
- ○ Silica Sand (4.4 mt)
- ◐ Gypsum (4.0 mt)
- □ China Clay (3.9 mt)
- ● Potash (0.8 mt)
- Pb Lead Ore (0.35 mt)
- Fe Iron Ore (0.008 mt)
- Sn Tin Ore (0.004 mt)

ELECTRICITY GENERATION 1:12 000 000

Power Stations (with capacity)

- ■ Coal-fired (over 1000 MW)
- ■ Peat-fired (over 400 MW)
- ■ Oil-fired (over 1000 MW in U.K., over 500 MW in Ireland)
- □ Nuclear (over 1000 MW)
- ■ Hydro-electric (over 40 MW)
- ▲ Pumped storage scheme

PRODUCTION OF PRIMARY FUELS IN THE U.K.

million tonnes of coal or coal equivalent

(Line graph, 1960–1992, values 0–250: Coal, Oil, Natural Gas, Hydro/Nuclear)

CONSUMPTION OF PRIMARY FUELS IN THE U.K.

- Hydro-electricity 0.7%
- Net imports of electricity 1.4%
- Nuclear energy 7.0%
- Oil 35.2%
- Natural gas 24.2%
- Coal 31.5%

Total consumption 1990 202.5 million tonnes of oil equivalent

NUMBER OF DEEP COALMINES IN THE U.K.

No. of mines

- 1966 (520 000 miners produce 188 mt in 480 mines)
- 1992 (58 100 miners produce 91 mt in 50 mines)

SCOTLAND | NORTH EAST | SELBY | SOUTH YORKSHIRE | NOTTS | MIDLANDS AND WALES

COPYRIGHT GEORGE PHILIP LTD.

ROADS AND FERRIES

- M6 — Motorways
- Main primary routes
- (56) Average 24 hour flow of vehicles at a selected point on a motorway. Figures are given in thousands
- --- Principal ferry routes
- --Oslo-- Long haul sea ferry destinations

RAILWAYS

- Electrified lines
- Other main lines

Furthest distances from London reached within a journey time of

	3 hours	6 hours
1950	▲	●
1990	▲	●

Channel tunnel
- --- Channel tunnel
- Proposed high speed rail link

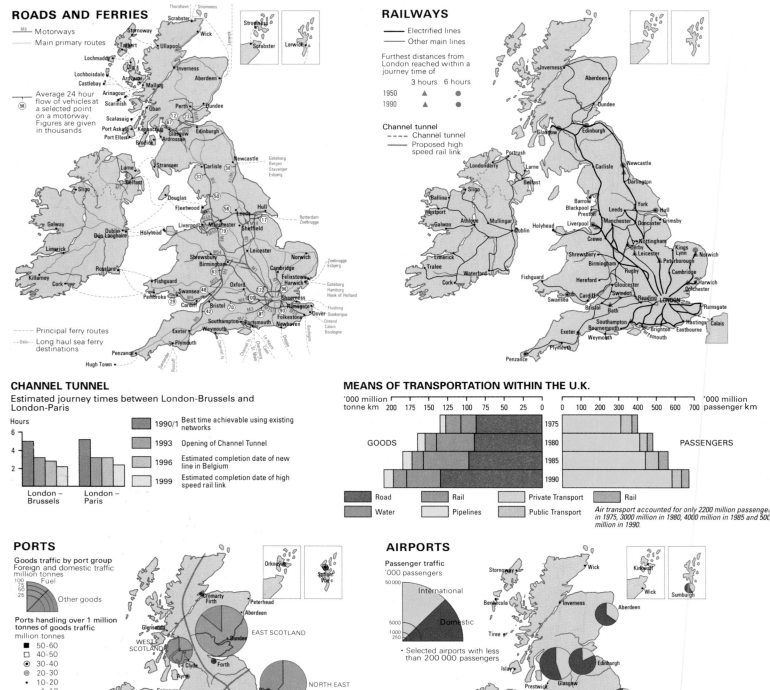

CHANNEL TUNNEL

Estimated journey times between London-Brussels and London-Paris

Hours (axis: 6, 4, 2)

- 1990/1 Best time achievable using existing networks
- 1993 Opening of Channel Tunnel
- 1996 Estimated completion date of new line in Belgium
- 1999 Estimated completion date of high speed rail link

London – Brussels   London – Paris

MEANS OF TRANSPORTATION WITHIN THE U.K.

'000 million tonne km   200 175 150 125 100 75 50 25 0

GOODS   (years: 1975, 1980, 1985, 1990)

0 100 200 300 400 500 600 700   '000 million passenger km

PASSENGERS

- Road
- Water
- Rail
- Pipelines
- Private Transport
- Public Transport
- Rail

Air transport accounted for only 2200 million passenger in 1975, 3000 million in 1980, 4000 million in 1985 and 500 million in 1990.

PORTS

Goods traffic by port group
Foreign and domestic traffic
million tonnes
100, 75, 50, 25 — Fuel
Other goods

Ports handling over 1 million tonnes of goods traffic
million tonnes
- ■ 50-60
- □ 40-50
- ◉ 30-40
- ◎ 20-30
- • 10-20
- · 1-10

- ● Ports where fuel represents over 75% of all goods handled
- *Hull* Ports handling over 1 million tonnes of unitized traffic
- Port group boundaries

The total figure for the Irish Rep. does not include domestic traffic

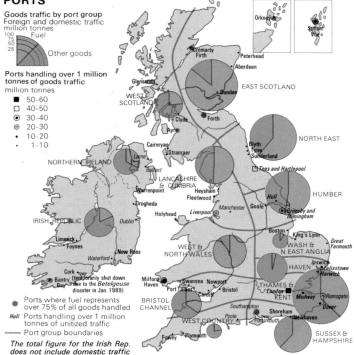

AIRPORTS

Passenger traffic
'000 passengers
50 000
International
5000
1000
250
Domestic

- · Selected airports with less than 200 000 passengers

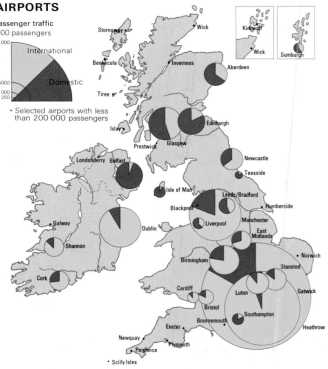

The DISTRICTS of Northern Ireland have been numbered and can be identified by reference to this table.

1	Londonderry	14	Craigavon
2	Limavady	15	Armagh
3	Coleraine	16	Newry & Mourne
4	Ballymoney	17	Banbridge
5	Moyle	18	Down
6	Larne	19	Lisburn
7	Ballymena	20	Antrim
8	Magherafelt	21	Newtownabbey
9	Cookstown	22	Carrickfergus
10	Strabane	23	North Down
11	Omagh	24	Ards
12	Fermanagh	25	Castlereagh
13	Dungannon	26	Belfast

ORKNEY

Kirkwall

HIGHLAND

SHETLAND

Lerwick

WESTERN ISLES

Stornoway

HIGHLAND

Inverness GRAMPIAN

SCOTLAND

Aberdeen

TAYSIDE

Dundee

FIFE
Glenrothes

CENTRAL
Stirling

Edinburgh
LOTHIAN

Glasgow

STRATHCLYDE

BORDERS

Newtown
St. Boswells

DUMFRIES
AND
GALLOWAY

Dumfries

NORTHUMBERLAND
Morpeth

Newcastle
TYNE AND
WEAR

Carlisle

Durham

CUMBRIA

DURHAM

CLEVELAND
Middlesbrough

Northallerton

NORTH
YORKSHIRE

ATLANTIC

OCEAN

ISLE OF
MAN

Douglas

North Channel

DONEGAL
Lifford

Londonderry

Antrim

NORTHERN
IRELAND

Tyrone

Belfast

Down

Sligo

Fermanagh

Monaghan

LEITRIM

SLIGO

Carrick-on-
Shannon

MONAGHAN

Cavan

CAVAN

Dundalk

LOUTH

MAYO

Castlebar

ROSCOMMON

Longford

LONGFORD

Roscommon

An Uaimh
(Navan)

Mullingar
WESTMEATH

MEATH

IRISH SEA

LANCASHIRE
Preston

WEST
YORKSHIRE

Wakefield

GREATER
MANCHESTER
MERSEYSIDE Manchester
Liverpool

Barnsley
SOUTH
YORKSHIRE

ENGLAND

Lincoln

HUMBERSIDE
Beverley

GALWAY

Galway

OFFALY
Tullamore

DUBLIN
Dublin

KILDARE

IRELAND

Port Laoise

Naas

Chester
CHESHIRE

DERBYSHIRE

Matlock

NOTT-
INGHAM-
SHIRE

Nottingham

LINCOLNSHIRE

Caernarfon

Mold

CLWYD

GWYNEDD

CLARE
Ennis

LAOIS

WICKLOW

Wicklow

NORFOLK
Norwich

Shrewsbury

SHROPSHIRE

Stafford
STAFFORD-
SHIRE

WEST
MIDLANDS
Birmingham

Leicester
LEICESTERSHIRE

CAMBRIDGE-
SHIRE

Cambridge

Ipswich

SUFFOLK

LIMERICK
Limerick

Kilkenny

KILKENNY

TIPPERARY

CARLOW
Carlow

Tralee

Clonmel

WEXFORD

Wexford

WATERFORD Waterford

WALES

POWYS

Llandrindod
Wells

HEREFORD
AND
WORCESTER

Warwick
WARWICK-
SHIRE

Worcester

NORTH-
AMPTON-
SHIRE
Northampton

Bedford
BEDFORD-
SHIRE

BUCK-
INGHAM-
SHIRE

Aylesbury

Hertford
HERTFORD-
SHIRE

ESSEX
Chelmsford

KERRY

CORK

Cork

DYFED

Carmarthen

Gloucester
GLOUCESTER-
SHIRE

Oxford
OXFORDSHIRE

GREATER
LONDON

Kingston

Maidstone

WEST
GLAMORGAN
Swansea

MID
GLAMORGAN

GWENT
Cwmbran

Cardiff
SOUTH
GLAMORGAN

Bristol

AVON

BERKSHIRE

Reading

SURREY

KENT

WILTSHIRE
Trowbridge

HAMPSHIRE
Winchester

WEST
SUSSEX

EAST
SUSSEX
Lewes

SOMERSET

Taunton

DORSET
Dorchester

Chichester

Newport
ISLE OF
WIGHT

DEVON

Exeter

CELTIC

SEA

CORNWALL

Truro

ENGLISH CHANNEL

NORTH

SEA

St. George's Channel

FRANCE

○ Norwich — Administrative headquarters

MERSEYSIDE — Metropolitan counties

Antrim — Former Northern Ireland counties

Projection: Conical with two standard parallels

West from Greenwich 0 East from Greenwich
COPYRIGHT. GEORGE PHILIP & SON. LTD.

1:4 000 000

20   0   20   40   60 miles
20 0 20 40 60 80 km

POPULATION DENSITY 1891 1 : 12 000 000

See map at right for reference to colours

Density in 1891 by country :
U.K. 142 people per km²
Ireland 49 people per km²

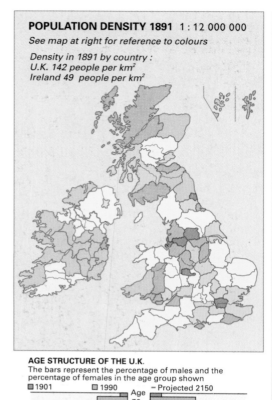

POPULATION DENSITY 1991

Persons per km²

- Over 1000
- 500-1000
- 200-500
- 100-200
- 50-100
- 25-50
- Under 25

The density for the whole of the U.K. is 223 people per km², the density for Ireland is 51.

1 : 7 000 000

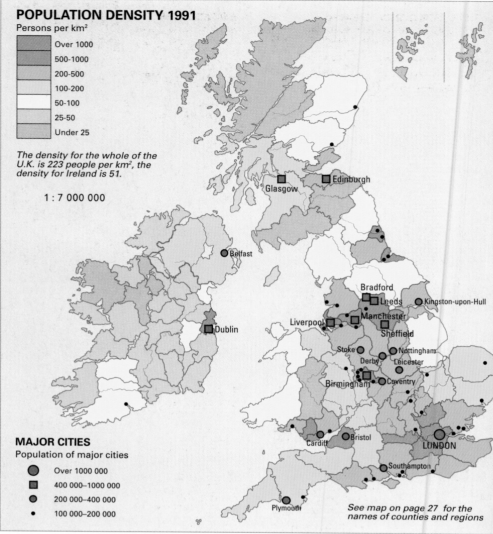

Glasgow Edinburgh

Belfast

Dublin

Bradford
Leeds Kingston-upon-Hull
Liverpool Manchester
Sheffield
Stoke Nottingham
Derby Leicester
Birmingham Coventry

Cardiff Bristol
LONDON
Southampton

Plymouth

See map on page 27 for the names of counties and regions

MAJOR CITIES

Population of major cities

- ⬤ Over 1000 000
- ⬛ 400 000–1000 000
- ● 200 000–400 000
- • 100 000–200 000

AGE STRUCTURE OF THE U.K.
The bars represent the percentage of males and the percentage of females in the age group shown

☐ 1901   ☐ 1990   — Projected 2150

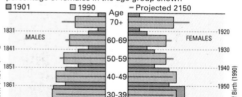

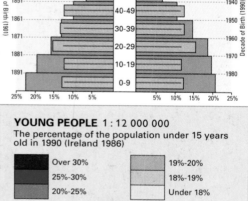

YOUNG PEOPLE 1 : 12 000 000
The percentage of the population under 15 years old in 1990 (Ireland 1986)

- Over 30%
- 25%-30%
- 20%-25%
- 19%-20%
- 18%-19%
- Under 18%

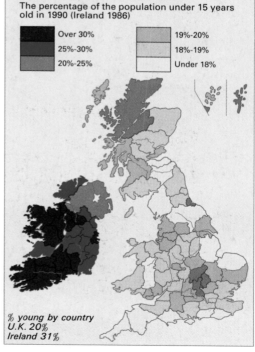

% young by country
U.K. 20%
Ireland 31%

OLD PEOPLE 1 : 12 000 000
The percentage of the population over pensionable age* in 1989

- Over 20%
- 17.5%-20%
- 15%-17.5%
- 12.5%-15%
- 10%-12.5%
- Under 10%

* Pensionable age is 65 for males, 60 for females

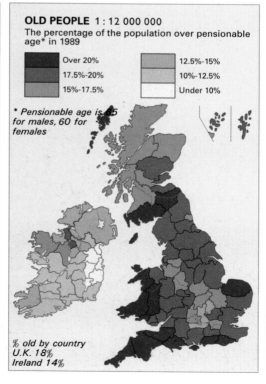

% old by country
U.K. 18%
Ireland 14%

URBANIZATION 1 : 12 000 000
The percentage of the population living in towns and cities (latest available year)

- Over 90%
- 80%-90%
- 70%-80%
- 60%-70%
- 50%-60%
- Under 50%

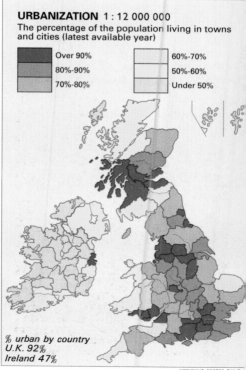

% urban by country
U.K. 92%
Ireland 47%

NATURAL POPULATION CHANGE

The difference between the number of births and the number of deaths per thousand inhabitants in 1990

- Over 10 more births
- 5-10 more births
- 2.5-5 more births
- 0-2.5 more births
- 0-2.5 more deaths
- Over 2.5 more deaths

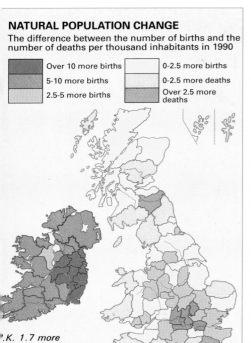

.K. 1.7 more
irths than deaths
eland 22.7 more
irths than deaths

ETHNIC GROUP

Ethnic minority groups

Thousands
500
100
50

Other
W. Indian/African
Indian/Pakistani/Bangladeshi

Ethnic minorities as a % of total population in each region named

- Over 6%
- 4%-6%
- 2%-4%
- 0-2%

No available data for Ireland or Northern Ireland

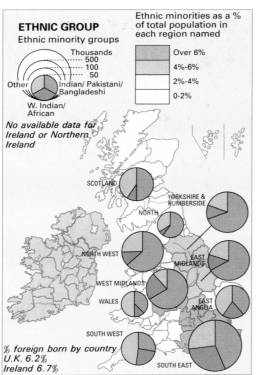

% foreign born by country
U.K. 6.2%
Ireland 6.7%

MIGRATION 1 : 12 000 000

The difference between the number moving in and the number moving away (per 1000 inhabitants)*

- Over 15 moved in
- 10-15 moved in
- 5-10 moved in
- 0-5 moved in
- 0-5 moved away
- 5-10 moved away

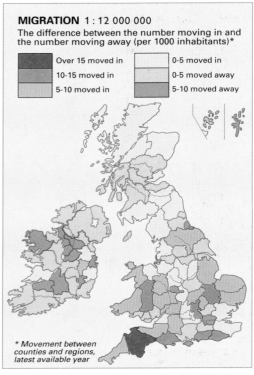

* Movement between counties and regions, latest available year

U.K. VITAL STATISTICS 1900-2000

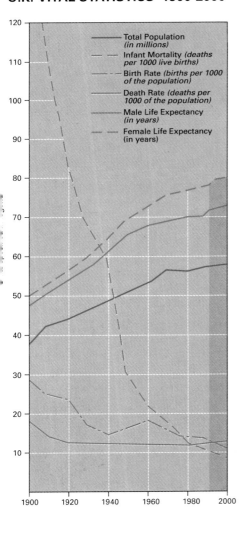

- Total Population (in millions)
- Infant Mortality (deaths per 1000 live births)
- Birth Rate (births per 1000 of the population)
- Death Rate (deaths per 1000 of the population)
- Male Life Expectancy (in years)
- Female Life Expectancy (in years)

POPULATION CHANGE 1961-1991

The percentage change in the number of people between 1961 and 1991

- Over 30% gain
- 25%-30% gain
- 20%-25% gain
- 15%-20% gain
- 10%-15% gain
- 5%-10% gain
- 0-5% gain
- 0-5% loss
- 5%-10% loss
- Over 10% loss

1 : 7 000 000

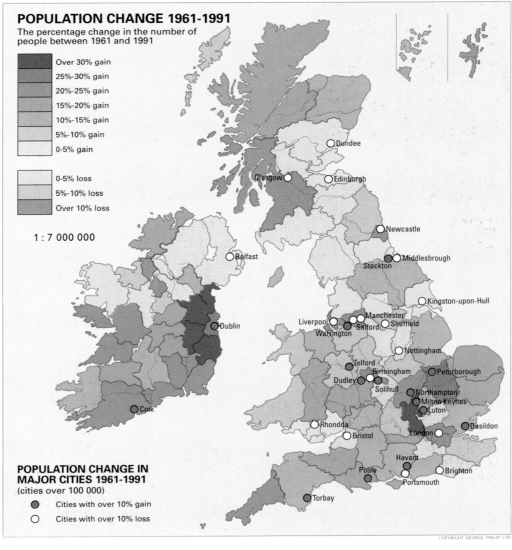

POPULATION CHANGE IN MAJOR CITIES 1961-1991
(cities over 100 000)

- Cities with over 10% gain
- Cities with over 10% loss

HOUSE OWNERSHIP 1 : 12 000 000

The percentage of dwellings which are owner-occupied in 1990 (Ireland 1985)

- Over 80%
- 70%-80%
- 60%-70%
- 50%-60%
- Under 50%

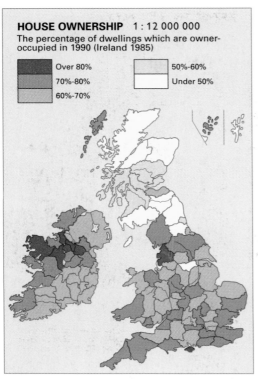

CAR OWNERSHIP 1 : 12 000 000

The number of new* cars per thousand people in 1990

- Over 50
- 40-50
- 30-40
- 20-30
- 10-20

No data

*First year of registration

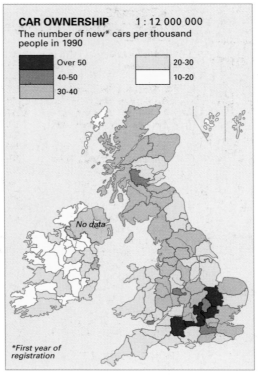

INCOME 1 : 12 000 000

The average gross weekly earnings of males in full employment in 1991 (U.K. only)*

- Over £375
- £350-£375
- £325-£350
- £300-£325
- £275-£300
- Under £275

*No data available for Ireland, Borders or Islands

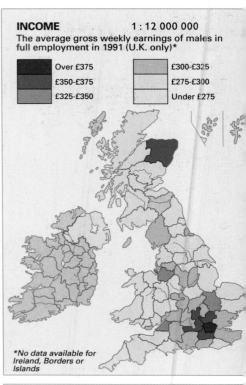

HEALTH 1 : 12 000 000

The number of doctors per 100 000 people (by health authority, latest available year)

- Over 90
- 80-90
- 70-80
- 60-70
- 50-60
- Under 50

Regional health authority boundaries

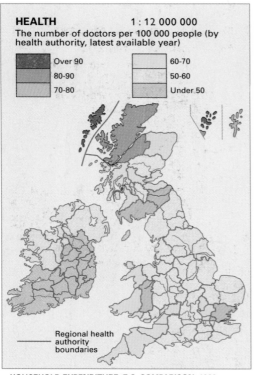

EDUCATION 1 : 12 000 000

The percentage of pupils aged 16 staying on in education in 1989 (U.K. only)

- Over 85%
- 80%-85%
- 75%-80%
- 70%-75%
- 65%-70%
- Under 65%

No comparable data

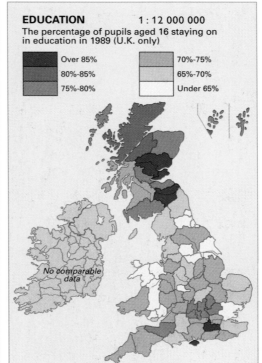

UNEMPLOYMENT 1 : 12 000 000

The percentage of the workforce unemployed in 1992

- Over 17.5%
- 15%-17.5%
- 12.5%-15%
- 10%-12.5%
- 7.5%-10%
- Under 7.5%

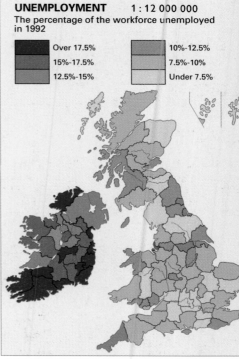

HOUSEHOLD EXPENDITURE: E.C. COMPARISON 1989

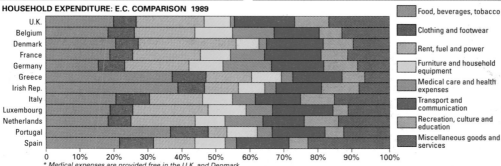

U.K.
Belgium
Denmark
France
Germany
Greece
Irish Rep.
Italy
Luxembourg
Netherlands
Portugal
Spain

0 10% 20% 30% 40% 50% 60% 70% 80% 90% 100%
* Medical expenses are provided free in the U.K. and Denmark

- Food, beverages, tobacco
- Clothing and footwear
- Rent, fuel and power
- Furniture and household equipment
- Medical care and health expenses
- Transport and communication
- Recreation, culture and education
- Miscellaneous goods and services

% OF U.K. HOUSEHOLDS OWNING DOMESTIC APPLIANCES

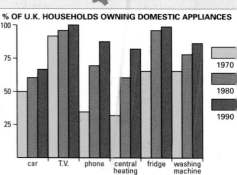

100
75
50
25

car T.V. phone central heating fridge washing machine

- 1970
- 1980
- 1990

U.K. TRADE
TOP TEN TRADING PARTNERS 1990

One container represents 1% of the total value of imports or 1% of the total value of exports

IMPORTS

- Germany £19.9b
- U.S.A. £14.4b
- France £11.7b
- Netherlands £10.5b
- Japan £6.7b
- Italy £6.7b
- Belgium/Lux. £5.7b
- Irish Republic £4.5b
- Switzerland £4.2b
- Norway £4.2b

Total Imports 1990 £126billion
Total Exports 1990 £104billion

EXPORTS

- Germany £13.1b
- U.S.A. £13.0b
- France £10.9b
- Netherlands £7.5b
- Belgium/Lux. £5.6b
- Italy £5.6b
- Irish Republic £5.3b
- Spain £3.7b
- Sweden £2.7b
- Japan £2.6b

TYPE OF GOODS
- Machinery and Transport Equipment
- • Road Vehicles
- Other manufactured Goods
- Chemicals
- Food and Live Animals
- Mineral fuels, Lubricants, etc.
- Other Goods

U.K. TOTAL FOREIGN TRADE 1970–1990 (£ million)

	Imports	Exports		Imports	Exports
1970	£9 051m	£8 063m	1982	£56 940m	£55 538m
1974	£23 117m	£16 494m	1986	£84 790m	£78 331m
1978	£40 969m	£37 368m	1990	£126 165m	£103 91m

TOURISM
TOP 20 TOURIST ATTRACTIONS (U.K. 1991)

- ● Theme Park
- ● Museum
- ○ Country Park
- ● Historic Property

Attraction	Visitors
● Blackpool Pleasure Beach	6 500 000
● British Museum, London	5 061 287
● National Gallery, London	4 280 139
○ Strathclyde Country Park	4 220 000
● Palace Pier, Brighton	3 500 000
● Pleasure Beach, Gt. Yarmouth	2 500 000
● Madame Tussauds, London	2 248 956
● Eastbourne Pier	2 200 000
● Alton Towers, Staffs.	1 968 000
● Tower of London	1 923 520
● Tate Gallery, London	1 816 421
● Pleasureland, Southport	1 750 000
● Natural History Museum, London	1 571 681
● St. Pauls Cathedral, London	1 500 000
● Chessington World of Adventures, Surrey	1 410 000
● Science Museum, London	1 327 503
○ Bradgate Park, Leics.	1 300 000
● Blackpool Tower	1 300 000
● Frontierland, Morecambe	1 300 000
○ Sandwell Valley Country Park	1 250 000

FOREIGN VISITORS TO THE U.K.

Nature of visit: Business, Leisure
Country of origin: North America, Western Europe, Other
No. of visits (millions)
Years: 1970, 1980, 1990

INCOME FROM TOURISM

The percentage of total U.K. income from tourism by region in 1990

- Over 25%
- 10%–25%
- 5%–10%
- 2.5%–5%
- 0–2.5%

Regions: SCOTLAND, NORTHERN IRELAND, CUMBRIA, NORTHUMBRIA, NORTH WEST, YORKSHIRE AND HUMBERSIDE, EAST MIDLANDS, HEART OF ENGLAND, WALES, EAST ANGLIA, THAMES AND CHILTERNS, WEST COUNTRY, SOUTHERN, LONDON, SOUTH EAST

Total income from tourism
U.K. 1990   £10.2 billion
Ireland 1990   £7.7 billion

VISITS ABROAD BY U.K. RESIDENTS
Top 10 destinations visited, 1990

No. of U.K. visitors ('000): 0 1000 2000 3000 4000 5000 6000 7000

- France
- Spain
- Irish Rep.
- U.S.A.
- Germany
- Greece
- Netherlands
- Italy
- Portugal
- Belgium

Total visits by area, 1990
North America	2 349 000
Western Europe EC	22 032 000
Western Europe (non EC)	3 786 000
Rest of World	3 016 000

DEPENDENCE ON TRADE WITH THE U.K.
Trade with the U.K. as a percentage of each country's total trade

- Over 10%
- 7.5%–10%
- 5.0%–7.5%
- 2.5%–5.0%
- 1.0%–2.5%
- Under 1.0%

CHANGES IN TRADE WITH THE U.K.
Percentage change in exports and imports for selected countries 1985–1990

Change: 1000%, 500%, 100%, 50%
Increase 1985–1990
Exports to U.K.   Imports from U.K.
Decrease 1985–1990

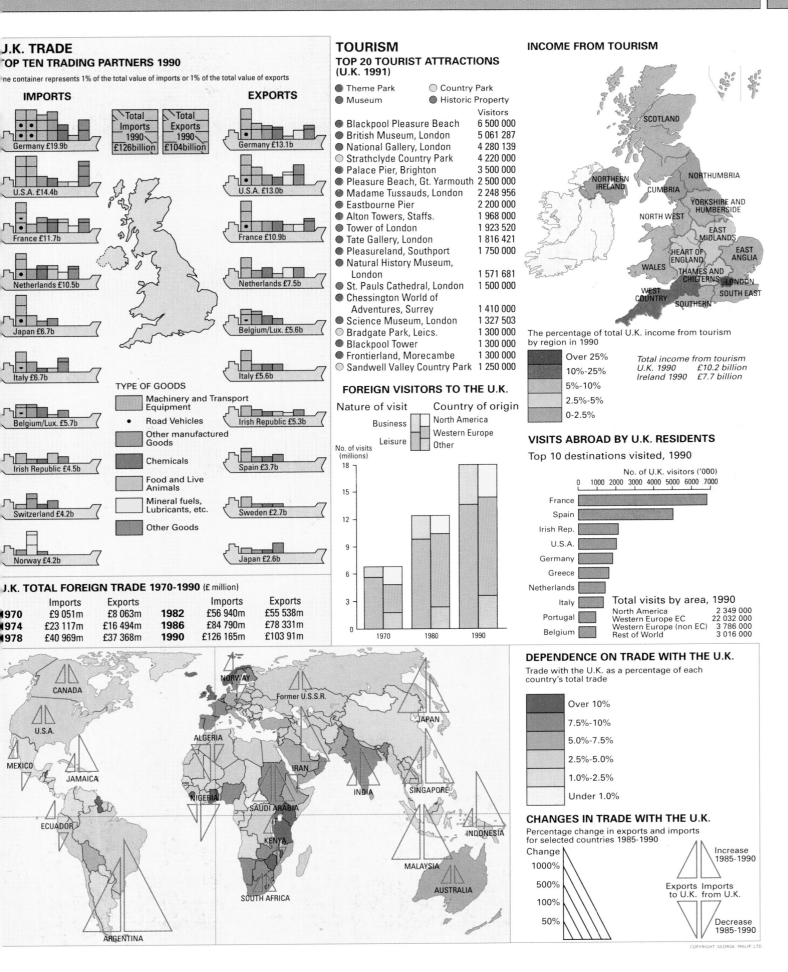

World map labels: CANADA, U.S.A., MEXICO, JAMAICA, ECUADOR, ARGENTINA, NORWAY, Former U.S.S.R., ALGERIA, NIGERIA, SAUDI ARABIA, KENYA, SOUTH AFRICA, IRAN, INDIA, JAPAN, SINGAPORE, INDONESIA, MALAYSIA, AUSTRALIA

TRADE ORGANIZATIONS & HIGH SPEED RAIL NETWORK

Proposals for a European High Speed Rail Network were put forward in 1989. Plans were initially limited to Western Europe, but have since been extended to Eastern Europe and links with Asia.

—— European High Speed Rail Network, Railway Lines proposed to be built or upgraded to at least 220km/h by 1995.

Projection: Bonne

LONDON Capital Cities

EMPLOYMENT 1989

Agriculture   Industry   Services

Bel. Den. Fra. Ger. Gre. Ire. Ita. Lux. Neth. Port. Spa. U.K.

PRODUCTION AND CONSUMPTION OF PRIMARY ENERGY WITHIN THE E.E.C. (million tonnes)

Consumption (Total 106.5)

2.0%
12.8%
3.2%
24.9%
22.7%
18.7%
44.9%
21.5%
27.7%
21.6%

Production (Total 106.5)

Oil
Coal
Natural gas
Nuclear energy
Electricity

E.E.C. (European Economic Community) H.Q. Brussels

The Six in 1957 (pop. 170 million)
The Nine in 1973 (pop. 256 million)
The Ten in 1981 (pop. 270 million)
The Twelve in 1990 (pop. 325 million)

E.F.T.A. (European Free Trade Association) H.Q. Geneva

E.E.C. Associate Members, negotiating for E.E.C. membership

No trade agreements currently established

STANDARDS OF LIVING

Gross Domestic Product (GDP) is a measure of a country's total production of goods and services.

NORWAY £50.9 b (2.7%)
FINLAND £67.4 b (3.1%)
U.K. £479.5 b (2.5%)
SWEDEN £105.0 b (1.8%)
DENMARK £58.9 b (2.1%)
NETH. £134.3 b (1.4%)
IRISH REP. £17.4 b (1.2%)
GERMANY £762.3 b (2.2%)
BELGIUM £80.3 b (1.2%)
AUSTRIA £75.3 b (2.0%)
FRANCE £570.8 b (1.7%)
SWITZERLAND £113.8 b (1.7%)
SPAIN £222.9 b (2.7%)
ITALY £503.6 b
PORTUGAL £26.3 b (2.4%)
GREECE £31.2 b (0.8%)

Gross National Product in 1990 in £ billions (% annual average growth 1980-1990 is given in brackets)

Gross Domestic Product per person in 1989

over 120
110-120
100-110
90-100
80-90
70-80
below 70

Indices : E.E.C. average = 100

DENSITY OF POPULATION

Inhabitants /km² 1990

over 350
300-350
250-300
200-250
150-200
100-150
50-100
25-50
under 25

● Urban areas with over 1 000 000 inhabitants

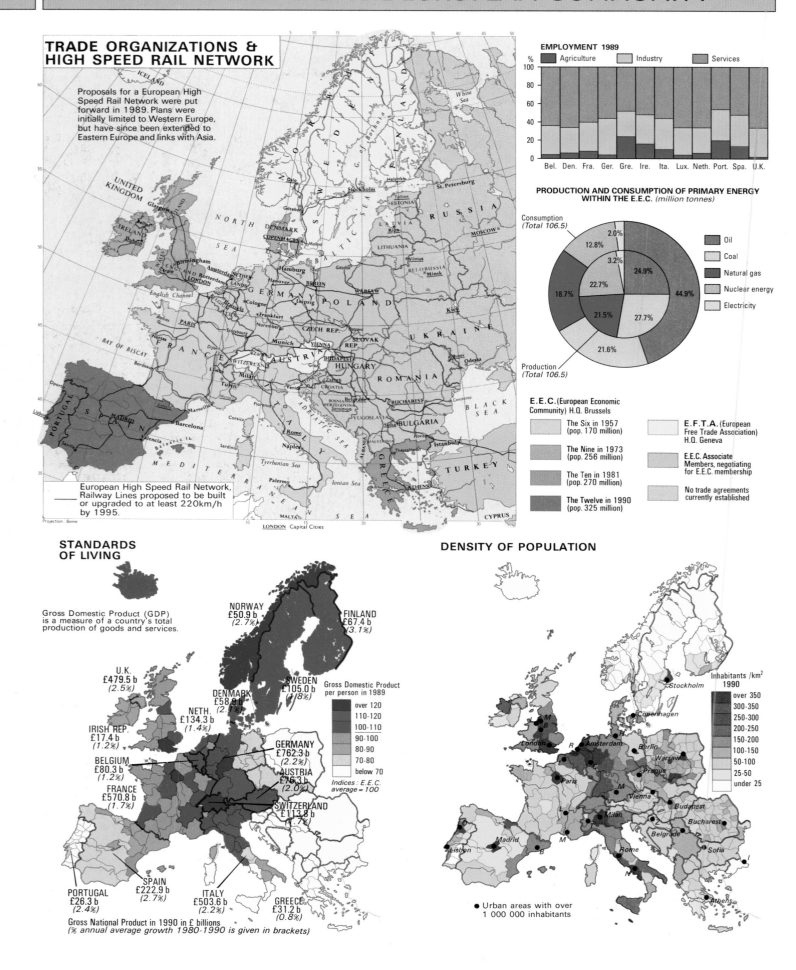

INDEX TO
BRITISH ISLES MAPS

This index lists all the placenames which appear on the large-scale maps of the British Isles (pages 4 – 15 with the orange band). Placenames for the rest of the world can be found in the World Index, with the turquoise band.

The first number beside each name in the index gives the map page on which that feature or place will be found. The letter and figure immediately after the page number give the grid square within which the feature is situated. The letter represents the latitude and the figure the longitude. In some cases the feature may fall within the specified square, while the name is outside. This is usually the case only with very large features. Rivers are indexed to their mouths or confluence.

The 'geographical co-ordinates' which follow the letter-figure references give the latitude and longitude of each place. The first co-ordinate indicates latitude – the distance north of the Equator. The second co-ordinate indicates longitude – the distance east or west of the Greenwich Meridian. Both latitude and longitude are measured in degrees and minutes (there are 60 minutes in a degree).

Thus the entry in the index for Runcorn reads:
Runcorn...........................8 **C3** 53 20N 2 44W
This indicates that Runcorn appears on map page 8 in grid square C3 at latitude 53 degrees, 20 minutes north and at longitude 2 degrees, 44 minutes west. To find Runcorn by using the geographical co-ordinates, look at the edges of the map. The degrees of latitude are indicated by blue figures on the left-hand edge of the map and the degrees of longitude are marked on the bottom edge of the map. The minutes can be calculated using the minute scales which are provided in the margin at the bottom and the side of the page. Runcorn will be found where lines extended from the two points on the map edge would cross on the map.

An open square □ indicates that the name refers to an administrative unit such as a county or region; rivers are indicated by an arrow ⤳. Names composed of a proper name (Wight) and a description (Isle of) are positioned alphabetically by the proper name. All names beginning St. are alphabetized under Saint. A list of abbreviations used can be found in the World Index at the end of the atlas.

A

Place	Ref	Lat	Long
Abbey Town	8 B2	54 50N	3 18W
Abbots Bromley	4 A3	52 50N	1 52W
Abbots Langley	5 B4	51 43N	0 25W
Abbotsbury	4 C2	50 40N	2 36W
Aberaeron	7 B2	52 15N	4 16W
Aberayron =			
Aberaeron	7 B2	52 15N	4 16W
Aberdare	7 C3	51 43N	3 27W
Aberdeen	13 D6	57 9N	2 6W
Aberdovey =			
Aberdyfi	7 B2	52 33N	4 3W
Aberdyfi	7 B2	52 33N	4 3W
Aberfeldy	13 E5	56 37N	3 50W
Abergavenny	7 C3	51 49N	3 1W
Aberystwyth	7 B2	52 25N	4 6W
Abingdon	4 B3	51 40N	1 17W
Aboyne	13 D6	57 4N	2 48W
Accrington	8 C3	53 46N	2 22W
Achill	14 C2	53 56N	9 55W
Achill Hd.	14 C1	53 59N	10 15W
Achill I.	14 C1	53 58N	10 5W
Achill Sd.	14 C2	53 53N	9 55W
Acle	5 A6	52 38N	1 32 E
Acton Burnell	4 A2	52 37N	2 41W
Addlestone	5 B4	51 22N	0 30W
Adlington	8 C3	53 36N	2 36W
Adwick le Street	9 C4	53 35N	1 12W
Ailsa Craig	10 B3	55 15N	5 7W
Ainsdale	8 C2	53 37N	3 2W
Airdrie	11 B5	55 53N	3 57W
Aire ⤳	9 C5	53 42N	0 55W
Aisgill	8 B3	54 23N	2 21W
Albrighton	4 A2	52 38N	2 17W
Alcester	4 A3	52 13N	1 52W
Aldborough	9 B4	54 6N	1 21W
Aldbourne	4 B3	51 28N	1 38W
Aldbrough	9 C5	53 50N	0 7W
Aldeburgh	5 A6	52 9N	1 35 E
Alderley Edge	8 C3	53 18N	2 15W
Alderbury	4 B3	51 4N	1 45W
Aldershot	5 B4	51 15N	0 43W
Aldingham	8 B2	54 8N	3 3W
Aldridge	4 A3	52 36N	1 55W
Alford, Gramp.	13 D6	57 13N	2 42W
Alford, Lincs.	9 C6	53 16N	0 10 E
Alfreton	9 C4	53 6N	1 22W
Alfriston	5 C5	50 48N	0 10 E
Allen, Bog of	15 C5	53 15N	7 0W
Allen, L.	14 B3	54 12N	8 5W
Alloa	11 A5	56 7N	3 49W
Allonby	8 B2	54 45N	3 27W
Almondsbury	4 B2	51 33N	2 34W
Alnwick	9 A4	55 25N	1 42W
Alrewas	4 A3	52 43N	1 44W
Alsager	8 C3	53 7N	2 20W
Alston	8 B3	54 48N	2 26W
Alton	5 B4	51 8N	0 59W
Altrincham	8 C3	53 25N	2 21W
Alvechurch	4 A3	52 22N	1 58W
Alyth	13 E5	56 38N	3 15W
Ambleside	8 B3	54 26N	2 58W
Amersham	5 B4	51 40N	0 38W
Amesbury	4 B3	51 10N	1 46W
Amlwch	7 A2	53 24N	4 21W
Ammanford	7 C2	51 48N	4 4W
Ampleforth	9 B4	54 13N	1 8W
Ampthill	5 A4	52 3N	0 30W
An Uaimh	14 C5	53 39N	6 40W
Ancaster	9 D5	52 59N	0 32W
Ancholme ⤳	9 C5	53 42N	0 32W
Andover	4 B3	51 13N	1 29W
Andreas	8 B1	54 23N	4 25W
Anglesey	7 A2	53 17N	4 20W
Angmering	5 C4	50 48N	0 28W
Angus, Braes of	13 E5	56 51N	3 10W
Annalee ⤳	14 B4	54 3N	7 15W
Annan	11 C5	54 57N	3 17W
Annan ⤳	11 C5	54 58N	3 18W
Annfield Plain	9 B4	54 52N	1 45W
Anstey	4 A3	52 41N	1 14W
Anstruther	11 A6	56 14N	2 40W
Antrim	14 B5	54 43N	6 13W
Antrim □	14 B5	54 55N	6 20W
Antrim, Mts. of	14 B5	54 57N	6 8W
Appleby	8 B3	54 35N	2 29W
Appledore	5 B5	51 2N	0 47 E
Aran I.	14 B3	55 0N	8 30W
Aran Is.	15 C2	53 5N	9 42W
Arbroath	13 E6	56 34N	2 35W
Ardee	14 C5	53 51N	6 32W
Ardgour	12 E3	56 45N	5 25W
Ardingly	5 B4	51 3N	0 3W
Ardnacrusha	15 D3	52 43N	8 38W
Ardnamurchan, Pt. of	12 E2	56 44N	6 14W
Ardrossan	10 B4	55 39N	4 50W
Ards □	14 B6	54 35N	5 30W
Ards Pen.	14 B6	54 30N	5 25W
Arisaig	12 E3	56 55N	5 50W
Arkaig, L.	12 E3	56 58N	5 10W
Arkle ⤳	8 B4	54 25N	1 55W
Arklow	15 D5	52 48N	6 10W
Armagh	14 B5	54 22N	6 40W
Armagh □	14 B5	54 18N	6 37W
Armthorpe	9 C4	53 32N	1 3W
Arnold	9 C4	53 0N	1 8W
Arnside	8 B3	54 12N	2 49W
Arran	10 B3	55 34N	5 12W
Arrow, L.	14 B3	54 3N	8 20W
Arun ⤳	5 C4	50 48N	0 33W
Arundel	5 C4	50 52N	0 32W
Ascot	5 B4	51 24N	0 41W
Asfordby	5 A4	52 45N	0 57W
Ash, Kent	5 B6	51 17N	1 16 E
Ash, Surrey	5 B4	51 14N	0 43W
Ashbourne	9 C4	53 2N	1 44W
Ashby de la Zouch	4 A3	52 45N	1 29W
Ashchurch	4 B2	52 0N	2 7W
Ashdown Forest	5 B5	51 4N	0 2 E
Ashford, Derby	9 C4	53 13N	1 43W
Ashford, Kent	5 B5	51 8N	0 53 E
Ashton-in-Makerfield	8 C3	53 29N	2 39W
Ashton under Lyne	8 C3	53 30N	2 8W
Ashurst	4 C3	50 53N	1 31W
Ashurstwood	5 B5	51 6N	0 2 E
Ashwell	5 A4	52 2N	0 9W
Ashwick	4 B2	51 13N	2 31W
Askrigg	8 B3	54 19N	2 6W
Aslackby	9 D5	52 53N	0 23W
Aspatria	8 B2	54 45N	3 20W
Assynt, L.	12 C3	58 25N	5 15W
Aston Clinton	5 B4	51 48N	0 44W
Astwood Bank	4 A3	52 15N	1 55W
Athboy	14 C5	53 37N	6 55W
Athenry	15 C3	53 18N	8 45W
Atherstone	4 A3	52 35N	1 32W
Atherton	8 C3	53 32N	2 30W
Athlone	14 C4	53 26N	7 57W
Atholl, Forest of	13 E5	56 51N	3 3W
Athy	15 D5	53 0N	7 0W
Attleborough	5 A6	52 32N	1 1 E
Audlem	8 D3	52 59N	2 31W
Austwick	8 B3	54 6N	2 21W
Avebury	4 B3	51 25N	1 52W
Avoca	15 D5	52 52N	6 13W
Avon □	4 B2	51 30N	2 40W
Avon ⤳, Avon	4 B2	51 30N	2 43W
Avon ⤳, Hants.	4 C3	50 44N	1 45W
Avon ⤳, Warks.	4 B2	51 57N	2 9W
Avonmouth	4 B2	51 30N	2 42W
Awe, L.	10 A3	56 15N	5 15W
Axbridge	4 B2	51 17N	2 50W
Axe ⤳	4 B2	51 17N	2 52W
Axe Edge	8 C4	53 14N	1 59W
Axholme, Isle of	9 C5	53 30N	0 55W
Axminster	6 B4	50 47N	3 1W
Aylesbury	5 B4	51 48N	0 49W
Aylesford	5 B5	51 18N	0 29 E
Aylesham	5 B6	51 14N	1 12 E
Aylsham	5 A6	52 48N	1 16 E
Aynho	4 B3	51 59N	1 15W
Ayr	10 B4	55 28N	4 37W
Ayr ⤳	10 B4	55 29N	4 40W
Ayre, Pt. of	8 B1	54 27N	4 21W
Aysgarth	8 B4	54 18N	2 0W
Ayton	9 B5	54 15N	0 29W

B

Place	Ref	Lat	Long
Bacton	5 A6	52 50N	1 29 E
Bacup	8 C3	53 42N	2 12W
Badenoch	13 E4	56 59N	4 15W
Bagenalstown = Muine Bheag	15 D5	52 42N	6 57W

34
INDEX TO BRITISH ISLES MAPS
Bagshot — Carrickmacross

Bagshot **5 B4** 51 22N 0 41W
Baildon **9 C4** 53 52N 1 46W
Baile Atha Cliath = Dublin **14 C5** 53 20N 6 18W
Bain → **9 C5** 53 10N 0 15W
Bainbridge **8 B3** 54 18N 2 7W
Bakewell **9 C4** 53 13N 1 40W
Bala, L. **7 B3** 52 53N 3 38W
Balbriggan **14 C5** 53 35N 6 10W
Balcombe **5 B4** 51 4N 0 8W
Balderton **9 C5** 53 3N 0 46W
Baldock **5 B4** 51 59N 0 11W
Ballachulish **12 E3** 56 40N 5 10W
Ballasalla **8 B1** 54 7N 4 36W
Ballater **13 D5** 57 2N 3 2W
Ballaugh **8 B1** 54 20N 4 32W
Ballina, *Mayo* **14 B2** 54 7N 9 10W
Ballina, *Tipp.* **15 D3** 52 49N 8 27W
Ballinasloe **15 C3** 53 20N 8 12W
Ballinrobe **14 C2** 53 36N 9 13W
Ballinskelligs B. **15 E1** 51 46N 10 11W
Ballycastle **14 A5** 55 12N 6 15W
Ballymena **14 B5** 54 53N 6 18W
Ballymena □ **14 B5** 54 53N 6 18W
Ballymoney **14 A5** 55 5N 6 30W
Ballymoney □ **14 A5** 55 5N 6 23W
Ballyshannon **14 B3** 54 30N 8 10W
Balmoral **13 D5** 57 3N 3 13W
Baltimore **15 E2** 51 29N 9 22W
Bamber Bridge **8 C3** 53 44N 2 39W
Bamford **9 C4** 53 21N 1 41W
Bampton **4 B3** 51 44N 1 33W
Banbridge **14 B5** 54 21N 6 17W
Banbridge □ **14 B5** 54 21N 6 16W
Banbury **4 A3** 52 4N 1 21W
Banchory **13 D6** 57 3N 2 30W
Bandon **15 E3** 51 44N 8 45W
Bandon → **15 E3** 51 40N 8 41W
Banff **13 D6** 57 40N 2 32W
Bangor, *Down* **14 B6** 54 40N 5 40W
Bangor, *Gwynedd* **7 A2** 53 13N 4 9W
Banham **5 A6** 52 27N 1 3 E
Bann →, *Down* **14 B5** 54 30N 6 31W
Bann →, *L'derry.* **14 A5** 55 10N 6 34W
Bannockburn **11 A5** 56 5N 3 55W
Banstead **5 B4** 51 19N 0 10W
Bantry **15 E2** 51 40N 9 28W
Bantry B. **15 E2** 51 35N 9 50W
Banwell **4 B2** 51 19N 2 51W
Bar Hill **5 A5** 52 15N 0 2 E
Bardney **9 C5** 53 13N 0 19W
Bardsey I. **7 B2** 52 46N 4 47W
Barford **4 A3** 52 15N 1 35W
Barham **5 B6** 51 12N 1 10 E
Barking **5 B5** 51 31N 0 10 E
Barlborough **9 C4** 53 17N 1 17W
Barlby **9 C4** 53 48N 1 3W
Barmby Moor **9 C5** 53 55N 0 47W
Barmouth **7 B2** 52 44N 4 3W
Barnard Castle **8 B4** 54 33N 1 55W
Barnet **5 B4** 51 37N 0 15W
Barnetby le Wold **9 C5** 53 34N 0 24W
Barnoldswick **8 C3** 53 55N 2 11W
Barnsley **9 C4** 53 33N 1 29W
Barnstaple **6 A3** 51 5N 4 3W
Barra **12 D1** 57 0N 7 30W
Barra, Sd. of **12 D1** 57 4N 7 25W
Barra Hd. **12 E1** 56 47N 7 40W
Barrow → **15 D5** 52 10N 6 57W
Barrow-in-Furness **8 B2** 54 8N 3 15W
Barrow upon Humber **9 C5** 53 41N 0 22W
Barrowford **8 C3** 53 51N 2 14W
Barry **7 C3** 51 23N 3 19W
Barton **9 B4** 54 28N 1 38W
Barton upon Humber **9 C5** 53 41N 0 27W
Barwell **4 A3** 52 35N 1 22W
Basildon **5 B5** 51 34N 0 29 E
Basingstoke **4 B3** 51 15N 1 5W
Bass Rock **11 A6** 56 5N 2 40W
Bassenthwaite L. **8 B2** 54 40N 3 14W
Baston **5 A4** 52 43N 0 19W
Bath **4 B2** 51 22N 2 22W
Bathford **4 B2** 51 23N 2 18W
Bathgate **11 B5** 55 54N 3 38W
Batley **9 C4** 53 43N 1 38W
Battle **5 C5** 50 55N 0 30 E
Bawdsey **5 A6** 52 1N 1 27 E
Bawtry **9 C4** 53 25N 1 1W
Beachley **4 B2** 51 37N 2 39W
Beachy Hd. **5 C5** 50 44N 0 16 E
Beaconsfield **5 B4** 51 36N 0 39W
Beaminster **4 C2** 50 48N 2 44W
Bear I. **15 E2** 51 38N 9 50W
Bearsted **5 B5** 51 15N 0 35 E
Beaulieu **4 C3** 50 49N 1 27W
Beauly **13 D4** 57 29N 4 27W
Beauly → **13 D4** 57 26N 4 28W
Beaumaris **7 A2** 53 16N 4 7W
Bebington **8 C2** 53 23N 3 1W
Beccles **5 A6** 52 27N 1 33 E
Beckermet **8 B2** 54 26N 3 31W
Beckfoot **8 B2** 54 50N 3 25W
Beckingham **9 C5** 53 24N 0 49W
Bedale **9 B4** 54 18N 1 35W
Bedford **5 A4** 52 8N 0 29W
Bedford Level **5 A5** 52 25N 0 5 E
Bedfordshire □ **5 A4** 52 4N 0 28W
Bedworth **4 A3** 52 28N 1 29W
Beeford **9 C5** 53 58N 0 18W
Beeston **9 D4** 52 55N 1 11W
Beighton **9 C4** 53 21N 1 21W
Belbroughton **4 A2** 52 23N 2 5W
Belfast **14 B6** 54 35N 5 56W
Belfast □ **14 B6** 54 35N 5 56W
Belfast L. **14 B6** 54 40N 5 50W
Belmullet **14 B2** 54 13N 9 58W
Belper **9 C4** 53 2N 1 29W
Belton, *Humber.* **9 C5** 53 33N 0 49W
Belton, *Norfolk* **5 A6** 52 35N 1 39 E
Belturbet **14 B4** 54 6N 7 28W
Bembridge **4 C3** 50 41N 1 4W
Ben Cruachan **10 A3** 56 26N 5 8W
Ben Dearg **13 D4** 57 47N 4 58W
Ben Hope **13 C4** 58 24N 4 36W
Ben Lawers **13 E4** 56 33N 4 13W
Ben Lomond **10 A4** 56 12N 4 39W
Ben Macdhui **13 D5** 57 4N 3 40W
Ben Mhor **12 D1** 57 16N 7 21W
Ben More, *Central* **10 A4** 56 23N 4 31W
Ben More, *Strath.* **10 A2** 56 26N 6 2W
Ben More Assynt **13 C4** 58 7N 4 51W
Ben Nevis **12 E4** 56 48N 4 58W
Ben Vorlich **10 A4** 56 22N 4 15W
Ben Wyvis **13 D4** 57 40N 4 35W
Benbecula **12 D1** 57 26N 7 21W
Benington **9 D6** 52 59N 0 5 E
Benson **4 B3** 51 37N 1 6W
Bentley, *Hants.* **5 B4** 51 12N 0 52W
Bentley, *S. Yorks.* **9 C4** 53 33N 1 9W
Bere Regis **4 C2** 50 45N 2 13W
Berkeley **4 B2** 51 41N 2 28W
Berkhamsted **5 B4** 51 45N 0 33W
Berkshire □ **4 B3** 51 30N 1 20W
Berkshire Downs **4 B3** 51 30N 1 30W
Berwick-upon-Tweed **9 A4** 55 47N 2 0W
Berwyn Mts. **7 B3** 52 54N 3 26W
Beverley **9 C5** 53 52N 0 26W
Bewdley **4 A2** 52 23N 2 19W
Bexhill **5 C5** 50 51N 0 29 E
Bexley **5 B5** 51 26N 0 10 E
Bibury **4 B3** 51 46N 1 50W
Bicester **4 B3** 51 53N 1 9W
Bicton **4 A2** 52 43N 2 47W
Biddenden **5 B5** 51 7N 0 40 E
Biddulph **8 C3** 53 8N 2 11W
Bideford **6 A3** 51 1N 4 13W
Bidford-on-Avon **4 A3** 52 9N 1 53W
Biggar **11 B5** 55 38N 3 31W
Biggleswade **5 A4** 52 6N 0 16W
Billericay **5 B5** 51 38N 0 25 E
Billesdon **5 A4** 52 38N 0 56W
Billingham **9 B4** 54 36N 1 18W
Billinghay **9 C5** 53 5N 0 17W
Billingshurst **5 B4** 51 2N 0 28W
Bilston **4 A2** 52 34N 2 5W
Binbrook **9 C5** 53 26N 0 9W
Bingham **9 D5** 52 57N 0 55W
Bingley **8 C4** 53 51N 1 50W
Birch **5 B5** 51 50N 0 54 E
Birchington **5 B6** 51 22N 1 18 E
Birdlip **4 B2** 51 50N 2 7W
Birkdale **8 C2** 53 38N 3 2W
Birkenhead **8 C2** 53 24N 3 1W
Birmingham **4 A3** 52 30N 1 55W
Birr **15 C4** 53 7N 7 55W
Bishop Auckland **9 B4** 54 40N 1 40W
Bishop's Castle **4 A2** 52 29N 3 0W
Bishop's Cleeve **4 B2** 51 56N 2 3W
Bishop's Frome **4 A2** 52 8N 2 29W
Bishop's Lydeard **4 B1** 51 4N 3 12W
Bishop's Stortford **5 B5** 51 52N 0 11 E
Bishop's Waltham **4 C3** 50 57N 1 13W
Bishopstoke **4 C3** 50 58N 1 19W
Bitton **4 B2** 51 25N 2 27W
Blaby **4 A3** 52 34N 1 10W
Black Combe **8 B2** 54 16N 3 20W
Black Mt. = Mynydd Du **7 C3** 51 45N 3 45W
Black Mts. **7 C3** 51 52N 3 5W
Blackburn **8 C3** 53 44N 2 30W
Blackdown Hills **4 C1** 50 57N 3 15W
Blackmoor Vale **4 C2** 50 54N 2 28W
Blackpool **8 C2** 53 48N 3 3W
Blacksod B. **14 B2** 54 6N 10 0W
Blackwater →, *Essex* **5 B5** 51 44N 0 53 E
Blackwater →, *Munst.* **15 E4** 51 55N 7 50W
Blackwater →, *Tyrone* **14 B5** 54 31N 6 35W
Blaenau Ffestiniog **7 B3** 52 59N 3 57W
Blagdon **4 B2** 51 19N 2 42W
Blair Atholl **13 E5** 56 46N 3 50W
Blairgowrie **13 E5** 56 36N 3 20W
Blakeney, *Gloucs.* **4 B2** 51 45N 2 29W
Blakeney, *Norfolk* **5 A6** 52 57N 1 1 E
Blandford Forum **4 C2** 50 52N 2 10W
Blarney **15 E3** 51 57N 8 35W
Blaydon **9 B4** 54 56N 1 47W
Bleadon **4 B2** 51 18N 2 57W
Blean **5 B6** 51 18N 1 3 E
Bleasdale Moors **8 C3** 53 57N 2 40W
Bletchingdon **4 B3** 51 51N 1 16W
Bletchley **5 B4** 51 59N 0 44W
Blewbury **4 B3** 51 33N 1 14W
Blidworth **9 C4** 53 6N 1 6W
Blisworth **5 A4** 52 11N 0 56W
Blockley **4 A3** 52 1N 1 45W
Blofield **5 A6** 52 38N 1 25 E
Bloody Foreland **14 A3** 55 10N 8 18W
Bloxham **4 A3** 52 1N 1 22W
Blue Stack Mts. **14 B3** 54 46N 8 5W
Blundeston **5 A6** 52 33N 1 42 E
Blyth, *Northumb.* **9 A4** 55 8N 1 32W
Blyth, *Notts.* **9 C4** 53 22N 1 2W
Blyth Bridge **8 D3** 52 58N 2 4W
Blyton **9 C5** 53 25N 0 42W
Bodenham **4 A2** 52 9N 2 41W
Bodiam **5 B5** 51 1N 0 33 E
Bodmin **6 B3** 50 28N 4 44W
Bodmin Moor **6 B3** 50 33N 4 36W
Boggeragh Mts. **15 D3** 52 2N 8 55W
Bognor Regis **5 C4** 50 47N 0 40W
Bollington **8 C3** 53 18N 2 8W
Bolney **5 C4** 51 0N 0 12W
Bolsover **9 C4** 53 14N 1 18W
Bolton **8 C3** 53 35N 2 26W
Bolton Abbey **8 C4** 53 59N 1 53W
Bolton by Bowland **8 C3** 53 56N 2 21W
Bolton le Sands **8 B3** 54 7N 2 49W
Bonchurch **4 C3** 50 36N 1 11W
Bo'ness **11 A5** 56 0N 3 38W
Boot **8 B2** 54 24N 3 18W
Bootle, *Cumb.* **8 B2** 54 17N 3 24W
Bootle, *Mersey.* **8 C2** 53 28N 3 1W
Borders □ **11 B6** 55 35N 2 50W
Bordon **5 B4** 51 6N 0 52W
Borehamwood **5 B4** 51 40N 0 15W
Boroughbridge **9 B4** 54 6N 1 23W
Borrowdale **8 B2** 54 31N 3 10W
Borth **7 B2** 52 29N 4 3W
Bosbury **4 A2** 52 5N 2 27W
Boscastle **6 B3** 50 42N 4 42W
Bosham **5 C4** 50 50N 0 51W
Boston **9 D5** 52 59N 0 2W
Bothel **8 B2** 54 43N 3 16W
Botley **4 B3** 51 45N 1 18W
Bottesford **9 D5** 52 57N 0 48W
Bourne **5 A4** 52 46N 0 22W
Bourne End **5 B4** 51 34N 0 42W
Bournemouth **4 C3** 50 43N 1 53W
Bourton-on-the-Water **4 B3** 51 53N 1 45W
Bovingdon **5 B4** 51 43N 0 32W
Bowes **8 B4** 54 31N 1 59W
Bowland, Forest of **8 C3** 54 0N 2 30W
Bowmore **10 B2** 55 45N 6 18W
Bowness-on-Solway **8 B2** 54 57N 3 13W
Bowness-on-Windermere **8 B3** 54 22N 2 56W
Box **4 B2** 51 24N 2 16W
Box Hill **5 B4** 51 16N 0 16W
Boxley **5 B5** 51 17N 0 34 E
Boyle **14 C3** 53 58N 8 19W
Boyne → **14 C5** 53 43N 6 15W
Bozeat **5 A4** 52 14N 0 41W
Brabourne Lees **5 B5** 51 8N 0 59 E
Bracadale, L. **12 D2** 57 20N 6 30W
Bracebridge Heath **9 C5** 53 13N 0 32W
Brackley **4 A3** 52 3N 1 9W
Bracknell **5 B4** 51 24N 0 45W
Bradda Hd. **8 B1** 54 6N 4 46W
Bradford **9 C4** 53 47N 1 45W
Bradford on Avon **4 B2** 51 20N 2 15W
Brading **4 C3** 50 41N 1 9W
Bradwell-on-Sea **5 B5** 51 44N 0 55 E
Braich-y-pwll **7 B2** 52 47N 4 46W
Brailsford **9 D4** 52 58N 1 35W
Braintree **5 B5** 51 53N 0 34 E
Bramford **5 A6** 52 5N 1 6 E
Bramley **5 B4** 51 11N 0 33W
Brampton, *Cambs.* **5 A4** 52 19N 0 13W
Brampton, *Cumb.* **8 B3** 54 56N 2 43W
Bramshott **5 B4** 51 5N 0 47W
Brancaster **5 A5** 52 58N 0 40 E
Brandon, *Durham* **9 B4** 54 46N 1 37W
Brandon, *Suffolk* **5 A5** 52 27N 0 37 E
Brandon B. **15 D1** 52 17N 10 8W
Brandon Mt. **15 D1** 52 15N 10 15W
Branston **9 C5** 53 13N 0 28W
Brasted **5 B5** 51 16N 0 8 E
Braunton **6 A3** 51 6N 4 9W
Bray, *Berks.* **5 B4** 51 30N 0 42W
Bray, *Dublin* **15 C5** 53 12N 6 6W
Breadalbane **10 A4** 56 30N 4 15W
Brechin **13 E6** 56 44N 2 40W
Breckland **5 A5** 52 30N 0 40 E
Brecon **7 C3** 51 57N 3 23W
Brecon Beacons **7 C3** 51 53N 3 27W
Brede **5 C5** 50 56N 0 37 E
Bredon Hill **4 A2** 52 3N 2 2W
Brendon Hills **4 B1** 51 6N 3 25W
Brent **5 B4** 51 33N 0 18W
Brentwood **5 B5** 51 37N 0 19 E
Bressay **12 A8** 60 10N 1 5W
Brewood **4 A2** 52 41N 2 10W
Bride **8 B1** 54 24N 4 23W
Bridge **5 B6** 51 14N 1 8 E
Bridgend **7 C3** 51 30N 3 35W
Bridgnorth **4 A2** 52 33N 2 25W
Bridgwater **4 B1** 51 7N 3 0W
Bridgwater B. **4 B1** 51 15N 3 15W
Bridlington **9 B5** 54 6N 0 11W
Bridlington B. **9 B5** 54 4N 0 10W
Bridport **4 C2** 50 43N 2 45W
Brierfield **8 C3** 53 49N 2 15W
Brierley Hill **4 A2** 52 29N 2 7W
Brigg **9 C5** 53 33N 0 30W
Brighouse **9 C4** 53 42N 1 47W
Brighstone **4 C3** 50 38N 1 23W
Brightlingsea **5 B6** 51 49N 1 1 E
Brighton **5 C4** 50 50N 0 9W
Brigstock **5 A4** 52 27N 0 38W
Brill **4 B3** 51 49N 1 3W
Brimfield **4 A2** 52 18N 2 42W
Brinklow **4 A3** 52 25N 1 22W
Brinkworth **4 B3** 51 33N 1 59W
Bristol **4 B2** 51 26N 2 35W
Bristol Channel **6 A3** 51 18N 4 30W
Briston **5 A6** 52 52N 1 4 E
Brixworth **5 A4** 52 20N 0 54W
Brize Norton **4 B3** 51 46N 1 35W
Broad B. **12 C2** 58 14N 6 16W
Broad Chalke **4 B3** 51 2N 1 54W
Broad Haven **14 B2** 54 20N 9 55W
Broad Law **11 B5** 55 30N 3 22W
Broads, The **5 A6** 52 45N 1 30 E
Broadstairs **5 B6** 51 21N 1 28 E
Broadway **4 A3** 52 2N 1 51W
Broadwey **4 C2** 50 57N 2 27W
Broadwindsor **4 C2** 50 49N 2 49W
Brockenhurst **4 C3** 50 49N 1 34W
Brockworth **4 B2** 51 51N 2 9W
Brodick **10 B3** 55 34N 5 9W
Bromborough **8 C3** 53 20N 3 0W
Bromfield **4 A2** 52 25N 2 45W
Bromham **4 B2** 51 23N 2 3W
Bromley **5 B5** 51 20N 0 5 E
Brompton **9 B4** 54 22N 1 25W
Bromsgrove **4 A2** 52 20N 2 3W
Bromyard **4 A2** 52 12N 2 30W
Broom, L. **12 D3** 57 55N 5 15W
Brora **13 C5** 58 3N 3 50W
Brora → **13 C5** 58 4N 3 52W
Broseley **4 A2** 52 36N 2 30W
Brosna → **15 C4** 53 8N 8 0W
Brothertoft **9 C5** 53 0N 0 5W
Brotton **9 B5** 54 34N 0 55W
Brough, *Cumb.* **8 B3** 54 32N 2 19W
Brough, *Humber.* **9 C5** 53 44N 0 35W
Broughton, *Humber.* **9 C5** 53 33N 0 36W
Broughton, *N. Yorks.* **9 B4** 54 26N 1 8W
Broughton, *Northants.* **5 A4** 52 22N 0 45W
Broughton-in-Furness **8 B2** 54 17N 3 12W
Broughty Ferry **11 A6** 56 29N 2 50W
Brown Willy **6 B3** 50 35N 4 34W
Brownhills **4 A3** 52 38N 1 57W
Brue → **4 B2** 51 10N 2 59W
Brundall **5 A6** 52 37N 1 26 E
Bruton **4 B2** 51 6N 2 28W
Buchan **13 D6** 57 32N 2 8W
Buchan Ness **13 D7** 57 29N 1 48W
Buckden **5 A4** 52 17N 0 16W
Buckhaven **11 A5** 56 10N 3 2W
Buckie **13 D6** 57 40N 2 58W
Buckingham **5 B4** 52 0N 0 59W
Buckinghamshire □ **5 B4** 51 50N 0 55W
Bude **6 B3** 50 49N 4 33W
Bugbrooke **5 A3** 52 12N 1 0W
Buglawton **8 C3** 53 12N 2 11W
Builth Wells **7 B3** 52 10N 3 26W
Bulford **4 B3** 51 11N 1 45W
Bulkington **4 A3** 52 29N 1 25W
Bulwell **9 C4** 53 1N 1 12W
Buncrana **14 A4** 55 8N 7 28W
Bundoran **14 B3** 54 24N 8 17W
Bungay **5 A6** 52 27N 1 26 E
Buntingford **5 B4** 51 57N 0 1W
Bunwell **5 A6** 52 30N 1 9 E
Burbage, *Derby* **8 C4** 53 15N 1 55W
Burbage, *Leics.* **4 A3** 52 31N 1 20W
Burbage, *Wilts.* **4 B3** 51 21N 1 40W
Bure → **5 A6** 52 38N 1 45 E
Burford **4 B3** 51 48N 1 38W
Burgess Hill **5 C4** 50 57N 0 7W
Burgh le Marsh **9 C6** 53 10N 0 15 E
Burley, *Hants.* **4 C3** 50 49N 1 41W
Burley, *N. Yorks.* **9 C4** 53 55N 1 46W
Burnham, *Bucks.* **5 B4** 51 32N 0 40W
Burnham, *Somst.* **4 B1** 51 14N 3 0W
Burnham Market **5 A5** 52 57N 0 43 E
Burnham-on-Crouch **5 B5** 51 37N 0 50 E
Burnley **8 C3** 53 47N 2 15W
Burntwood **4 A3** 52 41N 1 55W
Burry Port **7 C2** 51 41N 4 17W
Burscough Bridge **8 C3** 53 36N 2 52W
Burstwick **9 C5** 53 43N 0 6W
Burton **8 B3** 54 10N 2 43W
Burton Agnes **9 B5** 54 4N 0 18W
Burton Bradstock **4 C2** 50 41N 2 43W
Burton Fleming **9 B5** 54 8N 0 20W
Burton Latimer **5 A4** 52 23N 0 41W
Burton upon Stather **9 C5** 53 39N 0 41W
Burton upon Trent **4 A3** 52 48N 1 39W
Burwash **5 C5** 50 59N 0 24 E
Burwell **5 A5** 52 17N 0 20 E
Bury **8 C3** 53 36N 2 19W
Bury St. Edmunds **5 A5** 52 15N 0 42 E
Bushey **5 B4** 51 38N 0 20W
Bute **10 B3** 55 48N 5 2W
Buttermere **8 B2** 54 32N 3 17W
Buxton **8 C4** 53 16N 1 54W
Byfield **4 A3** 52 10N 1 15W
Byfleet **5 B4** 51 20N 0 28W

C

Cader Idris **7 B3** 52 43N 3 56W
Caenby Corner **9 C5** 53 23N 0 32W
Caernarfon **7 A2** 53 8N 4 17W
Caernarfon B. **7 A2** 53 4N 4 40W
Caernarvon = Caernarfon **7 A2** 53 8N 4 17W
Caerphilly **7 C3** 51 34N 3 13W
Caha Mts. **15 E2** 51 45N 9 40W
Caher **15 D4** 52 23N 7 56W
Cahersiveen **15 E1** 51 57N 10 13W
Cahore Pt. **15 D5** 52 34N 6 11W
Cairn Gorm **13 D5** 57 7N 3 40W
Cairn Toul **13 D5** 57 3N 3 44W
Cairngorm Mts. **13 D5** 57 6N 3 42W
Caister-on-Sea **5 A6** 52 38N 1 43 E
Caistor **9 C5** 53 29N 0 20W
Caithness, Ord of **13 C5** 58 9N 3 37W
Caldbeck **8 B2** 54 45N 3 3W
Calder → **9 C4** 53 44N 1 21W
Calder Bridge **8 B2** 54 27N 3 31W
Caldew → **8 B3** 54 54N 2 59W
Calf of Man **8 B1** 54 3N 4 49W
Callan **15 D4** 52 33N 7 25W
Callander **10 A4** 56 15N 4 14W
Calne **4 B3** 51 26N 2 0W
Calshot **4 C3** 50 49N 1 18W
Cam → **5 A5** 52 21N 0 16 E
Camber **5 C5** 50 55N 0 47 E
Camberley **5 B4** 51 20N 0 44W
Camborne **6 B2** 50 13N 5 18W
Cambrian Mts. **7 B3** 52 25N 3 52W
Cambridge **5 A5** 52 13N 0 8 E
Cambridgeshire □ **5 A5** 52 12N 0 7 E
Camden **5 B4** 51 33N 0 10W
Campbeltown **10 B3** 55 25N 5 36W
Canna **12 D2** 57 3N 6 33W
Cannington **4 B1** 51 8N 3 4W
Cannock **4 A2** 52 42N 2 2W
Cannock Chase **4 A3** 52 43N 2 0W
Canterbury **5 B6** 51 17N 1 5 E
Canvey **5 B5** 51 32N 0 35 E
Capel **5 B4** 51 8N 0 18W
Capel St. Mary **5 A6** 52 0N 1 3 E
Cardiff **7 C3** 51 28N 3 11W
Cardigan **7 B2** 52 6N 4 41W
Cardigan B. **7 B2** 52 30N 4 30W
Cardington **5 A4** 52 7N 0 23W
Carisbrooke **4 C3** 50 42N 1 19W
Cark **8 B3** 54 11N 2 59W
Carleton Rode **5 A6** 52 30N 1 6 E
Carlingford, L. **14 B5** 54 2N 6 5W
Carlisle **8 B3** 54 54N 2 55W
Carlow **15 D5** 52 50N 6 58W
Carlow □ **15 D5** 52 43N 6 50W
Carlton **9 D4** 52 58N 1 6W
Carlton Colville **5 A6** 52 27N 1 41 E
Carlton Miniott **9 B4** 54 13N 1 22W
Carmarthen **7 C2** 51 52N 4 20W
Carmarthen B. **7 C2** 51 40N 4 30W
Carndonagh **14 A4** 55 15N 7 16W
Carnforth **8 B3** 54 8N 2 47W
Carnsore Pt. **15 D5** 52 10N 6 20W
Carrauntoohill **15 D2** 52 0N 9 49W
Carrick-on-Shannon **14 C3** 53 57N 8 7W
Carrick-on-Suir **15 D4** 52 22N 7 30W
Carrickfergus **14 B6** 54 43N 5 50W
Carrickfergus □ **14 B6** 54 43N 5 49W
Carrickmacross **14 C5** 53 58N 6 43W

35
Carron
Edmondbyers

Carron → 12 D3 57 30N 5 30W
Carron, L. 12 D3 57 22N 5 35W
Carse of Gowrie 11 A5 56 30N 3 10W
Carstairs 11 B5 55 42N 3 41W
Carterton 4 B3 51 45N 1 35W
Cartmel 8 B3 54 13N 2 57W
Cashel 15 D4 52 31N 7 53W
Castle Acre 5 A5 52 42N 0 42 E
Castle Cary 4 B2 51 5N 2 32W
Castle Donington 4 A3 52 50N 1 20W
Castle Douglas 11 C5 54 57N 3 57W
Castle Eden 9 B4 54 45N 1 20W
Castlebar 14 C2 53 52N 9 17W
Castleblaney 14 B5 54 7N 6 44W
Castleford 9 C4 53 43N 1 21W
Castlereagh 14 C3 53 47N 8 30W
Castlereagh □ 14 B6 54 33N 5 53W
Castleside 8 B4 54 50N 1 52W
Castleton, *Derby* 9 C4 53 20N 1 47W
Castleton, *N. Yorks.* 9 B5 54 27N 0 57W
Castletown 8 B1 54 4N 4 40W
Castletown Bearhaven 15 E2 51 40N 9 54W
Caterham 5 B4 51 16N 0 4W
Caton 8 B3 54 5N 2 41W
Catsfield 5 C5 50 53N 0 28 E
Catterick 9 B4 54 23N 1 38W
Catterick Camp 9 B4 54 22N 1 43W
Cavan 14 C4 54 0N 7 22W
Cavan □ 14 C4 53 58N 7 10W
Cawood 9 C4 53 50N 1 7W
Cawston 5 A6 52 47N 1 10 E
Ceanannus Mor 14 C5 53 42N 6 53W
Celbridge 15 C5 53 20N 6 33W
Central □ 10 A4 56 10N 4 30W
Cerne Abbas 4 C2 50 49N 2 29W
Chadwell St. Mary 5 B5 51 28N 0 22 E
Chale 4 C3 50 35N 1 19W
Chalfont St. Peter 5 B4 51 36N 0 33W
Chandler's Ford 4 C3 50 59N 1 23W
Chapel en le Frith 8 C4 53 19N 1 54W
Chapel St. Leonards 9 C6 53 13N 0 19 E
Chard 4 C2 50 52N 2 59W
Charing 5 B5 51 12N 0 49 E
Charlbury 4 B3 51 52N 1 29W
Charleville = Rath Luirc 15 D3 52 21N 8 40W
Charlton Kings 4 B2 51 52N 2 3W
Charlwood 5 B4 51 8N 0 12W
Charminster 4 C2 50 43N 2 28W
Charmouth 4 C2 50 45N 2 54W
Charnwood Forest 4 A3 52 43N 1 18W
Chartham 5 B6 51 14N 1 1 E
Chatham 5 B5 51 22N 0 32 E
Chatteris 5 A5 52 27N 0 3 E
Cheadle, *Gt. Man.* 8 C3 53 23N 2 14W
Cheadle, *Staffs.* 8 D4 52 59N 1 59W
Cheadle Hulme 8 C3 53 22N 2 12W
Cheddar 4 B2 51 16N 2 47W
Cheddleton 8 C3 53 5N 2 2W
Chelmarsh 4 A2 52 29N 2 25W
Chelmer → 5 B5 51 45N 0 42 E
Chelmsford 5 B5 51 44N 0 29 E
Cheltenham 4 B2 51 55N 2 5W
Cheriton 4 B3 51 3N 1 9W
Chertsey 5 B4 51 23N 0 30W
Cherwell → 4 B3 51 46N 1 18W
Chesham 5 B4 51 42N 0 36W
Cheshire □ 8 C3 53 14N 2 30W
Cheshunt 5 B4 51 42N 0 1W
Chesil Beach 4 C2 50 37N 2 33W
Chester 8 C3 53 12N 2 53W
Chester-le-Street 9 B4 54 53N 1 34W
Chesterfield 9 C4 53 14N 1 26W
Cheviot, The 9 A3 55 29N 2 8W
Cheviot Hills 9 A3 55 20N 2 30W
Chew Magna 4 B2 51 21N 2 37W
Chichester 5 C4 50 50N 0 47W
Chiddingfold 5 B4 51 6N 0 37W
Chilcompton 4 B2 51 16N 2 31W
Chilham 5 B5 51 15N 0 59 E
Chiltern Hills 5 B4 51 44N 0 42W
Chinnor 5 B4 51 41N 0 54W
Chippenham 4 B2 51 27N 2 7W
Chipping Campden 4 A3 52 4N 1 48W
Chipping Norton 4 B3 51 56N 1 32W
Chipping Ongar 5 B5 51 42N 0 11 E
Chipping Sodbury 4 B2 51 31N 2 23W
Chirbury 4 A1 52 35N 3 6W
Chiseldon 4 B3 51 30N 1 44W
Chobham 5 B4 51 20N 0 36W
Cholsey 4 B3 51 34N 1 10W
Chorley 8 C3 53 39N 2 39W
Chorleywood 5 B4 51 39N 0 29W
Christchurch 4 C3 50 44N 1 45W
Church Stretton 4 A2 52 32N 2 49W
Churchdown 4 B2 51 53N 2 9W
Cinderford 4 B2 51 49N 2 30W
Cirencester 4 B3 51 43N 1 59W
Clacton-on-Sea 5 B6 51 47N 1 10 E
Clanfield 5 C4 50 56N 0 59W
Clara 15 C4 53 20N 7 38W
Clare 5 A5 52 5N 0 36 E
Clare □ 15 D3 52 45N 9 0W
Clare → 14 C2 53 22N 9 5W
Clare I. 14 C1 53 48N 10 0W
Claremorris 14 C2 53 45N 9 0W
Claverley 4 A2 52 32N 2 19W
Clay Cross 9 C4 53 11N 1 26W
Clay Hd. 8 B1 54 13N 4 23W
Claydon 5 A6 52 6N 1 7 E
Clear, C. 15 E2 51 26N 9 30W
Clear I. 15 E2 51 26N 9 30W
Cleator Moor 8 B2 54 30N 3 32W
Clee Hills 4 A2 52 26N 2 35W
Cleethorpes 9 C5 53 33N 0 2W
Cleeve Cloud 4 B3 51 56N 2 0W
Clent 4 A2 52 25N 2 6W
Cleobury Mortimer 4 A2 52 23N 2 28W
Clevedon 4 B2 51 26N 2 52W
Cleveland □ 9 B7 54 35N 1 8 E
Cleveland Hills 9 B4 54 25N 1 11W
Clew B. 14 C2 53 54N 9 50W
Cley 5 A6 52 57N 1 3 E
Clifden 14 C1 53 30N 10 2W
Cliffe 5 B5 51 27N 0 31 E
Clifford 4 A1 52 6N 3 6W
Clipston 5 A4 52 26N 0 58W
Clitheroe 8 C3 53 52N 2 23W
Clonakilty 15 E3 51 37N 8 53W
Clonakilty B. 15 E3 51 33N 8 50W
Clones 14 B4 54 10N 7 13W
Clonmel 15 D4 52 22N 7 42W
Cloughton 9 B5 54 20N 0 27W
Clowne 9 C4 53 18N 1 16W
Clun 4 A1 52 26N 3 2W
Clun Forest 4 A1 52 27N 3 7W
Clunbury 4 A2 52 25N 2 55W
Clwyd □ 7 A3 53 5N 3 20W
Clwyd → 7 A3 53 20N 3 30W
Clyde → 10 B4 55 56N 4 29W
Clyde, Firth of 10 B4 55 20N 5 0W
Clydebank 10 B4 55 54N 4 25W
Coalbrookdale 4 A2 52 38N 2 30W
Coalville 4 A3 52 43N 1 21W
Coatbridge 11 B4 55 52N 4 2W
Cóbh 15 E3 51 50N 8 18W
Cockerham 8 C3 53 58N 2 49W
Cockermouth 8 B2 54 40N 3 22W
Cockfield 5 A5 52 8N 0 47 E
Coddenham 5 A6 52 8N 1 8 E
Coggeshall 5 B5 51 53N 0 41 E
Colby 8 B1 54 6N 4 42W
Colchester 5 B5 51 54N 0 55 E
Cold Fell 8 B3 54 54N 2 40W
Coldstream 11 B6 55 39N 2 14W
Coleford 4 B2 51 46N 2 38W
Coleraine 14 A5 55 8N 6 40W
Coleraine □ 14 A5 55 8N 6 40W
Coleshill 4 A3 52 30N 1 42W
Coll 10 A2 56 40N 6 35W
Collier Law 8 B4 54 47N 1 59W
Collingbourne 4 B3 51 16N 1 39W
Collingham 9 C4 53 54N 1 24W
Collooney 14 B3 54 11N 8 28W
Colne 8 C3 53 51N 2 11W
Colne →, *Essex* 5 B5 51 55N 0 50 E
Colne →, *Herts.* 5 B4 51 36N 0 30W
Colonsay 10 A2 56 4N 6 12W
Colstorworth 5 A4 52 48N 0 37W
Coltishall 5 A6 52 44N 1 21 E
Colwich 4 A3 52 48N 1 58W
Colwyn Bay 7 A3 53 17N 3 44W
Comeragh Mts. 15 D4 52 17N 7 35W
Condover 4 A2 52 39N 2 46W
Congleton 8 C3 53 10N 2 12W
Congresbury 4 B2 51 20N 2 49W
Coningsby 9 C5 53 7N 0 9W
Conisbrough 9 C4 53 29N 1 12W
Coniston 8 B2 54 22N 3 6W
Coniston Water 8 B2 54 20N 3 5W
Conn, L. 14 B2 54 3N 9 15W
Connacht 14 C3 53 23N 8 40W
Connemara 14 C2 53 29N 9 45W
Cononbridge 13 D4 57 32N 4 30W
Consett 8 B4 54 52N 1 50W
Conway = Conwy 7 A3 53 17N 3 50W
Conway = Conwy → 7 A3 53 18N 3 50W
Conwy 7 A3 53 17N 3 50W
Conwy → 7 A3 53 18N 3 50W
Cookham 5 B4 51 33N 0 42W
Cookstown 14 B5 54 40N 6 43W
Cookstown □ 14 B5 54 40N 6 43W
Cootehill 14 B4 54 5N 7 5W
Coppall 8 C3 53 37N 2 39W
Copythorne 4 C3 50 56N 1 34W
Coquet → 9 A4 55 18N 1 45W
Corby 5 A4 52 29N 0 41W
Corby Glen 5 A4 52 49N 0 31W
Corfe Castle 4 C2 50 37N 2 3W
Corfe Mullen 4 C2 50 45N 2 0W
Cork 15 E3 51 54N 8 30W
Cork □ 15 E3 51 50N 8 50W
Cork Harbour 15 E3 51 46N 8 16W
Cornforth 9 B4 54 42N 1 28W
Cornwall □ 6 B3 50 26N 4 40W
Corrib, L. 14 C2 53 5N 9 10W
Corringham, *Essex* 5 B5 51 30N 0 26 E
Corringham, *Lincs.* 9 C5 53 25N 0 42W
Corsham 4 B2 51 25N 2 11W
Corsley 4 B2 51 12N 2 14W
Corton 5 A6 52 31N 1 46 E
Corve → 4 A2 52 22N 2 43W
Coseley 4 A2 52 33N 2 6W
Cosham 4 C3 50 51N 1 3W
Costessey 5 A6 52 40N 1 11 E
Cotherstone 8 B4 54 34N 1 59W
Cotswold Hills 4 B2 51 42N 2 10W
Cottenham 5 A5 52 18N 0 8 E
Coventry 4 A3 52 25N 1 31W
Cover → 8 B4 54 14N 1 45W
Cowdenbeath 11 A5 56 7N 3 20W
Cowes 4 C3 50 45N 1 18W
Cowfold 5 C4 50 58N 0 16W
Cowley 4 B3 51 43N 1 12W
Craigavon = Lurgan 14 B5 54 28N 6 20W
Cranborne 4 C3 50 55N 1 55W
Cranborne Chase 4 C2 50 56N 2 6W
Cranbrook 5 B5 51 6N 0 33 E
Cranleigh 5 B4 51 8N 0 29W
Cranwell 9 C5 53 4N 0 29W
Craven Arms 4 A2 52 27N 2 49W
Crawley 5 B4 51 7N 0 10W
Credenhill 4 A2 52 6N 2 49W
Cree → 10 C4 54 51N 4 24W
Crewe 8 C3 53 6N 2 28W
Crewkerne 4 C2 50 53N 2 48W
Crick 4 A3 52 22N 1 9W
Cricklade 4 B3 51 38N 1 50W
Crieff 11 A5 56 22N 3 50W
Croaghpatrick 14 C2 53 46N 9 40W
Croglin 8 B3 54 50N 2 37W
Cromarty 13 D4 57 40N 4 2W
Cromer 5 A6 52 56N 1 18 E
Crondall 5 B4 51 13N 0 51W
Crook 9 B4 54 43N 1 45W
Crooklands 8 B3 54 16N 2 43W
Crosby, *Cumb.* 8 B2 54 45N 3 25W
Crosby, *Mersey.* 8 C2 53 30N 3 2W
Crosby Ravensworth 8 B3 54 34N 2 35W
Cross Fell 8 B3 54 44N 2 29W
Crosshaven 15 E3 51 48N 8 19W
Croston 8 C3 53 40N 2 46W
Crouch → 5 B5 51 37N 0 53 E
Crow Hd. 15 E1 51 34N 10 9W
Crowborough 5 B5 51 3N 0 9 E
Crowland 5 A4 52 41N 0 10W
Crowle 9 C5 53 36N 0 49W
Crowthorne 5 B4 51 22N 0 50W
Croydon 5 B4 51 18N 0 5W
Crudgington 4 A2 52 46N 2 33W
Crummock Water 8 B2 54 33N 3 18W
Cuckfield 5 C4 51 0N 0 8W
Cuffley 5 B4 51 43N 0 9W
Cuillin Hills 12 D2 57 14N 6 15W
Cuillin Sd. 12 D2 57 4N 6 20W
Cullen 13 D6 57 45N 2 50W
Culloden Moor 13 D4 57 29N 4 7W
Cumbria □ 8 B3 54 35N 2 55W
Cumbrian Mts. 8 B2 54 30N 3 0W
Cumnock 10 B4 55 27N 4 18W
Cumnor 4 B3 51 44N 1 20W
Cumwhinton 8 B3 54 51N 2 49W
Cupar 11 A5 56 20N 3 3W
Curry Rivel 4 B2 51 2N 2 52W
Cwmbran 7 C3 51 39N 3 3W

D

Daingean 15 C4 53 18N 7 15W
Dalbeattie 11 C5 54 55N 3 50W
Dalkeith 11 B5 55 54N 3 5W
Dalmellington 10 B4 55 20N 4 25W
Dalton 9 B4 54 28N 1 32W
Dalton-in-Furness 8 B2 54 9N 3 10W
Damerham 4 C3 50 57N 1 52W
Danbury 5 B5 51 43N 0 34 E
Darent → 5 B5 51 22N 0 12 E
Darlaston 4 A2 52 35N 2 1W
Darlington 9 B4 54 33N 1 33W
Dart → 6 B4 50 24N 3 36W
Dartford 5 B5 51 26N 0 15 E
Dartmoor 6 B4 50 36N 4 0W
Dartmouth 6 B4 50 21N 3 35W
Darton 9 C4 53 36N 1 32W
Darwen 8 C3 53 42N 2 29W
Daventry 4 A3 52 16N 1 10W
Dawley 4 A2 52 40N 2 29W
Deal 5 B6 51 13N 1 25 E
Dean, Forest of 4 B2 51 50N 2 35W
Dearham 8 B2 54 43N 3 28W
Dearne 9 C4 53 32N 1 17W
Deben → 5 A6 52 4N 1 19 E
Debenham 5 A6 52 14N 1 10 E
Deddington 4 B3 51 58N 1 19W
Dee →, *Clwyd* 7 A3 53 15N 3 7W
Dee →, *Gramp.* 13 D6 57 4N 2 7W
Deeping Fen 5 A4 52 45N 0 15W
Deeping St. Nicholas 5 A4 52 44N 0 11W
Denbigh 7 A3 53 12N 3 26W
Denby Dale 9 C4 53 35N 1 40W
Dent 8 B3 54 17N 2 28W
Denton, *E. Susx.* 5 C5 50 48N 0 5 E
Denton, *Gt. Man.* 8 C3 53 26N 2 10W
Denton, *Lincs.* 9 D5 52 52N 0 42W
Derby 9 D4 52 55N 1 28W
Derbyshire □ 9 D4 52 55N 1 28W
Derg → 14 B4 54 42N 7 26W
Derg, L. 15 D3 53 0N 8 20W
Derry = Londonderry 14 A4 55 0N 7 23W
Derryveagh Mts. 14 B3 55 0N 8 4W
Dersingham 5 A5 52 51N 0 30 E
Derwent →, *Cumb.* 8 B2 54 42N 3 22W
Derwent →, *Derby* 9 D4 52 53N 1 17W
Derwent →, *N. Yorks.* 9 C5 53 45N 0 57W
Derwent Water 8 B2 54 35N 3 9W
Desborough 5 A4 52 27N 0 50W
Desford 4 A3 52 38N 1 19W
Deveron → 13 D6 57 40N 2 31W
Devizes 4 B3 51 21N 2 0W
Devon □ 6 B4 50 50N 3 40W
Devonport 6 B3 50 23N 4 11W
Dewsbury 9 C4 53 42N 1 38W
Didcot 4 B3 51 36N 1 14W
Dingle 15 D1 52 9N 10 17W
Dingle B. 15 D1 52 3N 10 20W
Dingwall 13 D4 57 36N 4 26W
Dinnington 9 C4 53 21N 1 12W
Diss 5 A6 52 23N 1 6 E
Distington 8 B2 54 35N 3 33W
Ditchingham 5 A6 52 28N 1 26 E
Ditchling 5 C4 50 55N 0 6W
Ditchling Beacon 5 C4 50 49N 0 7W
Ditton Priors 4 A2 52 30N 2 33W
Docking 5 A5 52 55N 0 39 E
Doddington 5 A5 52 29N 0 3 E
Dolgellau 7 B3 52 44N 3 53W
Dolgelley = Dolgellau 7 B3 52 44N 3 53W
Don →, *Gramp.* 13 D6 57 14N 2 5W
Don →, *S. Yorks.* 9 C5 53 41N 0 51W
Donaghadee 14 B6 54 38N 5 32W
Doncaster 9 C4 53 31N 1 9W
Donegal 14 B3 54 39N 8 8W
Donegal □ 14 B3 54 53N 8 0W
Donegal B. 14 B3 54 30N 8 35W
Donhead 4 B2 51 1N 2 8W
Donington 9 D5 52 54N 0 12W
Donna Nook 9 C6 53 29N 0 9 E
Doon → 10 B4 55 26N 4 41W
Dorchester, *Dorset* 4 C2 50 42N 2 28W
Dorchester, *Oxon.* 4 B3 51 38N 1 10W
Dorking 5 B4 51 14N 0 20W
Dornoch 13 D4 57 52N 4 5W
Dornoch Firth 13 D4 57 52N 4 0W
Dorridge 4 A3 52 22N 1 45W
Dorset □ 4 C2 50 48N 2 25W
Dorstone 4 A2 52 4N 3 0W
Douglas 8 B1 54 9N 4 29W
Douglas Hd. 8 B1 54 9N 4 28W
Dounreay 13 C5 58 34N 3 44W
Dove →, *N. Yorks.* 9 B5 54 20N 0 55W
Dove →, *Staffs.* 8 D4 52 51N 1 36W
Dove Dale 9 C4 53 10N 1 47W
Dover 5 B6 51 7N 1 19 E
Doveridge 8 D4 52 54N 1 49W
Dovey = Dyfi → 7 B3 52 32N 4 0W
Down □ 14 B6 54 20N 5 47W
Downham 5 A5 52 26N 0 15 E
Downham Market 5 A5 52 36N 0 22 E
Downpatrick 14 B6 54 20N 5 43W
Downpatrick Hd. 14 B2 54 20N 9 21W
Downton 4 C3 51 0N 1 44W
Driffield = Great Driffield 9 C5 54 0N 0 25W
Drogheda 14 C5 53 45N 6 20W
Droichead Nua 15 C5 53 11N 6 50W
Droitwich 4 A2 52 16N 2 10W
Dronfield 9 C4 53 18N 1 29W
Dublin 14 C5 53 20N 6 18W
Dublin □ 14 C5 53 24N 6 20W
Dublin B. 15 C5 53 18N 6 5W
Duddington 5 A4 52 36N 0 32W
Duddon → 8 B2 54 12N 3 15W
Dudley 4 A2 52 30N 2 5W
Duffield 9 D4 52 59N 1 30W
Dufftown 13 D5 57 26N 3 9W
Dukinfield 8 C3 53 29N 2 5W
Dulverton 4 B1 51 2N 3 33W
Dumbarton 10 B4 55 58N 4 35W
Dumfries 11 B5 55 4N 3 37W
Dumfries & Galloway □ 11 B4 55 5N 4 0W
Dun Laoghaire 15 C5 53 17N 6 9W
Dunbar 11 A6 56 0N 2 32W
Dunblane 11 A5 56 10N 3 58W
Dunchurch 4 A3 52 21N 1 19W
Dundalk 14 B5 54 1N 6 25W
Dundalk Bay 14 C5 53 55N 6 15W
Dundee 11 A6 56 29N 3 0W
Dundrum 14 B6 54 17N 5 50W
Dundrum B. 14 B6 54 12N 5 40W
Dunfermline 11 A5 56 5N 3 28W
Dungannon 14 B5 54 30N 6 47W
Dungannon □ 14 B5 54 30N 6 55W
Dungarvan 15 D4 52 6N 7 40W
Dungarvan Bay 15 D4 52 5N 7 35W
Dungeness 5 C5 50 54N 0 59 E
Dunkeld 13 E5 56 34N 3 36W
Dunkery Beacon 4 B1 51 15N 3 37W
Dúnleary = Dun Laoghaire 15 C5 53 17N 6 9W
Dunmanus B. 15 E2 51 31N 9 50W
Dunmore Hd. 15 D1 52 10N 10 35W
Dunnet Hd. 13 C5 58 38N 3 22W
Dunoon 10 B4 55 57N 4 56W
Duns 11 B6 55 47N 2 20W
Dunstable 5 B4 51 53N 0 31W
Dunster 4 B1 51 11N 3 28W
Dunston 4 A2 52 46N 2 7W
Durham 9 B4 54 47N 1 34W
Durham □ 8 B4 54 42N 1 45W
Durlston Hd. 4 C3 50 35N 1 58W
Durness 13 C4 58 34N 4 45W
Durrington 4 B3 51 12N 1 47W
Dursley 4 B2 51 41N 2 21W
Dyfed □ 7 B2 52 0N 4 30W
Dyfi → 7 B3 52 32N 4 0W
Dymchurch 5 B6 51 2N 1 0 E
Dymock 4 B2 51 58N 2 27W

E

Eaglescliffe 9 B4 54 32N 1 21W
Eakring 9 C5 53 9N 0 59W
Ealing 5 B4 51 30N 0 19W
Earby 8 C3 53 55N 2 8W
Eardisland 4 A2 52 14N 2 50W
Eardisley 4 A1 52 8N 3 0W
Earith 5 A5 52 21N 0 1 E
Earl Shilton 4 A3 52 35N 1 20W
Earl Soham 5 A6 52 14N 1 15 E
Earls Barton 5 A4 52 16N 0 44W
Earl's Colne 5 B5 51 56N 0 43 E
Earn → 11 A5 56 20N 3 19W
Earn, L. 10 A4 56 23N 4 14W
Easebourne 5 C4 51 0N 0 42W
Easington, *Durham* 9 B4 54 50N 1 24W
Easington, *Humber.* 9 C6 53 40N 0 7 E
Easington Colliery 9 B4 54 49N 1 19W
Easingwold 9 B4 54 8N 1 11W
East Anglian Hts. 5 A5 52 10N 0 17 E
East Bergholt 5 B6 51 58N 1 2 E
East Brent 4 B2 51 14N 2 55W
East Cowes 4 C3 50 45N 1 17W
East Dean 5 C5 50 45N 0 12 E
East Dereham 5 A5 52 40N 0 57 E
East Fen 9 C6 53 4N 0 5 E
East Grinstead 5 B4 51 8N 0 1W
East Harling 5 A5 52 26N 0 55 E
East Horsley 5 B4 51 15N 0 26W
East Ilsley 4 B3 51 33N 1 15W
East Markham 9 C5 53 15N 0 53W
East Moor 9 C4 53 15N 1 30W
East Retford 9 C5 53 19N 0 55W
East Sussex □ 5 C5 51 0N 0 20 E
East Wittering 5 C4 50 46N 0 53W
East Woodhay 4 B3 51 21N 1 26W
Eastbourne 5 C5 50 46N 0 18 E
Eastchurch 5 B5 51 23N 0 53 E
Eastfield 9 B5 54 14N 0 23W
Eastleigh 4 C3 50 58N 1 21W
Eastnor 4 A2 52 2N 2 22W
Easton, *Avon* 4 B2 51 28N 2 42W
Easton, *Dorset* 4 C2 50 32N 2 27W
Easton, *Northants.* 5 A4 52 37N 0 31W
Eastry 5 B6 51 15N 1 19 E
Eastwood 9 C4 53 2N 1 17W
Eaton 5 A4 52 52N 0 46W
Eaton Socon 5 A4 52 13N 0 18W
Ebberston 9 B5 54 14N 0 35W
Ebbw Vale 7 C3 51 47N 3 12W
Eccleshall 4 A2 52 52N 2 14W
Eckington 9 C4 53 19N 1 21W
Eday 13 B6 59 11N 2 47W
Eddrachillis B. 12 C3 58 16N 5 10W
Eddystone 6 B3 50 11N 4 16W
Eden → 8 B2 54 57N 3 2W
Edenbridge 5 B5 51 12N 0 4 E
Edenderry 15 C4 53 21N 7 3W
Edge Hill 4 A3 52 7N 1 28W
Edinburgh 11 B5 55 57N 3 12W
Edington 4 B2 51 17N 2 6W
Edmondbyers 8 B4 54 50N 1 59W

Egham **5 B4** 51 25N 0 33W
Egremont **8 B2** 54 28N 3 33W
Egton **9 B5** 54 27N 0 45W
Eigg **12 E2** 56 54N 6 10W
Eil, L. **12 E3** 56 50N 5 15W
Eire **15 D4** 53 0N 8 0W
Elgin **13 D5** 57 39N 3 20W
Elham **5 B6** 51 9N 1 7 E
Elland **9 C4** 53 41N 1 49W
Ellen → **8 B2** 54 44N 3 30W
Ellesmere **8 D3** 52 55N 2 53W
Ellesmere Port **8 C3** 53 17N 2 55W
Ellon **13 D6** 57 21N 2 5W
Elmswell **5 A5** 52 14N 0 53 E
Elstead **5 B4** 51 11N 0 42W
Elworth **8 C3** 53 9N 2 22W
Ely **5 A5** 52 24N 0 16 E
Enard B. **12 C3** 58 5N 5 20W
Enderby **4 A3** 52 35N 1 15W
Enfield **5 B4** 51 39N 0 4W
English Channel **5** 50 0N 2 0W
Ennerdale Water **8 B2** 54 32N 3 24W
Ennis **15 D3** 52 51N 8 59W
Enniscorthy **15 D5** 52 30N 6 35W
Enniskillen **14 B4** 54 20N 7 40W
Ennistimon **15 D2** 52 56N 9 18W
Enstone **4 B3** 51 55N 1 25W
Epping **5 B5** 51 42N 0 8 E
Epping Forest **5 B5** 51 40N 0 5 E
Epsom **5 B4** 51 19N 0 16W
Epworth **9 C5** 53 30N 0 50W
Eriboll, L. **13 C4** 58 28N 4 41W
Erne → **14 B3** 54 30N 8 16W
Erne, Lower L. **14 B4** 54 26N 7 46W
Erne, Upper L. **14 B4** 54 14N 7 22W
Errigal **14 A3** 55 2N 8 8W
Erris Hd. **14 B1** 54 19N 10 0W
Escrick **9 C4** 53 53N 1 3W
Esher **5 B4** 51 21N 0 22W
Esk →, *Cumb.* **8 B2** 54 23N 3 21W
Esk →, *Dumf. & Gall.* **11 C5** 54 58N 3 4W
Esk →, *N. Yorks.* **9 B5** 54 27N 0 36W
Essex □ **5 B5** 51 48N 0 30 E
Eston **9 B4** 54 33N 1 6W
Etchingham **5 B5** 51 0N 0 27 E
Etive, L. **10 A3** 56 30N 5 12W
Eton **5 B4** 51 29N 0 37W
Ettington **4 A3** 52 8N 1 38W
Ettrick Water → **11 B6** 55 31N 2 55W
Euxton **8 C3** 53 41N 2 42W
Evercreech **4 B2** 51 8N 2 30W
Evesham **4 A3** 52 6N 1 57W
Ewe, L. **12 D3** 57 49N 5 38W
Ewell **5 B4** 51 20N 0 15W
Ewhurst **5 B4** 51 9N 0 25W
Exe → **6 B4** 50 38N 3 27W
Exeter **6 B4** 50 43N 3 31W
Exford **4 B1** 51 8N 3 39W
Exmoor **6 A4** 51 10N 3 59W
Exmouth **6 B4** 50 37N 3 26W
Exton **5 A4** 52 42N 0 38W
Eyam **9 C4** 53 17N 1 40W
Eye, *Cambs.* **5 A4** 52 36N 0 11W
Eye, *Suffolk* **5 A6** 52 19N 1 9 E
Eyemouth **11 B6** 55 53N 2 5W
Eynsham **4 B3** 51 47N 1 21W

F

Fair Hd. **14 A5** 55 14N 6 10W
Fairford **4 B3** 51 42N 1 48W
Fairlight **5 C5** 50 53N 0 40 E
Fakenham **5 A5** 52 50N 0 51 E
Faldingworth **9 C5** 53 21N 0 22W
Falkirk **11 A5** 56 0N 3 47W
Falmouth **6 B2** 50 9N 5 5W
Fannich, L. **12 D3** 57 40N 5 0W
Fareham **4 C3** 50 52N 1 11W
Faringdon **4 B3** 51 39N 1 34W
Farnborough **5 B4** 51 17N 0 46W
Farne Is. **9 A4** 55 38N 1 37W
Farnham **5 B4** 51 13N 0 49W
Farnworth **8 C3** 53 33N 2 24W
Fastnet Rock **15 E2** 51 22N 9 37W
Faversham **5 B5** 51 18N 0 54 E
Fawley **4 C3** 50 49N 1 20W
Fazeley **4 A3** 52 36N 1 42W
Feale → **15 D2** 52 26N 9 40W
Felixstowe **5 B6** 51 58N 1 22 E
Felton **9 A4** 55 18N 1 42W
Feltwell **5 A5** 52 29N 0 32 E
Fenit **15 D2** 52 17N 9 51W
Fenny Bentley **9 C4** 53 4N 1 43W
Fenny Compton **4 A3** 52 9N 1 20W
Fenny Stratford **5 B4** 51 59N 0 42W
Fens, The **5 A5** 52 45N 0 2 E
Fermanagh □ **14 B4** 54 21N 7 40W
Fermoy **15 D3** 52 4N 8 18W
Ferndown **4 C3** 50 48N 1 53W
Fernhurst **5 B4** 51 3N 0 43W
Ferryhill **9 B4** 54 42N 1 32W
Fetlar **12 A9** 60 36N 0 52W
Ffestiniog **7 B3** 52 58N 3 56W
Fife □ **11 A5** 56 13N 3 2W
Fife Ness **11 A6** 56 17N 2 35W
Filby **5 A6** 52 40N 1 39 E
Filey **9 B5** 54 13N 0 18W
Filey B. **9 B5** 54 12N 0 15W
Filton **4 B2** 51 29N 2 34W
Fincham **5 A5** 52 38N 0 30 E
Findhorn → **13 D5** 57 38N 3 38W
Findon **5 C4** 50 53N 0 24W
Finedon **5 A4** 52 20N 0 40W
Fingest **5 B4** 51 35N 0 52W
Finn → **14 B4** 54 50N 7 55W
Fishguard **7 C2** 51 59N 4 59W
Fishtoft **9 D6** 52 27N 0 2 E
Flamborough **9 B5** 54 7N 0 7W
Flamborough Hd. **9 B5** 54 8N 0 4W
Fleet **5 B4** 51 16N 0 50W
Fleetwood **8 C2** 53 55N 3 1W
Flimby **8 B2** 54 42N 3 31W
Flint **7 A3** 53 15N 3 7W
Flitwick **5 B4** 51 59N 0 30W
Flodden **9 A3** 55 37N 2 8W
Folkestone **5 B6** 51 5N 1 11 E
Fordham **5 A5** 52 19N 0 23 E
Fordingbridge **4 C3** 50 56N 1 48W
Forest Row **5 B5** 51 6N 0 3 E
Forfar **13 E6** 56 40N 2 53W
Formby **8 C2** 53 33N 3 3W
Formby Pt. **8 C2** 53 33N 3 7W
Forres **13 D5** 57 37N 3 38W
Fort Augustus **13 D4** 57 9N 4 40W
Fort William **12 E3** 56 48N 5 8W
Forth, Firth of **11 A6** 56 5N 2 55W
Fortrose **13 D4** 57 35N 4 10W
Fortuneswell **4 C2** 50 33N 2 26W
Fothergill **8 B2** 54 43N 3 30W
Fotheringhay **5 A4** 52 32N 0 28W
Foulness I. **5 B5** 51 36N 0 55 E
Foulness Pt. **5 B5** 51 36N 0 59 E
Foulsham **5 A6** 52 48N 1 1 E
Fountains Abbey **9 B4** 54 8N 1 35W
Fovant **4 B2** 51 4N 2 0W
Fowey **6 B3** 50 20N 4 39W
Fownhope **4 A2** 52 0N 2 37W
Foxdale **8 B1** 54 12N 4 38W
Foyle, Lough **14 A4** 55 6N 7 8W
Foynes **15 D2** 52 37N 9 5W
Framlingham **5 A6** 52 14N 1 20 E
Frampton Cotterell **4 B2** 51 31N 2 29W
Frant **5 B5** 51 5N 0 17 E
Fraserburgh **13 D6** 57 41N 2 3W
Freckleton **8 C3** 53 45N 2 52W
Freshwater **4 C3** 50 42N 1 31W
Fridaythorpe **9 B5** 54 2N 0 40W
Frimley **5 B4** 51 18N 0 43W
Frinton-on-Sea **5 B6** 51 50N 1 16 E
Frizington **8 B2** 54 33N 3 30W
Frodsham **8 C3** 53 17N 2 45W
Frome **4 B2** 51 16N 2 17W
Frome → **4 C2** 50 44N 2 5W
Fulbourn **5 A5** 52 11N 0 12 E
Fulford **9 C4** 53 56N 1 3W
Fulwood **8 C3** 53 47N 2 41W
Furness **8 B2** 54 14N 3 8W
Fylde **8 C3** 53 50N 2 58W
Fylingdales Moor **9 B5** 54 22N 0 32W
Fyne, L. **10 B3** 56 0N 5 20W

G

Gainford **9 B4** 54 34N 1 44W
Gainsborough **9 C5** 53 23N 0 46W
Gairloch, L. **12 D3** 57 43N 5 45W
Galashiels **11 B6** 55 37N 2 50W
Galgate **8 C3** 53 59N 2 47W
Galley Hd. **15 E3** 51 32N 8 56W
Galloway **10 C4** 55 0N 4 25W
Galloway, Mull of **10 C4** 54 38N 4 50W
Galty Mts. **15 D3** 52 22N 8 10W
Galtymore **15 D3** 52 22N 8 12W
Galway **15 C2** 53 16N 9 4W
Galway □ **14 C2** 53 16N 9 3W
Galway B. **15 C2** 53 10N 9 20W
Gamlingay **5 A4** 52 9N 0 11W
Garboldisham **5 A5** 52 24N 0 57 E
Garforth **9 C4** 53 48N 1 22W
Gargrave **8 C3** 53 58N 2 7W
Garry → **13 E5** 56 47N 3 47W
Garsdale Head **8 B3** 54 19N 2 19W
Garstang **8 C3** 53 53N 2 47W
Garston **8 C3** 53 21N 2 55W
Gateshead **9 B4** 54 57N 1 37W
Gatley **8 C3** 53 25N 2 15W
Gawthwaite **8 B2** 54 16N 3 6W
Gayton **5 A5** 52 45N 0 35 E
Gaywood **5 A5** 52 46N 0 26 E
Gedney **5 A5** 52 47N 0 5 E
Gerrards Cross **5 B4** 51 35N 0 32W
Giants Causeway **14 A5** 55 15N 6 30W
Gibraltar Pt. **9 C6** 53 6N 0 20 E
Giggleswick **8 B3** 54 5N 2 19W
Gigha **10 B3** 55 42N 5 45W
Gillingham, *Dorset* **4 B2** 51 2N 2 15W
Gillingham, *Kent* **5 B5** 51 23N 0 34 E
Gilsland **8 B3** 55 0N 2 34W
Girdle Ness **13 D6** 57 9N 2 2W
Girton **5 A5** 52 14N 0 5 E
Girvan **10 B4** 55 15N 4 50W
Gisburn **8 C3** 53 56N 2 16W
Glasgow **10 B4** 55 52N 4 14W
Glastonbury **4 B2** 51 9N 2 42W
Glemsford **5 A5** 52 6N 0 41 E
Glen → **5 A4** 52 50N 0 7W
Glen Affric **12 D3** 57 15N 5 0W
Glen Coe **12 E4** 56 40N 5 0W
Glen Garry **12 D3** 57 3N 5 7W
Glen Helen **8 B1** 54 14N 4 35W
Glen Mor **13 D4** 57 12N 4 37W
Glen Moriston **12 D4** 57 10N 4 58W
Glen Orchy **10 A4** 56 27N 4 52W
Glen Spean **13 E4** 56 53N 4 40W
Glengarriff **15 E2** 51 45N 9 33W
Glenmaye **8 B1** 54 11N 4 42W
Glenrothes **11 A5** 56 12N 3 11W
Glenties **14 B3** 54 48N 8 18W
Glossop **8 C4** 53 27N 1 56W
Gloucester **4 B2** 51 52N 2 15W
Gloucestershire □ **4 B2** 51 44N 2 10W
Gnosall **4 A2** 52 48N 2 15W
Goat Fell **10 B3** 55 37N 5 11W
Goathland **9 B5** 54 24N 0 42W
Godalming **5 B4** 51 12N 0 37W
Godmanchester **5 A4** 52 19N 0 11W
Godshill **4 C3** 50 38N 1 13W
Godstone **5 B4** 51 15N 0 3W
Golden Vale **15 D3** 52 33N 8 17W
Golspie **13 D5** 57 58N 3 58W
Goodrich **4 B2** 51 52N 2 38W
Goodwood **5 C4** 50 53N 0 44W
Goole **9 C5** 53 42N 0 52W
Gorey **15 D5** 52 41N 6 18W
Goring **4 B3** 51 31N 1 8W
Goring-by-Sea **5 C4** 50 49N 0 26W
Gorleston **5 A6** 52 35N 1 44 E
Gort **15 C3** 53 4N 8 50W
Gosberton **9 D5** 52 52N 0 10W
Gosforth **8 B2** 54 24N 3 27W
Gosport **4 C3** 50 48N 1 8W
Goudhurst **5 B5** 51 7N 0 28 E
Gower **7 C2** 51 35N 4 10W
Gowna, L. **14 C4** 53 52N 7 35W
Grafham Water **5 A4** 52 18N 0 17W
Grainthorpe **9 C6** 53 27N 0 5 E
Grampian □ **13 D6** 57 20N 3 0W
Grampian Highlands = Grampian Mts. **13 E4** 56 50N 4 0W
Grampian Mts. **13 E4** 56 50N 4 0W
Granard **14 C4** 53 47N 7 30W
Grange-over-Sands **8 B3** 54 12N 2 55W
Grangemouth **11 A5** 56 1N 3 43W
Grangetown **9 B4** 54 36N 1 7W
Grantham **9 D5** 52 55N 0 39W
Grantown-on-Spey **13 D5** 57 19N 3 36W
Grasmere **8 B2** 54 28N 3 2W
Grasmere L. **8 B2** 54 28N 3 2W
Grassington **8 B4** 54 5N 2 0W
Gravesend **5 B5** 51 25N 0 22 E
Grayrigg **8 B3** 54 22N 2 40W
Grays **5 B5** 51 28N 0 23 E
Great Ayton **9 B4** 54 29N 1 8W
Great Baddow **5 B5** 51 43N 0 31 E
Great Bentley **5 B6** 51 51N 1 5 E
Great Blasket I. **15 D1** 52 5N 10 30W
Great Broughton **8 B2** 54 40N 3 26W
Great Chesterford **5 A5** 52 4N 0 11 E
Great Clifton **8 B2** 54 39N 3 29W
Great Driffield **9 C5** 54 0N 0 25W
Great Dunmow **5 B5** 51 52N 0 22 E
Great Harwood **8 C3** 53 47N 2 25W
Great Malvern **4 A2** 52 7N 2 19W
Great Massingham **5 A5** 52 47N 0 41 E
Great Missenden **5 B4** 51 42N 0 42W
Great Ormes Head **7 A3** 53 20N 3 52W
Great Ouse → **5 A5** 52 47N 0 22 E
Great Shefford **4 B3** 51 29N 1 27W
Great Shelford **5 A5** 52 9N 0 9 E
Great Shunner Fell **8 B3** 54 22N 2 16W
Great Stour = Stour → **5 B6** 51 15N 1 20 E
Great Waltham **5 B5** 51 47N 0 29 E
Great Whernside **8 B4** 54 9N 1 59W
Great Wyrley **4 A2** 52 40N 2 1W
Great Yarmouth **5 A6** 52 40N 1 45 E
Great Yeldham **5 A5** 52 1N 0 33 E
Greater London □ **5 B4** 51 31N 0 6W
Greater Manchester □ **8 C3** 53 30N 2 15W
Greatham **9 B4** 54 38N 1 14W
Green Hammerton **9 B4** 54 2N 1 17W
Greenock **10 B4** 55 57N 4 46W
Greenodd **8 B2** 54 14N 3 3W
Greenore **14 B5** 54 2N 6 8W
Greenore Pt. **15 D5** 52 15N 6 20W
Greenwich **5 B5** 51 28N 0 0 E
Greta → **8 B3** 54 9N 2 36W
Gretna Green **11 B5** 55 0N 3 3W
Gretton **5 A4** 52 33N 0 40W
Greystoke **8 B3** 54 39N 2 52W
Grimsby **9 C5** 53 35N 0 5W
Grizebeck **8 B2** 54 16N 3 10W
Grove **4 B3** 51 37N 1 25W
Guernsey **6 C5** 49 30N 2 35W
Guestling Green **5 C5** 50 53N 0 40 E
Guildford **5 B4** 51 14N 0 34W
Guisborough **9 B4** 54 32N 1 2W
Guiseley **9 C4** 53 52N 1 43W
Gweebarra B. **14 B3** 54 52N 8 21W
Gweedore **14 A3** 55 4N 8 15W
Gwent □ **7 C4** 51 45N 2 55W
Gwynedd □ **7 B2** 53 0N 4 0W

H

Hackney **5 B4** 51 33N 0 2W
Hackthorpe **8 B3** 54 37N 2 42W
Haddenham **5 B4** 51 46N 0 56W
Haddington **11 B6** 55 57N 2 48W
Hadleigh, *Essex* **5 B5** 51 33N 0 37 E
Hadleigh, *Suffolk* **5 A5** 52 3N 0 58 E
Hadley **4 A2** 52 42N 2 28W
Hadlow **5 B5** 51 12N 0 20 E
Hadrian's Wall **9 A3** 55 0N 2 30W
Hags Hd. **15 D2** 52 57N 9 30W
Hailsham **5 C5** 50 52N 0 17 E
Hainton **9 C5** 53 21N 0 13W
Hale **8 C3** 53 24N 2 21W
Halesowen **4 A2** 52 27N 2 2W
Halesworth **5 A6** 52 21N 1 30 E
Halifax **8 C4** 53 43N 1 51W
Hallow **4 A2** 52 14N 2 15W
Halstead **5 B5** 51 59N 0 39 E
Hambledon **4 C3** 50 56N 1 6W
Hambleton Hills **9 B4** 54 17N 1 12W
Hamilton **11 B4** 55 47N 4 2W
Hammersmith and Fulham **5 B4** 51 30N 0 15W
Hampshire □ **4 B3** 51 3N 1 20W
Hampshire Downs **4 B3** 51 10N 1 10W
Hampton in Arden **4 A3** 52 26N 1 42W
Hanningfield Water **5 B5** 51 40N 0 30 E
Harewood **9 C4** 53 54N 1 30W
Haringey **5 B4** 51 35N 0 7W
Harlech **7 B2** 52 52N 4 7W
Harleston **5 A6** 52 25N 1 18 E
Harlow **5 B5** 51 47N 0 9 E
Harpenden **5 B4** 51 48N 0 20W
Harrietsham **5 B5** 51 15N 0 41 E
Harrington **8 B2** 54 37N 3 40W
Harris **12 D2** 57 50N 6 55W
Harris, Sd. of **12 D1** 57 44N 7 6W
Harrogate **9 C4** 53 59N 1 32W
Harrow **5 B4** 51 35N 0 15W
Hartest **5 A5** 52 7N 0 41 E
Hartland Pt. **6 A3** 51 2N 4 32W
Hartlebury **4 A2** 52 20N 2 13W
Hartlepool **9 B4** 54 42N 1 11W
Hartpury **4 B2** 51 55N 2 18W
Harwell **4 B3** 51 40N 1 17W
Harwich **5 B6** 51 56N 1 18 E
Haslemere **5 B4** 51 5N 0 41W
Haslingden **8 C3** 53 43N 2 20W
Hassocks **5 C4** 50 55N 0 9W
Hastings **5 C5** 50 51N 0 36 E
Hatfield, *Herts.* **5 B4** 51 46N 0 11W
Hatfield, *S. Yorks.* **9 C5** 53 34N 0 59W
Hatfield Broad Oak **5 B5** 51 48N 0 16 E
Hathersage **9 C4** 53 20N 1 39W
Haughley **5 A5** 52 13N 0 59 E
Havant **5 C4** 50 51N 0 59W
Haverfordwest **7 C2** 51 48N 4 59W
Haverhill **5 A5** 52 6N 0 27 E
Haverigg **8 B2** 54 12N 3 16W
Havering **5 B5** 51 33N 0 20 E
Hawes **8 B3** 54 18N 2 12W
Haweswater **8 B3** 54 32N 2 48W
Hawick **11 B6** 55 25N 2 48W
Hawkesbury Upton **4 B2** 51 34N 2 19W
Hawkhurst **5 B5** 51 2N 0 31 E
Hawkshead **8 B3** 54 23N 3 0W
Haworth **8 C4** 53 50N 1 57W
Hawsker **9 B5** 54 27N 0 34W
Haxby **9 B4** 54 1N 1 4W
Hay-on-Wye **7 B3** 52 4N 3 9W
Hayburn Wyke **9 B5** 54 22N 0 28W
Haydock **8 C3** 53 27N 2 42W
Hayton **8 B3** 54 55N 2 45W
Haywards Heath **5 B4** 51 1N 0 6W
Hazel Grove **8 C3** 53 23N 2 7W
Heacham **5 A5** 52 55N 0 30 E
Headcorn **5 B5** 51 10N 0 39 E
Headley **5 B4** 51 7N 0 49W
Heanor **9 C4** 53 1N 1 20W
Heath End **4 B3** 51 21N 1 9W
Heathfield **5 C5** 50 58N 0 18 E
Hebden Bridge **8 C4** 53 45N 2 0W
Hebrides **12 D2** 57 30N 7 0W
Heckington **9 D5** 52 59N 0 17W
Hedge End **4 C3** 50 54N 1 17W
Hednesford **4 A3** 52 43N 2 0W
Hedon **9 C5** 53 44N 0 11W
Helensburgh **10 A4** 56 0N 4 44W
Hellifield **8 B3** 54 0N 2 13W
Helmsdale **13 C5** 58 7N 3 40W
Helmsley **9 B4** 54 15N 1 2W
Helperby **9 B4** 54 8N 1 20W
Helsby **8 C3** 53 16N 2 47W
Helston **6 B2** 50 7N 5 17W
Helvellyn **8 B2** 54 31N 3 1W
Hemel Hempstead **5 B4** 51 45N 0 28W
Hempton **5 A5** 52 50N 0 49 E
Hemsby **5 A6** 52 42N 1 42 E
Hemsworth **9 C4** 53 37N 1 21W
Henfield **5 C4** 50 56N 0 17W
Henley-in-Arden **4 A3** 52 18N 1 47W
Henley-on-Thames **5 B4** 51 32N 0 53W
Henlow **5 A4** 52 2N 0 18W
Henstridge **4 C2** 50 59N 2 24W
Hereford **4 A2** 52 4N 2 42W
Hereford and Worcester □ **4 A2** 52 10N 2 30W
Herm **6 C5** 49 30N 2 28W
Herne Bay **5 B6** 51 22N 1 8 E
Herstmonceux **5 C5** 50 53N 0 21 E
Hertford **5 B4** 51 47N 0 4W
Hertfordshire □ **5 B4** 51 51N 0 5W
Hessle **9 C5** 53 44N 0 28W
Heswall **8 C2** 53 19N 3 6W
Hethersett **5 A6** 52 35N 1 10 E
Hexham **9 B3** 54 58N 2 7W
Heybridge **5 B5** 51 44N 0 42 E
Heysham **8 B3** 54 5N 2 53W
Heytesbury **4 B2** 51 11N 2 7W
Heywood **8 C3** 53 36N 2 13W
High Bentham **8 B3** 54 8N 2 31W
High Borrow Bridge **8 B3** 54 26N 2 43W
High Ercall **4 A2** 52 46N 2 37W
High Hesket **8 B3** 54 47N 2 49W
High Pike **8 B2** 54 43N 3 4W
High Wycombe **5 B4** 51 37N 0 45W
Higham Ferrers **5 A4** 52 18N 0 36W
Highbridge **4 B2** 51 13N 2 59W
Highclere **4 B3** 51 20N 1 22W
Highland □ **12 D4** 57 30N 5 0W
Highley **4 A2** 52 25N 2 23W
Highworth **4 B3** 51 38N 1 42W
Hilgay **5 A5** 52 34N 0 23 E
Hillingdon **5 B4** 51 33N 0 29W
Hilpsford Pt. **8 B2** 54 4N 3 12W
Hinckley **4 A3** 52 33N 1 21W
Hinderwell **9 B5** 54 32N 0 45W
Hindhead **5 B4** 51 6N 0 42W
Hindley **8 C3** 53 32N 2 35W
Hingham **5 A5** 52 35N 0 59 E
Hinkley Pt. **4 C1** 50 59N 3 32W
Hinstock **4 A2** 52 50N 2 28W
Histon **5 A5** 52 15N 0 6 E
Hitchin **5 B4** 51 57N 0 16W
Hockley **5 B5** 51 35N 0 39 E
Hodder → **8 C3** 53 57N 2 27W
Hoddesdon **5 B4** 51 45N 0 1W
Hodge → **9 B5** 54 14N 0 55W
Hoff **8 B3** 54 34N 2 31W
Hog's Back **5 B4** 51 13N 0 40W
Holbeach **5 A5** 52 48N 0 1 E
Holbeach Marsh **5 A5** 52 52N 0 5 E
Holderness **9 C5** 53 45N 0 5W
Holkham **5 A5** 52 57N 0 48 E
Holland Fen **9 D5** 53 0N 0 8W
Holland on Sea **5 B6** 51 48N 1 12 E
Holme, *Humber.* **9 C5** 53 50N 0 48W
Holme, *W. Yorks.* **8 C4** 53 34N 1 50W
Holmes Chapel **8 C3** 53 13N 2 21W
Holmfirth **9 C4** 53 34N 1 48W
Holmwood **5 B4** 51 12N 0 19W
Holsworthy **6 B3** 50 48N 4 21W
Holt **5 A6** 52 55N 1 4 E
Holy I., *Gwynedd* **7 A2** 53 17N 4 37W
Holy I., *Northumb.* **9 A4** 55 42N 1 48W
Holyhead **7 A2** 53 18N 4 38W
Honington **9 D5** 52 58N 0 35W
Honiton **6 B4** 50 48N 3 11W
Hoo **5 B5** 51 25N 0 33 E
Hook **5 B4** 51 17N 0 55W
Hook Hd. **15 D5** 52 8N 6 57W
Horden **9 B4** 54 45N 1 17W
Horley **5 B4** 51 10N 0 10W
Horn Head **14 A3** 55 13N 8 0W
Horncastle **9 C5** 53 13N 0 8W
Horndean **5 C4** 50 50N 0 59W
Horningsham **4 B2** 51 11N 2 16W
Hornsea **9 C5** 53 55N 0 10W
Horsforth **9 C4** 53 50N 1 39W
Horsham **5 B4** 51 4N 0 20W
Horsham St. Faith **5 A6** 52 41N 1 15 E
Horsted Keynes **5 B4** 51 2N 0 1W
Horton in Ribblesdale **8 B3** 54 9N 2 19W
Horwich **8 C3** 53 37N 2 33W

37

Houghton-le- Spring Mask, L.

Houghton-le-Spring **9 B4** 54 51N 1 28W
Houghton Regis **5 B4** 51 54N 0 32W
Hounslow **5 B4** 51 29N 0 20W
Hove **5 C4** 50 50N 0 10W
Hoveton **5 A6** 52 45N 1 23 E
Hovingham **9 B5** 54 10N 0 59W
Howden **9 C5** 53 45N 0 52W
Howth Hd. **14 C5** 53 21N 6 3W
Hoxne **5 A6** 52 22N 1 11 E
Hoy **13 C5** 58 50N 3 15W
Hoylake **8 C2** 53 24N 3 11W
Hoyland Nether **9 C4** 53 30N 1 27W
Hucknall **9 C4** 53 3N 1 12W
Huddersfield **9 C4** 53 38N 1 49W
Hull = Kingston upon Hull **9 C5** 53 45N 0 20W
Hull → **9 C5** 53 43N 0 25W
Hullavington **4 B2** 51 31N 2 9W
Hullbridge **5 B5** 51 37N 0 37 E
Hulme End **8 C4** 53 8N 1 51W
Humber → **9 C5** 53 40N 0 10W
Humber, Mouth of the **9 C6** 53 32N 0 8 E
Humberside □ **9 C5** 53 50N 0 30W
Humberston **9 C5** 53 31N 0 2W
Hungerford **4 B3** 51 25N 1 30W
Hunmanby **9 B5** 54 12N 0 19W
Hunstanton **5 A5** 52 57N 0 30 E
Huntingdon **5 A4** 52 20N 0 11W
Huntly **13 D6** 57 27N 2 48W
Hursley **4 B3** 51 1N 1 23W
Hurstbourne Tarrant **4 B3** 51 17N 1 27W
Hurstpierpoint **5 C4** 50 56N 0 11W
Hurworth-on-Tees **9 B4** 54 29N 1 31W
Husband's Bosworth **4 A3** 52 27N 1 3W
Hutton Rudby **9 B4** 54 27N 1 17W
Huyton **8 C3** 53 25N 2 52W
Hyde **8 C3** 53 26N 2 6W
Hythe, *Hants.* **4 C3** 50 51N 1 23W
Hythe, *Kent* **5 B6** 51 4N 1 5 E

I

Ibstock **4 A3** 52 42N 1 23W
Idle → **9 C5** 53 27N 0 49W
Idmiston **4 B3** 51 8N 1 43W
Idsworth **5 C4** 50 56N 0 56W
Ilchester **4 C2** 51 0N 2 41W
Ilfracombe **6 A3** 51 13N 4 8W
Ilkeston **9 D4** 52 59N 1 19W
Ilkley **8 C4** 53 56N 1 49W
Ilminster **4 C2** 50 55N 2 56W
Immingham **9 C5** 53 37N 0 12W
Ince **8 C3** 53 32N 2 38W
Ingatestone **5 B5** 51 40N 0 28 E
Ingleborough **8 B3** 54 11N 2 23W
Ingleton **8 B3** 54 9N 2 29W
Ingoldmells Pt. **9 C6** 53 11N 0 21 E
Inishbofin **14 C1** 53 35N 10 12W
Inishmore **15 C2** 53 8N 9 45W
Inishowen **14 A4** 55 14N 7 15W
Inkberrow **4 A3** 52 13N 1 59W
Inkpen Beacon **4 B3** 51 22N 1 28W
Inner Hebrides **12 E2** 57 0N 6 30W
Inner Sound **12 D3** 57 30N 5 55W
Inny → **15 C4** 53 30N 7 50W
Inveraray **10 A3** 56 13N 5 5W
Inverbervie **13 E6** 56 50N 2 17W
Invergordon **13 D4** 57 41N 4 10W
Inverness **13 D4** 57 29N 4 12W
Inverurie **13 D6** 57 15N 2 21W
Iona **10 A2** 56 20N 6 25W
Ipswich **5 A6** 52 4N 1 9 E
Irchester **5 A4** 52 17N 0 40W
Ireland's Eye **14 C5** 53 25N 6 4W
Irish Republic **15 D4** 53 0N 8 0W
Irish Sea **8 C1** 54 0N 5 0W
Irlam **8 C3** 53 26N 2 27W
Ironbridge **4 A2** 52 38N 2 29W
Irt → **8 B2** 54 24N 3 25W
Irthlingborough **5 A4** 52 20N 0 37W
Irvine **10 B4** 55 37N 4 40W
Irvinestown **14 B4** 54 28N 7 38W
Isla → **13 E5** 56 32N 3 20W
Islay **10 B2** 55 46N 6 10W
Isle of Wight □ **4 C3** 50 40N 1 20W
Isleham **5 A5** 52 21N 0 24 E
Islip **4 B3** 51 49N 1 12W
Itchen → **4 C3** 50 57N 1 20W
Ivinghoe **5 B4** 51 50N 0 38W
Ixworth **5 A5** 52 18N 0 50 E

J

Jaywick **5 B6** 51 46N 1 7 E
Jedburgh **11 B6** 55 28N 2 33W
Jersey **6 C5** 49 13N 2 7W
Jervaulx **9 B4** 54 19N 1 41W
John o' Groats **13 C5** 58 39N 3 3W
Jura **10 B3** 56 0N 5 50W
Jura, Sd. of **10 B3** 55 57N 5 45W
Jurby Hd. **8 B1** 54 23N 4 31W

K

Kanturk **15 D3** 52 10N 8 55W
Katrine, L. **10 A4** 56 15N 4 30W
Keelby **9 C5** 53 34N 0 15W
Keele **8 C3** 53 0N 2 17W
Keeper Hill **15 D3** 52 46N 8 17W
Kegworth **4 A3** 52 50N 1 17W
Keighley **8 C4** 53 52N 1 54W
Keith **13 D6** 57 33N 2 58W
Keld **8 B3** 54 24N 2 11W
Kells = Ceanannus Mor **14 C5** 53 42N 6 53W
Kelsale **5 A6** 52 15N 1 30 E
Kelsall **8 C3** 53 14N 2 44W
Kelso **11 B6** 55 36N 2 27W
Kelvedon **5 B5** 51 50N 0 43 E
Kemble **4 B2** 51 40N 2 1W
Kempsey **4 A2** 52 8N 2 11W
Kempston **5 A4** 52 7N 0 30W
Kemsing **5 B5** 51 18N 0 14 E
Kendal **8 B3** 54 19N 2 44W
Kenilworth **4 A3** 52 22N 1 35W
Kenmare **15 E2** 51 52N 9 35W
Kenmare → **15 E2** 51 40N 10 0W
Kennet → **5 B4** 51 24N 0 58W
Kenninghall **5 A6** 52 26N 1 0 E
Kennington **4 B3** 51 43N 1 14W
Kent □ **5 B5** 51 12N 0 40 E
Kerry □ **15 D2** 52 7N 9 35W
Kerry Hd. **15 D2** 52 26N 9 56W
Kesgrave **5 A6** 52 4N 1 14 E
Kessingland **5 A6** 52 25N 1 41 E
Keswick **8 B2** 54 35N 3 9W
Kettering **5 A4** 52 24N 0 44W
Kettle Ness **9 B5** 54 32N 0 41W
Kettlewell **8 B3** 54 8N 2 2W
Kexby **9 C5** 53 21N 0 41W
Keyingham **9 C5** 53 42N 0 7W
Keymer **5 C4** 50 55N 0 5W
Keynsham **4 B2** 51 25N 2 30W
Keyworth **4 A3** 52 52N 1 8W
Kibworth Beauchamp **5 A4** 52 33N 0 59W
Kidderminster **4 A2** 52 24N 2 13W
Kidlington **4 B3** 51 49N 1 18W
Kidsgrove **8 C3** 53 6N 2 15W
Kidstones **8 B3** 54 15N 2 2W
Kielder Res. **9 A3** 55 10N 2 29W
Kildare **15 C5** 53 10N 6 50W
Kildare □ **15 C5** 53 10N 6 50W
Kilham **9 B5** 54 4N 0 22W
Kilkee **15 D2** 52 41N 9 40W
Kilkenny **15 D4** 52 40N 7 17W
Kilkenny □ **15 D4** 52 35N 7 15W
Kilkieran B. **15 C2** 53 18N 9 45W
Killala **14 B2** 54 13N 9 12W
Killala B. **14 B2** 54 20N 9 12W
Killaloe **15 D3** 52 48N 8 28W
Killarney **15 D2** 52 2N 9 30W
Killarney, Lakes of **15 E2** 52 0N 9 30W
Killary Harbour **14 C2** 53 38N 9 52W
Killiecrankie, Pass of **13 E5** 56 44N 3 46W
Killin **10 A4** 56 28N 4 20W
Killinghall **9 B4** 54 1N 1 33W
Killybegs **14 B3** 54 38N 8 26W
Kilmarnock **10 B4** 55 36N 4 30W
Kilrush **15 D2** 52 39N 9 30W
Kilsby **4 A3** 52 20N 1 11W
Kimbolton **5 A4** 52 17N 0 23W
Kinder Scout **8 C4** 53 24N 1 53W
Kineton **4 A3** 52 10N 1 30W
King's Lynn **5 A5** 52 45N 0 25 E
King's Sutton **4 A3** 52 1N 1 16W
King's Worthy **4 B3** 51 6N 1 18W
Kingsbridge **6 B4** 50 17N 3 46W
Kingsbury **4 A3** 52 33N 1 41W
Kingsclere **4 B3** 51 19N 1 15W
Kingscourt **14 C5** 53 55N 6 48W
Kingsland **4 A2** 52 15N 2 49W
Kingston upon Hull **9 C5** 53 45N 0 20W
Kingston-upon-Thames **5 B4** 51 23N 0 20W
Kingswood **4 B2** 51 26N 2 31W
Kington **4 A1** 52 12N 3 2W
Kingussie **13 D4** 57 5N 4 2W
Kinnairds Hd. **13 D7** 57 40N 2 0W
Kinross **11 A5** 56 13N 3 25W
Kinsale **15 E3** 51 42N 8 31W
Kinsale, Old Hd. of **15 E3** 51 37N 8 32W
Kintyre **10 B3** 55 30N 5 35W
Kintyre, Mull of **10 B3** 55 17N 5 55W
Kippure **15 C5** 53 11N 6 23W
Kirk Michael **8 B1** 54 17N 4 35W
Kirkbride **8 B2** 54 54N 3 13W
Kirkburton **9 C4** 53 36N 1 42W
Kirkby **8 C3** 53 29N 2 54W
Kirkby-in-Ashfield **9 C4** 53 6N 1 15W
Kirkby Lonsdale **8 B3** 54 13N 2 36W
Kirkby Malzeard **9 B4** 54 10N 1 38W
Kirkby Stephen **8 B3** 54 27N 2 23W
Kirkby Thore **8 B3** 54 38N 2 34W
Kirkbymoorside **9 B5** 54 16N 0 56W
Kirkcaldy **11 A5** 56 7N 3 10W
Kirkcudbright **11 C4** 54 50N 4 3W
Kirkham **8 C3** 53 47N 2 52W
Kirkintilloch **11 B4** 55 57N 4 10W
Kirkoswald **8 B3** 54 46N 2 41W
Kirkstone P. **8 B3** 54 29N 2 55W
Kirkwall **13 C6** 58 59N 2 59W
Kirriemuir **13 E6** 56 41N 2 58W
Kirtling **5 A5** 52 11N 0 27 E
Kirtlington **4 B3** 51 54N 1 9W
Kirton **9 D5** 52 56N 0 3W
Kirton in Lindsey **9 C5** 53 29N 0 35W
Knaresborough **9 B4** 54 1N 1 29W
Knebworth **5 B4** 51 52N 0 11W
Knighton **7 B3** 52 21N 3 2W
Knockmealdown Mts. **15 D4** 52 16N 8 0W
Knott End-on-Sea **8 C3** 53 55N 2 59W
Knottingley **9 C4** 53 42N 1 15W
Knowle **4 A3** 52 23N 1 43W
Knutsford **8 C3** 53 18N 2 22W
Kyle of Lochalsh **12 D3** 57 17N 5 43W

L

Laceby **9 C5** 53 32N 0 10W
Lacock **4 B2** 51 24N 2 8W
Lagan → **14 B6** 54 35N 5 55W
Lairg **13 C4** 58 1N 4 24W
Lake District **8 B2** 54 30N 3 10W
Lakenheath **5 A5** 52 25N 0 30 E
Lambay I. **14 C5** 53 30N 6 0W
Lamberhurst **5 B5** 51 5N 0 21 E
Lambeth **5 B4** 51 27N 0 7W
Lambourn **4 B3** 51 31N 1 31W
Lammermuir Hills **11 B6** 55 50N 2 40W
Lampeter **7 B2** 52 6N 4 6W
Lanark **11 B5** 55 40N 3 48W
Lancashire □ **8 C3** 53 40N 2 30W
Lancaster **8 B3** 54 3N 2 48W
Lanchester **9 B4** 54 50N 1 44W
Lancing **5 C4** 50 49N 0 19W
Land's End **6 B2** 50 4N 5 43W
Langholm **11 B6** 55 9N 2 59W
Langness **8 B1** 54 3N 4 37W
Langport **4 B2** 51 2N 2 51W
Langstrothdale Chase **8 B3** 54 14N 2 13W
Langtoft **5 A4** 52 42N 0 19W
Laois □ **15 D4** 53 0N 7 20W
Largs **10 B4** 55 48N 4 51W
Larkhill **4 B3** 51 12N 1 49W
Larne **14 B6** 54 52N 5 50W
Laskill **9 B4** 54 19N 1 6W
Launceston **6 B3** 50 38N 4 21W
Laune → **15 D2** 52 5N 9 40W
Laurencekirk **13 E6** 56 50N 2 30W
Lavendon **5 A4** 52 11N 0 39W
Lavenham **5 A5** 52 7N 0 48 E
Laxey **8 B1** 54 15N 4 23W
Laxfield **5 A6** 52 18N 1 23 E
Laxford, L. **12 C3** 58 25N 5 10W
Lazonby **8 B3** 54 45N 2 42W
Lea **9 C5** 53 22N 0 45W
Lea → **5 B4** 51 30N 0 10W
Leadenham **9 C5** 53 5N 0 33W
Leadgate **9 B4** 54 52N 1 48W
Leadhills **11 B5** 55 25N 3 47W
Leamington Spa = Royal Leamington Spa **4 A3** 52 18N 1 32W
Leasingham **9 C5** 53 1N 0 25W
Leatherhead **5 B4** 51 18N 0 20W
Lechlade **4 B3** 51 42N 1 40W
Ledbury **4 A2** 52 3N 2 25W
Lee → **15 E3** 51 50N 8 30W
Lee-on-Solent **4 C3** 50 47N 1 11W
Leeds **9 C4** 53 48N 1 34W
Leek **8 C3** 53 7N 2 2W
Leicester **4 A3** 52 39N 1 9W
Leicestershire □ **4 A3** 52 40N 1 10W
Leigh, *Gt. Man.* **8 C3** 53 29N 2 31W
Leigh, *Here. & Worcs.* **4 A2** 52 10N 2 21W
Leighton Buzzard **5 B4** 51 55N 0 39W
Leinster □ **15 C4** 53 0N 7 10W
Leinster, Mt. **15 D5** 52 38N 6 47W
Leintwardine **4 A2** 52 22N 2 51W
Leiston **5 A6** 52 13N 1 35 E
Leith **11 B5** 55 59N 3 10W
Leith Hill **5 B4** 51 10N 0 23W
Leitrim **14 B3** 54 0N 8 5W
Leitrim □ **14 B3** 54 8N 8 0W
Lenham **5 B5** 51 14N 0 44 E
Leominster **4 A2** 52 15N 2 43W
Lerwick **12 A8** 60 10N 1 10W
Letchworth **5 B4** 51 58N 0 13W
Letterkenny **14 B4** 54 57N 7 42W
Leven, *Fife* **11 A6** 56 12N 3 0W
Leven, *Humber.* **9 C5** 53 54N 0 18W
Leven → **9 B4** 54 27N 1 15W
Leven, L. **11 A5** 56 12N 3 22W
Lewes **5 C5** 50 53N 0 2 E
Lewis **12 C2** 58 10N 6 40W
Lewis, Butt of **12 C2** 58 30N 6 12W
Lewisham **5 B4** 51 27N 0 1W
Leyburn **9 B4** 54 19N 1 50W
Leyland **8 C3** 53 41N 2 42W
Leysdown on Sea **5 B5** 51 23N 0 57 E
Lichfield **4 A3** 52 40N 1 50W
Liffey → **15 C5** 53 21N 6 20W
Lifford **14 B4** 54 50N 7 30W
Lilleshall **4 A2** 52 45N 2 22W
Limavady **14 A5** 55 3N 6 58W
Limavady □ **14 B5** 55 0N 6 55W
Limerick **15 D3** 52 40N 8 38W
Limerick □ **15 D3** 52 30N 8 50W
Limpsfield **5 B5** 51 15N 0 1 E
Lincoln **9 C5** 53 14N 0 32W
Lincoln Wolds **9 C5** 53 20N 0 5W
Lincolnshire □ **9 C5** 53 14N 0 32W
Lindale **8 B3** 54 14N 2 54W
Lingfield **5 B4** 51 11N 0 1W
Linlithgow **11 B5** 55 58N 3 38W
Linnhe, L. **10 A3** 56 36N 5 25W
Linslade **5 B4** 51 55N 0 40W
Linton **5 A5** 52 6N 0 19 E
Lisburn **14 B5** 54 30N 6 9W
Liscannor, B. **15 D2** 52 57N 9 24W
Lismore **15 D4** 52 8N 7 58W
Liss **5 B4** 51 3N 0 53W
Listowel **15 D2** 52 27N 9 30W
Litcham **5 A5** 52 43N 0 49 E
Litherland **8 C3** 53 29N 3 0W
Little Minch **12 D2** 57 35N 6 45W
Little Ouse → **5 A5** 52 25N 0 50 E
Little Walsingham **5 A5** 52 53N 0 51 E
Littlehampton **5 C4** 50 48N 0 32W
Littleport **5 A5** 52 27N 0 18 E
Littlestone-on-Sea **5 C5** 50 59N 0 59 E
Liverpool **8 C3** 53 25N 3 0W
Lizard Pt. **6 C2** 49 57N 5 11W
Llandeilo **7 C2** 51 53N 4 3W
Llandovery **7 C3** 51 59N 3 49W
Llandrindod Wells **7 B3** 52 15N 3 23W
Llandudno **7 A3** 53 19N 3 51W
Llanelli **7 C2** 51 41N 4 11W
Llangollen **7 B3** 52 58N 3 10W
Llanidloes **7 B3** 52 28N 3 31W
Llanymynech **4 A1** 52 48N 3 6W
Lochaber **12 E3** 56 55N 5 0W
Lochcarron **12 D3** 57 25N 5 30W
Lochgelly **11 A5** 56 7N 3 18W
Lochgilphead **10 A3** 56 2N 5 37W
Lochinver **12 C3** 58 9N 5 15W
Lochnagar **13 E5** 56 57N 3 14W
Lochy → **12 E3** 56 52N 5 3W
Lockerbie **11 B5** 55 7N 3 21W
Loddon **5 A6** 52 32N 1 29 E
Loftus **9 B5** 54 33N 0 52W
Lomond, L. **10 A4** 56 8N 4 38W
London **5 B4** 51 30N 0 5W
London, Greater □ **5 B4** 51 30N 0 5W
London Colney **5 B4** 51 43N 0 18W
Londonderry **14 A4** 55 0N 7 23W
Londonderry □ **14 B4** 55 0N 7 20W
Long Bennington **9 D5** 52 59N 0 45W
Long Clawson **5 A4** 52 51N 0 56W
Long Crendon **5 B4** 51 47N 1 0W
Long Eaton **9 D4** 52 54N 1 16W
Long Itchington **4 A3** 52 16N 1 24W
Long Melford **5 A5** 52 5N 0 44 E
Long Mynd **4 A2** 52 35N 2 50W
Long Preston **8 B3** 54 0N 2 16W
Long Sutton **5 A5** 52 47N 0 9 E
Longford, *Gloucs.* **4 B2** 51 53N 2 14W
Longford, *Longf.* **14 C4** 53 43N 7 50W
Longford □ **14 C4** 53 42N 7 45W
Longhorsley **9 A4** 55 14N 1 46W
Longridge **8 C3** 53 50N 2 37W
Longton **8 C3** 53 43N 2 48W
Longtown, *Cumb.* **8 A3** 55 1N 2 59W
Longtown, *Here. & Worcs.* **4 B2** 51 58N 2 59W
Loop Hd. **15 D2** 52 34N 9 55W
Loose **5 B5** 51 15N 0 32 E
Lorn **10 A3** 56 26N 5 10W
Lorn, Firth of **10 A3** 56 20N 5 40W
Lossiemouth **13 D5** 57 43N 3 17W
Lothian □ **11 B6** 55 50N 3 0W
Loughborough **4 A3** 52 46N 1 11W
Loughrea **15 C3** 53 11N 8 33W
Loughros More B. **14 B3** 54 48N 8 30W
Loughton **5 B5** 51 38N 0 4 E
Louth, *Lincs.* **9 C5** 53 23N 0 0 E
Louth, *Louth* **14 C5** 53 47N 6 33W
Louth □ **14 C5** 53 55N 6 30W
Lower Beeding **5 B4** 51 2N 0 15W
Lower Shiplake **5 B4** 51 30N 0 53W
Lowes Water **8 B2** 54 35N 3 23W
Lowestoft **5 A6** 52 29N 1 44 E
Luce Bay **10 C4** 54 45N 4 48W
Ludgershall **4 B3** 51 15N 1 38W
Ludlow **4 A2** 52 23N 2 42W
Lugnaquilla **15 D5** 52 58N 6 28W
Lugwardine **4 A2** 52 4N 2 38W
Lundy **6 A3** 51 10N 4 41W
Lune → **8 B3** 54 0N 2 51W
Lurgan **14 B5** 54 28N 6 20W
Luton **5 B4** 51 53N 0 24W
Lutterworth **4 A3** 52 28N 1 12W
Lydd **5 C5** 50 57N 0 56 E
Lydham **4 A2** 52 31N 2 59W
Lydney **4 B2** 51 43N 2 32W
Lyme Regis **6 B5** 50 44N 2 57W
Lyminge **5 B6** 51 7N 1 6 E
Lymington **4 C3** 50 46N 1 32W
Lymm **8 C3** 53 23N 2 30W
Lympne **5 B6** 51 4N 1 2 E
Lyndhurst **4 C3** 50 53N 1 33W
Lyneham **4 B3** 51 30N 1 57W
Lynton **6 A4** 51 14N 3 50W
Lytchett Minster **4 C2** 50 44N 2 3W
Lytham St. Anne's **8 C3** 53 45N 2 58W
Lythe **9 B5** 54 30N 0 40W

M

Mablethorpe **9 C6** 53 21N 0 14 E
Macclesfield **8 C3** 53 16N 2 9W
Macduff **13 D6** 57 40N 2 30W
Macgillycuddy's Reeks **15 D2** 52 2N 9 45W
Machynlleth **7 B3** 52 36N 3 51W
Macroom **15 E3** 51 54N 8 57W
Madeley, *Shrops.* **4 A2** 52 38N 2 28W
Madeley, *Staffs.* **8 D3** 52 59N 2 20W
Madley **4 A2** 52 3N 2 51W
Maesteg **7 C3** 51 36N 3 40W
Magee, I. **14 B6** 54 48N 5 44W
Magherafelt **14 B5** 54 44N 6 37W
Maghull **8 C3** 53 31N 2 56W
Maiden Bradley **4 B2** 51 9N 2 18W
Maiden Newton **4 C2** 50 46N 2 35W
Maidenhead **5 B4** 51 31N 0 42W
Maidstone **5 B5** 51 16N 0 31 E
Main → **14 B5** 54 49N 6 20W
Maine → **15 D2** 52 10N 9 40W
Mainland, *Orkney* **13 C5** 59 0N 3 10W
Mainland, *Shet.* **12 A8** 60 15N 1 22W
Mal B. **15 D2** 52 50N 9 30W
Maldon **5 B5** 51 43N 0 41 E
Malham Tarn **8 B3** 54 6N 2 11W
Malin Hd. **14 A4** 55 18N 7 24W
Mallaig **12 E3** 57 0N 5 50W
Mallow **15 D3** 52 8N 8 40W
Malmesbury **4 B2** 51 35N 2 5W
Malpas **8 C3** 53 3N 2 47W
Maltby **9 C4** 53 25N 1 12W
Malton **9 B5** 54 9N 0 48W
Malvern Wells **4 A2** 52 4N 2 19W
Man, I. of **8 B1** 54 15N 4 30W
Manby **9 C6** 53 22N 0 6 E
Manchester **8 C3** 53 30N 2 15W
Manea **5 A5** 52 29N 0 10 E
Mangotsfield **4 B2** 51 29N 2 29W
Manningtree **5 B6** 51 56N 1 3 E
Mansfield **9 C4** 53 8N 1 12W
Mansfield Woodhouse **9 C4** 53 11N 1 11W
Manton **5 A4** 52 37N 0 41W
March **5 A5** 52 33N 0 5 E
Marden **4 A2** 52 7N 2 42W
Maree L. **12 D3** 57 40N 5 30W
Mareham le Fen **9 C5** 53 7N 0 3W
Maresfield **5 C5** 51 0N 0 5 E
Marfleet **9 C5** 53 45N 0 15W
Margate **5 B6** 51 23N 1 24 E
Market Bosworth **4 A3** 52 37N 1 24W
Market Deeping **5 A4** 52 40N 0 20W
Market Drayton **8 D3** 52 55N 2 30W
Market Harborough **5 A4** 52 29N 0 55W
Market Lavington **4 B3** 51 17N 1 59W
Market Rasen **9 C5** 53 24N 0 20W
Market Weighton **9 C5** 53 52N 0 40W
Markfield **4 A3** 52 42N 1 18W
Marks Tey **5 B5** 51 53N 0 48 E
Marlborough **4 B3** 51 26N 1 44W
Marlborough Downs **4 B3** 51 25N 1 55W
Marlow **5 B4** 51 34N 0 47W
Marnhull **4 C2** 50 58N 2 20W
Marple **8 C3** 53 23N 2 5W
Marshfield **4 B2** 51 27N 2 18W
Marske by the Sea **9 B5** 54 35N 1 0W
Marston Moor **9 C4** 53 58N 1 17W
Martham **5 A6** 52 42N 1 38 E
Martley **4 A2** 52 14N 2 22W
Martock **4 C2** 50 58N 2 47W
Maryborough = Port Laoise **15 C4** 53 2N 7 20W
Maryport **8 B2** 54 43N 3 30W
Masham **9 B4** 54 15N 1 40W
Mask, L. **14 C2** 53 36N 9 24W

Matlock **9 C4** 53 8N 1 32W
Maughold **8 B1** 54 18N 4 17W
Maughold Hd. **8 B1** 54 18N 4 17W
Mayfield, *Derby* **9 C4** 53 1N 1 47W
Mayfield, *E. Susx.* **5 B5** 51 1N 0 17 E
Mayland **5 B5** 51 40N 0 46 E
Maynooth **14 C5** 53 22N 6 38W
Mayo □ **14 C2** 53 47N 9 7W
Mealsgate **8 B2** 54 46N 3 14W
Measham **4 A3** 52 43N 1 30W
Meath □ **14 C5** 53 32N 6 40W
Medstead **4 B3** 51 7N 1 4W
Medway → **5 B5** 51 28N 0 45 E
Melbourn **5 A5** 52 5N 0 1 E
Melbourne **4 A3** 52 50N 1 25W
Melksham **4 B2** 51 22N 2 9W
Melmerby **8 B3** 54 44N 2 35W
Melrose **11 B6** 55 35N 2 44W
Melsonby **9 B4** 54 28N 1 41W
Meltham **8 C4** 53 35N 1 51W
Melton **5 A6** 52 6N 1 20 E
Melton Constable **5 A6** 52 52N 1 1 E
Melton Mowbray **5 A4** 52 46N 0 52W
Menai Strait **7 A2** 53 14N 4 10W
Mendip Hills **4 B2** 51 17N 2 40W
Mendlesham **5 A6** 52 15N 1 4 E
Mere **4 B2** 51 5N 2 16W
Meriden **4 A3** 52 27N 1 36W
Merrick **10 B4** 55 8N 4 30W
Merriott **4 C2** 50 55N 2 47W
Mersea I. **5 B5** 51 48N 0 55 E
Mersey → **8 C3** 53 20N 2 56W
Merseyside □ **8 C3** 53 25N 2 55W
Merthyr Tydfil **7 C3** 51 45N 3 23W
Merton **5 B4** 51 25N 0 13W
Metheringham **9 C5** 53 9N 0 22W
Methwold **5 A5** 52 30N 0 33 E
Mexborough **9 C4** 53 29N 1 18W
Micheldever **4 B3** 51 7N 1 17W
Mickle Fell **8 B3** 54 38N 2 16W
Mickleover **9 D4** 52 55N 1 32W
Mickleton, *Durham* **8 B3** 54 36N 2 3W
Mickleton, *Gloucs.* **4 A3** 52 5N 1 45W
Mid Glamorgan □ **7 C3** 51 40N 3 25W
Middleham **9 B4** 54 17N 1 49W
Middlemarsh **4 C2** 50 51N 2 29W
Middlesbrough **9 B4** 54 35N 1 14W
Middleton, *Gt. Man.* **8 C3** 53 33N 2 12W
Middleton, *Norfolk* **5 A5** 52 43N 0 29 E
Middleton Cheney **4 A3** 52 4N 1 17W
Middleton in Teesdale **8 B3** 54 38N 2 5W
Middleton-on-Sea **5 C4** 50 48N 0 37W
Middleton on the Wolds **9 C5** 53 56N 0 35W
Middlewich **8 C3** 53 12N 2 28W
Middlezoy **4 B2** 51 5N 2 54W
Midhurst **5 C4** 50 59N 0 44W
Midleton **15 E3** 51 52N 8 12W
Midsomer Norton **4 B2** 51 17N 2 29W
Milborne Port **4 C2** 50 57N 2 27W
Mildenhall **5 A5** 52 20N 0 30 E
Milford **5 B4** 51 10N 0 38W
Milford Haven **7 C1** 51 43N 5 2W
Milford on Sea **4 C3** 50 44N 1 36W
Millom **8 B2** 54 13N 3 16W
Milltown Malbay **15 D2** 52 51N 9 25W
Milnthorpe **8 B3** 54 14N 2 47W
Milton **13 D4** 57 18N 4 32W
Milton Keynes **5 A4** 52 3N 0 42W
Milverton **4 B1** 51 2N 3 15W
Minchinhampton **4 B2** 51 42N 2 10W
Minehead **4 B1** 51 12N 3 29W
Minster **5 B6** 51 20N 1 20 E
Minster-on-Sea **5 B5** 51 25N 0 50 E
Minsterley **4 A2** 52 38N 2 56W
Mirfield **9 C4** 53 37N 1 54W
Misterton, *Notts.* **9 C5** 53 27N 0 49W
Misterton, *Somst.* **4 C2** 50 51N 2 46W
Mistley **5 B6** 51 56N 1 4 E
Mitcheldean **4 B2** 51 51N 2 29W
Mitchelstown **15 D3** 52 16N 8 18W
Mizen Hd., *Cork* **15 E2** 51 27N 9 50W
Mizen Hd., *Wick.* **15 D5** 52 52N 6 4W
Moffat **11 B5** 55 20N 3 27W
Moidart, L. **12 E3** 56 47N 5 40W
Mold **7 A3** 53 10N 3 10W
Mole → **5 B4** 51 13N 0 15W
Monach Is. **12 D1** 57 32N 7 40W
Monadhliath Mts. **13 D4** 57 10N 4 4W
Monaghan **14 B5** 54 15N 6 58W
Monaghan □ **14 B5** 54 15N 7 0W
Monmouth **7 C4** 51 48N 2 43W
Monnow → **4 B2** 51 54N 2 48W
Montgomery **7 B3** 52 34N 3 9W
Montrose **13 E6** 56 43N 2 28W
Moorfoot Hills **11 B5** 55 44N 3 8W
Morar, L. **12 E3** 56 57N 5 40W
Moray Firth **13 D5** 57 50N 3 30W
Morecambe **8 B3** 54 5N 2 52W
Morecambe B. **8 B3** 54 7N 3 0W
Moreton-in-Marsh **4 B3** 51 59N 1 42W
Morley **9 C4** 53 45N 1 36W
Morpeth **9 A4** 55 11N 1 41W
Mortimer's Cross **4 A2** 52 17N 2 50W
Morton Fen **5 A4** 52 45N 0 23W
Morvern **10 A3** 56 38N 5 44W
Mossley **8 C3** 53 31N 2 1W
Motcombe **4 B2** 51 1N 2 12W
Motherwell **11 B5** 55 48N 4 0W
Mottisfont **4 B3** 51 2N 1 32W
Moulton, *Lincs.* **5 A4** 52 48N 0 4W
Moulton, *Northants.* **5 A4** 52 17N 0 51W
Mountmellick **15 C4** 53 7N 7 20W
Mountsorrel **4 A3** 52 43N 1 9W
Mourne → **14 B4** 54 45N 7 39W
Mourne Mts. **14 B5** 54 10N 6 0W
Moville **14 A4** 55 11N 7 3W
Moy → **14 B3** 54 5N 8 50W
Moyle □ **14 A5** 55 10N 6 15W
Much Dewchurch **4 B2** 51 58N 2 45W
Much Marcle **4 B2** 51 59N 2 27W
Much Wenlock **4 A2** 52 36N 2 34W
Muck **12 E2** 56 50N 6 15W
Muine Bheag **15 D5** 52 42N 6 57W
Mull **10 A3** 56 27N 6 0W
Mullet Pen. **14 B1** 54 10N 10 2W
Mullingar **14 C4** 53 31N 7 20W
Mundesley **5 A6** 52 53N 1 24 E
Munster □ **15 D3** 52 20N 8 40W
Murton **9 B4** 54 51N 1 22W
Musselburgh **11 B5** 55 57N 3 3W
Mweelrea **14 C2** 53 37N 9 48W
Myddle **4 A2** 52 49N 2 47W
Mynydd Du **7 C3** 51 45N 3 45W

N

Naas **15 C5** 53 12N 6 40W
Nafferton **9 B5** 54 1N 0 24W
Nailsea **4 B2** 51 25N 2 44W
Nailsworth **4 B2** 51 41N 2 12W
Nairn **13 D5** 57 35N 3 54W
Nantwich **8 C3** 53 5N 2 31W
Nappa **8 C3** 53 58N 2 14W
Narborough **4 A3** 52 34N 1 12W
Naseby **5 A4** 52 24N 0 59W
Navan = An Uaimh **14 C5** 53 39N 6 40W
Navenby **9 C5** 53 7N 0 32W
Naver → **13 C4** 58 34N 4 15W
Naze, The **5 B6** 51 53N 1 19 E
Neagh, Lough **14 B5** 54 35N 6 25W
Neath **7 C3** 51 39N 3 49W
Needham Market **5 A6** 52 9N 1 2 E
Needles, The **4 C3** 50 39N 1 35W
Nelson **8 C3** 53 50N 2 14W
Nenagh **15 D3** 52 52N 8 11W
Nene → **5 A5** 52 38N 0 13 E
Nephin **14 B2** 54 1N 9 21W
Ness, L. **13 D4** 57 15N 4 30W
Neston **8 C2** 53 17N 3 3W
Netley **4 C3** 50 53N 1 21W
Netley Marsh **4 C3** 50 55N 1 32W
Nettlebed **5 B4** 51 34N 0 54W
Nettleham **9 C5** 53 15N 0 28W
New Alresford **4 B3** 51 6N 1 10W
New Brighton **8 C2** 53 27N 3 2W
New Forest **4 C3** 50 53N 1 40W
New Holland **9 C5** 53 42N 0 22W
New Mills **8 C4** 53 22N 2 0W
New Milton **4 C3** 50 45N 1 40W
New Radnor **7 B3** 52 15N 3 10W
New Romney **5 C5** 50 59N 0 57 E
New Ross **15 D5** 52 24N 6 58W
New Rossington **9 C4** 53 30N 1 4W
New Scone **11 A5** 56 25N 3 26W
Newark-on-Trent **9 C5** 53 6N 0 48W
Newbury **4 B3** 51 24N 1 19W
Newby Bridge **8 B3** 54 16N 2 59W
Newcastle **14 B6** 54 13N 5 54W
Newcastle Emlyn **7 B2** 52 2N 4 29W
Newcastle-under-Lyme **8 C3** 53 2N 2 15W
Newcastle-upon-Tyne **9 B4** 54 59N 1 37W
Newent **4 B2** 51 56N 2 24W
Newham **5 B5** 51 31N 0 2 E
Newhaven **5 C5** 50 47N 0 4 E
Newick **5 C5** 50 58N 0 0 E
Newington, *Kent* **5 B6** 51 5N 1 8 E
Newington, *Kent* **5 B5** 51 21N 0 40 E
Newmarket, *Cork* **15 D3** 52 13N 9 0W
Newmarket, *Suffolk* **5 A5** 52 15N 0 23 E
Newnham **4 B2** 51 48N 2 27W
Newport, *Essex* **5 B5** 51 58N 0 13 E
Newport, *Gwent* **7 C4** 51 35N 3 0W
Newport, *I. of W.* **4 C3** 50 42N 1 18W
Newport, *Shrops.* **4 A2** 52 47N 2 22W
Newport Pagnell **5 A4** 52 5N 0 42W
Newquay **6 B2** 50 24N 5 6W
Newry **14 B5** 54 10N 6 20W
Newry & Mourne □ **14 B5** 54 10N 6 15W
Newton Abbot **6 B4** 50 32N 3 37W
Newton Arlosh **8 B2** 54 53N 3 15W
Newton Aycliffe **9 B4** 54 36N 1 33W
Newton le Willows **8 C3** 53 28N 2 40W
Newton Stewart **10 C4** 54 57N 4 30W
Newtonmore **13 D4** 57 4N 4 7W
Newtown **7 B3** 52 31N 3 19W
Newtownabbey □ **14 B6** 54 45N 6 0W
Newtownards **14 B6** 54 37N 5 40W
Nidd → **9 B4** 54 1N 1 32W
Nidderdale **9 B4** 54 5N 1 46W
Ninfield **5 C5** 50 53N 0 26 E
Nith → **11 B5** 55 20N 3 5W
Niton **4 C3** 50 35N 1 14W
Nordelph **5 A5** 52 34N 0 18 E
Norfolk □ **5 A6** 52 39N 1 0 E
Norfolk Broads **5 A6** 52 30N 1 15 E
Normanton **9 C4** 53 41N 1 26W
North Berwick **11 A6** 56 4N 2 44W
North Cerney **4 B3** 51 45N 1 58W
North Channel **10 B3** 55 0N 5 30W
North Collingham **9 C5** 53 8N 0 46W
North Dorset Downs **4 C2** 50 50N 2 30W
North Down □ **14 B6** 54 40N 5 45W
North Downs **5 B5** 51 17N 0 30 E
North Esk → **13 E6** 56 44N 2 25W
North Foreland **5 B6** 51 22N 1 28 E
North Hykeham **9 C5** 53 10N 0 35W
North Minch **12 C3** 58 5N 5 55W
North Petherton **4 B1** 51 6N 3 1W
North Ronaldsay **13 B6** 59 20N 2 30W
North Somercotes **9 C6** 53 28N 0 9 E
North Thoresby **9 C5** 53 27N 0 3W
North Tidworth **4 B3** 51 14N 1 40W
North Tyne → **9 B3** 54 59N 2 7W
North Uist **12 D1** 57 40N 7 15W
North Walsham **5 A6** 52 49N 1 22 E
North West Highlands **12 D3** 57 35N 5 2W
North York Moors **9 B5** 54 25N 0 50W
North Yorkshire □ **9 B4** 54 15N 1 25W
Northallerton **9 B4** 54 20N 1 26W
Northampton **5 A4** 52 14N 0 54W
Northamptonshire □ **5 A4** 52 16N 0 55W
Northern Ireland □ **14 B5** 54 45N 7 0W
Northfleet **5 B5** 51 26N 0 20 E
Northiam **5 C5** 50 59N 0 39 E
Northleach **4 B3** 51 49N 1 50W
Northrepps **5 A6** 52 53N 1 20 E
Northumberland □ **9 A4** 55 12N 2 0W
Northwich **8 C3** 53 16N 2 30W
Northwold **5 A5** 52 33N 0 37 E
Northwood **4 C3** 50 44N 1 18W
Norton, *N. Yorks.* **9 B5** 54 9N 0 48W
Norton, *Suffolk* **5 A5** 52 15N 0 52 E
Norton Fitzwarren **4 B1** 51 1N 3 10W
Norwich **5 A6** 52 38N 1 17 E
Noss Hd. **13 C5** 58 29N 3 4W
Nottingham **9 D4** 52 57N 1 10W
Nottinghamshire □ **9 C4** 53 10N 1 0W
Nuneaton **4 A3** 52 32N 1 29W
Nunney **4 B2** 51 13N 2 20W

O

Oadby **4 A3** 52 37N 1 7W
Oakengates **4 A2** 52 42N 2 29W
Oakham **5 A4** 52 40N 0 43W
Oban **10 A3** 56 25N 5 30W
Ochil Hills **11 A5** 56 14N 3 40W
Odiham **5 B4** 51 16N 0 56W
Offaly □ **15 C4** 53 15N 7 30W
Okehampton **6 B3** 50 44N 4 1W
Old Basing **4 B3** 51 16N 1 3W
Old Castle **14 C4** 53 46N 7 10W
Old Fletton **5 A4** 52 34N 0 13W
Old Leake **9 C6** 53 2N 0 6 E
Oldbury, *Avon* **4 B2** 51 38N 2 30W
Oldbury, *W. Mids.* **4 A3** 52 30N 2 0W
Oldham **8 C3** 53 33N 2 8W
Ollerton **9 C4** 53 12N 1 1W
Olney **5 A4** 52 9N 0 42W
Omagh **14 B4** 54 36N 7 20W
Omagh □ **14 B4** 54 35N 7 15W
Ombersley **4 A2** 52 17N 2 12W
Onchan **8 B1** 54 11N 4 27W
Onny → **4 A2** 52 30N 2 50W
Orford **5 A6** 52 6N 1 31 E
Orford Ness **5 A6** 52 6N 1 31 E
Orkney □ **13 C6** 59 0N 3 0W
Orkney Is. **13 C6** 59 0N 3 0W
Ormesby St. Margaret **5 A6** 52 39N 1 42 E
Ormskirk **8 C3** 53 35N 2 53W
Orton **8 B3** 54 28N 2 34W
Orwell → **5 A6** 52 2N 1 12 E
Osmotherley **9 B4** 54 22N 1 18W
Ossett **9 C4** 53 40N 1 35W
Oswaldtwistle **8 C3** 53 44N 2 27W
Oswestry **4 A1** 52 52N 3 3W
Otford **5 B5** 51 18N 0 11 E
Otley **9 C4** 53 54N 1 41W
Oulton **5 A6** 52 29N 1 40 E
Oulton Broad **5 A6** 52 28N 1 43 E
Oundle **5 A4** 52 28N 0 28W
Ouse →, *E. Susx.* **5 C5** 50 43N 0 3 E
Ouse →, *N. Yorks.* **9 B6** 54 3N 0 7 E
Outer Hebrides **12 D1** 57 30N 7 40W
Outwell **5 A5** 52 36N 0 14 E
Over Wallop **4 B3** 51 9N 1 35W
Overstrand **5 A6** 52 55N 1 20 E
Overton **4 B3** 51 14N 1 16W
Owston Ferry **9 C5** 53 28N 0 47W
Ox Mts. **14 B3** 54 6N 9 0W
Oxford **4 B3** 51 45N 1 15W
Oxfordshire □ **4 B3** 51 45N 1 15W
Oxted **5 B4** 51 14N 0 1W
Oykel → **13 D4** 57 55N 4 26W

P

Paddock Wood **5 B5** 51 13N 0 24 E
Padiham **8 C3** 53 48N 2 20W
Padstow **6 B3** 50 33N 4 57W
Paignton **6 B4** 50 26N 3 33W
Painshawfield **9 B4** 54 56N 1 54W
Painswick **4 B2** 51 47N 2 11W
Paisley **10 B4** 55 51N 4 27W
Palgrave **5 A6** 52 22N 1 7 E
Pangbourne **4 B3** 51 28N 1 5W
Pant → **5 B5** 51 45N 0 40 E
Parrett → **4 B2** 51 7N 2 58W
Partington **8 C3** 53 25N 2 25W
Partney **9 C6** 53 12N 0 7 E
Parton **8 B2** 54 34N 3 35W
Passage West **15 E3** 51 52N 8 20W
Patcham **5 C4** 50 52N 0 9W
Pateley Bridge **9 B4** 54 5N 1 45W
Patrick **8 B1** 54 13N 4 41W
Patrington **9 C5** 53 41N 0 1W
Patterdale **8 B3** 54 33N 2 55W
Paull **9 C5** 53 42N 0 12W
Peacehaven **5 C5** 50 47N 0 1 E
Peak, The = Kinder Scout **8 C4** 53 24N 1 53W
Peasedown St. John **4 B2** 51 18N 2 25W
Peasenhall **5 A6** 52 17N 1 24 E
Peebles **11 B5** 55 40N 3 12W
Peel **8 B1** 54 13N 4 41W
Pegwell Bay **5 B6** 51 18N 1 22 E
Pembridge **4 A2** 52 13N 2 54W
Pembroke **7 C2** 51 41N 4 57W
Pembury **5 B5** 51 8N 0 20 E
Pen-y-Ghent **8 B3** 54 10N 2 15W
Pendle Hill **8 C3** 53 53N 2 18W
Penicuik **11 B5** 55 50N 3 14W
Penistone **9 C4** 53 31N 1 38W
Penkridge **4 A2** 52 44N 2 8W
Pennines **8 B3** 54 50N 2 20W
Penrith **8 B3** 54 40N 2 45W
Penshurst **5 B5** 51 10N 0 12 E
Pentland Firth **13 C5** 58 43N 3 10W
Pentland Hills **11 B5** 55 48N 3 25W
Penwortham **8 C3** 53 45N 2 44W
Penzance **6 B2** 50 7N 5 32W
Perham Down Camp **4 B3** 51 14N 1 38W
Pershore **4 A2** 52 7N 2 4W
Perth **11 A5** 56 24N 3 27W
Peterborough **5 A4** 52 35N 0 14W
Peterchurch **4 A2** 52 3N 2 57W
Peterhead **13 D7** 57 30N 1 49W
Peterlee **9 B4** 54 45N 1 18W
Petersfield **5 C4** 51 0N 0 56W
Petworth **5 C4** 50 59N 0 37W
Pevensey **5 C5** 50 49N 0 20 E
Pevensey Levels **5 C5** 50 50N 0 20 E
Pewsey **4 B3** 51 20N 1 46W
Pewsey, Vale of **4 B3** 51 20N 1 46W
Pickering **9 B5** 54 15N 0 46W
Pickering, Vale of **9 B5** 54 14N 0 45W
Pidley **5 A4** 52 33N 0 4W
Pilling **8 C3** 53 55N 2 54W
Pilton **4 B2** 51 10N 2 35W
Pinchbeck **5 A4** 52 48N 0 9W
Pirbright **5 B4** 51 17N 0 40W
Pitlochry **13 E5** 56 43N 3 43W
Plymouth **6 B3** 50 23N 4 9W
Plynlimon = Pumlumon Fawr **7 B3** 52 29N 3 47W
Pocklington **9 C5** 53 56N 0 48W
Polden Hills **4 B2** 51 7N 2 50W
Polegate **5 C5** 50 49N 0 15 E
Polesworth **4 A3** 52 37N 1 37W
Pontefract **9 C4** 53 42N 1 19W
Pontrilas **4 B2** 51 56N 2 53W
Pontypool **7 C3** 51 42N 3 1W
Pontypridd **7 C3** 51 36N 3 21W
Poole **4 C3** 50 42N 1 58W
Poole Harbour **4 C3** 50 41N 2 0W
Pooley Bridge **8 B3** 54 37N 2 49W
Porlock **4 B1** 51 13N 3 36W
Porlock B. **4 B1** 51 14N 3 37W
Porlock Hill **4 B1** 51 12N 3 40W
Port Carlisle **8 B2** 54 56N 3 12W
Port Ellen **10 B2** 55 38N 6 10W
Port Erin **8 B1** 54 5N 4 45W
Port Glasgow **10 B4** 55 57N 4 40W
Port Laoise **15 C4** 53 2N 7 20W
Port St. Mary **8 B1** 54 5N 4 45W
Port Sunlight **8 C3** 53 22N 3 0W
Port Talbot **7 C3** 51 35N 3 48W
Portadown **14 B5** 54 27N 6 26W
Portarlington **15 C4** 53 10N 7 10W
Porthcawl **7 C3** 51 28N 3 42W
Portishead **4 B2** 51 29N 2 46W
Portland, I. of **4 C2** 50 32N 2 25W
Portland Bill **4 C2** 50 31N 2 27W
Porton **4 B3** 51 8N 1 42W
Portpatrick **10 C3** 54 50N 5 7W
Portree **12 D2** 57 25N 6 11W
Portrush **14 A5** 55 13N 6 40W
Portslade **5 C4** 50 50N 0 11W
Portsmouth **4 C3** 50 48N 1 6W
Portsoy **13 D6** 57 41N 2 41W
Portumna **15 C3** 53 5N 8 12W
Potter Heigham **5 A6** 52 44N 1 33 E
Potterne **4 B3** 51 19N 2 0W
Potters Bar **5 B4** 51 42N 0 11W
Potterspury **5 A4** 52 5N 0 52W
Potton **5 A4** 52 7N 0 12W
Poulaphouca Res. **15 C5** 53 8N 6 30W
Poulton le Fylde **8 C3** 53 51N 2 59W
Powick **4 A2** 52 9N 2 15W
Powys □ **7 B3** 52 20N 3 20W
Prees **8 D3** 52 54N 2 40W
Preesall **8 C3** 53 55N 2 58W
Prescot **8 C3** 53 27N 2 49W
Preshute **4 B3** 51 24N 1 45W
Prestbury **4 B2** 51 54N 2 2W
Presteigne **7 B3** 52 17N 3 0W
Preston, *Dorset* **4 C2** 50 38N 2 26W
Preston, *Lancs.* **8 C3** 53 46N 2 42W
Prestonpans **11 B6** 55 58N 2 58W
Prestwich **8 C3** 53 32N 2 18W
Prestwick **10 B4** 55 30N 4 38W
Prestwood **5 B4** 51 41N 0 44W
Princes Risborough **5 B4** 51 43N 0 50W
Puddletown **4 C2** 50 45N 2 21W
Pudsey **9 C4** 53 47N 1 40W
Pulborough **5 C4** 50 58N 0 30W
Pulham Market **5 A6** 52 25N 1 15 E
Pulham St. Mary **5 A6** 52 25N 1 14 E
Pumlumon Fawr **7 B3** 52 29N 3 47W
Purbeck, Isle of **4 C2** 50 40N 2 5W
Purfleet **5 B5** 51 29N 0 15 E
Purley **4 B3** 51 29N 1 4W
Purton **4 B3** 51 35N 1 52W
Pwllheli **7 B2** 52 54N 4 26W

Q

Quadring **9 D5** 52 53N 0 9W
Quainton **5 B4** 51 51N 0 53W
Quantock Hills **4 B1** 51 8N 3 10W
Queenborough **5 B5** 51 24N 0 46 E
Queensbury **8 C4** 53 46N 1 50W
Quorndon **4 A3** 52 45N 1 10W

R

Raasay **12 D2** 57 25N 6 4W
Raasay, Sd. of **12 D2** 57 30N 6 8W
Rackheath **5 A6** 52 41N 1 22 E
Radcliffe, *Gt. Man.* **8 C3** 53 35N 2 19W
Radcliffe, *Notts.* **9 D4** 52 57N 1 3W
Radlett **5 B4** 51 41N 0 19W
Radley **4 B3** 51 42N 1 14W
Radnor Forest **7 B3** 52 17N 3 10W
Radstock **4 B2** 51 17N 2 25W
Rainham **5 B5** 51 22N 0 36 E
Rainworth **9 C4** 53 8N 1 6W
Rampside **8 B2** 54 6N 3 10W
Ramsbottom **8 C3** 53 36N 2 20W
Ramsbury **4 B3** 51 26N 1 37W
Ramsey, *Cambs.* **5 A4** 52 27N 0 6W
Ramsey, *Essex* **5 B6** 51 55N 1 12 E
Ramsey, *I. of M.* **8 B1** 54 20N 4 21W

Ramsey Bay 8 B1 54 23N 4 20W
Ramsgate 5 B6 51 20N 1 25 E
Rannoch, L. 13 E4 56 41N 4 20W
Rannoch Moor 10 A4 56 38N 4 48W
Rath Luirc 15 D3 52 21N 8 40W
Rathdrum 15 D5 52 57N 6 13W
Rathkeale 15 D3 52 32N 8 57W
Rathlin 14 A5 55 18N 6 14W
Rathlin O'Birne I. 14 B3 54 40N 8 50W
Rattray Hd. 13 D7 57 38N 1 50W
Raunds 5 A4 52 20N 0 32W
Ravenglass 8 B2 54 21N 3 25W
Ravenshead 9 C4 53 5N 1 10W
Ravenstonedale 8 B3 54 26N 2 26W
Rawmarsh 9 C4 53 27N 1 20W
Rawtenstall 8 C3 53 42N 2 18W
Rayleigh 5 B5 51 36N 0 38 E
Reading 5 B4 51 27N 0 57W
Reculver 5 B6 51 22N 1 12 E
Red Dial 8 B2 54 48N 3 9W
Redbridge 5 B5 51 35N 0 7 E
Redcar 9 B4 54 37N 1 4W
Redditch 4 A3 52 18N 1 57W
Redhill 5 B4 51 14N 0 10W
Redlynch 4 C3 50 59N 1 42W
Redmile 9 D5 52 54N 0 48W
Redmire 8 B4 54 19N 1 55W
Redruth 6 B2 50 14N 5 14W
Ree, L. 14 C4 53 35N 8 0W
Reedham 5 A6 52 34N 1 33 E
Reepham 5 A6 52 46N 1 6 E
Reeth 8 B4 54 23N 1 56W
Reigate 5 B4 51 14N 0 11W
Renfrew 10 B4 55 52N 4 24W
Repton 4 A3 52 50N 1 32W
Reydon 5 A6 52 21N 1 40 E
Rhayader 7 B3 52 19N 3 30W
Rhondda 7 C3 51 39N 3 30W
Rhum 12 E2 57 0N 6 20W
Rhyl 7 A3 53 19N 3 29W
Rhymney 7 C3 51 45N 3 17W
Ribble → 8 B3 54 13N 2 20W
Riccall 9 C4 53 50N 1 4W
Richmond 9 B4 54 24N 1 43W
Richmond-upon-Thames 5 B4 51 28N 0 18W
Rickmansworth 5 B4 51 38N 0 28W
Rievaulx 9 B4 54 16N 1 7W
Rillington 9 B5 54 10N 0 41W
Ringmer 5 C5 50 53N 0 5 E
Ringwood 4 C3 50 50N 1 48W
Ripley, *Derby* 9 C4 53 3N 1 24W
Ripley, *N. Yorks.* 9 B4 54 3N 1 34W
Ripon 9 B4 54 8N 1 31W
Rishton 8 C3 53 46N 2 26W
Roade 5 A4 52 10N 0 53W
Roadhead 8 A3 55 4N 2 44W
Roag, L. 12 C2 58 10N 6 55W
Robe → 14 C2 53 38N 9 10W
Robin Hood's Bay 9 B5 54 26N 0 31W
Rocester 8 D4 52 56N 1 50W
Rochdale 8 C3 53 36N 2 10W
Rochester 5 B5 51 22N 0 30 E
Rochford 5 B5 51 36N 0 42 E
Rockcliffe 8 B3 54 58N 3 0W
Rockingham 5 A4 52 32N 0 43W
Rockingham Forest 5 A4 52 28N 0 42W
Roding → 5 B5 51 31N 0 7 E
Roe → 14 A5 55 10N 6 59W
Rogans Seat 8 B3 54 25N 2 10W
Rogate 5 B4 51 0N 0 51W
Romney Marsh 5 B5 51 4N 0 58 E
Romsey 4 C3 51 0N 1 29W
Rona 12 D3 57 33N 5 57W
Ropsley 9 D5 52 53N 0 31W
Roscommon 14 C3 53 38N 8 11W
Roscommon □ 14 C3 53 40N 8 15W
Roscrea 15 D4 52 58N 7 50W
Rosedale Abbey 9 B5 54 22N 0 51W
Ross-on-Wye 4 B2 51 55N 2 34W
Rossall Pt. 8 C2 53 55N 3 2W
Rossan Pt. 14 B3 54 42N 8 47W
Rosslare 15 D5 52 17N 6 23W
Rosyth 11 A5 56 2N 3 26W
Rother → 5 C5 50 59N 0 40 E
Rotherham 9 C4 53 26N 1 21W
Rothes 13 D5 57 31N 3 12W
Rothesay 10 B3 55 50N 5 3W
Rothwell, *Northants.* 5 A4 52 25N 0 48W
Rothwell, *W. Yorks.* 9 C4 53 46N 1 29W
Rottingdean 5 C4 50 48N 0 3W
Rousay 13 B5 59 10N 3 2W
Rowrah 8 B2 54 34N 3 26W
Roxby 9 C5 53 38N 0 37W
Royal Leamington Spa 4 A3 52 18N 1 32W
Royston, *Herts.* 5 A4 52 3N 0 1W
Royston, *S. Yorks.* 9 C4 53 36N 1 27W
Royton 8 C3 53 34N 2 7W
Rubery 4 A3 52 24N 1 59W
Rubh a' Mhail 10 B2 55 55N 6 10W
Rubha Hunish 12 D2 57 42N 6 20W
Rudgwick 5 B4 51 7N 0 54W
Rudston 9 B5 54 6N 0 19W
Rufford 8 C3 53 37N 2 50W
Rugby 4 A3 52 23N 1 16W
Rugeley 4 A3 52 47N 1 56W
Runcorn 8 C3 53 20N 2 44W
Rushden 5 A4 52 17N 0 37W
Ruskington 9 C5 53 5N 0 23W
Rutherglen 10 B4 55 50N 4 11W
Rutland Water 5 A4 52 38N 0 38W
Ryan, L. 10 C3 55 0N 5 2W
Rydal 8 B3 54 28N 2 59W
Ryde 4 C3 50 44N 1 9W
Rye 5 C5 50 57N 0 46 E
Rye → 9 B5 54 12N 0 53W
Rye Bay 5 C5 50 50N 0 50 E
Ryton 4 A3 52 23N 1 25W

S

Sacriston 9 B4 54 49N 1 38W
Saffron Walden 5 A5 52 2N 0 15 E
St. Abb's Head 11 B6 55 55N 2 10W
St. Albans 5 B4 51 44N 0 19W
St. Alban's Head 4 C2 50 34N 2 3W
St. Andrews 11 A6 56 20N 2 48W
St. Asaph 7 A3 53 15N 3 27W
St. Austell 6 B3 50 20N 4 48W
St. Bees 8 B2 54 29N 3 36W
St. Bee's Hd. 8 B2 54 30N 3 38W
St. Brides B. 7 C1 51 48N 5 15W
St. Catherine's Pt. 4 C3 50 34N 1 18W
St. David's 7 C1 51 54N 5 16W
St. David's Head 7 C1 51 55N 5 16W
St. George's Channel 15 E6 52 0N 6 0W
St. Helens, *I. of W.* 4 C3 50 42N 1 6W
St. Helens, *Mersey.* 8 C3 53 28N 2 44W
St. Helier 6 C5 49 11N 2 6W
St. Ives, *Cambs.* 5 A4 52 20N 0 5W
St. Ives, *Corn.* 6 B2 50 13N 5 29W
St. John's 8 B1 54 12N 4 38W
St. Johns Chapel 8 B3 54 43N 2 10W
St. Leonards, *Bucks.* 5 C5 50 51N 0 34 E
St. Leonards, *E. Susx.* 5 C5 50 51N 0 33 E
St. Margaret's-at-Cliffe 5 B6 51 10N 1 23 E
St. Mary Bourne 4 B3 51 16N 1 24W
St. Mary's 6 C1 49 55N 6 18W
St. Michael's Mount 6 B2 50 7N 5 30W
St. Neots 5 A4 52 14N 0 16W
St. Osyth 5 B6 51 47N 1 4 E
St. Peter Port 6 C5 49 27N 2 31W
Salcombe 6 B4 50 14N 3 47W
Sale 8 C3 53 26N 2 19W
Salford 8 C3 53 30N 2 17W
Salford Priors 4 A3 52 10N 1 52W
Salisbury 4 B3 51 4N 1 48W
Salisbury Plain 4 B3 51 13N 1 50W
Saltburn by the Sea 9 B5 54 35N 0 58W
Saltcoats 10 B4 55 38N 4 47W
Saltee Is. 15 D5 52 7N 6 37W
Saltergate 9 B5 54 20N 0 40W
Saltfleet 9 C6 53 25N 0 11 E
Saltfleetby 9 C6 53 23N 0 10 E
Saltwood 5 B6 51 4N 1 5 E
Sanday 13 B6 59 15N 2 30W
Sandbach 8 C3 53 9N 2 23W
Sandgate 5 B6 51 5N 1 9 E
Sandhurst 5 B4 51 21N 0 48W
Sandness 12 A8 60 18N 1 38W
Sandown 4 C3 50 39N 1 9W
Sandringham 5 A5 52 50N 0 30 E
Sandwich 5 B6 51 16N 1 21 E
Sandy 5 A4 52 8N 0 18W
Sanquhar 11 B5 55 21N 3 56W
Sark 6 C5 49 25N 2 20W
Sawbridgeworth 5 B5 51 49N 0 10 E
Sawel 14 B4 54 48N 7 5W
Sawston 5 A5 52 7N 0 11 E
Sawtry 5 A4 52 26N 0 17W
Saxilby 9 C5 53 16N 0 40W
Saxlingham Nethergate 5 A6 52 33N 1 16 E
Saxmundham 5 A6 52 13N 1 29 E
Scafell Pikes 8 B2 54 26N 3 14W
Scalby 9 B5 54 18N 0 26W
Scalby Ness 9 B5 54 18N 0 25W
Scalpay 12 D2 57 51N 6 40W
Scamblesby 9 C5 53 17N 0 5W
Scapa Flow 13 C5 58 52N 3 6W
Scarborough 9 B5 54 17N 0 24W
Scarning 5 A5 52 40N 0 53 E
Scilly, Isles of 6 C1 49 55N 6 15W
Scole 5 A6 52 22N 1 10 E
Scopwick 9 C5 53 6N 0 24W
Scotland □ 10 A4 57 0N 4 0W
Scunthorpe 9 C5 53 35N 0 38W
Seaford 5 C5 50 46N 0 8 E
Seamer 9 B5 54 14N 0 27W
Seascale 8 B2 54 24N 3 29W
Seaton 8 B2 54 40N 3 31W
Sedbergh 8 B3 54 20N 2 31W
Sedgefield 9 B4 54 40N 1 27W
Seend 4 B2 51 20N 2 2W
Selborne 5 B4 51 5N 0 55W
Selby 9 C4 53 47N 1 5W
Selkirk 11 B6 55 33N 2 50W
Selsey 5 C4 50 44N 0 47W
Selsey Bill 5 C4 50 44N 0 47W
Seph → 9 B4 54 17N 1 9W
Settle 8 B3 54 5N 2 18W
Seven → 9 B5 54 11N 0 51W
Sevenoaks 5 B5 51 16N 0 11 E
Severn → 4 B2 51 35N 2 38W
Severn Beach 4 B2 51 34N 2 39W
Severn Stoke 4 A2 52 5N 2 13W
Shaftesbury 4 C2 51 0N 2 12W
Shanklin 4 C3 50 39N 1 9W
Shannon → 15 D2 52 35N 9 30W
Shap 8 B3 54 32N 2 40W
Shapinsay 13 B6 59 2N 2 50W
Sharpness 4 B2 51 43N 2 28W
Shaw 8 C3 53 34N 2 5W
Shawbury 4 A2 52 48N 2 40W
Sheelin, L. 14 C4 53 48N 7 20W
Sheep Haven 14 A4 55 12N 7 55W
Sheerness 5 B5 51 26N 0 47 E
Sheffield 9 C4 53 23N 1 28W
Shefford 5 A4 52 2N 0 20W
Shelling Rocks 15 E1 51 45N 10 35W
Shenfield 5 B5 51 39N 0 21 E
Sheppey, I. of 5 B5 51 23N 0 50 E
Shepshed 4 A3 52 47N 1 18W
Shepton Mallet 4 B2 51 11N 2 31W
Sherborne 4 C2 50 56N 2 31W
Sherborne St. John 4 B3 51 18N 1 7W
Sherburn, *N. Yorks.* 9 B5 54 12N 0 32W
Sherburn, *N. Yorks.* 9 C4 53 47N 1 15W
Shere 5 B4 51 13N 0 28W
Sherfield English 4 B3 51 1N 1 35W
Sheriff Hutton 9 B5 54 5N 1 0W
Sheringham 5 A6 52 56N 1 11 E
Sherston 4 B2 51 35N 2 13W
Sherwood Forest 9 C4 53 5N 1 5W
Shetland □ 12 A8 60 30N 1 30W
Shetland Is. 12 A8 60 30N 1 30W
Shiel, L. 12 E3 56 48N 5 32W
Shifnal 4 A2 52 40N 2 23W
Shildon 9 B4 54 37N 1 39W
Shillelagh 15 D5 52 46N 6 32W
Shillingstone 4 C2 50 54N 2 15W
Shin, L. 13 C4 58 7N 4 30W
Shipbourne 5 B5 51 13N 0 19 E
Shipdham 5 A5 52 38N 0 53 E
Shipley 9 C4 53 50N 1 47W
Shipston-on-Stour 4 A3 52 4N 1 38W
Shipton under Wychwood 4 B3 51 51N 1 35W
Shirebrook 9 C4 53 13N 1 11W
Shoeburyness 5 B5 51 31N 0 49 E
Shoreham by Sea 5 C4 50 50N 0 17W
Shotley Gate 5 B6 51 57N 1 16 E
Shrewsbury 4 A2 52 42N 2 45W
Shrewton 4 B3 51 11N 1 55W
Shrivenham 4 B3 51 36N 1 39W
Shropshire □ 4 A2 52 36N 2 45W
Sible Hedingham 5 B5 51 58N 0 37 E
Sibsey 9 C6 53 3N 0 1 E
Sidlaw Hills 11 A5 56 32N 3 10W
Sidlesham 5 C4 50 46N 0 46W
Sidmouth 6 B4 50 40N 3 13W
Silloth 8 B2 54 53N 3 25W
Silsden 8 C4 53 55N 1 55W
Silverstone 4 A3 52 5N 1 3W
Simonsbath 4 B1 51 8N 3 45W
Singleton 5 C4 50 55N 0 45W
Sittingbourne 5 B5 51 20N 0 43 E
Sizewell 5 A6 52 13N 1 38 E
Skegness 9 C6 53 9N 0 20 E
Skellingthorpe 9 C5 53 14N 0 37W
Skelmersdale 8 C3 53 34N 2 49W
Skelton, *Cleve.* 9 B5 54 33N 0 59W
Skelton, *Cumb.* 8 B3 54 42N 2 50W
Skerries, The 7 A2 53 27N 4 40W
Skibbereen 15 E2 51 33N 9 16W
Skiddaw 8 B2 54 39N 3 9W
Skipsea 9 C5 53 58N 0 13W
Skipton 8 C3 53 57N 2 1W
Skull 15 E2 51 32N 9 40W
Skye 12 D2 57 15N 6 10W
Slaidburn 8 C3 53 57N 2 28W
Slaney → 15 D5 52 52N 6 45W
Sleaford 9 C5 53 0N 0 22W
Sleat, Sd. of 12 D3 57 5N 5 47W
Sledmere 9 B5 54 4N 0 35W
Sleights 9 B5 54 27N 0 40W
Slieve Aughty 15 C3 53 4N 8 30W
Slieve Bloom 15 C4 53 4N 7 40W
Slieve Donard 14 B6 54 10N 5 57W
Slieve Gullion 14 B5 54 8N 6 26W
Slieve Mish 15 D2 52 12N 9 50W
Slievenamon 15 D4 52 25N 7 37W
Sligo 14 B3 54 17N 8 28W
Sligo □ 14 B3 54 10N 8 35W
Sligo B. 14 B3 54 20N 8 40W
Slough 5 B4 51 30N 0 35W
Slyne Hd. 14 C1 53 25N 10 10W
Smethwick 4 A3 52 29N 1 58W
Smithfield 8 B3 54 59N 2 51W
Snaefell 8 B1 54 18N 4 26W
Snainton 9 B5 54 14N 0 33W
Snaith 9 C4 53 42N 1 1W
Snape 5 A6 52 11N 1 29 E
Snettisham 5 A5 52 52N 0 30 E
Snizort, L. 12 D2 57 33N 6 28W
Snodland 5 B5 51 19N 0 26 E
Snowdon 7 A2 53 4N 4 8W
Soham 5 A5 52 20N 0 20 E
Solent, The 4 C3 50 45N 1 25W
Solihull 4 A3 52 26N 1 47W
Solway Firth 8 B2 54 45N 3 38W
Somerby 5 A4 52 42N 0 49W
Somercotes 9 C4 53 4N 1 22W
Somerset □ 4 B2 51 9N 3 0W
Somersham 5 A4 52 24N 0 0 E
Somerton 4 B2 51 3N 2 45W
Sompting 5 C4 50 51N 0 20W
Sonning 5 B4 51 28N 0 53W
Sound, The 6 B3 50 20N 4 10W
South Barrule 8 B1 54 9N 4 36W
South Benfleet 5 B5 51 33N 0 34 E
South Cave 9 C5 53 46N 0 37W
South Dorset Downs 4 C2 50 40N 2 26W
South Downs 5 C4 50 53N 0 10W
South Elkington 9 C5 53 22N 0 5W
South Esk → 13 E6 56 44N 3 3W
South Foreland 5 B6 51 7N 1 23 E
South Glamorgan □ 7 C3 51 30N 3 20W
South Hayling 5 C4 50 47N 0 56W
South Kirkby 9 C4 53 35N 1 19W
South Molton 6 A4 51 1N 3 50W
South Petherton 4 C2 50 57N 2 49W
South Ronaldsay 13 C6 58 46N 2 58W
South Shields 9 B4 54 59N 1 26W
South Tyne → 9 B3 54 46N 2 25W
South Uist 12 D1 57 20N 7 15W
South Woodham Ferrers 5 B5 51 40N 0 37 E
South Yorkshire □ 9 C4 53 30N 1 20W
Southam 4 A3 52 16N 1 24W
Southampton 4 C3 50 54N 1 23W
Southampton Water 4 C3 50 52N 1 21W
Southborough 5 B5 51 10N 0 15 E
Southend-on-Sea 5 B5 51 32N 0 42 E
Southern Uplands 11 B5 55 30N 3 3W
Southery 5 A5 52 32N 0 23 E
Southminster 5 B5 51 40N 0 51 E
Southport 8 C2 53 38N 3 1W
Southwark 5 B4 51 29N 0 5W
Southwell 9 C5 53 4N 0 57W
Southwick 5 C4 50 50N 0 14W
Southwold 5 A6 52 19N 1 41 E
Sowerby 9 B4 54 13N 1 19W
Spalding 5 A4 52 47N 0 9W
Sparkford 4 B2 51 2N 2 33W
Speke 8 C3 53 21N 2 51W
Spennymoor 9 B4 54 43N 1 35W
Sperrin Mts. 14 B4 54 50N 7 0W
Spey → 13 D5 57 26N 3 25W
Spilsby 9 C6 53 10N 0 6 E
Spithead 5 50 43N 1 5W
Spofforth 9 C4 53 57N 1 28W
Sproatley 9 C5 53 46N 0 9W
Spurn Hd. 9 C6 53 34N 0 8 E
Staffa 10 A2 56 26N 6 21W
Stafford 4 A2 52 49N 2 9W
Staffordshire □ 4 A2 52 53N 2 10W
Staindrop 9 B4 54 35N 1 49W
Staines 5 B4 51 26N 0 30W
Stainforth 9 C5 53 37N 0 59W
Stainmore For. 8 B3 54 29N 2 5W
Stainton 9 C5 53 17N 0 23W
Staithes 9 B5 54 33N 0 47W
Stalbridge 4 C2 50 57N 2 22W
Stalham 5 A6 52 46N 1 31 E
Stallingborough 9 C5 53 36N 0 11W
Stalybridge 8 C3 53 29N 2 4W
Stamford 5 A4 52 39N 0 29W
Stamford Bridge 9 C5 53 59N 0 53W
Standish 8 C3 53 35N 2 39W
Standon 5 B5 51 53N 0 2 E
Stanford le Hope 5 B5 51 30N 0 25 E
Stanford on Teme 4 A2 52 17N 2 26W
Stanhope 8 B4 54 45N 2 0W
Stanley 9 B4 54 53N 1 42W
Stansted Mountfitchet 5 B5 51 54N 0 13 E
Stanwix 8 B3 54 54N 2 56W
Stapleford 9 D4 52 56N 1 16W
Staplehurst 5 B5 51 9N 0 35 E
Start Pt. 6 B4 50 13N 3 38W
Staunton 4 B2 51 58N 2 19W
Staveley, *Cumb.* 8 B3 54 24N 2 49W
Staveley, *Derby* 9 C4 53 16N 1 20W
Stevenage 5 B4 51 54N 0 11W
Steyning 5 C4 50 54N 0 19W
Stillington 9 B4 54 7N 1 5W
Stiperstones 4 A2 52 36N 2 57W
Stirling 11 A5 56 7N 3 57W
Stockbridge 4 B3 51 7N 1 30W
Stockport 8 C3 53 25N 2 11W
Stocksbridge 9 C4 53 30N 1 36W
Stockton-on-Tees 9 B4 54 34N 1 20W
Stoke 5 B5 51 26N 0 41 E
Stoke Ferry 5 A5 52 34N 0 31 E
Stoke Mandeville 5 B4 51 46N 0 47W
Stoke on Trent 8 C3 53 1N 2 11W
Stoke Prior 4 A2 52 18N 2 5W
Stokenchurch 5 B4 51 39N 0 54W
Stokesley 9 B4 54 27N 1 12W
Stone, *Bucks.* 5 B4 51 48N 0 52W
Stone, *Staffs.* 8 D3 52 55N 2 10W
Stonehaven 13 E6 56 58N 2 11W
Stonehenge 4 B3 51 9N 1 45W
Stonehouse 4 B2 51 45N 2 18W
Stonham Aspall 5 A6 52 11N 1 7 E
Stony Stratford 5 A4 52 4N 0 51W
Stornoway 12 C2 58 12N 6 23W
Storrington 5 C4 50 54N 0 27W
Stort → 5 B5 51 50N 0 7 E
Stotfold 5 A4 52 2N 0 13W
Stour →, *Dorset* 4 C2 50 48N 2 7W
Stour →, *Here. & Worcs.* 4 A2 52 25N 2 13W
Stour →, *Kent* 5 B6 51 15N 1 20 E
Stour →, *Suffolk* 5 B6 51 55N 1 5 E
Stourbridge 4 A2 52 28N 2 8W
Stourport-on-Severn 4 A2 52 21N 2 18W
Stow Bardolph 5 A5 52 38N 0 24 E
Stow-on-the-Wold 4 B3 51 55N 1 42W
Stowmarket 5 A5 52 11N 1 0 E
Strabane 14 B4 54 50N 7 28W
Strabane □ 14 B4 54 45N 7 25W
Stradbroke 5 A6 52 19N 1 16 E
Strangford L. 14 B6 54 30N 5 37W
Stranraer 10 C3 54 54N 5 0W
Stratford St. Mary 5 B5 51 58N 0 59 E
Stratford-upon-Avon 4 A3 52 12N 1 42W
Strath Spey 13 D5 57 15N 3 40W
Strathclyde □ 10 B4 56 0N 4 50W
Strathmore 13 E5 56 40N 3 4W
Strathpeffer 13 D4 57 35N 4 32W
Strathy Pt. 13 C4 58 35N 4 3W
Stratton, *Gloucs.* 4 B3 51 43N 1 58W
Stratton, *Wilts.* 4 B3 51 41N 1 45W
Stratton St. Margaret 4 B3 51 35N 1 45W
Streatley 4 B3 51 31N 1 9W
Street 4 B2 51 7N 2 43W
Strensall 9 B4 54 3N 1 2W
Stretford 8 C3 53 27N 2 19W
Stretton 8 C3 53 21N 2 34W
Stromeferry 12 D3 57 20N 5 33W
Stromness 13 C5 58 58N 3 18W
Stronsay 13 B6 59 8N 2 38W
Strood 5 B5 51 23N 0 30 E
Stroud 4 B2 51 44N 2 12W
Stubbington 4 C3 50 49N 1 12W
Studland 4 C3 50 39N 1 58W
Studley 4 A3 52 16N 1 54W
Sturminster Marshall 4 C2 50 48N 2 4W
Sturminster Newton 4 C2 50 56N 2 18W
Sturry 5 B6 51 18N 1 7 E
Sturton 9 C5 53 22N 0 39W
Sturton by Stow 9 C5 53 18N 0 39W
Suck → 15 C3 53 17N 8 18W
Sudbury, *Derby* 9 D4 52 53N 1 43W
Sudbury, *Suffolk* 5 A5 52 2N 0 44 E
Suffolk □ 5 A6 52 16N 1 0 E
Suir → 15 D4 52 15N 7 10W
Sulby 8 B1 54 18N 4 29W
Sumburgh Hd. 12 B8 59 52N 1 17W
Sunart, L. 12 E3 56 42N 5 43W
Sunderland 9 B4 54 54N 1 22W
Sunk Island 9 C5 53 38N 0 7W
Sunninghill 5 B4 51 25N 0 40W
Surrey □ 5 B4 51 16N 0 30W
Sussex, E. □ 5 C5 51 0N 0 20 E
Sussex, W. □ 5 C4 51 0N 0 30W
Sutterton 9 D5 52 54N 0 8W
Sutton 5 B4 51 22N 0 13W
Sutton Bridge 5 A5 52 46N 0 12 E
Sutton Coldfield 4 A3 52 33N 1 50W
Sutton Courtenay 4 B3 51 39N 1 16W
Sutton in Ashfield 9 C4 53 7N 1 20W
Sutton-on-Sea 9 C6 53 18N 0 18 E
Sutton Scotney 4 B3 51 9N 1 20W
Swadlincote 4 A3 52 47N 1 34W
Swaffham 5 A5 52 38N 0 42 E
Swale → 9 B4 54 5N 1 20W
Swanage 4 C3 50 36N 1 59W
Swanley 5 B5 51 23N 0 10 E
Swansea 7 C3 51 37N 3 57W
Sway 4 C3 50 47N 1 36W

40

INDEX TO BRITISH ISLES MAPS

Swilly, L. Ythan

Swilly, L. **14 A4** 55 12N 7 35W
Swindon **4 B3** 51 33N 1 47W
Swineshead **9 D5** 52 56N 0 11W
Swinton, *Gt. Man.* **8 C3** 53 31N 2 21W
Swinton, *S. Yorks.* **9 C4** 53 28N 1 20W
Swords **14 C5** 53 27N 6 15W
Symonds Yat **4 B2** 51 50N 2 38W
Syston **4 A3** 52 42N 1 5W

T

Tadcaster **9 C4** 53 53N 1 16W
Tadley **4 B3** 51 21N 1 8W
Tain **13 D4** 57 49N 4 4W
Takeley **5 B5** 51 52N 0 16 E
Tamar → **6 B3** 50 33N 4 15W
Tame → **4 A3** 52 43N 1 45W
Tamworth **4 A3** 52 38N 1 41W
Tanworth **4 A3** 52 20N 1 50W
Tarbat Ness **13 D5** 57 52N 3 48W
Tarbert, *Strath.* **10 B3** 55 55N 5 25W
Tarbert, *W. Isles* **12 D2** 57 54N 6 49W
Tarleton **8 C3** 53 41N 2 50W
Tarporley **8 C3** 53 10N 2 42W
Tarvin **8 C3** 53 11N 2 46W
Tattenhall **8 C3** 53 7N 2 47W
Taunton **4 B1** 51 1N 3 7W
Tavistock **6 B3** 50 33N 4 9W
Taw → **6 A3** 51 4N 4 11W
Tay → **11 A5** 56 37N 3 38W
Tay, Firth of **11 A5** 56 25N 3 8W
Tay, L. **11 A4** 56 30N 4 10W
Tayport **11 A6** 56 27N 2 52W
Tayside □ **11 A5** 56 25N 3 30W
Tebay **8 B3** 54 25N 2 35W
Tees → **9 B4** 54 36N 1 25W
Tees B. **9 B4** 54 38N 1 8W
Teesdale **8 B3** 54 37N 2 10W
Teesside **9 B4** 54 37N 1 13W
Tegid, L. = Bala, L. **7 B3** 52 53N 3 38W
Teifi → **7 B2** 52 4N 4 14W
Teign → **6 B4** 50 41N 3 42W
Teignmouth **6 B4** 50 33N 3 30W
Telford **4 A2** 52 42N 2 31W
Teme → **4 A2** 52 23N 2 15W
Temple Combe **4 C2** 51 0N 2 25W
Temple Ewell **5 B6** 51 9N 1 15 E
Temple Sowerby **8 B3** 54 38N 2 33W
Templemore **15 D4** 52 48N 7 50W
Tenbury **4 A2** 52 18N 2 35W
Tenby **7 C2** 51 40N 4 42W
Tenterden **5 B5** 51 4N 0 42 E
Terrington St. Clement **5 A5** 52 45N 0 17 E
Test → **4 B3** 51 7N 1 30W
Tetbury **4 B2** 51 37N 2 9W
Tetney **9 C5** 53 30N 0 1W
Tettenhall **4 A2** 52 35N 2 7W
Teviot → **11 B6** 55 21N 2 51W
Tewkesbury **4 B2** 51 59N 2 8W
Teynham **5 B5** 51 19N 0 50 E
Thame **5 B4** 51 44N 0 58W
Thame → **4 B3** 51 35N 1 8W
Thames → **5 B5** 51 30N 0 35 E
Thanet, I. of **5 B6** 51 21N 1 20 E
Thatcham **4 B3** 51 24N 1 17W
Thaxted **5 B5** 51 57N 0 20 E
Theale **4 B3** 51 26N 1 5W
Thetford **5 A5** 52 25N 0 44 E
Thirlmere **8 B2** 54 32N 3 4W
Thirsk **9 B4** 54 15N 1 20W
Thornaby on Tees **9 B4** 54 36N 1 19W
Thornbury **4 B2** 51 36N 2 31W
Thorndon **5 A6** 52 16N 1 8 E
Thorne **9 C5** 53 36N 0 56W
Thorney **5 A4** 52 37N 0 8W
Thornham **5 A5** 52 59N 0 35 E
Thornthwaite **8 B2** 54 36N 3 13W
Thornton **8 C3** 53 52N 2 29W
Thornton Dale **9 B5** 54 14N 0 41W
Thorpe **5 A6** 52 38N 1 20 E
Thorpe le Soken **5 B6** 51 50N 1 11 E
Thrapston **5 A4** 52 24N 0 32W
Threlkeld **8 B2** 54 37N 3 2W
Threshfield **8 B3** 54 5N 2 2W
Thurcroft **9 C4** 53 24N 1 13W
Thurlby **5 A4** 52 45N 0 21W
Thurles **15 D4** 52 40N 7 53W
Thurmaston **4 A3** 52 40N 1 8W
Thursby **8 B2** 54 40N 3 3W
Thurso **13 C5** 58 34N 3 31W
Ticehurst **5 B5** 51 2N 0 23 E
Tickhill **9 C4** 53 25N 1 8W
Tideswell **9 C4** 53 17N 1 46W
Tilbury **5 B5** 51 27N 0 24 E
Till → **9 A3** 55 35N 2 3W
Tilmanstone **5 B6** 51 13N 1 18 E
Tilt → **13 E5** 56 50N 3 50W
Tingewick **4 B3** 51 59N 1 4W
Tipperary **15 D3** 52 28N 8 10W
Tipperary □ **15 D4** 52 37N 7 55W
Tipton **4 A2** 52 32N 2 4W
Tiptree **5 B5** 51 48N 0 46 E
Tiree **10 A2** 56 31N 6 55W
Tisbury **4 B2** 51 4N 2 4W
Titchfield **4 C3** 50 51N 1 13W
Tiverton **6 B4** 50 54N 3 30W
Tobermory **10 A2** 56 37N 6 4W
Toddington **5 B4** 51 57N 0 31W
Todmorden **8 C3** 53 43N 2 7W
Tollesbury **5 B5** 51 46N 0 51 E
Tomnavoulin **13 D5** 57 19N 3 18W
Tonbridge **5 B5** 51 12N 0 18 E
Tong **4 A2** 52 39N 2 18W
Tongue **13 C4** 58 29N 4 25W
Torbay **6 B4** 50 26N 3 31W
Torquay **6 B4** 50 27N 3 31W
Torridge → **6 B3** 50 51N 4 10W
Torridon, L. **12 D3** 57 35N 5 50W
Torver **8 B2** 54 20N 3 7W
Tory I. **14 A3** 55 17N 8 12W
Totland **4 C3** 50 41N 1 32W
Totley **9 C4** 53 18N 1 32W
Totnes **6 B4** 50 26N 3 41W
Totton **4 C3** 50 55N 1 29W
Towcester **5 A4** 52 7N 0 56W
Tralee **15 D2** 52 16N 9 42W
Tralee B. **15 D2** 52 17N 9 55W
Tramore **15 D4** 52 10N 7 10W
Tredegar **7 C3** 51 47N 3 16W
Tregaron **7 B3** 52 14N 3 56W
Trent → **9 C5** 53 33N 0 44W
Trentham **8 D3** 52 59N 2 12W
Trim **14 C5** 53 34N 6 48W
Trimdon **9 B4** 54 43N 1 23W
Trimley **5 B6** 51 59N 1 19 E
Tring **5 B4** 51 47N 0 39W
Troon **10 B4** 55 33N 4 40W
Trossachs, The **10 A4** 56 14N 4 24W
Trostan **14 A5** 55 4N 6 10W
Trotternish **12 D2** 57 32N 6 15W
Trowbridge **4 B2** 51 18N 2 12W
Trull **4 C1** 50 58N 3 8W
Trumpington **5 A5** 52 11N 0 6 E
Truro **6 B2** 50 17N 5 2W
Tuam **14 C3** 53 30N 8 50W
Tullamore **15 C4** 53 17N 7 30W
Tullow **15 D5** 52 48N 6 45W
Tummel, L. **13 E5** 56 43N 3 55W
Tunbridge Wells **5 B5** 51 7N 0 16 E
Tunstall **5 A6** 52 7N 1 28 E
Turriff **13 D6** 57 32N 2 28W
Tuskar Rock **15 D5** 52 12N 6 10W
Tutbury **4 A3** 52 52N 1 41W
Tuxford **9 C5** 53 14N 0 52W
Tweed → **11 B7** 55 42N 1 59W
Twenty **5 A4** 52 43N 0 20W
Twyford, *Berks.* **5 B4** 51 29N 0 51W
Twyford, *Hants.* **4 B3** 51 1N 1 19W
Tydd St. Mary **5 A5** 52 45N 0 9 E
Tyldesley **8 C3** 53 31N 2 29W
Tyne → **9 B4** 54 58N 1 28W
Tyne & Wear □ **9 B4** 54 55N 1 35W
Tynemouth **9 A4** 55 1N 1 27W
Tywi → **7 C2** 51 48N 4 20W
Tywyn **7 B2** 52 36N 4 5W

U

Uckfield **5 C5** 50 58N 0 6 E
Ufford **5 A6** 52 6N 1 22 E
Ulceby Cross **9 C6** 53 14N 0 6 E
Ullapool **12 D3** 57 54N 5 10W
Ullswater **8 B3** 54 35N 2 52W
Ulster □ **14 B5** 54 35N 6 30W
Ulverston **8 B2** 54 13N 3 7W
Unst **12 A9** 60 50N 0 55W
Upavon **4 B3** 51 17N 1 49W
Upper Heyford **4 B3** 51 54N 1 16W
Uppingham **5 A4** 52 36N 0 43W
Upton **8 C3** 53 14N 2 52W
Upton-upon-Severn **4 A2** 52 4N 2 12W
Upwey **4 C2** 50 40N 2 29W
Ure → **9 B4** 54 20N 1 25W
Urmston **8 C3** 53 28N 2 22W
Usk → **7 C4** 51 37N 2 56W
Usselby **9 C5** 53 25N 0 21W
Uttoxeter **8 D4** 52 53N 1 50W

V

Valentia Harbour **15 E1** 51 56N 10 17W
Valentia I. **15 E1** 51 54N 10 22W
Ventnor **4 C3** 50 35N 1 12W
Verwood **4 C3** 50 53N 1 53W
Vickerstown **8 B2** 54 8N 3 17W
Virginia Water **5 B4** 51 23N 0 33W
Vyrnwy, L. **7 B3** 52 48N 3 30W

W

Waddesdon **5 B4** 51 50N 0 54W
Waddingham **9 C5** 53 28N 0 31W
Waddington **9 C5** 53 10N 0 31W
Wadhurst **5 B5** 51 3N 0 21 E
Wainfleet All Saints **9 C6** 53 7N 0 16 E
Wakefield **9 C4** 53 41N 1 31W
Walberswick **5 A6** 52 18N 1 39 E
Walbury Hill **4 B3** 51 22N 1 28W
Waldron **5 C5** 50 56N 0 13 E
Wales □ **7 B3** 52 30N 3 30W
Wallasey **8 C2** 53 26N 3 2W
Wallingford **4 B3** 51 36N 1 8W
Wallsend **9 B4** 54 59N 1 30W
Walmer **5 B6** 51 12N 1 23 E
Walney, I. of **8 B2** 54 5N 3 15W
Walpole **5 A5** 52 44N 0 13 E
Walsall **4 A3** 52 36N 1 59W
Walsoken **5 A5** 52 41N 0 12 E
Waltham **9 C5** 53 32N 0 6W
Waltham Abbey **5 B5** 51 40N 0 1 E
Waltham Forest **5 B5** 51 37N 0 2 E
Waltham on the Wolds **5 A4** 52 49N 0 48W
Walton-on-Thames **5 B4** 51 21N 0 22W
Walton-on-the-Naze **5 B6** 51 52N 1 17 E
Wanborough **4 B3** 51 33N 1 40W
Wandsworth **5 B4** 51 28N 0 15W
Wantage **4 B3** 51 35N 1 25W
Warboys **5 A4** 52 25N 0 5W
Wardington **4 A3** 52 8N 1 17W
Wardle **8 C3** 53 7N 2 35W
Ward's Stone **8 B3** 54 2N 2 39W
Ware **5 B4** 51 48N 0 2W
Wareham **4 C2** 50 41N 2 8W
Warley **4 A3** 52 30N 1 58W
Warlingham **5 B4** 51 18N 0 3W
Warminster **4 B2** 51 12N 2 11W
Warrenpoint **14 B5** 54 7N 6 15W
Warrington **8 C3** 53 25N 2 38W
Warsop **9 C4** 53 13N 1 9W
Warwick **4 A3** 52 17N 1 36W
Warwickshire □ **4 A3** 52 20N 1 30W
Wash, The **9 D6** 52 58N 0 20 E
Washford **4 B1** 51 9N 3 22W
Washingborough **9 C5** 53 13N 0 27W
Wast Water **8 B2** 54 26N 3 18W
Watchet **4 B1** 51 10N 3 20W
Watchfield **4 B3** 51 37N 1 39W
Waterbeach **5 A5** 52 16N 0 11 E
Waterford **15 D4** 52 16N 7 8W
Waterford □ **15 D4** 52 10N 7 40W
Waterford Harbour **15 D5** 52 10N 6 58W
Watford **5 B4** 51 38N 0 23W
Wath **9 C4** 53 29N 1 20W
Wath upon Dearne **9 C4** 53 30N 1 21W
Watlington, *Norfolk* **5 A5** 52 40N 0 24 E
Watlington, *Oxon.* **5 B3** 51 38N 1 0W
Watton **5 A5** 52 35N 0 50 E
Waveney → **5 A6** 52 24N 1 20 E
Waver → **8 B2** 54 50N 3 15W
Weald, The **5 B5** 51 7N 0 29 E
Wear → **9 B4** 54 55N 1 22W
Weardale **8 B3** 54 44N 2 5W
Wearhead **8 B3** 54 45N 2 14W
Weaver → **8 C3** 53 17N 2 35W
Weaverham **8 C3** 53 15N 2 30W
Wedmore **4 B2** 51 14N 2 50W
Wednesbury **4 A2** 52 33N 2 1W
Wednesfield **4 A2** 52 36N 2 3W
Weedon Bec **4 A3** 52 14N 1 6W
Welford, *Berks.* **4 B3** 51 28N 1 24W
Welford, *Northants.* **4 A3** 52 26N 1 5W
Welland → **5 A4** 52 43N 0 10W
Wellingborough **5 A4** 52 18N 0 41W
Wellington, *Shrops.* **4 A2** 52 42N 2 31W
Wellington, *Somst.* **4 C1** 50 58N 3 13W
Wellow **4 B2** 51 20N 2 22W
Wells, *Norfolk* **5 A5** 52 57N 0 51 E
Wells, *Somst.* **4 B2** 51 12N 2 39W
Welney **5 A5** 52 31N 0 15 E
Welshpool **7 B3** 52 40N 3 9W
Welton **9 C5** 53 19N 0 29W
Welwyn Garden City **5 B4** 51 49N 0 11W
Wem **4 A2** 52 52N 2 45W
Wendover **5 B4** 51 46N 0 45W
Wenhaston **5 A6** 52 17N 1 35 E
Wenlock Edge **4 A2** 52 30N 2 43W
Wensleydale **8 B4** 54 18N 2 0W
Wensum → **5 A6** 52 37N 1 22 E
Weobley **4 A2** 52 9N 2 52W
West Auckland **9 B4** 54 38N 1 42W
West Bergholt **5 B5** 51 54N 0 51 E
West Bridgford **9 D4** 52 56N 1 8W
West Bromwich **4 A2** 52 32N 2 1W
West Coker **4 C2** 50 55N 2 40W
West End **4 C3** 50 55N 1 20W
West Fen **9 C5** 53 5N 0 5W
West Glamorgan □ **7 C3** 51 40N 3 55W
West Grinstead **5 C4** 50 58N 0 19W
West Haddon **4 A3** 52 21N 1 5W
West Kirby **8 C2** 53 22N 3 11W
West Lulworth **4 C2** 50 37N 2 14W
West Malling **5 B5** 51 16N 0 25 E
West Meon **4 B3** 51 2N 1 3W
West Mersea **5 B5** 51 46N 0 55 E
West Midlands □ **4 A3** 52 30N 1 55W
West Moors **4 C3** 50 49N 1 50W
West Rasen **9 C5** 53 23N 0 23W
West Sussex □ **5 C4** 50 55N 0 30W
West Yorkshire □ **9 C4** 53 45N 1 40W
Westbourne **5 C4** 50 53N 0 55W
Westbury, *Shrops.* **4 A2** 52 40N 2 57W
Westbury, *Wilts.* **4 B2** 51 16N 2 11W
Westbury-on-Severn **4 B2** 51 49N 2 24W
Westerham **5 B5** 51 16N 0 5 E
Western Isles □ **12 D1** 57 30N 7 10W
Westfield **5 C5** 50 53N 0 30 E
Westhoughton **8 C3** 53 34N 2 30W
Westmeath □ **14 C4** 53 30N 7 30W
Weston-super-Mare **4 B2** 51 20N 2 59W
Weston upon Trent **4 A2** 52 50N 2 2W
Westport **14 C2** 53 44N 9 31W
Westray **13 B5** 59 18N 3 0W
Wetheral **8 B3** 54 52N 2 50W
Wetherby **9 C4** 53 56N 1 23W
Wetwang **9 B5** 54 2N 0 35W
Wexford **15 D5** 52 20N 6 28W
Wexford □ **15 D5** 52 20N 6 25W
Wexford Harbour **15 D5** 52 20N 6 25W
Wey → **5 B4** 51 19N 0 29W
Weybourne **5 A6** 52 57N 1 9 E
Weybridge **5 B4** 51 22N 0 28W
Weymouth **4 C2** 50 36N 2 28W
Whaley Bridge **8 C4** 53 20N 2 0W
Whalley **8 C3** 53 49N 2 25W
Whalsay **12 A9** 60 22N 1 0W
Whaplode **5 A4** 52 42N 0 3W
Wharfe → **9 C4** 53 55N 1 30W
Wharfedale **8 B3** 54 7N 2 4W
Wheatley **4 B3** 51 45N 1 8W
Wheatley Hill **9 B4** 54 45N 1 23W
Wheaton Aston **4 A2** 52 43N 2 13W
Whernside **8 B3** 54 14N 2 24W
Whicham **8 B2** 54 14N 3 22W
Whipsnade **5 B4** 51 51N 0 32W
Whissendine **5 A4** 52 43N 0 46W
Whitby **9 B5** 54 29N 0 37W
Whitchurch, *Hants.* **4 B3** 51 14N 1 20W
Whitchurch, *Here. & Worcs.* **4 B2** 51 51N 2 41W
Whitchurch, *Shrops.* **8 D3** 52 58N 2 42W
White Horse Hill **4 B3** 51 35N 1 35W
Whitehaven **8 B2** 54 33N 3 35W
Whitehorse, Vale of **4 B3** 51 37N 1 30W
Whithorn **10 C4** 54 44N 4 25W
Whitstable **5 B6** 51 21N 1 2 E
Whittington, *Derby* **9 C4** 53 17N 1 26W
Whittington, *Shrops.* **4 A2** 52 53N 3 0W
Whittlesey **5 A4** 52 34N 0 8W
Whittlesford **5 A5** 52 6N 0 9 E
Whitton **9 C5** 53 42N 0 39W
Whitwell, *Derby* **9 C4** 53 16N 1 11W
Whitwell, *I. of W.* **4 C3** 50 35N 1 19W
Whitwick **4 A3** 52 45N 1 23W
Whitworth **8 C3** 53 40N 2 11W
Whixley **9 B4** 54 2N 1 19W
Wick **13 C5** 58 26N 3 5W
Wickford **5 B5** 51 37N 0 31 E
Wickham **4 C3** 50 54N 1 11W
Wickham Market **5 A6** 52 9N 1 21 E
Wicklow **15 D5** 53 0N 6 2W
Wicklow □ **15 D5** 52 59N 6 25W
Wicklow Hd. **15 D5** 52 59N 6 3W
Wickwar **4 B2** 51 35N 2 23W
Widnes **8 C3** 53 22N 2 44W
Wigan **8 C3** 53 33N 2 38W
Wight, I. of □ **4 C3** 50 40N 1 20W
Wigmore **4 A2** 52 19N 2 51W
Wigston **4 A3** 52 35N 1 6W
Wigton **8 B2** 54 50N 3 9W
Wigtown **10 C4** 54 52N 4 27W
Wigtown B. **10 C4** 54 46N 4 15W
Willaston **8 C3** 53 17N 2 59W
Willenhall **4 A2** 52 36N 2 3W
Willesborough **5 B5** 51 8N 0 55 E
Willingdon **5 C5** 50 47N 0 17 E
Williton **4 B1** 51 9N 3 20W
Willoughby **9 C6** 53 14N 0 12 E
Wilmslow **8 C3** 53 19N 2 14W
Wilnecote **4 A3** 52 36N 1 40W
Wilton **4 B3** 51 5N 1 52W
Wiltshire □ **4 B3** 51 20N 2 0W
Wimblington **5 A5** 52 31N 0 5 E
Wimborne Minster **4 C3** 50 48N 2 0W
Wincanton **4 B2** 51 3N 2 24W
Winchcombe **4 B3** 51 57N 1 57W
Winchelsea **5 C5** 50 55N 0 43 E
Winchester **4 B3** 51 4N 1 19W
Windermere **8 B3** 54 24N 2 56W
Windermere, L. **8 B3** 54 20N 2 57W
Windrush → **4 B3** 51 48N 1 35W
Windsor **5 B4** 51 28N 0 36W
Wing **5 B4** 51 54N 0 41W
Wingham **5 B6** 51 16N 1 12 E
Winsford **8 C3** 53 12N 2 31W
Winslow **5 B4** 51 57N 0 52W
Winster **9 C4** 53 9N 1 42W
Winston **9 B4** 54 32N 1 47W
Winterborne Abbas **4 C2** 50 43N 2 30W
Winterton, *Humber.* **9 C5** 53 39N 0 37W
Winterton, *Norfolk* **5 A6** 52 43N 1 43 E
Wirksworth **9 C4** 53 5N 1 34W
Wirral **8 B3** 53 25N 3 0W
Wisbech **5 A5** 52 39N 0 10 E
Wisborough Green **5 B4** 51 2N 0 30W
Wishaw **11 B5** 55 46N 3 55W
Wiske → **9 B4** 54 26N 1 27W
Witham **5 B5** 51 48N 0 39 E
Witham → **9 C5** 53 3N 0 8W
Withern **9 C6** 53 19N 0 9 E
Withernsea **9 C6** 53 43N 0 2 E
Witley **5 B4** 51 9N 0 39W
Witney **4 B3** 51 47N 1 29W
Wittersham **5 B5** 51 1N 0 42 E
Wiveliscombe **4 B1** 51 2N 3 20W
Wivenhoe **5 B5** 51 51N 0 59 E
Woburn **5 B4** 51 59N 0 37W
Woburn Sands **5 A4** 52 1N 0 38W
Woking **5 B4** 51 18N 0 33W
Wokingham **5 B4** 51 25N 0 50W
Wollaston **5 A4** 52 15N 0 39W
Wolsingham **8 B4** 54 44N 1 52W
Wolverhampton **4 A2** 52 35N 2 6W
Wolverton **5 A4** 52 3N 0 48W
Wolviston **9 B4** 54 39N 1 25W
Wombwell **9 C4** 53 31N 1 23W
Wonston **4 B3** 51 9N 1 18W
Woodbridge **5 A6** 52 6N 1 19 E
Woodchurch **5 B5** 51 5N 0 47 E
Woodhall Spa **9 C5** 53 10N 0 12W
Woodhouse **9 C4** 53 23N 1 21W
Woodley **5 B4** 51 26N 0 54W
Woodstock **4 B3** 51 51N 1 20W
Wookey **4 B2** 51 13N 2 41W
Wookey Hole **4 B2** 51 13N 2 41W
Wool **4 C2** 50 41N 2 13W
Wootton Bassett **4 B3** 51 32N 1 55W
Wootton Wawen **4 A3** 52 16N 1 47W
Worcester **4 A2** 52 12N 2 12W
Worfield **4 A2** 52 34N 2 22W
Workington **8 B2** 54 39N 3 34W
Worksop **9 C4** 53 19N 1 9W
Worplesdon **5 B4** 51 16N 0 36W
Worsbrough **9 C4** 53 31N 1 29W
Wortham **5 A6** 52 22N 1 3 E
Worthing **5 C4** 50 49N 0 21W
Wotton under Edge **4 B2** 51 37N 2 20W
Wragby **9 C5** 53 17N 0 18W
Wrangle **9 C6** 53 3N 0 9 E
Wrath, C. **12 C3** 58 38N 5 0W
Wrekin, The **4 A2** 52 41N 2 35W
Wrentham **5 A6** 52 24N 1 39 E
Wrexham **7 A4** 53 5N 3 0W
Writtle **5 B5** 51 44N 0 27 E
Wrotham **5 B5** 51 18N 0 20 E
Wroughton **4 B3** 51 31N 1 47W
Wroxham **5 A6** 52 42N 1 23 E
Wye **5 B5** 51 11N 0 56 E
Wye → **4 B2** 51 36N 2 40W
Wylye → **4 B3** 51 8N 1 53W
Wymondham, *Leics.* **5 A4** 52 45N 0 42W
Wymondham, *Norfolk* **5 A6** 52 34N 1 7 E
Wyre → **8 C3** 53 52N 2 57W
Wyre Forest **4 A2** 52 24N 2 24W

Y

Yare → **5 A6** 52 36N 1 28 E
Yarm **9 B4** 54 31N 1 21W
Yarmouth **4 C3** 50 42N 1 29W
Yate **4 B2** 51 32N 2 26W
Yatton **4 B2** 51 23N 2 50W
Yaxley **5 A4** 52 31N 0 14W
Yeadon **9 C4** 53 52N 1 40W
Yell **12 A8** 60 35N 1 5W
Yell Sd. **12 A8** 60 33N 1 15W
Yeo → **4 B2** 51 10N 3 0W
Yeovil **4 C2** 50 57N 2 38W
Yes Tor **6 B4** 50 41N 3 59W
York **9 C4** 53 58N 1 7W
York, Vale of **9 B4** 54 15N 1 25W
Yorkshire Wolds **9 B5** 54 0N 0 30W
Youghal **15 E4** 51 58N 7 51W
Youghal B. **15 E4** 51 55N 7 50W
Youlgreave **9 C4** 53 12N 1 50W
Yoxall **4 A3** 52 45N 1 49W
Yoxford **5 A6** 52 16N 1 30 E
Ythan → **13 D7** 57 26N 2 0W

WORLD MAPS

SETTLEMENTS

⬡ PARIS   ■ Berne   ◉ Livorno   ◉ Brugge   ◎ Algeciras   ○ Frejus   ○ Oberammergau   ○ Thira

Settlement symbols and type styles vary according to the scale of each map and indicate the importance of towns on the map rather than specific population figures

∴ Ruins or Archæological Sites   ᵕ Wells in Desert

ADMINISTRATION

——— International Boundaries

— — — International Boundaries (Undefined or Disputed)

·········· Internal Boundaries

National Parks

Country Names

NICARAGUA

Administrative Area Names

KENT

CALABRIA

International boundaries show the *de facto* situation where there are rival claims to territory

COMMUNICATIONS

——— Principal Roads

⌒ Other Roads

·-·-· Trails and Seasonal Roads

≍ Passes

✿ Airfields

⌒ Principal Railways

·-·-· Railways Under Construction

⌒ Other Railways

⌐---⌐ Railway Tunnels

·········· Principal Canals

PHYSICAL FEATURES

⌒ Perennial Streams

········· Intermittent Streams

⬭ Perennial Lakes

⬮ Intermittent Lakes

Swamps and Marshes

Permanent Ice and Glaciers

▲ 8848 Elevations in metres

▼ 8050 Sea Depths in metres

1133 Height of Lake Surface Above Sea Level in metres

ELEVATION AND DEPTH TINTS

Height of Land Above Sea Level	Land Below Sea Level	Depth of Sea

in metres   6000   4000   3000   2000   1500   1000   400   200   0   6000   12 000   15 000   18 000   24 000   in feet

in feet   18 000   12 000   9000   6000   4500   3000   1200   600   0   200   2000   4000   5000   6000   8000   in metres

Some of the maps have different contours to highlight and clarify the principal relief features

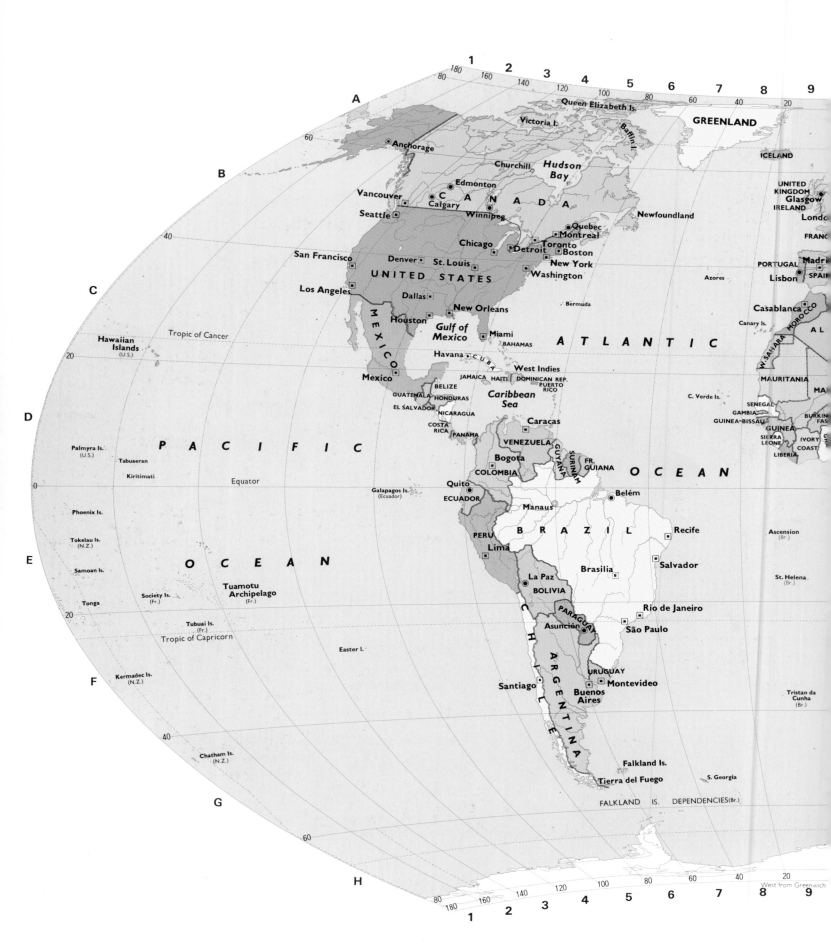

A

B

C

D

E

F

G

H

1 2 3 4 5 6 7 8 9

GREENLAND

ICELAND

Queen Elizabeth Is.

Victoria I.

Baffin I.

Anchorage

Churchill

Hudson Bay

Edmonton

Vancouver

C A N A D A

Calgary

Winnipeg

Seattle

Newfoundland

Quebec

Montreal

Chicago

Toronto

Detroit

Boston

San Francisco

Denver

St. Louis

New York

Washington

UNITED   STATES

Los Angeles

Dallas

M
E
X
I
C
O

Houston

New Orleans

Tropic of Cancer

Gulf of Mexico

Miami

BAHAMAS

Havana

CUBA

A T L A N T I C

Bermuda

Hawaiian Islands
(U.S.)

West Indies

Mexico

JAMAICA HAITI DOMINICAN REP.
PUERTO
RICO

Caribbean Sea

BELIZE

GUATEMALA

HONDURAS

EL SALVADOR

NICARAGUA

COSTA
RICA

PANAMA

Caracas

VENEZUELA

GUYANA

SURINAM

FR.
GUIANA

O C E A N

P A C I F I C

Palmyra Is.
(U.S.)

Tabuaeran

Kiritimati

Equator

Galapagos Is.
(Ecuador)

Bogota

COLOMBIA

Quito

ECUADOR

Belém

Manaus

Phoenix Is.

B R A Z I L

Recife

Ascension
(Br.)

Tokelau Is.
(N.Z.)

PERU

Lima

O   C   E   A   N

Samoan Is.

Brasilia

Salvador

St. Helena
(Br.)

Society Is.
(Fr.)

Tuamotu
Archipelago
(Fr.)

La Paz

BOLIVIA

Tonga

Rio de Janeiro

PARAGUAY

Tubuai Is.
(Fr.)

Asunción

São Paulo

Tropic of Capricorn

Easter I.

C
H
I
L
E

A
R
G
E
N
T
I
N
A

URUGUAY

Montevideo

Kermadec Is.
(N.Z.)

Santiago

Buenos
Aires

Tristan da
Cunha
(Br.)

Chatham Is.
(N.Z.)

Falkland Is.

Tierra del Fuego

S. Georgia

FALKLAND IS. DEPENDENCIES(Br.)

UNITED
KINGDOM

Glasgow

IRELAND

London

FRANC

PORTUGAL

Madri

SPAIN

Lisbon

Azores

Casablanca

MOROCCO

AL

Canary Is.

W. SAHARA

MAURITANIA

MA

C. Verde Is.

SENEGAL

GAMBIA

GUINEA-BISSAU

GUINEA

BURKIN
FAS

SIERRA
LEONE

IVORY
COAST

LIBERIA

180 160 140 120 100 80 60 40 20

60

40

20

0

20

40

60

West from Greenwich

Projection: Hammer Equal Area

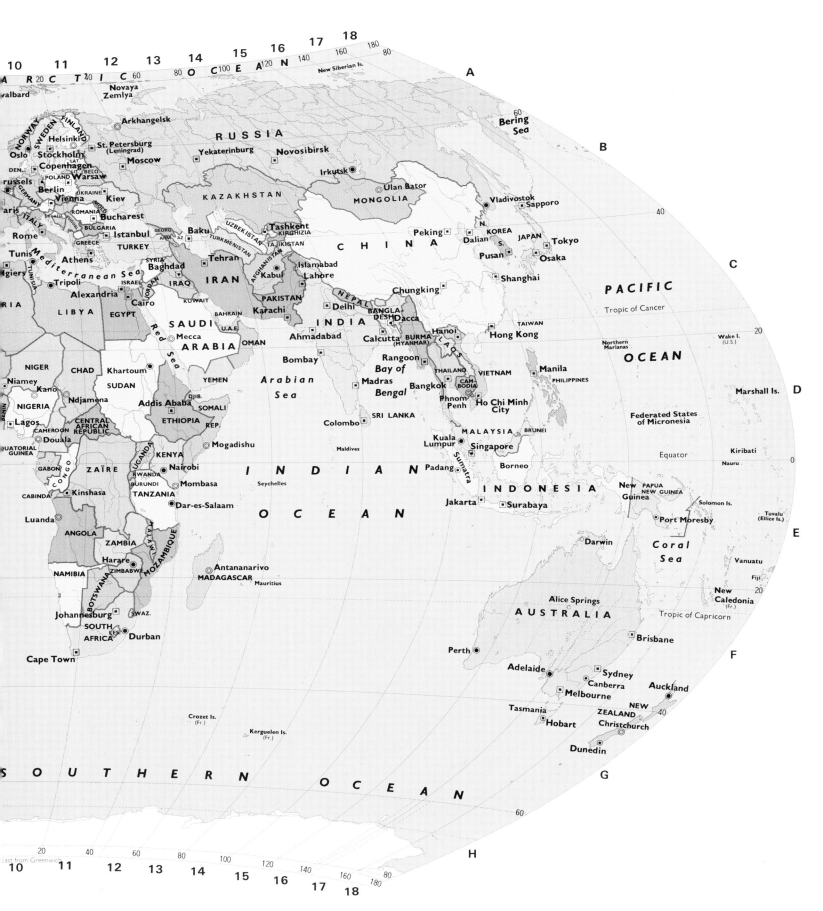

10 11 12 13 14 15 16 17 18

20 40 60 80 100 120 140 160 180 80

RUSSIA

Svalbard
Novaya Zemlya

NORWAY SWEDEN FINLAND
Arkhangelsk

New Siberian Is.

Bering Sea

Oslo Helsinki
Stockholm St. Petersburg (Leningrad)
Copenhagen Yekaterinburg Novosibirsk

DEN. Moscow
Brussels POLAND Warsaw
Berlin Irkutsk
Vienna BELO. KAZAKHSTAN Ulan Bator
GERMANY UKRAINE Kiev MONGOLIA Vladivostok Sapporo
Paris ROMANIA Bucharest
CROATIA YUGOS. MOLD. Peking N. KOREA JAPAN Tokyo
Rome BULGARIA Istanbul Baku UZBEKISTAN Tashkent Dalian S. Osaka
ITALY GEORG. KIRGHIZIA C H I N A Pusan
GREECE TURKEY ARM. AZ. TURKMENISTAN TAJIKISTAN Shanghai
Tunis Athens SYRIA Tehran AFGHANISTAN Chungking
Algiers Mediterranean Sea Baghdad Kabul
TUNISIA ISRAEL IRAQ I R A N Islamabad
Tripoli JORDAN Lahore NEPAL
Alexandria KUWAIT PAKISTAN Delhi BANGLA- Hanoi Hong Kong
Cairo BAHRAIN Karachi DESH Dacca
LIBYA EGYPT SAUDI U.A.E. I N D I A Calcutta BURMA LAOS TAIWAN
Mecca (MYANMAR)
ARABIA OMAN Ahmadabad Rangoon
Red Sea Bombay Bay of THAILAND VIETNAM Manila
NIGER CHAD Khartoum YEMEN Arabian Madras Bengal Bangkok CAM- PHILIPPINES
Niamey Kano SUDAN Sea Phnom BODIA
NIGERIA Ndjamena DJIB. Penh Ho Chi Minh
Lagos CAMEROON Addis Ababa SOMALI Colombo City
CENTRAL ETHIOPIA REP. SRI LANKA MALAYSIA BRUNEI
Douala AFRICAN Kuala Singapore
EQUATORIAL REPUBLIC Mogadishu Maldives Lumpur Borneo
GUINEA UGANDA KENYA Nairobi I N D I A N Padang Sumatra
GABON ZAIRE RWANDA Seychelles I N D O N E S I A
CONGO BURUNDI Mombasa Jakarta Surabaya
CABINDA Kinshasa TANZANIA Dar-es-Salaam O C E A N
Luanda
ANGOLA ZAMBIA Antananarivo
NAMIBIA Harare MADAGASCAR Mauritius
Johannesburg ZIMBABWE MOZAMBIQUE SWAZ.
SOUTH LES.
AFRICA Durban
Cape Town

PACIFIC
OCEAN

Tropic of Cancer

Wake I. (U.S.)

Northern Marianas

Marshall Is.

Federated States of Micronesia

Equator
Kiribati
Nauru

PAPUA
NEW GUINEA
New Guinea Solomon Is.

Tuvalu (Ellice Is.)

Port Moresby

Darwin Coral Sea

Vanuatu
Fiji

New Caledonia (Fr.)

Alice Springs
A U S T R A L I A

Tropic of Capricorn

Brisbane

Perth
Adelaide Sydney
Canberra Auckland
Melbourne
Tasmania NEW
ZEALAND
Hobart Christchurch

Dunedin

Crozet Is. (Fr.)

Kerguelen Is. (Fr.)

S O U T H E R N   O C E A N

East from Greenwich
10 11 12 13 14 15 16 17 18
20 40 60 80 100 120 140 160 180 80

60

40

20

0

20

40

60

A
B
C
D
E
F
G
H

1:80 000 000

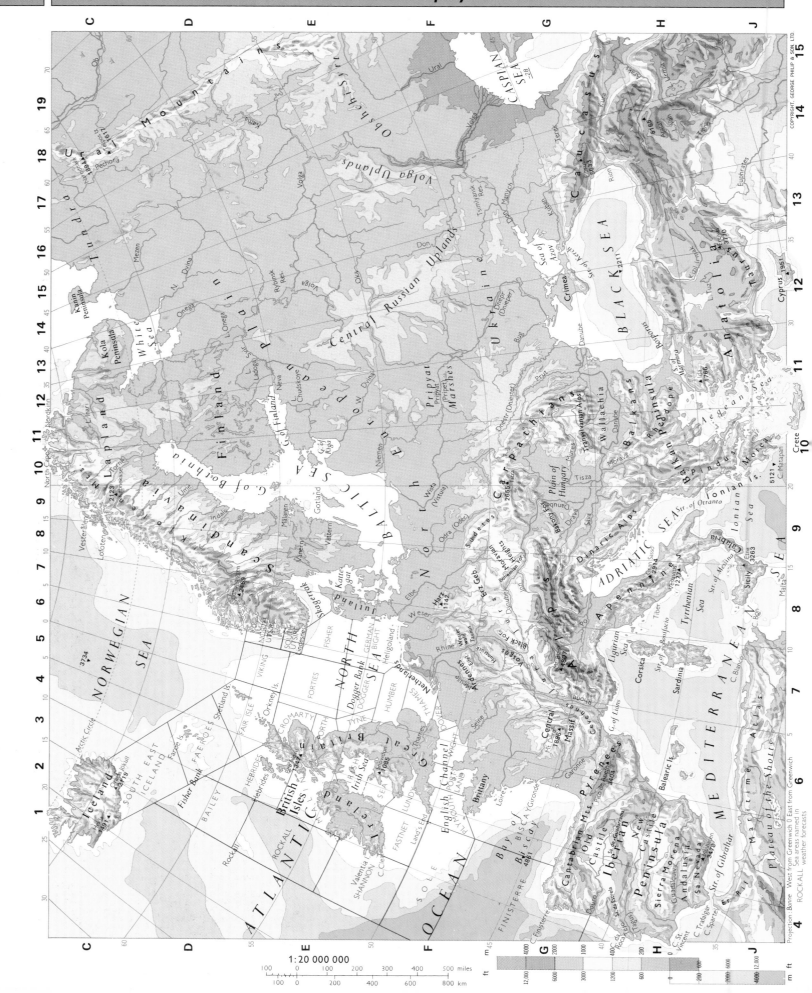

1:20 000 000

Projection: Bonne. West from Greenwich 0 East from Greenwich
ROCKALL Sea areas named in weather forecasts

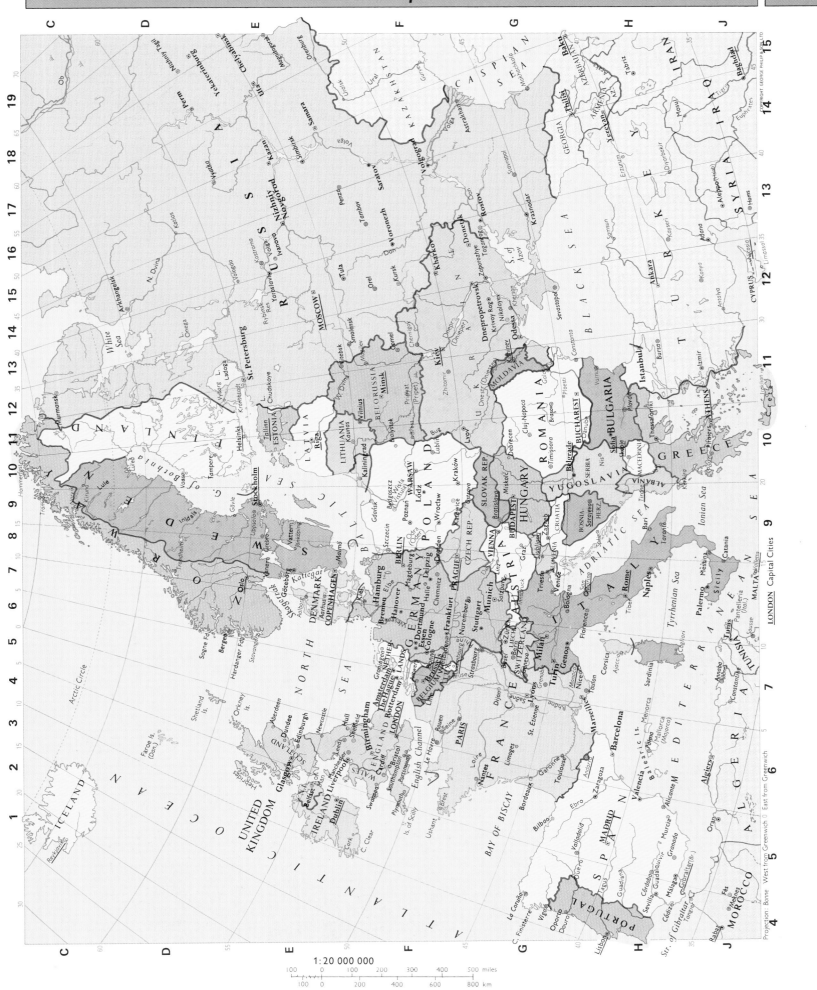

1:20 000 000

100   0   100   200   300   400   500 miles

100   0   200   400   600   800 km

ICELAND
On the same scale   West from Greenwich

ARCTIC OCEAN

ATLANTIC OCEAN

N O R W A Y

S W E D E N

FINLAND

Lapland

Norrland

Svealand

Götaland

Kola Peninsula

White Sea

Karelia

R U S S I A

ESTONIA

LATVIA

LITHUANIA

BELORUSSIA

DENMARK

GERMANY

POLAND

CZECH REP.

UKRAINE

BALTIC SEA

Gulf of Bothnia

Gulf of Finland

Skagerrak

Kattegat

Projection: Conical with two standard parallels

1:10 000 000

East from Greenwich

COPYRIGHT. GEORGE PHILIP & SON. LTD.

50   0   50   100   150   200   250 miles
50   0   50 100 150 200 250 300 350 400 km

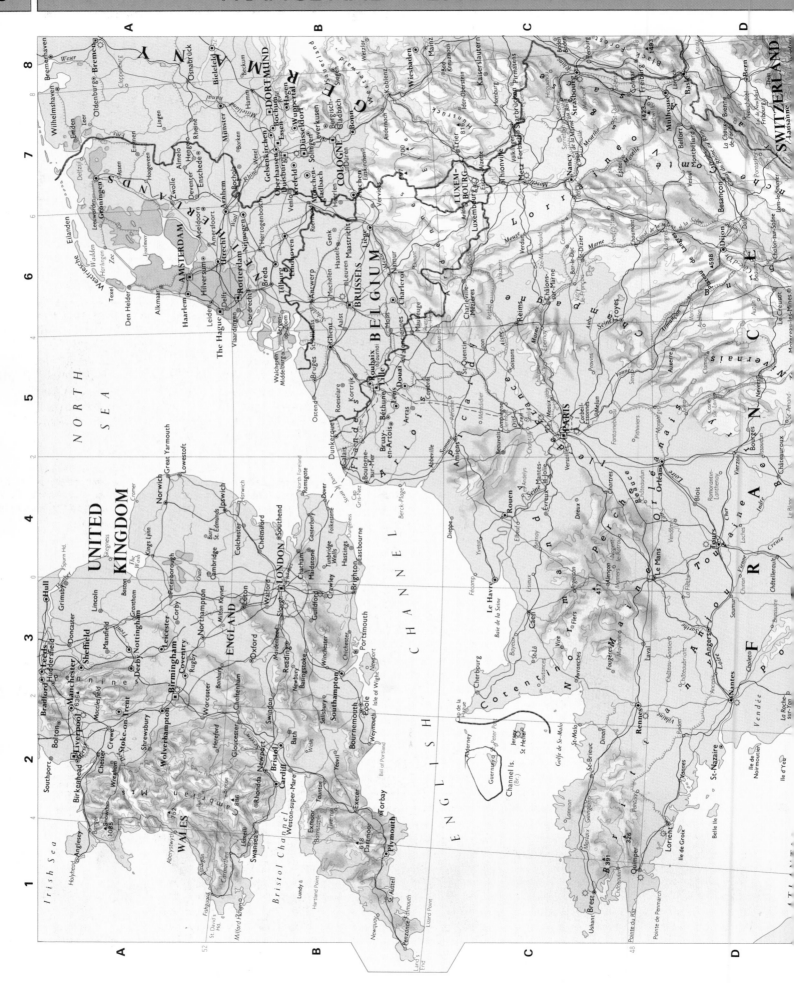

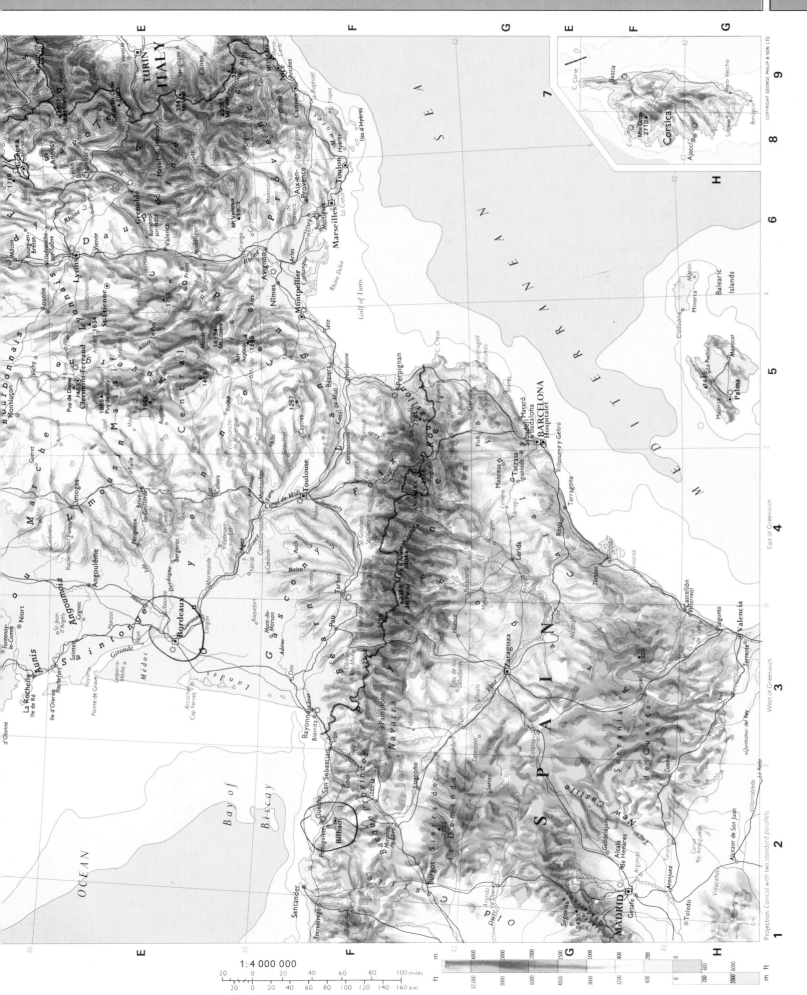

Corsica

Balearic Islands

MEDITERRANEAN SEA

Gulf of Lions

COPYRIGHT GEORGE PHILIP & SON LTD

ITALY
TURIN

FRANCE

Bay of Biscay

OCEAN

SPAIN

Bordeaux
Toulouse
Marseilles
Toulon
Perpignan
BARCELONA
Zaragoza
Valencia
MADRID
Bilbao
San Sebastian
Bayonne
Lyons
Grenoble
Clermont-Ferrand
St-Étienne
Limoges
Nîmes
Montpellier
Avignon
Aix-en-Provence
Cannes
Nice
Angoulême
La Rochelle
Vittoria
Pamplona
Lérida
Tarragona
Palma
Majorca
Minorca

Projection: Conical with two standard parallels

1 : 4 000 000

20   0   20   40   60   80   100 miles
20 0 20 40 60 80 100 120 140 160 km

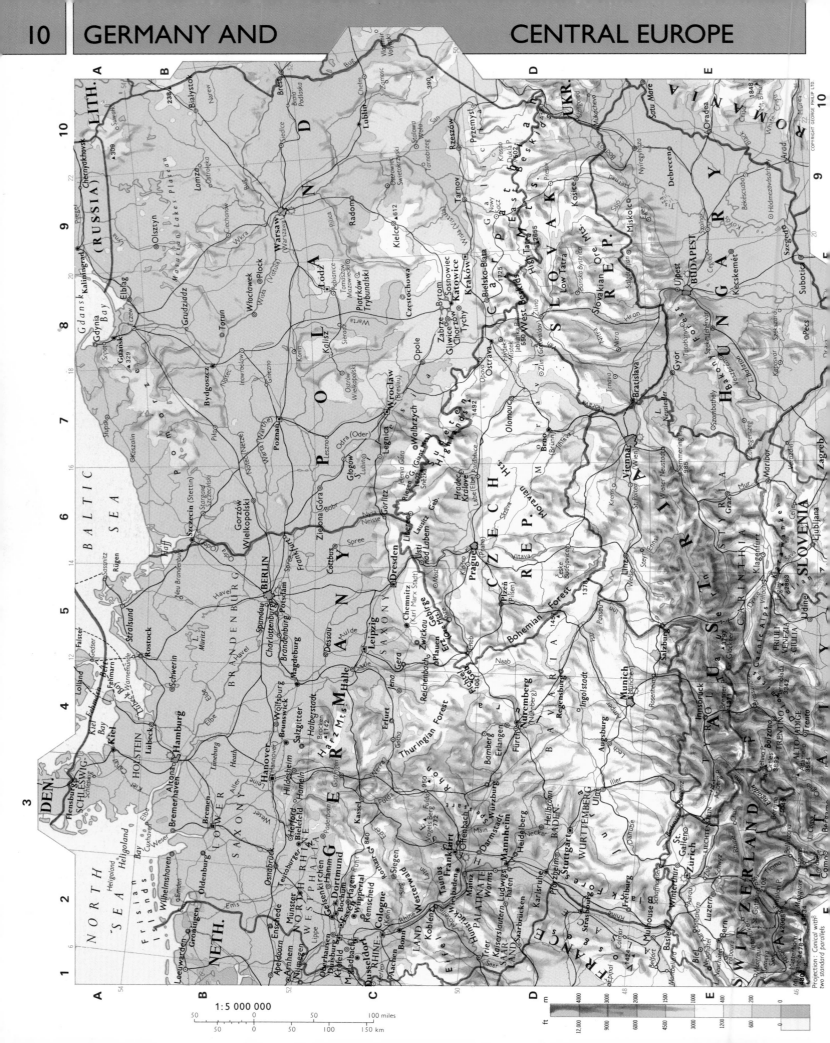

Projection: Conical with
two standard parallels

1:5 000 000

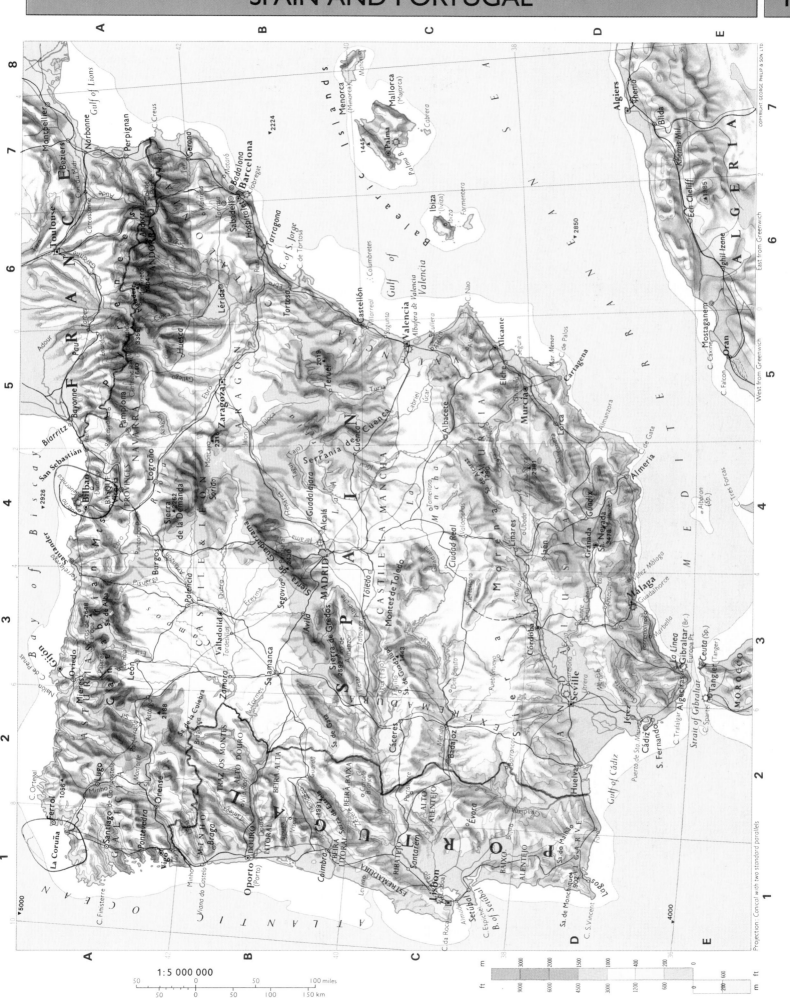

1 : 5 000 000

Projection: Conical with two standard parallels

Countries and regions: FRANCE, SWITZERLAND, SLOVENIA, CROATIA, ALGERIA, TUNISIA, MALTA

Italian regions: PIEDMONT, LOMBARDY, TRENTINO ALTO ADIGE, FRIULI VENEZIA GIULIA, VENETO, EMILIA ROMAGNA, TUSCANY, UMBRIA, MARCHES, ABRUZZI, MOLISE, LAZIO, CAMPANIA, BASILICATA, CALABRIA, PROVENCE, DAUPHINÉ, V. D'AOSTA

Seas: LIGURIAN SEA, ADRIATIC SEA, TYRRHENIAN SEA, MEDITERRANEAN, Gulf of Venice, G. of Genoa, G. of Manfredónia, G. of Táranto

Cities and towns:
Lyons, Geneva, Grenoble, Valence, Montélimar, Avignon, Aix, Marseilles, Toulon, Cannes, Nice, Chambéry, Vienne, Annecy, Briançon

Turin (Torino), Cuneo, Susa, Alessandria, Asti, Novara, Vercelli, Pavia, Milan (Milano), Bergamo, Brescia, Como, Varese, Cremona, Mantua (Mantova), Piacenza, Parma, Reggio, Modena, Bologna, Ferrara, Ravenna, Forlì, Cesena, Rimini, Pesaro

Genoa (Genova), Savona, La Spezia, Imperia, Massa, Carrara, Pistoia, Lucca, Prato, Pisa, Leghorn (Livorno), Florence (Firenze), Arezzo, Siena, Grosseto, Viterbo, Terni, Rieti, Perugia, Ancona, Macerata, Ascoli Piceno, Teramo, Pescara, Chieti, L'Aquila

ROME (Roma), Ostia, Anzio, Latina, Frosinone, Isernia, Campobasso, Foggia, Benevento, Caserta, Avellino, Naples (Napoli), Salerno, Potenza, Matera, Bari, Barletta, Andria, Cerignola, Taranto, Cosenza, Catanzaro, Reggio

Trieste, Udine, Pordenone, Treviso, Padua (Padova), Venice (Venezia), Verona, Vicenza, Rovigo, Trento, Bolzano, Bellano, Sondrio, Locarno, Lugano

Ljubljana, Zagreb, Maribor, Klagenfurt, Villach, Celje, Rijeka, Pula (Pola), Zadar, Šibenik, Split, Banja Luka, Sisak, Karlovac

Sardinia: SARDINIA, Sassari, Cagliari, Oristano, Nuoro, Olbia (Terranova), Alghero, Iglesias, Carbonia, Asinara, C. Falcone, C. Carbonara, C. Spartivento, G. of Oristano, G. of Cagliari, G. of Palmas, G. of Asinara

Corsica: CORSICA, Ajaccio, Bastia, Calvi, Aleria, Bonifacio, Mte. Cinto 2710, Portoferraio, Elba, Capraia, C. Corse

Sicily: SICILY, Palermo, Messina, Catánia, Siracusa (Syracuse), Ragusa, Trapani, Marsala, Castelvetrano, Sciacca, Agrigento, Licata, Gela, Caltanissetta, Caltagirone, Enna, Termini, Milazzo, Giarre, Paternò, Lentini, Augusta, Alcamo, Favara, Vittória, Módica, Nébrodi Mts., Mt. Etna 3340, Lipari Is., Stromboli, Salina, Vulcano, Ustica, Egadi Is., Erice, C. Peloro, C. Passero, Str. of Messina

North Africa: Tunis, Bizerte, Béja, Nabeul, Sousse, Kairouan, Annaba, Skikda, Constantine, Tébessa, Khenchela, Sfax, C. Bon, G. de Tunis, G. de Hammamet, Galite Is.

Malta: Valletta, Mdina, Gozo

Islands: Pantelleria (Ital.), Lampedusa (Ital.), Palagruža (Yugoslavia), Dugi Otok, Krk, Cres, Lošinj, Pag, Brač, Hvar, Vis, Korčula, Lastovo, Pontine Is., Capri, Capraia, Asinara, Caprera, Iles d'Hyères

Mountains and peaks: Mt. Blanc 4807, Matterhorn, Mte. Rosa, Gran Paradiso 4061, Mt. Viso 3841, Mt. Pelvoux 4103, Mte. Amiata 1738, Mte. Cimone 2165, Gran Sasso 2914, Monti Vettore 2478, Mt. Amaro 2795, Mt. Gargano 1056, Vesuvius 1277, Mt. Gennargentu 1834, Mt. Cenis 3052, Marmolada 3342, Adamello 3554, Ortles 3899, Stelvio P., Brenner P. 1371, Bernina, St. Gotthard P., Gt. St. Bernard, Mte. Santo, Adamello, Mt. Peloux

Rivers/lakes: Rhône, Isère, Po, Tanaro, Ticino, Adda, Chiese, Adige, Reno, Arno, Ombrone, Fiora, Tiber, Garigliano, Volturno, Sele, Sinni, Agri, Ofanto, Drave, Sava, Kupa, Una, L. Maggiore, L. Como, L. Garda, L. Trasimeno, L. Bolsena, L. Bracciano, L. Bilancino

Scale bar (elevation):
ft / m: 12,000 / 4000, 9000 / 3000, 6000 / 2000, 4500 / 1500, 3000 / 1000, 1200 / 400, 600 / 200, 0 / 0

Projection: Conical with two standard parallels

8　　　　　9　　　　　10　　　　　11　　　　　12　　　　　13

Kaposvár Szekszárd

Baja

Pécs

Drava

Hódmezővásárhely

Szeged Arad Mt. Bihor 1848 T r a n s y l v a n i a UKRAINE

Subotica White Alba-Iulia Sfîntu Gheorghe Bârlad Sasyk

Sombor Kikinda Mures Deva ROMANIA Sibiu Focşani Galati Izmail B

Osijek Timişoara Brasov Sireth (Sereth) Braila Tulcea

Vukovar YUGO Zrenjanin Vojvodina B a n a t T r a n s y l v a n i a n Red 350 Mt. Negoiu 2535 (Orasul Stalin) Buzău Buzău

Novi Sad (Petrovgrad) 2509 Tower Peleaga 2518 Parîngul-Mare Tîrgu-Jiu Rîmnicu Vîlcea Tîrgovişte Prahova Ploeşti D o b r o d j a

Pancevo S L Iron Gate Dobreta-Turnu- Pitesti Ialomita Danube

BOSNIA- Belgrade Smederevo A Orsova Severin W a l l a c h i a Dâmbovita Bucharest Călăraşi Constanţa 44

HERCE- (Beograd) V Danube Argeş (Bucureşti) Trajan's

Tuzla Sava I Craiova Slatina Vedea Silistra Wall

GOVINA Drina A Morava Vidin Olt Giurgiu Tutrakon Ruse (Ruschuk) Dobrich C

Mostar Kragujevac Danube Oryakhovo Somovit Svishtov (Tolbukhin) C. Kaliakra

Durmitor 2522 Cacak Tara Bulgaria Balkan Pleven Sumen Varna B L A C K

Sarajevo J Krusevac S Nis 2168 Gabrovo Sliven (Kolarovgrad) S E A

MONTENEGRO U Leskovac Juzna Morava Vezhen Shipka P. Stara Zagora Burgas

Podgorica G Kopaonik Kosovska Dragoman Sofia 2198 Yambol

Prizren O Mitrovica Pristina Pernik Trajan's Gate BULGARIA C. Igneada

Shkoder S Pec Kosovo Pl. Musala Maritsa Pazardzhik Plovdiv Khaskovo Istranca Mts. 1018 Bosporus

L. Shkoder Prizren L Korab Sar Pl. Kyustendil Rhodope Arda Edirne Istanbul Üsküdar D

A A Tetovo 2496 Skopje 2925 Mountains Dhidhimotikhon TURKEY Sea of Marmara Bursa

V Kumanovo Struma Ergene Marmara Imrali I 2543

Durres I Jablanica Solunska Vardar Petrich Kamotini THRACE Enez Bandirma

Tirane 2289 A Prilep 2540 M A C E D O N I A Drama Axánthi Alexandroúpolis Cangkkale

Elbasan Bitola Serrai Kavalla Gökçeada Ida 1766 Balikesir

Ohridsko L. (Monastir) Florina Edhessa 1127 Thásos Samothráki 1600 G. of Saros Gallipoli Troy

Tomorrit 2480 Prespa 2917 Veroia C. Plati Dardanelles Ayvalik 2181

Korce Olympus M Thessaloniki C. Psevdhókavos Límnos (Hellespont) Bozca Ada Mytilíni 968

Vlore Kastoria Kozáni G. of Thessaloniki G. of Toronaïos Áyios Evstrátios C. Baba Edremit E

Vjose Smolikas Larisa 1978 Singitikós G. Mt. Áthos 2033 Lésvos Manisa 2157

2637 Ossa Volos G. of Volos N. Sporades Skíros Turgutlu

Ioannina G Trikkala THESSALY Rílion 1575 Áyios Izmir 2308

Préveza Pindus Mts. Iliodhrómia Skíros 1297 Khíos (Smyrna) Aydin Menderes

C. Otranto Árta Lamia N. Sporades Khíos 2294

Preveza Aetolikón Dhírfis 1743 (Chios) F

Brindisi Levkás (Sta. Maura) G. of Pátrai P. of Thermopylae Évvoia (Euboea) Samos G. of Kerme

Lecce Giona 2510 Khalkis C. Kafirévs Ándros Ikaria Ródhos

C. St. Maria di Leuca Kefallinía (Cephalonia) Parnassos 2457 1398 Tínos Míkonos Ródhos (Rhodes) 4486

Mesolóngion Athens (Athinai) Kéa Kíthnos Rínia Páros KIKLÁDHES (Cyclades) 1001 Náxos Amorgós Kálimnos G. of

Zákinthos Erímanthos 2224 Killini Corinth Piraiévs (Piraeus) Sériphos Sífnos Íos Astipálaia Kos F

Zákinthos Olympia PELOPONNESE 2376 Mycenae G. of Alvíno Sikinos Míkonos Tilos

Pírgos Kiparissía G. Trípolis Návplion G. of Argolis Síkinos Kásos

5121 Sparti Taïyetos Mts. Ídhra Thíra Karpáthos

Kalamata G. of Messini Yíthion G. of Lakonia C. Malea R R A N E A N S E A Kíthira (Cerigo) 1215 G

C. Spatha Khaníon B. C R E T E 1215

Andikíthira Khaniá Soúdhas B. Rethimnon C. Dia Iráklion (Candia) Knossos Kásos

Lévka Óri 2452 Mt. Ídhi 2456 Dhíkti 2148 Mérabéllou B. COPYRIGHT. GEORGE PHILIP & SON. LTD.

C. Lithinon

East from Greenwich

1:5 000 000

CASPIAN SEA

BLACK SEA

MEDITERRANEAN SEA

Sea of Azov

KAZAKHSTAN

Kirgiz Steppe

KALMYK REP.

UKRAINE

ROMANIA

MOLDAVIA

BULGARIA

GEORGIA

ARMENIA

AZERBAIJAN

DAGESTAN REP.

CAUCASUS Mts.

TURKEY

Canik (Pontine) Mts.

Taurus Mountains

SYRIA

IRAQ

I R A N

Elburz

LEBANON

CYPRUS

Dodecanese

Crimea

Levant

Syrian Desert

Kurdistan

1 Kabardino-Balkar Rep.
2 North Ossetian Rep.
3 Nakhichevan Rep. (Azer)
4 Checheno-Ingush Rep.

Karagiye Depression

Kara Bogaz Gol.

−28m below sea-level

MOSCOW / cities: Actyubinsk, Aktyubinsk, Oktabrsk, Kuldary, Makát, Kalmykovo, Aleksandrov Gai, Guryev, Fort Shevchenko, Bandar Torkeman, Krasnovodsk, TEHRAN, Qom, Ardq, Bakhtaran, Hamadan, Rasht, Qazvin, BAKU, Lenkoran, Kirkuk, Erbil, Mosul, BAGHDAD, Damascus, Aleppo, Beirut, Homs, Hama, Latakia, Tripoli, Adana, Mersin, Tarsus, Iskenderun, Antakya, Gaziantep, Şanlıurfa, Diyarbakır, Malatya, Elazığ, Erzurum, Erzincan, Sivas, Kayseri, ANKARA, Konya, Bursa, ISTANBUL, İzmir, Denizli, Antalya, Rhodes, Nicosia, Limassol, Famagusta, Larnaca

Volgograd (Stalingrad), Volzhskiy, Astrakhan, Saratov, Balta, Kamyshin, Elista, Stavropol, Pyatigorsk, Kislovodsk, Nalchik, Grozny, Vladikavkaz, Ordzhonikidze, Makhachkala, Derbent, Kizlyar, Budennovsk, Armavir, Maykop, Kropotkin, Tikhoretsk, Krasnodar, Novorossiysk, Sochi, Sukhumi, Batumi, Kutaisi, TBILISI, YEREVAN, Gyandzha, Mingechaur Res., Kuba, Sheki, Nakhichevan, Trabzon, Rize

Rostov, Taganrog, Novocherkassk, Shakhty, Novoshakhtinsk, Lugansk (Voroshilovgrad), Kadiyevka (Stakhanov), Kramatorsk, DONETSK, Makeyevka, Gorlovka, Zdanov (Mariupol), Berdyansk, Melitopol, Zaporozhye, Krivoy Rog, Dnepropetrovsk, DNEPROPETROVSK, Dneprodzerzhinsk, KHARKOV, Belgorod, Sumy, Poltava, Kremenchug, Cherkassy, KIEV, Zhitomir, Vinnitsa, Berdichev, Nikolayev (Kirovograd), Kherson, Yevpatoriya, Simferopol, Sevastopol, Yalta, Balaklava

OKS: Sea of Marmara, Dardanelles, G. of Iskenderun, G. of Antalya, Küçükkuyu, Konya, Tuz Gölü, Beyşehir Gölü, Eğridir Gölü, Burdur, Kütahya, Manisa, Aydın, Muğla, Mersin

L. Manych-Gudilo, Tsimlyansk Res., Kakhovka Res., G. of Karkinitsk, C. Tarkhankut, Constanta, Varna, Burgas, Edirne, Tekirdağ, Çanakkale, Gelibolu (Gallipoli), İzmit, Adapazarı, Bolu, Zonguldak, Samsun, Sinop, C. İnce, Ordu, Giresun, Kastamonu, Çorum, Yozgat, Kırıkkale, Kırşehir, Nevşehir, Niğde, Karaman, Silifke, Alanya, Manavgat

Ergeni Heights

Volga, Don, Dnepr, Dnestr, Prut, Siret, Danube, Kuban, Ural, Emba

Kara Su, Aras, Kura, L. Sevan, L. Van, L. Urmia, Zagros Mts., Great Zab, Little Zab, Tigris, Euphrates

Elbruz 5633, 5047, Ararat 5165, Aragats, Demavend 5604, 4824, 4488, 4168, 3937, 3770, 3086, 2211, 2565, 2535, 2102, 3083, 2814, 4486

MOUNTAINS: 995, 132

ABKHAZIA, ADZHAR, OSSETIA, Sukhumi

Nezhin, Belaya Tserkov, Yelizavetgrad (Kirovograd), S. Bug, Vinnitsa, Kishinev, Tiraspol, ODESSA, Sulina, Galati, Braila, BUCHAREST (București), Ploești, Brașov, Pitești, Prut, Nistru (Dniestr), Iași, Chernovtsy, Ivano-Frankovsk, Lvov, Khmelnitskiy

COPYRIGHT GEORGE PHILIP & SON, LTD.

East from Greenwich

Division between Greeks and Turks
in Cyprus, Turks to the North

Projection: Conical with two standard parallels

1:10 000 000

50   0   50   100 150 200 250 miles
50 0 50 100 150 200 250 300 350 400 km

ft   m   m   ft
12,000 4000   0   0
6000   3000   200   600
        1200   1000   3000
        600   2000   6000
        200   4000   12,000
0   0

Projection: Bonne

1:50 000 000

200 0 200 400 600 800 1000 miles

200 0 400 800 1200 1600 km

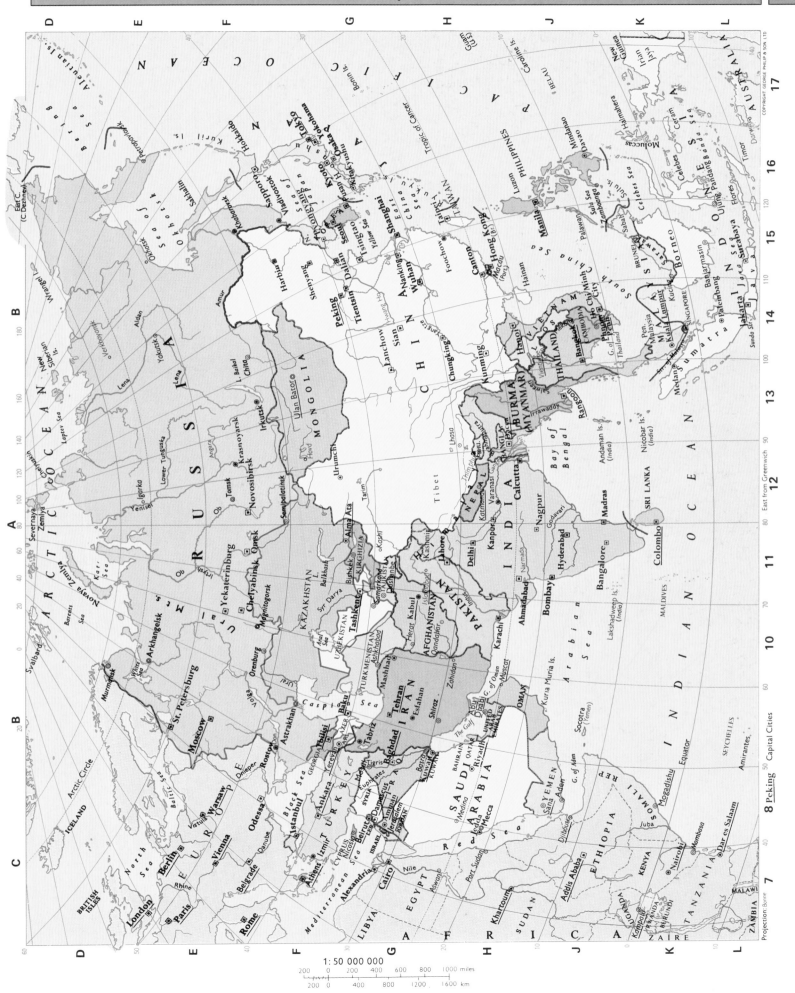

Projection: Bonne

1:50 000 000

200   0   200   400   600   800   1000 miles

200   0   400   800   1200   1600 km

8 Peking   50 Capital Cities

East from Greenwich

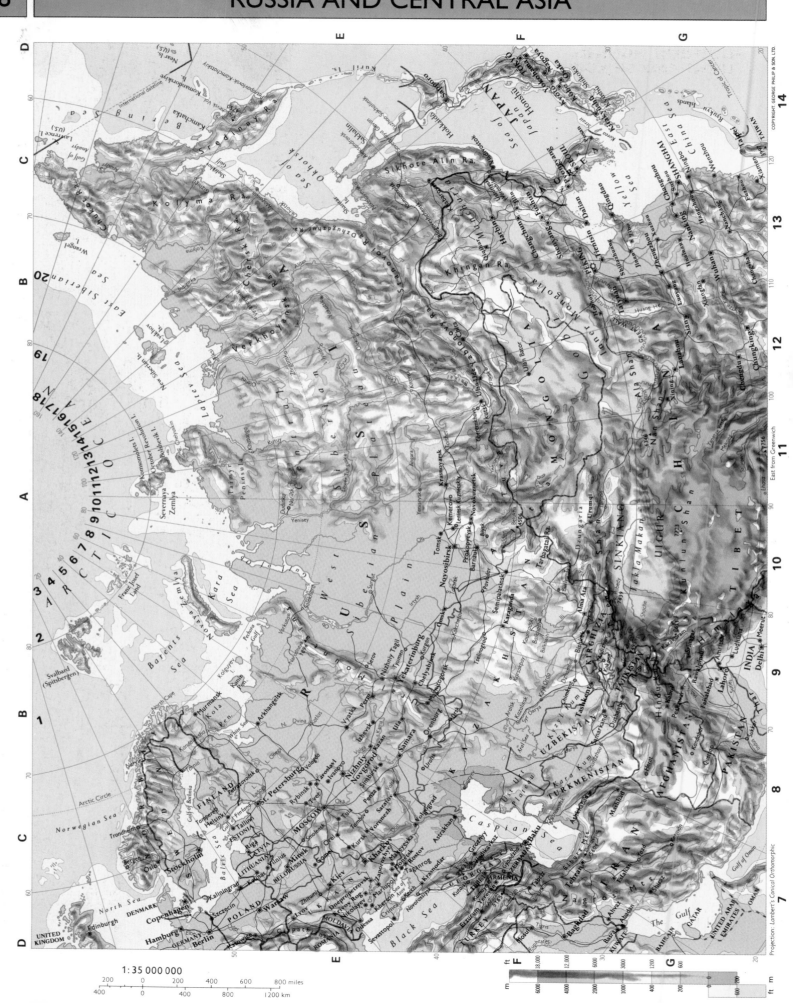

1 : 35 000 000

Projection: Lambert's Conical Orthomorphic

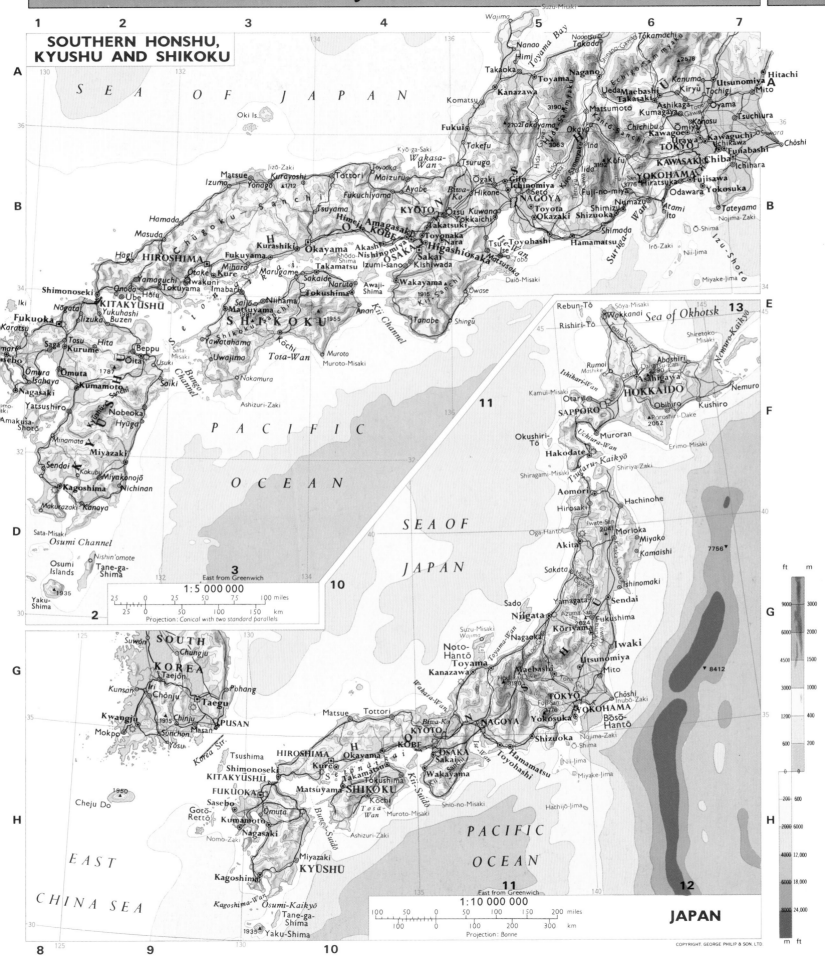

SOUTHERN HONSHU, KYUSHU AND SHIKOKU

1 : 5 000 000
Projection : Conical with two standard parallels

1 : 10 000 000
Projection : Bonne

JAPAN

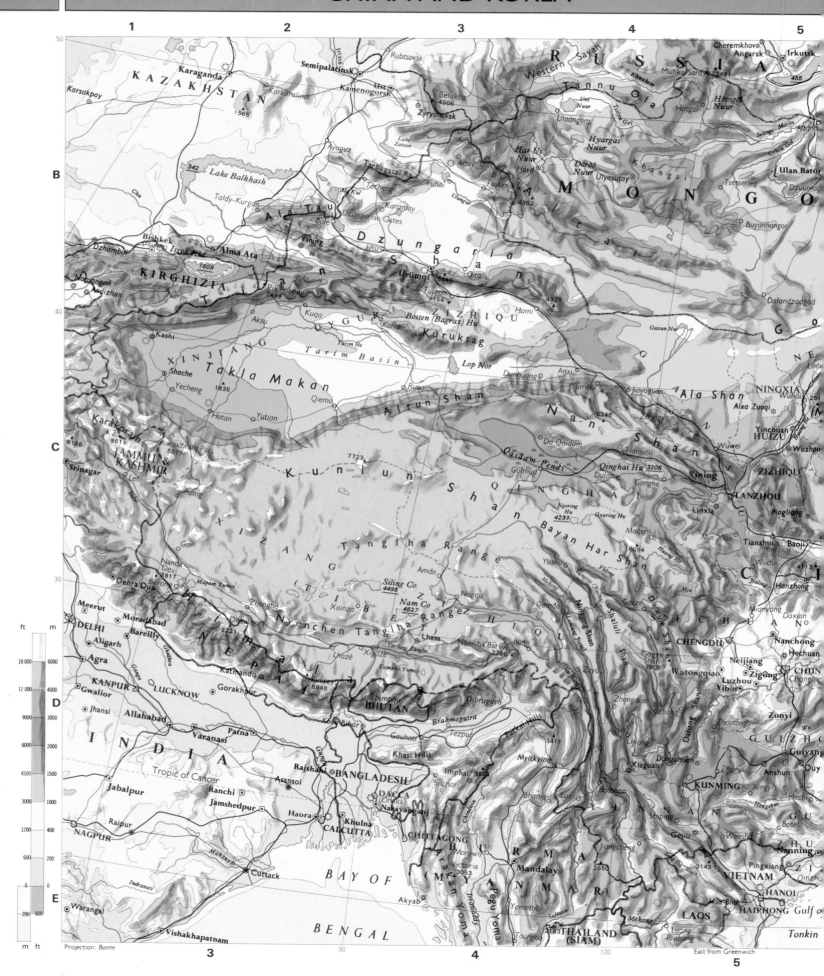

Projection: Bonne

East from Greenwich

7

6　　　　　　8　　　　　9

Lake Baykal　Chita
Ulan Ude　Yablonovyy Range
Khta　Nerchinsk
Borzya
Manzhouli
Hentiyn Nuruu　Choybalsan
Buir Nur
Hulun Nur
Hailar
Oroqen Zizhiqi
Nenjiang
Blagoveshchensk
Svobodny
Chegdomyn
Aihui
Amur
Komsomolsk
L. Bolon
Poronaysk　C. Terpeniya
Sakhalin
Aleksandrovsk
Khabarovsk
Yuzhno-Sakhalinsk

B

LIA
Saynshand
Dzamin Üüd　Erenhot
Abagnar Qi
1949
INNER MONGOLIA
b
Butha Qi
Bei'an
Yichun
Jiamusi
Hegang
Shuangyashan
Qiqihar
Anda
Suihua
Songhua
Jixi
Mishan
Lake Khanka
Sikhote Alin Ra.
Wakkanai
Asahigawa
2290
Hokkaido
SAPPORO
Otaru
Kushiro
C. Erimo
La Perouse Str.

HEILONGJIANG
Great Khingan Mts.
Little Khingan Mts.
Horqin Youyi Qianqi
HARBIN
Manchuria
Tao'an
JILIN
CHANGCHUN
Shuangliao
Mudanjiang
Ussuriysk
Vladivostok
Nakhodka
Hakodate
Tsugaru Strait
Aomori
Hachinohe
Morioka

40

Saynshand
Hohhot
Jining
Zhangjiakou
Chengde
Jinzhou
Chifeng
Chaoyang
Fuxin
Liaoyang
FUSHUN
SHENYANG
Mukden
Benxi
2744
Tonghua
Siping
Liaoyuan
Yanji
Chongjin
Tongliao
Songhua Lake
SEA OF JAPAN
Akita
Sado
Niigata
Sendai
Kōriyama
Utsunomiya

Baotou
Datong
Xuanhua
Qinhuangdao
G. of Liaodong
Liaodong
ANSHAN
Yingkou
Dandong
Yalu
NORTH
Hungnam
Wŏnsan
Toyama
Kanazawa
NAGOYA
TOKYO
KAWASAKI
YOKOHAMA
Yokosuka
Fuji-san
3776
Shizuoka

C

Ordos
Us mo)
GREAT WALL
PEKING (Beijing)
Baoding
3058
HEBEI
TIENTSIN (Tianjin)
Cangzhou
DALIAN (Lüda)
Korea Bay
Haeju
YONGYANG
Kaesong
SEOUL
INCHON
SOUTH
KOBE
KYOTO
OSAKA
Sakai
Wakayama
Okayama
Hiroshima
Shikoku
Kochi
Matsuyama

TAIYUAN
Yangquan
Shijiazhuang
G. of Chihli (Bo Hai)
Yantai
Weihai
Taejon
TAEGU
PUSAN
Masan
1915
Kwangju
Shimonoseki
KITAKYUSHU
FUKUOKA
Sasebo

Yuci
Fenyang
Dezhou
Ye Xian
Weifang
YELLOW
SEA
KOREA
JAPAN
Nagasaki
Kumamoto
Kyushu

an'an
Tongchuan
JINAN
Handan
Anyang
Tai'an
Zibo
Jining
QINGDAO
SHANDONG
Xinxiang
Huang He
Cheju Do
1950
Kagoshima
Tanega

SIAN (Xi'an)
Luoyang
Kaifeng
ZHENGZHOU
HENAN
Pingdingshan
Nanyang
Shangqiu
Xuzhou
Qingjiang
Hongze Hu
JIANGSU

30

Ankang
Han Shui
Zhumadian
Shangshui
Huaian
Bengbu
NANKING (Nanjing)
Zhenjiang
Changzhou
Nantong
Wuxi
Suzhou
SHANGHAI

aba Shan
Xiangfan
Dable Shan
ANHUI
Hefei
Wuhu
Tongling
Hangzhou
Hangzhou Wan

WUHAN
Anqing
Yangtze
Ningbo
EAST CHINA
SEA
Amami-ō-Shima

Wanxian
Yichang
Shashi
Huangshi
Hujiang
Tunxi
Shaoxing
Jinhua
Jingdezhen
Shangrao

ING
Changde
Dongting L.
Yiyang
Nanchang
Poyang L.
ZHEJIANG
Wenzhou
Ryukyu Islands
Okinawa
Naha
PACIFIC

Changsha
Xiangtan
Zhuzhou
JIANGXI
Wuyi Shan
2120
D
583
HUNAN
Shaoyang
Hengyang
Jian
Sanming
Nanping
Min
Nanchang

Xiang
Guilin
Ganzhou
FUJIAN
Fuzhou
Sakishima Gunto
Formosa Strait
Tropic of Cancer

Nan Ling
iuzhou
Shaoguan
Zhangzhou
Quanzhou
Chilung
TAIPEI
Taichung

NGXI
Wuzhou
GUANGDONG
Mei Xian
Chao'an
Xiamen (Amoy)
Chiai
Yu Shan
3997
TAIWAN

GZU
Foshan
CANTON (Guangzhou)
Shantou
Tainan
KAOHSIUNG

liqu
Jiangmen
Macau (Port.)
HONG KONG (Br.)
20

eihai
Maoming
Batan Is.

E

eizhou Penin.
Zhanjiang
SOUTH CHINA
SEA
Babuyan Is.

HAINAN
1879
Hainan Str.
Haikou

110

6　　　　　　120　　　　　7　　　　　　130　　　　　8

COPYRIGHT GEORGE PHILIP & SON LTD

1:15 000 000

100　　0　　100　　200　　300　　400 miles
100　0　100　200　300　400　500　600 km

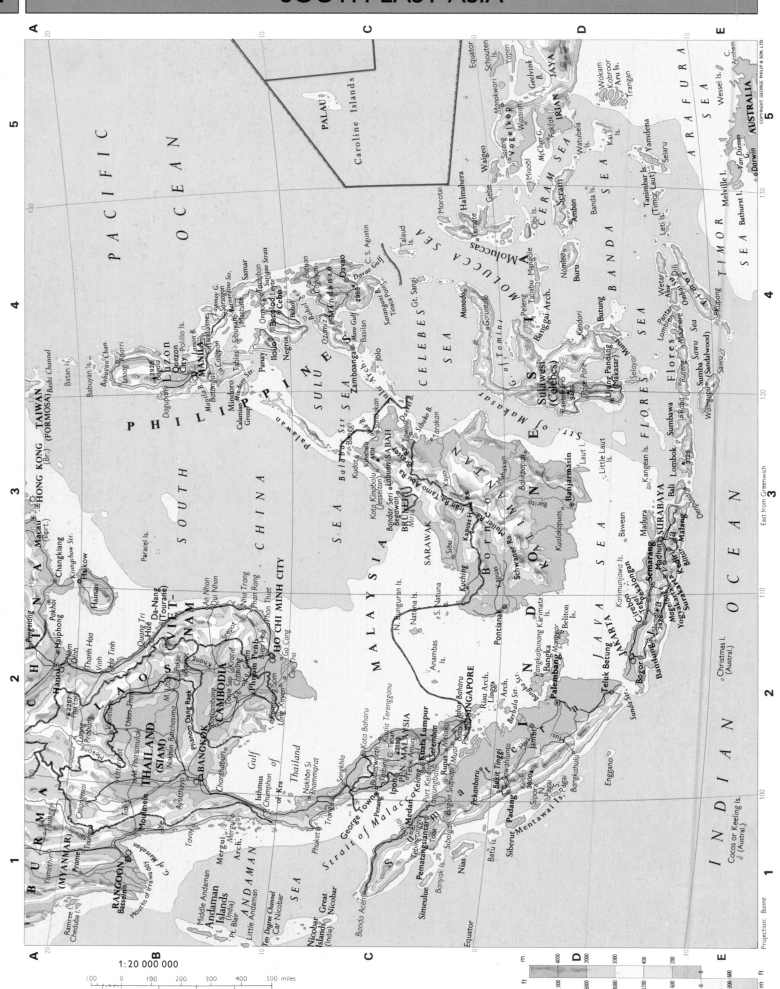

Projection: Bonne

COPYRIGHT GEORGE PHILIP & SON LTD.

East from Greenwich

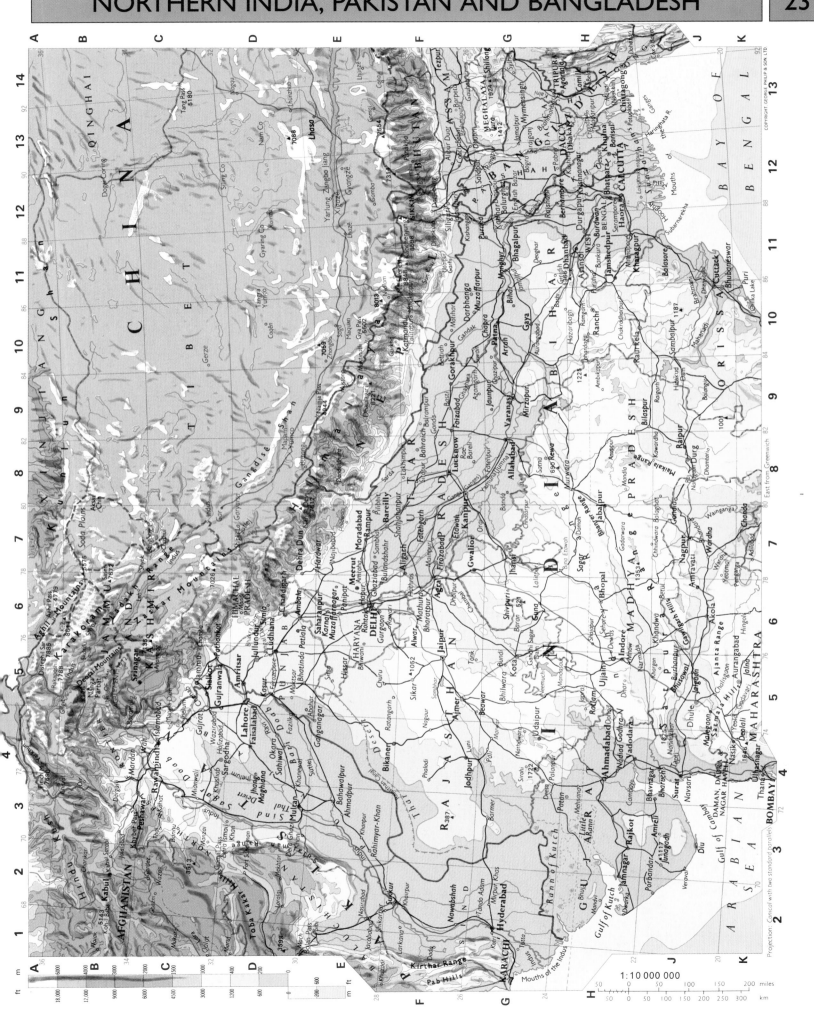

Projection: Conical with two standard parallels

1:10 000 000

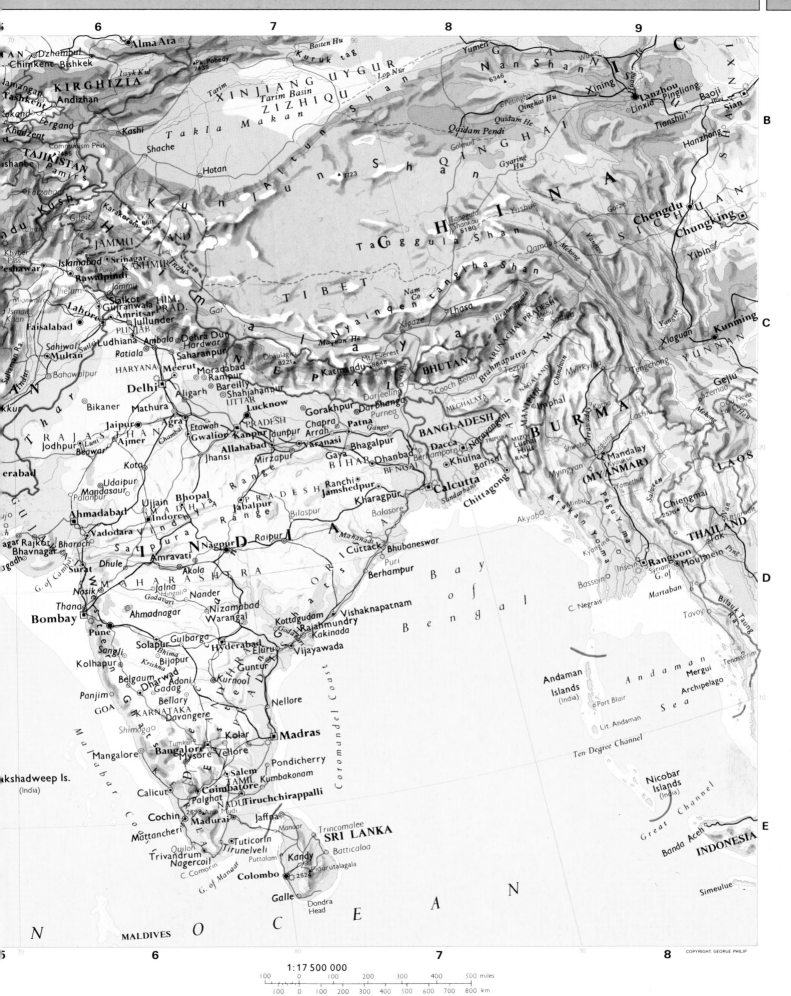

1:17 500 000

100   0   100   200   300   400   500 miles

100 0 100 200 300 400 500 600 700 800 km

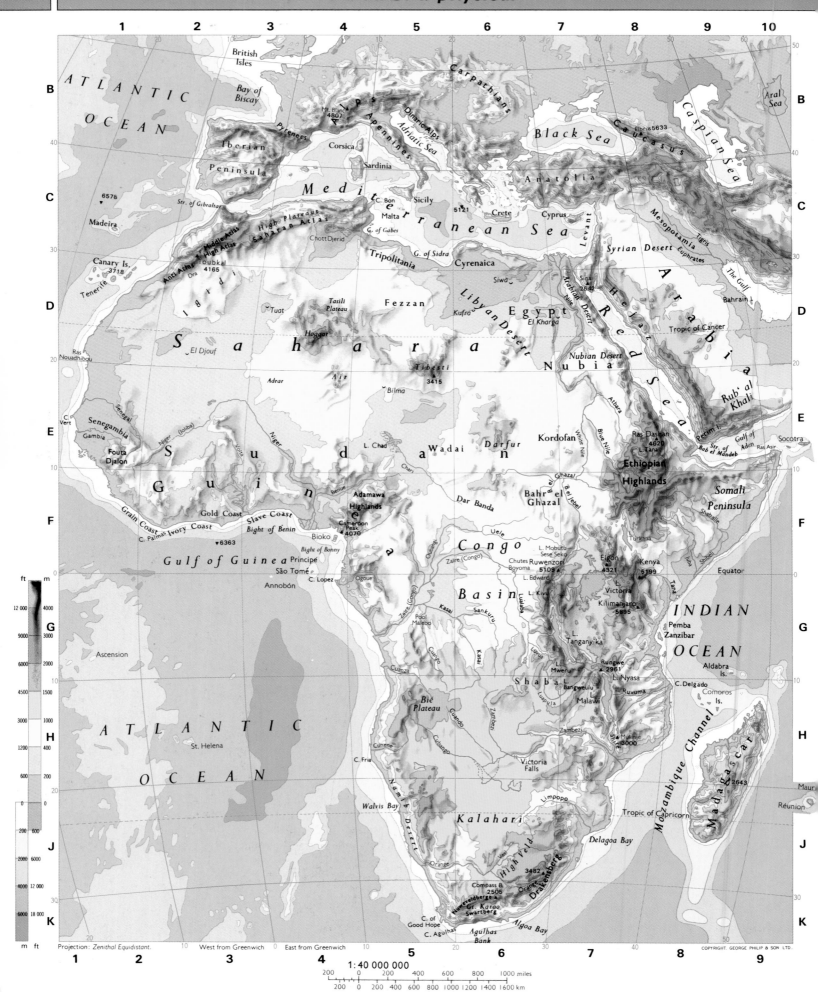

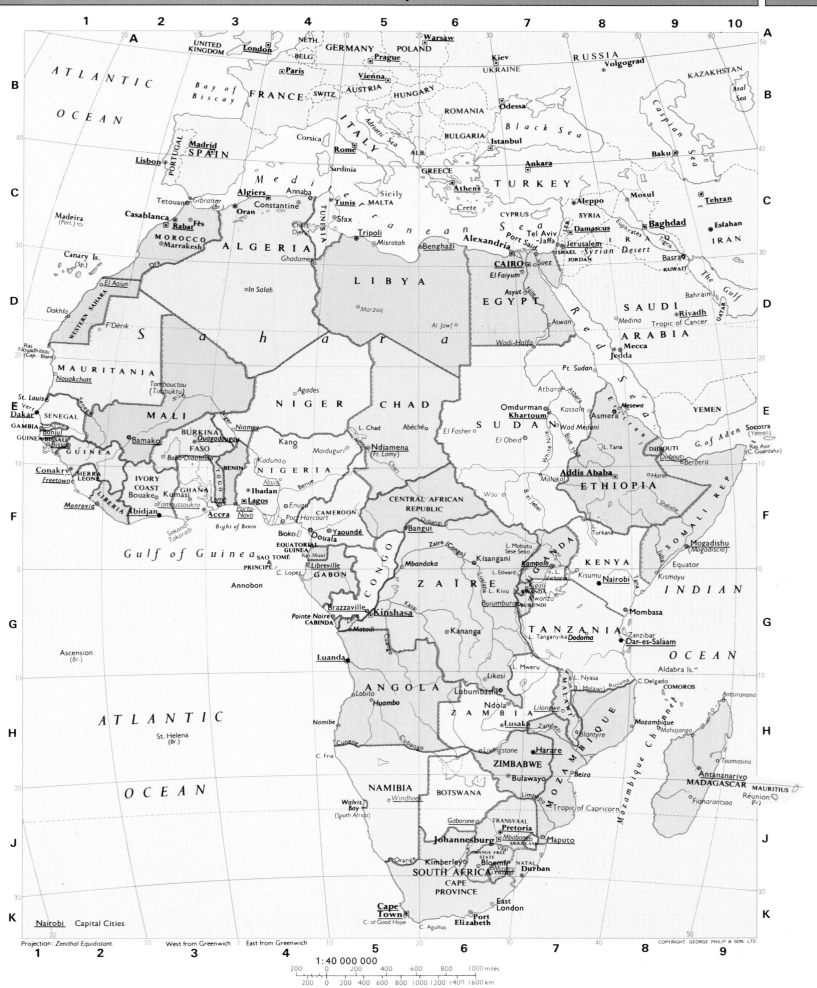

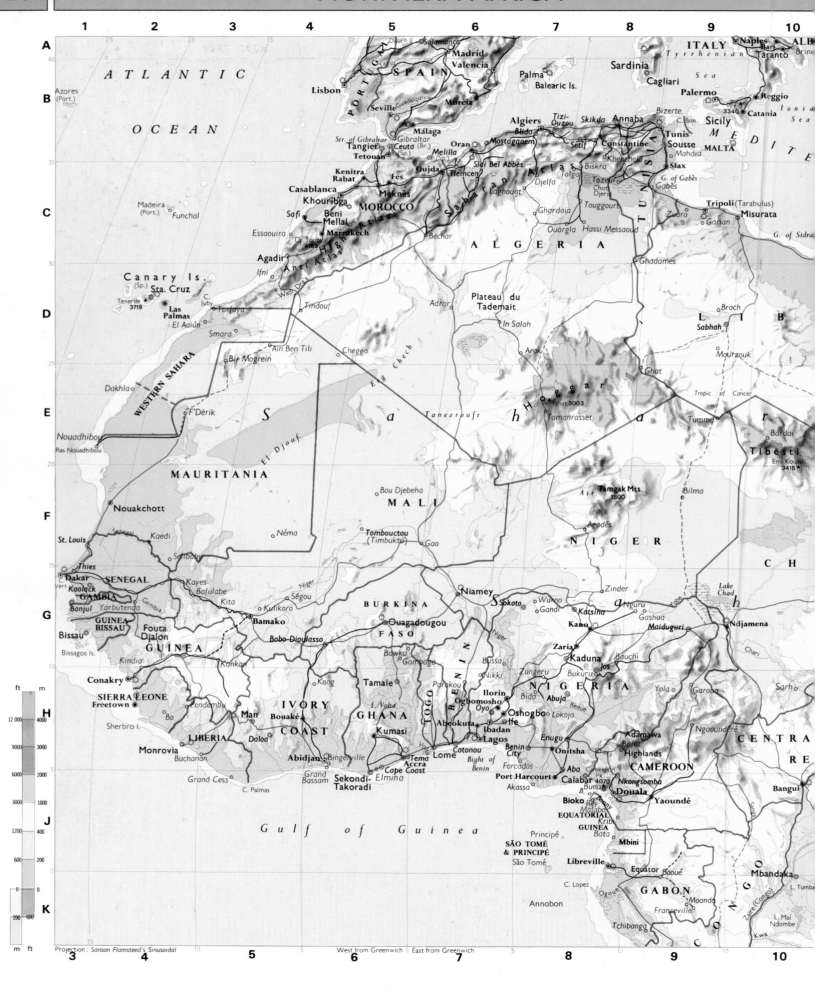

ATLANTIC

OCEAN

Azores
(Port.)

Madeira
(Port.)
Funchal

ITALY
Naples ALB
Bari
Taranto Brine

Tyrrhenian

Sea

Sardinia
Cagliari

Palermo
Etna
3340 Reggio
Sicily Catania Ionian
Sea
Bizerte MALTA
MEDITE

Douro
Salamanca
Madrid
Valencia
SPAIN
PORTUGAL
Lisbon
Guadalquivir
Seville
Murcia
Palma
Balearic Is.

Málaga
Str. of Gibraltar
Tangier Gibraltar
Ceuta (Br.)
Tetouan (Sp.)
Melilla
Kenitra
Rabat Fès Oujda
Casablanca Meknès
Khouribga
MOROCCO
Safi
Beni
Mellal
Marrakech
Essaouira
Dj Toubkal
185

Algiers Tizi-
Blida Ouzou
Mostaganem
Oran
Sidi Bel Abbès
Tlemcen
Djelfa
Laghouat
Skikda Annaba
Setif Constantine
Khenchela
Biskra
Tolga
Tozeur
Chott
Djerid
TUNISIA
Tunis
Sousse
Mahdia
Sfax
G. of Gabès
Gabès

Tripoli (Tarabulus)
Misurata
Garian
Zuara

G. of Sidra

Agadir
Anti Atlas
Ifni
High Atlas
Wad Draa
Saharan Atlas
Béchar

Ghardaia
Ouargla
Touggourt
Hassi Messaoud
Ghadames

ALGERIA

LIB

Canary Is.
(Sp.)
Sta. Cruz
Tenerife
3718
Las
Palmas
El Aaiún
Smara

C. Juby
Tarfaya
Tindouf

Plateau du
Tademait
Adrar
In Salah
Arak
Ghat
Brach
Sabhah

B

Dakhla

WESTERN SAHARA

Nouadhibou
Ras Nouadhibou

F'Dérik

Ain Ben Tili
Bir Mogrein
Chegga
El Djouf

Eg Chech

S a

Tanezrouft

h a

Oued
Tahat 3003
Tamanrasset

Hoggar

Tummo

r a

Mourzouk

Tropic of Cancer

Bardai

Tibesti
Emi Koussi
3415

MAURITANIA

Nouakchott
Senegal
Kaedi
Selibaby

Bou Djebeha

MALI

Néma

Tombouctou
(Timbuktu)
Gao

Air
Tamgak Mts.
1800

Bilma

Agadés

NIGER

CH

St. Louis
Thies
Dakar
C. Vert
Kaolack
GAMBIA
Banjul
Yarbutenda
GUINEA
BISSAU
Bissau
Bissagos Is.

SENEGAL
Kayes
Bafulabe
Kita
Kindia

Kaolack

Gambia

Niger
Ségou
Kulikoro
Bamako
Bobo-Dioulasso
Fouta
Djalon
GUINEA
Kankan

BURKINA
FASO
Ouagadougou
Bawku
Gambaga

Niamey
Sokoto
Wurno
Gandi
Zinder

Nguru
Katsina
Kano
Gashua

Lake Chad

Ndjamena
Maiduguri

Chari

Conakry
SIERRA LEONE
Freetown
Bo
Pendembu
Sherbro I.
Man
Bouaké
Daloa
LIBERIA
Monrovia
Buchanan
Grand Cess
C. Palmas

IVORY
COAST
Kong
Tamale
L. Volta
GHANA
Kumasi
Grand
Bassam
Sekondi-
Takoradi
Elmina
Cape Coast
Abidjan
Bingerville
Tema
Accra
Lome
TOGO

Parakou
BENIN
Nikki
Bussa
Zungeru
Ilorin
Oyo
Oshogbo
Oyo
Abeokuta
Ibadan
Lagos
Cotonou
Benin
City
Forcados
Akassa
Bight of
Benin

Bida
Abuja
NIGERIA
Bukuru
Jos
Kaduna
Zaria
Bauchi
Lokoja
Benue
Yola
Enugu
Onitsha
Aba
Port Harcourt
Calabar
Buea
Cameroon Pk.
4070
Bioko
Malabo

Garoba
Ngaoundéré

Adamawa
Bofut
Highlands

CAMEROON
Nkongsomba
Douala
Yaoundé

CENTRA
RE

Bangui

Gulf of Guinea

Principé
SÃO TOMÉ
& PRINCIPE
São Tomé

EQUATORIAL
GUINEA
Bata
Mbini
Kribi

Libreville
Equator Boué
GABON
Moando
Franceville
Tchibanga
Annobon
C. Lopez
Ogooué

Bangui

Mbandaka
L. Tumba
CONGO
Zaire (Congo)
L. Mai
Ndombe
Kwa

ft m
12 000 4000
9000 3000
6000 2000
3000 1000
1200 400
600 200
0 0
200 600
m ft

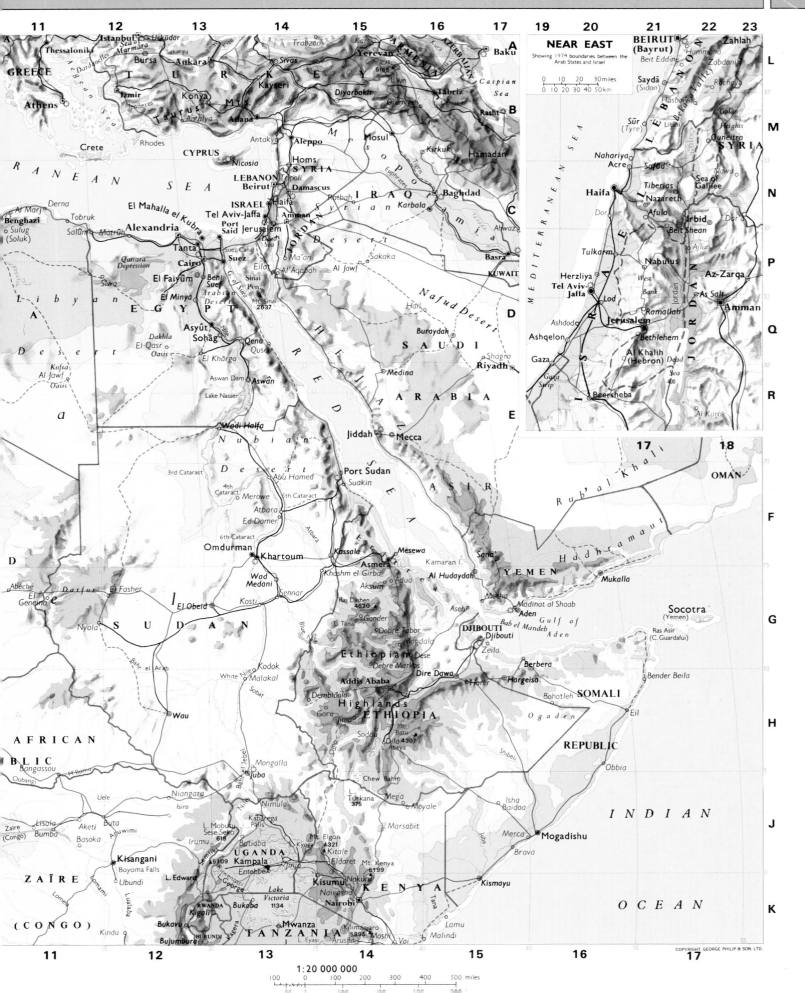

Main Map Labels

11 12 13 14 15 16 17 19 20 21 22 23

Thessaloniki
Istanbul · Üsküdar
GREECE
Sea of Marmara
Bursa · Ankara
Sakarya
Trabzon
Kars
Yerevan
ARMENIA
Ararat 5165
AZERBAIJAN
Baku
A

Athens
Izmir
Konya
Kayseri
Sivas
TURKEY
Diyarbakir
Van
Orumiyeh
Tabriz
Rasht
Caspian Sea
B

Crete
Rhodes
Antalya
Taurus Mts.
Adana
Antakya
Aleppo
Mosul
Kirkuk
Hamadan
CYPRUS
Nicosia
Homs
SYRIA
Tripoli
M
e
s
o
p
o
t
a
m
i
a
Tigris

RANEAN SEA
LEBANON
Beirut
Damascus
Baghdad
Karbala
N

Al Marj
Derna
Tobruk
Salûm
Matrûh
El Mahalla el Kubra
ISRAEL
Haifa
Tel Aviv-Jaffa
Amman
JORDAN
Rutbah
IRAQ
Basra
KUWAIT
C

Benghazi
Sulug (Soluk)
Alexandria
Tanta
Port Said
Jerusalem
Suez Canal
Ma'an
Sakaka
Ahwaz
Syrian Desert

NEAR EAST
Showing 1974 boundaries between the Arab States and Israel

0 10 20 30 miles
0 10 20 30 40 50 km

BEIRUT (Bayrut)
Hammana
Zahlah
Beit Eddine
Zabdani
Rachaya
Saydâ (Sidon)
L

Sûr (Tyre)
Litani
Golan Heights
Quneitra
SYRIA
Nawa
M

Nahariya
Acre
Safad
Sea of Galilee
Haifa
Tiberias
Nazareth
Irbid
Dora
N

Dor
Afula
Beit Shean
Ajlun
Tulkarm
Nabulus
As Salt
West Bank
P

Herzliya
Tel Aviv-Jaffa
Lod
Ramallah
Amman
Jordan
Az-Zarqa
Ashdod
Ashqelon
Jerusalem
Bethlehem
Gaza
Gaza Strip
Al Khalih (Hebron)
Dead Sea 400
Q

Beersheba
Al Kurak
R

Egypt / Africa section:
Cairo
El Faiyûm
Beni Suef
Qattara Depression
Siwa
Libyan Desert
EGYPT
Arabian Desert
Eilat
Al 'Aqabah
Al Jawf
Hail
Nafud Desert
SAUDI
D

Asyût
Sohâg
El Qasr
Dakhla Oasis
El Khârga
Qena
Quseir
Medina
Buraydah
Shaqra
Riyadh
ARABIA
E

Aswan Dam
Aswân
Lake Nasser
Nile
Mt Sinai 2637
Sinai Pen.
G. of Suez
RED SEA
HEJAZ
Kufra
Al Jawf Oasis
Desert
a

Wadi Halfa
Nubian Desert
3rd Cataract
4th Cataract
Merowe
5th Cataract
Jiddah
Mecca
ASIR
F

Port Sudan
Suakin
Abu Hamed
Atbara
Ed Damer
6th Cataract
Kamaran I.
Sana'
Mukalla
YEMEN
Hadhramaut
Rub' al Khali
OMAN
17 18

Omdurman
Khartoum
Kassala
Mesewa
Asmera
Al Hudaydah
Aden
Madinat al Shaab
Socotra (Yemen)
Ras Asir (C. Guardafui)
G

Abéché
El Geneina
El Fasher
Wad Medani
Sennar
Khashm el Girba
Adua
Aksum
Mocha
Aseb
Bab el Mandeb
Gulf of Aden
Bender Beila
D

Nyala
El Obeid
Kosti
SUDAN
Ras Dashen 4620
Gonder
L. Tana
Debre Tabor
Magdala
DJIBOUTI
Djibouti
Zeila
Berbera
Hargeisa
SOMALI
G

Darfur
Bahr el Arab
White Nile
Kodok
Malakal
Sobat
Blue Nile
Debre Markos
Dese
Dire Dawa
Harer
Bohotleh
Eil
H

AFRICAN
BLIC
Bangassou
M'Bomu
Oubangi
Wau
Bahr el Jebel
Addis Ababa
Ethiopian Highlands
ETHIOPIA
Gore
Jimma
Sodo
Mt Batu
Dila 4307
L. Abaya
Ogaden
REPUBLIC
Obbia
H

Lisala
Zaire (Congo)
Bumba
Aketi
Basoka
Buta
Aduwimi
Uele
Isiro
Niangara
Mongalla
Juba
Nimule
Chew Bahir
L. Turkana 375
Mega
Moyale
Isha Baidoa
Merca
Mogadishu
INDIAN
J

Kisangani
Boyoma Falls
Ubundi
Irumu
Butiaba
L. Mobutu Sese Seko 619
Kabarega Falls
L. Kyoga
UGANDA
Kampala
Entebbe
Jinja
Mt Elgon 4321
Kitale
Eldoret
Mt Kenya 5199
Marsabit
Brava
ZAÏRE
K

ZAÏRE
Lomami
Kindu
Bukavu
RWANDA
Kigali
L. Edward
Ruwenzori Mt 5109
Gorge
L. Kivu
Bukoba
Lake Victoria 1134
Kisumu
Nakuru
Naivasha
KENYA
Nairobi
Kismayu
OCEAN
K

(CONGO)
Lualaba
BURUNDI
Bujumbura
TANZANIA
Mwanza
L. Eyasi
Kilimanjaro 5895
Moshi
Arusha
Voi
Lamu
Malindi
Tana

1:20 000 000
100 0 100 200 300 400 500 miles

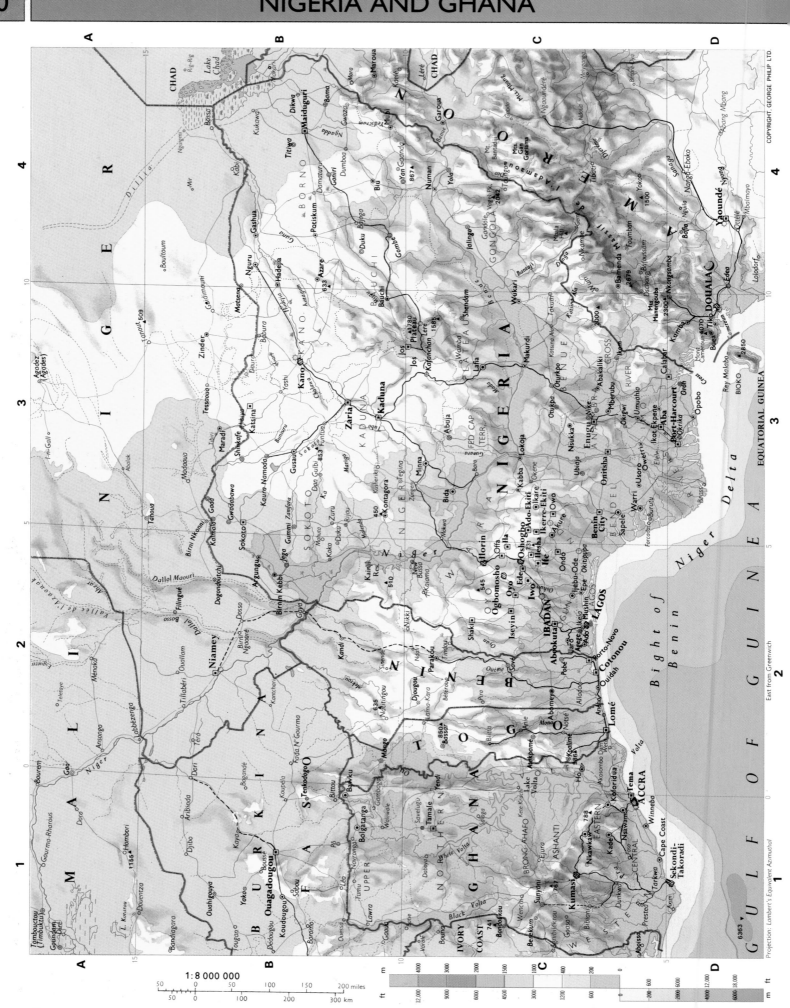

Projection: Lambert's Equivalent Azimuthal

1 : 8 000 000

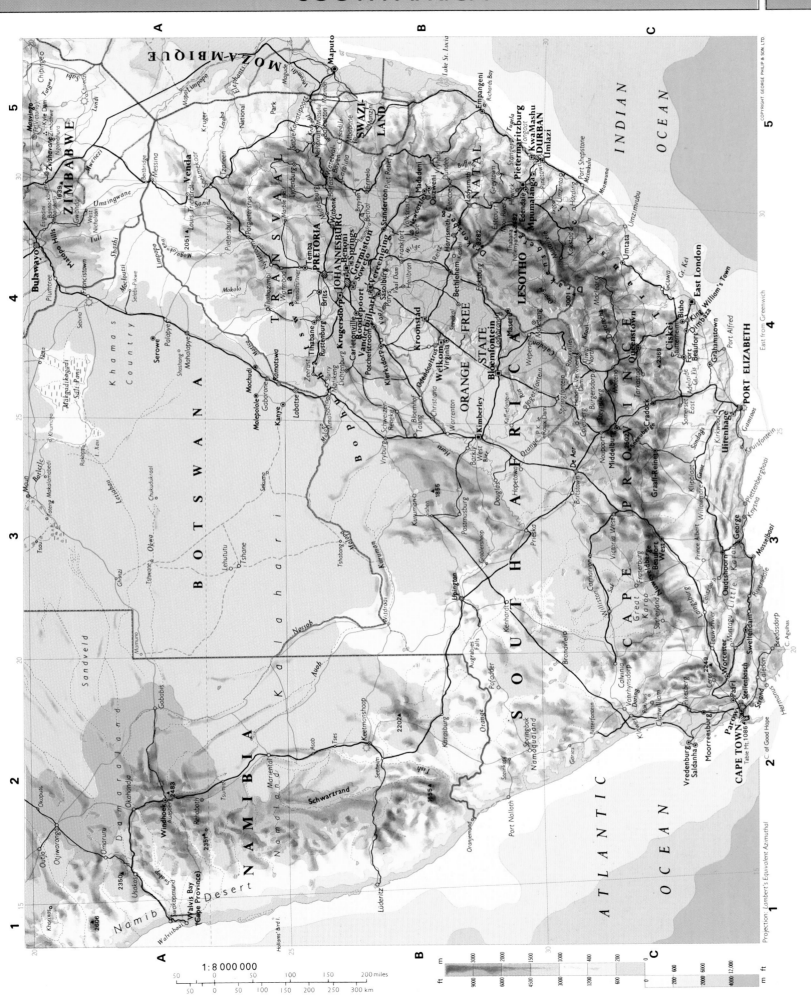

Projection: Lambert's Equivalent Azimuthal

East from Greenwich

1 : 8 000 000

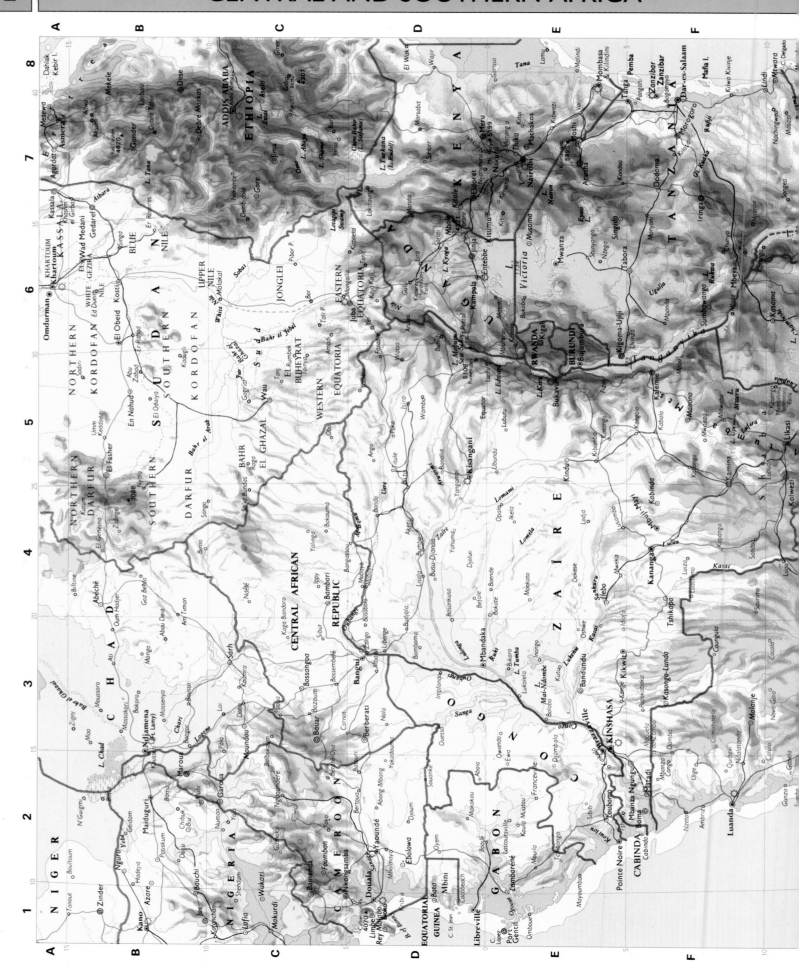

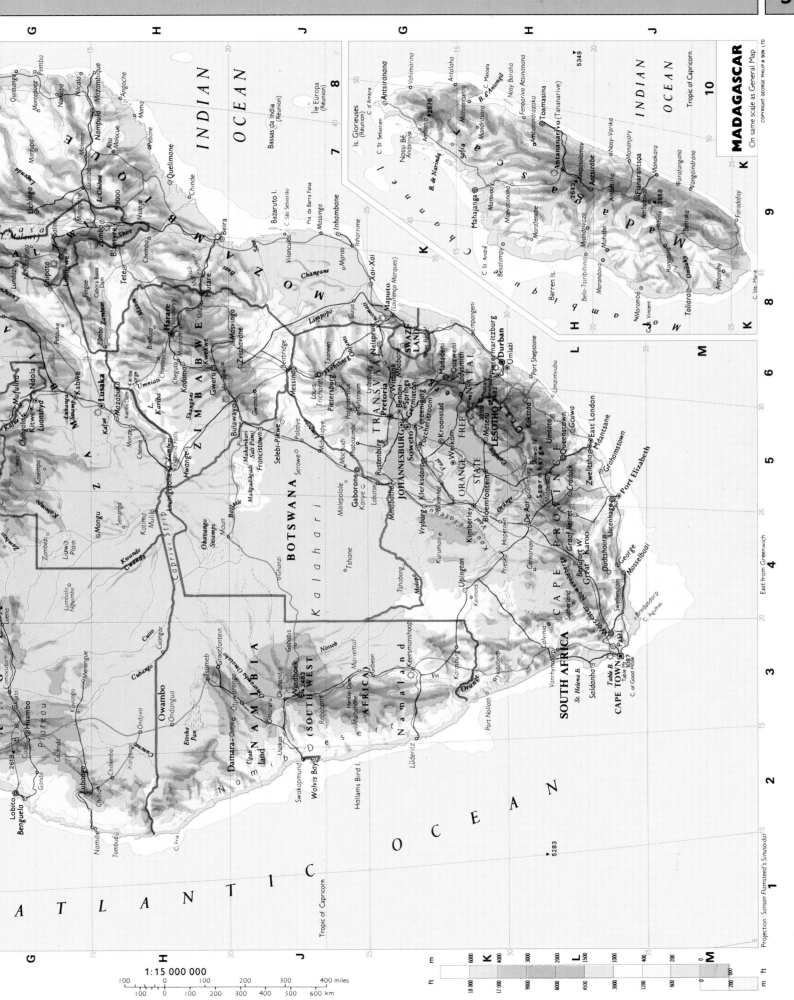

MADAGASCAR
On same scale as General Map

COPYRIGHT GEORGE PHILIP & SON LTD

1:15 000 000

100   0   100   200   300   400 miles
100 0 100 200 300 400 500 600 km

Projection : Sanson Flamsteed's Sinusoidal

INDONESIA

Maluku

Sulawesi (Celebes)

Buru
Ceram
Ambon
Butung
Kendari
5300

Vogelkop Peninsula
Sorong
Misool
Fakfak
Biak

Irian Barat
Pegunungan Maoke
Puncak Jaya
5020
Jayapura

PAPUA NEW GUINEA

NEW GUINEA
Wewak
Madang
Mount Hagen
4508
Mt. Wilhelm
Lae
Owen Stanley Range

Bismarck Archipelago
Rabaul
New Ireland
Kaweng
New Britain
91

Solomon Sea

Banda Sea
7260 Kep. Kai
3350
Kep. Aru

Fly
Gulf of Papua

Port Moresby

D'Entrecastea
Louisiade Archipelago

Ujung Pandang (Makasar)

Wetar
Leti Babar
Kep. Tanimbar

Pulau Yos Sudarso

Torres Strait

Flores Sea
Alor

Arafura Sea

Sumbawa
Flores
Ende
Kupang
6204

Timor

Timor Sea
3310

C. York

C. Croker
C. Arnhem
Weipa
Cape York
Coral Sea

Sumba
Babar
Dili

Melville

Darwin

Arnhem Land

Gulf of Carpenteria

Wellesley

Cape York Peninsula

Cooktown

Coral Sea Islands Territory

C. Londonderry

Kimberley Plateau
Wyndham
Cambridge G.
Daly Waters
Larrimah

Mitchell
Normanton
Forsayth
1611
Bartle Frere
Cairns

Derby

Barkly Tableland

NORTHERN

Flinders
Kajaabi

Townsville
Charters Towers

Great Barrier Reef

Coral Sea

Broome

Tanami Desert
Tennant Creek

Mount Isa

Hughenden

Mackay

Great Sandy Desert

TERRITORY

Winton

QUEENSLAND
Rockhampton
Gladstone

Port Hedland
Dampier
L. Mackay
Macdonnell Ranges
1510 Mt. Ziel
Alice Springs

Longreach
Yaraka
Diamantina

Great Dividing Range
Bundab

N.W. Cape

Lake Disappointment
Gibson Desert

Simpson Desert

Charleville
Roma
Maryborough
Gympie

Mt. Bruce
1726
Newman
Hamersley Range

AUSTRALIA

Ayers Rock
Mt. Woodroffe
4440
Musgrave Ranges

Cooper Creek

Grey Range
Quilpie
Cunnamulla
Thargomindah

BRISBAN
Toowoomba
Ipswic

Carnarvon

WESTERN

L. Carnegie

Great Victoria Desert

SOUTH

Lake Eyre

Warrego

Dirrabandi

Lism
1615
Round Mt.

Meekatharra
Leonora

AUSTRALIA

Marree

Bourke
Walgett
Cobar

Tamworth
Taree

Murchison

Kalgoorlie-Boulder

Tarcoola

Broken Hill

Darling

NEW SOUTH

WALES
Newcastle
Orange
Bathurst
SYDNEY
Wollongon
Shellharbour

Geraldton
Lake Barlee
Deakin
Nullarbor Plain
Penong
Port Augusta
Whyalla
Port Pirie

Dubbo

Northam
Narseman
Spencer Gulf

Murray
Mildura

Wagga Wagga
Canberra
CAPITAL TERRITORY

Perth
Bunbury

Darling Range

Esperance

Great Australian Bight

Port Lincoln
5632

Adelaide

Shepparton
Albury

Murray Kosciusko
2237
Australian Alps
Bombala

C. Leeuwin
Augusta
Albany

Horsham
Bendigo

VICTORIA
Ballarat
MELBOURNE
Geelong

Eombla
C. Howe

Mount Gambier
Warrnambool

Encounter B.

Bass Strait
King I.
Furneaux Group

INDIAN OCEAN

Burnie
1617
Mt. Ossa
TASMANIA
Launceston
Hobart

S.E. Cape

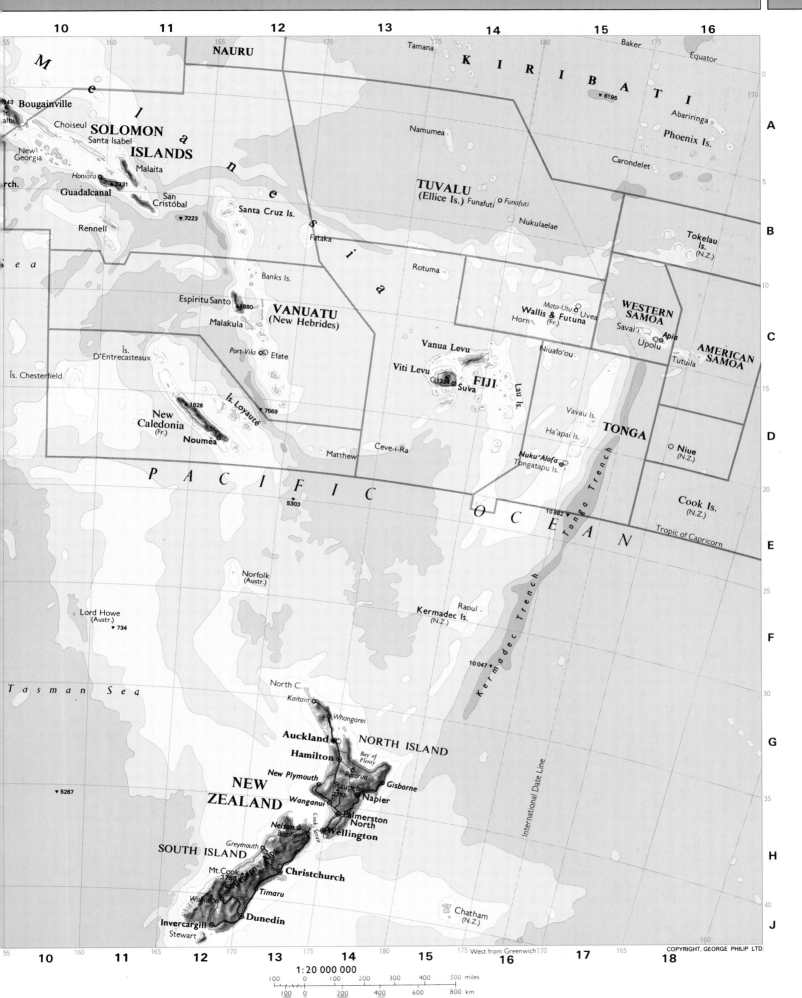

10   **11**   **12**   **13**   **14**   **15**   **16**

NAURU

Tamana

K I R I B A T I

Baker   Equator

M
e
l
a
n
e
s
i
a

▼243 Bougainville

Choiseul

SOLOMON

Santa Isabel

ISLANDS

New
Georgia

Malaita

Honiara ○ ▼2331

Guadalcanal

San
Cristóbal

Rennell

Namumea

▼6195

Abariringa

Phoenix Is.

Carondelet

A

Sea

▼7223

Santa Cruz Is.

Fataka

TUVALU

(Ellice Is.) *Funafuti* ○ *Funafuti*

Nukulaelae

Tokelau
Is.
(N.Z.)

B

Banks Is.

Rotuma

Espíritu Santo ▼1880

VANUATU
(New Hebrides)

Malakula

Îs.
D'Entrecasteaux

Mata-Utu ○ *Uvea*

Wallis & Futuna

Horn **(Fr.)**

Savai'i

WESTERN
SAMOA

Upolu Apia ○

AMERICAN
SAMOA

Tutuila

C

Îs. Chesterfield

Port-Vila ○ ○ Efate

Vanua Levu

Viti Levu

▼1324 ○ **FIJI**
Suva ○

Niuafo'ou

Lau Is.

▼1628

Is. Loyauté

▼7569

New
Caledonia
(Fr.)

Nouméa ○

Matthew

Ceve-i-Ra

Vavau Is.

Ha'apai Is.

TONGA

Niue
(N.Z.)

D

P A C I F I C

▼5303

Nuku'Alofa ○
Tongatapu Is.

▼10 882

Tonga Trench

Cook Is.
(N.Z.)

Tropic of Capricorn

O C E A N

E

Norfolk
(Austr.)

Lord Howe
(Austr.)

▼734

Kermadec Is.
(N.Z.)

Raoul

▼10 047

Kermadec Trench

F

T a s m a n   S e a

North C.

Kaitaia

Whangarei ○

Auckland ○

NORTH ISLAND

International Date Line

G

Hamilton ○

Bay of
Plenty

▼5267

NEW
ZEALAND

New Plymouth ○

Rotorua

Raupehu
▼2797

Napier ○

Gisborne ○

Wanganui ○

Palmerston
North ○

Wellington ○

Chatham
(N.Z.)

35

Nelson ○
Blenheim ○

Cook Strait

H

Greymouth ○

Southern Alps

SOUTH ISLAND

Mt.Cook
▼3753

Christchurch ○

Wakatipu

Timaru ○

40

Invercargill ○

Dunedin ○

Stewart

J

10   **11**   **12**   **13**   **14**   **15** *West from Greenwich* **16**   **17**   **18**

1:20 000 000

100 0 100 200 300 400 500 miles

100 0 200 400 600 800 km

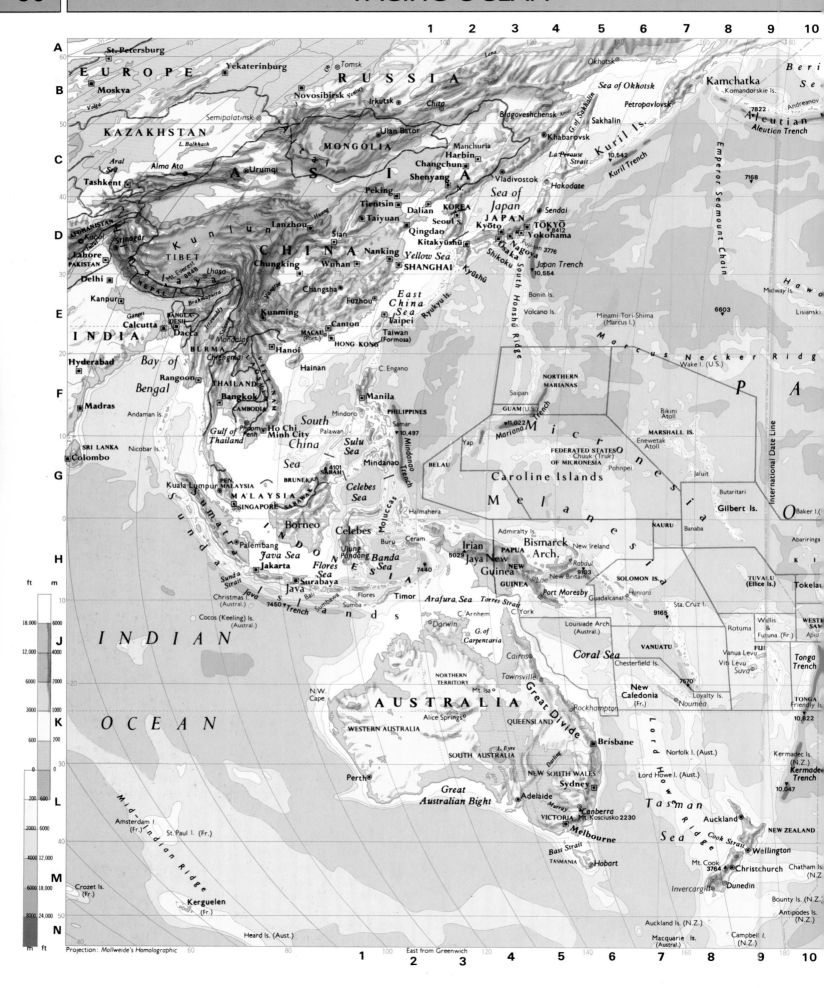

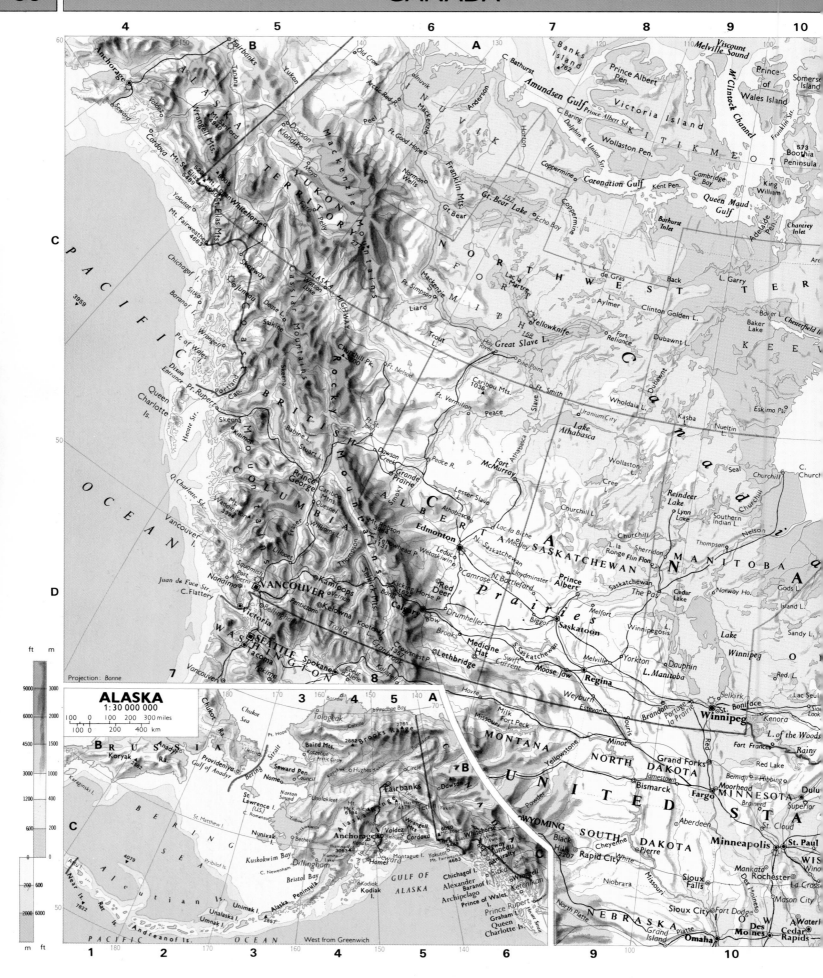

CANADA

Projection: Bonne

ALASKA
1 : 30 000 000

100 0   100 200 300 miles
100 0   200 400 km

West from Greenwich

11   **12**   **13**   **14**   **15**   **16**

Devon Island
Lancaster Sound
Baffin Bay
2136
Bylot I.
Pond Inlet
Brodeur
Peninsula
Svartenhuk
Peninsula
Disko I.
C. Hewett
Home B.
Sondre Stromfjord
GREENLAND
King Frederick VI Coast
Angmagssalik

A T L A N T I C

Melville
Peninsula
Prince
Charles
Foxe
2591
Cumberland
Peninsula
C. Dyer
Davis Strait
Godthaab
Frederikshaab
Sydproven

Committee B.
Melville
Peninsula
Foxe
Basin
Nettilling
L.
Cumberland Sd.
C. Mercy

Wager
B.
C. Dorchester
Amadjuak
L.
Frobisher
Bay
C. Farewell

Foxe
Channel
Foxe
Penin.
Frobisher Bay
Resolution I.

Southampton
I.

Hudson Strait

Coats
I.
C. Chidley

Mansel
I.
Ivujivik
Maricourt
(Wakeham
Bay)
Koartac
Akpatok
I.
Port Nouveau-Quebec
(George R.)

Hudson
Bay
Payne
(Payne Bay)
Bellin
Ungava Bay
Nain

257
Ungava
Peninsula
Payne L.
Leaf
Koksoak
George
NEW
Hopedale
C. Harrison
Indian Harbour

Ottawa
Isls.
Kuujjuaq
L. Minto
Kaniapiskau
Rigolet
L. Melville
Cartwright

King George Is.
Clearwater
L.
Lac Bienville
Schefferville
Petitsikapau
L.
LABRADOR
Michikamau
Happy Valley
Goose Bay
Battle Hbr.

Belcher
Is.
Poste de
la Baleine
(Great Whale River)
Kaniapiskau
Churchill
Str. of Belle Isle

C. Henrietta
Maria
Ft. George
Clearwater
Labrador City
Q U E B E C
Grand
Falls
Gander
Bonavista

Severn
Winisk
1128
Gagnon
NEWFOUNDLAND
Carbonear
St. John's

Big
Trout
L.
James Bay
Eastmain
Manicouagan
Sept Iles
Port Cartier
Mingan
Natashquan
Anticosti
I.
Corner
Brook
C. Race

Attawapiskat
Akimiski
I.
Fort Rupert
(Rupert
House)
Rupert
Baie Comeau
R. St. Lawrence
Gaspé
C. Gaspé
Gulf of
St. Lawrence
Ray
Channel-Port
aux Basques

St. Joseph
Albany
Moosonee
Eastmain
Mistassini
St. John
Matane
Gaspé Pen.
Campbellton
Cabot Str.
PR. EDWARD I.
Cape Breton
ST. PIERRE
& MIQUELON
(Fr.)

Missinaibi
Harricanaw
Chibougamau
Saguenay
Rimouski
Bathurst
Chatham
Summerside
Charlottetown
Glace Bay
Sydney

Nipigon
Geraldton
Hearst
Gouin
Reservoir
Riviere
du Loup
NEW
BRUNSWICK
Moncton
Northumberland Str.
NOVA
New Glasgow
Truro

L.
Nipigon
Oba
Timmins
Rouyn
Val d'Or
La Tuque
Jonquiere
Chicoutimi
Edmundston
Amherst
SCOTIA
Sable I.
(Nova Scotia)

Thunder Bay
Geraldton
Kirkland Lake
1190
Quebec
Fredericton
Saint
John
Dartmouth
Halifax

Marquette
Sault Ste.
Marie
Sudbury
North
Bay
Shawinigan
Trois Rivieres
Thetford Mines
St. Hyacinthe
Sherbrooke
Bangor
B. of Fundy
Bridgewater

Sault Ste. Marie
Cabonga
Reservoir
MONTREAL
Hull
Cornwall
Burlington
Lewiston
Portland
Yarmouth
C. Sable

Wausau
Green
Bay
Georgian
Bay
North
Ottawa
Ottawa
Kingston
L. Champlain
1917
NEW
HAMPSHIRE
Concord
Manchester

Appleton
Traverse
City
Peterboro
Orillia
L. Ontario
Rochester
Syracuse
Springfield
MASS.
BOSTON
C. Cod

London
Kitchener
TORONTO
Oshawa
Niagara Falls
Buffalo
Albany
NEW
YORK
CONN.
RHODE I.
Providence

Milwaukee
Grand
Rapids
Saginaw
Hamilton
St. Catharines
L. Erie
Binghamton
Scranton
New Haven

DETROIT
Windsor
Erie
Newark
NEW JERSEY
NEW YORK

CHICAGO
Gary
INDIANA
Toledo
Akron
CLEVELAND
OHIO
PENNSYLVANIA
Allentown

1:15 000 000

100   0   100   200   300   400 miles
100   0   100   200   300   400   500   600 km

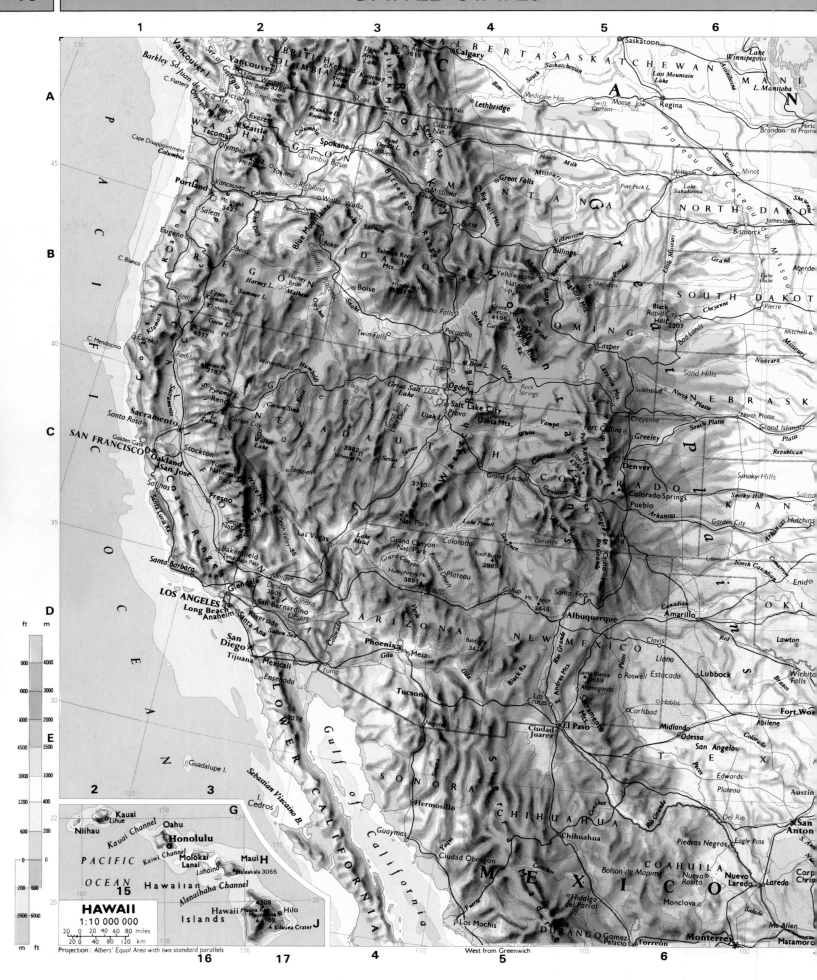

HAWAII
1:10 000 000

Projection: Albers' Equal Area with two standard parallels

West from Greenwich

1:12 000 000

50   0   50   100   150   200   250   300 miles

50   0   50 100 150 200 250 300 350 400 450 500 km

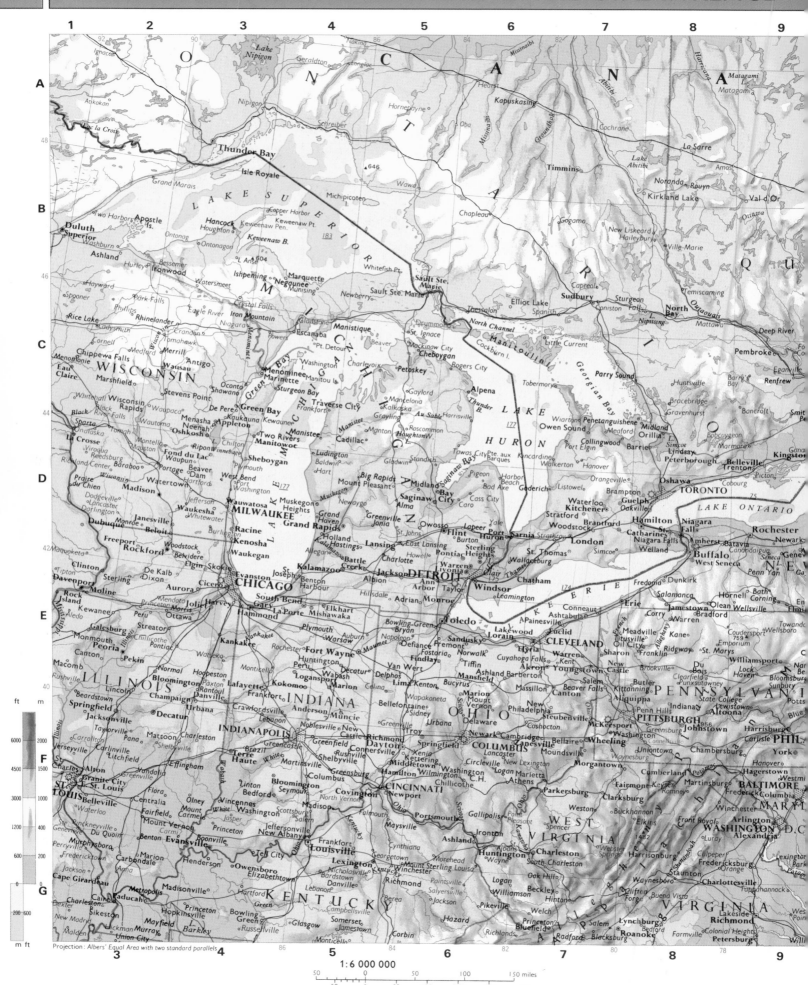

Projection: Albers' Equal Area with two standard parallels

1:6 000 000

ft m

6000 2000

4500 1500

3000 1000

1200 400

600 200

0 0

200 600

m ft

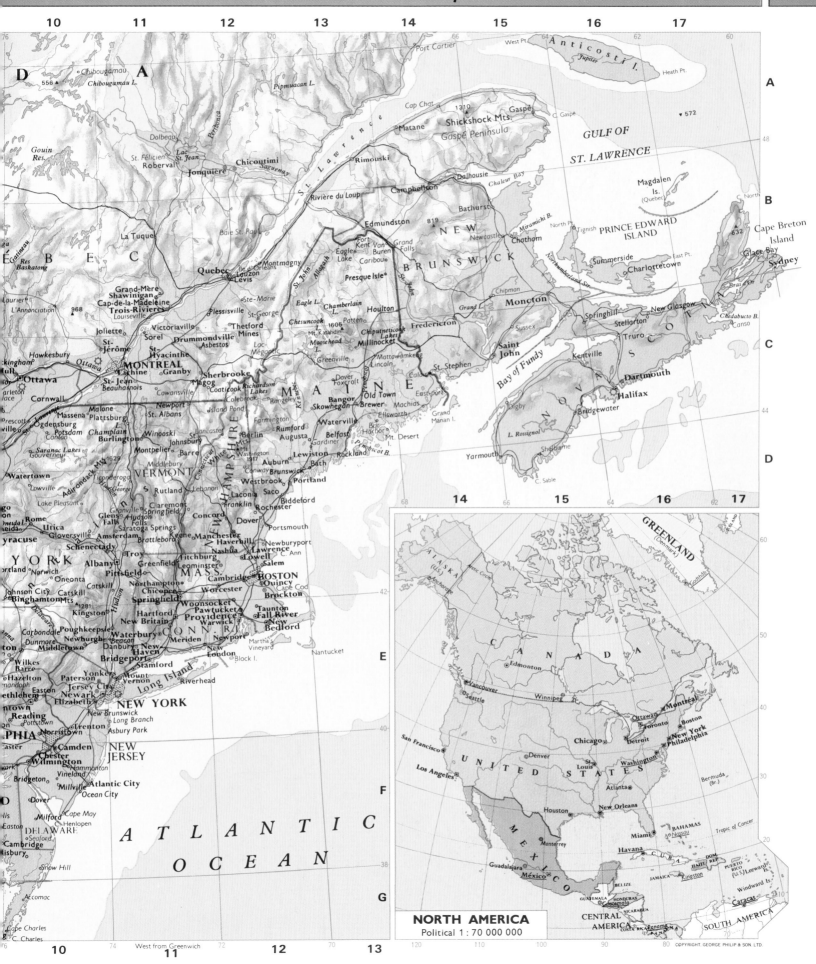

PANAMA CANAL
1 : 1 000 000

JAMAICA
1 : 5 000 000

TRINIDAD AND TOBAGO
1 : 5 000 000

LEEWARD ISLANDS
1 : 5 000 000

WINDWARD ISLANDS
1 : 5 000 000

Projection : Bonne

A

ATLANTIC OCEAN

B

Colombus C. Fear
Atlanta
Macon Charleston Augusta
lombus
Savannah
Albany
llahassee Jacksonville
Daytona Beach
Orlando C. Canaveral
Tampa West Palm Beach
etersburg Grand
L. Okeechobee Bahama Freeport Gt. Abaco I.
I. New Providence I.
Miami Fort Eleuthera I.
C. Sable Lauderdale Nassau Cat I.
Key West Andros I. S. Salvador Tropic of Cancer C

BAHAMAS

Havana Matanzas Sagua la Grande Long I.
Rio Cárdenas Mayaguana
C Sta. Clara Acklins Turks &
U Ciego de Ávila Morón I. Caicos Is.
Cienfuegos B Camagüey Gt. Inagua (Br.)
I. de Juventud Sancti Spíritus Holguín I.
G Manzanillo Ciego de Ávila Cap Haïtien Santiago San Francisco de Macorís PUERTO RICO (U.S.A.)
R 2000 Bayamo Guantánamo Gonaïves de Macorís St. Thomas (U.S.A.) Anguilla
E Santiago DOMINICAN Charlotte Amalie St. Martin (Fr. & Neth.)
Grand Cayman A de Cuba Windward Passage La Romana San Juan Virgin Is. (Br.) ST. CHRISTOPHER-NEVIS
(Br.) T 2280 REP. Barahona Ponce 1338 St. Croix ANTIGUA & (St. Kitts)
Montego Bay E Santo Domingo Caguas (U.S.A.) BARBUDA D
Les Cayes H Bani Mayagüez St. John's
JAMAICA R A Port au Prince Hispaniola Montserrat Guadeloupe (Fr.)
Kingston I Leeward Pointe à Pitre
T Islands
I DOMINICA
L LESSER
L E
S
Caratasca Lagoon Fort de France Martinique (Fr.)
C. Gracias á Dios ANTILLES
CARIBBEAN SEA ST. LUCIA
Providencia ANTILLES Windward BARBADOS
(Col.) ST. VINCENT Bridgetown
San Andrés & GRENADA
(Col.) Pta. Gallinas Gulf of Venezuela THE GRENADINES Islands
Bluefields Aruba (Neth.) Curaçao La Blanquilla
Pen. de la Willemstad (Ven.) Tobago
Santa Marta Guajira Bonaire Margarita Carúpano Port of Spain
BARRANQUILLA Coro La Tortuga Cumaná TRINIDAD & TOBAGO
Cartagena Punto Pen de NETH. (Ven.) G. of San Fernando
Fijo Paraguana ANTILLES Paria
5800 MARACAIBO Barcelona 2596 Delta of the
Colón Sierra Nevada Cabimas Maracay Maturín Orinoco
Limón de Santa Marta Valencia CARACAS El Tigre
Vol. Barú L. de Barquisimeto GUYANA Georgetown
3374 Maracaibo Valera El Tigre New
David Panama Mérida Barinas Orinoco Ciudad Guayana Amsterdam
Coiba Cúcuta Cord. de Mérida Ciudad Angel Cuyuni
Azuero 4100 San Cristóbal Apure San Fernando Bolívar Falls 2560
Pen. G. of Bucaramanga Arauca de Apure 2560 Roraima SURINAM
Panama Cauca VENEZUELA Pto. Ayacucho 2285 2810
Medellín Barrancabermeja Meta Sa. Parima 1280
Quibdó COLOMBIA Sierra Pacaraima
Manizales Tunja Casiquiare
Pereira Bogotá
Buenaventura Armenia Girardot BRAZIL
Cali Guaviare
Popayán

COPYRIGHT. GEORGE PHILIP & SON. LTD.

1:15 000 000

100 0 100 200 300 400 miles
100 0 100 200 300 400 500 600 km

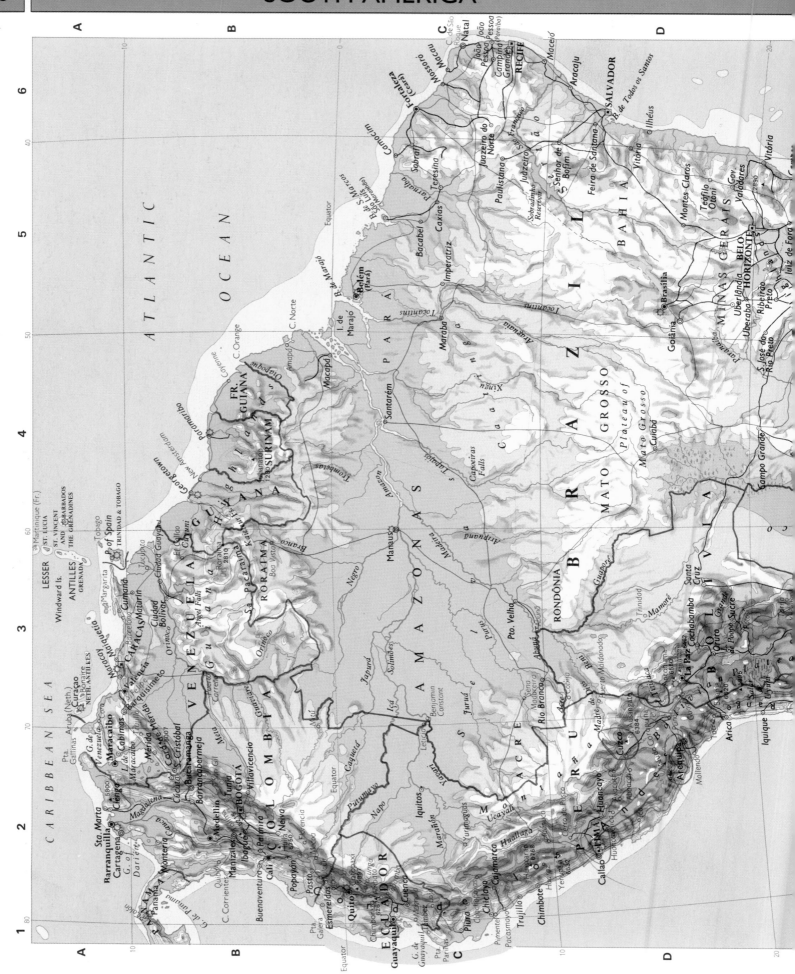

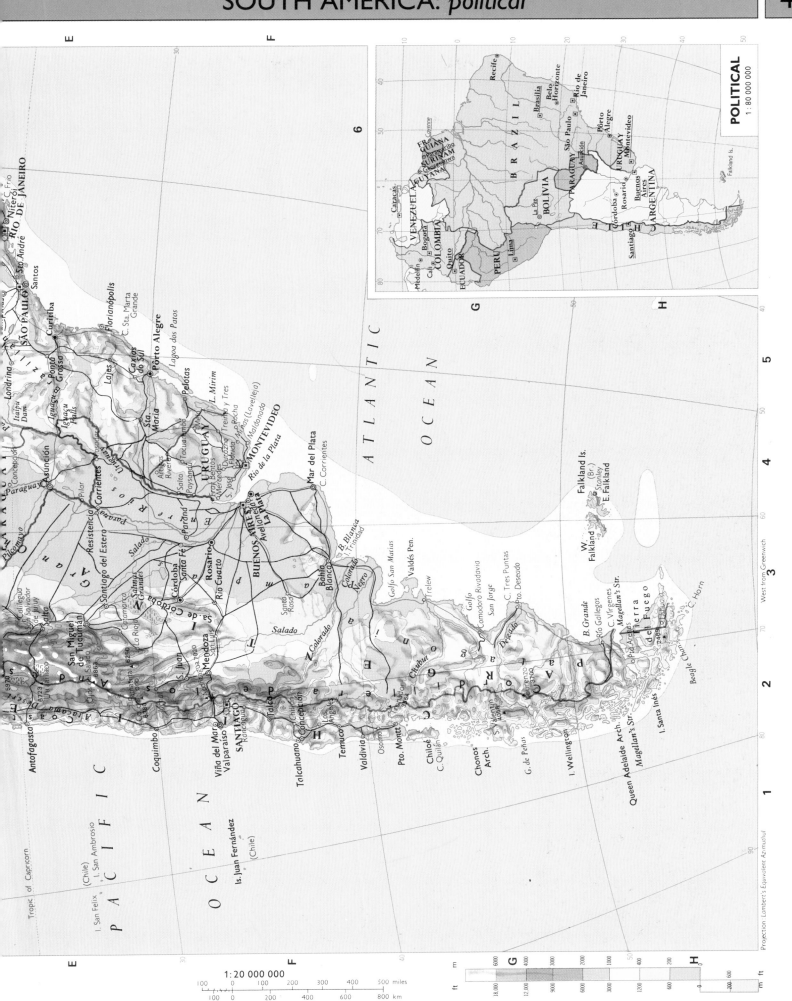

Projection: Lambert's Equivalent Azimuthal

1 : 20 000 000

100   0   100   200   300   400   500 miles
100   0   200   400   600   800 km

POLITICAL
1 : 80 000 000

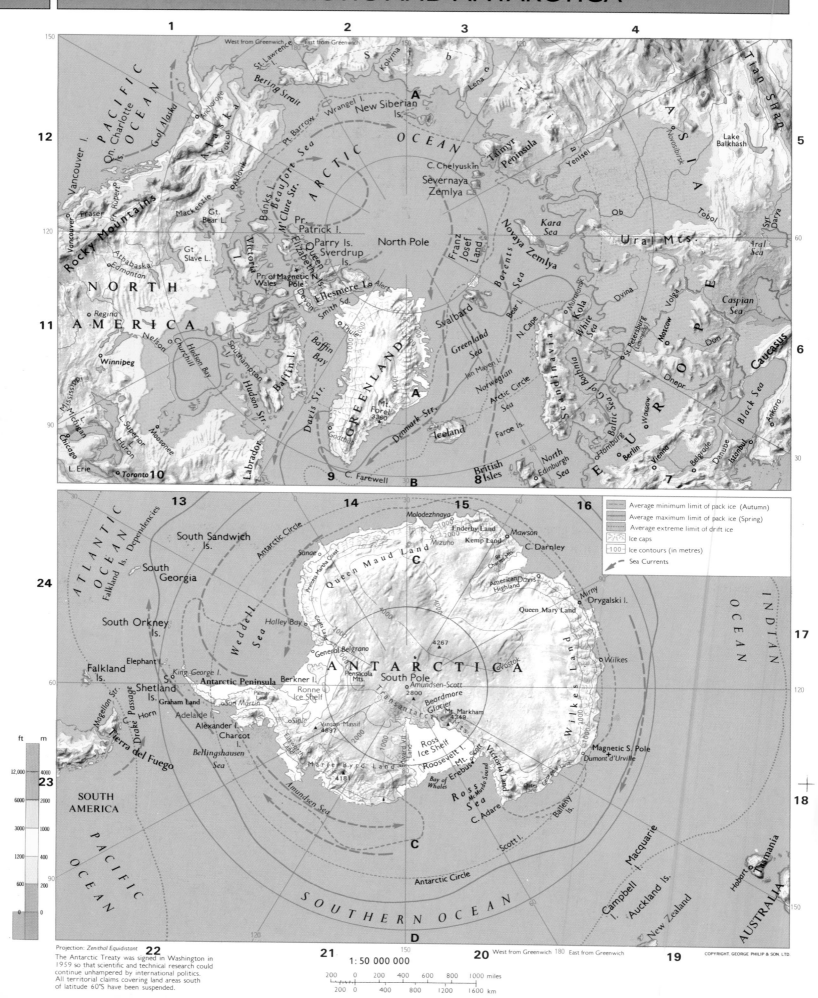

THE ARCTIC (upper map)

150   1   West from Greenwich   East from Greenwich   2   3   4   150

S   Kolyma   b   Lena   Tian Shan

St. Lawrence I.   Bering Strait   Wrangel I.   New Siberian Is.   A   ASIA

12   PACIFIC OCEAN   Qn. Charlotte Is.   Anchorage   G. of Alaska   ALASKA   Yukon   Pt. Barrow   Beaufort Sea   ARCTIC OCEAN   C. Chelyuskin   Taimyr Peninsula   Novosibirsk   Lake Balkhash   5

Vancouver I.   Oakland   Banks I.   M'Clure Str.   Severnaya Zemlya   Yenisei   Ob

Fraser   Vancouver   Rocky Mountains   Mackenzie   Gt. Bear L.   Pr. Patrick I.   Victoria I.   Queen Elizabeth   Parry Is.   Sverdrup Is.   NORTH POLE   Franz Josef Land   Kara Sea   Novaya Zemlya   Ural Mts.   Aral Sea

120   Athabaska   Edmonton   Gt. Slave L.   Pr. of Wales   Magnetic N. Pole   Devon   Barents Sea   Tobol   Ishim   Irtysh   60

NORTH   Regina   Ellesmere I.   Alert   Bear I.   N. Cape   Murmansk   Kola   Dvina   Caspian Sea

11   AMERICA   Nelson   Churchill   Southampton I.   Smith Sd.   Thule   Svalbard   Greenland Sea   White Sea   St. Petersburg (Leningrad)   Moscow   Volga   Caucasus   6

Winnipeg   Hudson Bay   Baffin Bay   Baffin I.   GREENLAND   Jan Mayen I.   Norwegian Sea   Scandinavia   G. of Bothnia   Don   Dnepr

Mississippi   L. Michigan   L. Superior   Moosonee   Hudson Str.   Davis Str.   Denmark Str.   Mt. Forel 3360   Iceland   Faroe Is.   Baltic Sea   Warsaw   Berlin   Vienna   Belgrade   Danube   Black Sea   Ankara   30

90   L. Huron   Chicago   L. Erie   Toronto   10   Labrador   9   C. Farewell   Godthab   B   British Isles   North Sea   Edinburgh   Hamburg   EUROPE   Istanbul   7

THE ANTARCTIC (lower map)

13   30   14   15   60   16   Average minimum limit of pack ice (Autumn)

ATLANTIC OCEAN   South Sandwich Is.   Antarctic Circle   Molodezhnaya   Enderby Land   Mawson   Average maximum limit of pack ice (Spring)

Sanae   Princess Martha Coast   Mizuho   Kemp Land   C. Darnley   Average extreme limit of drift ice

South Georgia   Falkland Is. Dependencies   Halley Bay   Queen Maud Land   C   American Highland   Davis   Ice caps

24   South Orkney Is.   Weddell Sea   Coats Land   4000   1000   Queen Mary Land   Mirny   Drygalski I.   100   Ice contours (in metres)

Elephant I.   King George I.   General Belgrano   4267   Vostok   Wilkes   Sea Currents

Falkland Is.   S. Shetland Is.   Antarctic Peninsula   Berkner I.   Pensacola Mts.   ANTARCTICA   South Pole   17

60   Graham Land   San Martin   Ronne Ice Shelf   Amundsen-Scott 2800   Wilkes Land   1000   120

SOUTH AMERICA   Magellan Str.   Drake Passage   Horn   Adelaide I.   Alexander I.   Charcot I.   Siple   Vinson Massif 4897   Transantarctic Mts.   Beardmore Glacier   Mt. Markham 4349   Magnetic S. Pole   Dumont d'Urville

Tierra del Fuego   Bellingshausen Sea   Marie Byrd Land   4181   Ross Ice Shelf   Roosevelt I.   Mt. Erebus   Victoria Land   Balleny Is.   18

23   PACIFIC OCEAN   Amundsen Sea   Bay of Whales   Ross Sea   McMurdo Sound   C. Adare   Oates Land   Macquarie I.   INDIAN OCEAN

22   Antarctic Circle   Scott I.   Campbell I.   Auckland Is.   Hobart   Tasmania

SOUTHERN OCEAN   New Zealand   AUSTRALIA

ft   m   12,000   4000   6000   2000   3000   1000   1200   400   600   200   0   0

Projection: Zenithal Equidistant   22

The Antarctic Treaty was signed in Washington in 1959 so that scientific and technical research could continue unhampered by international politics. All territorial claims covering land areas south of latitude 60°S have been suspended.

21   150   20   West from Greenwich   180   East from Greenwich   19

1 : 50 000 000

200   0   200   400   600   800   1000 miles
200   0   400   800   1200   1600 km

WORLD THEMATIC MAPS

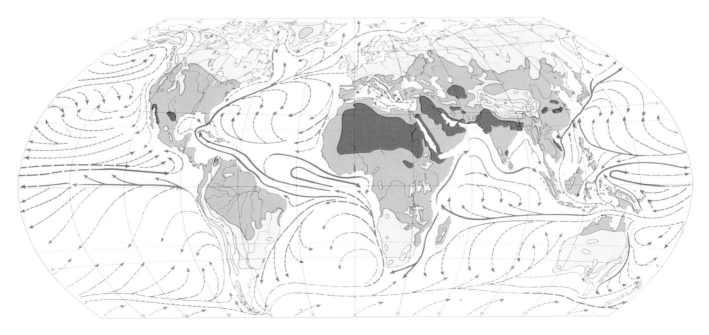

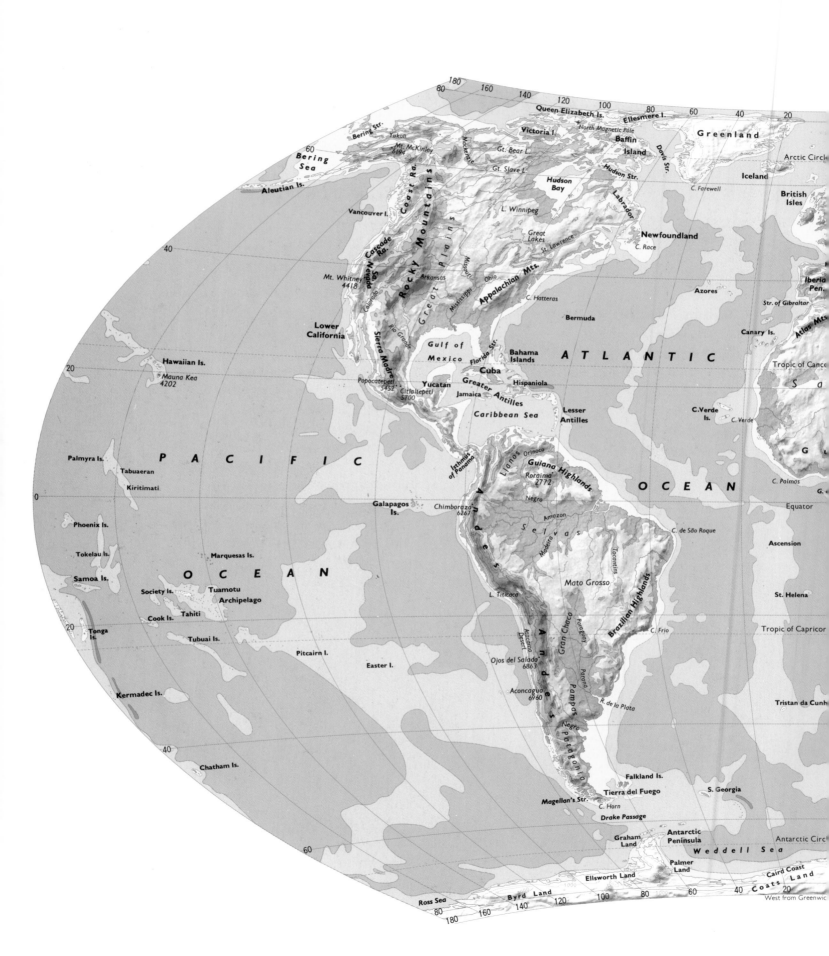

180 160 140 120 100 80 60 40 20

Queen Elizabeth Is.   Ellesmere I.   Greenland   Arctic Circle
Bering Str.   Yukon   North Magnetic Pole
60   Victoria I.   Baffin   Davis Str.   Iceland
Mt. McKinley   Gt. Bear L.   Island
Bering   6194   Mackenzie   Hudson Str.   C. Farewell   British
Sea   Gt. Slave L.   Hudson   Isles
Aleutian Is.   Bay   Labrador

Vancouver I.   L. Winnipeg   Newfoundland
40   Great   St. Lawrence   C. Race
Lakes
Mt. Whitney   Arkansas   Missouri   Ohio   Appalachian Mts.   Azores   Iberia
4418   Mississippi   C. Hatteras   Pen.
Lower   Str. of Gibraltar
California   Rio Grande   Bermuda   Canary Is.   Atlas Mts.
Sierra Madre   Gulf of   ATLANTIC   Tropic of Cancer
20   Mauna Kea   Mexico   Florida Str.   Bahama   Sa
Hawaiian Is.   4202   Popocatepetl   Yucatan   Islands
5452   Cuba   Hispaniola   C.Verde
Citlaltepetl   Greater Antilles   Is.   C. Verde   G
5700   Jamaica   Lesser
Palmyra Is.   Caribbean Sea   Antilles   OCEAN   C. Palmas
PACIFIC   Orinoco   Guiana Highlands
Tabuaeran   Isthmus   Llanos   Roraima   G.
0   Kiritimati   of Panama   2772   Equator
Galapagos   Chimborazo   Negro   C. de São Roque
Is.   6267   Amazon   Ascension
Phoenix Is.   Madeira   Selvas   Tocantins
Marquesas Is.   St. Helena
Tokelau Is.   Mato Grosso
OCEAN   Brazilian Highlands
Samoa Is.   Society Is.   Tuamotu   L. Titicaca   Gran Chaco   C. Frio
Cook Is.   Archipelago   Andes   Paraguay   Tropic of Capricorn
20   Tonga   Tahiti   Atacama   Parana
Is.   Tubuai Is.   Desert   Ojos del Salado   R. de la Plata   Tristan da Cunh
6863   Pampas
Pitcairn I.   Easter I.   Aconcagua   Negro
Kermadec Is.   6960   Patagonia
Falkland Is.
40   Chatham Is.   Magellan's Str.   Tierra del Fuego   S. Georgia
C. Horn
Drake Passage
Antarctic
Graham   Peninsula   Antarctic Circle
Land   Palmer   Weddell Sea
60   Land   Caird Coast
Ellsworth Land   Coats Land
Ross Sea   Byrd Land   120   100   80   60   40   20
80   West from Greenwich
180 160 140

Projection: Hammer Equal Area

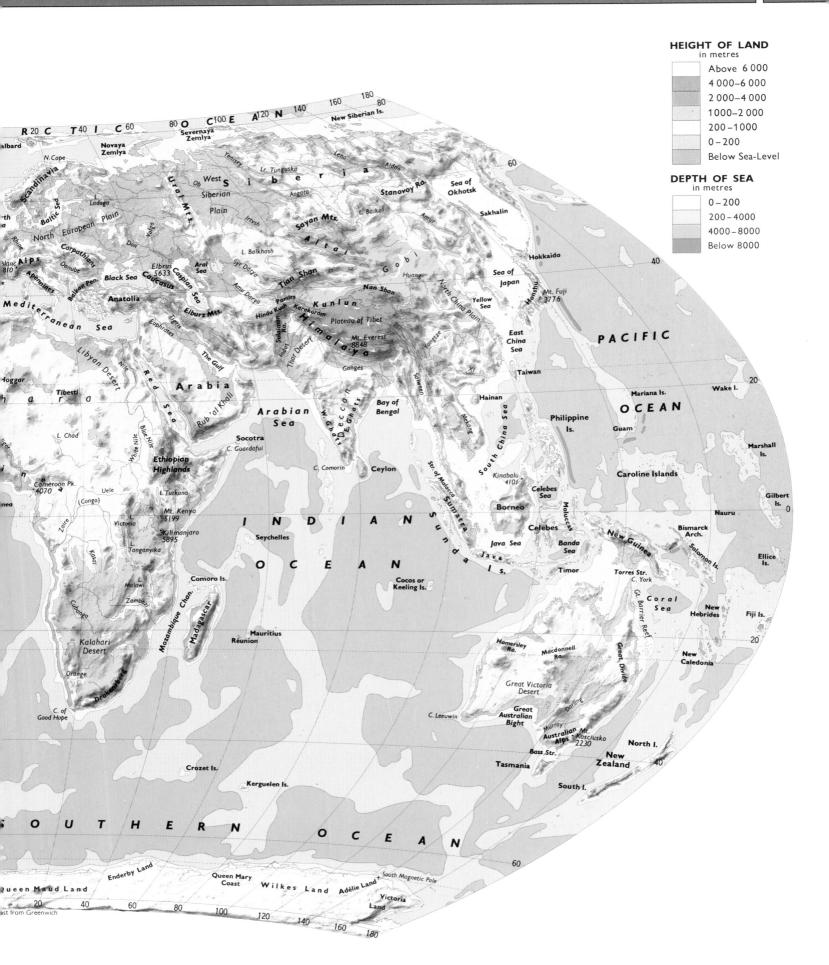

HEIGHT OF LAND
in metres

Above 6 000
4 000–6 000
2 000–4 000
1000–2 000
200–1000
0 – 200
Below Sea-Level

DEPTH OF SEA
in metres

0 – 200
200 – 4000
4000 – 8000
Below 8000

1 : 80 000 000

Copyright. George Philip & Son, Ltd.

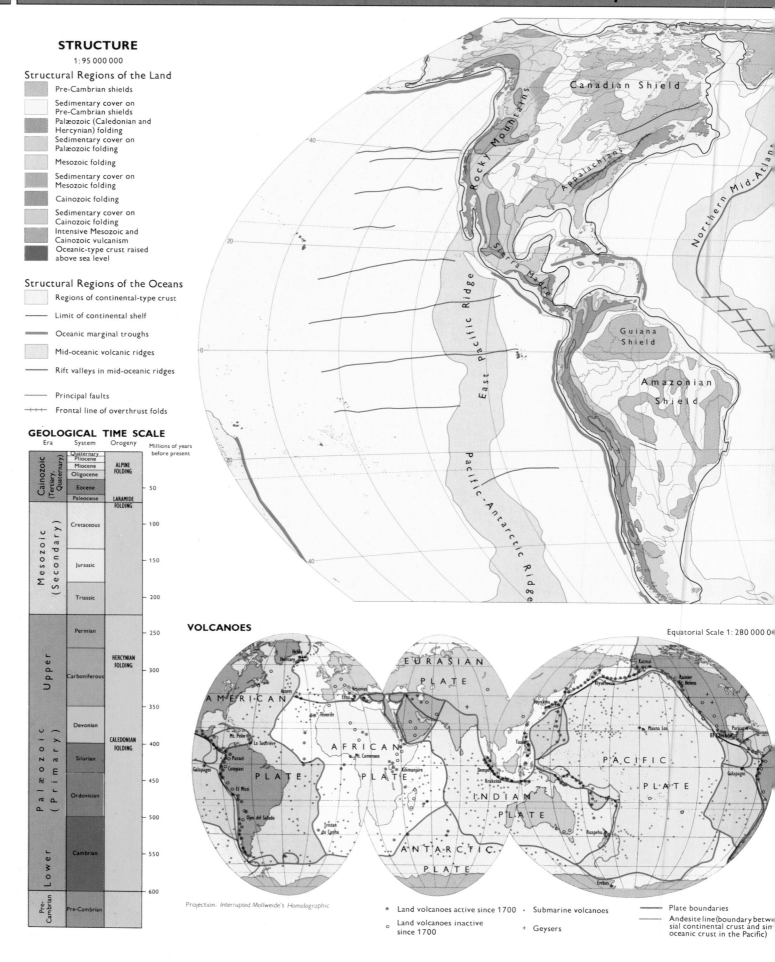

STRUCTURE

1:95 000 000

Structural Regions of the Land

- Pre-Cambrian shields
- Sedimentary cover on Pre-Cambrian shields
- Palæozoic (Caledonian and Hercynian) folding
- Sedimentary cover on Palæozoic folding
- Mesozoic folding
- Sedimentary cover on Mesozoic folding
- Cainozoic folding
- Sedimentary cover on Cainozoic folding
- Intensive Mesozoic and Cainozoic vulcanism
- Oceanic-type crust raised above sea level

Structural Regions of the Oceans

- Regions of continental-type crust
- Limit of continental shelf
- Oceanic marginal troughs
- Mid-oceanic volcanic ridges
- Rift valleys in mid-oceanic ridges
- Principal faults
- Frontal line of overthrust folds

GEOLOGICAL TIME SCALE

Era	System	Orogeny	Millions of years before present
Cainozoic (Tertiary, Quaternary)	Quaternary (Pliocene)	ALPINE FOLDING	
	Miocene		
	Oligocene		
	Eocene		50
	Paleocene	LARAMIDE FOLDING	
Mesozoic (Secondary)	Cretaceous		100
	Jurassic		150
	Triassic		200
Palæozoic (Primary) — Upper	Permian		250
	Carboniferous	HERCYNIAN FOLDING	300
	Devonian		350
	Silurian	CALEDONIAN FOLDING	400
Palæozoic (Primary) — Lower	Ordovician		450
	Cambrian		500
			550
Pre-Cambrian	Pre-Cambrian		600

VOLCANOES

Equatorial Scale 1: 280 000 000

Projection: *Interrupted Mollweide's Homolographic*

- • Land volcanoes active since 1700
- ○ Land volcanoes inactive since 1700
- · Submarine volcanoes
- + Geysers
- — Plate boundaries
- — Andesite line (boundary between sial continental crust and simatic oceanic crust in the Pacific)

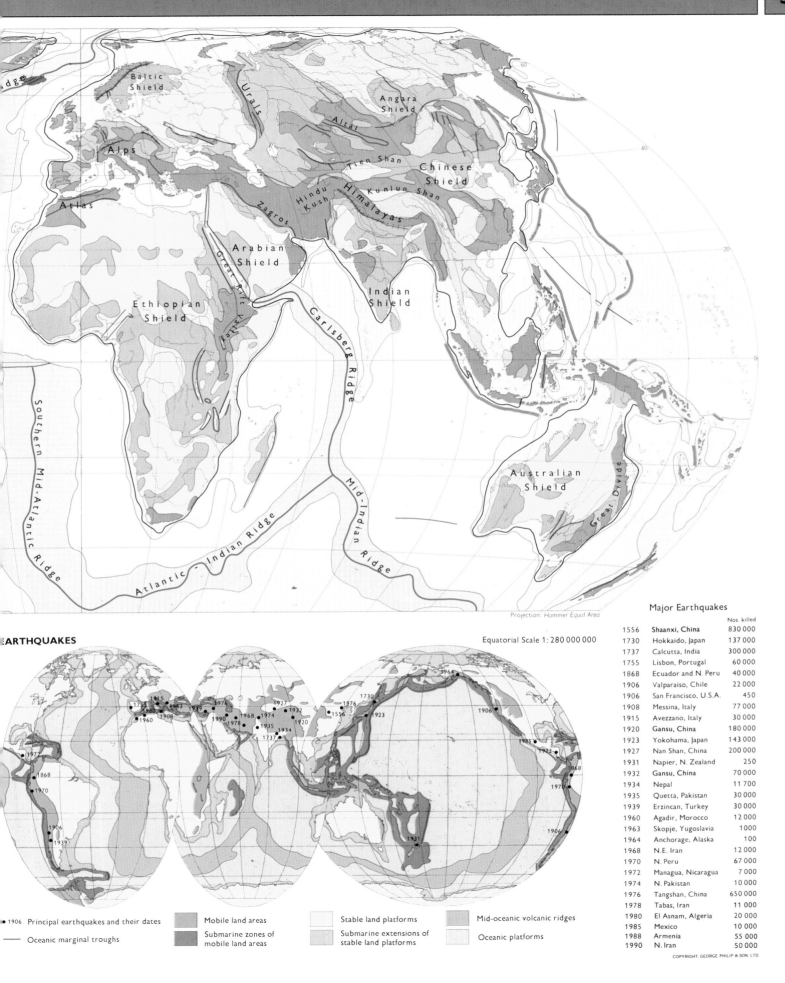

Baltic Shield
Urals
Angara Shield
Altai
Alps
Tien Shan
Chinese Shield
Atlas
Zagros
Hindu Kush
Kunlun Shan
Himalayas
Arabian Shield
Great Rift Valley
Indian Shield
Carlsberg Ridge
Ethiopian Shield
Southern Mid-Atlantic Ridge
Australian Shield
Great Divide
Atlantic – Indian Ridge
Mid-Indian Ridge

Projection: Hammer Equal Area

EARTHQUAKES

Equatorial Scale 1: 280 000 000

• 1906 Principal earthquakes and their dates

— Oceanic marginal troughs

Mobile land areas

Submarine zones of mobile land areas

Stable land platforms

Submarine extensions of stable land platforms

Mid-oceanic volcanic ridges

Oceanic platforms

Major Earthquakes

		Nos. killed
1556	Shaanxi, China	830 000
1730	Hokkaido, Japan	137 000
1737	Calcutta, India	300 000
1755	Lisbon, Portugal	60 000
1868	Ecuador and N. Peru	40 000
1906	Valparaiso, Chile	22 000
1906	San Francisco, U.S.A.	450
1908	Messina, Italy	77 000
1915	Avezzano, Italy	30 000
1920	Gansu, China	180 000
1923	Yokohama, Japan	143 000
1927	Nan Shan, China	200 000
1931	Napier, N. Zealand	250
1932	Gansu, China	70 000
1934	Nepal	11 700
1935	Quetta, Pakistan	30 000
1939	Erzincan, Turkey	30 000
1960	Agadir, Morocco	12 000
1963	Skopje, Yugoslavia	1 000
1964	Anchorage, Alaska	100
1968	N.E. Iran	12 000
1970	N. Peru	67 000
1972	Managua, Nicaragua	7 000
1974	N. Pakistan	10 000
1976	Tangshan, China	650 000
1978	Tabas, Iran	11 000
1980	El Asnam, Algeria	20 000
1985	Mexico	10 000
1988	Armenia	55 000
1990	N. Iran	50 000

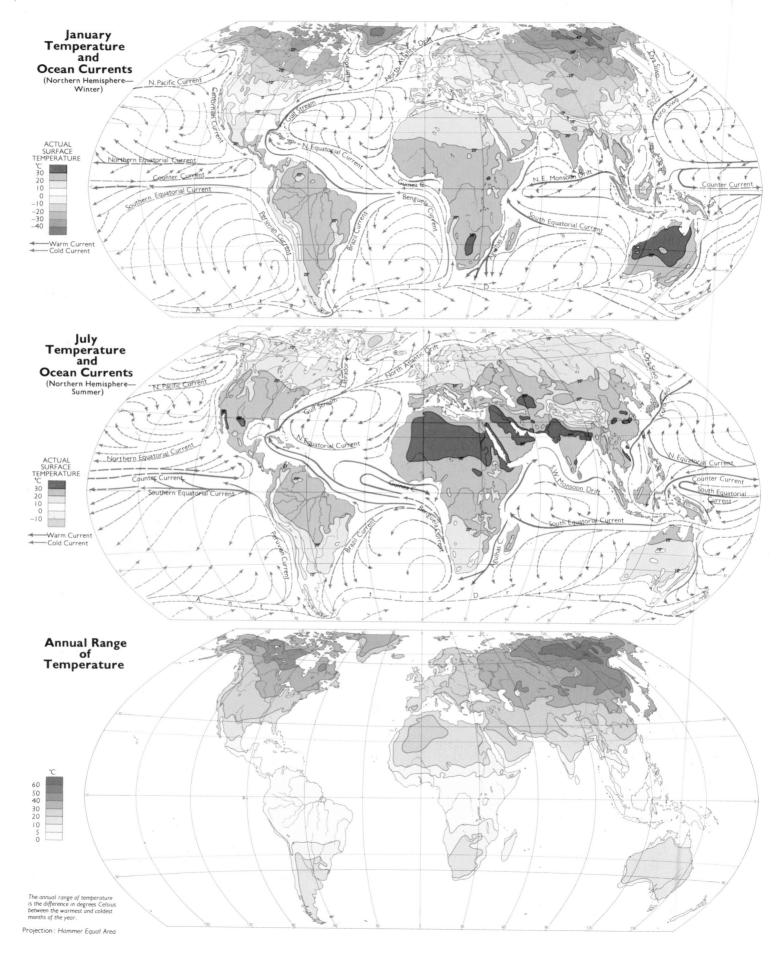

**January
Temperature
and
Ocean Currents**
(Northern Hemisphere—
Winter)

ACTUAL
SURFACE
TEMPERATURE
°C
30
20
10
0
−10
−20
−30
−40

← Warm Current
← Cold Current

**July
Temperature
and
Ocean Currents**
(Northern Hemisphere—
Summer)

ACTUAL
SURFACE
TEMPERATURE
°C
30
20
10
0
−10

← Warm Current
← Cold Current

**Annual Range
of
Temperature**

°C
60
50
40
30
20
10
5
0

*The annual range of temperature
is the difference in degrees Celsius
between the warmest and coldest
months of the year.*

Projection: *Hammer Equal Area*

1:190 000 000

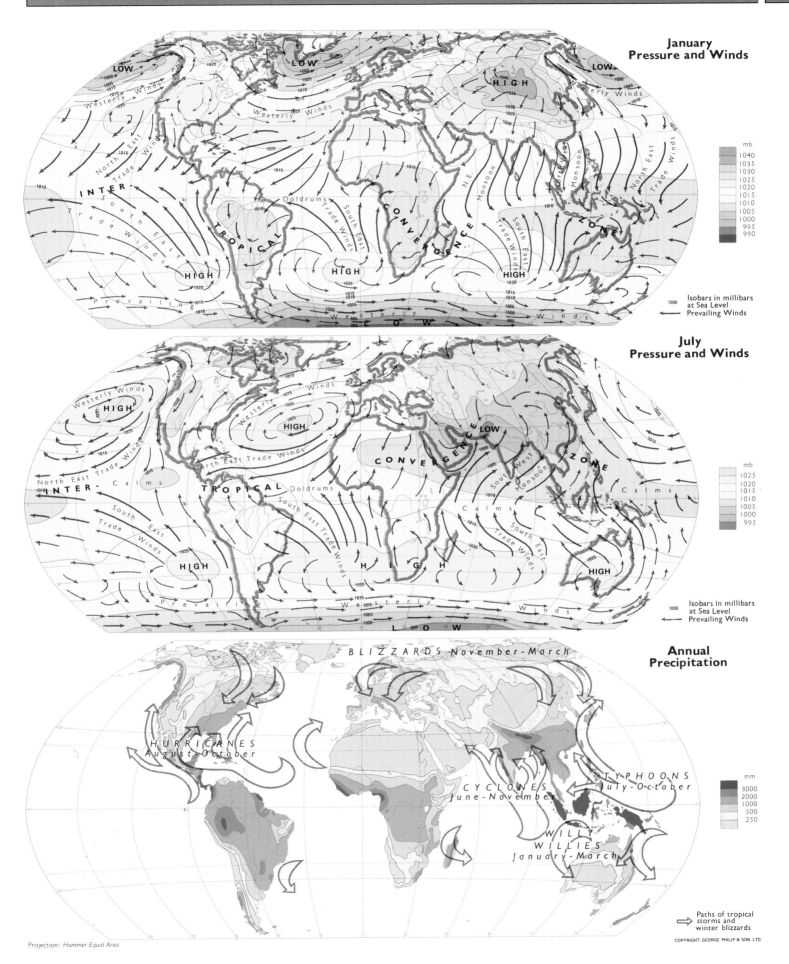

**January
Pressure and Winds**

	mb
	1040
	1035
	1030
	1025
	1020
	1015
	1010
	1005
	1000
	995
	990

1000 Isobars in millibars
at Sea Level
Prevailing Winds

**July
Pressure and Winds**

	mb
	1025
	1020
	1015
	1010
	1005
	1000
	995

1000 Isobars in millibars
at Sea Level
Prevailing Winds

**Annual
Precipitation**

BLIZZARDS November-March

HURRICANES
August-October

CYCLONES
June-November

TYPHOONS
July-October

WILLY
WILLIES
January-March

	mm
	3000
	2000
	1000
	500
	250

Paths of tropical
storms and
winter blizzards

Projection: *Hammer Equal Area*

COPYRIGHT. GEORGE PHILIP & SON. LTD.

1:190 000 000

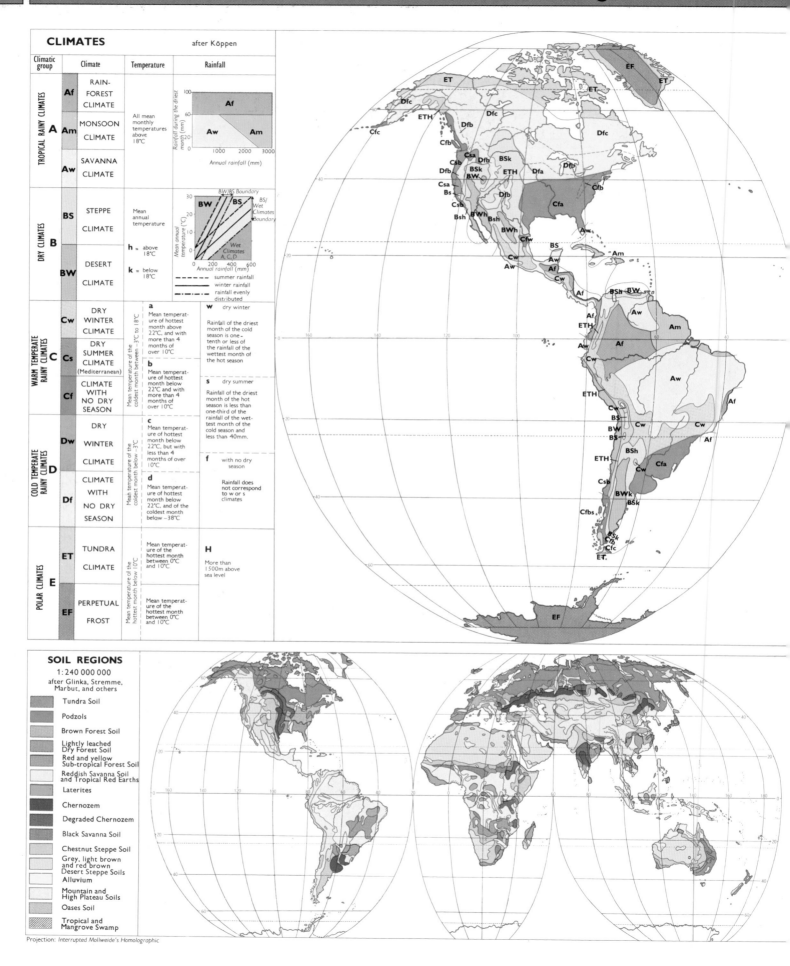

CLIMATES

after Köppen

Climatic group		Climate	Temperature	Rainfall
A TROPICAL RAINY CLIMATES	**Af**	RAIN-FOREST CLIMATE	All mean monthly temperatures above 18°C	*Af / Aw / Am chart*
	Am	MONSOON CLIMATE		
	Aw	SAVANNA CLIMATE		
B DRY CLIMATES	**BS**	STEPPE CLIMATE	Mean annual temperature	*BW / BS chart*
	BW	DESERT CLIMATE	**h** = above 18°C **k** = below 18°C	
C WARM TEMPERATE RAINY CLIMATES	**Cw**	DRY WINTER CLIMATE	Mean temperature of the coldest month between −3°C to 18°C	**a** Mean temperature of hottest month above 22°C, and with more than 4 months of over 10°C
	Cs	DRY SUMMER CLIMATE (Mediterranean)		**b** Mean temperature of hottest month below 22°C and with more than 4 months of over 10°C
	Cf	CLIMATE WITH NO DRY SEASON		**w** dry winter — Rainfall of the driest month of the cold season is one-tenth or less of the rainfall of the wettest month of the hot season
D COLD TEMPERATE RAINY CLIMATES	**Dw**	DRY WINTER CLIMATE	Mean temperature of the coldest month below −3°C	**c** Mean temperature of hottest month below 22°C, but with less than 4 months of over 10°C
	Df	CLIMATE WITH NO DRY SEASON		**d** Mean temperature of hottest month below 22°C, and of the coldest month below −38°C **s** dry summer — Rainfall of the driest month of the hot season is less than one-third of the rainfall of the wettest month of the cold season and less than 40mm.
E POLAR CLIMATES	**ET**	TUNDRA CLIMATE	Mean temperature of the hottest month below 10°C	Mean temperature of the hottest month between 0°C and 10°C — **f** with no dry season — Rainfall does not correspond to w or s climates
	EF	PERPETUAL FROST		Mean temperature of the hottest month between 0°C and 10°C — **H** More than 1500m above sea level

BW/BS Boundary
BS/Wet Climates Boundary
Wet Climates A, C, D
Mean annual temperature (°C)
Annual rainfall (mm)
— summer rainfall
--- winter rainfall
-·- rainfall evenly distributed

Rainfall during the driest month (mm)
Annual rainfall (mm)

SOIL REGIONS

1:240 000 000
after Glinka, Stremme, Marbut, and others

- Tundra Soil
- Podzols
- Brown Forest Soil
- Lightly leached Dry Forest Soil
- Red and yellow Sub-tropical Forest Soil
- Reddish Savanna Soil and Tropical Red Earths
- Laterites
- Chernozem
- Degraded Chernozem
- Black Savanna Soil
- Chestnut Steppe Soil
- Grey, light brown and red brown Desert Steppe Soils
- Alluvium
- Mountain and High Plateau Soils
- Oases Soil
- Tropical and Mangrove Swamp

Projection: Interrupted Mollweide's Homolographic

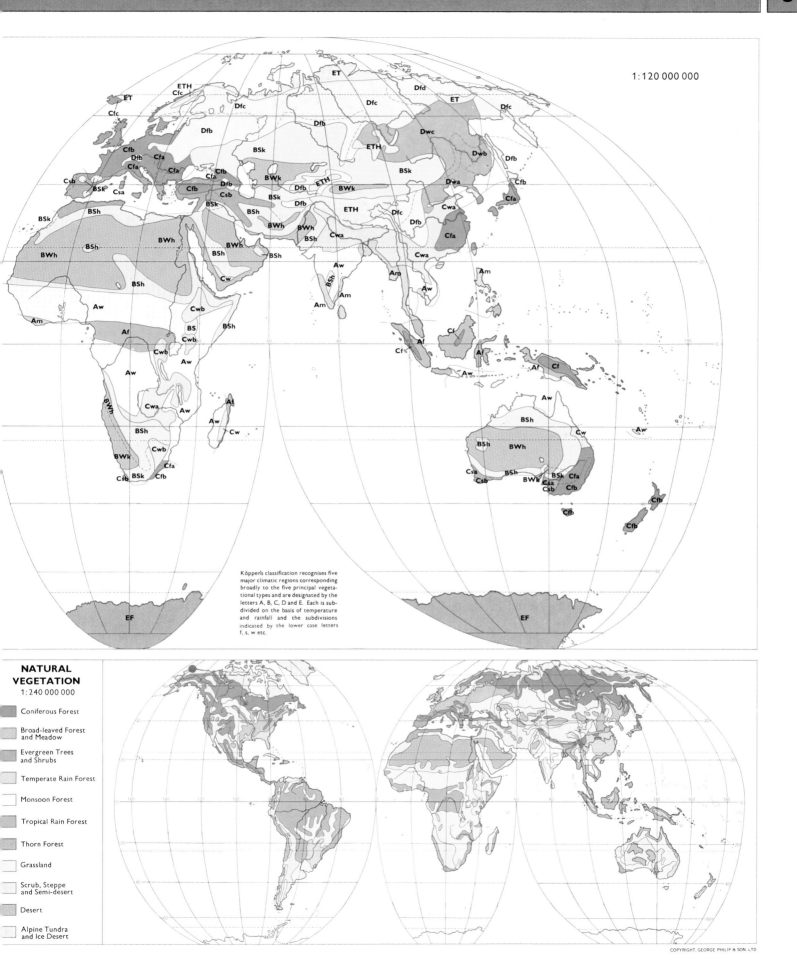

1:120 000 000

Köppen's classification recognises five
major climatic regions corresponding
broadly to the five principal vegeta-
tional types and are designated by the
letters A, B, C, D and E. Each is subdivided on the basis of temperature
and rainfall and the subdivisions
indicated by the lower case letters
f, s, w etc.

NATURAL VEGETATION
1:240 000 000

- Coniferous Forest
- Broad-leaved Forest and Meadow
- Evergreen Trees and Shrubs
- Temperate Rain Forest
- Monsoon Forest
- Tropical Rain Forest
- Thorn Forest
- Grassland
- Scrub, Steppe and Semi-desert
- Desert
- Alpine Tundra and Ice Desert

COPYRIGHT. GEORGE PHILIP & SON. LTD.

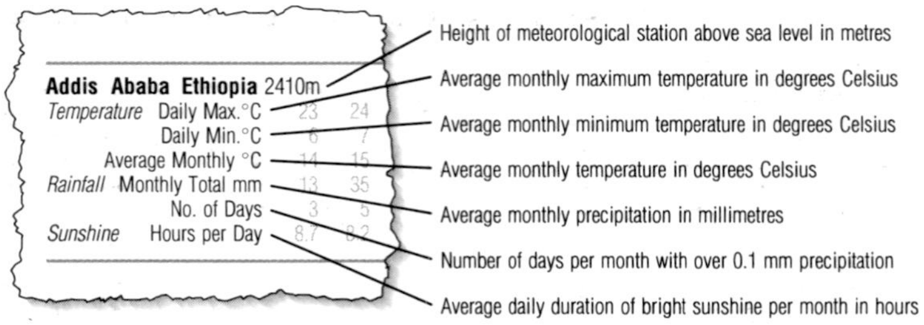
Addis Ababa Ethiopia 2410m
Temperature Daily Max.°C 23 24
Daily Min.°C 6 7
Average Monthly °C 14 15
Rainfall Monthly Total mm 13 35
No. of Days 3 5
Sunshine Hours per Day 8.7 8.2
Height of meteorological station above sea level in metres
Average monthly maximum temperature in degrees Celsius
Average monthly minimum temperature in degrees Celsius
Average monthly temperature in degrees Celsius
Average monthly precipitation in millimetres
Number of days per month with over 0.1 mm precipitation
Average daily duration of bright sunshine per month in hours

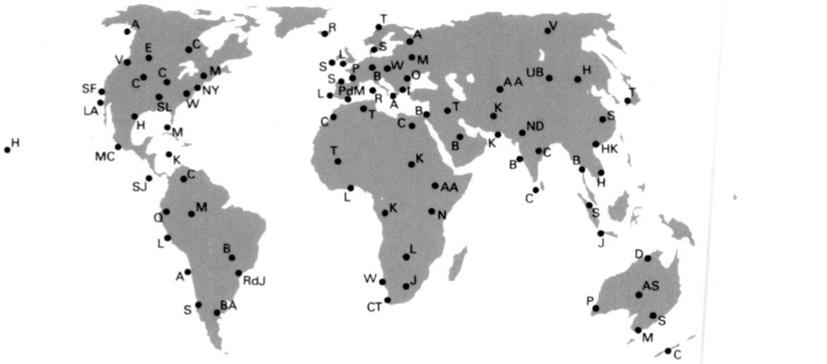

Addis Ababa Ethiopia 2410m

	Jan	Feb	Mar	Apr	May	June	July	Aug	Sep	Oct	Nov	Dec	Year
Temperature Daily Max.°C	23	24	25	24	25	23	20	20	21	22	23	22	23
Daily Min.°C	6	7	9	10	9	10	11	11	10	7	5	5	8
Average Monthly °C	14	15	17	17	17	16	16	15	15	15	14	14	15
Rainfall Monthly Total mm	13	35	67	91	81	117	247	255	167	29	8	5	1115
No. of Days	3	5	10	12	10	20	27	28	21	7	2	1	146
Sunshine Hours per Day	8.7	8.2	7.6	8.1	6.5	4.8	2.8	3.2	5.2	7.6	6.7	7	6.4

Alice Springs Australia 580m

	Jan	Feb	Mar	Apr	May	June	July	Aug	Sep	Oct	Nov	Dec	Year
Temperature Daily Max.°C	35	35	32	27	23	19	19	23	27	31	33	35	28
Daily Min.°C	21	20	17	12	8	5	4	6	10	15	18	20	13
Average Monthly °C	28	27	25	20	15	12	12	14	18	23	25	27	21
Rainfall Monthly Total mm	44	33	27	10	15	13	7	8	7	18	29	38	249
No. of Days	4	3	3	2	2	2	1	2	1	3	4	4	31
Sunshine Hours per Day	10.3	10.4	9.3	9.2	8	8	8.9	9.8	10	9.7	10.1	10	9.5

Alma Ata Kazakhstan 848m

	Jan	Feb	Mar	Apr	May	June	July	Aug	Sep	Oct	Nov	Dec	Year
Temperature Daily Max.°C	-3	-2	6	17	22	27	29	28	19	14	5	-1	13
Daily Min.°C	-14	-13	-6	3	9	13	16	14	5	1	-7	-12	1
Average Monthly °C	-9	-7	0	10	15	20	22	21	12	8	-1	-6	7
Rainfall Monthly Total mm	26	32	64	89	99	59	35	23	25	46	48	35	581
No. of Days	8	8	11	12	11	10	9	6	5	7	9	9	105
Sunshine Hours per Day	3.7	3.8	4.5	6.3	7.8	9.1	10.2	9.6	8	6.4	4.2	3.6	6.6

Anchorage USA 183m

	Jan	Feb	Mar	Apr	May	June	July	Aug	Sep	Oct	Nov	Dec	Year
Temperature Daily Max.°C	-7	-3	0	7	13	18	19	17	13	6	-2	-6	-6
Daily Min.°C	-15	-12	-9	-2	4	8	10	9	5	-2	-9	-14	-2
Average Monthly °C	-11	-7	-4	3	9	13	15	13	9	2	-5	-10	-4
Rainfall Monthly Total mm	20	18	13	11	13	25	47	64	64	47	28	24	374
No. of Days	5	10	7	7	7	9	13	13	13	11	10	11	116
Sunshine Hours per Day	2.4	4.1	6.6	8.3	8.3	9.2	8.5	6	4.4	3.1	2.6	1.6	5.4

Antofagasta Chile 95m

	Jan	Feb	Mar	Apr	May	June	July	Aug	Sep	Oct	Nov	Dec	Year
Temperature Daily Max.°C	25	25	24	21	20	19	17	17	18	19	21	22	21
Daily Min.°C	17	17	16	15	13	11	11	11	12	13	15	16	14
Average Monthly °C	21	21	20	18	16	15	5	14	15	16	18	19	17
Rainfall Monthly Total mm	0	0	0	1	1	3	5	3	1	3	1	0	18
No. of Days	0	0	0	0.1	0.1	0.2	0.5	0.4	0.5	0.2	0.3	0	2.3
Sunshine Hours per Day	10.5	10.3	8	7.3	6.3	6.1	6	5.5	6	5.5	6.5	8.9	7.2

Archangel Russia 4m

	Jan	Feb	Mar	Apr	May	June	July	Aug	Sep	Oct	Nov	Dec	Year
Temperature Daily Max.°C	-9	-8	-2	5	11	18	22	17	13	6	-2	-7	6
Daily Min.°C	-17	-17	-14	-7	0	6	9	10	3	-3	-8	-14	-4
Average Monthly °C	-13	-12	-8	-1	6	12	16	13	8	1	-5	-10	1
Rainfall Monthly Total mm	33	28	28	28	39	59	63	57	66	55	44	39	539
No. of Days	22	19	19	15	14	14	12	14	19	21	21	23	213
Sunshine Hours per Day	0.2	1.3	3.9	6	7.2	9.2	9.8	7.4	3.3	1.9	0.6	0.1	4.3

Athens Greece 107m

	Jan	Feb	Mar	Apr	May	June	July	Aug	Sep	Oct	Nov	Dec	Year
Temperature Daily Max.°C	13	14	16	20	25	30	33	33	29	24	19	15	23
Daily Min.°C	6	7	8	11	16	20	23	23	19	15	12	8	14
Average Monthly °C	10	10	12	16	20	25	28	28	24	20	15	11	18
Rainfall Monthly Total mm	62	37	37	23	23	14	6	7	15	51	56	71	402
No. of Days	6	11	11	9	8	4	2	3	4	8	12	15	103
Sunshine Hours per Day	3.9	5.2	5.8	7.7	8.9	10.7	11.9	11.5	9.4	6.8	4.8	3.8	7.3

Bahrain City Bahrain 2m

	Jan	Feb	Mar	Apr	May	June	July	Aug	Sep	Oct	Nov	Dec	Year
Temperature Daily Max.°C	20	21	25	29	33	36	37	38	36	32	27	22	30
Daily Min.°C	14	15	18	22	25	29	31	32	29	25	22	16	23
Average Monthly °C	17	18	21	25	29	32	34	35	32	29	25	19	26
Rainfall Monthly Total mm	18	12	10	9	2	0	0	0	0	0.4	3	16	70
No. of Days	3	3	3	2	1	0	0	0	0	0	0.1	3	15
Sunshine Hours per Day	5.9	6.9	7.9	8.8	10.6	13.2	12.1	12	12	10.3	7.7	6.4	9.5

Bangkok Thailand 10m

	Jan	Feb	Mar	Apr	May	June	July	Aug	Sep	Oct	Nov	Dec	Year
Temperature Daily Max.°C	32	33	34	35	34	33	32	32	32	31	31	31	33
Daily Min.°C	20	23	24	26	25	25	25	24	24	24	23	20	24
Average Monthly °C	26	28	29	30	30	29	28	28	28	28	27	26	28
Rainfall Monthly Total mm	9	30	36	82	165	153	168	183	310	239	55	8	1438
No. of Days	2	2	4	5	14	16	19	21	23	17	7	1	131
Sunshine Hours per Day	8.2	8	8	10	7.5	6.1	4.7	5.2	5.2	6.1	7.3	7.8	7

Beirut Lebanon 35m

	Jan	Feb	Mar	Apr	May	June	July	Aug	Sep	Oct	Nov	Dec	Year
Temperature Daily Max.°C	16	17	19	22	26	29	31	32	30	27	23	19	24
Daily Min.°C	11	11	12	15	18	21	23	24	23	20	16	13	17
Average Monthly °C	13	14	16	19	22	25	27	28	26	24	20	16	21
Rainfall Monthly Total mm	195	156	94	51	17	3	0.5	0.5	7	48	130	185	887
No. of Days	16	14	11	6	3	1	0.1	0.2	1	4	9	14	79
Sunshine Hours per Day	4.8	5.4	6.3	7.5	9.9	12.1	11.9	11.3	9.2	8.2	6.6	4.7	8.2

Berlin Germany 55m

	Jan	Feb	Mar	Apr	May	June	July	Aug	Sep	Oct	Nov	Dec	Year
Temperature Daily Max.°C	2	3	8	14	19	22	24	23	20	13	7	3	13
Daily Min.°C	-4	-3	0	4	8	11	13	13	9	5	2	-1	5
Average Monthly °C	-1	0	4	9	14	17	19	18	14	9	4	1	9
Rainfall Monthly Total mm	43	40	31	41	46	62	70	68	46	47	46	41	581
No. of Days	11	9	8	9	9	9	11	9	8	9	10	9	111
Sunshine Hours per Day	1.6	2.5	4.3	5.3	6.9	7.8	7.1	6.6	5.7	3.4	1.6	1.1	4.5

Bombay India 10m

	Jan	Feb	Mar	Apr	May	June	July	Aug	Sep	Oct	Nov	Dec	Year
Temperature Daily Max.°C	28	28	30	32	33	31	30	29	30	32	32	30	31
Daily Min.°C	19	20	22	24	27	26	25	24	24	24	23	21	23
Average Monthly °C	24	24	26	28	30	29	27	27	27	28	27	25	27
Rainfall Monthly Total mm	2	1	0	3	16	520	709	419	297	88	21	2	2078
No. of Days	0	0	0	0	1	16	26	20	14	3	1	0	81
Sunshine Hours per Day	9	9.3	9	9.1	9.3	5	3.1	2.5	5.4	7.7	9.7	9.6	7.4

Brasilia Brazil 910m

	Jan	Feb	Mar	Apr	May	June	July	Aug	Sep	Oct	Nov	Dec	Year
Temperature Daily Max.°C	28	28	28	28	27	27	27	29	30	29	28	27	28
Daily Min.°C	18	18	18	17	15	13	13	14	16	18	18	18	16
Average Monthly °C	23	23	23	22	21	20	20	21	23	24	23	22	22
Rainfall Monthly Total mm	252	204	227	93	17	3	6	3	30	127	255	343	1560
No. of Days	21	16	18	13	5	2	1	3	7	12	19	23	140
Sunshine Av. Monthly Dur.	5.8	5.7	6	7.4	8.7	9.3	9.6	9.8	7.9	6.5	4.8	4.4	7.2

Buenos Aires Argentina 25m

	Jan	Feb	Mar	Apr	May	June	July	Aug	Sep	Oct	Nov	Dec	Year
Temperature Daily Max.°C	30	29	26	22	18	14	14	16	18	21	25	28	22
Daily Min.°C	17	17	16	12	9	5	6	6	8	10	14	16	11
Average Monthly °C	23	23	21	17	13	10	10	11	13	15	19	22	16
Rainfall Monthly Total mm	79	71	109	89	76	61	56	61	79	86	84	99	950
No. of Days	7	6	7	8	7	7	8	9	8	9	9	8	93
Sunshine Hours per Day	9.2	8.5	7.5	6.8	4.9	3.5	3.8	5.2	6	6.8	8.1	8.5	6.6

Cairo Egypt 75m

	Jan	Feb	Mar	Apr	May	June	July	Aug	Sep	Oct	Nov	Dec	Year
Temperature Daily Max.°C	19	21	24	28	32	35	35	35	33	30	26	21	28
Daily Min.°C	9	9	12	14	18	20	22	22	20	18	14	10	16
Average Monthly °C	14	15	18	21	25	28	29	28	26	24	20	16	22
Rainfall Monthly Total mm	4	4	3	1	2	1	0	0	1	1	3	7	25
No. of Days	3	2	1	1	1	0	0	0	1	1	1	2	12
Sunshine Hours per Day	6.9	8.4	8.7	9.7	10.5	11.9	11.7	11.3	10.4	9.4	8.3	6.4	9.5

Calcutta India 5m

	Jan	Feb	Mar	Apr	May	June	July	Aug	Sep	Oct	Nov	Dec	Year
Temperature Daily Max.°C	27	29	34	36	35	34	32	32	32	32	29	26	31
Daily Min.°C	13	15	21	24	25	26	26	26	26	23	18	13	21
Average Monthly °C	20	22	27	30	30	30	29	29	29	28	23	20	26
Rainfall Monthly Total mm	10	30	34	44	140	297	325	332	253	114	20	5	1604
No. of Days	3	4	3	5	9	17	23	23	18	9	1	1	116
Sunshine Hours per Day	8.6	8.7	8.9	9	8.7	5.4	4.1	4.1	5.1	6.5	8.3	8.4	7.1

Cape Town South Africa 44m

	Jan	Feb	Mar	Apr	May	June	July	Aug	Sep	Oct	Nov	Dec	Year
Temperature Daily Max.°C	26	26	25	23	20	18	17	18	19	21	24	25	22
Daily Min.°C	15	15	14	11	9	7	7	7	8	10	13	15	11
Average Monthly °C	21	20	20	17	14	13	12	12	14	16	18	20	16
Rainfall Monthly Total mm	12	19	17	42	67	98	68	76	36	45	12	13	505
No. of Days	5	5	5	9	13	12	12	13	10	9	5	5	103
Sunshine Hours per Day	11.4	10.2	9.4	7.7	6.1	5.7	6.4	6.6	7.6	8.6	10.2	10.9	8.4

Caracas Venezuela 1040m

	Jan	Feb	Mar	Apr	May	June	July	Aug	Sep	Oct	Nov	Dec	Year
Temperature Daily Max.°C	24	25	26	27	27	26	26	26	27	26	25	26	26
Daily Min.°C	14	14	15	16	17	17	16	16	16	16	16	15	16
Average Monthly °C	19	19	20	21	22	21	21	21	21	21	20	20	21
Rainfall Monthly Total mm	23	10	15	33	79	102	109	109	107	109	94	46	836
No. of Days	6	2	3	4	9	14	15	15	13	12	13	10	116
Sunshine Hours per Day	7.6	7.8	7.5	6.4	6.4	6.4	7.3	7.4	7.2	6.8	6.9	6.7	7

Casablanca Morocco 59m

	Jan	Feb	Mar	Apr	May	June	July	Aug	Sep	Oct	Nov	Dec	Year
Temperature Daily Max.°C	17	18	20	21	22	24	26	26	26	24	21	18	22
Daily Min.°C	8	9	11	12	15	18	19	20	18	15	12	10	14
Average Monthly °C	13	13	15	16	18	21	23	23	22	20	17	14	18
Rainfall Monthly Total mm	78	61	54	37	20	3	0	1	6	28	58	94	440
No. of Days	11	8	9	5	4	2	0	1	2	6	9	10	67
Sunshine Hours per Day	5.2	6.3	7.3	9	9.4	9.7	10.2	9.7	9.1	7.4	5.9	5.3	7.9

Cheyenne USA 1869m

	Jan	Feb	Mar	Apr	May	June	July	Aug	Sep	Oct	Nov	Dec	Year
Temperature Daily Max.°C	3	4	6	12	18	24	29	28	23	16	8	5	15
Daily Min.°C	-9	-9	-7	-2	4	9	12	12	7	1	-5	-7	1
Average Monthly °C	-3	-2	0	5	11	16	21	20	15	9	2	-1	8
Rainfall Monthly Total mm	13	14	31	48	64	55	46	37	28	21	16	11	384
No. of Days	6	7	10	10	13	11	11	10	7	5	6	5	101
Sunshine Hours per Day	6	6.9	7.8	8	8.4	10.3	10.1	9.2	9.1	8	6	5.5	7.9

Chicago USA 186m

	Jan	Feb	Mar	Apr	May	June	July	Aug	Sep	Oct	Nov	Dec	Year
Temperature Daily Max.°C	0.6	1.5	6.4	14.1	20.6	26.4	28.9	28	23.8	17.4	8.4	2.1	14.9
Daily Min.°C	-7	-6	-2	5	11	16	20	19	14	8	0	-5	-6
Average Monthly °C	-3	-2	2	9	16	21	24	23	19	13	4	-2	4
Rainfall Monthly Total mm	47	41	70	77	96	103	86	80	69	71	56	48	843
No. of Days	10	10	12	12	13	11	9	9	8	8	10	10	122
Sunshine Hours per Day	4	5	6.6	6.9	8.9	10.2	10	9.2	8.2	6.9	4.5	3.7	7

Christchurch New Zealand 5m

	Jan	Feb	Mar	Apr	May	June	July	Aug	Sep	Oct	Nov	Dec	Year
Temperature Daily Max.°C	21	21	19	17	13	11	10	11	14	17	19	21	16
Daily Min.°C	12	12	10	7	4	2	1	3	5	7	8	11	7
Average Monthly °C	16	16	15	12	9	6	6	7	9	12	13	16	11
Rainfall Monthly Total mm	56	46	43	46	76	69	61	58	51	51	51	61	669
No. of Days	10	8	9	10	12	13	14	11	10	11	10	11	129
Sunshine Hours per Day	7	6.5	5.6	4.7	4.3	3.9	4.1	4.7	5.6	6.1	6.9	6.3	5.5

Churchill Canada 35m

	Jan	Feb	Mar	Apr	May	June	July	Aug	Sep	Oct	Nov	Dec	Year
Temperature Daily Max.°C	-24	-22	-15	-7	1	10	17	16	9	2	-7	-18	-3
Daily Min.°C	-32	-31	-24	-15	-5	2	7	8	3	-4	-15	-26	-11
Average Monthly °C	-28	-27	-19	-11	-2	6	12	12	6	-1	-11	-22	-7
Rainfall Monthly Total mm	14	16	18	30	34	44	30	62	53	42	42	25	410
No. of Days	9	9	10	13	11	10	12	13	15	16	17	14	149
Sunshine Hours per Day	2.6	6.6	6.1	6.2	5.6	7.1	9.2	7.5	3.4	2.2	1.6	1.9	4.8

Colombo Sri Lanka 10m

	Jan	Feb	Mar	Apr	May	June	July	Aug	Sep	Oct	Nov	Dec	Year
Temperature Daily Max.°C	30	31	31	31	30	30	29	29	30	29	29	30	30
Daily Min.°C	22	22	23	24	25	25	25	25	25	24	23	22	24
Average Monthly °C	26	26	27	28	28	27	27	27	27	27	26	26	27
Rainfall Monthly Total mm	101	66	118	230	394	220	140	102	174	348	333	142	2368
No. of Days	10	6	11	17	23	22	16	14	17	22	20	12	190
Sunshine Hours per Day	7.9	9	8.1	7.2	6.4	5.4	6.1	6.3	6.2	6.5	6.4	7.8	6.9

Darwin Australia 30m

	Jan	Feb	Mar	Apr	May	June	July	Aug	Sep	Oct	Nov	Dec	Year
Temperature Daily Max.°C	32	32	33	33	33	31	31	32	33	34	34	33	33
Daily Min.°C	25	25	25	24	23	21	19	21	23	25	26	26	24
Average Monthly °C	29	29	29	29	28	26	25	26	28	29	30	29	28
Rainfall Monthly Total mm	405	309	279	77	8	2	0	1	15	48	108	214	1466
No. of Days	20	18	17	6	1	1	0.1	0.1	2	5	10	15	95
Sunshine Hours per Day	5.8	5.8	6.6	9.8	9.3	10	9.9	10.4	10.1	9.4	9.6	6.8	8.6

Edmonton Canada 676m

	Jan	Feb	Mar	Apr	May	June	July	Aug	Sep	Oct	Nov	Dec	Year
Temperature Daily Max.°C	-9	-7	0	10	17	20	24	22	17	11	0	-5	8
Daily Min.°C	-19	-17	-10	-2	4	8	11	9	5	-1	-9	-14	-3
Average Monthly °C	-14	-12	-5	4	11	14	17	15	11	5	-4	-10	3
Rainfall Monthly Total mm	24	22	20	26	42	77	82	70	34	21	20	22	460
No. of Days	11	11	10	8	9	13	13	12	9	7	8	11	122
Sunshine Hours per Day	2.9	4.1	5.3	7.3	8.5	8.4	9.8	8.5	6.3	5.1	3.5	2.6	6

Harbin China 175m

	Jan	Feb	Mar	Apr	May	June	July	Aug	Sep	Oct	Nov	Dec	Year
Temperature Daily Max.°C	-14	-9	0	12	21	26	29	27	20	12	-1	-11	9
Daily Min.°C	-26	-23	-12	-1	7	14	18	16	8	0	-12	-22	-3
Average Monthly °C	-20	-16	-6	6	14	20	23	22	14	6	-7	-17	3
Rainfall Monthly Total mm	4	6	17	23	44	92	167	119	52	36	12	5	577
No. of Days	5	5	6	7	11	15	16	13	12	7	6	6	109
Sunshine Hours per Day	6.4	7.8	8	7.8	8.3	8.6	8.6	8.2	7.2	6.9	6.1	5.7	7.5

Ho Chi Minh Vietnam 10m

	Jan	Feb	Mar	Apr	May	June	July	Aug	Sep	Oct	Nov	Dec	Year
Temperature Daily Max.°C	32	33	34	35	33	32	31	31	31	31	31	31	32
Daily Min.°C	21	22	23	24	24	24	24	24	23	23	23	22	23
Average Monthly °C	26	27	29	30	29	28	28	28	27	27	27	26	28
Rainfall Monthly Total mm	16	3	13	42	220	331	314	269	336	269	115	56	1984
No. of Days	2	1	2	5	17	22	23	21	22	20	11	7	153
Sunshine Hours per Day	6.3	7.1	6.8	6.7	5.1	5	3.9	5	4	4.5	5.2	5.7	5.4

Hong Kong Hong Kong 35m

	Jan	Feb	Mar	Apr	May	June	July	Aug	Sep	Oct	Nov	Dec	Year
Temperature Daily Max.°C	18	18	20	24	28	30	31	31	30	27	24	20	25
Daily Min.°C	13	13	16	19	23	26	26	26	25	23	19	15	20
Average Monthly °C	16	15	18	22	25	28	28	28	27	25	21	17	23
Rainfall Monthly Total mm	30	60	70	133	332	479	286	415	364	33	46	17	2265
No. of Days	6	8	11	11	16	21	19	17	15	8	5	5	142
Sunshine Hours per Day	4.7	3.5	3.1	3.8	5	5.4	6.8	6.5	6.6	7	6.2	5.5	5.3

Honolulu Hawaii 5m

	Jan	Feb	Mar	Apr	May	June	July	Aug	Sep	Oct	Nov	Dec	Year
Temperature Daily Max.°C	26	26	26	27	28	29	29	29	30	29	28	26	28
Daily Min.°C	19	19	19	20	21	22	23	23	23	22	21	20	21
Average Monthly °C	23	22	23	23	24	26	26	26	26	26	24	23	24
Rainfall Monthly Total mm	96	84	73	33	25	8	11	23	25	47	55	76	556
No. of Days	10	10	9	9	6	6	8	7	7	10	10	11	103
Sunshine Hours per Day	7.3	7.7	8.3	8.6	8.8	9.1	9.4	9.3	9.2	8.3	7.5	6.2	8.3

Houston USA 12m

	Jan	Feb	Mar	Apr	May	June	July	Aug	Sep	Oct	Nov	Dec	Year
Temperature Daily Max.°C	17	18	22	25	29	32	34	34	31	28	21	18	26
Daily Min.°C	8	9	12	16	20	23	24	24	22	17	12	9	16
Average Monthly °C	12	14	17	21	25	28	29	29	27	22	16	14	21
Rainfall Monthly Total mm	94	82	61	87	113	97	131	90	97	91	103	104	1150
No. of Days	11	10	9	8	7	8	10	9	9	6	8	10	105
Sunshine Hours per Day	5.1	5.6	6.6	7.3	9.3	10.9	10.4	9.7	8.7	8.3	6.6	5.5	7.8

Istanbul Turkey 40m

	Jan	Feb	Mar	Apr	May	June	July	Aug	Sep	Oct	Nov	Dec	Year
Temperature Daily Max.°C	9	9	11	16	21	26	29	29	25	21	15	11	18
Daily Min.°C	3	2	3	7	12	16	18	20	15	12	8	5	10
Average Monthly °C	6	6	7	12	16	21	23	24	20	16	12	8	14
Rainfall Monthly Total mm	88	80	61	37	32	27	27	22	49	61	87	96	667
No. of Days	18	15	14	9	8	5	4	3	6	10	13	17	122
Sunshine Hours per Day	2.6	3.8	4.5	6.3	8.6	10.6	11.6	10.9	8.2	5.3	3.7	2.8	6.6

Jakarta Indonesia 10m

	Jan	Feb	Mar	Apr	May	June	July	Aug	Sep	Oct	Nov	Dec	Year
Temperature Daily Max.°C	29	29	30	31	31	31	31	31	31	31	30	29	30
Daily Min.°C	23	23	23	24	24	23	23	23	23	23	23	23	23
Average Monthly °C	26	26	27	27	27	27	27	27	27	27	27	26	27
Rainfall Monthly Total mm	300	300	211	147	114	97	64	43	66	112	142	203	1799
No. of Days	18	17	15	11	9	7	5	4	5	8	12	14	125
Sunshine Av. Monthly Dur.	6.1	6.5	7.7	8.5	8.4	8.5	9.1	9.5	9.6	9	7.7	7.1	8.1

Johannesburg South Africa 1692m

	Jan	Feb	Mar	Apr	May	June	July	Aug	Sep	Oct	Nov	Dec	Year
Temperature Daily Max.°C	25	25	24	21	19	16	17	19	23	24	24	25	22
Daily Min.°C	14	14	13	10	7	4	4	6	9	11	13	14	10
Average Monthly °C	20	20	18	16	13	10	10	13	16	18	18	19	16
Rainfall Monthly Total mm	112	97	75	61	22	9	8	5	25	69	116	111	710
No. of Days	15	11	10	10	5	2	1	2	3	10	15	15	99
Sunshine Av. Monthly Dur.	8.4	8.3	7.9	9.1	8.8	8.8	9.2	9.7	9.5	8.9	8.3	8.4	

Kabul Afghanistan 1791 m

	Jan	Feb	Mar	Apr	May	June	July	Aug	Sep	Oct	Nov	Dec	Year
Temperature Daily Max.°C	2	4	12	19	26	31	33	33	30	22	17	8	20
Daily Min.°C	-8	-6	1	6	11	13	16	15	11	6	1	-3	5
Average Monthly °C	-3	-1	6	13	18	22	25	24	20	14	9	3	12
Rainfall Monthly Total mm	28	61	72	117	33	1	7	1		1	37	14	372
No. of Days	6	7	9	11	8	3	2	1	1	3	2	5	58
Sunshine Av. Monthly Dur.	5.9	6	5.7	6.8	10.1	11.5	11.4	11.2	9.8	9.4	7.8	6.1	8.5

Karachi Pakistan 5m

	Jan	Feb	Mar	Apr	May	June	July	Aug	Sep	Oct	Nov	Dec	Year
Temperature Daily Max.°C	24	25	28	30	31	32	31	30	30	31	30	26	29
Daily Min.°C	14	16	20	23	26	28	27	26	25	23	19	16	22
Average Monthly °C	19	21	24	27	29	30	29	28	27	27	25	21	26
Rainfall Monthly Total mm	13	10	8	3	3	18	81	41	13	0.5	3	5	198
No. of Days	2	3	1	1	0.1	1	6	3	1	0.2	0.4	1.3	20
Sunshine Av. Monthly Dur.	8.8	9.3	9	9.9	10.1	7.8	4.4	4.8	7.1	9.3	9.3	8.7	8.2

Khartoum Sudan 380m

	Jan	Feb	Mar	Apr	May	June	July	Aug	Sep	Oct	Nov	Dec	Year
Temperature Daily Max.°C	32	33	37	40	42	41	38	36	38	39	35	32	37
Daily Min.°C	16	17	20	23	26	27	26	25	25	25	21	17	22
Average Monthly °C	24	25	28	32	34	34	32	30	32	32	28	25	30
Rainfall Monthly Total mm	0	0	0	1	7	5	56	80	28	2	0	0	179
No. of Days	0	0	0	0	1	1	6	8	3	1	0	0	20
Sunshine Av. Monthly Dur.	10.6	11.2	10.4	10.8	10.4	10.1	8.6	8.6	9.6	10.3	10.8	10.6	10.2

Kingston Jamaica 35m

	Jan	Feb	Mar	Apr	May	June	July	Aug	Sep	Oct	Nov	Dec	Year
Temperature Daily Max.°C	30	30	30	31	31	32	32	32	32	31	31	31	31
Daily Min.°C	20	20	20	21	22	24	23	23	23	23	22	21	22
Average Monthly °C	25	25	25	26	26	28	28	28	27	27	26	26	26
Rainfall Monthly Total mm	23	15	23	31	102	89	38	91	99	180	74	36	801
No. of Days	3	3	2	3	4	5	4	7	6	9	5	4	55
Sunshine Av. Monthly Dur.	8.3	8.8	8.7	8.7	8.3	7.8	8.5	8.5	7.6	7.3	8.3	7.7	8.2

Kinshasa Zaire 311m

	Jan	Feb	Mar	Apr	May	June	July	Aug	Sep	Oct	Nov	Dec	Year
Temperature Daily Max.°C	31	31	32	32	31	28	27	29	30	31	31	30	30
Daily Min.°C	22	22	22	22	22	19	17	18	20	21	21	22	21
Average Monthly °C	26	26	27	27	26	24	22	23	25	26	26	26	25
Rainfall Monthly Total mm	128	142	173	222	129	4	3	3	46	145	246	161	1402
No. of Days	9	10	13	15	10	1	0	1	5	10	16	13	103
Sunshine Av. Monthly Dur.	4.3	4.8	4.8	5.5	4.5	4.6	4	4.7	4.3	4.7	4.4	4.6	4.6

Lagos Nigeria 40m

	Jan	Feb	Mar	Apr	May	June	July	Aug	Sep	Oct	Nov	Dec	Year
Temperature Daily Max.°C	32	33	33	32	31	29	28	28	29	30	31	32	31
Daily Min.°C	22	23	23	23	23	22	22	21	22	22	23	22	22
Average Monthly °C	27	28	28	28	27	26	25	24	25	26	27	27	26
Rainfall Monthly Total mm	28	41	99	99	203	300	180	56	180	190	63	25	1464
No. of Days	1	4	7	8	14	18	14	9	16	16	7	2	116
Sunshine Av. Monthly Dur.	5.9	6.8	6.3	6.1	5.6	3.8	2.8	3.3	3	5.1	6.6	6.5	5.2

Lima Peru 120m

	Jan	Feb	Mar	Apr	May	June	July	Aug	Sep	Oct	Nov	Dec	Year
Temperature Daily Max.°C	28	29	29	27	24	20	20	19	20	22	24	26	24
Daily Min.°C	19	20	19	17	16	15	14	14	14	15	16	17	16
Average Monthly °C	24	24	24	22	20	17	17	16	17	18	20	21	20
Rainfall Monthly Total mm	1	1	1	1	5	5	8	8	8	3	3	1	45
No. of Days	1	0	0	0	1	1	1	2	1	0	0	0	7
Sunshine Av. Monthly Dur.	6.3	6.8	6.9	6.7	4	1.4	1.1	1	1.1	2.5	4.1	5	3.9

Lisbon Portugal 77m

	Jan	Feb	Mar	Apr	May	June	July	Aug	Sep	Oct	Nov	Dec	Year
Temperature Daily Max.°C	14	15	17	20	21	25	27	28	26	22	17	15	21
Daily Min.°C	8	8	10	12	13	15	17	17	17	14	11	9	13
Average Monthly °C	11	12	14	16	17	20	22	23	21	18	14	12	17
Rainfall Monthly Total mm	111	76	109	54	44	16	3	4	33	62	93	103	708
No. of Days	15	12	14	10	10	5	2	2	6	9	13	15	113
Sunshine Av. Monthly Dur.	4.7	5.9	6	8.3	9.1	10.6	11.4	10.7	8.4	6.7	5.2	4.6	7.7

London (Kew) United Kingdom 5m

	Jan	Feb	Mar	Apr	May	June	July	Aug	Sep	Oct	Nov	Dec	Year
Temperature Daily Max.°C	6	7	10	13	17	20	22	21	19	14	10	7	14
Daily Min.°C	2	2	3	6	8	12	14	13	11	8	5	4	7
Average Monthly °C	4	5	7	9	12	16	18	17	15	11	8	5	11
Rainfall Monthly Total mm	54	40	37	37	46	45	57	59	49	57	64	48	593
No. of Days	15	13	11	12	12	11	12	11	13	13	15	15	153
Sunshine Av. Monthly Dur.	1.7	2.3	3.5	5.7	6.7	7	6.6	6	5	3.3	1.9	1.4	4.3

Los Angeles USA 30m

	Jan	Feb	Mar	Apr	May	June	July	Aug	Sep	Oct	Nov	Dec	Year
Temperature Daily Max.°C	18	18	18	19	20	22	24	24	24	23	22	19	21
Daily Min.°C	7	8	9	11	13	15	17	17	16	14	11	9	12
Average Monthly °C	12	13	14	15	17	18	21	21	20	18	16	14	17
Rainfall Monthly Total mm	69	74	46	28	3	3	0	0	5	10	28	61	327
No. of Days	7	6	5	4	1	1	0	1	1	2	3	6	37
Sunshine Av. Monthly Dur.	6.9	8.2	8.9	8.8	9.5	10.3	11.7	11	10.1	8.6	8.2	7.6	9.2

Lusaka Zambia 1154m

	Jan	Feb	Mar	Apr	May	June	July	Aug	Sep	Oct	Nov	Dec	Year
Temperature Daily Max.°C	26	26	26	27	25	23	23	26	29	31	29	27	27
Daily Min.°C	17	17	16	15	12	10	9	11	15	18	18	17	15
Average Monthly °C	22	22	21	21	18	17	16	19	22	25	23	22	21
Rainfall Monthly Total mm	224	173	90	19	3	1	0	1	1	17	85	196	810
No. of Days	19	18	12	3	1	0	0	0	0	3	10	18	84
Sunshine Av. Monthly Dur.	5.1	5.4	6.9	8.9	9	9	9.1	9.6	9.5	9	7	5.5	7.8

Manaus Brazil 45m

	Jan	Feb	Mar	Apr	May	June	July	Aug	Sep	Oct	Nov	Dec	Year
Temperature Daily Max.°C	31	31	31	31	31	31	32	33	34	34	33	32	32
Daily Min.°C	24	24	24	24	24	24	24	24	24	25	25	24	24
Average Monthly °C	28	28	28	27	28	28	28	29	29	29	29	28	28
Rainfall Monthly Total mm	278	278	300	287	193	99	61	41	62	112	165	220	2096
No. of Days	20	19	20	19	18	11	8	6	7	11	12	16	167
Sunshine Av. Monthly Dur.	3.9	4	3.6	3.9	5.4	6.9	7.9	8.2	7.5	6.6	5.9	4.9	5.7

Melbourne Australia 35m

	Jan	Feb	Mar	Apr	May	June	July	Aug	Sep	Oct	Nov	Dec	Year
Temperature Daily Max.°C	26	26	24	20	17	14	13	15	17	19	22	24	20
Daily Min.°C	14	14	13	11	8	7	6	6	8	9	11	12	10
Average Monthly °C	20	20	18	15	13	10	9	11	13	14	16	18	15
Rainfall Monthly Total mm	47	50	56	57	48	52	48	51	55	66	58	60	648
No. of Days	9	8	9	13	14	16	17	17	15	14	13	11	156
Sunshine Av. Monthly Dur.	8.3	8.4	6.7	5.3	4.4	3.6	4.1	4.9	5.7	6.4	7.6	7.9	6.1

Mexico City Mexico 2309m

	Jan	Feb	Mar	Apr	May	June	July	Aug	Sep	Oct	Nov	Dec	Year
Temperature Daily Max.°C	21	23	26	27	26	25	23	24	23	22	21	21	24
Daily Min.°C	5	6	7	9	10	11	11	11	11	9	6	5	8
Average Monthly °C	13	15	16	18	18	18	17	17	17	16	14	13	16
Rainfall Monthly Total mm	8	4	9	23	57	111	160	149	119	46	16	7	709
No. of Days	2	3	4	6	14	17	22	22	20	11	3	3	127
Sunshine Av. Monthly Dur.	7.3	8.1	8.5	8.1	7.8	7	6.2	6.4	5.6	6.3	7	7.3	7.1

Miami USA 2m

	Jan	Feb	Mar	Apr	May	June	July	Aug	Sep	Oct	Nov	Dec	Year
Temperature Daily Max.°C	24	25	27	28	30	31	32	32	31	29	27	25	28
Daily Min.°C	14	15	16	19	21	23	24	24	24	22	18	15	20
Average Monthly °C	19	20	21	23	25	27	28	28	27	25	22	20	24
Rainfall Monthly Total mm	51	48	58	99	163	188	170	178	241	208	71	43	1518
No. of Days	6	6	6	8	10	13	17	16	19	15	9	7	132
Sunshine Av. Monthly Dur.	7.7	8.3	8.7	9.4	8.9	8.5	8.7	8.4	7.1	6.5	7.5	7.1	8.1

Montreal Canada 57m

	Jan	Feb	Mar	Apr	May	June	July	Aug	Sep	Oct	Nov	Dec	Year
Temperature Daily Max.°C	-6	-4	2	11	18	23	26	25	20	14	5	-3	11
Daily Min.°C	-13	-11	-5	2	9	14	17	16	11	6	0	-9	3
Average Monthly °C	-9	-8	-2	6	13	19	22	20	16	10	3	-6	7
Rainfall Monthly Total mm	87	76	86	83	81	91	98	87	96	84	89	89	1047
No. of Days	17	15	15	14	13	12	13	10	13	12	15	17	166
Sunshine Av. Monthly Dur.	2.8	3.4	4.5	5.2	6.7	7.7	8.2	7.7	5.6	4.3	2.4	2.2	5.1

Moscow Russia 156m

	Jan	Feb	Mar	Apr	May	June	July	Aug	Sep	Oct	Nov	Dec	Year
Temperature Daily Max.°C	-6	-4	1	9	18	22	24	22	17	10	1	-5	9
Daily Min.°C	-14	-16	-11	-1	5	9	12	9	4	-2	-6	-12	-2
Average Monthly °C	-10	-10	-5	4	12	15	18	16	10	4	-2	-8	4
Rainfall Monthly Total mm	31	28	33	35	52	67	74	74	58	51	36	36	575
No. of Days	17	15	14	13	12	15	16	16	17	16	17	19	187
Sunshine Av. Monthly Dur.	1	1.9	3.7	5.2	7.8	8.3	8.4	7.1	4.4	2.4	1	0.6	4.4

Nairobi Kenya 1616m

	Jan	Feb	Mar	Apr	May	June	July	Aug	Sep	Oct	Nov	Dec	Year
Temperature Daily Max.°C	27	28	28	26	25	24	23	23	26	27	25	25	25
Daily Min.°C	13	13	14	15	14	12	11	12	12	13	14	14	13
Average Monthly °C	20	21	21	20	19	18	17	17	19	20	19	19	19
Rainfall Monthly Total mm	49	36	85	153	126	32	13	18	21	48	132	75	788
No. of Days	5	4	8	16	14	5	4	5	4	7	16	11	99
Sunshine Av. Monthly Dur.	8.8	9.4	8.7	7.3	5.9	5.9	4.3	4.2	5.8	7.1	7	8.1	6.9

New Delhi India 220m

	Jan	Feb	Mar	Apr	May	June	July	Aug	Sep	Oct	Nov	Dec	Year
Temperature Daily Max.°C	21	24	29	36	41	39	35	34	34	34	28	23	32
Daily Min.°C	6	10	14	20	26	28	27	26	24	17	11	7	18
Average Monthly °C	14	17	22	28	33	34	31	30	29	26	20	15	25
Rainfall Monthly Total mm	25	21	13	8	13	77	178	184	123	10	2	11	665
No. of Days	3	4	2	2	2	6	14	11	7	0.4	0.3	2	54
Sunshine Av. Monthly Dur.	7.7	8.2	8.2	8.7	9.2	7.9	6	6.3	6.9	9.4	8.7	8.3	8

New York USA 3m

	Jan	Feb	Mar	Apr	May	June	July	Aug	Sep	Oct	Nov	Dec	Year
Temperature Daily Max.°C	4	4	9	15	21	26	28	27	24	18	12	6	16
Daily Min.°C	-3	-2	1	6	12	17	20	19	16	10	4	-1	8
Average Monthly °C	1	1	5	11	16	21	24	23	20	14	8	2	12
Rainfall Monthly Total mm	89	74	104	89	91	86	102	119	89	84	89	84	1100
No. of Days	11	10	12	11	12	10	10	10	8	8	9	10	121
Sunshine Av. Monthly Dur.	4.9	5.9	6.7	7.1	8.1	10	9.9	8.9	7.9	7	5.7	5.1	7.3

Odessa Ukraine 64m

	Jan	Feb	Mar	Apr	May	June	July	Aug	Sep	Oct	Nov	Dec	Year
Temperature Daily Max.°C	1	2	6	12	19	24	27	26	21	15	8	4	14
Daily Min.°C	-6	-7	-2	4	11	15	18	17	12	8	1	-4	6
Average Monthly °C	-3	-2	2	8	15	19	22	21	17	11	5	0	10
Rainfall Monthly Total mm	28	26	20	27	34	45	34	37	29	35	43	31	389
No. of Days	11	10	10	9	9	9	7	6	6	8	10	11	106
Sunshine Av. Monthly Dur.	2.3	2.6	4.6	6.7	9	9.9	11.3	10.4	8.2	5.7	2.2	1.9	6.3

Palma Spain 93m

	Jan	Feb	Mar	Apr	May	June	July	Aug	Sep	Oct	Nov	Dec	Year
Temperature Daily Max.°C	13	14	16	18	21	25	28	28	25	21	16	13	20
Daily Min.°C	6	7	9	11	14	18	21	21	19	15	11	8	13
Average Monthly °C	10	10	12	15	18	22	24	24	22	18	13	10	17
Rainfall Monthly Total mm	31	39	48	43	54	37	27	49	76	86	52	45	587
No. of Days	5	5	8	9	8	6	4	6	7	9	6	6	79
Sunshine Av. Monthly Dur.	4.8	5.9	5.7	7.1	8.1	9.3	10.1	8.8	6.7	5.7	5	4.3	6.8

Paris France 75m

	Jan	Feb	Mar	Apr	May	June	July	Aug	Sep	Oct	Nov	Dec	Year
Temperature Daily Max.°C	6	7	12	16	20	23	25	24	21	16	10	7	16
Daily Min.°C	1	1	4	6	10	13	15	14	12	8	5	2	8
Average Monthly °C	3	4	8	11	15	18	20	19	17	12	7	4	12
Rainfall Monthly Total mm	56	46	35	42	57	54	59	64	55	50	51	50	619
No. of Days	17	14	12	13	12	12	12	13	13	13	15	16	162
Sunshine Av. Monthly Dur.	2	2.9	4.9	6.6	7.3	7.2	7.3	6.6	6	4	2.1	1.5	4.9

Perth Australia 60m

	Jan	Feb	Mar	Apr	May	June	July	Aug	Sep	Oct	Nov	Dec	Year
Temperature Daily Max.°C	29	30	27	25	21	18	17	18	19	21	25	27	23
Daily Min.°C	17	18	16	14	12	10	9	9	10	11	14	16	13
Average Monthly °C	23	24	22	19	16	14	13	13	15	16	19	22	18
Rainfall Monthly Total mm	8	13	22	44	128	189	177	145	84	58	19	13	900
No. of Days	3	3	5	8	15	17	19	19	15	12	7	5	128
Sunshine Av. Monthly Dur.	10.4	9.8	8.8	7.5	5.7	4.8	5.4	6	7.2	8.1	9.6	10.4	7.8

Quito Ecuador 2875m

	Jan	Feb	Mar	Apr	May	June	July	Aug	Sep	Oct	Nov	Dec	Year
Temperature Daily Max.°C	22	22	22	21	21	22	22	23	23	22	22	22	22
Daily Min.°C	8	9	9	9	9	7	7	7	7	8	7	8	8
Average Monthly °C	15	15	15	15	15	14	14	15	15	15	15	15	15
Rainfall Monthly Total mm	119	131	154	185	130	54	20	25	81	134	96	104	1233
No. of Days	16	17	20	22	21	12	7	9	14	18	14	16	186
Sunshine Av. Monthly Dur.	5.4	5	4.2	4.5	5.2	6.3	7.2	7.1	6.1	5.4	5.6	5.6	5.6

Reykjavik Iceland 18m

	Jan	Feb	Mar	Apr	May	June	July	Aug	Sep	Oct	Nov	Dec	Year
Temperature Daily Max.°C	2	3	5	6	10	13	15	14	12	8	5	4	8
Daily Min.°C	-3	-3	-1	1	4	7	9	8	6	3	0	-2	3
Average Monthly °C	0	0	2	4	7	10	12	11	9	5	3	1	5
Rainfall Monthly Total mm	89	64	62	56	42	42	50	56	67	94	78	79	779
No. of Days	20	17	18	18	16	15	15	16	19	21	18	20	213
Sunshine Av. Monthly Dur.	0.8	2	3.6	4.5	5.9	6.1	5.8	5.4	3.5	2.3	1.1	0.3	3.7

Rio de Janeiro Brazil 60m

	Jan	Feb	Mar	Apr	May	June	July	Aug	Sep	Oct	Nov	Dec	Year
Temperature Daily Max.°C	29	30	29	27	25	25	24	25	24	25	26	28	26
Daily Min.°C	23	23	22	21	19	18	17	18	19	19	20	22	20
Average Monthly °C	26	26	25	24	22	21	21	21	21	22	23	25	23
Rainfall Monthly Total mm	125	122	130	107	79	53	41	43	66	79	104	137	1086
No. of Days	13	11	12	10	10	7	7	7	11	13	13	14	128
Sunshine Av. Monthly Dur.	6.9	6.9	6.8	6.3	6.2	6.3	6.5	6.6	5.1	5.1	5.7	5.6	6.2

Rome Italy 46m

	Jan	Feb	Mar	Apr	May	June	July	Aug	Sep	Oct	Nov	Dec	Year
Temperature Daily Max.°C	11	12	15	19	23	27	30	30	26	21	16	12	20
Daily Min.°C	4	4	7	9	13	17	19	19	16	13	8	6	11
Average Monthly °C	7	8	11	14	18	22	25	25	21	17	12	9	16
Rainfall Monthly Total mm	76	89	77	73	63	48	14	22	70	128	117	107	882
No. of Days	7	6	8	9	6	4	2	2	5	6	8	8	68
Sunshine Av. Monthly Dur.	4.3	4.7	6.6	7	8.6	9.4	10.8	9.9	8.1	6.4	4.1	3.3	6.9

St Denis Réunion 10m

	Jan	Feb	Mar	Apr	May	June	July	Aug	Sep	Oct	Nov	Dec	Year
Temperature Av. Daily Max.	30	30	29	28	27	26	25	25	25	26	27	29	27
Av. Daily Min.	23	23	23	21	20	18	17	17	17	19	20	22	20
Av. Monthly	26	26	26	25	23	22	21	21	21	22	24	25	24
Rainfall Monthly Total mm	263	216	290	160	81	75	70	49	47	44	95	151	1541
No. of Days	19	17	18	13	14	14	17	16	14	12	13	16	183
Sunshine Av. Monthly Dur.	7.7	7.7	6.7	7.4	7.6	7.3	7.2	7.1	7.2	7.1	7.1	7	7.3

St Louis USA 172m

	Jan	Feb	Mar	Apr	May	June	July	Aug	Sep	Oct	Nov	Dec	Year
Temperature Daily Max.°C	5	7	12	19	24	30	32	31	27	21	12	6	19
Daily Min.°C	-5	-4	0	7	12	17	19	19	14	8	1	-3	7
Average Monthly °C	0	2	6	13	18	23	26	25	21	15	7	2	13
Rainfall Monthly Total mm	50	52	78	94	95	109	84	77	70	73	65	50	897
No. of Days	7	8	10	11	10	9	9	7	9	8	8	9	105
Sunshine Av. Monthly Dur.	4.4	5.3	6.8	7.7	9.2	9.9	10.6	9.4	8.8	7.9	5.7	4.3	7.6

San Francisco USA 5m

	Jan	Feb	Mar	Apr	May	June	July	Aug	Sep	Oct	Nov	Dec	Year
Temperature Daily Max.°C	13	15	16	17	17	18	18	18	21	20	18	14	17
Daily Min.°C	8	9	9	10	11	12	12	12	13	12	11	9	11
Average Monthly °C	10	12	13	13	14	15	15	15	17	16	14	0	14
Rainfall Monthly Total mm	116	93	74	37	16	4	0.3	1	6	23	51	108	528
No. of Days	11	10	10	6	3	1	1	1	1	4	8	11	67
Sunshine Av. Monthly Dur.	4.9	6.9	7.9	9.1	9.6	11	9.3	8.3	8.8	7.5	6.3	4.6	7.9

San Jose Costa Rica 1145m

	Jan	Feb	Mar	Apr	May	June	July	Aug	Sep	Oct	Nov	Dec	Year
Temperature Daily Max.°C	24	25	26	26	27	26	25	26	26	25	25	24	25
Daily Min.°C	15	15	15	17	17	17	17	16	16	16	16	15	16
Average Monthly °C	19	20	21	21	22	21	21	21	21	20	20	19	20
Rainfall Monthly Total mm	8	5	10	37	244	284	230	233	342	333	172	46	1944
No. of Days	3	1	2	7	19	22	23	24	24	25	14	6	170
Sunshine Av. Monthly Dur.	7	7.8	8	7	5.2	4	4	4.4	5	4.4	4.5	5.9	5.6

Santander Spain 66m

	Jan	Feb	Mar	Apr	May	June	July	Aug	Sep	Oct	Nov	Dec	Year
Temperature Daily Max.°C	12	12	14	15	17	20	22	22	21	18	15	13	17
Daily Min.°C	7	7	8	10	11	14	16	16	15	12	10	8	11
Average Monthly °C	9	9	11	12	14	17	19	19	18	15	12	10	14
Rainfall Monthly Total mm	119	88	78	83	89	63	54	84	114	133	125	159	1189
No. of Days	16	14	13	13	14	13	11	14	14	14	15	18	169
Sunshine Av. Monthly Dur.	2.7	3.5	4.5	5.5	6	6.7	6.8	6.4	5.2	4.3	3.2	2.4	4.8

Santiago Chile 520m

	Jan	Feb	Mar	Apr	May	June	July	Aug	Sep	Oct	Nov	Dec	Year
Temperature Daily Max.°C	30	29	27	24	19	15	15	17	19	22	26	29	23
Daily Min.°C	12	11	10	7	5	3	3	4	6	7	9	11	7
Average Monthly °C	21	20	18	15	12	9	9	10	12	15	17	20	15
Rainfall Monthly Total mm	3	3	5	13	64	84	76	56	31	15	8	5	363
No. of Days	0	0	1	1	5	6	6	5	3	3	1	0	31
Sunshine Av. Monthly Dur.	10.8	8.9	8.5	5.5	3.6	3.3	3.3	3.6	4.8	6.1	8.7	10.1	6.4

Shanghai China 5m

	Jan	Feb	Mar	Apr	May	June	July	Aug	Sep	Oct	Nov	Dec	Year
Temperature Daily Max.°C	8	8	13	19	24	28	32	32	27	23	17	10	20
Daily Min.°C	-1	0	4	9	14	19	23	23	19	13	7	2	11
Average Monthly °C	3	4	8	14	19	23	27	27	23	18	12	6	15
Rainfall Monthly Total mm	48	59	84	94	94	180	147	142	130	71	51	36	1136
No. of Days	10	10	12	13	12	14	11	11	12	9	8	8	130
Sunshine Av. Monthly Dur.	4	3.7	4.4	4.8	5.4	4.7	6.9	7.5	5.3	5.6	4.7	4.5	5.1

Shannon Ireland 2m

	Jan	Feb	Mar	Apr	May	June	July	Aug	Sep	Oct	Nov	Dec	Year
Temperature Daily Max.°C	8	9	11	13	16	19	19	20	17	14	11	9	14
Daily Min.°C	2	2	4	5	7	10	12	12	10	7	5	3	7
Average Monthly °C	5	5	7	9	12	14	16	16	14	11	8	6	10
Rainfall Monthly Total mm	94	67	56	53	61	57	77	79	86	86	96	117	929
No. of Days	15	11	11	11	11	11	14	14	14	14	15	18	159
Sunshine Av. Monthly Dur.	1.8	2.6	3.4	5.1	6.8	5.8	4.9	5.1	3.7	2.8	2.1	1.4	3.8

Singapore Singapore 10m

	Jan	Feb	Mar	Apr	May	June	July	Aug	Sep	Oct	Nov	Dec	Year
Temperature Daily Max.°C	31	31	31	31	31	31	31	31	30	31	30	30	31
Daily Min.°C	23	23	24	24	24	25	25	24	24	24	24	23	24
Average Monthly °C	27	27	27	27	28	28	28	27	27	27	27	27	27
Rainfall Monthly Total mm	252	175	200	196	173	171	165	191	178	206	251	265	2423
No. of Days	17	12	14	15	15	13	13	15	14	16	19	19	182
Sunshine Av. Monthly Dur.	5.1	5.7	6	5.8	5.7	5.7	5.9	5.7	5.6	5	4.6	4.3	5.4

Stockholm Sweden 44m

	Jan	Feb	Mar	Apr	May	June	July	Aug	Sep	Oct	Nov	Dec	Year
Temperature Daily Max.°C	-1	-1	2	8	15	19	22	20	15	9	5	2	10
Daily Min.°C	-5	-6	-4	1	6	10	14	13	9	5	1	-2	4
Average Monthly °C	-3	-3	-1	5	10	15	18	17	12	7	3	0	7
Rainfall Monthly Total mm	46	32	27	33	36	45	61	77	59	50	56	50	572
No. of Days	10	7	6	7	7	8	9	10	9	9	10	11	103
Sunshine Av. Monthly Dur.	1.3	2.4	5	6.8	8.7	9.6	9.1	7.3	5.6	2.8	1.3	0.7	5.1

Sydney Australia 40m

	Jan	Feb	Mar	Apr	May	June	July	Aug	Sep	Oct	Nov	Dec	Year
Temperature Daily Max.°C	26	26	25	22	19	17	17	18	20	22	24	25	22
Daily Min.°C	18	19	17	14	11	9	8	9	11	13	16	17	14
Average Monthly °C	22	22	21	18	15	13	12	13	16	18	20	21	18
Rainfall Monthly Total mm	89	101	127	135	127	117	117	76	74	71	74	74	1182
No. of Days	13	13	14	13	13	12	12	11	12	12	12	13	150
Sunshine Av. Monthly Dur.	7.5	7	6.4	6.1	5.7	5.3	6.1	7	7.3	7.5	7.5	7.5	6.8

Tehran Iran 1191m

	Jan	Feb	Mar	Apr	May	June	July	Aug	Sep	Oct	Nov	Dec	Year
Temperature Daily Max.°C	9	11	16	21	29	30	37	36	29	24	16	11	22
Daily Min.°C	-1	1	4	10	16	20	23	23	18	12	6	1	11
Average Monthly °C	4	6	10	15	22	25	30	29	23	18	11	6	17
Rainfall Monthly Total mm	37	23	36	31	14	2	1	1	1	5	29	27	207
No. of Days	4	4	3	6	3	0.6	0.2	0.3	0.4	2	4	5	32
Sunshine Av. Monthly Dur.	5.9	6.7	7.5	7.4	8.6	11.6	11.2	11	10.1	7.6	6.9	6.3	8.4

Timbuktu Mali 269m

	Jan	Feb	Mar	Apr	May	June	July	Aug	Sep	Oct	Nov	Dec	Year
Temperature Daily Max.°C	31	35	38	41	43	42	38	35	38	40	37	31	37
Daily Min.°C	13	16	18	22	26	27	25	24	24	23	18	14	21
Average Monthly °C	22	25	28	31	34	34	32	30	31	31	28	23	29
Rainfall Monthly Total mm	0	0	0	1	4	20	54	93	31	3	0	0	206
No. of Days	0	0	0	0	1	4	8	10	5	1	0	0	29
Sunshine Av. Monthly Dur.	9.1	9.6	9.6	9.7	9.8	9.4	9.6	9	9.3	9.5	9.5	8.9	9.4

Tokyo Japan 5m

	Jan	Feb	Mar	Apr	May	June	July	Aug	Sep	Oct	Nov	Dec	Year
Temperature Daily Max.°C	9	9	12	18	22	25	29	30	27	20	16	11	19
Daily Min.°C	-1	-1	3	4	13	17	22	23	19	13	7	1	10
Average Monthly °C	4	4	8	11	18	21	25	26	23	17	11	6	14
Rainfall Monthly Total mm	48	73	101	135	131	182	146	147	217	220	101	61	1562
No. of Days	6	7	10	11	12	12	11	10	13	12	8	5	117
Sunshine Av. Monthly Dur.	6	5.9	5.7	6	6.2	5	5.8	6.6	4.5	4.4	4.8	5.4	5.5

Tromsø Norway 100m

	Jan	Feb	Mar	Apr	May	June	July	Aug	Sep	Oct	Nov	Dec	Year
Temperature Daily Max.°C	-2	-2	0	3	7	12	16	14	10	5	2	0	5
Daily Min.°C	-6	-6	-5	-2	1	6	9	8	5	1	-2	-4	0
Average Monthly °C	-4	-4	-3	0	4	9	13	11	7	3	0	-2	3
Rainfall Monthly Total mm	96	79	91	65	61	59	56	80	109	115	88	95	994
No. of Days	14	12	15	12	11	11	10	14	15	16	13	13	156
Sunshine Av. Monthly Dur.	0.1	1.6	2.9	6.1	5.7	6.9	7.9	4.8	3.5	1.7	0.3	0	3.5

Tunis Tunisia 65m

	Jan	Feb	Mar	Apr	May	June	July	Aug	Sep	Oct	Nov	Dec	Year
Temperature Daily Max.°C	15	16	18	21	25	29	32	33	30	25	20	16	23
Daily Min.°C	7	7	9	11	14	18	20	21	19	15	11	7	13
Average Monthly °C	11	12	13	16	19	23	26	27	25	20	15	12	18
Rainfall Monthly Total mm	65	49	43	40	22	10	2	7	34	56	54	62	444
No. of Days	13	12	11	9	6	5	2	3	7	9	11	14	102
Sunshine Av. Monthly Dur.	5.6	6.7	7.2	7.8	9.9	10.6	12.1	11.3	8.6	7	6.1	5.3	8.2

Ulan Bator Mongolia 1305m

	Jan	Feb	Mar	Apr	May	June	July	Aug	Sep	Oct	Nov	Dec	Year
Temperature Daily Max.°C	-19	-13	-4	7	13	21	22	21	14	6	-6	-16	104
Daily Min.°C	-32	-29	-22	-8	-2	7	11	8	2	-8	-20	-28	-10
Average Monthly °C	-26	-21	-13	-1	6	14	16	14	8	-1	-13	-22	47
Rainfall Monthly Total mm	1	1	2	5	10	28	76	51	23	5	5	2	209
No. of Days	1	1	2	2	4	5	10	8	3	2	2	1	41
Sunshine Av. Monthly Dur.	6.4	7.8	8	7.8	8.3	8.6	8.6	8.2	7.2	6.9	6.1	5.7	7.5

Vancouver Canada 5m

	Jan	Feb	Mar	Apr	May	June	July	Aug	Sep	Oct	Nov	Dec	Year
Temperature Daily Max.°C	6	7	10	14	17	20	23	22	19	14	9	7	14
Daily Min.°C	0	1	3	5	8	11	13	12	10	7	3	2	6
Average Monthly °C	3	4	6	9	13	16	18	17	14	10	6	4	10
Rainfall Monthly Total mm	214	161	151	90	69	65	39	44	83	172	198	243	1529
No. of Days	20	16	17	13	10	10	7	7	10	15	18	21	164
Sunshine Av. Monthly Dur.	1.6	3	3.8	5.9	7.5	7.4	9.5	8.2	6	3.7	2	1.4	5

Verkhoyansk Russia 137m

	Jan	Feb	Mar	Apr	May	June	July	Aug	Sep	Oct	Nov	Dec	Year
Temperature Daily Max.°C	-47	-40	-20	-1	11	21	24	21	12	-8	-33	-42	-8
Daily Min.°C	-51	-48	-40	-25	-7	4	6	1	-6	-20	-39	-50	-23
Average Monthly °C	-49	-44	-30	-13	2	12	15	11	3	-14	-36	-46	-16
Rainfall Monthly Total mm	7	5	5	4	5	25	33	30	13	11	10	7	155
No. of Days	9	8	7	5	6	10	9	9	8	10	12	11	104
Sunshine Av. Monthly Dur.	0	2.6	6.9	9.6	9.7	10	9.7	7.5	4.1	2.4	0.6	0	5.4

Warsaw Poland 110m

	Jan	Feb	Mar	Apr	May	June	July	Aug	Sep	Oct	Nov	Dec	Year
Temperature Daily Max.°C	0	0	6	12	20	23	24	23	19	13	6	2	12
Daily Min.°C	-6	-6	-2	3	9	12	15	14	10	5	1	-3	4
Average Monthly °C	-3	-3	2	7	14	17	19	18	14	9	3	0	8
Rainfall Monthly Total mm	27	32	27	37	46	69	96	65	43	38	31	44	555
No. of Days	15	14	11	13	11	13	16	13	12	12	12	16	158
Sunshine Av. Monthly Dur.	1.7	2	3.7	5.3	8.1	8.1	7.1	6.9	5.3	3.8	1.6	1.3	4.6

Washington USA 22m

	Jan	Feb	Mar	Apr	May	June	July	Aug	Sep	Oct	Nov	Dec	Year
Temperature Daily Max.°C	7	8	12	19	25	29	31	30	26	20	14	8	19
Daily Min.°C	-1	-1	2	8	13	18	21	20	16	10	4	-1	9
Average Monthly °C	3	3	7	13	19	24	26	25	21	15	9	4	14
Rainfall Monthly Total mm	84	68	96	85	103	88	108	120	100	78	75	75	1080
No. of Days	11	9	12	10	12	10	11	10	9	8	9	10	121
Sunshine Av. Monthly Dur.	4.4	5.7	6.7	7.4	8.2	8.8	8.6	8.2	7.5	6.5	5.3	4.5	6.8

Windhoek Namibia 1728m

	Jan	Feb	Mar	Apr	May	June	July	Aug	Sep	Oct	Nov	Dec	Year
Temperature Daily Max.°C	30	29	27	26	23	20	21	24	27	29	30	30	26
Daily Min.°C	17	17	15	13	9	7	7	9	12	15	16	17	13
Average Monthly °C	24	23	21	19	16	13	14	16	20	22	23	24	20
Rainfall Monthly Total mm	71	76	77	41	5	2	1	1	3	13	35	39	364
No. of Days	12	11	10	5	2	0	0	0	1	3	7	7	58
Sunshine Av. Monthly Dur.	8.9	8.6	8.3	9.5	10	10	10	10.5	10.4	10.2	9.7	9.8	9.7

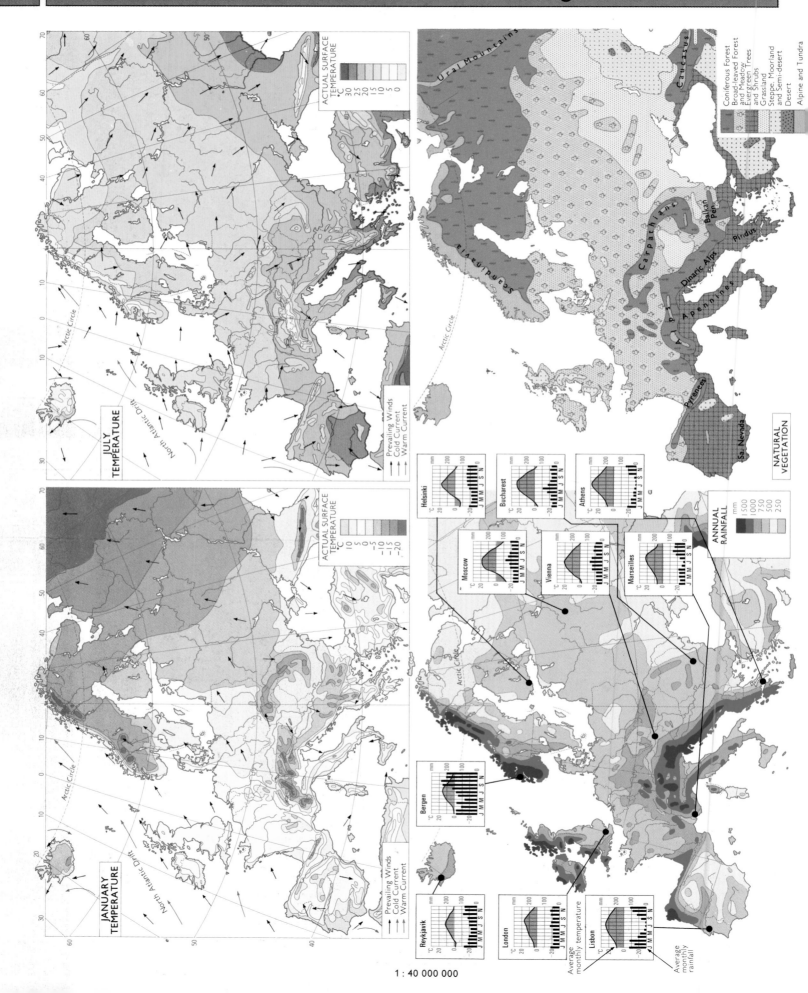

JULY TEMPERATURE

ACTUAL SURFACE TEMPERATURE
°C
30
25
20
15
10
5
0

Prevailing Winds
Cold Current
Warm Current

North Atlantic Drift

Arctic Circle

JANUARY TEMPERATURE

ACTUAL SURFACE TEMPERATURE
°C
10
5
0
-5
-15
-20

Prevailing Winds
Cold Current
Warm Current

North Atlantic Drift

Arctic Circle

NATURAL VEGETATION

Coniferous Forest
Broad-leaved Forest and Meadow
Evergreen Trees and Shrubs
Grassland
Steppe, Moorland and Semi-desert
Desert
Alpine and Tundra

Ural Mountains
Caucasus
Scandinavia
Carpathians
Balkan Pen.
Pindus
Dinaric Alps
Alps
Apennines
Pyrenees
Sa. Nevada

ANNUAL RAINFALL

mm
1500
1000
750
500
250

Helsinki
Bucharest
Athens
Moscow
Vienna
Marseilles
Bergen
Reykjavik
London
Lisbon

Average monthly temperature
Average monthly rainfall

1 : 40 000 000

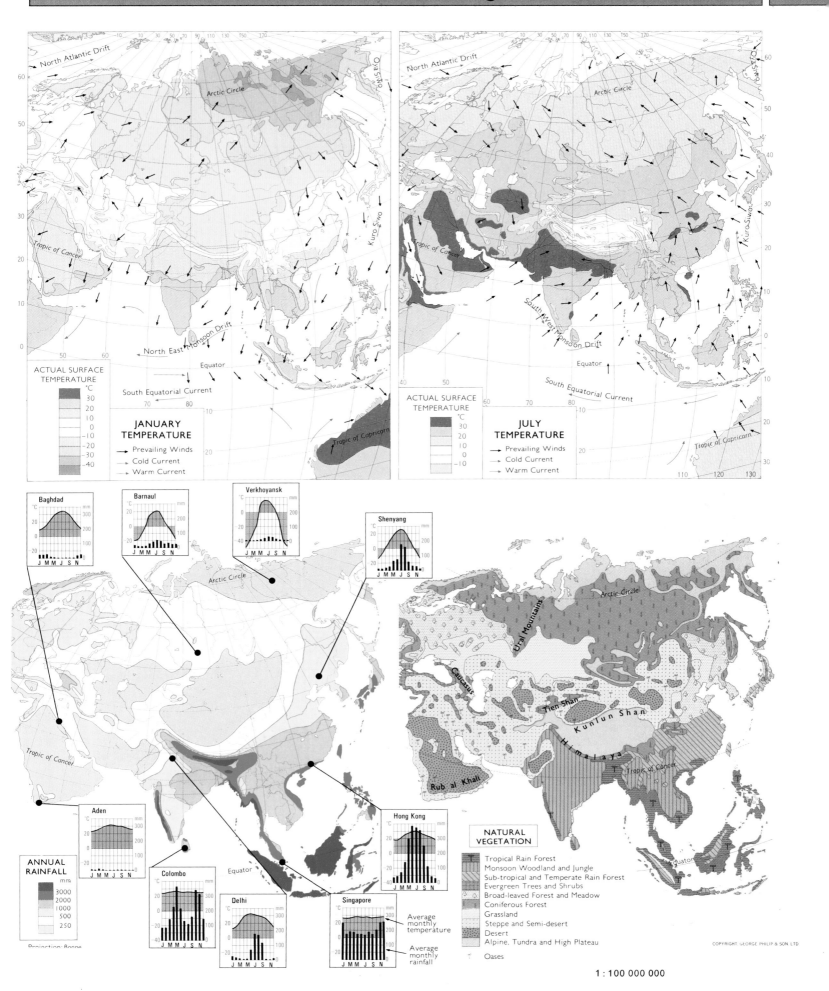

ACTUAL SURFACE
TEMPERATURE
°C
30
20
10
0
-10
-20
-30
-40

JANUARY TEMPERATURE

→ Prevailing Winds
→ Cold Current
→ Warm Current

ACTUAL SURFACE
TEMPERATURE
°C
30
20
10
0
-10

JULY TEMPERATURE

→ Prevailing Winds
→ Cold Current
→ Warm Current

North Atlantic Drift
Arctic Circle
Kuro Siwo
Tropic of Cancer
North East Monsoon Drift
Equator
South Equatorial Current
Tropic of Capricorn

South West Monsoon Drift
South Equatorial Current

Baghdad
Barnaul
Verkhoyansk
Shenyang
Aden
Colombo
Delhi
Singapore
Hong Kong

Arctic Circle
Tropic of Cancer
Equator

ANNUAL
RAINFALL
mm
3000
2000
1000
500
250

Average
monthly
temperature

Average
monthly
rainfall

NATURAL VEGETATION

Tropical Rain Forest
Monsoon Woodland and Jungle
Sub-tropical and Temperate Rain Forest
Evergreen Trees and Shrubs
Broad-leaved Forest and Meadow
Coniferous Forest
Grassland
Steppe and Semi-desert
Desert
Alpine, Tundra and High Plateau

T   Oases

Ural Mountains
Caucasus
Tien Shan
Kunlun Shan
Himalaya
Rub al Khali
Arctic Circle
Tropic of Cancer
Equator

Projection: Bonne

COPYRIGHT GEORGE PHILIP & SON LTD

1 : 100 000 000

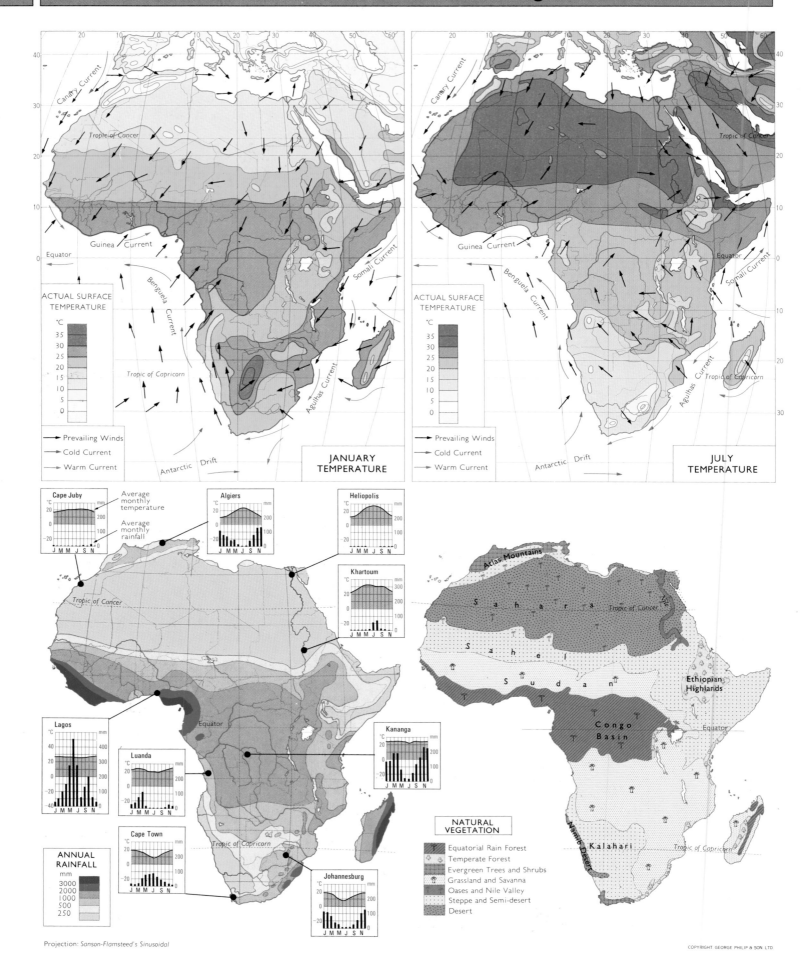

JANUARY TEMPERATURE

ACTUAL SURFACE TEMPERATURE

°C
35
30
25
20
15
10
5
0

→ Prevailing Winds
→ Cold Current
→ Warm Current

JULY TEMPERATURE

ACTUAL SURFACE TEMPERATURE

°C
35
30
25
20
15
10
5
0

→ Prevailing Winds
→ Cold Current
→ Warm Current

Cape Juby — Average monthly temperature / Average monthly rainfall
Algiers
Heliopolis
Khartoum
Lagos
Luanda
Kananga
Cape Town
Johannesburg

ANNUAL RAINFALL

mm
3000
2000
1000
500
250

NATURAL VEGETATION

Equatorial Rain Forest
Temperate Forest
Evergreen Trees and Shrubs
Grassland and Savanna
Oases and Nile Valley
Steppe and Semi-desert
Desert

Atlas Mountains
Sahara
Sahel
Sudan
Ethiopian Highlands
Congo Basin
Kalahari
Namib Desert

Projection: Sanson-Flamsteed's Sinusoidal

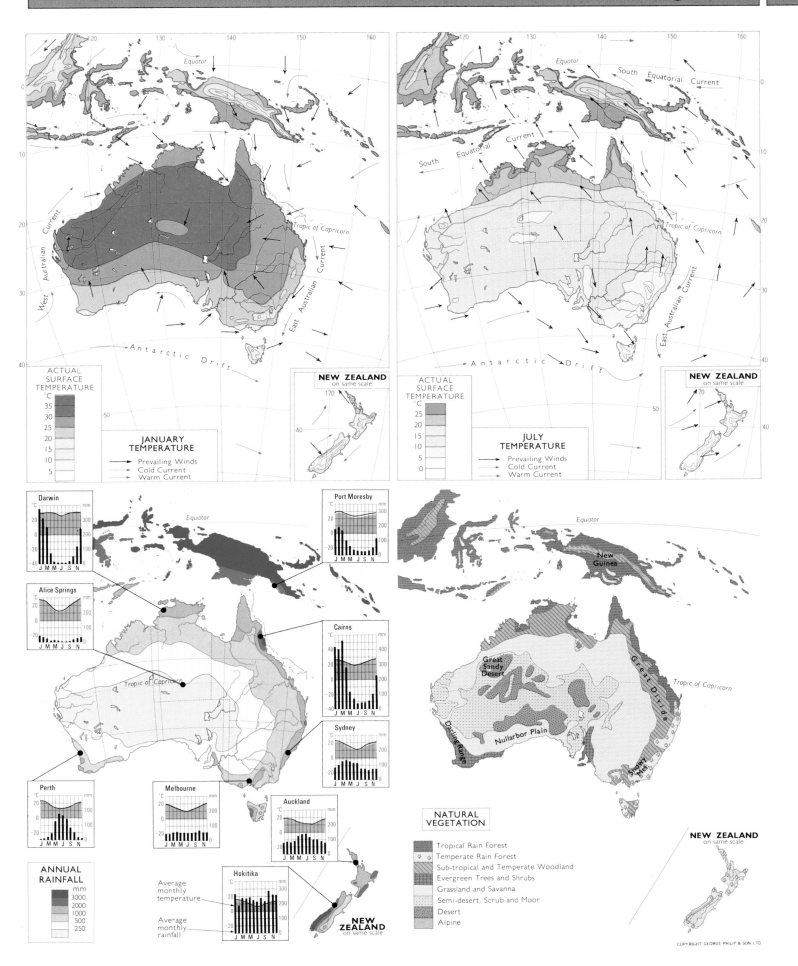

ACTUAL SURFACE TEMPERATURE °C
35
30
25
20
15
10
5

JANUARY TEMPERATURE
→ Prevailing Winds
→ Cold Current
→ Warm Current

NEW ZEALAND
on same scale

ACTUAL SURFACE TEMPERATURE °C
25
20
15
10
5
0

JULY TEMPERATURE
→ Prevailing Winds
→ Cold Current
→ Warm Current

NEW ZEALAND
on same scale

Darwin
Port Moresby
Alice Springs
Cairns
Sydney
Perth
Melbourne
Auckland
Hokitika

Average monthly temperature
Average monthly rainfall

NEW ZEALAND
on same scale

ANNUAL RAINFALL
mm
3000
2000
1000
500
250

New Guinea

Great Sandy Desert
Great Divide
Darling Range
Nullarbor Plain
Snowy Mts
Tropic of Capricorn
Equator

NATURAL VEGETATION
Tropical Rain Forest
Temperate Rain Forest
Sub-tropical and Temperate Woodland
Evergreen Trees and Shrubs
Grassland and Savanna
Semi-desert, Scrub and Moor
Desert
Alpine

NEW ZEALAND
on same scale

COPYRIGHT GEORGE PHILIP & SON LTD

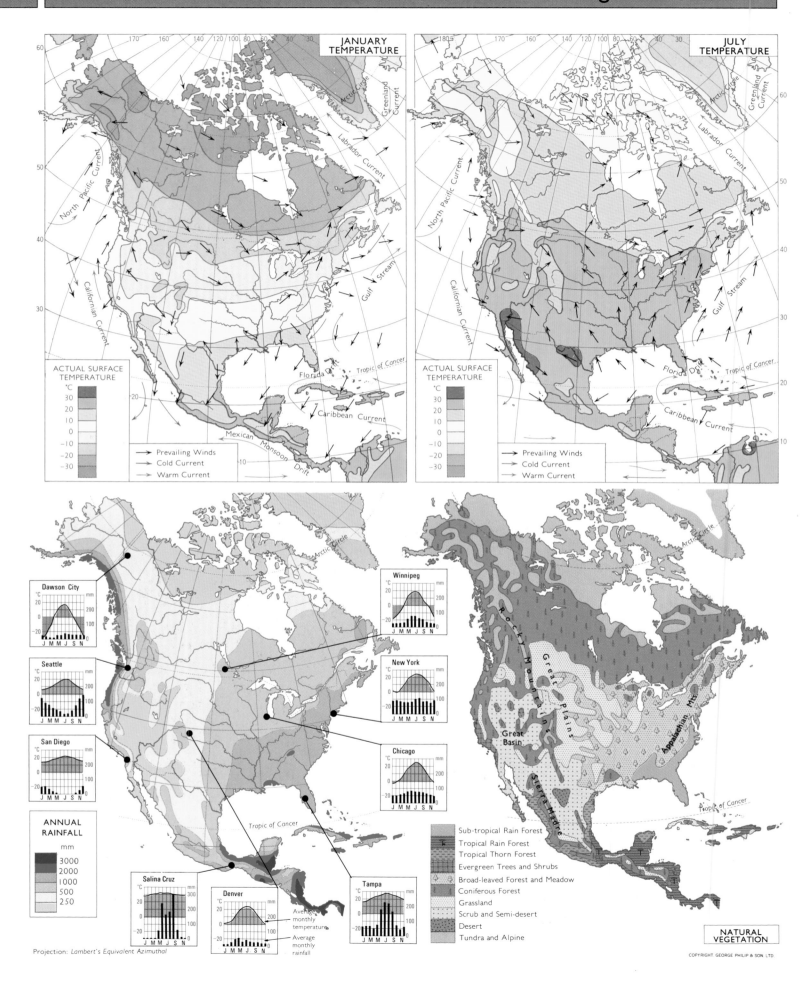

JANUARY TEMPERATURE

ACTUAL SURFACE TEMPERATURE
°C
30
20
10
0
-10
-20
-30

→ Prevailing Winds
→ Cold Current
→ Warm Current

JULY TEMPERATURE

ACTUAL SURFACE TEMPERATURE
°C
30
20
10
0
-10
-20
-30

→ Prevailing Winds
→ Cold Current
→ Warm Current

Dawson City
Seattle
San Diego
Salina Cruz
Denver
Tampa
Winnipeg
New York
Chicago

ANNUAL RAINFALL

mm
3000
2000
1000
500
250

Average monthly temperature
Average monthly rainfall

Projection: *Lambert's Equivalent Azimuthal*

NATURAL VEGETATION

Sub-tropical Rain Forest
Tropical Rain Forest
Tropical Thorn Forest
Evergreen Trees and Shrubs
Broad-leaved Forest and Meadow
Coniferous Forest
Grassland
Scrub and Semi-desert
Desert
Tundra and Alpine

Rocky Mountains
Great Plains
Great Basin
Appalachian Mts
Sierra Madre

COPYRIGHT GEORGE PHILIP & SON, LTD.

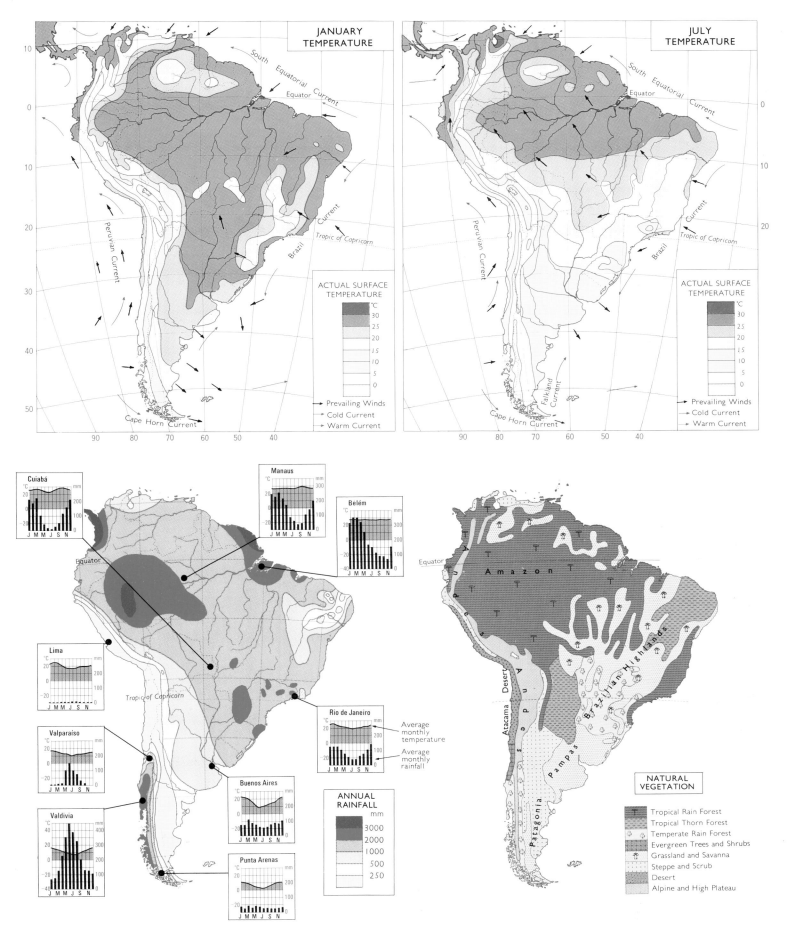

JANUARY TEMPERATURE

South Equatorial Current

Equator

Tropic of Capricorn

Peruvian Current

Brazil Current

Cape Horn Current

ACTUAL SURFACE TEMPERATURE
°C
30
25
20
15
10
5
0

→ Prevailing Winds
→ Cold Current
→ Warm Current

JULY TEMPERATURE

South Equatorial Current

Equator

Tropic of Capricorn

Peruvian Current

Brazil Current

Falkland Current

Cape Horn Current

ACTUAL SURFACE TEMPERATURE
°C
30
25
20
15
10
5
0

→ Prevailing Winds
→ Cold Current
→ Warm Current

Cuiabá

Manaus

Belém

Equator

Lima

Tropic of Capricorn

Valparaíso

Rio de Janeiro

Average monthly temperature

Average monthly rainfall

Valdivia

Buenos Aires

Punta Arenas

ANNUAL RAINFALL
mm
3000
2000
1000
500
250

Amazon

Andes

Atacama Desert

Brazilian Highlands

Pampas

Patagonia

NATURAL VEGETATION

Tropical Rain Forest
Tropical Thorn Forest
Temperate Rain Forest
Evergreen Trees and Shrubs
Grassland and Savanna
Steppe and Scrub
Desert
Alpine and High Plateau

Projection: *Lambert's Equivalent Azimuthal*

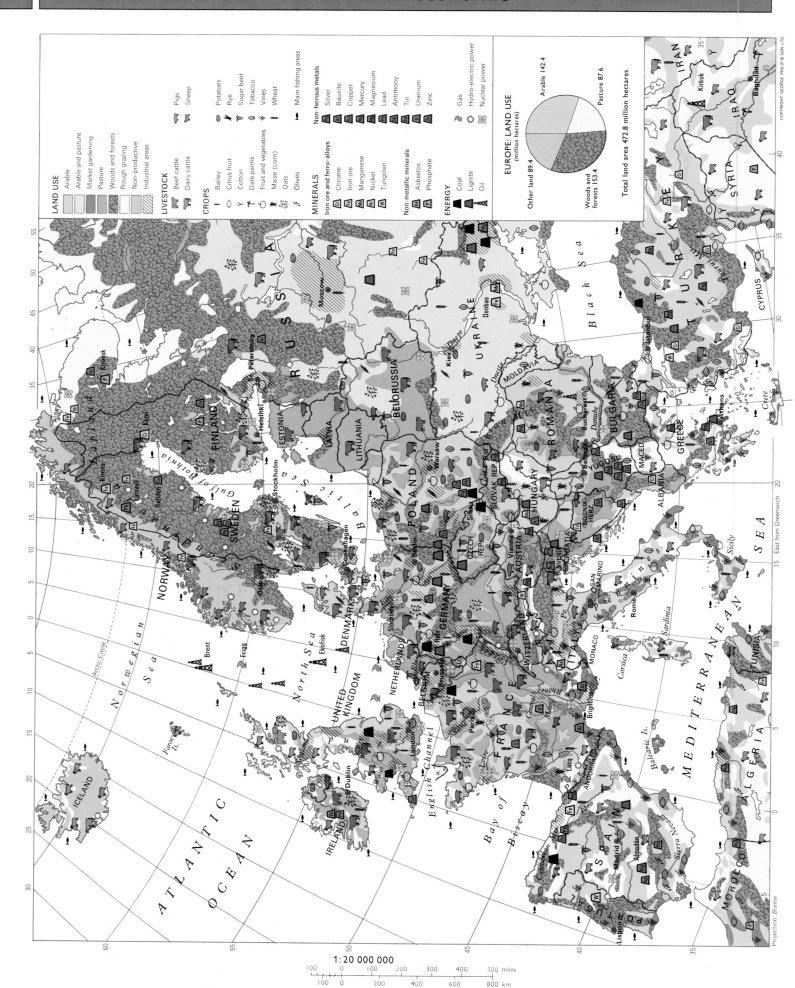

LAND USE
- Arable
- Arable and pasture
- Market gardening
- Pasture
- Woods and forests
- Rough grazing
- Non-productive
- Industrial areas

LIVESTOCK
- Beef cattle
- Dairy cattle
- Pigs
- Sheep

CROPS
- Barley
- Citrus fruit
- Cotton
- Date palms
- Fruit and vegetables
- Maize (corn)
- Oats
- Olives
- Potatoes
- Rye
- Sugar beet
- Tobacco
- Vines
- Wheat
- Main fishing areas

MINERALS

Iron ore and ferro-alloys
- Chrome
- Iron ore
- Manganese
- Nickel
- Tungsten

Non-ferrous metals
- Silver
- Bauxite
- Copper
- Mercury
- Magnesium
- Lead
- Antimony
- Tin
- Uranium
- Zinc

Non-metallic minerals
- Asbestos
- Phosphate

ENERGY
- Coal
- Lignite
- Oil
- Gas
- Hydro-electric power
- Nuclear power

EUROPE: LAND USE
(million hectares)

Arable 142.4
Pasture 87.6
Woods and forests 153.4
Other land 89.4

Total land area 472.8 million hectares

Scale 1:20 000 000

Projection: Bonne

East from Greenwich

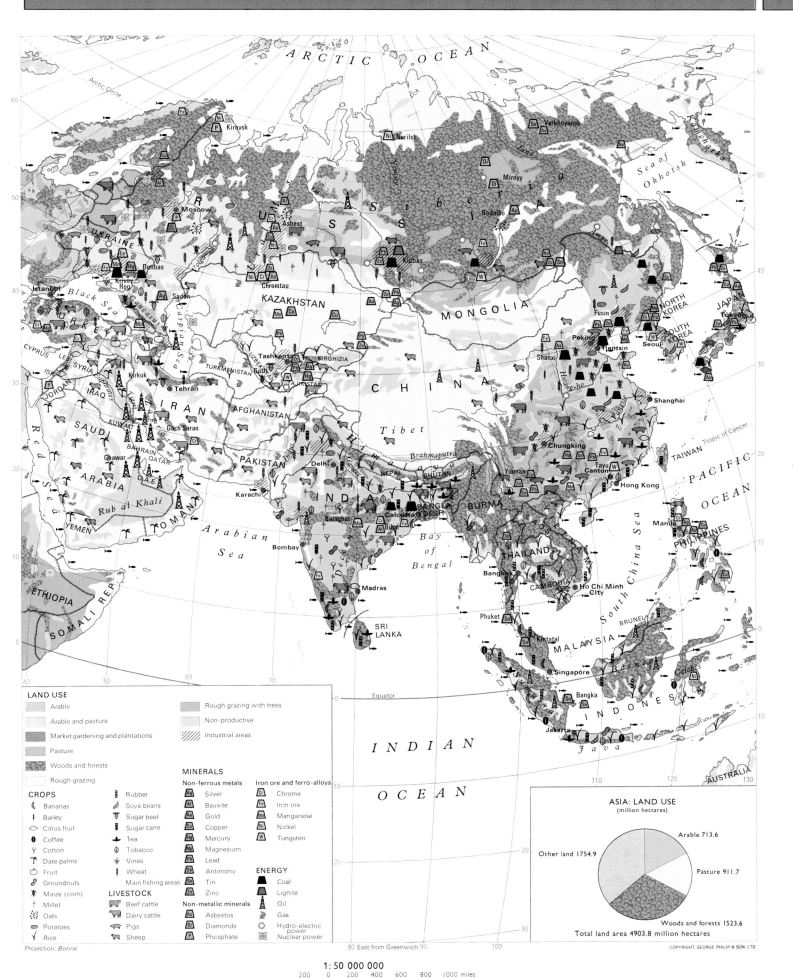

LAND USE

- Arable
- Arable and pasture
- Market gardening and plantations
- Pasture
- Woods and forests
- Rough grazing
- Rough grazing with trees
- Non-productive
- Industrial areas

CROPS

Bananas	Rubber
Barley	Soya beans
Citrus fruit	Sugar beet
Coffee	Sugar cane
Cotton	Tea
Date palms	Tobacco
Fruit	Vines
Groundnuts	Wheat
Maize (corn)	Main fishing areas
Millet	
Oats	LIVESTOCK
Potatoes	Beef cattle
Rice	Dairy cattle
	Pigs
	Sheep

MINERALS

Non-ferrous metals

			Iron ore and ferro-alloys	
Ag	Silver		Cr	Chrome
Al	Bauxite		Fe	Iron ore
Au	Gold		Mn	Manganese
Cu	Copper		Ni	Nickel
Hg	Mercury		W	Tungsten
Mg	Magnesium			
Pb	Lead		ENERGY	
Sb	Antimony			Coal
Sn	Tin			Lignite
Zn	Zinc			Oil

Non-metallic minerals

As	Asbestos			Gas
Di	Diamonds			Hydro-electric power
P	Phosphate			Nuclear power

ASIA: LAND USE
(million hectares)

- Arable 713.6
- Pasture 911.7
- Woods and forests 1523.6
- Other land 1754.9

Total land area 4903.8 million hectares

Projection: *Bonne*

80 East from Greenwich 90   100

COPYRIGHT GEORGE PHILIP & SON. LTD

1:50 000 000

200 0 200 400 600 800 1000 miles

200 0 400 800 1200 1600 km

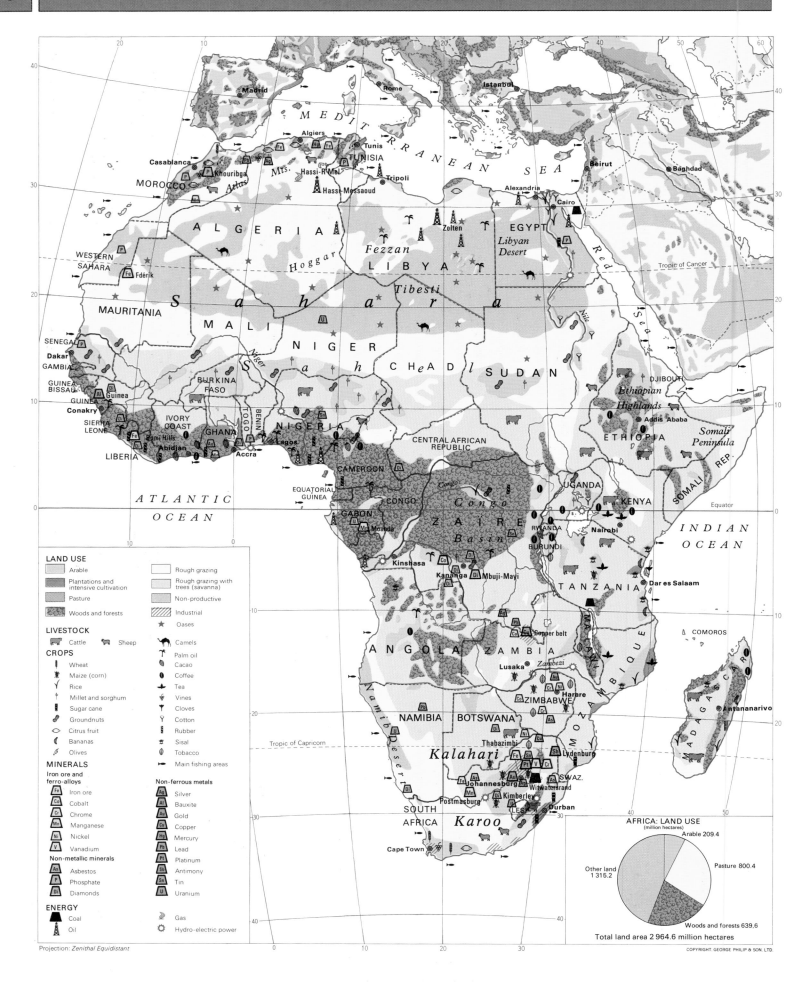

LAND USE

Arable

Plantations and intensive cultivation

Pasture

Woods and forests

Rough grazing

Rough grazing with trees (savanna)

Non-productive

Industrial

★ Oases

LIVESTOCK

Cattle   Sheep   Camels

CROPS

Wheat

Maize (corn)

Rice

Millet and sorghum

Sugar cane

Groundnuts

Citrus fruit

Bananas

Olives

Palm oil

Cacao

Coffee

Tea

Vines

Cloves

Cotton

Rubber

Sisal

Tobacco

Main fishing areas

MINERALS

Iron ore and ferro-alloys

Fe Iron ore
Co Cobalt
Cr Chrome
Mn Manganese
Ni Nickel
V   Vanadium

Non-metallic minerals

As Asbestos
P   Phosphate
Di Diamonds

Non-ferrous metals

Ag Silver
Al Bauxite
Au Gold
Cu Copper
Hg Mercury
Pb Lead
Pt Platinum
Sb Antimony
Sn Tin
U   Uranium

ENERGY

Coal

Oil

Gas

Hydro-electric power

AFRICA: LAND USE
(million hectares)

Arable 209.4

Pasture 800.4

Other land 1 315.2

Woods and forests 639.6

Total land area 2 964.6 million hectares

Projection: *Zenithal Equidistant*

COPYRIGHT. GEORGE. PHILIP & SON. LTD.

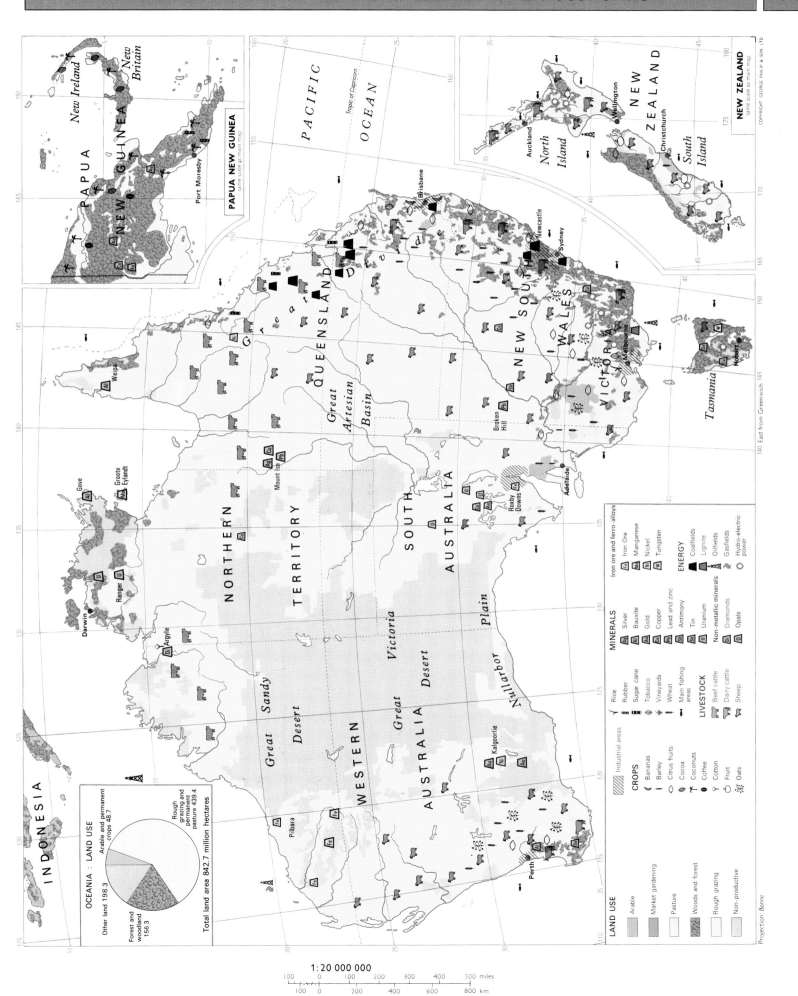

PAPUA NEW GUINEA
same scale as main map

NEW ZEALAND
same scale as main map

COPYRIGHT GEORGE PHILIP & SON, LTD

PACIFIC OCEAN

Tropic of Capricorn

New Ireland
New Britain
PAPUA NEW GUINEA
Port Moresby
INDONESIA

NEW ZEALAND
North Island
South Island
Auckland
Wellington
Christchurch

Brisbane
Newcastle
Sydney
NEW SOUTH WALES
VICTORIA
Melbourne
Broken Hill
Adelaide
Roxby Downs
SOUTH AUSTRALIA
QUEENSLAND
Great Artesian Basin
NORTHERN TERRITORY
WESTERN AUSTRALIA
Great Sandy Desert
Great Victoria Desert
Nullarbor Plain
Kalgoorlie
Perth
Pilbara
Argyle
Darwin
Ranger
Gove
Groote Eylandt
Weipa
Mount Isa
Tasmania
Hobart

140 East from Greenwich 145

OCEANIA : LAND USE

Other land 198.3

Arable and permanent crops 48.7

Rough grazing and permanent pasture 439.4

Forest and woodland 156.3

Total land area 842.7 million hectares

Projection: Bonne

Iron ore and ferro-alloys
- Fe Iron Ore
- Mn Manganese
- Ni Nickel
- W Tungsten

MINERALS
- Ag Silver
- Al Bauxite
- Au Gold
- Pb Lead and zinc
- Sb Antimony
- Sn Tin
- U Uranium
- Non-metallic minerals
- Diamonds
- Opals

ENERGY
- Coalfields
- Lignite
- Oilfields
- Gasfields
- Hydro-electric power

CROPS
- Industrial areas
- Bananas
- Barley
- Citrus fruits
- Cocoa
- Coconuts
- Coffee
- Cotton
- Fruit
- Oats
- Rice
- Rubber
- Sugar cane
- Tobacco
- Vineyards
- Wheat
- Main fishing areas

LIVESTOCK
- Beef cattle
- Dairy cattle
- Sheep

LAND USE
- Arable
- Market gardening
- Pasture
- Woods and forest
- Rough grazing
- Non-productive

1 : 20 000 000

100 0 100 200 300 400 500 miles
100 0 200 400 600 800 km

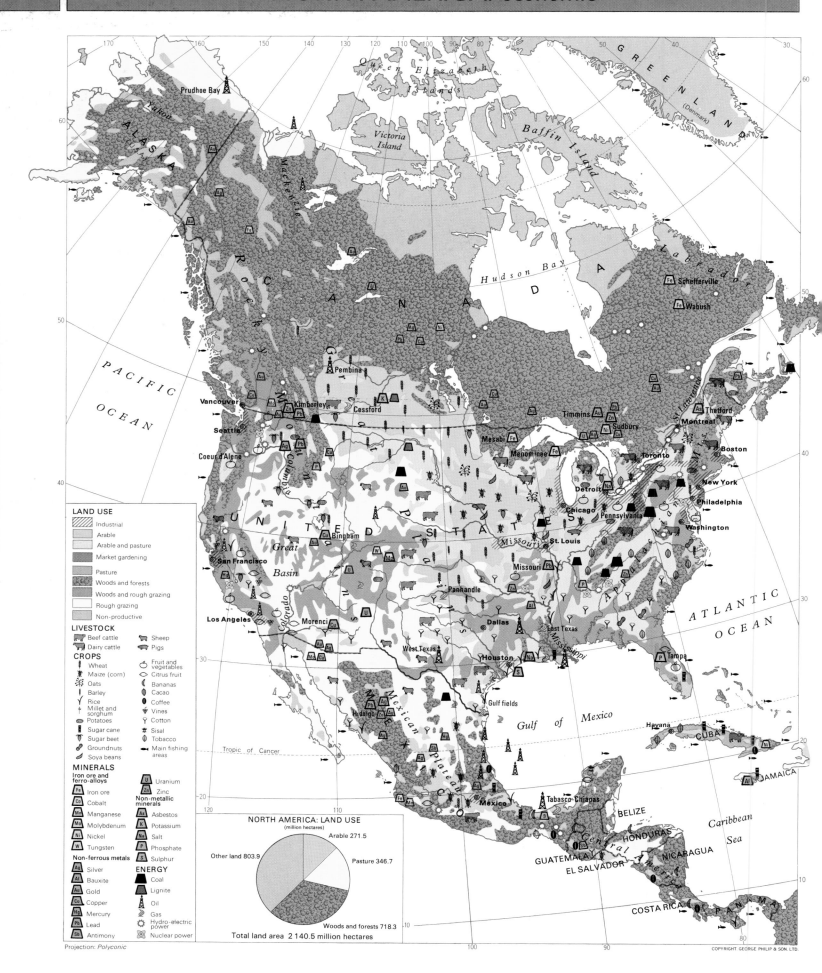

LAND USE

- Industrial
- Arable
- Arable and pasture
- Market gardening
- Pasture
- Woods and forests
- Woods and rough grazing
- Rough grazing
- Non-productive

LIVESTOCK

- Beef cattle
- Dairy cattle
- Sheep
- Pigs

CROPS

- Wheat
- Maize (corn)
- Oats
- Barley
- Rice
- Millet and sorghum
- Potatoes
- Sugar cane
- Sugar beet
- Groundnuts
- Soya beans
- Fruit and vegetables
- Citrus fruit
- Bananas
- Cacao
- Coffee
- Vines
- Cotton
- Sisal
- Tobacco
- Main fishing areas

MINERALS

Iron ore and ferro-alloys

- Fe Iron ore
- Co Cobalt
- Mn Manganese
- Mo Molybdenum
- Ni Nickel
- W Tungsten

Non-ferrous metals

- Ag Silver
- Al Bauxite
- Au Gold
- Cu Copper
- Hg Mercury
- Pb Lead
- Sb Antimony
- U Uranium
- Zn Zinc

Non-metallic minerals

- As Asbestos
- K Potassium
- Ne Salt
- P Phosphate
- S Sulphur

ENERGY

- Coal
- Lignite
- Oil
- Gas
- Hydro-electric power
- Nuclear power

NORTH AMERICA: LAND USE
(million hectares)

- Arable 271.5
- Pasture 346.7
- Other land 803.9
- Woods and forests 718.3

Total land area 2 140.5 million hectares

Projection: *Polyconic*

SOUTH AMERICA: LAND USE
(million hectares)

Other land 283.5
Arable 104.1
Pasture 441.8
Woods and forests 924.3

Total land area 1 753.7 million hectares

LAND USE

- Industrial
- Arable
- Market gardening and plantations
- Pasture
- Woods and forests
- Rough grazing
- Non-productive

LIVESTOCK

- Beef cattle
- Sheep
- Dairy cattle
- Pigs

CROPS

- Wheat
- Coconut palms
- Maize (corn)
- Cacao
- Rice
- Coffee
- Millet and sorghum
- Tea
- Potatoes
- Vines
- Sugar cane
- Cotton
- Groundnuts
- Rubber
- Fruit and vegetables
- Tobacco
- Citrus fruit
- Main fishing areas
- Bananas

MINERALS

Iron ore and ferro-alloys
- Fe Iron ore
- Cr Chrome
- Mn Manganese
- Mo Molybdenum
- W Tungsten

Non-metallic minerals
- Saltpetre

Non-ferrous metals
- Ag Silver
- Al Bauxite
- Au Gold
- Cu Copper
- Pb Lead
- Sb Antimony
- Sn Tin
- Zn Zinc

ENERGY

- Coal
- Nuclear power
- Oil
- Gas
- Hydro-electric power

Projection: *Lambert's Equivalent Azimuthal*

COPYRIGHT GEORGE PHILIP & SON LTD

Wheat

The most important grain crop in the temperate regions though it is also grown in a variety of climates e.g. in Monsoon lands as a winter crop.

World production 1990
595.7 million tonnes

Oats

Widely grown in temperate regions with the limit fixed by early autumn frosts. Mainly fed to cattle. The best quality oats are used for oatmeal, porridge and breakfast foods.

World production 1990
43.8 million tonnes

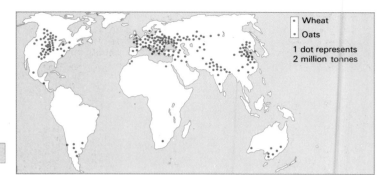

Wheat
Oats
1 dot represents
2 million tonnes

Rye

The hardiest of cereals and more resistant to cold, pests and disease than wheat. An important foodstuff in Central and E. Europe.

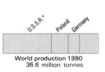

World production 1990
36.6 million tonnes

Maize (or Corn)

Needs plenty of sunshine, summer rain or irrigation and frost free for 6 months. Important as animal feed and for human food in Africa, Latin America and as a vegetable and breakfast cereal.

World production 1990
468.8 million tonnes

Rye
Maize
1 dot represents
2 million tonnes

Barley

Has the widest range of cultivation requiring only 8 weeks between seed time and harvest. Used mainly as animal-feed and by the malting industry.

World production 1990
181.2 million tonnes

Rice

The staple food of half the human race. The main producing areas are the flood plains and hill terraces of S. and E. Asia where water is abundant in the growing season.

World production 1990
520.5 million tonnes

Barley
Rice
1 dot represents
2 million tonnes

Millets

The name given to a number of related members of the grass family, of which sorghum is one of the most important. They provide nutritious grain.

World production 1990
89.2 million tonnes

Potatoes

An important food crop though less nutritious weight for weight than grain crops. Requires a temperate climate with a regular and plentiful supply of rain.

World production 1990
268.4 million tonnes

Millets
Potatoes
1 dot represents
2 million tonnes

Vegetable oilseeds and oils

Despite the increasing use of synthetic chemical products and animal and marine fats, vegetable oils extracted from these crops grow in quantity, value and importance. Food is the major use- in margarine and cooking fats.

Groundnuts are also a valuable subsistence crop and the meal is used as animal feed. Soya-bean meal is a growing source of protein for humans and animals. The Mediterranean lands are the prime source of olive oil.

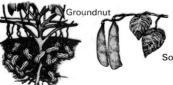

Groundnut

Soya bean

Sunflower

Groundnuts
Soya beans
Sunflower seed
1 dot represents
1 million tonnes

Statistics for each of the new republics of the former U.S.S.R. and Yugoslavia are not yet available.

Tea and cacao
Tea requires plentiful rainfall and well-drained, sloping ground, whereas cacao prefers a moist heavy soil. Both are grown mainly for export.

Coffee
Prefers a hot climate, wet and dry seasons and an elevated location. It is very susceptible to frost, drought and market fluctuations.

Brazil / Colombia / Indonesia
World production 1990
6.0 million tonnes

Tea
Cacao
Coffee
1 dot represents 100 000 tonnes

Sugar beet
Requires a deep, rich soil and a temperate climate. Europe produces over 90 % of the world's beets mainly for domestic consumption.

U.S.S.R.* / France / Germany / U.S.A.
World production 1990
307.7 million tonnes

Sugar cane
Also requires deep and rich soil but a tropical climate. It produces a much higher yield per hectare than beet and is grown primarily for export.

Brazil / India / Cuba
World production 1990
1044.3 million tonnes

Sugar beet
Sugar cane
1 dot represents 10 million tonnes

Fruit
With the improvements in canning, drying and freezing, and in transport and marketing, the international trade and consumption of deciduous and soft fruits, citrus fruits and tropical fruits has greatly increased. Recent developments in the use of the peel will give added value to some of the fruit crops.

Fish
Commercial fishing requires large shoals of fish of one species within reach of markets. Freshwater fishing is also important. A rich source of protein, fish will become an increasingly valuable food source.

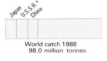

Japan / U.S.S.R.* / China
World catch 1988
98.0 million tonnes

Temperate fruit
Citrus fruit
Principal fishing grounds

Beef cattle
Australia, New Zealand and Argentina provide the major part of international beef exports. Western U.S.A. and Europe have considerable production of beef for their local high demand.

U.S.A. / U.S.S.R.* / Argentina
World production 1989
49.4 million tonnes of meat

Dairy cattle
The need of herds for a rich diet and for nearby markets result in dairying being characteristic of densely-populated areas of the temperate zones – U.S.A., N.W. Europe, and S.E. Australia.

U.S.S.R.* / U.S.A. / Germany
World production 1989
474.0 million tonnes of milk

Cattle
1 dot represents 10 million head
Dairy produce

Sheep
Raised mostly for wool and meat, their skins and the cheese from their milk are important products in some countries. The merino yields a fine wool and crossbreeds are best for meat.

U.S.S.R.* / New Zealand
World production 1990
6.5 million tonnes of meat

Pigs
Can be reared in most climates from monsoon to cool temperate. They are abundant in China, the Corn Belt of the U.S.A. N.W. and C. Europe, Brazil and Russia.

China / U.S.A. / U.S.S.R.* / Germany
World production 1990
67.1 million tonnes of meat

Sheep
Pigs
1 dot represents 10 million head

COPYRIGHT GEORGE PHILIP & SON LTD.

*Statistics for each of the new republics of the former U.S.S.R. and Yugoslavia are not yet available.

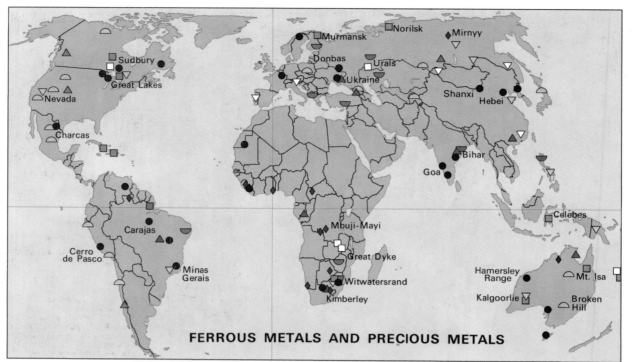

FERROUS METALS AND PRECIOUS METALS

Projection: *Modified Hammer Equal Area*

Precious Metals

▽ **Gold**
World total (1990)
1 750 tonnes

South Africa	34.9%
U.S.A.	16.9%
U.S.S.R.	16.0%
Australia	13.8%
Canada	9.4%

⌂ **Silver**
World total (1990)
14 654 tonnes

Mexico	15.7%
U.S.A.	13.7%
Peru	12.6%
U.S.S.R.	10.2%
Canada	8.9%

◆ **Diamonds**
World total (1990)
108 000 000 carats

Australia	33.3%
Zaire	22.2%
Botswana	16.0%
U.S.S.R.	13.9%
South Africa	7.9%

● **Iron Ore** World total (1990) 962 000 000 tonnes	■ **Nickel** World total (1990) 865 000 tonnes	◗ **Chrome** World total (1990) 12 000 tonnes	▲ **Manganese** World total (1990) 24 000 tonnes	☐ **Cobalt** World total (1988) 43 900 tonnes	▲ **Molybdenum** World total (1988) 94 700 tonnes	▽ **Tungsten** World total (1990) 45 000 tonnes
U.S.S.R. 14.8%	U.S.S.R. 24.3%	South Africa 35.0%	U.S.S.R. 37.5%	Zaire 57.9%	U.S.A. 45.4%	China 44.4%
Brazil 10.9%	Canada 23.5%	U.S.S.R. 31.7%	South Africa 15.8%	Zambia 15.3%	Chile 18.0%	U.S.S.R. 15.6%
China 8.8%	New Caledonia 11.1%	India 6.3%	China 11.3%	U.S.S.R. 6.6%	Canada 13.1%	Mongolia 3.3%
Australia 7.3%	Australia 7.5%	Albania 5.8%	Australia 9.6%	Canada 5.7%	U.S.S.R. 12.1%	Austria 3.1%
U.S.A. 3.6%	Indonesia 6.9%	Turkey 5.0%	Gabon 9.2%	New Caledonia 4.8%	Mexico 4.5%	Portugal 3.1%

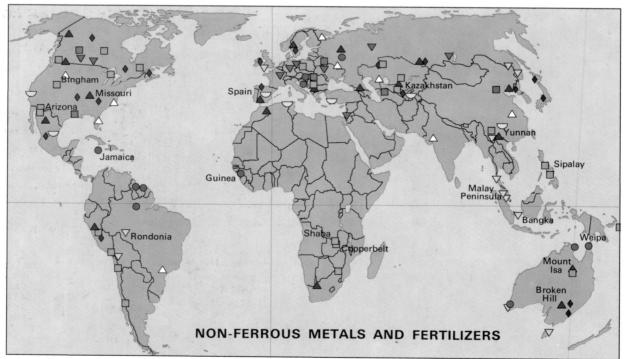

NON-FERROUS METALS AND FERTILIZERS

Fertilizers

■ **Nitrates**
World total (1989)
85 151 000 tonnes

U.S.S.R.	18.3%
China	16.4%
U.S.A.	14.9%
Hungary	7.9%
Canada	3.2%

△ **Phosphates**
World total (1989)
41 532,000 tonnes

U.S.A.	22.9%
U.S.S.R.	22.0%
China	9.1%
India	5.5%
Brazil	3.4%

▽ **Potash**
World total (1989)
31 151 000 tonnes

U.S.S.R.	36.3%
Canada	26.0%
Germany	18.5%
France	4.5%
Israel	3.9%

☐ **Copper** World total (1989) 9 129 000 tonnes	▲ **Lead** World total (1989) 3 341 000 tonnes	● **Bauxite** World total (1989) 106 560 000 tonnes	▽ **Tin** World total (1989) 223 000 tonnes	◆ **Zinc** World total (1989) 7 138 000 tonnes	◗ **Mercury** World total (1990) 5 541 tonnes
Chile 17.6%	U.S.S.R. 15.0%	Australia 36.2%	Brazil 22.5%	Canada 17.0%	U.S.S.R. 45.1%
U.S.A. 17.3%	Australia 14.8%	Guinea 16.4%	China 14.8%	U.S.S.R. 13.2%	China 18.8%
U.S.S.R. 10.4%	U.S.A. 12.5%	Jamaica 8.8%	Malaysia 14.3%	Australia 11.2%	Spain 12.9%
Canada 8.0%	China 10.2%	Brazil 7.4%	Indonesia 14.0%	China 8.7%	Algeria 12.6%
Zambia 5.5%	Canada 8.2%	U.S.S.R. 5.4%	Bolivia 7.1%	Peru 8.4%	Mexico 3.5%

Statistics for each of the new republics of the former U.S.S.R. and Yugoslavia are not yet available.

Some countries are highly dependent upon minerals. The following are dependent on metals and minerals for over 50% of the value of their exports:
Zambia 93%,
New Caledonia 81%,
Zaire 55%.

ENERGY PRODUCTION

Primary energy production
expressed in kilograms
of coal equivalent per
person 1989

Over 10 000 kg per person

1 000-10 000 kg per person

100-1 000 kg per person

10-100 kg per person

Under 10 kg per person

● Oil

▽ Natural gas

▲ Coal and lignite

◇ Uranium *(the fuel used to generate nuclear power)*

In developing countries traditional fuels are still very important. Sometimes called biomass fuels, they include wood, charcoal and dried dung. The pie graph for Nigeria at the foot of the page shows their importance.

Projection: Modified Hammer Equal Area

Top 5 producers for each primary energy source with percentage of World production 1990

Oil World total (1990) 3 150 000 000 tonnes		Natural Gas World total (1990) 3 007 075 tonnes		Coal (bituminous) World total (1990) 3 562 000 000 tonnes		Brown Coal (lignite) World total (1990) 1 176 000 000 tonnes		Uranium World total (1990) 37 000 tonnes		Nuclear Power World total (1990) 461 100 000 tonnes of oil equivalent		Hydro-Electric Power World total (1990) 540 600 000 tonnes of oil equivalent	
U.S.S.R.	18.1%	U.S.S.R.	37.2%	China	29.5%	Germany	30.4%	Canada	23.0%	U.S.A.	33.8%	U.S.A.	13.3%
U.S.A.	13.2%	U.S.A.	25.2%	U.S.A.	24.2%	U.S.S.R.	13.4%	U.S.S.R.	12.5%	France	13.3%	Canada	11.8%
Saudi Arabia	10.4%	Canada	5.0%	U.S.S.R.	13.3%	Czechoslovakia	7.3%	Germany	11.8%	Japan	10.6%	U.S.S.R.	10.3%
Iran	4.9%	Netherlands	3.1%	India	5.6%	U.S.A.	7.0%	U.S.A.	10.4%	U.S.S.R.	9.4%	Brazil	8.8%
China	4.4%	U.K.	2.3%	South Africa	5.1%	China	9.6%	Australia	7.4%	Germany	7.2%	China	5.8%

ENERGY CONSUMPTION

Primary energy consumption
expressed in kilograms
of coal equivalent per
person 1989

Over 10 000 kg per person

5 000-10 000 kg per person

1 000-5 000 kg per person

100-1 000 kg per person

Under 100 kg per person

Energy Consumption by Continent 1990

		Change 1989-90
Europe*	38.5%	(-2.6%)
North America	27.6%	(-0.2%)
Asia	23.9%	(+4.9%)
South America	5.9%	(+3.7%)
Africa	2.8%	(+2.6%)
Australasia	1.3%	(+2.7%)
*includes U.S.S.R.		

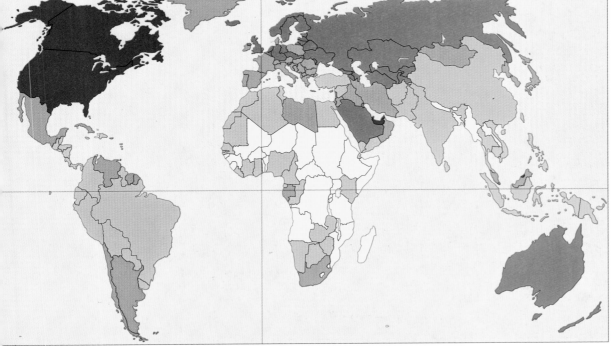

TYPE OF ENERGY CONSUMED BY SELECTED COUNTRIES

Coal and Lignite / Oil / Natural Gas / Hydro-electricity / Nuclear electricity / Traditional Fuels

NIGERIA · CHINA · JAPAN · FRANCE · U.S.A. · NORWAY

Statistics for each of the new republics of the former U.S.S.R. and Yugoslavia are not yet available.

COPYRIGHT GEORGE PHILIP LTD

AGE DISTRIBUTION PYRAMIDS

The bars represent the percentage of the total population (males plus females) in the age group shown.
Developed countries such as the U.K. have populations evenly spread across age groups and usually a growing percentage of elderly people. Developing countries such as Kenya have the great majority of their people in the younger age groups, about to enter their most fertile years.

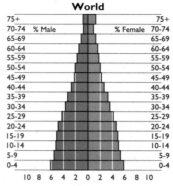

World

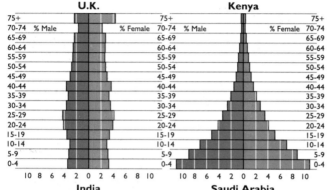

U.K.   **Kenya**

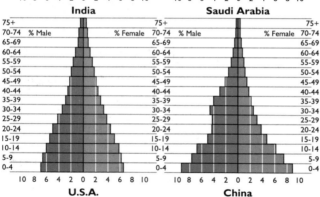

India   **Saudi Arabia**

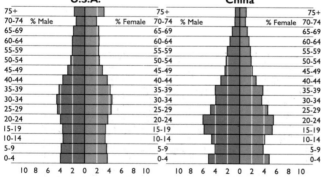

U.S.A.   **China**

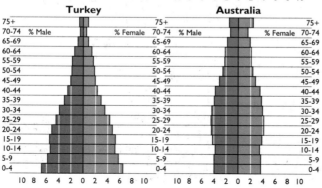

Turkey   **Australia**

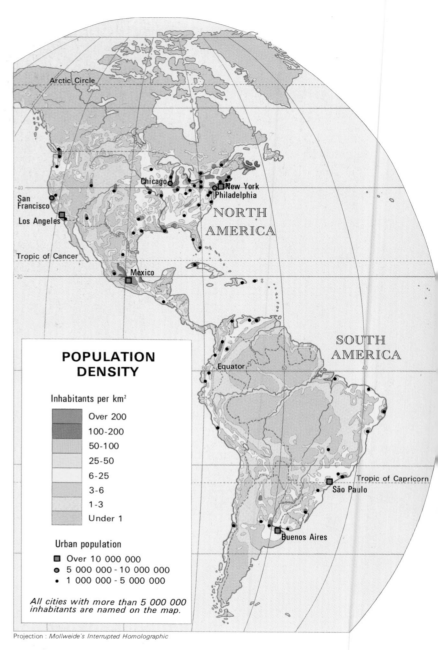

POPULATION DENSITY

Inhabitants per km²

- Over 200
- 100-200
- 50-100
- 25-50
- 6-25
- 3-6
- 1-3
- Under 1

Urban population

- ■ Over 10 000 000
- ◉ 5 000 000 - 10 000 000
- • 1 000 000 - 5 000 000

All cities with more than 5 000 000 inhabitants are named on the map.

Projection : *Mollweide's Interrupted Homolographic*

POPULATION CHANGE 1930-2020   Population totals are in millions

Figures in italics represent the percentage average annual increase for the period show

	1930	1930– 1960	1960	1960– 1990	1990	1990– 2020	2020
World	2013	*1.4%*	3019	*1.9%*	5292	*1.4%*	8062
Africa	155	*2.0%*	281	*2.8%*	648	*2.7%*	1441
North America	135	*1.3%*	199	*1.1%*	276	*0.6%*	327
Latin America*	129	*1.8%*	218	*2.4%*	448	*1.6%*	719
Asia	1073	*1.5%*	1669	*2.1%*	3108	*1.4%*	4680
Europe	355	*0.6%*	425	*0.5%*	498	*0.1%*	514
Oceania	10	*1.4%*	16	*1.7%*	27	*1.1%*	37
C.I.S. †	176	*0.7%*	214	*1.0%*	288	*0.6%*	343

* South America plus Central America, Mexico and the West Indies
† Commonwealth of Independent States, formerly the U.S.S.R.

1 : 105 000 000

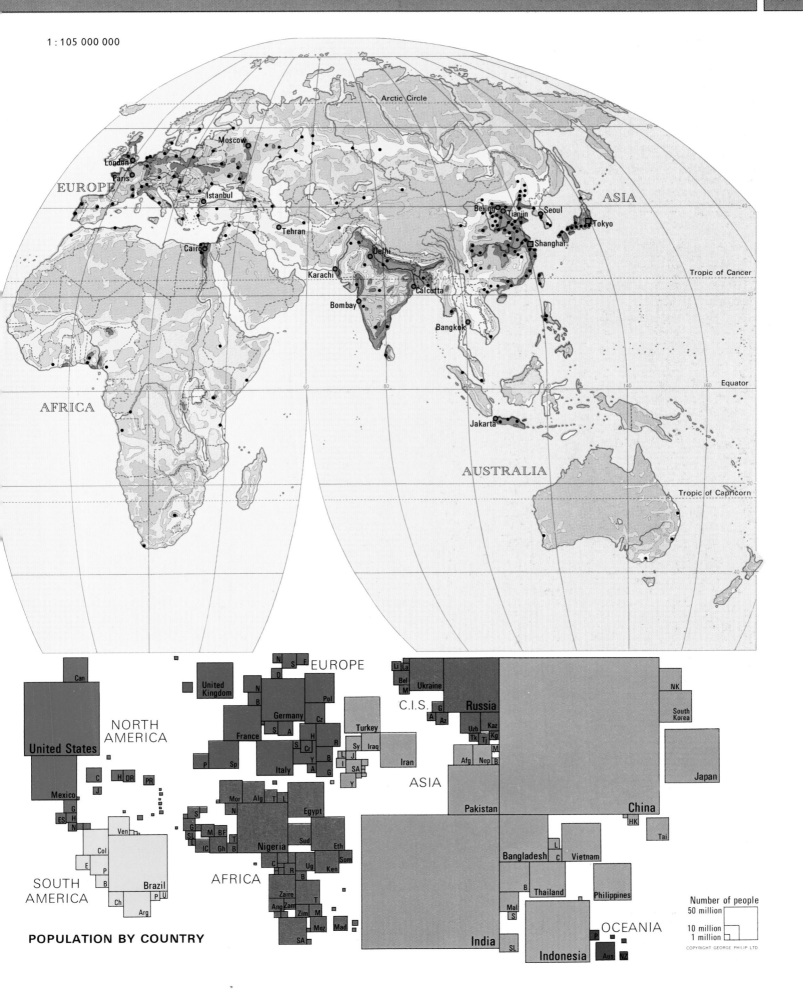

EUROPE

Moscow

London
Paris

Istanbul

Tehran

Cairo

ASIA

Beijing
Tianjin
Seoul
Tokyo
Shanghai

Delhi

Karachi

Calcutta

Bombay

Bangkok

AFRICA

Jakarta

AUSTRALIA

Arctic Circle

Tropic of Cancer

Equator

Tropic of Capricorn

POPULATION BY COUNTRY

NORTH AMERICA

Can

United States

Mexico

United Kingdom

EUROPE

Germany

France

Italy

Turkey

Iran

C.I.S.

Ukraine

Russia

ASIA

Pakistan

China

Japan

South Korea

NK

SOUTH AMERICA

Brazil

Ven

Col

AFRICA

Nigeria

Egypt

Sud

Eth

India

Bangladesh

Vietnam

Thailand

Philippines

Indonesia

OCEANIA

Number of people

50 million

10 million

1 million

COPYRIGHT GEORGE PHILIP LTD.

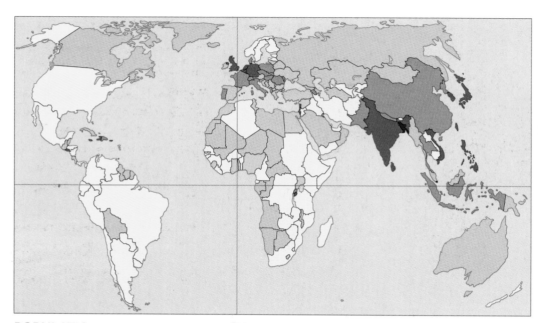

POPULATION DENSITY BY COUNTRY

Density of people per square kilometre 1991*

▮	Over 500 people per km²
▮	200-500 people per km²
▮	100-200 people per km²
▮	50-100 people per km²
▯	10-50 people per km²
▯	Under 10 people per km²

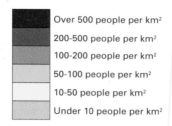

Top 5 countries		Bottom 5 countries	
Macau	24 850 per km²	Mauritania	2.0 per km²
Hong Kong	5 960 per km²	Mongolia	1.5 per km²
Singapore	4 667 per km²	French Guiana	1.1 per km²
Gibraltar	3 000 per km²	Congo	0.7 per km²
Malta	1 333 per km²	Greenland	0.2 per km²

U.K. 238 per km²

POPULATION CHANGE 1990-2000

Expected percentage population change between 1990 and 2000*

▮	Over 40% population gain
▮	30 - 40% population gain
▮	20 - 30% population gain
▯	10 - 20% population gain
▯	0 - 10% population gain
▮	No change or population loss

Top 5 countries		Bottom 5 countries	
Afghanistan	+60%	Hungary	-0.2%
Mali	+56%	Singapore	-0.2%
Tanzania	+55%	Grenada	-2.4%
Ivory Coast	+47%	Tonga	-3.2%
Saudi Arabia	+46%	Germany	-3.2%

U.K. +2.0%

URBAN POPULATION

Percentage of total population living in towns and cities 1990*

▮	Over 80%
▮	60 - 80%
▮	40 - 60%
▯	20 - 40%
▯	Under 20%

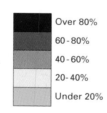

Most urbanized		Least urbanized	
Singapore	100%	Nepal	10%
Belgium	97%	Burkina Faso	9%
Kuwait	96%	Rwanda	8%
Hong Kong	93%	Burundi	7%
U.K.	93%	Bhutan	5%

Projection: Modified Hammer Equal Area

* Statistics for each of the new republics of the former U.S.S.R. and Yugoslavia are not yet available. The map shows the statistics for the entire U.S.S.R. and Yugoslavia.

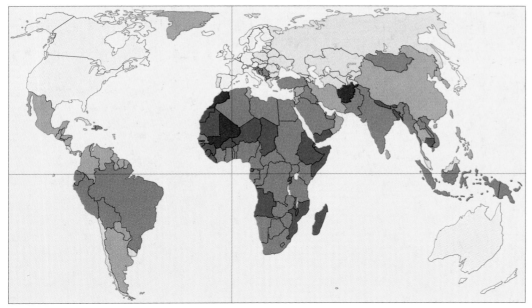

CHILD MORTALITY

The number of babies who will die
under the age of one, per 1 000 births
(average 1990-95)*

Over 150 deaths per 1 000 births

100-150 deaths per 1 000 births

50-100 deaths per 1 000 births

20-50 deaths per 1 000 births

10-20 deaths per 1 000 births

Under 10 deaths per 1 000 births

Highest child mortality		Lowest child mortality	
Afghanistan	162 deaths	Hong Kong	6 deaths
Mali	159 deaths	Denmark	6 deaths
Sierra Leone	143 deaths	Japan	5 deaths
Guinea-Bissau	140 deaths	Iceland	5 deaths
Malawi	138 deaths	Finland	5 deaths
		U.K.	8 deaths

LIFE EXPECTANCY

Average expected lifespan in years
of babies born in the period 1990-95*

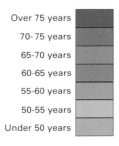

Over 75 years

70-75 years

65-70 years

60-65 years

55-60 years

50-55 years

Under 50 years

Highest life expectancy		Lowest life expectancy	
Japan	79 years	Gambia	45 years
Iceland	78 years	Guinea	45 years
Sweden	78 years	Afghanistan	44 years
Hong Kong	78 years	Guinea-Bissau	44 years
Switzerland	78 years	Sierra Leone	43 years
		U.K.	76 years

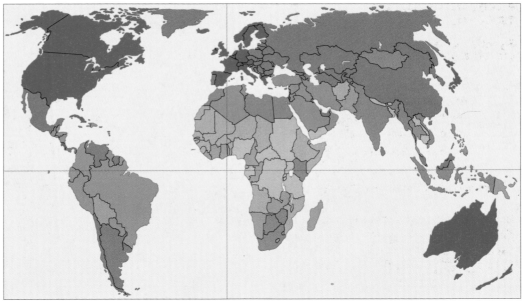

FAMILY SIZE

The average number of children a woman
can expect to bear during her lifetime 1990*

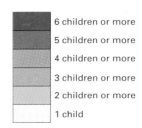

6 children or more

5 children or more

4 children or more

3 children or more

2 children or more

1 child

*In the U.K. the average family size is 1.8
children per family, whilst in Kenya
the average size is 6.8 children.*

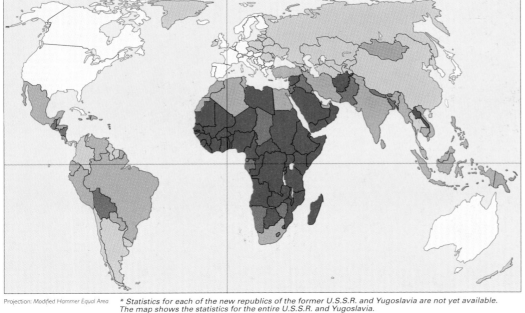

Projection: Modified Hammer Equal Area   * Statistics for each of the new republics of the former U.S.S.R. and Yugoslavia are not yet available.
The map shows the statistics for the entire U.S.S.R. and Yugoslavia.

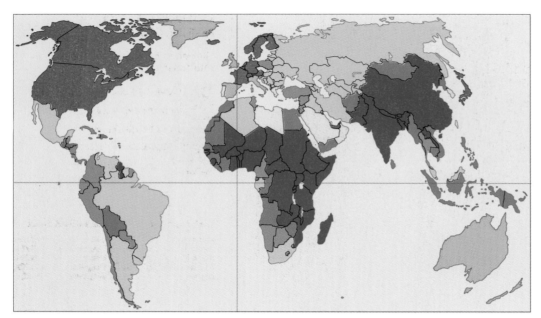

WEALTH

The value of total production divided by population 1989*
(Gross National Product per capita)

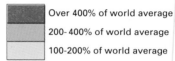

- Over 400% of world average
- 200- 400% of world average
- 100-200% of world average

World average wealth per person = US$ 3 980

- 50-100% of world average
- 25-50% of world average
- 10-25% of world average
- Under 10% of world average

Richest 5 countries		Poorest 5 countries	
Switzerland	$30 270	Nepal	$170
Luxembourg	$24 860	Somalia	$170
Japan	$23 730	Ethiopia	$120
Finland	$22 060	Tanzania	$120
Norway	$21 850	Mozambique	$80
		U.K.	$14 570

INTERNATIONAL AID

Aid provided or received, divided by total population (latest available year)*

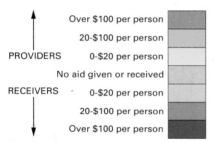

	Over $100 per person
	20-$100 per person
PROVIDERS	0-$20 per person
	No aid given or received
RECEIVERS	0-$20 per person
	20-$100 per person
	Over $100 per person

Top 5 providers		Top 5 receivers	
Norway	$218	Seychelles	$515
Sweden	$212	Vanuatu	$333
Denmark	$184	São Tomé & Principe	$311
Finland	$141	Samoa	$308
Netherlands	$139	Djibouti	$293
U.K.	$45		

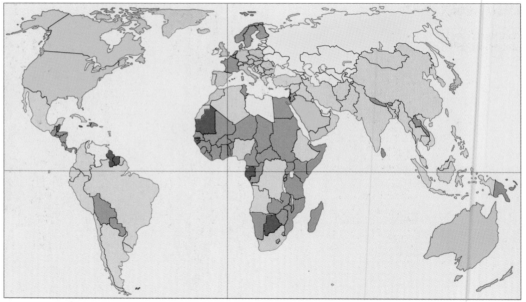

ILLITERACY

Percentage of total population unable to read or write (latest available year)*

- Over 75% of population illiterate
- 50 - 75% of population illiterate
- 25-50% of population illiterate
- 10 - 25% of population illiterate
- Under 10% of population illiterate

Most illiterate countries		Least illiterate countries	
Somalia	88%	Canada	5%
Burkina Faso	87%	Denmark	5%
Niger	86%	Finland	5%
Bhutan	85%	Guyana	4%
Mali	83%	Trinidad & Tob.	4%
		U.K.	1%

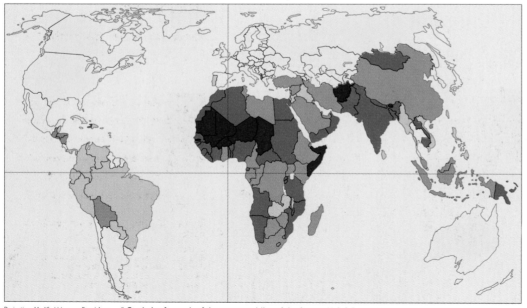

Projection: Modified Hammer Equal Area

* Statistics for each of the new republics of the former U.S.S.R. and Yugoslavia are not yet available. The map shows the statistics for the entire U.S.S.R. and Yugoslavia.

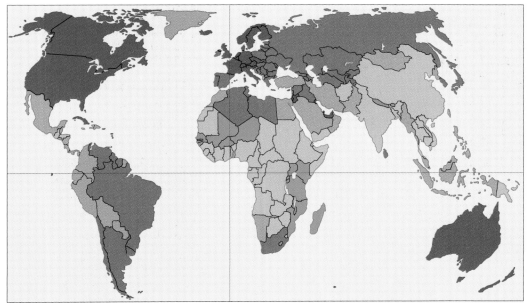

THE IMPORTANCE OF AGRICULTURE

The percentage of the total population who depend on agriculture 1990*

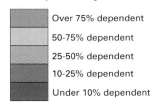

Over 75% dependent

50-75% dependent

25-50% dependent

10-25% dependent

Under 10% dependent

Top 5 countries		Bottom 5 countries	
Nepal	92%	U.K.	2.0%
Rwanda	91%	Belgium	1.8%
Burundi	91%	Bahrain	1.7%
Bhutan	91%	Hong Kong	1.2%
Niger	87%	Singapore	1.0%

FOOD CONSUMPTION

Daily food intake in calories per person 1986-88 average*

Over 3 500 calories per person per day

3 000-3 500 calories per person per day

2 500-3 000 calories per person per day

2 000-2 500 calories per person per day

Under 2 000 calories per person per day

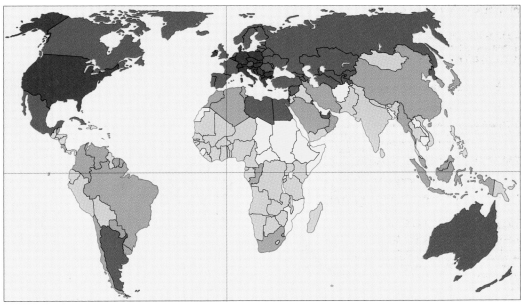

Top 5 countries		Bottom 5 countries	
Belgium	3 901 cal.	Bangladesh	1 925 cal.
Greece	3 702 cal.	Rwanda	1 817 cal.
Ireland	3 688 cal.	Sierra Leone	1 813 cal.
Bulgaria	3 650 cal.	Somalia	1 781 cal.
Germany	3 650 cal.	Mozambique	1 604 cal.

U.K.   3 256 cal.

HEALTH CARE

Number of people per doctor 1990*

Over 25 000 people per doctor

10 000-25 000 people per doctor

5 000-10 000 people per doctor

1 000-5 000 people per doctor

500-1 000 people per doctor

Under 500 people per doctor

Most people per doctor		Fewest people per doctor	
Ethiopia	60 000	Hungary	310
Burkina Faso	57 220	Czechoslovakia	280
Guinea	46 420	Bulgaria	280
Niger	39 730	Former U.S.S.R.	250
Chad	38 360	Italy	230

U.K.   620

Projection: *Modified Hammer Equal Area*   * *Statistics for each of the new republics of the former U.S.S.R. and Yugoslavia are not yet available. The map shows the statistics for the entire U.S.S.R. and Yugoslavia.*

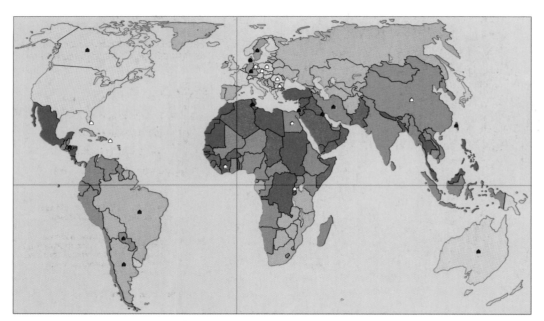

HOUSING

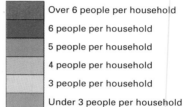

Number of people per household
(latest available year)*

	Over 6 people per household
	6 people per household
	5 people per household
	4 people per household
	3 people per household
	Under 3 people per household

Expenditure on housing and energy as a
percentage of total consumer spending

▲　　Over 20% spent

△　　Under 5% spent

WATER SUPPLY

Percentage of total population
with access to safe drinking water
(latest available year)*

Over 90% with safe water	
75-90% with safe water	
60-75% with safe water	
45-60% with safe water	
30-45% with safe water	
Under 30% with safe water	

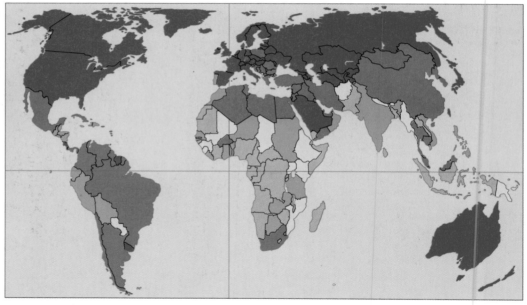

CAR OWNERSHIP

Number of people per car
(latest available year)*

	Over 1000 people per car
	500-1000 people per car
	100-500 people per car
	25-100 people per car
	5-25 people per car
	Under 5 people per car

Most people per car		Most cars (millions)	
China	4300	U.S.A.	140.7
Mauritania	3400	Japan	30.8
Bangladesh	2053	Germany	29.2
Nepal	2000	France	27.0
Togo	1237	Italy	23.5

Projection: Modified Hammer Equal Area

* Statistics for each of the new republics of the former U.S.S.R. and Yugoslavia are not yet available.
The map shows the statistics for the entire U.S.S.R. and Yugoslavia.

TYPE OF WORK

Percentage of total workforce employed in agriculture† (latest available year)*

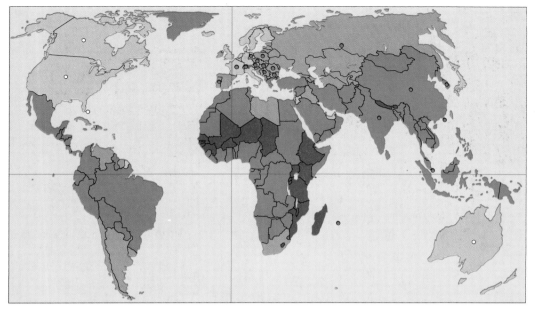

	Over 75% in agriculture
	50 - 75% in agriculture
	25 - 50% in agriculture
	10 - 25% in agriculture
	Under 10% in agriculture

● Over 25% of total workforce employed in manufacturing

○ Over 75% of total workforce employed in service industries (work in offices, shops, tourism, transport, construction and government)

† Includes forestry and fishing

WOMEN IN THE WORKFORCE

Working women as a percentage of the total workforce (latest available year)*

Over 40% are women	
30 - 40% are women	
20 - 30% are women	
10 - 20% are women	
Under 10% are women	

Most women in the workforce		Fewest women in the workforce	
Burundi	48%	U.A.E.	6%
Former U.S.S.R.	48%	Saudi Arabia	7%
Mozambique	48%	Bangladesh	7%
Tanzania	48%	Qatar	7%
Benin	48%	Algeria	8%
	U.K.	39%	

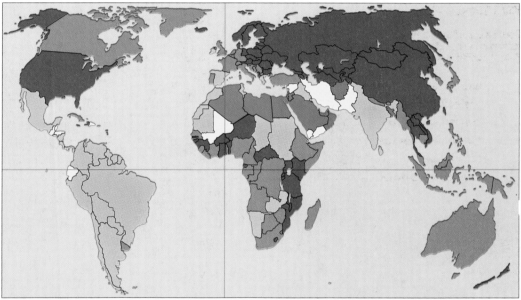

SELF SUFFICIENCY IN FOOD

Balance of trade in food products as a percentage of total trade in food products 1988*

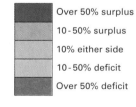

	Over 50% surplus
	10 - 50% surplus
	10% either side
	10 - 50% deficit
	Over 50% deficit

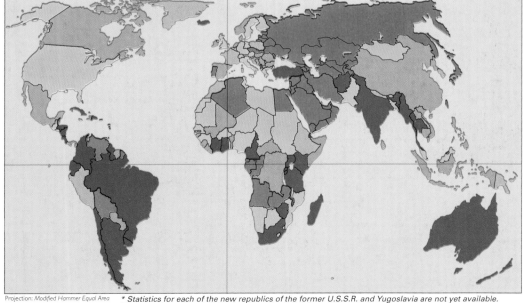

Projection: Modified Hammer Equal Area

* Statistics for each of the new republics of the former U.S.S.R. and Yugoslavia are not yet available. The map shows the statistics for the entire U.S.S.R. and Yugoslavia.

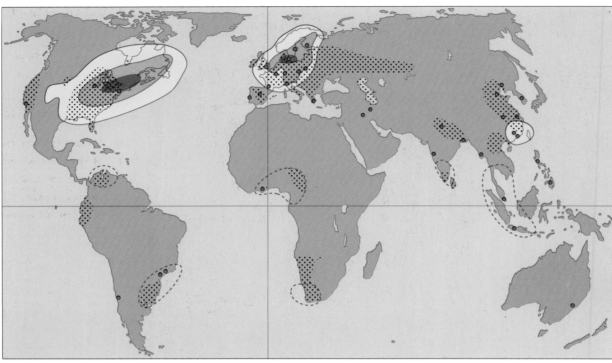

ACID RAIN

Acid rain is caused by high levels of sulphur and nitrogen in the atmosphere. They combine with water vapour and oxygen to form acids (H_2SO_4 and HNO_3) which fall as precipitation.

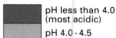 Main areas of sulphur and nitrogen emissions (from the burning of fossil fuels)

• Major cities with high levels of air pollution (including sulphur and nitrogen emissions)

Areas of acid deposition

(pH numbers measure acidity: normal rain is pH 5.6)

pH less than 4.0 (most acidic)

pH 4.0 - 4.5

pH 4.5 - 5.0

Potential problem areas

GLOBAL WARMING

Global warming is caused by high levels of carbon dioxide and other gases in the atmosphere (the Greenhouse Effect). It is estimated that by 2020 the world could be approximately 1.3°C warmer than now.

Carbon dioxide (CO_2) emissions in tonnes per person per year*

Over 10 tonnes

5 - 10 tonnes

1 - 5 tonnes

Under 1 tonne

Coastal areas vulnerable to rising sea levels caused by global warming

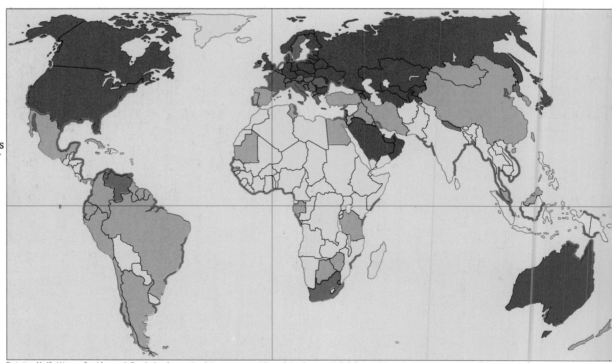

Projection: Modified Hammer Equal Area

*Statistics for each of the new republics of the former U.S.S.R. and Yugoslavia are not yet available. The map shows the statistics for the entire U.S.S.R. and Yugoslavia.

THE GREENHOUSE EFFECT

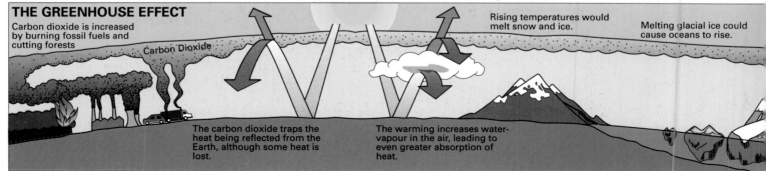

Carbon dioxide is increased by burning fossil fuels and cutting forests

Carbon Dioxide

Rising temperatures would melt snow and ice.

Melting glacial ice could cause oceans to rise.

The carbon dioxide traps the heat being reflected from the Earth, although some heat is lost.

The warming increases water-vapour in the air, leading to even greater absorption of heat.

WATER POLLUTION

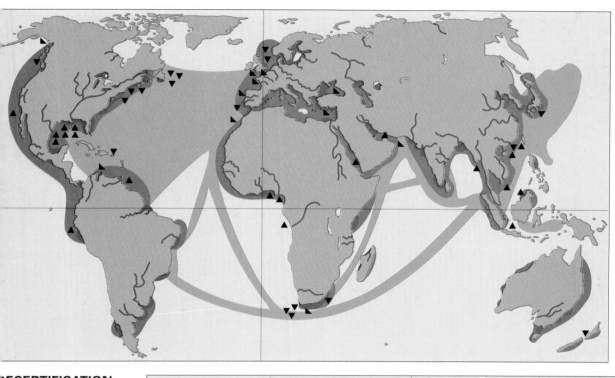

	Severely polluted sea areas and lakes
	Other polluted sea areas and lakes
	Sea areas of frequent oil pollution from shipping

◣ Major oil tanker spills

▲ Major oil rig blow-outs

▼ Offshore dumpsites for industrial and municipal waste

— Severely polluted rivers

DESERTIFICATION

Existing deserts

Areas with a high risk of desertification

Areas with a moderate risk of desertification

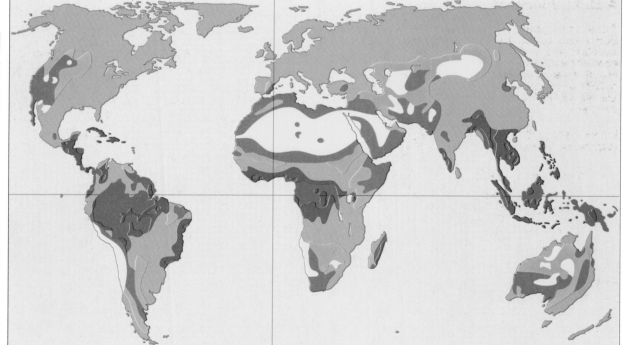

DEFORESTATION IN THE TROPICS

Former areas of rainforest

Existing rainforest

RATE OF DEFORESTATION

(Forest area remaining is given in brackets in thousands of square kilometres)

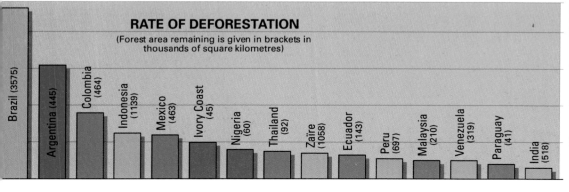

Forest area lost each year in the 1980s
20 000km²

15 000km²

10 000km²

5 000km²

Rate of deforestation (% each year)

Over 2.5%

1.0 - 2.5%

0 - 1.0%

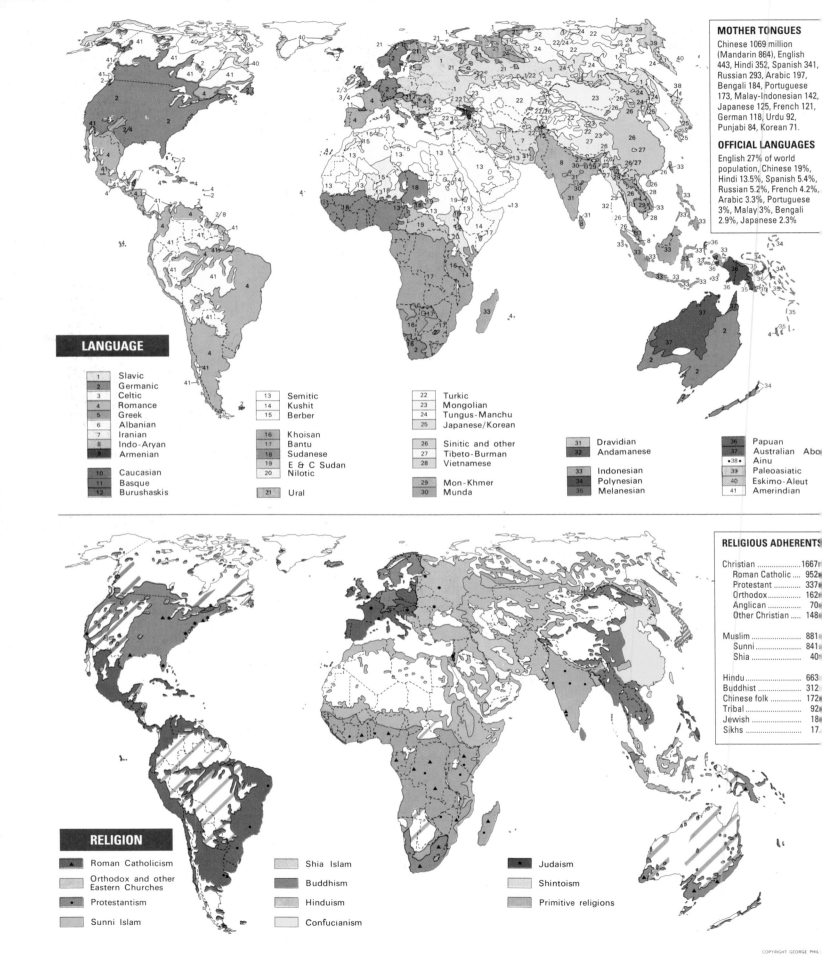

COPYRIGHT GEORGE PHIL

MOTHER TONGUES

Chinese 1069 million (Mandarin 864), English 443, Hindi 352, Spanish 341, Russian 293, Arabic 197, Bengali 184, Portuguese 173, Malay-Indonesian 142, Japanese 125, French 121, German 118, Urdu 92, Punjabi 84, Korean 71.

OFFICIAL LANGUAGES

English 27% of world population, Chinese 19%, Hindi 13.5%, Spanish 5.4%, Russian 5.2%, French 4.2%, Arabic 3.3%, Portuguese 3%, Malay 3%, Bengali 2.9%, Japanese 2.3%

LANGUAGE

1	Slavic		13	Semitic
2	Germanic		14	Kushit
3	Celtic		15	Berber
4	Romance			
5	Greek		16	Khoisan
6	Albanian		17	Bantu
7	Iranian		18	Sudanese
8	Indo-Aryan		19	E & C Sudan
9	Armenian		20	Nilotic
10	Caucasian		21	Ural
11	Basque			
12	Burushaskis			

22	Turkic		31	Dravidian
23	Mongolian		32	Andamanese
24	Tungus-Manchu			
25	Japanese/Korean		33	Indonesian
26	Sinitic and other		34	Polynesian
27	Tibeto-Burman		35	Melanesian
28	Vietnamese		36	Papuan
29	Mon-Khmer		37	Australian Abo
30	Munda		•38•	Ainu
			39	Paleoasiatic
			40	Eskimo-Aleut
			41	Amerindian

RELIGIOUS ADHERENTS

Christian	1667m
Roman Catholic	952m
Protestant	337m
Orthodox	162m
Anglican	70m
Other Christian	148m
Muslim	881m
Sunni	841m
Shia	40m
Hindu	663m
Buddhist	312m
Chinese folk	172m
Tribal	92m
Jewish	18m
Sikhs	17m

RELIGION

- ▲ Roman Catholicism
- Orthodox and other Eastern Churches
- • Protestantism
- Sunni Islam
- Shia Islam
- Buddhism
- Hinduism
- Confucianism
- • Judaism
- Shintoism
- Primitive religions

UNITED NATIONS

Created in 1945 to promote peace and cooperation and based in New York, the United Nations is the world's largest international organization, with over 160 members and an annual budget exceeding two billion US dollars. Each member of the General Assembly has one vote, while the permanent members of the 15-nation Security Council - USA, Russia, China, UK and France - hold a veto. The 54 members of the Economic and Social Council are responsible for economic, social, cultural, educational, health and related matters. The Secretariat is the UN's chief administrative arm; the only territory now administered by the Trusteeship Council is Belau (by the USA). The UN has 24 specialized agencies - based in Canada, France, Switzerland and Italy as well as the USA - which help members in fields such as economic development (UNDP), education (UNESCO), agriculture (FAO) and medicine (WHO).

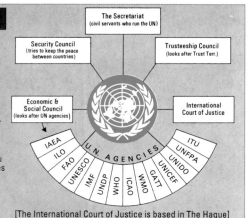

The Secretariat (civil servants who run the UN)

Security Council (tries to keep the peace between countries)

Trusteeship Council (looks after Trust Terr.)

Economic & Social Council (looks after UN agencies)

International Court of Justice

U.N. AGENCIES: IAEA, ILO, FAO, UNESCO, IMF, UNDP, OHM, ICAO, WMO, GATT, UNICEF, UNIDO, UNFPA, ITU

[The International Court of Justice is based in The Hague]

Membership: There are 13 independent states who are not members of the UN - Andorra, Kiribati, Liechtenstein, N. Korea, S. Korea, Monaco, Nauru, San Marino, Switzerland, Taiwan, Tonga, Tuvalu and Vatican City. By 1992, the successor states of the former USSR had either joined or planned to. There were 51 members in 1945. Official languages are Chinese, English, French, Russian, Spanish and Arabic.

Funding: The UN budget for 1988-1989 was US $ 1,788,746,000. Contributions are assessed by members' ability to pay, with the maximum 25% of the total, the minimum 0.01%. Contributions for 1988-1989 were: USA 25%, Japan 11.38%, USSR 9.99%, W. Germany 8.08%, France 6.25%, UK 4.86%, Italy 3.99%, Canada 3.09%, Spain 1.95%, Netherlands 1.65% (others 23.75%).

Peacekeeping: The UN has been involved in 18 peacekeeping operations worldwide since 1945, five of which (Afghanistan/Pakistan, Iran/Iraq, Angola, Namibia and Honduras) were initiated in 1988-1989. In June 1991 UN personnel totalling over 11,000 were working in eight separate areas.

EFTA: European Free Trade Association (formed in 1960). Portugal left the 'Seven' in 1989 to join the EEC.
ACP: African-Caribbean-Pacific (1963).
COMECON: Council for Mutual Economic Assistance. Founded in 1949 by Joseph Stalin, it has been largely moribund since the political upheavals of 1989-92.

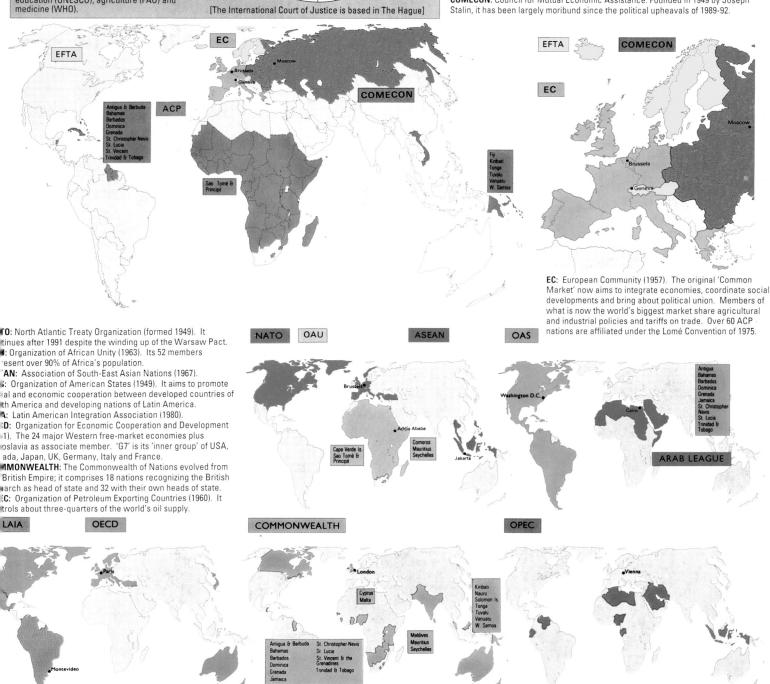

EC: European Community (1957). The original 'Common Market' now aims to integrate economies, coordinate social developments and bring about political union. Members of what is now the world's biggest market share agricultural and industrial policies and tariffs on trade. Over 60 ACP nations are affiliated under the Lomé Convention of 1975.

TO: North Atlantic Treaty Organization (formed 1949). It tinues after 1991 despite the winding up of the Warsaw Pact.
J: Organization of African Unity (1963). Its 52 members esent over 90% of Africa's population.
AN: Association of South-East Asian Nations (1967).
S: Organization of American States (1949). It aims to promote al and economic cooperation between developed countries of th America and developing nations of Latin America.
A: Latin American Integration Association (1980).
D: Organization for Economic Cooperation and Development 1). The 24 major Western free-market economies plus oslavia as associate member. 'G7' is its 'inner group' of USA, ada, Japan, UK, Germany, Italy and France.
MMONWEALTH: The Commonwealth of Nations evolved from British Empire; it comprises 18 nations recognizing the British arch as head of state and 32 with their own heads of state.
C: Organization of Petroleum Exporting Countries (1960). It rols about three-quarters of the world's oil supply.

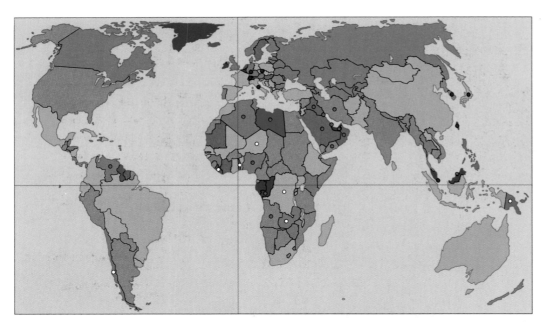

DEPENDENCE ON TRADE

Value of exports as a percentage of G.D.P. (Gross Domestic Product) 1988*

Over 50% G.D.P.

40 - 50% G.D.P.

30 - 40% G.D.P.

20 - 30% G.D.P.

10 - 20% G.D.P.

Under 10% G.D.P.

- • Most dependent on industrial exports (over 75% of total exports)

- • Most dependent on fuel exports (over 75% of total exports)

- ○ Most dependent on metal and mineral exports (over 75% of total exports)

BALANCE OF TRADE

Value of exports in proportion to the value of imports 1988*

Exports exceed imports by:

More than 50%

10 - 50%

10% either side

10 - 50%

More than 50%

Imports exceed exports by:

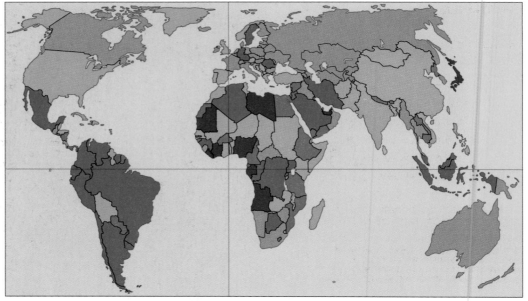

SHARE OF WORLD TRADE

Percentage share of total world exports by value 1988*

Over 10% of world trade

5 - 10% of world trade

1 - 5% of world trade

0.5 - 1% of world trade

0.25 - 0.5% of world trade

Under 0.25% of world trade

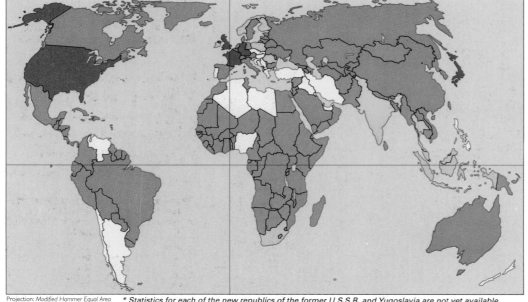

Projection: *Modified Hammer Equal Area*

* Statistics for each of the new republics of the former U.S.S.R. and Yugoslavia are not yet available. The map shows the statistics for the entire U.S.S.R. and Yugoslavia.

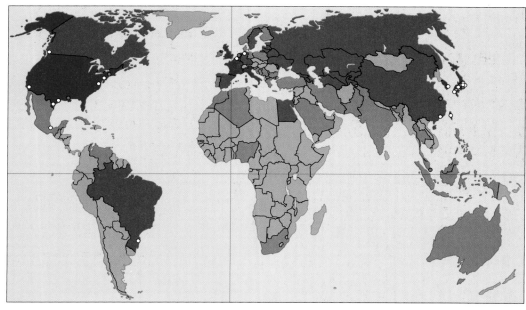

SHIPPING

Freight unloaded in
millions of tonnes 1988*

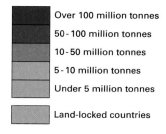

- Over 100 million tonnes
- 50 - 100 million tonnes
- 10 - 50 million tonnes
- 5 - 10 million tonnes
- Under 5 million tonnes
- Land-locked countries

Major Seaports

- •   Handling over 100 million tonnes p.a.
- ○   Handling 50-100 million tonnes p.a.

AIR TRAVEL

Passenger kilometres†flown 1988*

- Over 100 000 million
- 50 000 - 100 000 million
- 10 000 - 50 000 million
- 1 000 - 10 000 million
- 500 - 1 000 million
- Under 500 million

Major airports (handling over
20 million passengers in 1988)   ○

† Passenger kilometres are the number of
passengers (international and domestic)
multiplied by the distance flown by each
passenger from the airport of origin.

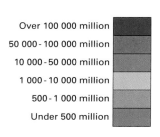

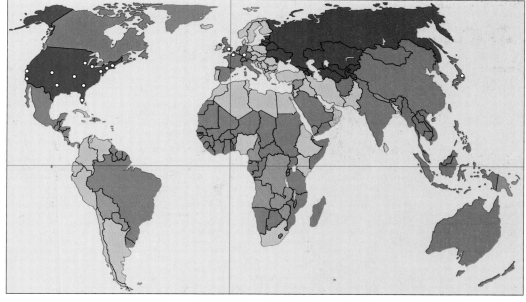

TOURISM

Tourism receipts as a percentage of
G.N.P. (Gross National Product) 1988*

- Over 10% of G.N.P. from tourism
- 5 - 10% of G.N.P. from tourism
- 2.5 - 5% of G.N.P. from tourism
- 1 - 2.5% of G.N.P. from tourism
- 0.5 - 1% of G.N.P. from tourism
- Under 0.5% of G.N.P. from tourism

Largest percentage share of total world spending on tourism 1988		Largest percentage share of total world receipts from tourism 1988	
Germany	16%	U.S.A.	10%
U.S.A.	14%	Spain	9%
U.K.	8%	Italy	8%
Japan	7%	France	8%
France	6%	U.K.	6%

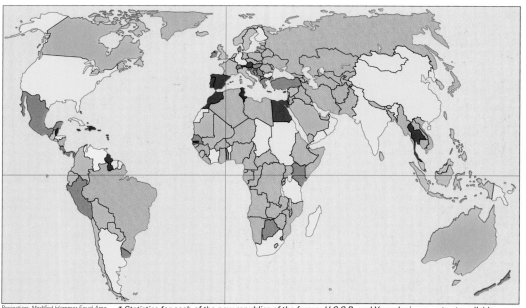

Projection: Modified Hammer Equal Area   * Statistics for each of the new republics of the former U.S.S.R. and Yugoslavia are not yet available.
The map shows the statistics for the entire U.S.S.R. and Yugoslavia.

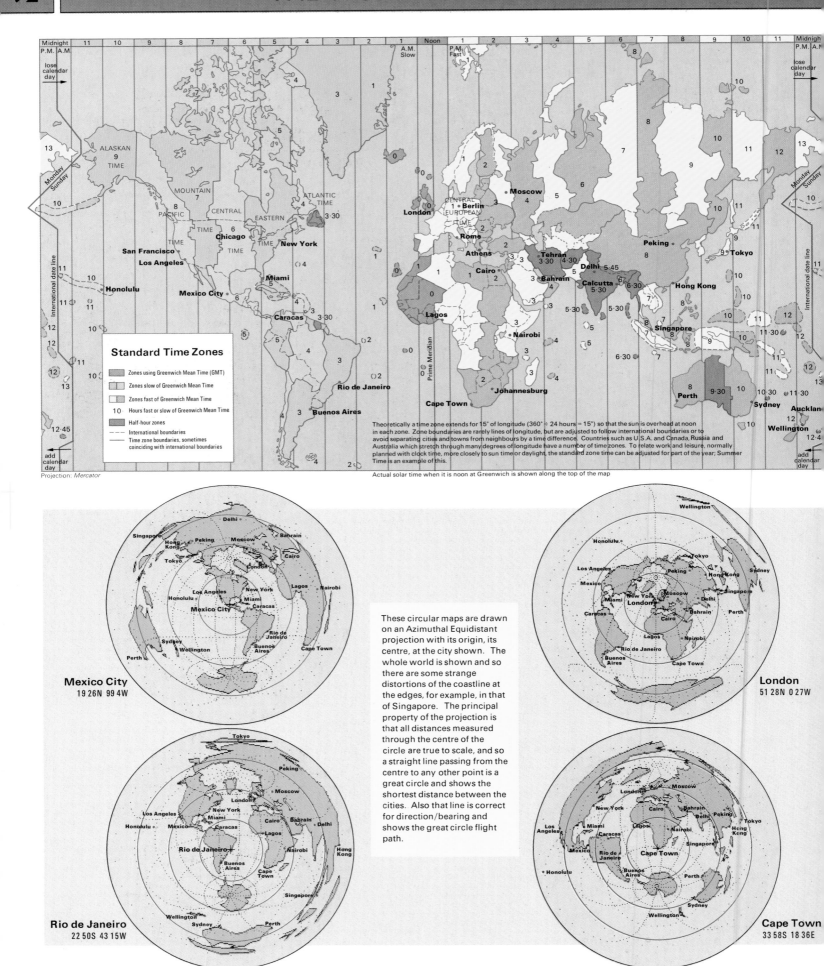

Standard Time Zones

- Zones using Greenwich Mean Time (GMT)
- Zones slow of Greenwich Mean Time
- Zones fast of Greenwich Mean Time
- 10   Hours fast or slow of Greenwich Mean Time
- Half-hour zones
- - - - International boundaries
- ——— Time zone boundaries, sometimes coinciding with international boundaries

Projection: *Mercator*

Theoretically a time zone extends for 15° of longitude (360° ÷ 24 hours = 15°) so that the sun is overhead at noon in each zone. Zone boundaries are rarely lines of longitude, but are adjusted to follow international boundaries or to avoid separating cities and towns from neighbours by a time difference. Countries such as U.S.A. and Canada, Russia and Australia which stretch through many degrees of longitude have a number of time zones. To relate work and leisure, normally planned with clock time, more closely to sun time or daylight, the standard zone time can be adjusted for part of the year; Summer Time is an example of this.

Actual solar time when it is noon at Greenwich is shown along the top of the map

These circular maps are drawn on an Azimuthal Equidistant projection with its origin, its centre, at the city shown. The whole world is shown and so there are some strange distortions of the coastline at the edges, for example, in that of Singapore. The principal property of the projection is that all distances measured through the centre of the circle are true to scale, and so a straight line passing from the centre to any other point is a great circle and shows the shortest distance between the cities. Also that line is correct for direction/bearing and shows the great circle flight path.

Mexico City 19 26N 99 4W

London 51 28N 0 27W

Rio de Janeiro 22 50S 43 15W

Cape Town 33 58S 18 36E

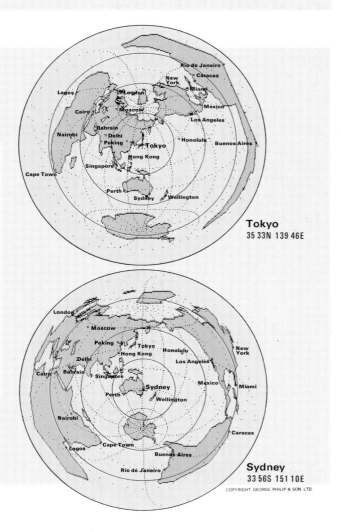

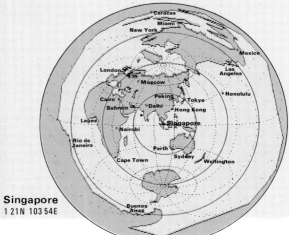

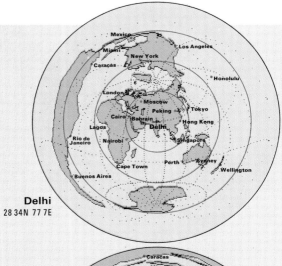

These distances are in kilometres and are the great circle distances between the cities (international airports). Great circle distances are the shortest distances between two points on the globe. They are the normal flight paths for aircraft where they are free from the restrictions of air corridors or national airspace.

	Bahrain	Buenos Aires	Cairo	Cape Town	Caracas	Delhi	Hong Kong	Honolulu	Lagos	London	Los Angeles	Mexico	Miami	Moscow	Nairobi	New York	Peking	Perth	Rio de Janeiro	Singapore	Sydney	Tokyo
Buenos Aires	13 291																					
Cairo	1 927	11 845																				
Cape Town	7 496	6 880	7 246																			
Caracas	12 121	5 124	10 200	10 254																		
Delhi	2 618	15 784	4 400	9 278	14 186																	
Hong Kong	6 387	18 442	8 121	11 852	16 340	3 768																
Honolulu	13 882	12 158	14 195	18 555	9 671	11 984	8 911															
Lagos	5 454	7 932	3 926	4 783	7 722	8 071	11 832	16 286														
London	5 089	11 128	3 528	9 672	7 465	6 726	9 637	11 617	4 998													
Los Angeles	13 210	9 854	12 206	16 067	5 813	12 863	11 634	4 105	12 408	8 752												
Mexico	13 962	7 391	12 360	13 701	3 572	14 651	12 121	6 096	11 043	8 898	2 498											
Miami	12 182	7 113	10 441	12 334	2 190	13 495	14 430	7 806	9 045	7 102	3 759	2 050										
Moscow	3 466	13 488	2 909	10 150	9 900	4 359	7 148	11 289	6 250	2 505	9 748	10 682	9 191									
Nairobi	3 398	10 413	3 542	4 096	11 545	5 413	8 750	17 255	3 828	6 835	15 560	14 812	12 771	6 365								
New York	10 613	8 526	9 009	12 551	3 402	11 747	12 956	8 000	8 437	5 535	3 968	3 361	1 751	7 476	11 828							
Peking	6 180	19 273	7 526	12 956	14 356	3 804	1 985	8 124	11 452	8 146	10 030	12 426	12 475	5 789	9 217	10 971						
Perth	9 467	12 562	11 256	8 684	17 610	7 874	6 030	10 886	12 517	14 495	14 986	16 247	18 281	12 236	8 889	18 699	8 000					
Rio de Janeiro	11 462	1 990	9 897	6 080	4 522	14 054	17 688	13 330	6 022	9 248	10 132	7 659	6 713	11 528	8 937	7 724	17 306	13 527				
Singapore	6 319	15 860	8 246	9 650	18 332	4 148	2 581	10 789	11 149	10 867	14 099	16 593	16 951	8 437	7 446	15 330	4 489	3 909	15 729			
Sydney	12 502	11 760	14 391	10 982	15 341	10 424	7 370	8 163	15 514	17 005	12 052	12 973	15 012	14 501	12 125	16 001	8 956	3 274	13 512	6 294		
Tokyo	8 271	18 338	9 552	14 710	14 154	5 852	2 874	6 185	13 475	9 584	8 806	11 304	11 991	7 487	11 243	10 869	2 089	7 896	18 557	5 300	7 809	
Wellington	14 678	9 943	16 503	11 287	13 119	12 647	9 424	7 508	16 047	18 816	10 787	11 099	13 054	16 547	13 643	14 406	10 782	5 246	11 865	8 521	2 226	9 258

The three circles are drawn at radius 5 000, 10 000 and 15 000 km from the central city

•   Cities shown on the distance table

The co-ordinates given are for the airport of each city

Delhi
28 34N 77 7E

Tokyo
35 33N 139 46E

Singapore
1 21N 103 54E

Sydney
33 56S 151 10E

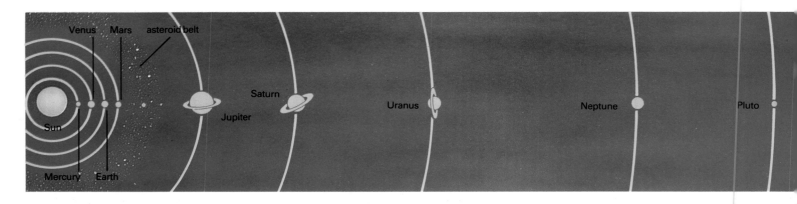

THE SOLAR SYSTEM

A minute part of one of the billions of galaxies (collections of stars) that comprise the Universe, the Solar System lies some 27,000 light-years from the centre of our own galaxy, the 'Milky Way'. Thought to be over 4,700 million years old, it consists of a central sun with nine planets and their moons revolving around it, attracted by its gravitational pull. The planets orbit the Sun in the same direction – anti-clockwise when viewed from the Northern Heavens – and almost in the same plane. Their orbital paths, however, vary enormously.

The Sun's diameter is 109 times that of Earth, and the temperature at its core – caused by continuous thermonuclear fusions of hydrogen into helium – is estimated to be 15 million degrees Celsius. It is the Solar System's only source of light and heat.

PROFILE OF THE PLANETS

	Mean distance from Sun (million km)	Mass (Earth = 1)	Period of orbit	Period of rotation (in days)	Diameter (km)	Number of known satellites
Mercury	58.3	0.06	88 days	58.67	4,878	0
Venus	107.7	0.8	224.7 days	243.0	12,104	0
Earth	149.6	1.0	365.24 days	0.99	12,756	1
Mars	227.3	0.1	1.88 years	1.02	6,794	2
Jupiter	777.9	317.8	11.86 years	0.41	142,800	16
Saturn	1427.1	95.2	29.63 years	0.42	120,000	17
Uranus	2872.3	14.5	83.97 years	0.45	52,000	15
Neptune	4502.7	17.2	164.8 years	0.67	48,400	8
Pluto	5894.2	0.002	248.63 years	6.38	2,400	1

All planetary orbits are elliptical in form, but only Pluto and Mercury follow paths that deviate noticeably from a circular one. Near Perihelion - its closest approach to the Sun - Pluto actually passes inside the orbit of Neptune, an event that last occurred in 1983. Pluto will not regain its station as outermost planet until February 1999.

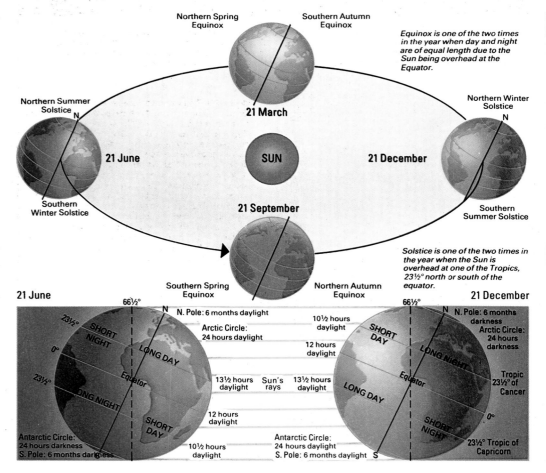

Equinox is one of the two times in the year when day and night are of equal length due to the Sun being overhead at the Equator.

Solstice is one of the two times in the year when the Sun is overhead at one of the Tropics, 23½° north or south of the equator.

THE SEASONS

The Earth revolves around the Sun once a year in an 'anti-clockwise' direction, tilted at a constant angle 66½°. In June, the northern hemisphere is tilted towards the Sun: as a result it receives more hours of sunshine in a day and therefore has its warmest season, summer. By December, the Earth has rotated halfway round the Sun so that the southern hemisphere is tilted towards the Sun and has its summer; the hemisphere that is tilted away from the Sun has winter. On 21 June the Sun is directly overhead at the Tropic of Cancer (23½° N), and this is midsummer in the northern hemisphere. Midsummer in the southern hemisphere occurs on 21 December, when the Sun is overhead at the Tropic of Capricorn (23½° S).

DAY & NIGHT

The Sun appears to rise in the east, reach its highest point at noon, and then set in the west, to be followed by night. In reality it is not the Sun that is moving but the Earth revolving from west to east. Due to the tilting of the Earth the length of day and night varies from place to place and month to month.

At the summer solstice in the northern hemisphere (21 June), the Arctic has total daylight and the Antarctic total darkness. The opposite occurs at the winter solstice (21 December). At the equator, the length of day and night are almost equal all year, at latitude 30° the length of day varies from about 14 hours to 10 hours, and at latitude 50° from about 16 hours to about 8 hours.

TIME

Year: the time taken by the Earth to revolve around the Sun, or 365.24 days.

Month: the approximate time taken by the Moon to revolve around the Earth. The 12 months of the year in fact vary from 28 (29 in a Leap Year) to 31 days.

Week: an artificial period of 7 days, not based on astronomical time.

Day: the time taken by the Earth to complete one rotation on its axis.

Hour: 24 hours make one day. Usually the day is divided into hours AM (ante meridiem or before noon) and PM (post meridiem or after noon), although most timetables now use the 24-hour system, from midnight to midnight.

SUNRISE

SUNSET

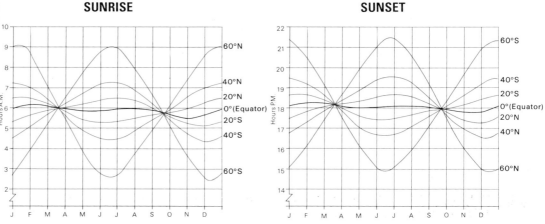

THE MOON

Distance from Earth: 356,410 km - 406,685 km; Mean diameter: 3,475.1 km;   Mass: approx. 1/81 that of Earth;
Surface gravity: one sixth of Earth's; Daily range of temperature at lunar equator: 200°C; Average orbital speed: 3,683 km/h

PHASES OF THE MOON

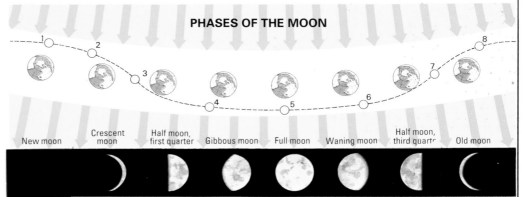

New moon | Crescent moon | Half moon, first quarter | Gibbous moon | Full moon | Waning moon | Half moon, third quarter | Old moon

The Moon rotates more slowly than the Earth, making one complete turn on its axis in just over 27 days. Since this corresponds to its period of revolution around the Earth, the Moon always presents the same hemisphere or face to us, and we never see 'the dark side'. The interval between one full Moon and the next (and between new Moons) is about 29½ days - a lunar month. The apparent changes in the shape of the Moon are caused by its changing position in relation to the Earth; like the planets, it produces no light of its own and shines only by reflecting the rays of the Sun.

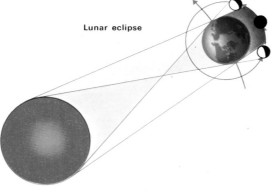

Partial eclipse (1)

Lunar eclipse

Total eclipse (2)

ECLIPSES

When the Moon passes between the Sun and the Earth it causes a partial eclipse of the Sun (1) if the Earth passes through the Moon's outer shadow (P), or a total eclipse (2) if the inner cone shadow crosses the Earth's surface. In a lunar eclipse, the Earth's shadow crosses the Moon and, again, provides either a partial or total eclipse. Eclipses of the Sun and the Moon do not occur every month because of the 5° difference between the plane of the Moon's orbit and the plane in which the Earth moves. In the 1990s only 14 lunar eclipses are possible, for example, seven partial and seven total; each is visible only from certain, and variable, parts of the world. The same period witnesses 13 solar eclipses - six partial (or annular) and seven total.

TIDES

The daily rise and fall of the ocean's tides are the result of the gravitational pull of the Moon and that of the Sun, though the effect of the latter is only 46.6% as strong as that of the Moon. This effect is greatest on the hemisphere facing the Moon and causes a tidal 'bulge'. When lunar and solar forces pull together, with Sun, Earth and Moon in line (near new and full Moons), higher 'spring tides' (and lower low tides) occur; when lunar and solar forces are least coincidental with the Sun and Moon at an angle (near the Moon's first and third quarters), 'neap tides' occur, which have a small tidal range.

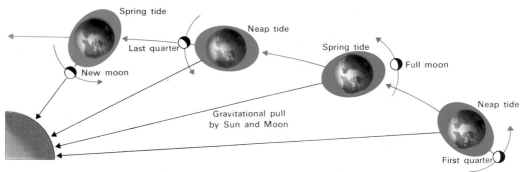

Spring tide | Neap tide | Last quarter | New moon | Spring tide | Full moon | Neap tide | Gravitational pull by Sun and Moon | First quarter

MAP PROJECTIONS

A map projection is the systematic depiction on a plane surface of the imaginary lines of latitude or longitude from a globe of the earth. This network of lines is called the graticule and forms the framework upon which an accurate depiction of the earth is made. The map graticule, which is the basis of any map, is constructed sometimes by graphical means, but often by using mathematical formulae to give the intersections of the graticule plotted as x and y co-ordinates. The choice between projections is based upon which properties the cartographer wishes the map to possess, the map scale and also the extent of the area to be mapped. Since the globe is three dimensional, it is not possible to depict its surface on a two dimensional plane without distortion. Preservation of one of the basic properties listed below can only be secured at the expense of the others and the choice of projection is often a compromise solution.

Correct Area

In these projections the areas from the globe are to scale on the map. For example, if you look at the diagram at the top right, areas of 10° x 10° are shown from the equator to the poles. The proportion of this area at the extremities are approximately 11:1. An equal area projection will retain that proportion in its portrayal of those areas. This is particularly useful in the mapping of densities and distributions. Projections with this property are termed **Equal Area, Equivalent or Homolographic.**

Correct Distance

In these projections the scale is correct along the meridians, or in the case of the Azimuthal Equidistant scale is true along any line drawn from the centre of the projection. They are called **Equidistant.**

Correct Shape

This property can only be true within small areas as it is achieved only by having a uniform scale distortion along both x and y axes of the projection. The projections are called **Conformal** or **Orthomorphic.**

In order to minimise the distortions at the edges of some projections, central portions of them are often selected for atlas maps. Below are listed some of the major types of projection.

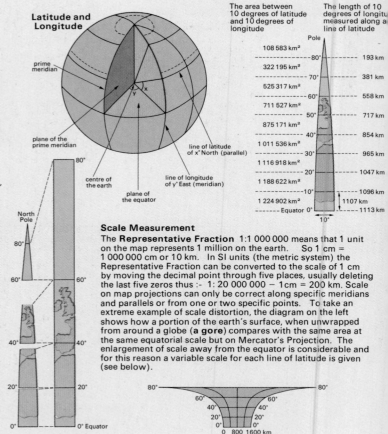

Latitude and Longitude

prime meridian

plane of the prime meridian

centre of the earth

plane of the equator

line of latitude of x° North (parallel)

line of longitude of y° East (meridian)

The area between 10 degrees of latitude and 10 degrees of longitude	The length of 10 degrees of longitude measured along a line of latitude
	Pole
108 583 km² --- 80° ---	193 km
322 195 km² --- 70° ---	381 km
525 317 km² --- 60° ---	558 km
711 527 km² --- 50° ---	717 km
875 171 km² --- 40° ---	854 km
1 011 536 km² --- 30° ---	965 km
1 116 918 km² --- 20° ---	1047 km
1 188 622 km² ---10° ---	1096 km
1 224 902 km² --- Equator 0° ---	1107 km / 1113 km
	10°

Scale Measurement

The **Representative Fraction** 1:1 000 000 means that 1 unit on the map represents 1 million on the earth. So 1 cm = 1 000 000 cm or 10 km. In SI units (the metric system) the Representative Fraction can be converted to the scale of 1 cm by moving the decimal point through five places, usually deleting the last five zeros thus :- 1: 20 000 000 – 1cm = 200 km. Scale on map projections can only be correct along specific meridians and parallels or from one or two specific points. To take an extreme example of scale distortion, the diagram on the left shows how a portion of the earth's surface, when unwrapped from around a globe (**a gore**) compares with the same area at the same equatorial scale but on Mercator's Projection. The enlargement of scale away from the equator is considerable and for this reason a variable scale for each line of latitude is given (see below).

0 800 1600 km

AZIMUTHAL OR ZENITHAL PROJECTIONS

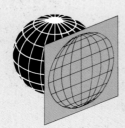

These are constructed by the projection of part of the graticule from the globe onto a plane tangential to any single point on it. This plane may be tangential to the equator (**equatorial case**), the poles (**polar case**) or any other point (**oblique case**). Any straight line drawn from the point at which the plane touches the globe is the shortest distance from that point and is known as a **great circle.** In its **Gnomonic** construction *any* straight line on the map is a great circle, but there is great exaggeration towards the edges and this reduces its general uses. There are five different ways of transferring the graticule onto the plane and these are shown on the right. The central diagram below shows how the graticules vary, using the polar case as the example.

Equidistant   **Equal-Area**   **Orthographic**   **Gnomonic**   **Stereographic (conformal)**

Oblique Case

The plane touches the globe at any point between the equator and poles. The oblique orthographic uses the distortion in azimuthal projections away from the centre to give a graphic depiction of the earth as seen from any desired point in space. It can also be used in both Polar and Equatorial cases. It is used not only for the earth but also for the moon and planets.

Polar Case

The polar case is the simplest to construct and the diagram below shows the differing effects of all five methods of construction comparing their coverage, distortion etc., using North America as the example.

Equatorial Case

The example shown here is Lambert's Equivalent Azimuthal. It is the only projection which is both equal area and where bearing is true from the centre.

Stereographic

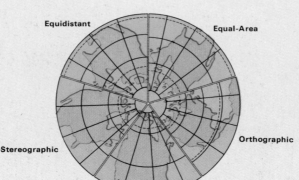

Equidistant   Equal-Area   Orthographic   Gnomonic

CONICAL PROJECTIONS

These use the projection of the graticule from the globe onto a cone which is tangential to a line of latitude (termed the **standard parallel**). This line is always an arc and scale is always true along it. Because of its method of construction it is used mainly for depicting the temperate latitudes around the standard parallel i.e. where there is least distortion. To reduce the distortion and include a larger range of latitudes, the projection may be constructed with the cone bisecting the surface of the globe so that there are two standard parallels each of which is true to scale. The distortion is thus spread more evenly between the two chosen parallels.

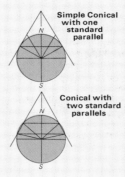

Bonne
This is a modification of the simple conic whereby the true scale along the meridians is sacrificed to enable the accurate representation of areas. However scale is true along each parallel but shapes are distorted at the edges.

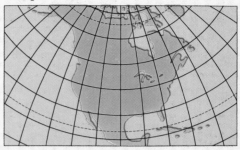

Simple Conic
Scale is correct not only along the standard parallel but also along all meridians. The selection of the standard parallel used is crucial because of the distortion away from it. The projection is usually used to portray regions or continents at small scales.

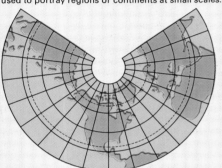

Lambert's Conformal Conic
This projection uses two standard parallels but instead of being equal area as Albers, it is Conformal. Because it has comparatively small distortion, direction and distances can be readily measured and it is therefore used for some navigational charts.

Albers Conical Equal Area
This projection uses two standard parallels and once again the selection of the two specific ones relative to the land area to be mapped is very important. It is equal area and is especially useful for large land masses oriented East-West, for example the U.S.A.

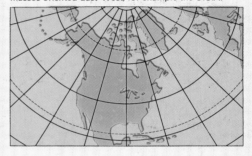

CYLINDRICAL AND OTHER WORLD PROJECTIONS

This group of projections are those which permit the whole of the Earth's surface to be depicted on one map. They are a very large group of projections and the following are only a few of them. Cylindrical projections are constructed by the projection of the graticule from the globe onto a cylinder tangential to the globe. In the examples shown here the cylinder touches the equator, but it can be moved through 90° so it touches the poles - this is called the **Transverse Aspect**. If the cylinder is twisted so that it touches anywhere between the equator and poles it is called the **Oblique Aspect**. Although cylindrical projections can depict all the main land masses, there is considerable distortion of shape and area towards the poles. One cylindrical projection, **Mercator** overcomes this shortcoming by possessing the unique navigational property that any straight drawn on it is a line of constant bearing (**loxodrome**), i.e. a straight line route on the globe crosses the parallels and meridians on the map at the same angles as on the globe. It is used for maps and charts between 15° either side of the equator. Beyond this enlargement of area is a serious drawback, although it is used for navigational charts at all latitudes.

Simple Cylindrical

Mercator

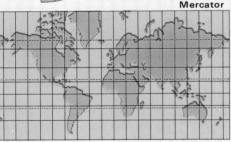

Mollweide

Sanson-Flamsteed

Hammer
This is not a cylindrical projection, but is developed from the Lambert Azimuthal Equal Area by doubling all the East-West distances along the parallels from the central meridian. Like both Sanson-Flamsteed and Mollweide it is distorted towards its edges but has curved parallels to lessen the distortion.

Mollweide and Sanson-Flamsteed
Both of these projections are termed **pseudo-cylindrical**. They are basically cylindrical projections where parallels have been progressively shortened and drawn to scale towards the poles. This allows them to overcome the gross distortions exhibited by the ordinary cylindrical projections and they are in fact Equal Area, Mollweide's giving a slightly better shape. To improve the shape of the continents still further they, like some other projections can be **Interrupted** as can be seen below, but this is at the expense of contiguous sea areas. These projections can have any central meridian and so can be 'centred' on the Atlantic, Pacific, Asia, America etc. In this form both projections are suitable for any form of mapping statistical distributions.

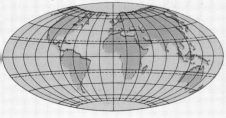

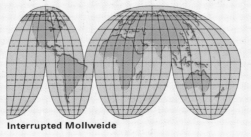

Interrupted Mollweide

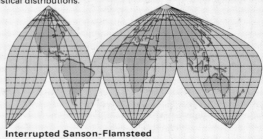

Interrupted Sanson-Flamsteed

	Population									Land and Agriculture					Energy	Trade	
	Population Total 1991	Population Density 1991	Change 1970-80	Change 1980-90	Birth Rate	Death Rate	Fertility Rate	Life Expectancy	Urban Population	Land Area	Arable and Permanent Crops	Permanent grassland	Forest	Agric. Population	Comm. Consumpt. 1989	Imports per capita	Exports per capita
	millions	persons per km²	%	%	births per thousand	deaths per thousand	children	years	%	thousand km²	% of land area	% of land area	% of land area	% of active pop.	gigajoules	US $	US $
Afghanistan	17.7	27	18	3	52	22	6.8	44	22	652	12	46	3	55	7	58	15
Albania	3.3	122	25	21	22	6	2.7	73	35	27	26	15	38	48	37	...	...
Algeria	25.7	11	36	33	35	7	4.9	66	45	2,382	3	13	2	24	27	313	345
Angola	10.3	8.3	38	30	47	10	6.3	47	28	1,247	3	23	42	70	3	48	233
Argentina	32.7	12	18	14	20	9	2.8	71	86	2,737	13	52	22	10	57	126	380
Australia	17.1	2.2	17	15	14	8	1.8	77	86	7,618	6	55	14	5	211	2,223	2,410
Austria	7.6	93	1	0	12	12	1.5	75	58	82	19	24	39	6	117	6,488	5,254
Bahamas	0.26	26	23	20	19	5	2.2	69	59	10	1	0	32	6	76	12,004	11,144
Bangladesh	119	914	32	31	41	14	5.1	53	14	130	71	5	15	69	2	27	13
Barbados	0.26	593	4	2	16	9	1.8	75	45	0.43	77	9	0	7	47	2,692	804
Belgium	9.8	321	2	0	12	12	1.7	76	97	31	25	21	21	2	168	11,875	11,602
Benin	4.9	44	28	34	49	18	7.1	48	42	111	17	4	32	61	1	103	20
Bolivia	7.6	7.0	29	31	41	12	5.8	56	51	1,084	3	25	51	42	11	124	113
Botswana	1.4	2.5	45	45	44	10	6.4	61	24	567	2	58	19	63	...	...	...
Brazil	153	18	27	24	26	8	3.2	66	77	8,457	9	20	65	24	23	134	209
Bulgaria	9	81	4	2	12	12	1.8	73	70	111	38	18	35	12	144	1,434	1,485
Burkina Faso	9.3	34	25	29	47	17	6.5	49	9	274	13	37	24	84	1	57	17
Burma	42.6	65	27	20	30	9	3.7	63	25	658	15	1	49	47	2	14	10
Burundi	5.6	218	17	32	47	16	6.8	50	7	26	52	36	3	91	1	43	14
Cambodia	8.5	48	-8	29	37	15	4.4	51	12	177	17	3	76	70	1	...	...
Cameroon	12.2	26	31	37	47	13	6.9	55	49	465	15	18	53	61	7	115	84
Canada	26.7	2.9	13	10	13	8	1.7	77	76	9,221	5	4	39	3	321	4,376	4,699
Central Africa	3.1	5.0	25	31	45	16	6.2	51	47	623	3	5	57	63	1	51	45
Chad	5.8	4.6	23	27	43	18	5.8	48	33	1,259	3	36	10	75	1	78	26
Chile	13.4	18	17	18	23	6	2.7	72	86	749	6	18	12	13	35	552	652
China	1,131	121	20	14	21	7	2.3	71	21	9,326	10	34	14	68	23	55	63
Colombia	33.6	32	26	23	26	6	2.9	69	70	1,039	5	39	49	27	24	169	205
Congo	2.3	6.73	32	36	46	13	6.3	55	42	342	0	29	62	60	10	238	414
Costa Rica	3.1	61	32	32	26	4	3.0	75	54	51	10	45	32	24	16	684	466
Cuba	10.7	97	14	10	17	7	1.9	76	75	110	30	27	25	19	45	728	530
Cyprus	0.71	77	2	11	17	8	2.2	77	53	9.2	17	1	13	21	74	3,664	1,356
Czechoslovakia	15.7	126	7	2	14	11	2.0	72	69	125	41	13	37	9	175	837	759
Denmark	5.1	121	4	0	11	11	1.5	76	86	42	60	5	12	5	130	6,276	6,967
Dominican Republic	7.3	152	29	26	26	6	3.3	68	60	48	30	43	13	36	12	249	102
Ecuador	10.9	39	34	30	31	7	3.9	67	57	277	10	18	40	30	19	249	295
Egypt	53.6	54	24	30	31	9	4.0	62	49	995	3	0	0	41	22	173	49
El Salvador	5.4	270	26	16	36	7	4.5	66	44	20	35	29	5	37	7	172	79
Ethiopia	50.7	46	27	27	48	18	6.8	47	13	1,101	13	41	25	75	1	21	6
Finland	5	16	4	4	12	10	1.7	76	68	305	8	0	76	8	169	4,257	4,532
France	56.3	102	6	4	13	10	1.8	77	74	550	35	21	27	5	115	4,075	3,767
Gabon	1.2	4.7	60	45	43	16	5.3	54	46	258	2	18	78	68	37	691	1,215
Gambia	0.88	88	38	34	45	20	6.2	45	23	10	18	9	16	81	4	233	48
Germany	79.5	228	1	2	11	12	1.5	75	84	349	35	16	30	5	200	4,734	4,849
Ghana	15.5	67	25	40	44	12	6.3	56	33	230	12	22	35	50	3	64	72
Greece	10.1	77	10	4	12	10	1.7	77	63	131	30	40	20	24	91	1,954	792
Guatemala	9.5	88	32	33	39	8	5.4	65	42	108	17	13	35	51	6	177	130
Guinea	5.9	24	14	29	51	20	7.0	45	26	246	3	25	60	74	3	...	...
Guinea-Bissau	0.98	35	51	21	43	21	5.8	44	20	28	12	38	38	79	2	69	14
Guyana	0.80	4.1	7	5	24	7	2.4	65	34	197	3	6	83	22	11	640	319
Haiti	6.6	244	18	21	35	12	4.8	57	30	27	33	18	1	64	2	56	16
Honduras	5.3	47	39	40	37	7	4.9	66	44	112	16	23	30	55	5	198	184
Hong Kong	5.9	5,960	28	16	12	6	1.4	78	93	0.99	7	1	12	1	58	16,992	16,708
Hungary	10.5	114	4	-1	12	13	1.8	72	60	92	57	13	18	12	107	831	920
Iceland	0.26	2.6	12	11	15	7	1.9	78	91	100	0	23	1	7	165	6,615	5,977
India	871	293	24	20	31	10	4.1	60	28	2,973	57	4	22	67	9	28	22
Indonesia	188	104	26	19	27	9	3.1	63	29	1,812	12	7	63	49	8	122	143
Iran	55.8	34	37	40	33	7	4.7	67	55	1,636	9	27	11	28	45	306	353
Iraq	19.6	45	42	42	41	7	5.9	66	74	437	12	9	4	21	31	670	2,021

Wealth							Social Indicators						Aid		
GNP 1990	GNP per capita 1990	Rate of change 1980-90	GDP share agriculture	GDP share industry	GDP share services	Real GDP per capita 1989	Human Development Index	Food Intake	Population per doctor 1984	% of GNP spent on education 1989	% of age-group in secondary education	Adult Illiteracy	Per capita 1989	% of GNP 1990	
million US $	US $	%	%	%	%	US $		calories per day	persons	%	%	%	US $	%	
7,200	450	2.6	65	20	15	710	0.065	2,000	5,200	1.8	8	71	10	...	Afghanistan
3,255	1,000	1.8	60	28	12	4,270	0.791	2,500	1,230	...	...	15	3	...	Albania
51,585	2,060	-0.3	16	44	40	3,088	0.533	2,818	2,340	9.4	61	43	9	0.3	Algeria
6,207	620	6.1	75	10	15	1,225	0.169	2,000	17,790	3.4	11	58	21	3.5	Angola
76,491	2,370	-1.8	14	33	53	4,310	0.833	3,110	370	1.5	74	5	6.7	0.4	Argentina
290,522	17,080	1.7	4	32	64	15,266	0.971	3,186	440	5.7	79	1	*59.6	*0.38	Australia
147,016	19,240	2	3	37	60	13,063	0.95	3,496	390	6	...	1	*37.2	*0.23	Austria
2,913	11,510	1.7	...	...	...	11,293	0.875	2,791	1,100	6.2	...	1	12	0.1	Bahamas
22,579	200	1	44	14	42	820	0.185	1,996	6,730	2.2	17	65	16.2	8.9	Bangladesh
1,680	6,540	1.4	7	15	78	8,351	0.927	3,247	1,150	6.9	93	1	12	0.2	Barbados
154,688	15,440	1.2	2	31	67	13,313	0.95	3,947	330	5.4	89	1	*71.7	*0.46	Belgium
1,716	360	-1	46	12	42	1,030	0.111	2,245	15,940	3.5	16	77	53.8	14.7	Benin
4,526	620	-2.6	24	30	46	1,531	0.394	1,968	1,540	2.3	34	22	60.8	9.6	Bolivia
2,561	2,040	6.3	3	57	40	3,180	0.534	2,368	6,900	8.2	37	26	116	6.5	Botswana
402,788	2,680	0.6	9	43	48	4,951	0.739	2,722	1,080	3.7	38	19	1.3	0.05	Brazil
19,875	2,210	2.3	11	59	30	5,064	0.865	3,683	280	3.5	59	7	...	...	Bulgaria
2,955	330	1.4	32	26	42	617	0.074	2,286	57,220	2.3	7	82	32.4	11.1	Burkina Faso
20,805	500	2.1	51	10	39	595	0.385	2,474	3,740	2.2	24	19	5.4	1.1	Burma
1,151	210	1.3	56	15	29	611	0.165	1,995	21,120	3.2	4	50	37.3	18.6	Burundi
2,475	300	2.5	75	10	15	1,000	0.178	2,500	...	...	...	65	4	...	Cambodia
11,233	940	-0.3	27	27	46	1,699	0.313	2,195	14,000	3.3	26	46	40.7	4.2	Cameroon
542,774	20,450	2.4	3	21	76	18,635	0.982	3,462	510	7.2	93	1	*86.9	*0.44	Canada
1,194	390	-1.3	42	15	43	770	0.159	2,004	23,530	2.9	11	62	75	17.1	Central Africa
1,074	190	3.3	36	20	44	582	0.088	1,800	38,360	2	7	70	55	30.3	Chad
25,504	1,940	1.1	8	30	62	4,987	0.863	2,553	1,230	3.6	75	7	7	0.2	Chile
415,884	370	7.9	32	48	20	2,656	0.612	2,634	1,000	2.4	44	27	2	0.5	China
40,805	1,240	1.1	17	36	47	4,068	0.758	2,571	1,240	2.9	52	13	3	0.2	Colombia
2,296	1,010	-0.2	14	35	51	2,382	0.372	2,603	8,320	5.1	...	43	92	10.2	Congo
5,342	1,910	0.6	18	27	56	4,413	0.842	2,791	960	4.4	41	7	76	4.3	Costa Rica
21,250	2,000	1.1	12	36	52	2,500	0.732	3,153	560	6.6	89	6	3	0.1	Cuba
5,633	8,040	4.9	7	27	66	9,368	0.912	3,250	1,100	3.6	88	6	49	0.7	Cyprus
49,225	3,140	1.3	6	57	37	7,420	0.897	3,609	280	4	86	1	...	...	Czechoslovakia
113,515	22,090	2.1	5	29	66	13,751	0.953	3,622	400	7.3	84	1	*183.7	*0.94	Denmark
5,847	820	-0.4	15	26	59	2,537	0.595	2,342	1,760	1.5	74	17	13	2.1	Dominican Republic
10,112	960	-0.8	15	39	46	3,012	0.641	2,518	820	2.6	56	14	15.7	1.6	Ecuador
31,381	600	2.1	19	30	51	1,934	0.385	3,326	770	6.8	81	52	107	17.2	Egypt
5,767	1,100	-0.6	21	21	58	1,897	0.498	2,200	2,830	2	26	27	65	7.6	El Salvador
6,041	120	-1.2	42	16	42	392	0.173	1,750	60,000	4.4	15	34	18	11.6	Ethiopia
129,823	26,070	3.1	7	36	57	14,598	0.953	3,144	440	5.7	83	1	*141.2	*0.63	Finland
1,099,750	19,480	1.7	4	29	67	14,164	0.969	3,449	320	6.6	83	1	*132.3	*0.78	France
3,654	3,220	-2.6	11	47	42	4,735	0.545	2,500	2,790	5.6	...	39	121.3	3.9	Gabon
229	260	-0.3	34	12	54	886	0.083	2,351	11,600	4	16	73	109	48	Gambia
1,468,871	22,730	2.2	3	37	60	14,507	0.955	3,650	380	4.5	85	1	*62.3	*0.41	Germany
5,824	390	-0.6	50	17	33	1,005	0.31	2,246	14,890	3.4	39	40	37.6•	10.3	Ghana
60,245	6,000	0.8	16	29	55	6,764	0.901	3,793	350	3.1	85	7	3.3	0.1	Greece
8,309	900	-2.1	18	26	56	2,531	0.485	2,229	2,180	1.8	21	45	21	3.1	Guatemala
2,756	480	2.5	30	33	37	602	0.052	2,193	46,420	3	9	76	48	12.6	Guinea
176	180	1.7	47	16	37	820	0.088	2,500	7,500	2.8	7	63	122	68.2	Guinea-Bissau
293	370	-3.2	25	31	44	1,453	0.539	2,736	6,200	8.8	64	4	133	42.7	Guyana
2,400	370	-2.3	31	38	31	962	0.276	2,011	7,180	1.8	19	47	31.1	8.4	Haiti
3,023	590	-1.2	21	25	54	1,504	0.473	2,229	1,510	4.9	32	27	87	9.9	Honduras
66,666	11,540	5.5	0	28	72	15,180	0.913	2,817	1,070	2.8	73	10	8	0.03	Hong Kong
30,047	2,780	1.5	14	36	50	6,245	0.893	3,638	310	4	73	3	...	...	Hungary
5,456	21,150	1.2	10	15	75	14,210	0.958	3,518	460	3.7	85	1	...	...	Iceland
294,816	350	3.2	32	29	39	910	0.297	2,196	2,520	3.2	43	52	2.3	0.7	India
101,151	560	4.1	24	37	39	2,034	0.491	2,708	9,460	0.9	47	23	10.3	1.9	Indonesia
139,120	2,450	-0.8	25	15	60	3,120	0.547	3,300	2,690	3.1	53	46	1.7	0.1	Iran
37,828	2,000	3.6	25	20	55	3,510	0.589	3,000	1,740	3.7	47	40	3	0.01	Iraq

	Population									Land and Agriculture					Energy	Trade	
	Population Total 1991	Population Density 1991	Change 1970-80	Change 1980-90	Birth Rate	Death Rate	Fertility Rate	Life Expectancy	Urban Population	Land Area	Arable and Permanent Crops	Permanent grassland	Forest	Agric. Population	Comm. Consumpt. 1989	Imports per capita	Exports per capita
	millions	persons per km²	%	%	births per thousand	deaths per thousand	children	years	%	thousand km²	% of land area	% of land area	% of land area	% of active pop.	gigajoules	US $	US $
Ireland	3.8	56	15	9	18	8	2.4	75	59	68	14	68	5	14	112	5,922	6,797
Israel	4.7	235	30	19	21	7	2.8	76	92	20	21	7	5	4	89	3,241	2,484
Italy	57.1	194	5	1	11	11	1.4	76	69	294	41	17	23	7	111	3,113	2,931
Ivory Coast	12.5	39	49	46	50	13	7.4	55	47	318	12	41	24	56	5	189	251
Jamaica	2.5	231	14	15	22	6	2.4	74	52	11	25	18	17	27	25	770	461
Japan	124	329	12	6	12	8	1.7	79	77	377	12	2	67	6	118	1,901	2,538
Jordan	4.2	48	27	37	39	5	5.5	68	68	88	4	9	1	6	29	649	230
Kenya	24.9	44	45	44	47	10	6.8	61	24	570	4	67	4	77	3	93	44
Korea, North	22.2	185	25	19	25	5	2.4	71	67	120	17	0	74	34	83	...	...
Korea, South	43.2	441	19	12	15	6	1.7	71	72	98	22	1	66	25	65	1,629	1,517
Laos	4.3	19	18	29	44	15	6.7	51	19	231	4	3	55	72	1	...	...
Lebanon	2.8	280	8	1	30	8	3.4	67	84	10	29	1	8	9	42	846	197
Lesotho	1.8	59	26	32	40	11	5.8	59	20	30	11	66	0	80	...	...	...
Liberia	2.7	28	35	37	47	14	6.7	56	44	96	4	59	18	70	4	131	163
Libya	4.7	2.7	53	49	43	8	6.7	63	70	1,760	1	8	0	14	117	1,559	1,773
Luxembourg	0.40	155	7	2	12	11	1.5	75	84	2.6	...	...	...	...	361	...	...
Madagascar	12.4	21	30	37	45	13	6.5	56	25	582	5	58	27	77	1	29	27
Malawi	9.1	97	37	42	55	19	7.6	49	15	94	26	20	40	75	1	69	50
Malaysia	18.3	56	27	30	28	5	3.5	71	42	329	15	0	58	32	41	2,028	1,899
Mali	9.5	7.8	25	19	51	19	7.1	46	19	1,220	2	25	6	81	1	70	33
Malta	0.40	1,333	12	-3	13	9	1.9	74	87	0.30	41	0	0	4	60	5,580	3,217
Mauritania	2.1	2.0	27	30	46	18	6.5	48	42	1,025	0	38	5	64	21	178	229
Mexico	90.5	47	33	22	27	5	3.1	70	73	1,909	13	39	23	30	51	348	308
Mongolia	2.3	1.5	32	32	34	8	4.7	64	51	1,567	1	79	9	30	57	...	...
Morocco	25.7	58	27	29	33	8	4.2	63	49	446	21	47	18	37	11	276	170
Mozambique	16.1	21	29	29	44	17	6.2	49	27	782	4	49	23	82	1	48	7
Namibia	1.8	2.2	29	36	42	11	5.7	59	57	823	1	64	22	35	...		
Nepal	19.6	143	29	29	36	13	5.5	54	10	137	19	15	18	92	1	36	11
Netherlands	15.1	458	9	6	13	9	1.6	78	89	33	28	32	9	4	195	8,360	8,868
New Zealand	3.4	13	10	9	16	8	2.0	76	84	268	2	51	27	9	151	2,514	2,867
Nicaragua	4	34	35	40	39	7	5.0	66	60	119	11	45	29	38	8	264	86
Niger	8	6.3	34	38	51	19	7.1	47	20	1,267	3	7	2	87	2	52	32
Nigeria	88.5	97	39	38	47	14	6.6	53	35	911	34	44	13	65	6	40	95
Norway	4.2	14	5	3	13	11	1.7	78	74	307	3	0	27	5	209	5,954	8,027
Pakistan	126	164	30	31	42	11	5.9	59	32	771	27	6	5	50	8	73	56
Panama	2.5	33	28	24	25	5	2.9	73	55	76	8	20	44	25	17	615	133
Papua New Guinea	3.96	8.7	27	26	33	11	4.8	56	16	453	1	0	84	67	9	348	308
Paraguay	4.4	11	34	36	33	6	4.3	67	48	397	6	52	36	46	6	167	280
Peru	22	17	31	29	29	8	3.6	65	70	1,280	3	21	54	35	15	134	152
Philippines	63.9	214	29	29	30	7	3.9	65	42	298	27	4	35	47	9	212	133
Poland	38.6	127	9	8	15	10	2.1	72	63	304	48	13	29	21	134	373	378
Portugal	10.6	115	8	5	13	10	1.7	74	33	92	41	8	32	16	53	2,380	1,552
Puerto Rico	3.6	406	18	9	18	8	2.1	76	74	8.9	14	38	20	3	82	...	...
Romania	23.4	102	10	5	15	11	2.0	72	50	230	45	19	28	20	132	241	177
Rwanda	7.5	313	38	40	50	16	8.0	51	8	24	47	19	23	91	1	55	15
Saudi Arabia	14.7	6.8	63	51	42	7	7.1	66	77	2,150	1	40	1	39	186	1,466	1,967
Senegal	7.5	39	33	32	44	16	6.2	49	38	193	27	30	31	78	6	148	88
Sierra Leone	4.3	61	23	27	48	22	6.5	43	32	71	25	31	29	62	2	40	35
Singapore	2.8	4,667	16	24	16	6	1.8	75	100	0.60	2	0	5	1	146	20,262	17,580
Somalia	7.7	12	46	40	47	18	6.6	47	36	627	2	69	14	71	2	19	15
South Africa	36.1	30	26	25	31	9	4.2	63	59	1,221	11	67	4	14	77	484	538
Spain	39.3	79	11	4	13	9	1.7	77	78	499	41	20	31	11	73	2,391	1,542
Sri Lanka	17.4	272	18	16	21	6	2.5	72	21	64	29	7	27	52	3	155	113
Sudan	25.9	11	35	35	43	14	6.3	52	22	2,376	6	6	6	60	2	45	21
Surinam	0.43	2.8	-5	20	25	6	2.6	70	48	156	0	0	95	16	35	735	753
Swaziland	0.82	48	34	40	47	11	6.5	58	33	17	10	69	6	66	...	...	...
Sweden	8.5	21	3	2	13	12	1.9	78	84	412	7	1	68	4	147	5,759	6,381
Switzerland	6.6	169	2	5	12	10	1.6	78	60	39	10	40	26	4	107	9,796	9,063

| Wealth | | | | | | | Social Indicators | | | | | | Aid | | |
| GNP 1990 | GNP per capita 1990 | Rate of change 1980-90 | GDP share agriculture | GDP share industry | GDP share services | Real GDP per capita 1989 | Human Development Index | Food Intake | Population per doctor 1984 | % of GNP spent on education 1989 | % of age-group in secondary education | Adult Illiteracy | Per capita 1989 | % of GNP 1990 | |
million US $	US $	%	%	%	%	US $		calories per day	persons	%	%	%	US $	%	
33,467	9,550	1.1	10	10	80	7,481	0.921	3,779	680	6.2	79	1	*12.9	*0.17	Ireland
50,866	10,970	1.5	5	22	73	10,448	0.939	3,150	350	...	83	4	264.4	2.6	Israel
970,619	16,850	2.2	4	34	62	13,608	0.922	3,508	230	3.9	77	3	*62.3	*0.42	Italy
8,920	730	-3.7	46	24	30	1,381	0.289	2,580	15,000	7	20	46	56	7.2	Ivory Coast
3,606	1,510	-0.4	6	45	49	2,787	0.722	2,622	2,040	6.6	61	2	113	9.2	Jamaica
3,140,948	25,430	3.5	3	41	56	14,311	0.981	2,909	660	6.5	96	1	*72.2	*0.32	Japan
3,924	1,240	-3.9	6	29	65	2,415	0.586	3,000	1,140	5.9	46	20	221	16.7	Jordan
8,958	370	0.3	31	20	49	1,023	0.366	2,159	9,970	6.5	23	31	41.1	11.7	Kenya
50,000	2,000	1.8	...	...	...	2,172	0.654	2,909	500	...	87	4	5	1	Korea, North
231,132	5,400	8.9	10	44	46	6,117	0.871	2,853	1,160	3.6	87	4	1	1	Korea, South
848	200	0.7	70	10	20	1,025	0.24	2,400	1,360	1.2	27	46	34.8	22.5	Laos
5,400	2,000	0.3	8	35	57	2,250	0.561	3,000	680	...	67	20	50	...	Lebanon
832	470	-0.9	24	30	46	1,646	0.423	2,326	18,610	4	26	22	78	16.9	Lesotho
1,280	500	3.2	37	28	35	937	0.227	2,404	9,340	5.7	17	60	37	4.5	Liberia
26,367	5,800	-9.2	5	50	45	4,927	0.659	3,350	690	10.1	...	36	2	0.52	Libya
10,875	28,770	3.9	3	41	56	16,537	0.929	...	570	2.8	60	1	...	...	Luxembourg
2,710	230	-2.3	31	14	55	690	0.325	2,177	9,780	1.8	19	20	28.4	12.6	Madagascar
1,662	200	-0.1	35	19	46	620	0.166	2,098	11,330	3.3	4	53	47.9	30.5	Malawi
41,524	2,340	2.5	23	42	35	5,649	0.789	2,754	1,930	5.6	59	22	26	1.3	Malaysia
2,292	270	1.2	50	12	38	576	0.081	2,234	25,390	3.3	6	68	50	22.6	Mali
2,342	6,630	3.6	4	41	55	8,231	0.854	3,238	850	3.6	75	13	15	0.2	Malta
987	500	-1.8	37	24	39	1,092	0.141	2,599	12,120	6	16	66	101.8	19.4	Mauritania
214,500	2,490	-0.9	9	32	59	5,691	0.804	3,048	1,240	3.8	53	13	1.1	0.1	Mexico
850	400	2.7	40	25	35	2,000	0.574	2,449	570	...	92	7	5	0.05	Mongolia
23,788	950	1.6	16	34	50	2,298	0.429	3,005	15,580	7.3	36	50	39	4.4	Morocco
1,208	80	-4.1	64	22	14	1,060	0.153	1,665	37,960	...	5	67	59	77.4	Mozambique
1,780	1,000	3.1	11	38	51	1,500	0.295	2,200	...	1.9	...	60	35	2.3	Namibia
3,289	170	1.8	58	14	28	896	0.168	2,074	32,710	2.8	30	74	20	11.9	Nepal
258,804	17,330	1.4	5	31	64	13,351	0.968	3,163	450	6.8	82	1	*138.7	*0.94	Netherlands
43,185	12,680	0.6	10	28	62	11,155	0.947	3,389	580	4.9	86	1	*25.6	*0.22	New Zealand
3,082	800	-1.4	29	23	48	1,463	0.496	2,500	1,500	3.9	37	19	81	7.4	Nicaragua
2,365	310	-4.5	35	13	52	634	0.078	2,297	39,730	3.1	6	72	39.8	14.5	Niger
31,285	270	-3	31	44	25	1,160	0.241	2,306	7,990	1.5	19	49	3	1.1	Nigeria
98,079	23,120	2.7	4	34	62	16,838	0.978	3,338	450	6.7	85	1	*218.3	*1.04	Norway
42,649	380	2.9	27	24	49	1,789	0.305	2,197	2,910	2.6	20	65	10.2	2.8	Pakistan
4,414	1,830	-2	10	15	75	3,231	0.731	2,537	980	6.2	59	12	38	2.2	Panama
3,372	860	-0.5	28	30	42	1,834	0.321	...	6,070	5	13	48	97	9.5	Papua New Guinea
4,796	1,110	-1.3	29	22	49	2,742	0.637	2,755	1,460	1.5	29	10	12	2.2	Paraguay
25,149	1,160	-2	8	30	62	2,731	0.6	2,244	1,040	3.5	70	15	14.2	1	Peru
43,954	730	-1.5	23	33	44	2,269	0.6	2,342	6,700	2.9	73	10	20	3	Philippines
64,480	1,700	1.2	14	50	36	4,770	0.874	3,464	490	3.6	76	3	...	...	Poland
50,692	4,890	2.4	9	37	54	6,259	0.85	3,414	410	4.1	37	15	7.6	0.2	Portugal
21,346	6,470	2.1	2	40	58	...	...	...	...	...	...	...	...	...	Puerto Rico
38,025	1,640	1.1	14	53	33	3,000	0.733	3,252	570	2.7	79	4	...	...	Romania
2,214	310	-2.2	37	23	40	680	0.186	1,945	34,680	4.2	7	50	34.5	11	Rwanda
92,839	6,230	-5.6	8	45	47	10,330	0.687	2,842	690	7.6	46	38	81.2	1.46	Saudi Arabia
5,260	710	0	22	31	47	1,208	0.178	2,374	13,060	4.6	16	62	90.5	14	Senegal
981	240	-1.5	46	11	43	1,061	0.062	1,841	13,630	3.8	18	79	16	10.5	Sierra Leone
33,512	12,310	5.7	0	37	63	15,108	0.848	3,249	1,310	3.4	69	12	35.4	0.3	Singapore
946	150	-1.8	65	10	25	861	0.088	1,932	16,080	0.4	10	76	58	38.9	Somalia
90,410	2,520	-0.9	6	44	50	4,958	0.674	3,104	2,000	4.6	...	30	...	...	South Africa
429,404	10,920	2.7	6	9	85	8,723	0.916	3,567	320	3.2	79	6	*6	*0.1	Spain
7,971	470	2.4	26	27	47	2,253	0.651	2,299	5,520	3	74	12	33.2	9.1	Sri Lanka
11,300	450	1.1	36	15	49	1,042	0.157	2,028	10,100	4.8	20	73	31		Sudan
1,365	3,050	-5	11	26	63	3,907	0.749	2,908	1,400	9.5	53	5	135	4.3	Surinam
645	820	1.1	23	40	37	2,405	0.458	2,612	23,000	6.2	50	28	69	7.9	Swaziland
202,498	23,680	1.8	4	34	62	14,817	0.976	2,945	390	7.5	86	1	*211.6	*0.97	Sweden
219,337	32,790	1.7	4	42	54	18,590	0.977	3,565	700	5.2	86	1	*84.5	*0.3	Switzerland

	Population									Land and Agriculture					Energy	Trade	
	Population Total 1991	Population Density 1991	Change 1970-80	Change 1980-90	Birth Rate	Death Rate	Fertility Rate	Life Expectancy	Urban Population	Land Area	Arable and Permanent Crops	Permanent grassland	Forest	Agric. Population	Comm. Consumpt. 1989	Imports per capita	Exports per capita
	millions	persons per km²	%	%	births per thousand	deaths per thousand	children	years	%	thousand km²	% of land area	% of land area	% of land area	% of active pop.	gigajoules	US $	US $
Syria	12.8	70	41	42	43	6	6.3	67	52	184	30	43	4	24	28	208	335
Taiwan	20.5	569	21	13	17	5	1.7	70	76	36	13	11	52		...	...	...
Tanzania	28.4	32	40	36	50	13	7.1	55	33	886	6	40	46	81	1	62	14
Thailand	56.5	111	31	22	20	7	2.2	67	23	511	43	2	28	64	18	584	403
Togo	3.6	67	29	35	45	13	6.6	55	26	54	27	33	30	70	2	161	85
Trinidad & Tobago	1.3	253	11	18	23	6	2.7	72	69	5.1	23	2	43	8	165	994	1,666
Tunisia	8.4	54	25	28	27	6	3.4	68	54	155	30	19	4	24	21	641	458
Turkey	58.5	76	26	32	27	8	3.3	66	48	770	36	11	26	48	28	396	230
Uganda	19.5	98	34	43	52	14	7.3	53	10	200	34	9	28	81	1	31	16
USSR (CIS)	282	13	9	9	17	10	2.3	71	66	22,098	10	17		13	191	417	360
United Kingdom	57.6	238	1	2	14	12	1.8	76	93	242	28	46	10	2	147	3,659	3,227
United States	251	27	11	9	14	9	1.9	76	74	9,167	21	26	32	2	295	20,293	16,792
Uruguay	3.1	18	4	6	17	10	2.3	73	86	175	7	77	4	14	23	433	546
Venezuela	20.2	23	42	31	28	5	3.5	70	91	882	4	20	35	11	83	323	891
Vietnam	65.2	201	26	24	30	8	3.7	64	22	325	20	1	30	61	3	...	...
Yemen	12.1	23	21	47	51	14	7.6	52	32	528	3	30	8	56	20	2	...
Yugoslavia	23.9	94	9	7	14	9	1.9	73	50	255	30	25	37	22	75	793	601
Zaïre	36.7	16	33	36	45	13	6.1	54	40	2,267	3	7	77	66	2	25	28
Zambia	8.8	12	37	47	50	12	7.2	55	56	743	7	40	39	69	6	154	111
Zimbabwe	10	26	35	36	40	9	5.3	61	28	387	7	13	50	68	20	197	184

As yet, for the new divisions of Czechoslovakia, USSR and Yugoslavia, many of the statistics shown in the main table are not available. The area and population of the new republics are shown in the second table, opposite, which lists the area and population of the smaller countries and territories.

Many figures for Luxembourg are included in those for Belgium.

For trade and energy the figures for South Africa include those for Botswana, Lesotho, Swaziland and Namibia.

The sign ... means that figures are not available.

Population Total. This is the UN estimate for the mid-year, 1991.

Population Density. This is the total population divided by the land area, both quoted in the table.

Population Change. This shows the percentage change over ten years 1970-80 and 1980-90.

Birth and Death Rates and Life Expectancy. These are UN estimates for the current period. The Birth and Death rates are the number of these occurrences per year, per thousand population. Life Expectancy is the number of years that a child born today can expect to live if the levels of mortality of today last throughout its life. The figure is the average of that for men and women.

Fertility Rate. This is the average number of children born to a woman in her lifetime.

Urban Population. This is the percentage of the total population living in urban areas. The definition of urban is that of the individual nations and often includes quite small towns.

Land Area. This is the total area of the country less the area covered by major lakes and rivers.

Arable Land and Permanent Crops. This excludes fallow land but includes temporary pasture.

Forest and Woodland. This includes natural and planted woodland and land recently cleared of timber which will be replanted.

Agricultural Population. This is the percentage of the economically active population working in agriculture. It includes those working in forestry, hunting and fishing.

Energy. All forms of energy have been expressed in gigajoules, which is a measure of their calorific value. A gigajoule = 24 kg of oil equivalent.

Trade. The trade figures are for 1991 or 1990. In a few cases the figure is older than this but is the latest available. The total Import and Export figures have been divided by the population to give a figure in US $ per capita.

Gross Natural Product (GNP). This figure is an estimate of the value of a country's production and the average production per person for 1990, in US $. The GNP measures the value of goods and services produced in a country, plus the balance, positive or negative, of income from abroad, for example, from investments, interest on capital, money returned from workers abroad, etc. The average annual rate of change is for the GNP per capita during the period 1980-90. The

GDP, the Gross Domestic Product, is the GNP less the foreign balances. The adjoining three columns show the percentage contribution to the GDP made by the agricultural, mining and manufacturing and service sectors of the economy.

Real GDP per capita. Using exchange rates to convert national currencies into $ US makes no attempt to reflect the varying domestic purchasing powers of the local currency. The UN has made these estimates of Real GDP taking into account these local purchasing values.

Human Development Index. This is a calculation made by the UN Development Programme, using 1990 data, and takes into account not only national income, but also life expectancy, adult literacy and the years in education. It is a measure of national human progress. The wealthy developed countries have an index approaching 1, and the figures range down to some of the poorer with an index of less than 0.100.

Food Intake. The figures are the average intake per person in calories per day.

Adult Illiteracy. This is the percentage of the population aged 15 and over who cannot read or write a simple sentence.

Aid. The bulk of the table is concerned with aid received but aid given is shown by an asterisk.

To convert square kilometres to square miles multiply by 0.39.

Wealth · Social Indicators · Aid

GNP 1990 (million US$)	GNP per capita 1990 (US$)	Rate of change 1980-90 (%)	GDP share agriculture (%)	GDP share industry (%)	GDP share services (%)	Real GDP per capita 1989 (US$)	Human Development Index	Food Intake (calories per day)	Population per doctor 1984 (persons)	% of GNP spent on education 1989 (%)	% of age-group in secondary education (%)	Adult Illiteracy (%)	Per capita 1989 (US$)	% of GNP 1990 (%)	
12,404	990	-2.1	38	23	39	4,348	0.665	3,074	1,260	4.1	54	35	51	5.2	Syria
132,660	6,600	6.4	6	46	48	...	...	3,000	1,000	...	...	...	...	...	Taiwan
2,779	120	-0.7	66	7	27	557	0.268	2,209	26,200	3.7	4	35	38.5	32	Tanzania
79,044	1,420	5.6	17	38	45	3,569	0.685	2,312	6,290	...	28	7	12.6	1	Thailand
1,474	410	-1.7	34	23	43	752	0.218	2,141	8,700	5.2	22	57	58	13.6	Togo
4,458	3,470	-6	3	41	56	6,266	0.876	2,913	950	4.9	83	4	8	0.3	Trinidad & Tobago
11,592	1,420	0.9	13	33	54	3,329	0.582	3,081	2,150	6.3	44	35	30.9	2.5	Tunisia
91,742	1,630	3	17	35	48	4,002	0.671	3,170	1,380	1.8	51	19	23	1.7	Turkey
3,814	220	0.8	17	7	76	499	0.192	2,136	21,900	3.4	13	52	30	13.2	Uganda
1,435,000	5,000	0.8	23	42	35	6,270	0.873	3,380	250	...	...	1	14	...	USSR (CIS)
923,959	16,070	2.5	2	37	61	13,732	0.962	3,181	620	5	79	1	*44.9	*0.31	United Kingdom
5,445,825	21,700	2.2	2	29	69	20,998	0.976	3,676	470	6.8	88	1	*30.6	*0.15	United States
7,929	2,560	-0.9	11	28	61	5,805	0.88	2,697	520	3.1	77	4	15	0.5	Uruguay
50,574	2,560	-2	6	46	48	5,908	0.824	2,620	700	4.2	56	12	4	0.2	Venezuela
19,942	300	2.1	70	20	10	1,000	0.464	2,250	1,000	...	42	12	2.1	...	Vietnam
6,432	640	3.4	24	25	51	1,560	0.232	2,300	5,639	6.1	21	61	33	5.4	Yemen
72,800	3,060	0.9	14	42	44	5,095	0.857	3,620	550	3.6	80	7	1.8	0.1	Yugoslavia
8,117	230	-1.5	30	32	38	380	0.262	2,061	12,940	0.9	24	28	23	6.6	Zaïre
3,391	420	2.9	14	47	39	767	0.315	2,054	7,150	5.5	20	27	49.6	14.1	Zambia
6,313	640	0.8	13	39	47	1,469	0.397	2,288	6,700	8.5	52	33	27.9	4.5	Zimbabwe

	Land Area (thousand km²)	Population 1991 (millions)
American Samoa	0.20	0.038
Andorra	0.49	0.050
Anguilla	0.096	0.007
Antigua & Barbuda	0.44	0.076
Armenia	30	3.3
Aruba	0.19	0.059
Ascension I.	0.090	0.002
Azerbaijan	87	7.1
Bahrain	0.70	0.53
Belize	22	0.19
Belorussia	208	10.3
Bermuda	0.050	0.058
Bhutan	47	1.6
Bosnia-Herzegovina	51	4.4
Brunei	5.3	0.27
Cape Verde Is.	4.0	0.38
Cayman Is.	0.26	0.030
Cocos Is.	0.014	0.001
Comoros	2.2	0.57
Cook Is.	0.24	0.020
Croatia	57	4.7
Czech Republic	79	10.4
Djibouti	23	0.42
Dominica	0.75	0.083
Equatorial Guinea	28	0.36
Estonia	45	1.6
Falkland Is.	12	0.002
Faroe Is.	1.4	0.050
Fiji	18	0.78
French Guiana	88	0.10
French Polynesia	3.7	0.21
Georgia	70	5.5
Gibraltar	0.010	0.030
Greenland	342	0.056
Grenada	0.34	0.084
Guadeloupe	1.7	0.35
Guam	0.54	0.12
Kazakhstan	2,717	16.7
Kirghizia	199	4.4
Kiribati	0.73	0.066
Kuwait	17	2.2
Latvia	64	2.7
Liechtenstein	0.16	0.028
Lithuania	65	3.8
Macau	0.020	0.50
Macedonia	26	2.1
Maldives	0.30	0.22
Martinique	1.1	0.34
Mauritius	1.9	1.1
Micronesia	0.71	0.18
Moldavia	34	4.4
Monaco	0.002	0.030
Montenegro	14	0.63
Montserrat	0.100	0.012
Nauru	0.020	0.009
Netherlands Antilles	0.99	0.19
New Caledonia	18	0.17
Niue	0.26	0.003
Norfolk I.	0.036	0.002
Northern Marianas	0.48	0.020
Oman	212	1.6
Palau	0.46	0.015
Qatar	11	0.38
Reunion	2.5	0.61
Russia	17,068	147
St Christopher-Nevis	0.36	0.044
St Helena	0.122	0.007
St Lucia	0.61	0.15
St Pierre & Miquelon	0.24	0.006
St Vincent & the Grenadines	0.39	0.12
San Marino	0.060	0.020
São Tomé & Principe	0.96	0.12
Serbia	88	9.8
Seychelles	0.30	0.069
Slovenia	20	1.9
Slovak Republic	49	5.3
Solomon Is.	28	0.33
Svalbard	62	0.004
Tajikistan	143	5.3
Tokelau	0.010	0.002
Tonga	0.75	0.094
Tristan da Cunha	0.104	0.0003
Turkmenistan	488	3.6
Turks & Caicos Is.	0.43	0.010
Tuvalu	0.030	0.009
Ukraine	604	51.8
United Arab Emirates	83	1.6
Uzbekistan	447	20.3
Vanuatu	12	0.16
Vatican	0.0004	0.001
Virgin Is. [Br.]	0.150	0.010
Virgin Is. [US]	0.34	0.12
Wallis & Futuna	0.20	0.018
Western Sahara	266	0.18
Western Samoa	2.8	0.17

This list shows the principal cities with more than 500,000 inhabitants (for Brazil, China, India, Japan and USA only cities with more than 1 million are included). The figures are taken from the most recent census or estimate available, and as far as possible are the population of the metropolitan area, eg greater New York, Mexico or London. All the figures are in thousands. The top 20 world cities are indicated with their rank in brackets following the name.

Population in thousands.

Afghanistan
- Kabul — 1,127

Algeria
- Algiers — 1,722
- Oran — 664

Angola
- Luanda — 1,200

Argentina
- Buenos Aires [8] — 10,728
- Cordoba — 1,055
- Rosario — 1,016
- Mendoza — 668
- La Plata — 611
- San Miguel de Tucuman — 571

Armenia
- Yerevan — 1,199

Australia
- Sydney — 3,531
- Melbourne — 2,965
- Brisbane — 1,215
- Perth — 1,083
- Adelaide — 1,013

Austria
- Vienna — 1,483

Azerbaijan
- Baku — 1,757

Bangladesh
- Dacca — 4,770
- Chittagong — 1,840
- Khulna — 860
- Rajshahi — 430

Belgium
- Brussels — 970
- Antwerp — 500

Belorussia
- Minsk — 1,589
- Gomel — 500

Bolivia
- La Paz — 993

Brazil
- São Paulo [3] — 16,832
- Rio de Janeiro [7] — 11,141
- Belo Horizonte — 3,446
- Recife — 2,945
- Pôrto Alegre — 2,924
- Salvador — 2,362
- Fortaleza — 2,169
- Çuritiba — 1,926
- Brasilia — 1,557
- Nova Iguaçu — 1,325
- Belem — 1,296
- Santos — 1,200

Bulgaria
- Sofia — 1,129

Burma
- Rangoon — 2,459
- Mandalay — 533

Cambodia
- Phnom Penh — 500

Cameroon
- Douala — 1,030
- Yaoundé — 654

Central African Rep.
- Bangui — 597

Chad
- Ndjamena — 512

Canada
- Toronto — 3,427
- Montréal — 2,921
- Vancouver — 1,381
- Ottawa-Hull — 819
- Edmonton — 785
- Calgary — 671
- Winnipeg — 623
- Québec — 603
- Hamilton — 557

Chile
- Santiago — 4,858

China
- Shanghai [5] — 12,320
- Peking [10] — 9,750
- Tientsin — 5,459
- Shenyang — 4,285
- Wuhan — 3,493
- Canton — 3,359
- Chungking — 2,832
- Harbin — 2,668
- Chengdu — 2,642
- Sian — 2,387
- Zibo — 2,329
- Nanking — 2,290
- Nanchang — 2,289
- Lupanshui — 2,247
- Taiyuan — 1,929
- Changchun — 1,908
- Dalian — 1,682
- Zhaozhuang — 1,612
- Zhengzhou — 1,610
- Kunming — 1,516
- Jinan — 1,464
- Tangshan — 1,410
- Guiyang — 1,403
- Lanzhou — 1,391
- Linyi — 1,385
- Pingxiang — 1,305
- Qiqihar — 1,301
- Anshan — 1,298
- Qingdao — 1,273
- Xintao — 1,272
- Hangzhou — 1,271
- Fushun — 1,270
- Yangcheng — 1,265
- Yulin — 1,255
- Dongguang — 1,230
- Chao'an — 1,227
- Xiaogan — 1,219
- Fuzhou — 1,205
- Suining — 1,195
- Changsha — 1,193
- Shijiazhuang — 1,187
- Jilin — 1,169
- Xintai — 1,167
- Puyang — 1,125
- Baotou — 1,119
- Bozhou — 1,112
- Zhongshan — 1,073
- Luoyang — 1,063
- Laiwu — 1,054
- Leshan — 1,039
- Urumqi — 1,038
- Ningbo — 1,033
- Datong — 1,020
- Huainan — 1,019
- Heze — 1,017
- Handan — 1,014
- Linhai — 1,012
- Macheng — 1,010
- Changshu — 1,004

Colombia
- Bogotá — 4,185
- Medellin — 1,506
- Cali — 1,397
- Barranquilla — 920
- Cartagena — 560

Congo
- Brazzaville — 596

Croatia
- Zagreb — 1,175

Cuba
- Havana — 2,059

Czech Republic
- Prague — 1,194

Denmark
- Copenhagen — 1,339

Dominican Rep.
- Santo Domingo — 1,313

Ecuador
- Guayaquil — 1,301
- Quito — 1,110

Egypt
- Cairo [18] — 6,325
- Alexandria — 2,893
- El Giza — 1,858
- Shubra el Kheima — 711

El Salvador
- San Salvador — 973

Ethiopia
- Addis Ababa — 1,686

Finland
- Helsinki — 987

France
- Paris [13] — 8,510
- Lyons — 1,170
- Marseilles — 1,080
- Lille — 935
- Bordeaux — 628
- Toulouse — 523

Georgia
- Tbilisi — 1,194

Germany
- Berlin — 3,301
- Hamburg — 1,594
- Munich — 1,189
- Cologne — 928
- Essen — 623
- Frankfurt — 619
- Dortmund — 584
- Düsseldorf — 563
- Stuttgart — 552
- Leipzig — 545
- Bremen — 533
- Duisburg — 525
- Dresden — 518
- Hanover — 500

Ghana
- Accra — 965

Greece
- Athens — 3,027
- Thessalonika — 872

Guatemala
- Guatemala — 2,000

Guinea
- Conakry — 705

Haiti
- Port-au-Prince — 1,144

Honduras
- Tegucigalpa — 605

Hong Kong
- Kowloon — 2,302
- Hong Kong — 1,176
- Tsuen Wan — 690

Hungary
- Budapest — 2,115

India
- Calcutta [11] — 9,194
- Bombay [14] — 8,243
- Delhi — 5,729
- Madras — 4,289
- Bangalore — 2,922
- Ahmadabad — 2,548
- Hyderabad — 2,546
- Poona — 1,686
- Kanpur — 1,639
- Nagpur — 1,302
- Jaipur — 1,015
- Lucknow — 1,008

Indonesia
- Jakarta [17] — 7,348
- Surabaya — 2,224
- Medan — 1,806
- Bandung — 1,567
- Semarang — 1,026
- Palembang — 787
- Ujung Pandang — 709
- Malang — 512

Iran
- Tehran [19] — 6,043
- Mashhad — 1,464
- Esfahan — 987
- Tabriz — 971
- Shiraz — 848
- Ahvaz — 580
- Bakhtaran — 561
- Qom — 543

Iraq
- Baghdad — 4,649
- Basra — 617
- Mosul — 571

Ireland
- Dublin — 921

Italy
- Rome — 2,817
- Milan — 1,464
- Naples — 1,203
- Turin — 1,012
- Palermo — 731
- Genoa — 712

Ivory Coast
- Abidjan — 1,850
- Bouaké — 640

Jamaica
- Kingston — 525

Japan
- Tokyo [6] — 11,829
- Yokohama — 2,993
- Osaka — 2,636
- Nagoya — 2,116
- Sapporo — 1,543
- Kyoto — 1,479
- Kobe — 1,411
- Fukuoka — 1,160
- Kawasaki — 1,089
- Kitakyushu — 1,056
- Hiroshima — 1,044

Jordan
- Amman — 1,160
- Irbid — 680

Kazakhstan
- Alma Ata — 1,108
- Karaganda — 614
- Astrakhan — 509

Kenya
- Nairobi — 1,429
- Mombasa — 500

Kirghizia
- Bishkek — 616

Korea, North
- Pyongyang — 2,639
- Hamhung — 775
- Chongjin — 754
- Chinnampo — 691
- Sinuiju — 500

Korea, South
- Seoul [9] — 10,513
- Pusan — 3,754
- Taegu — 2,206
- Inchon — 1,604
- Kwangju — 1,165
- Taejon — 866
- Ulsan — 551

Latvia
- Riga — 915

Lebanon
- Beirut — 702

Libya
- Tripoli — 980
- Benghazi — 650

Lithuania
- Vilnius — 582

Macedonia
- Skopje — 505

Madagascar
- Antananarivo — 703

Malaysia
- Kuala Lumpur — 1,103

Mali
- Bamako — 646

Mauritania
- Nouakchott — 500

Mexico
- Mexico City [1] — 18,748
- Guadalajara — 2,587
- Monterrey — 2,335
- Puebla — 1,218
- León — 947
- Torreón — 730
- San Luis Potosi — 602
- Ciudad Juárez — 596
- Mérida — 580
- Culiacán Rosales — 560
- Mexicali — 511

Moldavia
- Kishinev — 565

Mongolia
- Ulan Bator — 500

Morocco
- Casablanca — 2,158
- Rabat-Salé — 893
- Fès — 548

Mozambique
- Maputo — 1,070

Netherlands
- Rotterdam — 1,040
- Amsterdam — 1,038
- The Hague — 684
- Utrecht — 526

New Zealand
- Auckland — 851

Nicaragua
- Managua — 682

Nigeria
- Lagos — 1,097
- Ibadan — 1,060
- Ogbomosho — 527

Norway
- Oslo — 643

Pakistan
- Karachi — 5,208
- Lahore — 2,953
- Faisalabad — 1,104
- Rawalpindi — 795
- Hyderabad — 752
- Multan — 722
- Gujranwala — 659
- Peshawar — 556

Panama
- Panama City — 625

Paraguay
- Asunción — 708

Peru
- Lima-Callao — 4,605
- Arequipa — 592

Philippines
- Manila — 1,728
- Quezon City — 1,326
- Cebu — 552
- Caloocan — 524

Poland
- Warsaw — 1,671
- Lodz — 852
- Krakow — 744
- Wroclaw — 640
- Poznan — 586

Portugal
- Lisbon — 1,612
- Oporto — 1,315

Puerto Rico
- San Juan — 1,816

Romania
- Bucharest — 2,014

Russia
- Moscow [12] — 8,967
- St Petersburg — 5,020
- Nizhniy Novgorod — 1,438
- Novosibirsk — 1,436
- Yekaterinburg — 1,367
- Samara — 1,257
- Chelyabinsk — 1,179
- Omsk — 1,148
- Kazan — 1,094
- Perm — 1,091
- Ufa — 1,083
- Rostov — 1,020
- Volgograd — 999
- Krasnoyarsk — 912
- Saratov — 905
- Voronezh — 887
- Vladivostok — 648
- Izhevsk — 635
- Yaroslavl — 633
- Togliatti — 630
- Irkutsk — 626
- Simbirsk — 625
- Krasnodar — 620
- Barnaul — 602
- Khaborovsk — 601
- Novokuznetsk — 600
- Orenburg — 547
- Penza — 543
- Tula — 540
- Kemerovo — 520
- Ryazan — 515
- Tomsk — 502
- Naberezhniye-Chelni — 501

Saudi Arabia
- Riyadh — 2,000
- Jedda — 1,400
- Mecca — 618
- Medina — 500

Senegal
- Dakar — 1,382

Serbia
- Belgrade — 1,470

Singapore
- Singapore — 2,600

Somali Rep.
- Mogadishu — 1,000

South Africa
- Cape Town — 1,912
- Johannesburg — 1,762
- East Rand — 1,038
- Durban — 982
- Pretoria — 823
- Port Elizabeth — 652
- West Rand — 647
- Vereeniging — 540

Spain
- Madrid — 3,123
- Barcelona — 1,694
- Valencia — 739
- Seville — 668
- Zaragoza — 596
- Malaga — 595

Sri Lanka
- Colombo — 1,412

Sudan
- Omdurman — 600
- Khartoum — 510

Sweden
- Stockholm — 1,471
- Gothenburg — 720
- Malmö — 500

Switzerland
- Zurich — 839

Syria
- Damascus — 1,361
- Aleppo — 1,308

Taiwan
- Taipei — 2,680
- Kaohsiung — 1,343
- Taichung — 715
- Tainan — 657
- Panchiao — 506

Tajikistan
- Dushanbe — 595

Tanzania
- Dar es Salaam — 1,100

Thailand
- Bangkok — 5,609

Tunisia
- Tunis — 774

Turkey
- Istanbul — 5,495
- Ankara — 2,252
- Izmir — 1,490
- Adana — 776
- Bursa — 614

Uganda
- Kampala — 500

Ukraine
- Kiev — 2,587
- Kharkhov — 1,611
- Dnepropetrovsk — 1,179
- Odessa — 1,115
- Donetsk — 1,110
- Zaporozhye — 884
- Lvov — 790
- Krivoy Rog — 713
- Mariupol — 529
- Lugansk — 509
- Nikolayev — 503

United Kingdom
- London [17] — 6,378
- Manchester — 1,669
- Birmingham — 1,400
- Liverpool — 1,060
- Glasgow — 730
- Newcastle — 617

Uruguay
- Montevideo — 1,248

United States
- New York [2] — 18,120
- Los Angeles [4] — 13,770
- Chicago [15] — 8,181
- San Francisco [20] — 6,042
- Philadelphia — 5,963
- Detroit — 4,620
- Dallas — 3,766
- Boston — 3,736
- Washington — 3,734
- Houston — 3,642
- Miami — 3,001
- Cleveland — 2,769
- Atlanta — 2,737
- Saint Louis — 2,467
- Seattle — 2,421
- Minneapolis-SP. — 2,388
- San Diego — 2,370
- Baltimore — 2,343
- Pittsburgh — 2,284
- Phoenix — 2,030
- Tampa — 1,995
- Denver — 1,858
- Cincinnati — 1,729
- Kansas City — 1,575
- Milwaukee — 1,572
- Portland — 1,414
- Sacramento — 1,385
- Norfolk — 1,380
- Columbus — 1,344
- San Antonio — 1,323
- New Orleans — 1,307
- Indianapolis — 1,237
- Buffalo — 1,176
- Providence — 1,118
- Charlotte — 1,112
- Hartford — 1,108
- Salt Lake City — 1,065

Uzbekistan
- Tashkent — 2,073

Venezuela
- Caracas — 3,247
- Maracaibo — 1,295
- Valencia — 1,135
- Maracay — 857
- Barquisimeto — 718

Vietnam
- Ho Chi Minh — 3,900
- Hanoi — 3,100
- Haiphong — 1,279
- Da-Nang — 500

Yemen
- San'a — 500

Zaïre
- Kinshasa — 2,654
- Lubumbashi — 543

Zambia
- Lusaka — 900

Zimbabwe
- Harare — 681
- Bulawayo — 500

INDEX TO WORLD MAPS

The index contains the names of all the principal places and features shown on the World Maps. Each name is followed by an additional entry in italics giving the country or region within which it is located. The alphabetical order of names composed of two or more words is governed primarily by the first word and then by the second. This is an example of the rule:

New South Wales □, *Australia*.. **34 G8** 33 0S 146 0E
New York □, *U.S.A.* **43 D10** 42 40N 76 0W
New York City, *U.S.A.* **43 E11** 40 45N 74 0W
New Zealand ■, *Oceania*............ **35 J13** 40 0S 176 0E
Newark, *U.S.A.* **43 F10** 39 42N 75 45W

Physical features composed of a proper name (Erie) and a description (Lake) are positioned alphabetically by the proper name. The description is positioned after the proper name and is usually abbreviated:

Erie, L., *N. Amer.* **42 D7** 42 15N 81 0W

Where a description forms part of a settlement or administrative name, however, it is always written in full and put in its true alphabetical position:

Mount Isa, *Australia*...................... **34 E6** 20 42S 139 26E

Names beginning with M' and Mc are indexed as if they were spelt Mac. Names beginning St. are alphabetized under Saint, but Santa and San are all spelt in full and are alphabetized accordingly. If the same placename occurs two or more times in the index and all are in the same country, each is followed by the name of the administrative subdivision in which it is located. The names are placed in the alphabetical order of the subdivision. For example:

Columbus, Ga., *U.S.A.* **41 D10** 32 30N 84 58W
Columbus, Ind., *U.S.A.* **42 F5** 39 14N 85 55W
Columbus, Ohio, *U.S.A.* **42 F6** 39 57N 83 1W

The number in bold type which follows each name in the index refers to the number of the map page where that feature or place will be found. This is usually the largest scale at which the place or feature appears.

The letter and figure which are in bold type immediately after the page number give the grid square on the map page, within which the feature is situated. The letter represents the latitude and the figure the longitude. In some cases the feature itself may fall within the specified square, while the name is outside.

For a more precise location, the geographical co-ordinates which follow the letter-figure references give the latitude and the longitude of each place. The first set of figures represent the latitude, which is the distance north or south of the Equator measured as an angle at the centre of the Earth. The Equator is latitude 0°, the North Pole is 90°N, and the South Pole 90°S.

The second set of figures represent the longitude, which is the distance east or west of the prime meridian, which runs through Greenwich, England. Longitude is also measured as an angle at the centre of the Earth and is given east or west of the prime meridian, from 0° to 180° in either direction.

The unit of measurement for latitude and longitude is the degree, which is subdivided into 60 minutes. Each index entry states the position of a place in degrees and minutes, a space being left between the degrees and the minutes. The latitude is followed by N(orth) or S(outh) and the longitude by E(ast) or W(est).

Rivers are indexed to their mouths or confluences, and carry the symbol ⤳ after their names. A solid square ■ follows the name of a country, while an open square □ refers to a first order administrative area.

ABBREVIATIONS USED IN THE INDEX

Afghan. – Afghanistan
Ala. – Alabama
Alta. – Alberta
Amer. – America(n)
Arch. – Archipelago
Ariz. – Arizona
Ark. – Arkansas
Atl. Oc. – Atlantic Ocean
B. – Baie, Bahia, Bay, Bucht, Bugt
B.C. – British Columbia
Bangla. – Bangladesh
C. – Cabo, Cap, Cape, Coast
C.A.R. – Central African Republic
C. Prov. – Cape Province
Calif. – California
Cent. – Central
Chan. – Channel
Colo. – Colorado

Conn. – Connecticut
Cord. – Cordillera
Cr. – Creek
D.C. – District of Columbia
Del. – Delaware
Domin. – Dominica
Dom. Rep. – Dominican Republic
E. – East
El Salv. – El Salvador
Eq. Guin. – Equatorial Guinea
Fla. – Florida
Falk. Is. – Falkland Is.
G. – Golfe, Golfo, Gulf
Ga. – Georgia
Guinea-Biss. – Guinea–Bissau
Hd. – Head
Hts. – Heights
I.(s). – Ile, Ilha, Insel,

Isla, Island, Isle(s)
Ill. – Illinois
Ind. – Indiana
Ind. Oc. – Indian Ocean
Ivory C. – Ivory Coast
Kans. – Kansas
Ky. – Kentucky
L. – Lac, Lacul, Lago, Lagoa, Lake, Limni, Loch, Lough
La. – Louisiana
Lux. – Luxembourg
Madag. – Madagascar
Man. – Manitoba
Mass.– Massachusetts
Md. – Maryland
Me. – Maine
Medit. S. – Mediterranean Sea
Mich. – Michigan
Minn. – Minnesota
Miss. – Mississippi

Mo. – Missouri
Mont. – Montana
Mozam.– Mozambique
Mt.(s).– Mont, Monte, Monti, Montaña, Mountain
N. – Nord, Norte, North, Northern
N.B. – New Brunswick
N.C. – North Carolina
N. Cal. – New Caledonia
N. Dak. – North Dakota
N.H. – New Hampshire
N.J. – New Jersey
N. Mex. – New Mexico
N.S. – Nova Scotia
N.S.W. – New South Wales
N.W.T. – North West Territory
N.Y. – New York
N.Z. – New Zealand

Nebr. – Nebraska
Neths. – Netherlands
Nev. – Nevada
Nfld. – Newfoundland
Nic. – Nicaragua
O.F.S. – Orange Free State
Okla. – Oklahoma
Ont. – Ontario
Oreg. – Oregon
P.E.I. – Prince Edward Island
Pa. – Pennsylvania
Pac. Oc. – Pacific Ocean
Papua N.G. – Papua New Guinea
Pen. – Peninsula, Peninsule
Phil. – Philippines
Pk. – Park, Peak
Plat. – Plateau
Prov. – Province,

Provincial
Pt. – Point
Pta. – Ponta, Punta
Pte. – Pointe
Qué. – Québec
Queens. – Queensland
R. – Rio, River
R.I. – Rhode Island
Ra.(s). – Range(s)
Reg. – Region
Rep. – Republic
Res. – Reserve, Reservoir
S. – San, South
Si. Arabia – Saudi Arabia
S.C. – South Carolina
S. Dak. – South Dakota
S. Leone – Sierra Leone
Sa. – Serra, Sierra
Sask. – Saskatchewan
Scot. – Scotland
Sd. – Sound

Sib. – Siberia
St. – Saint, Sankt, Sint
Str. – Strait, Stretto
Switz. – Switzerland
Tas. – Tasmania
Tenn. – Tennessee
Tex. – Texas
Trin. & Tob. – Trinidad & Tobago
U.A.E. – United Arab Emirates
U.K. – United Kingdom
U.S.A. – United States of America
Va. – Virginia
Vic. – Victoria
Vol. – Volcano
Vt. – Vermont
W. – West
W. Va. – West Virginia
Wash. – Washington
Wis. – Wisconsin

106 INDEX TO WORLD MAPS

Aachen — Balkhash, L.

A

Aachen, *Germany* **10 C2** 50 47N 6 4 E
Aalborg, *Denmark* **6 G9** 57 2N 9 54 E
Aalst, *Belgium* **8 B6** 50 56N 4 2 E
Aarau, *Switz.* **10 E3** 47 23N 8 4 E
Aare →, *Switz.* **10 E3** 47 33N 8 14 E
Aarhus, *Denmark* **6 G10** 56 8N 10 11 E
Abadan, *Iran* **24 B3** 30 22N 48 20 E
Abbeville, *France* **8 B4** 50 6N 1 49 E
Abéché, *Chad* **29 G11** 13 50N 20 35 E
Abeokuta, *Nigeria* **30 C2** 7 3N 3 19 E
Aberdeen, *U.K.* **7 D5** 57 9N 2 6W
Aberystwyth, *U.K.* **7 F4** 52 25N 4 6W
Abidjan, *Ivory C.* **28 H6** 5 26N 3 58W
Abitibi, L., *Canada* **42 A8** 48 40N 79 40W
Abkhaz Republic □, *Georgia* **15 F7** 43 0N 41 0 E
Abohar, *India* **23 D5** 30 10N 74 10 E
Abu Dhabi, *U.A.E.* **24 C4** 24 28N 54 22 E
Abuja, *Nigeria* **30 C3** 9 16N 7 2 E
Acapulco, *Mexico* **44 D5** 16 51N 99 56W
Accomac, *U.S.A.* **43 G10** 37 43N 75 40W
Accra, *Ghana* **30 C1** 5 35N 0 6W
Achill I., *Ireland* **7 F1** 53 58N 10 5W
Acklins I., *Bahamas* **45 C10** 22 30N 74 0W
Aconcagua, *Argentina* **47 F3** 32 39S 70 0W
Acre, *Israel* **29 N21** 32 55N 35 4 E
Acre □, *Brazil* **46 C2** 9 1S 71 0W
Adamawa Highlands, *Cameroon* **28 H9** 7 20N 12 20 E
Adana, *Turkey* **15 G6** 37 0N 35 16 E
Adapazarı, *Turkey* **15 F5** 40 48N 30 25 E
Adare, C., *Antarctica* **48 C19** 71 0S 171 0 E
Addis Ababa, *Ethiopia* **29 H14** 9 2N 38 42 E
Adelaide, *Australia* **34 G6** 34 52S 138 30 E
Adelaide, *S. Africa* **31 C4** 32 42S 26 20 E
Adelaide I., *Antarctica* **48 C23** 67 15S 68 30W
Adélie Land, *Antarctica* **48 C18** 68 0S 140 0 E
Aden, *Yemen* **24 D3** 12 45N 45 0 E
Aden, G. of, *Asia* **24 D3** 12 30N 47 30 E
Adirondack Mts., *U.S.A.* **43 D10** 44 0N 74 15W
Admiralty Is., *Papua N. G.* **36 H6** 2 0S 147 0 E
Ado Ekiti, *Nigeria* **30 C3** 7 38N 5 12 E
Adoni, *India* **25 D6** 15 33N 77 18 E
Adour →, *France* **9 F3** 43 32N 1 32W
Adrar, *Algeria* **28 D6** 27 51N 0 11W
Adrian, *U.S.A.* **42 E5** 41 55N 84 5W
Adriatic Sea, *Europe* **12 C6** 43 0N 16 0 E
Adzhar Republic □, *Georgia* **15 F7** 41 30N 42 0 E
Ægean Sea, *Europe* **13 E11** 38 30N 25 0 E
Afghanistan ■, *Asia* **24 B5** 33 0N 65 0 E
'Afif, *Si. Arabia* **24 C3** 23 53N 42 56 E
Agadès, *Niger* **30 A3** 16 58N 7 59 E
Agadir, *Morocco* **28 C5** 30 28N 9 55W
Agartala, *India* **23 H13** 23 50N 91 23 E
Agen, *France* **9 E4** 44 12N 0 38 E
Agra, *India* **23 F6** 27 17N 77 58 E
Agrigento, *Italy* **12 F5** 37 19N 13 33 E
Aguascalientes, *Mexico* **44 C4** 21 53N 102 12W
Agulhas, C., *S. Africa* **31 C3** 34 52S 20 0 E
Ahmadabad, *India* **23 H4** 23 0N 72 40 E
Ahmadnagar, *India* **25 D6** 19 7N 74 46 E
Ahmadpur, *Pakistan* **23 E3** 29 12N 71 10 E
Ahvaz, *Iran* **24 B3** 31 20N 48 40 E
Ahvenanmaa Is., *Finland* **6 F11** 60 15N 20 0 E
Aigoual, Mt., *France* **9 E5** 44 8N 3 35 E
Ain →, *France* **9 E6** 45 45N 5 11 E
Aïr, *Niger* **28 F8** 18 30N 8 0 E
Aisne →, *France* **8 C5** 49 26N 2 50 E
Aix-en-Provence, *France* **9 F6** 43 32N 5 27 E
Aix-les-Bains, *France* **9 E6** 45 41N 5 53 E
Ajaccio, *France* **9 G8** 41 55N 8 40 E
Ajanta Ra., *India* **23 J5** 20 28N 75 50 E
Ajmer, *India* **23 F5** 26 28N 74 37 E
Akashi, *Japan* **19 B4** 34 45N 134 58 E
Akita, *Japan* **19 G12** 39 45N 140 7 E
Akola, *India* **23 J6** 20 42N 77 2 E
Akranes, *Iceland* **6 B2** 64 19N 22 5W
Akron, *U.S.A.* **42 E7** 41 7N 81 31W
Aksai Chih, *India* **23 B7** 35 15N 79 55 E
Aktyubinsk, *Kazakhstan* **15 D10** 50 17N 57 10 E
Akure, *Nigeria* **30 C3** 7 15N 5 5 E
Akureyri, *Iceland* **6 B4** 65 40N 18 6W
Akyab, *Burma* **25 C8** 20 18N 92 45 E
Al Ḥudaydah, *Yemen* **24 D3** 14 50N 43 0 E
Al Hufūf, *Si. Arabia* **24 C3** 25 25N 49 45 E
Al Jawf, *Si. Arabia* **24 C2** 29 55N 39 40 E
Al Kut, *Iraq* **24 B3** 32 30N 46 0 E
Al Qatif, *Si. Arabia* **24 C3** 26 35N 50 0 E
Al 'Ula, *Si. Arabia* **24 C2** 26 35N 38 0 E
Alabama □, *U.S.A.* **41 D9** 33 0N 87 0W
Aland Is., *Sweden* **6 G11** 60 0N 19 30 E
Alaska □, *U.S.A.* **38 B5** 65 0N 150 0W
Alaska, G. of, *Pac. Oc.* **38 C5** 58 0N 145 0W
Alaska Pen., *U.S.A.* **38 C4** 56 0N 160 0W
Alaska Range, *U.S.A.* **38 B4** 62 50N 151 0W
Alba Iulia, *Romania* **13 A10** 46 8N 23 39 E
Albacete, *Spain* **11 C5** 39 0N 1 50W
Albania ■, *Europe* **13 D9** 41 0N 20 0 E
Albany, *Australia* **34 H2** 35 1S 117 58 E
Albany, *Ga., U.S.A.* **41 D10** 31 40N 84 10W
Albany, *N.Y., U.S.A.* **43 D11** 42 35N 73 47W
Albany →, *Canada* **39 C11** 52 17N 81 31W
Alberta □, *Canada* **38 C8** 54 40N 115 0W
Albertville, *France* **9 E7** 45 40N 6 22 E
Albi, *France* **9 F5** 43 56N 2 9 E
Albion, *U.S.A.* **42 D5** 42 15N 84 45W
Albuquerque, *U.S.A.* **40 C5** 35 5N 106 47W
Albury, *Australia* **34 H8** 36 3S 146 56 E
Alcalá de Henares, *Spain* **11 B4** 40 28N 3 22W
Aldabra Is., *Seychelles* **27 G8** 9 22S 46 28 E
Aldan →, *Russia* **18 C14** 63 28N 129 35 E
Alderney, *Chan. Is.* **8 C2** 49 42N 2 12W
Aleksandrovsk-Sakhalinskiy, *Russia* **18 D16** 50 50N 142 20 E
Alençon, *France* **8 C4** 48 27N 0 4 E
Aleppo, *Syria* **24 B2** 36 10N 37 15 E
Alès, *France* **9 E6** 44 9N 4 5 E
Alessandria, *Italy* **12 B3** 44 54N 8 37 E
Ålesund, *Norway* **6 F9** 62 28N 6 12 E
Aleutian Is., *Pac. Oc.* **36 B10** 52 0N 175 0W
Alexander Arch., *U.S.A.* **38 C6** 57 0N 135 0W
Alexander I., *Antarctica* **48 C23** 69 0S 70 0W
Alexandria, *Egypt* **29 C13** 31 0N 30 0 E
Alexandria, *La., U.S.A.* **41 D8** 31 20N 92 30W
Alexandria, *Va., U.S.A.* **42 F9** 38 47N 77 1W
Algarve, *Portugal* **11 D1** 36 58N 8 20W
Algeciras, *Spain* **11 D3** 36 9N 5 28W
Algeria ■, *Africa* **28 D7** 28 30N 2 0 E
Algiers, *Algeria* **28 B7** 36 42N 3 8 E
Alicante, *Spain* **11 C5** 38 23N 0 30W
Alice Springs, *Australia* **34 E5** 23 40S 133 50 E
Aligarh, *India* **23 F7** 27 55N 78 10 E
Alipur Duar, *India* **23 F12** 26 30N 89 35 E
Aliquippa, *U.S.A.* **42 E7** 40 38N 80 18W
Aliwal North, *S. Africa* **31 C4** 30 45S 26 45 E
Alkmaar, *Neths.* **8 A6** 52 37N 4 45 E
Allahabad, *India* **23 G8** 25 25N 81 58 E
Allegan, *U.S.A.* **42 D5** 42 32N 85 52W
Allegheny →, *U.S.A.* **42 E8** 40 27N 80 0W
Allegheny Plateau, *U.S.A.* **42 G7** 38 0N 80 0W
Allentown, *U.S.A.* **43 E10** 40 36N 75 30W
Alleppey, *India* **25 E6** 9 30N 76 28 E
Allier →, *France* **8 D5** 46 57N 3 4 E
Alma, *U.S.A.* **42 D5** 43 25N 84 40W
Alma Ata, *Kazakhstan* **18 E9** 43 15N 76 57 E
Almelo, *Neths.* **8 A7** 52 22N 6 42 E
Almería, *Spain* **11 D4** 36 52N 2 27W
Alor, *Indonesia* **22 D4** 8 15S 124 30 E
Alpena, *U.S.A.* **42 C6** 45 6N 83 24W
Alps, *Europe* **4 F7** 46 30N 9 30 E
Alsace, *France* **8 C7** 48 15N 7 25 E
Altai, *Mongolia* **20 B4** 46 40N 92 45 E
Altay, *China* **20 B3** 47 48N 88 10 E
Altoona, *U.S.A.* **42 E8** 40 32N 78 24W
Altun Shan, *China* **20 C3** 38 30N 88 0 E
Alwar, *India* **23 F6** 27 38N 76 34 E
Amadjuak L., *Canada* **39 B12** 65 0N 71 8W
Amagasaki, *Japan* **19 B4** 34 42N 135 20 E
Amarillo, *U.S.A.* **40 C6** 35 14N 101 46W
Amazon →, *S. Amer.* **46 C5** 0 5S 50 0W
Ambala, *India* **23 D6** 30 23N 76 56 E
Ambert, *France* **9 E5** 45 33N 3 44 E
Ambikapur, *India* **23 H9** 23 15N 83 15 E
Ambon, *Indonesia* **22 D4** 3 35S 128 20 E
American Highland, *Antarctica* **48 C16** 73 0S 75 0 E
American Samoa ■, *Pac. Oc.* **35 C17** 14 20S 170 40W
Amersfoort, *Neths.* **8 A6** 52 9N 5 23 E
Amiens, *France* **8 C5** 49 54N 2 16 E
Amman, *Jordan* **24 B2** 31 57N 35 52 E
Amos, *Canada* **42 A8** 48 35N 78 5W
Amravati, *India* **23 J6** 20 55N 77 45 E
Amreli, *India* **23 J3** 21 35N 71 17 E
Amritsar, *India* **23 D5** 31 35N 74 57 E
Amroha, *India* **23 E7** 28 53N 78 30 E
Amsterdam, *Neths.* **8 A6** 52 23N 4 54 E
Amsterdam, *U.S.A.* **43 D10** 42 58N 74 10W
Amu Darya →, *Uzbekistan* **18 E7** 43 40N 59 0 E
Amundsen Gulf, *Canada* **38 A7** 71 0N 124 0W
Amundsen Sea, *Antarctica* **48 C22** 72 0S 115 0W
Amur →, *Russia* **18 D16** 52 56N 141 10 E
An Najaf, *Iraq* **24 B3** 32 3N 44 15 E
An Nasiriyah, *Iraq* **24 B3** 31 0N 46 15 E
An Nhon, *Vietnam* **22 B2** 13 55N 109 7 E
Anadyr, *Russia* **18 C19** 64 35N 177 20 E
Anadyr, G. of, *Russia* **18 C20** 64 0N 180 0 E
Anaheim, *U.S.A.* **40 D3** 33 50N 118 0W
Anambas Is., *Indonesia* **22 C2** 3 20N 106 30 E
Anantnag, *India* **23 C5** 33 45N 75 10 E
Anar, *Iran* **24 B4** 30 55N 55 13 E
Anatolia, *Turkey* **15 G5** 39 0N 30 0 E
Ancenis, *France* **8 D3** 47 21N 1 10W
Anchorage, *U.S.A.* **38 B5** 61 10N 149 50W
Ancona, *Italy* **12 C5** 43 37N 13 30 E
Anda, *China* **21 B7** 46 24N 125 19 E
Andalusia □, *Spain* **11 D3** 37 35N 5 0W
Andaman Is., *Ind. Oc.* **25 D8** 12 30N 92 30 E
Anderson, *U.S.A.* **42 E5** 40 5N 85 40W
Andes, *S. Amer.* **46 E3** 20 0S 68 0W
Andhra Pradesh □, *India* **25 D6** 18 0N 79 0 E
Andorra ■, *Europe* **11 A6** 42 30N 1 30 E
Andreanof Is., *U.S.A.* **38 C2** 52 0N 178 0W
Andria, *Italy* **12 D7** 41 13N 16 17 E
Andros I., *Bahamas* **45 C9** 24 30N 78 0W
Angara →, *Russia* **18 D11** 58 5N 94 20 E
Ånge, *Sweden* **6 F11** 62 31N 15 35 E
Angel Falls, *Venezuela* **46 B3** 5 57N 62 30W
Angerman →, *Sweden* **6 F11** 62 40N 18 0 E
Angers, *France* **8 D3** 47 30N 0 35W
Anglesey, *U.K.* **7 F4** 53 17N 4 20W
Angola ■, *Africa* **33 G3** 12 0S 18 0 E
Angoulême, *France* **9 E4** 45 39N 0 10 E
Angoumois, *France* **9 E4** 45 50N 0 25 E
Anguilla, *W. Indies* **44 J18** 18 14N 63 5W
Anhui □, *China* **21 C6** 32 0N 117 0 E
Anjou, *France* **8 D3** 47 20N 0 15W
Ankara, *Turkey* **15 G5** 39 57N 32 54 E
Ann, C., *U.S.A.* **43 D12** 42 39N 70 37W
Ann Arbor, *U.S.A.* **42 D6** 42 17N 83 45W
Annaba, *Algeria* **28 B8** 36 50N 7 46 E
Annapolis, *U.S.A.* **42 F9** 39 0N 76 30W
Annecy, *France* **9 E7** 45 55N 6 8 E
Annemasse, *France* **9 D7** 46 12N 6 16 E
Annobón, *Atl. Oc.* **28 K8** 1 25S 5 36 E
Anshan, *China* **21 B7** 41 5N 122 58 E
Anshun, *China* **20 D5** 26 18N 105 57 E
Antalya, *Turkey* **15 G5** 36 52N 30 45 E
Antananarivo, *Madag.* **33 H9** 18 55S 47 31 E
Antarctic Pen., *Antarctica* **48 C24** 67 0S 60 0W
Antarctica **48 C24** 90 0S 0 0 E
Antibes, *France* **9 F7** 43 34N 7 6 E
Anticosti I., *Canada* **43 A16** 49 30N 63 0W
Antigua & Barbuda ■, *W. Indies* **44 K20** 17 20N 61 48W
Antofagasta, *Chile* **47 E2** 23 50S 70 30W
Antrim, *U.K.* **7 E3** 54 43N 6 13W
Antrim, Mts. of, *U.K.* **7 E3** 54 57N 6 8W
Antsiranana, *Madag.* **33 G9** 12 25S 49 20 E
Antwerp, *Belgium* **8 B6** 51 13N 4 25 E
Anyang, *China* **21 C6** 36 5N 114 21 E
Aomori, *Japan* **19 F12** 40 45N 140 45 E
Aparri, *Phil.* **22 B4** 18 22N 121 38 E
Apeldoorn, *Neths.* **8 A6** 52 13N 5 57 E
Apennines, *Italy* **12 C4** 44 0N 10 0 E
Apia, *W. Samoa* **35 C16** 13 50S 171 50W
Appalachian Mts., *U.S.A.* **42 G7** 38 0N 80 0W
Appleton, *U.S.A.* **42 C3** 44 17N 88 25W
Ar Ramadi, *Iraq* **24 B3** 33 25N 43 20 E
Arabia, *Asia* **16 G8** 25 0N 45 0 E
Arabian Gulf = Gulf, The, *Asia* **24 C4** 27 0N 50 0 E
Arabian Sea, *Ind. Oc.* **24 D5** 16 0N 65 0 E
Aracaju, *Brazil* **46 D6** 10 55S 37 4W
Arad, *Romania* **10 E9** 46 10N 21 20 E
Arafura Sea, *E. Indies* **22 D5** 9 0S 135 0 E
Aragón □, *Spain* **11 B5** 41 25N 0 40W
Araguaia →, *Brazil* **46 C5** 5 21S 48 41W
Arakan Yoma, *Burma* **25 C8** 20 0N 94 40 E
Aral Sea, *Asia* **18 E8** 44 30N 60 0 E
Aralsk, *Kazakhstan* **18 E8** 46 50N 61 20 E
Aran I., *Ireland* **7 E2** 55 0N 8 30W
Araq, *Iran* **24 B3** 34 0N 49 40 E
Arbroath, *U.K.* **7 D5** 56 34N 2 35W
Arcachon, *France* **9 E3** 44 40N 1 10W
Archangel = Arkhangelsk, *Russia* **14 B7** 64 40N 41 0 E
Arctic Ocean, *Arctic* **48 A1** 78 0N 160 0W
Arctic Red River, *Canada* **38 B6** 67 15N 134 0W
Ardebil, *Iran* **24 B3** 38 15N 48 18 E
Ardennes, *Belgium* **8 C6** 49 50N 5 5 E
Arendal, *Norway* **6 G9** 58 28N 8 46 E
Arequipa, *Peru* **46 D2** 16 20S 71 30W
Argentan, *France* **8 C3** 48 45N 0 1W
Argentina ■, *S. Amer.* **47 F3** 35 0S 66 0W
Arima, *Trin. & Tob.* **44 S20** 10 38N 61 17W
Arizona □, *U.S.A.* **40 D4** 34 20N 111 30W
Arkansas □, *U.S.A.* **41 D8** 35 0N 92 30W
Arkansas →, *U.S.A.* **41 D8** 33 48N 91 4W
Arkhangelsk, *Russia* **14 B7** 64 40N 41 0 E
Arklow, *Ireland* **7 F3** 52 48N 6 10W
Arlberg Pass, *Austria* **10 E4** 47 9N 10 12 E
Arles, *France* **9 F6** 43 41N 4 40 E
Arlington, *U.S.A.* **42 F9** 38 52N 77 5W
Arlon, *Belgium* **8 C6** 49 42N 5 49 E
Armagh, *U.K.* **7 E3** 54 22N 6 40W
Armançon →, *France* **8 D5** 47 59N 3 30 E
Armenia ■, *Asia* **15 F7** 40 20N 45 0 E
Arnhem, *Neths.* **8 B6** 51 58N 5 55 E
Arnhem Land, *Australia* **34 C5** 13 10S 134 30 E
Arnprior, *Canada* **42 C9** 45 26N 76 21W
Arrah, *India* **23 G10** 25 35N 84 32 E
Arran, *U.K.* **7 E4** 55 34N 5 12W
Arras, *France* **8 B5** 50 17N 2 46 E
Artois, *France* **8 B5** 50 20N 2 30 E
Aru Is., *Indonesia* **22 D5** 6 0S 134 30 E
Arunachal Pradesh □, *India* **25 C8** 28 0N 95 0 E
Arusha, *Tanzania* **32 E7** 3 20S 36 40 E
As Salt, *Jordan* **29 P22** 32 2N 35 43 E
Asab, *Namibia* **31 B2** 25 30S 18 0 E
Asahigawa, *Japan* **19 F12** 43 46N 142 22 E
Asansol, *India* **23 H11** 23 40N 87 1 E
Asbestos, *Canada* **43 C12** 45 47N 71 58W
Asbury Park, *U.S.A.* **43 E10** 40 15N 74 1W
Ascension I., *Atl. Oc.* **2 E9** 8 0S 14 15W
Ashford, *U.K.* **7 G7** 51 8N 0 53 E
Ashkhabad, *Turkmenistan* **18 F7** 38 0N 57 50 E
Ashland, *Ky., U.S.A.* **42 F6** 38 25N 82 40W
Ashland, *Ohio, U.S.A.* **42 E6** 40 52N 82 20W
Ashqelon, *Israel* **29 Q20** 31 42N 34 35 E
Ashtabula, *U.S.A.* **42 E7** 41 52N 80 50W
Asifabad, *India* **23 K7** 19 20N 79 24 E
Asir □, *Si. Arabia* **29 F15** 18 40N 42 30 E
Asir, Ras, *Somali Rep.* **29 G17** 11 55N 51 10 E
Asmara, *Ethiopia* **29 F14** 15 19N 38 55 E
Assam □, *India* **23 F13** 26 0N 93 0 E
Assen, *Neths.* **8 A7** 53 0N 6 35 E
Asti, *Italy* **12 B3** 44 54N 8 11 E
Astrakhan, *Russia* **15 E8** 46 25N 48 5 E
Asturias □, *Spain* **11 A2** 43 15N 6 0W
Asunción, *Paraguay* **47 E4** 25 10S 57 30W
Aswân, *Egypt* **29 E13** 24 4N 32 57 E
Atacama Desert, *Chile* **47 E3** 24 0S 69 20W
Atbara →, *Sudan* **29 F13** 17 40N 33 56 E
Athabasca, L., *Canada* **38 C9** 59 15N 109 15W
Athens, *Greece* **13 F10** 37 58N 23 46 E
Athens, *U.S.A.* **42 F6** 39 25N 82 6W
Athlone, *Ireland* **7 F3** 53 26N 7 57W
Atikokan, *Canada* **42 A2** 48 45N 91 37W
Atlanta, *U.S.A.* **41 D10** 33 50N 84 24W
Atlantic City, *U.S.A.* **43 F10** 39 25N 74 25W
Atlantic Ocean **2 E9** 0 0 20 0W
Au Sable →, *U.S.A.* **42 C6** 44 25N 83 20W
Aube →, *France* **8 C5** 48 34N 3 43 E
Auburn, *Ind., U.S.A.* **42 E5** 41 20N 85 5W
Auburn, *N.Y., U.S.A.* **42 D9** 42 57N 76 39W
Aubusson, *France* **9 E5** 45 57N 2 11 E
Auch, *France* **9 F4** 43 39N 0 36 E
Auckland, *N.Z.* **35 H13** 36 52S 174 46 E
Aude →, *France* **9 F5** 43 13N 3 14 E
Augrabies Falls, *S. Africa* **31 B3** 28 35S 20 20 E
Augsburg, *Germany* **10 D4** 48 22N 10 54 E
Augusta, *Ga., U.S.A.* **41 D10** 33 29N 81 59W
Augusta, *Maine, U.S.A.* **43 C13** 44 20N 69 46W
Aunis, *France* **9 D3** 46 5N 0 50W
Aurangabad, *Bihar, India* **23 G10** 24 45N 84 18 E
Aurangabad, *Maharashtra, India* **23 K5** 19 50N 75 23 E
Aurillac, *France* **9 E5** 44 55N 2 26 E
Aurora, *U.S.A.* **42 E3** 41 42N 88 12W
Austin, *U.S.A.* **40 D7** 30 20N 97 45W
Australia ■, *Oceania* **34 E5** 23 0S 135 0 E
Australian Alps, *Australia* **34 H8** 36 30S 148 30 E
Australian Capital Territory □, *Australia* **34 H8** 35 30S 149 0 E
Austria ■, *Europe* **10 E6** 47 0N 14 0 E
Autun, *France* **8 D6** 46 58N 4 17 E
Auvergne, *France* **9 E5** 45 20N 3 15 E
Auxerre, *France* **8 D5** 47 48N 3 32 E
Avallon, *France* **8 D5** 47 30N 3 53 E
Avellino, *Italy* **12 D6** 40 54N 14 46 E
Avesnes-sur-Helpe, *France* **8 B5** 50 8N 3 55 E
Aveyron →, *France* **9 E4** 44 5N 1 16 E
Avignon, *France* **9 F6** 43 57N 4 50 E
Ávila, *Spain* **11 B3** 40 39N 4 43W
Avranches, *France* **8 C3** 48 40N 1 20W
Ayers Rock, *Australia* **34 F5** 25 23S 131 5 E
Aylesbury, *U.K.* **7 G6** 51 48N 0 49W
Ayr, *U.K.* **7 E4** 55 28N 4 37W
Azamgarh, *India* **23 F9** 26 5N 83 13 E
Azerbaijan ■, *Asia* **15 F8** 40 20N 48 0 E
Azores, *Atl. Oc.* **28 B1** 38 44N 29 0W
Azov, Sea of, *Europe* **15 E6** 46 0N 36 30 E
Azuero, Pen., *Panama* **45 F8** 7 30N 80 30W

B

Babol, *Iran* **24 B4** 36 40N 52 50 E
Babuyan Chan., *Phil.* **22 B4** 18 40N 121 30 E
Bacolod, *Phil.* **22 B4** 10 40N 122 57 E
Bad Axe, *U.S.A.* **42 D6** 43 48N 82 59W
Badajoz, *Spain* **11 C2** 38 50N 6 59W
Badalona, *Spain* **11 B7** 41 26N 2 15 E
Baden-Württemberg □, *Germany* **10 D3** 48 40N 9 0 E
Baffin B., *Canada* **48 A10** 72 0N 64 0W
Baffin I., *Canada* **39 B12** 68 0N 75 0W
Baghdad, *Iraq* **24 B3** 33 20N 44 30 E
Bagnères-de-Bigorre, *France* **9 F4** 43 5N 0 9 E
Baguio, *Phil.* **22 B4** 16 26N 120 34 E
Bahamas ■, *N. Amer.* **45 C10** 24 0N 75 0W
Bahawalpur, *Pakistan* **23 E3** 29 24N 71 40 E
Bahía = Salvador, *Brazil* **46 D6** 13 0S 38 30W
Bahia □, *Brazil* **46 D5** 12 0S 42 0W
Bahía Blanca, *Argentina* **47 F3** 38 35S 62 13W
Bahraich, *India* **23 F8** 27 38N 81 37 E
Bahrain ■, *Asia* **24 C4** 26 0N 50 35 E
Baie-St-Paul, *Canada* **43 B12** 47 28N 70 32W
Baikal, L., *Russia* **18 D12** 53 0N 108 0 E
Baile Atha Cliath = Dublin, *Ireland* **7 F3** 53 20N 6 18W
Baja California = Lower California, *Mexico* **44 B2** 31 10N 115 12W
Bakersfield, *U.S.A.* **40 C3** 35 25N 119 0W
Bakhtaran, *Iran* **24 B3** 34 23N 47 0 E
Bakony Forest, *Hungary* **10 E7** 47 10N 17 30 E
Baku, *Azerbaijan* **15 F8** 40 25N 49 45 E
Balabac Str., *E. Indies* **22 C3** 7 53N 117 5 E
Balaghat, *India* **23 J8** 21 49N 80 12 E
Balasore, *India* **23 J11** 21 35N 87 3 E
Balaton, L., *Hungary* **10 E7** 46 50N 17 40 E
Balboa, *Panama* **44 H14** 9 0N 79 30W
Baldwin, *U.S.A.* **42 D5** 43 54N 85 53W
Balearic Is., *Spain* **11 C7** 39 30N 3 0 E
Bali, *Indonesia* **22 D3** 8 20S 115 0 E
Balıkeşir, *Turkey* **15 G4** 39 35N 27 58 E
Balikpapan, *Indonesia* **22 D3** 1 10S 116 55 E
Balkan Mts., *Bulgaria* **13 C10** 43 15N 23 0 E
Balkan Peninsula, *Europe* **4 G10** 42 0N 23 0 E
Balkhash, *Kazakhstan* **18 E9** 46 50N 74 50 E
Balkhash, L., *Kazakhstan* **18 E9** 46 0N 74 50 E

Ballarat   **Bruce, Mt.**

Bruges   **Colorado Springs**

109
Columbia Eleuthera

Columbia, *U.S.A.* **41 D10** 34 0N 81 0W
Columbia →, *N. Amer.* **40 A2** 46 15N 124 5W
Columbia, District of □, *U.S.A.* **42 F9** 38 55N 77 0W
Columbus, *Ga., U.S.A.* **41 D10** 32 30N 84 58W
Columbus, *Ind., U.S.A.* **42 F5** 39 14N 85 55W
Columbus, *Ohio, U.S.A.* **42 F6** 39 57N 83 1W
Comilla, *Bangla.* **23 H13** 23 28N 91 10 E
Commercy, *France* **8 C6** 48 43N 5 34 E
Commonwealth of Independent States ■, *Eurasia* **18 C11** 60 0N 100 0 E
Communism Pk., *Tajikistan* **18 F9** 39 0N 72 2 E
Como, *Italy* **12 B3** 45 48N 9 5 E
Como, L., *Italy* **12 A3** 46 5N 9 17 E
Comodoro Rivadavia, *Argentina* **47 G3** 45 50S 67 40W
Comorin, C., *India* **25 E6** 8 3N 77 40 E
Comoro Is. ■, *Ind. Oc.* **27 H8** 12 10S 44 15 E
Compiègne, *France* **8 C5** 49 24N 2 50 E
Conakry, *Guinea* **28 H4** 9 29N 13 49W
Concepción, *Chile* **47 F2** 36 50S 73 0W
Conchos →, *Mexico* **44 B4** 29 32N 105 0W
Concord, *U.S.A.* **43 D12** 43 12N 71 30W
Condom, *France* **9 F4** 43 57N 0 22 E
Confolens, *France* **9 D4** 46 2N 0 40 E
Congo ■, *Africa* **32 E3** 1 0S 16 0 E
Congo = Zaïre →, *Africa* **32 F2** 6 4S 12 24 E
Congo Basin, *Africa* **26 G6** 0 10S 24 30 E
Coniston, *Canada* **42 B7** 46 29N 80 51W
Conn, L., *Ireland* **7 E2** 54 3N 9 15W
Conneaut, *U.S.A.* **42 E7** 41 55N 80 32W
Connecticut □, *U.S.A.* **43 E11** 41 40N 72 40W
Connecticut →, *U.S.A.* **43 E11** 41 17N 72 21W
Connellsville, *U.S.A.* **42 E8** 40 3N 79 32W
Connemara, *Ireland* **7 F2** 53 29N 9 45W
Connersville, *U.S.A.* **42 F5** 39 40N 85 10W
Constance, L., *Europe* **10 E3** 47 35N 9 25 E
Constanţa, *Romania* **13 B13** 44 14N 28 38 E
Constantine, *Algeria* **28 B8** 36 25N 6 42 E
Conway, *U.S.A.* **43 D12** 43 58N 71 8W
Cooch Behar, *India* **23 F12** 26 22N 89 29 E
Cook, Mt., *N.Z.* **35 J13** 43 36S 170 9 E
Cook Is., *Pac. Oc.* **35 D18** 17 0S 160 0W
Cook Strait, *N.Z.* **35 J13** 41 15S 174 29 E
Copenhagen, *Denmark* **6 G10** 55 41N 12 34 E
Copper Harbor, *U.S.A.* **42 B4** 47 31N 87 55W
Coppermine, *Canada* **38 B8** 67 50N 115 5W
Coppermine →, *Canada* **38 B8** 67 49N 116 4W
Coral Sea, *Pac. Oc.* **36 J7** 15 0S 150 0 E
Corbeil-Essonnes, *France* **8 C5** 48 36N 2 26 E
Corbin, *U.S.A.* **42 G5** 37 0N 84 3W
Corby, *U.K.* **7 F6** 52 29N 0 41W
Córdoba, *Argentina* **47 F3** 31 20S 64 10W
Córdoba, *Spain* **11 D3** 37 50N 4 50W
Cordova, *U.S.A.* **38 B5** 60 36N 145 45W
Corfu = Kérkira, *Greece* **13 E8** 39 38N 19 50 E
Corinth, G. of, *Greece* **13 E10** 38 16N 22 30 E
Cork, *Ireland* **7 G2** 51 54N 8 30W
Corner Brook, *Canada* **39 D14** 48 57N 57 58W
Corning, *U.S.A.* **42 D9** 42 10N 77 3W
Cornwall, *Canada* **43 C10** 45 2N 74 44W
Coromandel Coast, *India* **25 D7** 12 30N 81 0 E
Coronation Gulf, *Canada* **38 B8** 68 25N 110 0W
Corpus Christi, *U.S.A.* **40 E7** 27 50N 97 28W
Corrib, L., *Ireland* **7 F2** 53 5N 9 10W
Corrientes, *Argentina* **47 E4** 27 30S 58 45W
Corry, *U.S.A.* **42 E8** 41 55N 79 39W
Corse, C., *France* **9 E9** 43 1N 9 25 E
Corsica, *France* **9 F8** 42 0N 9 0 E
Corte, *France* **9 F9** 42 19N 9 11 E
Cortland, *U.S.A.* **43 D9** 42 35N 76 11W
Cosenza, *Italy* **12 E7** 39 17N 16 14 E
Coshocton, *U.S.A.* **42 E7** 40 17N 81 51W
Cosne-sur-Loire, *France* **8 D5** 47 24N 2 54 E
Costa Rica ■, *Cent. Amer.* **45 F8** 10 0N 84 0W
Côte-d'Ivoire = Ivory Coast ■, *Africa* **28 H6** 7 30N 5 0W
Côte d'Or, *France* **8 D6** 47 10N 4 50 E
Cotentin, *France* **8 C3** 49 15N 1 30W
Cotonou, *Benin* **30 C2** 6 20N 2 25 E
Cotopaxi, *Ecuador* **46 C2** 0 40S 78 30W
Cotswold Hills, *U.K.* **7 G5** 51 42N 2 10W
Cottbus, *Germany* **10 C6** 51 44N 14 20 E
Coudersport, *U.S.A.* **42 E8** 41 45N 78 1W
Council Bluffs, *U.S.A.* **41 B7** 41 20N 95 50W
Coutances, *France* **8 C3** 49 3N 1 28W
Coventry, *U.K.* **7 F6** 52 25N 1 31W
Covington, *U.S.A.* **42 F5** 39 5N 84 30W
Cox's Bazar, *Bangla.* **23 J13** 21 26N 91 59 E
Cradock, *S. Africa* **31 C4** 32 8S 25 36 E
Craiova, *Romania* **13 B10** 44 21N 23 48 E
Cranbrook, *Canada* **38 D8** 49 30N 115 46W
Crawfordsville, *U.S.A.* **42 E4** 40 2N 86 51W
Creil, *France* **8 C5** 49 15N 2 29 E
Cremona, *Italy* **12 B4** 45 8N 10 2 E
Crete, *Greece* **13 G11** 35 15N 25 0 E
Creuse →, *France* **9 D4** 47 0N 0 34 E
Crewe, *U.K.* **7 F5** 53 6N 2 28W
Crimea, *Ukraine* **15 E5** 45 0N 34 0 E
Crişu, Black →, *Romania* **10 E9** 46 42N 21 16 E
Crişu, White →, *Romania* **10 E9** 46 42N 21 17 E
Croatia ■, *Europe* **12 B7** 45 20N 16 0 E
Crocodile →, *Mozam.* **31 B5** 25 14S 32 18 E
Crystal Falls, *U.S.A.* **42 B3** 46 9N 88 11W
Cuba ■, *W. Indies* **45 C9** 22 0N 79 0W
Cúcuta, *Colombia* **46 B2** 7 54N 72 31W
Cuenca, *Ecuador* **46 C2** 2 50S 79 9W
Cuenca, *Spain* **11 B4** 40 5N 2 10W
Cuernavaca, *Mexico* **44 D5** 18 55N 99 15W
Cuiabá, *Brazil* **46 D4** 15 30S 56 0W
Culiacán, *Mexico* **44 C3** 24 50N 107 23W
Culpeper, *U.S.A.* **42 F9** 38 29N 77 59W
Cumberland, *U.S.A.* **42 F8** 39 40N 78 43W
Cumberland Plateau, *U.S.A.* **41 C10** 36 0N 84 30W
Cumbrian Mts., *U.K.* **7 E5** 54 30N 3 0W
Cuneo, *Italy* **12 B2** 44 23N 7 31 E
Cupar, *U.K.* **7 D5** 56 20N 3 3W
Curitiba, *Brazil* **47 E5** 25 20S 49 10W
Cuttack, *India* **23 J10** 20 25N 85 57 E
Cuxhaven, *Germany* **10 B3** 53 51N 8 41 E
Cuyahoga Falls, *U.S.A.* **42 E7** 41 8N 81 30W
Cuzco, *Peru* **46 D2** 13 32S 72 0W
Cyclades = Kikládhes, *Greece* **13 F11** 37 20N 24 30 E
Cynthiana, *U.S.A.* **42 F5** 38 23N 84 10W
Cyprus ■, *Medit. S.* **24 B2** 35 0N 33 0 E
Czech Rep. ■, *Europe* **10 D6** 50 0N 15 0 E
Częstochowa, *Poland* **10 C8** 50 49N 19 7 E

D

Da Nang, *Vietnam* **22 B2** 16 4N 108 13 E
Dacca, *Bangla.* **23 H13** 23 43N 90 26 E
Dacca □, *Bangla.* **23 G13** 24 25N 90 25 E
Dadra and Nagar Haveli □, *India* **23 J4** 20 5N 73 0 E
Dadu, *Pakistan* **23 F1** 26 45N 67 45 E
Dagestan Republic □, *Russia* **15 F8** 42 30N 47 0 E
Dagupan, *Phil.* **22 B4** 16 3N 120 20 E
Dahod, *India* **23 H5** 22 50N 74 15 E
Dakar, *Senegal* **28 G3** 14 34N 17 29W
Dakhla, *W. Sahara* **28 E3** 23 50N 15 53W
Dalhousie, *Canada* **43 A14** 48 5N 66 26W
Dalian, *China* **21 C7** 38 50N 121 40 E
Dallas, *U.S.A.* **41 D7** 32 50N 96 50W
Dalmatia □, *Croatia* **12 C7** 43 20N 17 0 E
Daloa, *Ivory C.* **28 H5** 7 0N 6 30W
Damaraland, *Namibia* **31 A2** 21 0S 17 0 E
Damascus, *Syria* **24 B2** 33 30N 36 18 E
Dammam, *Si. Arabia* **24 C4** 26 20N 50 5 E
Dampier, *Australia* **34 E2** 20 41S 116 42 E
Danbury, *U.S.A.* **43 E11** 41 23N 73 29W
Dandeldhura, *Nepal* **23 E8** 29 20N 80 35 E
Dandong, *China* **21 B7** 40 10N 124 20 E
Dannemora, *Sweden* **6 F11** 60 12N 17 51 E
Danube →, *Europe* **13 B13** 45 20N 29 40 E
Danville, *Ill., U.S.A.* **42 E4** 40 10N 87 40W
Danville, *Ky., U.S.A.* **42 G5** 37 40N 84 45W
Dar-es-Salaam, *Tanzania* **32 F7** 6 50S 39 12 E
Dar'ā, *Syria* **29 C14** 32 36N 36 7 E
Darbhanga, *India* **23 F10** 26 15N 85 55 E
Dardanelles, *Turkey* **13 D12** 40 17N 26 32 E
Dargai, *Pakistan* **23 B3** 34 25N 71 55 E
Darjeeling, *India* **23 F12** 27 3N 88 18 E
Darling →, *Australia* **34 G7** 34 4S 141 54 E
Darling Ra., *Australia* **34 G2** 32 30S 116 0 E
Darlington, *U.K.* **7 E6** 54 33N 1 33W
Darmstadt, *Germany* **10 D3** 49 51N 8 40 E
Darnley, C., *Antarctica* **48 C16** 68 0S 69 0 E
Dartmoor, *U.K.* **7 G5** 50 36N 4 0W
Dartmouth, *Canada* **43 C16** 44 40N 63 30W
Darwin, *Australia* **34 C5** 12 25S 130 51 E
Dasht →, *Pakistan* **24 C5** 25 10N 61 40 E
Dasht-e Lūt, *Iran* **24 B4** 31 30N 58 0 E
Datong, *China* **21 B6** 40 6N 113 18 E
Daulpur, *India* **23 F6** 26 45N 77 59 E
Dauphin, *Canada* **38 C9** 51 9N 100 5W
Dauphiné, *France* **9 E6** 45 15N 5 25 E
Davao, *Phil.* **22 C4** 7 0N 125 40 E
Davao G., *Phil.* **22 C4** 6 30N 125 48 E
Davenport, *U.S.A.* **41 B8** 41 30N 90 40W
David, *Panama* **45 F8** 8 30N 82 30W
Davis Str., *N. Amer.* **39 B14** 65 0N 58 0W
Dawson, *Canada* **38 B6** 64 10N 139 30W
Dawson Creek, *Canada* **38 C7** 55 45N 120 15W
Dax, *France* **9 F3** 43 44N 1 3W
Dayton, *U.S.A.* **42 F5** 39 45N 84 10W
De Aar, *S. Africa* **31 C3** 30 39S 24 0 E
De Pere, *U.S.A.* **42 C3** 44 28N 88 1W
Dead Sea, *Asia* **29 Q21** 31 30N 35 30 E
Dease Lake, *Canada* **38 C6** 58 25N 130 6W
Death Valley, *U.S.A.* **40 C3** 36 19N 116 52W
Debrecen, *Hungary* **10 E9** 47 33N 21 42 E
Decatur, *U.S.A.* **42 E5** 40 50N 84 56W
Deccan, *India* **25 D6** 18 0N 79 0 E
Dee →, *Clwyd, U.K.* **7 F5** 53 15N 3 7W
Dee →, *Gramp., U.K.* **7 D5** 57 4N 2 7W
Defiance, *U.S.A.* **42 E5** 41 20N 84 20W
Dehra Dun, *India* **23 D7** 30 20N 78 4 E
Delaware, *U.S.A.* **42 E6** 40 20N 83 5W
Delaware □, *U.S.A.* **43 F10** 39 0N 75 40W
Delaware →, *U.S.A.* **43 F10** 39 20N 75 25W
Delft, *Neths.* **8 A6** 52 1N 4 22 E
Delfzijl, *Neths.* **8 A7** 53 20N 6 55 E
Delhi, *India* **23 E6** 28 38N 77 17 E
Delphos, *U.S.A.* **42 E5** 40 51N 84 17W
Demavand, *Iran* **24 B4** 35 47N 52 0 E
Den Haag = The Hague, *Neths.* **8 A6** 52 7N 4 17 E
Den Helder, *Neths.* **8 A6** 52 57N 4 45 E
Denizli, *Turkey* **15 G4** 37 42N 29 2 E
Denmark ■, *Europe* **6 G9** 55 30N 9 0 E
Denmark Str., *Atl. Oc.* **48 A8** 66 0N 30 0W
Denpasar, *Indonesia* **22 D3** 8 45S 115 14 E
Denver, *U.S.A.* **40 C5** 39 45N 105 0W
Deoghar, *India* **23 G11** 24 30N 86 42 E
Deolali, *India* **23 K4** 19 58N 73 50 E
Deosai Mts., *Pakistan* **23 B5** 35 40N 75 0 E
Dera Ghazi Khan, *Pakistan* **23 D3** 30 5N 70 43 E
Dera Ismail Khan, *Pakistan* **23 D3** 31 50N 70 50 E
Derby, *U.K.* **7 F6** 52 55N 1 28W
Derg, L., *Ireland* **7 F2** 53 0N 8 20W
Derryveagh Mts., *Ireland* **7 E2** 55 0N 8 4W
Des Moines, *U.S.A.* **41 B8** 41 35N 93 37W
Des Moines →, *U.S.A.* **41 B8** 40 23N 91 25W
Dessau, *Germany* **10 C5** 51 49N 12 15 E
Detour, Pt., *U.S.A.* **42 C4** 45 37N 86 35W
Detroit, *U.S.A.* **42 D6** 42 23N 83 5W
Deventer, *Neths.* **8 A7** 52 15N 6 10 E
Devon I., *Canada* **48 A10** 75 10N 85 0W
Dewas, *India* **23 H6** 22 59N 76 3 E
Dhamtari, *India* **23 J8** 20 42N 81 35 E
Dhanbad, *India* **23 H11** 23 50N 86 30 E
Dhankuta, *Nepal* **23 F11** 26 55N 87 40 E
Dhar, *India* **23 H5** 22 35N 75 26 E
Dharwad, *India* **25 D6** 15 22N 75 15 E
Dhaulagiri, *Nepal* **23 E9** 28 39N 83 28 E
Dhenkanal, *India* **23 J10** 20 45N 85 35 E
Dhuburi, *India* **23 F12** 26 2N 89 59 E
Dhule, *India* **23 J5** 20 58N 74 50 E
Diamantina →, *Australia* **34 F6** 26 45S 139 10 E
Dieppe, *France* **8 C4** 49 54N 1 4 E
Digby, *Canada* **43 C15** 44 38N 65 50W
Digne, *France* **9 E7** 44 5N 6 12 E
Dijon, *France* **8 D6** 47 20N 5 3 E
Dili, *Indonesia* **22 D4** 8 39S 125 34 E
Dillingham, *U.S.A.* **38 C4** 59 5N 158 30W
Dimbaza, *S. Africa* **31 C4** 32 50S 27 14 E
Dinajpur, *Bangla.* **23 G12** 25 33N 88 43 E
Dinan, *France* **8 C2** 48 28N 2 2W
Dinant, *Belgium* **8 B6** 50 16N 4 55 E
Dinaric Alps, *Croatia* **12 C7** 44 0N 16 30 E
Dingwall, *U.K.* **7 D4** 57 36N 4 26W
Dir, *Pakistan* **23 B3** 35 8N 71 59 E
Disteghil Sar, *Pakistan* **23 A5** 36 20N 75 12 E
Diu, *India* **23 J3** 20 45N 70 58 E
Diyarbakır, *Turkey* **15 G7** 37 55N 40 18 E
Djakarta = Jakarta, *Indonesia* **22 D2** 6 9S 106 49 E
Djerid, Chott, *Tunisia* **28 C8** 33 42N 8 30 E
Djibouti ■, *Africa* **29 G15** 12 0N 43 0 E
Dneprodzerzhinsk, *Ukraine* **15 E5** 48 32N 34 37 E
Dnepropetrovsk, *Ukraine* **15 E5** 48 30N 35 0 E
Dnieper →, *Ukraine* **15 E5** 46 30N 32 18 E
Dniester →, *Europe* **15 E5** 46 18N 30 17 E
Dobreta-Turnu-Severin, *Romania* **13 B10** 44 39N 22 41 E
Dodecanese, *Greece* **13 F12** 36 35N 27 0 E
Dodoma, *Tanzania* **32 F7** 6 8S 35 45 E
Dogger Bank, *N. Sea* **4 E6** 54 50N 2 0 E
Doha, *Qatar* **24 C4** 25 15N 51 35 E
Dohazari, *Bangla.* **23 H14** 22 10N 92 5 E
Dolbeau, *Canada* **43 A11** 48 53N 72 18W
Dole, *France* **8 D6** 47 7N 5 31 E
Dolomites, *Italy* **12 A4** 46 30N 11 40 E
Dominica ■, *W. Indies* **44 M20** 15 20N 61 20W
Dominican Rep. ■, *W. Indies* **45 D10** 19 0N 70 30W
Don →, *Russia* **15 E6** 47 4N 39 18 E
Don →, *U.K.* **7 D5** 57 14N 2 5W
Doncaster, *U.K.* **7 F6** 53 31N 1 9W
Dondra Head, *Sri Lanka* **25 E7** 5 55N 80 40 E
Donetsk, *Ukraine* **15 E6** 48 0N 37 45 E
Dongting, L., *China* **21 D6** 29 18N 112 45 E
Donostia = San Sebastián, *Spain* **11 A5** 43 17N 1 58W
Dorchester, *U.K.* **7 G5** 50 42N 2 28W
Dordogne →, *France* **9 E3** 45 2N 0 36W
Dordrecht, *Neths.* **8 B6** 51 48N 4 39 E
Dordrecht, *S. Africa* **31 C4** 31 20S 27 3 E
Doring →, *S. Africa* **31 C2** 31 54S 18 39 E
Dortmund, *Germany* **10 C2** 51 32N 7 28 E
Douai, *France* **8 B5** 50 21N 3 4 E
Douala, *Cameroon* **30 D3** 4 0N 9 45 E
Doubs →, *France* **8 D6** 46 53N 5 1 E
Douglas, *S. Africa* **31 B3** 29 4S 23 46 E
Douglas, *U.K.* **7 E4** 54 9N 4 29W
Douro →, *Europe* **11 B1** 41 8N 8 40W
Dover, *U.K.* **7 G7** 51 7N 1 19 E
Dover, *Del., U.S.A.* **43 F10** 39 10N 75 31W
Dover, *N.H., U.S.A.* **43 D12** 43 12N 70 51W
Dover, Str. of, *Europe* **8 B4** 51 0N 1 30 E
Dover-Foxcroft, *U.S.A.* **43 C13** 45 14N 69 14W
Dovrefjell, *Norway* **6 F9** 62 15N 9 33 E
Drac →, *France* **9 E6** 45 12N 5 42 E
Draguignan, *France* **9 F7** 43 32N 6 27 E
Drake Passage, *S. Ocean* **48 D23** 58 0S 68 0W
Drakensberg, *S. Africa* **31 C4** 31 0S 28 0 E
Drammen, *Norway* **6 G10** 59 42N 10 12 E
Drava →, *Croatia* **13 B8** 45 33N 18 55 E
Dresden, *Germany* **10 C5** 51 2N 13 45 E
Dreux, *France* **8 C4** 48 44N 1 23 E
Drina →, *Bos.-H., Yug.* **13 B8** 44 53N 19 21 E
Drogheda, *Ireland* **7 F3** 53 45N 6 20W
Dronne →, *France* **9 E3** 45 2N 0 9W
Drumheller, *Canada* **38 C8** 51 25N 112 40W
Drummond I., *U.S.A.* **42 B5** 46 0N 83 40W
Drummondville, *Canada* **43 C11** 45 55N 72 25W
Drygalski I., *Antarctica* **48 C17** 66 0S 92 0 E
Du Bois, *U.S.A.* **42 E8** 41 8N 78 46W
Dubai, *U.A.E.* **24 C4** 25 18N 55 20 E
Dubbo, *Australia* **34 G8** 32 11S 148 35 E
Dublin, *Ireland* **7 F3** 53 20N 6 18W
Dubrovnik, *Croatia* **13 C8** 42 39N 18 6 E
Dudinka, *Russia* **18 C10** 69 30N 86 13 E
Duisburg, *Germany* **10 C2** 51 27N 6 42 E
Duluth, *U.S.A.* **41 A8** 46 48N 92 10W
Dumbarton, *U.K.* **7 E4** 55 58N 4 35W
Dumfries, *U.K.* **7 E5** 55 4N 3 37W
Dun Laoghaire, *Ireland* **7 F3** 53 17N 6 9W
Dunbar, *U.K.* **7 E5** 56 0N 2 32W
Dundalk, *Ireland* **7 E3** 54 1N 6 25W
Dundee, *S. Africa* **31 B5** 28 11S 30 15 E
Dundee, *U.K.* **7 D5** 56 29N 3 0W
Dunedin, *N.Z.* **35 K13** 45 50S 170 33 E
Dunfermline, *U.K.* **7 D5** 56 5N 3 28W
Dunkerque, *France* **8 B5** 51 2N 2 20 E
Dunkirk, *U.S.A.* **42 D8** 42 30N 79 18W
Dunmore, *U.S.A.* **43 E10** 41 27N 75 38W
Durango, *Mexico* **44 C4** 24 3N 104 39W
Durban, *S. Africa* **31 B5** 29 49S 31 1 E
Durg, *India* **23 J8** 21 15N 81 22 E
Durgapur, *India* **23 H11** 23 30N 87 20 E
Durham, *U.K.* **7 E6** 54 47N 1 34W
Durham, *U.S.A.* **41 C11** 36 0N 78 55W
Durrës, *Albania* **13 D8** 41 19N 19 28 E
Dushanbe, *Tajikistan* **18 F8** 38 33N 68 48 E
Düsseldorf, *Germany* **10 C2** 51 15N 6 46 E
Duyun, *China* **20 D5** 26 18N 107 29 E
Dvina, N. →, *Russia* **14 B7** 64 32N 40 30 E
Dwarka, *India* **23 H2** 22 18N 69 8 E
Dzerzhinsk, *Russia* **14 C7** 56 14N 43 30 E
Dzhambul, *Kazakhstan* **18 E9** 42 54N 71 22 E
Dzhugdzhur Ra., *Russia* **18 D15** 57 30N 138 0 E
Dzungaria, *China* **20 B3** 44 30N 86 0 E

E

Eagle L., *U.S.A.* **43 B13** 46 23N 69 22W
East Beskids, *Europe* **10 D9** 49 20N 22 0 E
East China Sea, *Asia* **21 C7** 30 5N 126 0 E
East Indies, *Asia* **16 K15** 0 0 120 0 E
East Lansing, *U.S.A.* **42 D5** 42 44N 84 29W
East London, *S. Africa* **31 C4** 33 0S 27 55 E
East Pt., *Canada* **43 B17** 46 27N 61 58W
East Siberian Sea, *Russia* **18 B18** 73 0N 160 0 E
Eastbourne, *U.K.* **7 G7** 50 46N 0 18 E
Easter Dal →, *Sweden* **6 F10** 61 30N 13 45 E
Easter Islands, *Pac. Oc.* **37 K17** 27 0S 109 0W
Eastern Ghats, *India* **25 D6** 14 0N 78 50 E
Easton, *Md., U.S.A.* **43 F9** 38 47N 76 7W
Easton, *Pa., U.S.A.* **43 E10** 40 41N 75 15W
Eastport, *U.S.A.* **43 C14** 44 57N 67 0W
Eau Claire, *U.S.A.* **41 B8** 44 46N 91 30W
Ebro →, *Spain* **11 B6** 40 43N 0 54 E
Echo Bay, *Canada* **38 B8** 66 5N 117 55W
Ecuador ■, *S. Amer.* **46 C2** 2 0S 78 0W
Ede, *Nigeria* **30 C2** 7 45N 4 29 E
Edendale, *S. Africa* **31 B5** 29 39S 30 18 E
Edinburgh, *U.K.* **7 E5** 55 57N 3 12W
Edmonton, *Canada* **38 C8** 53 30N 113 30W
Edmundston, *Canada* **43 B13** 47 23N 68 20W
Edward, L., *Africa* **32 E5** 0 25S 29 40 E
Edward VII Land, *Antarctica* **48 C21** 80 0S 150 0W
Effingham, *U.S.A.* **42 F3** 39 8N 88 30W
Eganville, *Canada* **42 C9** 45 32N 77 5W
Eger, *Hungary* **10 E9** 47 53N 20 27 E
Egersund, *Norway* **6 G9** 58 26N 6 1 E
Egypt ■, *Africa* **29 D13** 28 0N 31 0 E
Eifel, *Germany* **10 C2** 50 10N 6 45 E
Eindhoven, *Neths.* **8 B6** 51 26N 5 28 E
El Aaiún, *W. Sahara* **28 D4** 27 9N 13 12W
El Faiyum, *Egypt* **29 D13** 29 19N 30 50 E
El Fasher, *Sudan* **29 G12** 13 33N 25 26 E
El Iskandarîya = Alexandria, *Egypt* **29 C13** 31 0N 30 0 E
El Mahalla el Kubra, *Egypt* **29 C13** 31 0N 31 0 E
El Minya, *Egypt* **29 D13** 28 7N 30 33 E
El Obeid, *Sudan* **29 G13** 13 8N 30 10 E
El Paso, *U.S.A.* **40 D5** 31 50N 106 30W
El Qâhira = Cairo, *Egypt* **29 C13** 30 1N 31 14 E
El Salvador ■, *Cent. Amer.* **44 E7** 13 50N 89 0W
Elba, *Italy* **12 C4** 42 48N 10 15 E
Elbasan, *Albania* **13 D9** 41 9N 20 9 E
Elbe →, *Europe* **10 B3** 53 50N 9 0 E
Elbeuf, *France* **8 C4** 49 17N 1 2 E
Elblag, *Poland* **10 A8** 54 10N 19 25 E
Elbrus, *Asia* **15 F7** 43 21N 42 30 E
Elburz Mts., *Iran* **24 B4** 36 0N 52 0 E
Elche, *Spain* **11 C5** 38 15N 0 42W
Eldoret, *Kenya* **32 D7** 0 30N 35 17 E
Elephant I., *Antarctica* **48 C24** 61 0S 55 0W
Elephants →, *Mozam.* **31 A5** 24 10S 32 40 E
Eleuthera, *Bahamas* **45 C9** 25 0N 76 20W

110 INDEX TO WORLD MAPS

Elgin — Great Barrier Reef

Elgin, *U.K.* **7 D5** 57 39N 3 20W
Elgin, *U.S.A.* **42 D3** 42 5N 88 20W
Elizabeth, *U.S.A.* **43 E10** 40 37N 74 12W
Elizabethtown, *U.S.A.* **42 G5** 37 40N 85 54W
Elkhart, *U.S.A.* **42 E5** 41 42N 85 55W
Elkins, *U.S.A.* **42 F8** 38 53N 79 53W
Ellesmere I., *Canada* **48 A10** 79 30N 80 0W
Elliot Lake, *Canada* **42 B6** 46 25N 82 35W
Ellsworth Land, *Antarctica* **48 C23** 76 0S 89 0W
Elmira, *U.S.A.* **42 D9** 42 8N 76 49W
Eluru, *India* **25 D7** 16 48N 81 8 E
Elyria, *U.S.A.* **42 E6** 41 22N 82 8W
Emamrud, *Iran* **24 B4** 36 30N 55 0 E
Emden, *Germany* **10 B2** 53 22N 7 12 E
Emmen, *Neths.* **8 A7** 52 48N 6 57 E
Empangeni, *S. Africa* **31 B5** 28 50S 31 52 E
Emporium, *U.S.A.* **42 E8** 41 30N 78 17W
Empty Quarter = Rub' al Khali, *Si. Arabia* **24 D3** 18 0N 48 0 E
Ems →, *Germany* **10 B2** 53 22N 7 15 E
Enderbury I., *Kiribati* **36 H10** 3 8S 171 5W
Enderby Land, *Antarctica* **48 C15** 66 0S 53 0 E
Endicott, *U.S.A.* **43 D9** 42 6N 76 2W
Engadin, *Switz.* **10 E4** 46 45N 10 10 E
Enggano, *Indonesia* **22 D2** 5 20S 102 40 E
England □, *U.K.* **7 F6** 53 0N 2 0W
English Bazar, *India* **23 G12** 24 58N 88 10 E
English Channel, *Europe* **8 C2** 50 0N 2 0W
Ennis, *Ireland* **7 F2** 52 51N 8 59W
Enniskillen, *U.K.* **7 E3** 54 20N 7 40W
Enns →, *Austria* **10 D6** 48 14N 14 32 E
Enschede, *Neths.* **8 A7** 52 13N 6 53 E
Ensenada, *Mexico* **44 A1** 31 50N 116 50W
Entebbe, *Uganda* **32 D6** 0 4N 32 28 E
Enugu, *Nigeria* **30 C3** 6 20N 7 30 E
Épernay, *France* **8 C5** 49 3N 3 56 E
Épinal, *France* **8 C7** 48 10N 6 27 E
Equatorial Guinea ■, *Africa* **28 J8** 2 0N 8 0 E
Erbil, *Iraq* **24 B3** 36 15N 44 5 E
Erebus, Mt., *Antarctica* **48 C19** 77 35S 167 0 E
Erfurt, *Germany* **10 C4** 50 58N 11 2 E
Erie, *U.S.A.* **42 D7** 42 10N 80 7W
Erie, L., *N. Amer.* **42 D7** 42 15N 81 0W
Eritrea □, *Ethiopia* **29 G14** 14 0N 38 30 E
Erlangen, *Germany* **10 D4** 49 35N 11 2 E
Ermelo, *S. Africa* **31 B4** 26 31S 29 59 E
Erne, Lower L., *U.K.* **7 E3** 54 26N 7 46W
Erode, *India* **25 D6** 11 24N 77 45 E
Erz Gebirge, *Germany* **10 C5** 50 25N 13 0 E
Erzurum, *Turkey* **15 G7** 39 57N 41 15 E
Esbjerg, *Denmark* **6 G9** 55 29N 8 29 E
Escanaba, *U.S.A.* **42 C4** 45 44N 87 5W
Esch-sur-Alzette, *Lux.* **8 C7** 49 32N 6 0 E
Esfahan, *Iran* **24 B4** 33 0N 51 30 E
Eskilstuna, *Sweden* **6 G11** 59 22N 16 32 E
Eskimo Pt., *Canada* **38 B10** 61 10N 94 15W
Eskişehir, *Turkey* **15 G5** 39 50N 30 35 E
Esperance, *Australia* **34 G3** 33 45S 121 55 E
Essen, *Germany* **10 C2** 51 28N 6 59 E
Estcourt, *S. Africa* **31 B4** 29 0S 29 53 E
Estonia ■, *Europe* **14 C4** 58 30N 25 30 E
Etawah, *India* **23 F7** 26 48N 79 6 E
Ethiopia ■, *Africa* **29 H15** 8 0N 40 0 E
Ethiopian Highlands, *Ethiopia* **26 E7** 10 0N 37 0 E
Etna, *Italy* **12 F6** 37 45N 15 0 E
Euclid, *U.S.A.* **42 E7** 41 32N 81 31W
Eugene, *U.S.A.* **40 B2** 44 0N 123 8W
Euphrates →, *Asia* **24 B3** 31 0N 47 25 E
Evanston, *U.S.A.* **42 D4** 42 0N 87 40W
Evansville, *U.S.A.* **42 G4** 37 55N 87 35W
Everest, Mt., *Nepal* **23 E11** 28 5N 86 58 E
Évora, *Portugal* **11 C2** 38 33N 7 57W
Évreux, *France* **8 C4** 49 3N 1 8 E
Évvoia, *Greece* **13 E11** 38 30N 24 0 E
Exeter, *U.K.* **7 G5** 50 43N 3 31W
Exmoor, *U.K.* **7 G5** 51 10N 3 59W
Extremadura □, *Spain* **11 C2** 39 30N 6 5W
Eyre, L., *Australia* **34 F6** 29 30S 137 26 E

F

Fair Isle, *U.K.* **7 C6** 59 30N 1 40W
Fairbanks, *U.S.A.* **38 B5** 64 50N 147 50W
Fairfield, *U.S.A.* **42 F3** 38 20N 88 20W
Fairmont, *U.S.A.* **42 F7** 39 29N 80 10W
Faisalabad, *Pakistan* **23 D4** 31 30N 73 5 E
Faizabad, *India* **23 F9** 26 45N 82 10 E
Fakfak, *Indonesia* **22 D5** 3 0S 132 15 E
Falkirk, *U.K.* **7 E5** 56 0N 3 47W
Falkland Is., *Atl. Oc.* **47 H4** 51 30S 59 0W
Fall River, *U.S.A.* **43 E12** 41 45N 71 5W
Falmouth, *U.K.* **7 G4** 50 9N 5 5W
Falmouth, *U.S.A.* **42 F5** 38 40N 84 20W
Falun, *Sweden* **6 F11** 60 37N 15 37 E
Farah, *Afghan.* **24 B5** 32 20N 62 7 E
Farewell C., *Greenland* **48 B9** 59 48N 43 55W
Farmville, *U.S.A.* **42 G8** 37 19N 78 22W
Faroe Is., *Atl. Oc.* **5 C4** 62 0N 7 0W
Fatehgarh, *India* **23 F7** 27 25N 79 35 E
Fatehpur, *India* **23 G8** 25 56N 81 13 E
Fayetteville, *U.S.A.* **41 C11** 35 0N 78 58W
Fazilka, *India* **23 D5** 30 27N 74 2 E
F'Dérik, *Mauritania* **28 E4** 22 40N 12 45W
Fécamp, *France* **8 C4** 49 45N 0 22 E
Fehmarn, *Germany* **10 A4** 54 26N 11 10 E
Fehmarn Belt, *Denmark* **10 A4** 54 35N 11 20 E
Feira de Santana, *Brazil* **46 D6** 12 15S 38 57W
Fens, The, *U.K.* **7 F7** 52 45N 0 2 E
Fermoy, *Ireland* **7 F2** 52 4N 8 18W
Fernando Póo = Bioko, *Eq. Guin.* **30 D3** 3 30N 8 40 E
Ferozepore, *India* **23 D5** 30 55N 74 40 E
Ferrara, *Italy* **12 B4** 44 50N 11 36 E
Ferret, C., *France* **9 E3** 44 38N 1 15W
Fès, *Morocco* **28 C6** 34 0N 5 0W
Fianarantsoa, *Madag.* **33 J9** 21 26S 47 5 E
Fichtel Gebirge, *Germany* **10 C5** 50 10N 12 0 E
Ficksburg, *S. Africa* **31 B4** 28 51S 27 53 E
Figeac, *France* **9 E5** 44 37N 2 2 E
Fiji ■, *Pac. Oc.* **35 D14** 17 20S 179 0 E
Findlay, *U.S.A.* **42 E6** 41 5N 83 41W
Finisterre, C., *Spain* **11 A1** 42 50N 9 19W
Finland ■, *Europe* **6 F13** 63 0N 27 0 E
Finland, G. of, *Europe* **6 G12** 60 0N 26 0 E
Firenze = Florence, *Italy* **12 C4** 43 47N 11 15 E
Firozabad, *India* **23 F7** 27 10N 78 25 E
Fish →, *Namibia* **31 B2** 28 7S 17 10 E
Fishguard, *U.K.* **7 G4** 51 59N 4 59W
Fitchburg, *U.S.A.* **43 D12** 42 35N 71 47W
Flanders □, *Belgium* **8 B5** 51 0N 3 0 E
Flensburg, *Germany* **10 A3** 54 46N 9 28 E
Flers, *France* **8 C3** 48 47N 0 33W
Flinders →, *Australia* **34 D7** 17 36S 140 36 E
Flinders Ras., *Australia* **34 G6** 31 30S 138 30 E
Flint, *U.S.A.* **42 D6** 43 5N 83 40W
Flint →, *U.S.A.* **41 D10** 30 52N 84 38W
Flora, *U.S.A.* **42 F3** 38 40N 88 30W
Florence, *Italy* **12 C4** 43 47N 11 15 E
Flores, *Indonesia* **22 D4** 8 35S 121 0 E
Florianópolis, *Brazil* **47 E5** 27 30S 48 30W
Florida □, *U.S.A.* **41 E10** 28 30N 82 0W
Florida, Straits of, *U.S.A.* **45 C9** 25 0N 80 0W
Florida Keys, *U.S.A.* **41 F10** 24 45N 80 40W
Florø, *Norway* **6 F9** 61 35N 5 1 E
Foggia, *Italy* **12 D6** 41 28N 15 31 E
Foix, *France* **9 F4** 42 58N 1 38 E
Folkestone, *U.K.* **7 G7** 51 5N 1 11 E
Fontainebleau, *France* **8 C5** 48 24N 2 40 E
Fontenay-le-Comte, *France* **9 D3** 46 28N 0 48W
Forbach, *France* **8 C7** 49 10N 6 52 E
Forel, Mt., *Greenland* **48 A9** 66 52N 36 55W
Forfar, *U.K.* **7 D5** 56 40N 2 53W
Fort Beaufort, *S. Africa* **31 C4** 32 46S 26 40 E
Fort Collins, *U.S.A.* **40 B5** 40 30N 105 4W
Fort-Coulonge, *Canada* **42 C9** 45 50N 76 45W
Fort-de-France, *Martinique* **44 N20** 14 36N 61 2W
Fort Kent, *U.S.A.* **43 B13** 47 12N 68 30W
Fort Lauderdale, *U.S.A.* **41 E10** 26 10N 80 5W
Fort McMurray, *Canada* **38 C8** 56 44N 111 7W
Fort Sandeman, *Pakistan* **23 D2** 31 20N 69 31 E
Fort Smith, *U.S.A.* **41 C8** 35 25N 94 25W
Fort Wayne, *U.S.A.* **42 E5** 41 5N 85 10W
Fort William, *U.K.* **7 D4** 56 48N 5 8W
Fort Worth, *U.S.A.* **41 D7** 32 45N 97 25W
Fortaleza, *Brazil* **46 C6** 3 45S 38 35W
Forth, Firth of, *U.K.* **7 D5** 56 5N 2 55W
Foshan, *China* **21 D6** 23 4N 113 5 E
Fostoria, *U.S.A.* **42 E6** 41 8N 83 25W
Fougères, *France* **8 C3** 48 21N 1 14W
Foula, *U.K.* **7 A5** 60 10N 2 5W
Fourmies, *France* **8 B6** 50 1N 4 2 E
Foxe Chan., *Canada* **39 B11** 65 0N 80 0W
France ■, *Europe* **8 D5** 47 0N 3 0 E
Franche-Comté, *France* **8 D6** 46 50N 5 55 E
Francistown, *Botswana* **31 A4** 21 7S 27 33 E
Frankfort, *S. Africa* **31 B4** 27 17S 28 30 E
Frankfort, *Ind., U.S.A.* **42 E4** 40 20N 86 33W
Frankfort, *Ky., U.S.A.* **42 F5** 38 12N 84 52W
Frankfort, *Mich., U.S.A.* **42 C4** 44 38N 86 14W
Frankfurt am Main, *Germany* **10 C3** 50 7N 8 40 E
Frankfurt an der Oder, *Germany* **10 B6** 52 20N 14 31 E
Franklin, *N.H., U.S.A.* **43 D12** 43 28N 71 39W
Franklin, *Pa., U.S.A.* **42 E8** 41 22N 79 45W
Franz Josef Land, *Russia* **18 A7** 82 0N 55 0 E
Fraser →, *Canada* **38 D7** 49 7N 123 11W
Fraserburg, *S. Africa* **31 C3** 31 55S 21 30 E
Fraserburgh, *U.K.* **7 D5** 57 41N 2 3W
Frederick, *U.S.A.* **42 F9** 39 25N 77 23W
Fredericksburg, *U.S.A.* **42 F9** 38 16N 77 29W
Fredericton, *Canada* **43 C14** 45 57N 66 40W
Fredonia, *U.S.A.* **42 D8** 42 26N 79 20W
Fredrikstad, *Norway* **6 G10** 59 13N 10 57 E
Freetown, *S. Leone* **28 H4** 8 30N 13 17W
Freiburg, *Germany* **10 E2** 48 0N 7 52 E
Fremont, *U.S.A.* **42 E6** 41 20N 83 5W
French Cr. →, *U.S.A.* **42 E8** 41 22N 79 50W
French Guiana ■, *S. Amer.* **46 B4** 4 0N 53 0W
French Polynesia ■, *Pac. Oc.* **37 J13** 20 0S 145 0W
Fresnillo, *Mexico* **44 C4** 23 10N 103 0W
Fresno, *U.S.A.* **40 C3** 36 47N 119 50W
Frisian Is., *Europe* **10 A2** 53 30N 6 0 E
Frobisher B., *Canada* **39 B13** 62 30N 66 0W
Front Royal, *U.S.A.* **42 F8** 38 55N 78 10W
Frunze = Bishkek, *Kirghizia* **18 E9** 42 54N 74 46 E
Frýdek-Místek, *Czech.* **10 D8** 49 40N 18 20 E
Fuji-San, *Japan* **19 B6** 35 22N 138 44 E
Fujian □, *China* **21 D6** 26 0N 118 0 E
Fukui, *Japan* **19 A5** 36 5N 136 10 E
Fukuoka, *Japan* **19 C2** 33 39N 130 21 E
Fukushima, *Japan* **19 G12** 37 44N 140 28 E
Fukuyama, *Japan* **19 B3** 34 35N 133 20 E
Fulda, *Germany* **10 C3** 50 32N 9 41 E
Fulda →, *Germany* **10 C3** 51 27N 9 40 E
Fulton, *U.S.A.* **42 D9** 43 20N 76 22W
Funafuti, *Pac. Oc.* **35 B14** 8 30S 179 0 E
Fundy, B. of, *Canada* **43 C15** 45 0N 66 0W
Furneaux Group, *Australia* **34 J8** 40 10S 147 50 E
Fürth, *Germany* **10 D4** 49 29N 11 0 E
Fury and Hecla Str., *Canada* **39 B11** 69 56N 84 0W
Fushun, *China* **21 B7** 41 50N 123 56 E
Fuxin, *China* **21 B7** 42 5N 121 48 E
Fuzhou, *China* **21 D6** 26 5N 119 16 E
Fyn, *Denmark* **6 G10** 55 20N 10 30 E

G

Gabès, *Tunisia* **28 C9** 33 53N 10 2 E
Gabon ■, *Africa* **32 E2** 0 10S 10 0 E
Gaborone, *Botswana* **31 A4** 24 45S 25 57 E
Gabrovo, *Bulgaria* **13 C11** 42 52N 25 19 E
Gadag, *India* **25 D6** 15 30N 75 45 E
Gadarwara, *India* **23 H7** 22 50N 78 50 E
Gainesville, *U.S.A.* **41 E10** 29 38N 82 20W
Galápagos, *Pac. Oc.* **37 H18** 0 0 91 0W
Galashiels, *U.K.* **7 E5** 55 37N 2 50W
Galaţi, *Romania* **13 B13** 45 27N 28 2 E
Galdhøpiggen, *Norway* **6 F9** 61 38N 8 18 E
Galicia □, *Spain* **11 A2** 42 43N 7 45W
Galle, *Sri Lanka* **25 E7** 6 5N 80 10 E
Gallipolis, *U.S.A.* **42 F6** 38 50N 82 10W
Gällivare, *Sweden* **6 E12** 67 9N 20 40 E
Galveston, *U.S.A.* **41 E8** 29 15N 94 48W
Galway, *Ireland* **7 F2** 53 16N 9 4W
Galway B., *Ireland* **7 F2** 53 10N 9 20W
Gambia ■, *W. Afr.* **28 G3** 13 25N 16 0W
Gan Jiang →, *China* **21 D6** 29 15N 116 0 E
Gananoque, *Canada* **43 C9** 44 20N 76 10W
Gandak →, *India* **23 G10** 25 39N 85 13 E
Gandhi Sagar Dam, *India* **23 G5** 24 40N 75 40 E
Ganganagar, *India* **23 E4** 29 56N 73 56 E
Gangdisê Shan, *China* **23 D8** 31 20N 81 0 E
Ganges →, *India* **23 H13** 23 20N 90 30 E
Gangtok, *India* **23 F12** 27 20N 88 37 E
Gansu □, *China* **20 C5** 36 0N 104 0 E
Gao, *Mali* **28 F6** 16 15N 0 5W
Gap, *France* **9 E7** 44 33N 6 5 E
Garda, L. di, *Italy* **12 B4** 45 40N 10 40 E
Gardēz, *Afghan.* **23 C2** 33 37N 69 9 E
Garies, *S. Africa* **31 C2** 30 32S 17 59 E
Garonne →, *France* **9 E3** 45 2N 0 36W
Garoua, *Cameroon* **30 C4** 9 19N 13 21 E
Gary, *U.S.A.* **42 E4** 41 35N 87 20W
Garzê, *China* **20 C5** 31 38N 100 1 E
Gascony, *France* **9 F4** 43 45N 0 20 E
Gaspé, *Canada* **43 A15** 48 52N 64 30W
Gaspé, C., *Canada* **43 A15** 48 48N 64 7W
Gaspé Pen., *Canada* **43 A15** 48 45N 65 40W
Gateshead, *U.K.* **7 E6** 54 57N 1 37W
Gatineau →, *Canada* **43 C10** 45 27N 75 42W
Gatun, *Panama* **44 H14** 9 16N 79 55W
Gatun, L., *Panama* **44 H14** 9 7N 79 56W
Gauhati, *India* **23 F13** 26 10N 91 45 E
Gävle, *Sweden* **6 F11** 60 40N 17 9 E
Gawilgarh Hills, *India* **23 J6** 21 15N 76 45 E
Gaya, *India* **23 G10** 24 47N 85 4 E
Gaylord, *U.S.A.* **42 C5** 45 1N 84 41W
Gaza, *Egypt* **29 Q19** 31 30N 34 28 E
Gaziantep, *Turkey* **15 G6** 37 6N 37 23 E
Gcuwa, *S. Africa* **31 C4** 32 20S 28 11 E
Gdańsk, *Poland* **10 A8** 54 22N 18 40 E
Gdańsk B., *Poland* **10 A8** 54 30N 19 20 E
Gdynia, *Poland* **10 A8** 54 35N 18 33 E
Gebe, *Indonesia* **22 C4** 0 5N 129 25 E
Gedser, *Denmark* **6 H10** 54 35N 11 55 E
Geelong, *Australia* **34 H7** 38 10S 144 22 E
Gejiu, *China* **20 D5** 23 20N 103 10 E
Gelsenkirchen, *Germany* **10 C2** 51 30N 7 5 E
Geneva, *Switz.* **9 D7** 46 12N 6 9 E
Geneva, *U.S.A.* **42 D9** 42 53N 77 0W
Genk, *Belgium* **8 B6** 50 58N 5 32 E
Gennargentu, Mti. del, *Italy* **12 E3** 40 0N 9 10 E
Genoa, *Italy* **12 B3** 44 24N 8 56 E
George, *S. Africa* **31 C3** 33 58S 22 29 E
George Town, *Malaysia* **22 C2** 5 25N 100 15 E
George V Land, *Antarctica* **48 C18** 69 0S 148 0 E
Georgetown, *Guyana* **46 B4** 6 50N 58 12W
Georgetown, *U.S.A.* **42 F5** 38 13N 84 33W
Georgia □, *U.S.A.* **41 D10** 32 0N 82 0W
Georgia ■, *Asia* **15 F7** 42 0N 43 0 E
Georgian B., *Canada* **42 C7** 45 15N 81 0W
Gera, *Germany* **10 C5** 50 53N 12 11 E
Geraldton, *Australia* **34 F1** 28 48S 114 32 E
Geraldton, *Canada* **42 A4** 49 44N 86 59W
Germany ■, *Europe* **10 C4** 51 0N 10 0 E
Germiston, *S. Africa* **31 B4** 26 15S 28 10 E
Gerona, *Spain* **11 B7** 41 58N 2 46 E
Ghaghara →, *India* **23 G10** 25 45N 84 40 E
Ghana ■, *W. Afr.* **30 C1** 8 0N 1 0W
Ghanzi, *Botswana* **31 A3** 21 50S 21 34 E
Ghazâl, Bahr el →, *Sudan* **32 C6** 9 31N 30 25 E
Ghaziabad, *India* **23 E6** 28 42N 77 26 E
Ghazipur, *India* **23 G9** 25 38N 83 35 E
Ghazni, *Afghan.* **23 C2** 33 30N 68 28 E
Ghent, *Belgium* **8 B5** 51 2N 3 42 E
Gibraltar, *Europe* **11 D3** 36 7N 5 22W
Gibraltar, Str. of, *Medit. S.* **11 E3** 35 55N 5 40W
Gibson Desert, *Australia* **34 E4** 24 0S 126 0 E
Gien, *France* **8 D5** 47 40N 2 36 E
Gifu, *Japan* **19 B5** 35 30N 136 45 E
Gijón, *Spain* **11 A3** 43 32N 5 42W
Gilgit, *India* **23 B5** 35 50N 74 15 E
Gillingham, *U.K.* **7 G7** 51 23N 0 34 E
Giridih, *India* **23 G11** 24 10N 86 21 E
Gironde →, *France* **9 E3** 45 32N 1 7W
Gisborne, *N.Z.* **35 H14** 38 39S 178 5 E
Gizhiga, *Russia* **18 C18** 62 3N 160 30 E
Glace Bay, *Canada* **43 B18** 46 11N 59 58W
Gladstone, *Australia* **34 E9** 23 52S 151 16 E
Gladstone, *U.S.A.* **42 C4** 45 52N 87 1W
Gladwin, *U.S.A.* **42 D5** 43 59N 84 29W
Glåma →, *Norway* **6 G10** 59 12N 10 57 E
Glasgow, *U.K.* **7 E4** 55 52N 4 14W
Glasgow, *U.S.A.* **42 G5** 37 2N 85 55W
Glencoe, *S. Africa* **31 B5** 28 11S 30 11 E
Glendale, *U.S.A.* **40 D3** 34 7N 118 18W
Glens Falls, *U.S.A.* **43 D11** 43 20N 73 40W
Gliwice, *Poland* **10 C8** 50 22N 18 41 E
Głogów, *Poland* **10 C7** 51 37N 16 5 E
Gloucester, *U.K.* **7 G5** 51 52N 2 15W
Gloversville, *U.S.A.* **43 D10** 43 5N 74 18W
Gniezno, *Poland* **10 B7** 52 30N 17 35 E
Go Cong, *Vietnam* **22 B2** 10 22N 106 40 E
Goa □, *India* **25 D6** 15 33N 73 59 E
Gobabis, *Namibia* **31 A2** 22 30S 19 0 E
Gobi, *Asia* **21 B6** 44 0N 111 0 E
Godavari →, *India* **25 D7** 16 25N 82 18 E
Goderich, *Canada* **42 D7** 43 45N 81 41W
Godhra, *India* **23 H4** 22 49N 73 40 E
Godthåb, *Greenland* **48 A9** 64 10N 51 35W
Gogama, *Canada* **42 B7** 47 35N 81 43W
Goiânia, *Brazil* **46 D5** 16 43S 49 20W
Gold Coast, *Australia* **34 F9** 28 0S 153 25 E
Gomel, *Belorussia* **14 D5** 52 28N 31 0 E
Gómez Palacio, *Mexico* **44 B4** 25 40N 104 0W
Gonabad, *Iran* **24 B4** 34 15N 58 45 E
Gonda, *India* **23 F8** 27 9N 81 58 E
Gonder, *Ethiopia* **29 G14** 12 39N 37 30 E
Gondia, *India* **23 J8** 21 23N 80 10 E
Good Hope, C. of, *S. Africa* **31 C2** 34 24S 18 30 E
Gorakhpur, *India* **23 F9** 26 47N 83 23 E
Gorkiy = Nizhniy Novgorod, *Russia* **14 C7** 56 20N 44 0 E
Görlitz, *Germany* **10 C6** 51 10N 14 59 E
Gorontalo, *Indonesia* **22 C4** 0 35N 123 5 E
Gorzów Wielkopolski, *Poland* **10 B6** 52 43N 15 15 E
Gota Canal, *Sweden* **6 G11** 58 30N 15 58 E
Göteborg, *Sweden* **6 G10** 57 43N 11 59 E
Gotha, *Germany* **10 C4** 50 56N 10 42 E
Gotland, *Sweden* **6 G11** 57 30N 18 33 E
Göttingen, *Germany* **10 C3** 51 31N 9 55 E
Gouin Res., *Canada* **43 A10** 48 35N 74 40W
Goulburn, *Australia* **34 G8** 34 44S 149 44 E
Gourdon, *France* **9 E4** 44 44N 1 23 E
Governador Valadares, *Brazil* **46 D5** 18 15S 41 57W
Gozo, *Malta* **12 F6** 36 3N 14 13 E
Graaff-Reinet, *S. Africa* **31 C3** 32 13S 24 32 E
Graham Land, *Antarctica* **48 C23** 65 0S 64 0W
Grahamstown, *S. Africa* **31 C4** 33 19S 26 31 E
Grampian Mts., *U.K.* **7 D5** 56 50N 4 0W
Gran Chaco, *S. Amer.* **47 E3** 25 0S 61 0W
Granada, *Spain* **11 D4** 37 10N 3 35W
Granby, *Canada* **43 C11** 45 25N 72 45W
Grand Bahama I., *Bahamas* **45 B9** 26 40N 78 30W
Grand Canyon, *U.S.A.* **40 C4** 36 3N 112 9W
Grand Canyon National Park, *U.S.A.* **40 C4** 36 15N 112 20W
Grand Cayman, *Cayman Is.* **45 D8** 19 20N 81 20W
Grand Haven, *U.S.A.* **42 D4** 43 3N 86 13W
Grand L., *Canada* **43 C14** 45 57N 66 7W
Grand Manan I., *Canada* **43 C14** 44 45N 66 52W
Grand-Mère, *Canada* **43 B11** 46 36N 72 40W
Grand Rapids, *U.S.A.* **42 D4** 42 58N 85 40W
Grande →, *U.S.A.* **41 E7** 25 57N 97 9W
Grande de Santiago →, *Mexico* **44 C3** 21 36N 105 26W
Grande Prairie, *Canada* **38 C8** 55 10N 118 50W
Grantham, *U.K.* **7 F6** 52 55N 0 39W
Granville, *U.S.A.* **43 D11** 43 24N 73 16W
Grasse, *France* **9 F7** 43 38N 6 56 E
Graulhet, *France* **9 F4** 43 45N 1 59 E
Grave, Pte. de, *France* **9 E3** 45 34N 1 4W
's-Gravenhage = The Hague, *Neths.* **8 A6** 52 7N 4 17 E
Grayling, *U.S.A.* **42 C5** 44 40N 84 42W
Graz, *Austria* **10 E6** 47 4N 15 27 E
Great Abaco I., *Bahamas* **45 B9** 26 25N 77 10W
Great Australian Bight, *Australia* **34 G4** 33 30S 130 0 E
Great Barrier Reef, *Australia* **34 D8** 18 0S 146 50 E

Great Basin   **Istanbul**

113

Kualakapuas — Malacca, Str. of

Kualakapuas, *Indonesia* **22 D3** 2 55S 114 20 E
Kuching, *Malaysia* **22 C3** 1 33N 110 25 E
Kudat, *Malaysia* **22 C3** 6 55N 116 55 E
Kumanovo, *Macedonia, Yug.* **13 C9** 42 9N 21 42 E
Kumasi, *Ghana* **30 C1** 6 41N 1 38W
Kumayri, *Armenia* **15 F7** 40 47N 43 50 E
Kumbakonam, *India* **25 D6** 10 58N 79 25 E
Kunlun Shan, *Asia* **20 C3** 36 0N 86 30 E
Kunming, *China* **20 D5** 25 1N 102 41 E
Kuopio, *Finland* **6 F13** 62 53N 27 35 E
Kupang, *Indonesia* **22 E4** 10 19S 123 39 E
Kura →, *Azerbaijan* **15 G8** 39 50N 49 20 E
Kurashiki, *Japan* **19 B3** 34 40N 133 50 E
Kurdistan, *Asia* **24 B3** 37 20N 43 30 E
Kure, *Japan* **19 B3** 34 14N 132 32 E
Kurgan, *Russia* **18 D8** 55 26N 65 18 E
Kuril Is., *Russia* **18 E17** 45 0N 150 0 E
Kurnool, *India* **25 D6** 15 45N 78 0 E
Kursk, *Russia* **14 D6** 51 42N 36 11 E
Kuruman, *S. Africa* **31 B3** 27 28S 23 28 E
Kuruman →, *S. Africa* **31 B3** 26 56S 20 39 E
Kurume, *Japan* **19 C2** 33 15N 130 30 E
Kushiro, *Japan* **19 F12** 43 0N 144 25 E
Kushtia, *Bangla.* **23 H12** 23 55N 89 5 E
Kütahya, *Turkey* **15 G5** 39 30N 30 2 E
Kutaisi, *Georgia* **15 F7** 42 19N 42 40 E
Kutch, Gulf of, *India* **23 H2** 22 50N 69 15 E
Kutch, Rann of, *India* **23 G2** 24 0N 70 0 E
Kuwait, *Kuwait* **24 C3** 29 30N 48 0 E
Kuwait ■, *Asia* **24 C3** 29 30N 47 30 E
Kuybyshev = Samara, *Russia* **14 D9** 53 8N 50 6 E
KwaMashu, *S. Africa* **31 B5** 29 45S 30 58 E
Kwangju, *S. Korea* **21 C7** 35 9N 126 54 E
Kyōto, *Japan* **19 B4** 35 0N 135 45 E
Kyūshū, *Japan* **19 C2** 33 0N 131 0 E
Kyzyl Kum, *Uzbekistan* **18 E8** 42 30N 65 0 E
Kzyl-Orda, *Kazakhstan* **18 E8** 44 48N 65 28 E

L

La Chorrera, *Panama* **44 H14** 8 50N 79 50W
La Ciotat, *France* **9 F6** 43 10N 5 37 E
La Coruña, *Spain* **11 A1** 43 20N 8 25W
La Flèche, *France* **8 D3** 47 42N 0 4W
La Habana = Havana, *Cuba* **45 C8** 23 8N 82 22W
La Mancha, *Spain* **11 C4** 39 10N 2 54W
La Paz, *Bolivia* **46 D3** 16 20S 68 10W
La Perouse Str., *Asia* **16 E18** 45 40N 142 0 E
La Plata, *Argentina* **47 F4** 35 0S 57 55W
La Porte, *U.S.A.* **42 E4** 41 36N 86 43W
La Roche-sur-Yon, *France* **8 D3** 46 40N 1 25W
La Sarre, *Canada* **42 A8** 48 45N 79 15W
La Spezia, *Italy* **12 B3** 44 8N 9 50 E
La Tour-du-Pin, *France* **9 E6** 45 33N 5 27 E
La Tuque, *Canada* **43 B11** 47 30N 72 50W
Labrador, Coast of, *Canada* **39 C13** 53 20N 61 0W
Labuk B., *Malaysia* **22 C3** 6 10N 117 50 E
Lac-Mégantic, *Canada* **43 C12** 45 35N 70 53W
Laccadive Is. = Lakshadweep Is., *Ind. Oc.* **25 D6** 10 0N 72 30 E
Lachine, *Canada* **43 C11** 45 30N 73 40W
Laconia, *U.S.A.* **43 D12** 43 32N 71 30W
Ladakh Ra., *India* **23 B6** 34 0N 78 0 E
Ladoga, L., *Russia* **14 B5** 61 15N 30 30 E
Ladybrand, *S. Africa* **31 B4** 29 9S 27 29 E
Ladysmith, *S. Africa* **31 B4** 28 32S 29 46 E
Lae, *Papua N. G.* **34 B8** 6 40S 147 2 E
Lafayette, *Ind., U.S.A.* **42 E4** 40 25N 86 54W
Lafayette, *La., U.S.A.* **41 D8** 30 18N 92 0W
Lagos, *Nigeria* **30 C2** 6 25N 3 27 E
Lagos, *Portugal* **11 D1** 37 5N 8 41W
Lahn →, *Germany* **10 C2** 50 17N 7 38 E
Lahore, *Pakistan* **23 D5** 31 32N 74 22 E
Lahti, *Finland* **6 F13** 60 58N 25 40 E
Laingsburg, *S. Africa* **31 C3** 33 9S 20 52 E
Lake Charles, *U.S.A.* **41 D8** 30 15N 93 10W
Lakewood, *U.S.A.* **42 E7** 41 28N 81 50W
Lakshadweep Is., *Ind. Oc.* **25 D6** 10 0N 72 30 E
Lalitapur, *Nepal* **23 F10** 27 40N 85 20 E
Lamon Bay, *Phil.* **22 B4** 14 30N 122 20 E
Lancaster, *U.K.* **7 E5** 54 3N 2 48W
Lancaster, *N.H., U.S.A.* **43 C12** 44 27N 71 33W
Lancaster, *Pa., U.S.A.* **42 E9** 40 4N 76 19W
Lancaster Sd., *Canada* **39 A11** 74 13N 84 0W
Landes, *France* **9 E3** 44 0N 1 0W
Land's End, *U.K.* **7 G4** 50 4N 5 43W
Langon, *France* **9 E3** 44 33N 0 16W
Langres, *France* **8 D6** 47 52N 5 20 E
Langres, Plateau de, *France* **8 D6** 47 45N 5 3 E
Lannion, *France* **8 C2** 48 46N 3 29W
L'Annonciation, *Canada* **43 B10** 46 25N 74 55W
L'Anse, *U.S.A.* **42 B3** 46 45N 88 28W
Lansing, *U.S.A.* **42 D5** 42 47N 84 40W
Lanzhou, *China* **20 C5** 36 1N 103 52 E
Laoag, *Phil.* **22 B4** 18 7N 120 34 E
Laon, *France* **8 C5** 49 33N 3 35 E
Laos ■, *Asia* **22 B2** 17 45N 105 0 E
Lapeer, *U.S.A.* **42 D6** 43 3N 83 20W
Lapland, *Europe* **6 E12** 68 7N 24 0 E
Laptev Sea, *Russia* **18 B14** 76 0N 125 0 E
Laredo, *U.S.A.* **40 E7** 27 34N 99 29W
Largentière, *France* **9 E6** 44 34N 4 18 E
Larisa, *Greece* **13 E10** 39 49N 22 28 E
Larne, *U.K.* **7 E4** 54 52N 5 50W
Larvik, *Norway* **6 G10** 59 4N 10 4 E
Las Palmas, *Canary Is.* **28 D3** 28 7N 15 26W
Las Vegas, *U.S.A.* **40 C3** 36 10N 115 5W
Lashio, *Burma* **25 C8** 22 56N 97 45 E
Latakia, *Syria* **24 B2** 35 30N 35 45 E
Latina, *Italy* **12 D5** 41 26N 12 53 E
Latvia ■, *Europe* **14 C3** 56 50N 24 0 E
Launceston, *Australia* **34 J8** 41 24S 147 8 E
Laurentian Plateau, *Canada* **39 C13** 52 0N 70 0W
Lausanne, *Switz.* **8 D7** 46 32N 6 38 E
Laut, *Indonesia* **22 C2** 4 45N 108 0 E
Lauzon, *Canada* **43 B12** 46 48N 71 10W
Laval, *France* **8 C3** 48 4N 0 48W
Lawrence, *U.S.A.* **43 D12** 42 40N 71 9W
Layla, *Si. Arabia* **24 C3** 22 10N 46 40 E
Le Creusot, *France* **8 D6** 46 48N 4 24 E
Le Havre, *France* **8 C4** 49 30N 0 5 E
Le Mans, *France* **8 D4** 48 0N 0 10 E
Le Puy, *France* **9 E5** 45 3N 3 52 E
Leamington, *Canada* **42 D6** 42 3N 82 36W
Lebanon, *Ind., U.S.A.* **42 E4** 40 3N 86 28W
Lebanon, *Ky., U.S.A.* **42 G5** 37 35N 85 15W
Lebanon, *Pa., U.S.A.* **42 E9** 40 20N 76 28W
Lebanon ■, *Asia* **24 B2** 34 0N 36 0 E
Lecce, *Italy* **13 D8** 40 20N 18 10 E
Leduc, *Canada* **38 C8** 53 15N 113 30W
Leeds, *U.K.* **7 F6** 53 48N 1 34W
Leeuwarden, *Neths.* **8 A6** 53 15N 5 48 E
Leeuwin, C., *Australia* **34 G2** 34 20S 115 9 E
Leeward Is., *Atl. Oc.* **44 L18** 16 30N 63 30W
Leghorn, *Italy* **12 C4** 43 32N 10 18 E
Legnica, *Poland* **10 C7** 51 12N 16 10 E
Leh, *India* **23 B6** 34 9N 77 35 E
Lehututu, *Botswana* **31 A3** 23 54S 21 55 E
Leicester, *U.K.* **7 F6** 52 39N 1 9W
Leiden, *Neths.* **8 A6** 52 9N 4 30 E
Leine →, *Germany* **10 B3** 52 20N 9 50 E
Leipzig, *Germany* **10 C5** 51 20N 12 23 E
Leith, *U.K.* **7 E5** 55 59N 3 10W
Leitrim, *Ireland* **7 F2** 54 0N 8 5W
Lena →, *Russia* **18 B14** 72 52N 126 40 E
Leningrad = St. Petersburg, *Russia* **14 C5** 59 55N 30 20 E
Leninsk-Kuznetskiy, *Russia* **18 D10** 54 44N 86 10 E
Lens, *France* **8 B5** 50 26N 2 50 E
Leominster, *U.S.A.* **43 D12** 42 32N 71 45W
León, *Mexico* **44 C4** 21 7N 101 30W
León, *Guanajuato, Mexico* **44 C4** 21 7N 101 40W
León, *Spain* **11 A3** 42 38N 5 34W
Lérida, *Spain* **11 B6** 41 37N 0 39 E
Lerwick, *U.K.* **7 A6** 60 10N 1 10W
Les Andelys, *France* **8 C4** 49 15N 1 25 E
Les Sables-d'Olonne, *France* **9 D3** 46 30N 1 45W
Leskovac, *Serbia, Yug.* **13 C9** 43 0N 21 58 E
Lesotho ■, *Africa* **31 B4** 29 40S 28 0 E
Lesparre-Médoc, *France* **9 E3** 45 18N 0 57W
Lesvos, *Greece* **13 E12** 39 10N 26 20 E
Leszno, *Poland* **10 C7** 51 50N 16 30 E
Lethbridge, *Canada* **38 D8** 49 45N 112 45W
Leti Is., *Indonesia* **22 D4** 8 10S 128 0 E
Letiahau →, *Botswana* **31 A3** 21 16S 24 0 E
Leuven, *Belgium* **8 B6** 50 52N 4 42 E
Lévis, *Canada* **43 B12** 46 48N 71 9W
Lewes, *U.K.* **7 G7** 50 53N 0 2 E
Lewis, *U.K.* **7 C3** 58 10N 6 40W
Lewiston, *U.S.A.* **43 C12** 44 3N 70 10W
Lewistown, *U.S.A.* **42 E9** 40 37N 77 33W
Lexington, *U.S.A.* **42 F5** 38 6N 84 30W
Lexington Park, *U.S.A.* **42 F9** 38 16N 76 27W
Leyte, *Phil.* **22 B4** 11 0N 125 0 E
Lhasa, *China* **20 D4** 29 25N 90 58 E
Liaoning □, *China* **21 B7** 41 40N 122 30 E
Liaoyang, *China* **21 B7** 41 15N 122 58 E
Liaoyüan, *China* **21 B7** 42 58N 125 2 E
Liberec, *Czech.* **10 C6** 50 47N 15 7 E
Liberia ■, *W. Afr.* **28 H5** 6 30N 9 30W
Libourne, *France* **9 E3** 44 55N 0 14W
Libreville, *Gabon* **32 D1** 0 25N 9 26 E
Libya ■, *N. Afr.* **28 D10** 27 0N 17 0 E
Lichinga, *Mozam.* **33 G7** 13 13S 35 11 E
Lichtenburg, *S. Africa* **31 B4** 26 8S 26 8 E
Liechtenstein ■, *Europe* **10 E3** 47 8N 9 35 E
Liège, *Belgium* **8 B6** 50 38N 5 35 E
Liepāja, *Latvia* **14 C3** 56 30N 21 0 E
Ligurian Sea, *Italy* **12 C3** 43 20N 9 0 E
Likasi, *Zaïre* **32 G5** 10 55S 26 48 E
Lille, *France* **8 B5** 50 38N 3 3 E
Lillehammer, *Norway* **6 F10** 61 8N 10 30 E
Lilongwe, *Malawi* **33 G6** 14 0S 33 48 E
Lim Fjord, *Denmark* **6 G9** 56 55N 9 0 E
Lima, *Peru* **46 D2** 12 0S 77 0W
Lima, *U.S.A.* **42 E5** 40 42N 84 5W
Limerick, *Ireland* **7 F2** 52 40N 8 38W
Límnos, *Greece* **13 E11** 39 50N 25 5 E
Limoges, *France* **9 E4** 45 50N 1 15 E
Limousin, *France* **9 E4** 45 30N 1 30 E
Limoux, *France* **9 F5** 43 4N 2 12 E
Limpopo →, *Africa* **33 K6** 25 5S 33 30 E
Linares, *Spain* **11 C4** 38 10N 3 40W
Lincoln, *U.K.* **7 F6** 53 14N 0 32W
Lincoln, *Maine, U.S.A.* **43 C13** 45 27N 68 29W
Lincoln, *Nebr., U.S.A.* **41 B7** 40 50N 96 42W
Lindsay, *Canada* **42 C8** 44 22N 78 43W
Lingga Arch., *Indonesia* **22 D2** 0 10S 104 30 E
Linköping, *Sweden* **6 G11** 58 28N 15 36 E
Linton, *U.S.A.* **42 F4** 39 0N 87 10W
Linxia, *China* **20 C5** 35 36N 103 10 E
Linz, *Austria* **10 D6** 48 18N 14 18 E
Lions, G. of, *France* **9 F5** 43 10N 4 0 E
Lipari Is., *Italy* **12 E6** 38 30N 14 50 E
Lipetsk, *Russia* **14 D6** 52 37N 39 35 E
Lippe →, *Germany* **10 C2** 51 39N 6 38 E
Lisbon, *Portugal* **11 C1** 38 42N 9 10W
Lisburn, *U.K.* **7 E3** 54 30N 6 9W
Lisieux, *France* **8 C4** 49 10N 0 12 E
Lismore, *Australia* **34 F9** 28 44S 153 21 E
Listowel, *Canada* **42 D7** 43 44N 80 58W
Lithuania ■, *Europe* **14 C3** 55 30N 24 0 E
Little Current, *Canada* **42 C7** 45 55N 82 0W
Little Karoo, *S. Africa* **31 C3** 33 45S 21 0 E
Little Laut Is., *Indonesia* **22 D3** 4 45S 115 40 E
Little Rock, *U.S.A.* **41 D8** 34 41N 92 10W
Liuzhou, *China* **21 D5** 24 22N 109 22 E
Liverpool, *U.K.* **7 F5** 53 25N 3 0W
Livingstone, *Zambia* **33 H5** 17 46S 25 52 E
Livonia, *U.S.A.* **42 D6** 42 25N 83 23W
Livorno = Leghorn, *Italy* **12 C4** 43 32N 10 18 E
Ljubljana, *Slovenia* **12 A6** 46 4N 14 33 E
Ljusnan →, *Sweden* **6 F11** 61 12N 17 8 E
Llandudno, *U.K.* **7 F5** 53 19N 3 51W
Llanelli, *U.K.* **7 G4** 51 41N 4 11W
Llanos, *S. Amer.* **46 B2** 5 0N 71 35W
Lobatse, *Botswana* **31 B4** 25 12S 25 40 E
Lobito, *Angola* **33 G2** 12 18S 13 35 E
Loches, *France* **8 D4** 47 7N 1 0 E
Lock Haven, *U.S.A.* **42 E9** 41 7N 77 31W
Lodève, *France* **9 F5** 43 44N 3 19 E
Łódź, *Poland* **10 C8** 51 45N 19 27 E
Lofoten, *Norway* **6 E10** 68 30N 15 0 E
Logan, *Ohio, U.S.A.* **42 F6** 39 25N 82 22W
Logan, *W. Va., U.S.A.* **42 G7** 37 51N 81 59W
Logan, Mt., *Canada* **38 B5** 60 31N 140 22W
Logansport, *U.S.A.* **42 E4** 40 45N 86 21W
Logroño, *Spain* **11 A4** 42 28N 2 27W
Lohardaga, *India* **23 H10** 23 27N 84 45 E
Loir →, *France* **8 D3** 47 33N 0 32W
Loire →, *France* **8 D2** 47 16N 2 10W
Lombardy □, *Italy* **12 B3** 45 35N 9 45 E
Lomblen, *Indonesia* **22 D4** 8 30S 123 32 E
Lombok, *Indonesia* **22 D3** 8 45S 116 30 E
Lomé, *Togo* **30 C2** 6 9N 1 20 E
Lomond, L., *U.K.* **7 D4** 56 8N 4 38W
Łomza, *Poland* **10 B10** 53 10N 22 2 E
London, *Canada* **42 D7** 42 59N 81 15W
London, *U.K.* **7 G6** 51 30N 0 5W
Londrina, *Brazil* **47 E4** 23 18S 51 10W
Long Beach, *U.S.A.* **40 D3** 33 46N 118 12W
Long Branch, *U.S.A.* **43 E11** 40 19N 74 0W
Long I., *Bahamas* **45 C9** 23 20N 75 10W
Long I., *U.S.A.* **43 E11** 40 50N 73 20W
Long Xuyen, *Vietnam* **22 B2** 10 19N 105 28 E
Longlac, *Canada* **42 A4** 49 45N 86 25W
Lons-le-Saunier, *France* **8 D6** 46 40N 5 31 E
Lop Nor, *China* **20 B4** 40 20N 90 10 E
Lorain, *U.S.A.* **42 E6** 41 28N 82 55W
Loralai, *Pakistan* **23 D2** 30 20N 68 41 E
Lorca, *Spain* **11 D5** 37 41N 1 42W
Lorient, *France* **8 D2** 47 45N 3 23W
Lorn, Firth of, *U.K.* **7 D4** 56 20N 5 40W
Lorraine, *France* **8 C6** 48 53N 6 0 E
Los Angeles, *Chile* **47 F2** 37 28S 72 23W
Los Angeles, *U.S.A.* **40 D3** 34 0N 118 10W
Los Mochis, *Mexico* **44 B3** 25 45N 108 57W
Lot →, *France* **9 E4** 44 18N 0 20 E
Louis Trichardt, *S. Africa* **31 A4** 23 1S 29 43 E
Louisa, *U.S.A.* **42 F6** 38 5N 82 40W
Louiseville, *Canada* **43 B11** 46 20N 72 56W
Louisiana □, *U.S.A.* **41 D8** 30 50N 92 0W
Louisville, *U.S.A.* **42 F5** 38 15N 85 45W
Lourdes, *France* **9 F3** 43 6N 0 3W
Low Tatra, *Slovakia* **10 D8** 48 55N 19 30 E
Lowell, *U.S.A.* **43 D12** 42 38N 71 19W
Lower California, *Mexico* **44 B2** 31 10N 115 12W
Lower Tunguska →, *Russia* **18 C10** 65 48N 88 4 E
Lowestoft, *U.K.* **7 F7** 52 29N 1 44 E
Lowville, *U.S.A.* **43 D10** 43 48N 75 30W
Luanda, *Angola* **32 F2** 8 50S 13 15 E
Luanshya, *Zambia* **33 G5** 13 3S 28 28 E
Lubbock, *U.S.A.* **40 D6** 33 40N 101 53W
Lübeck, *Germany* **10 B4** 53 52N 10 41 E
Lublin, *Poland* **10 C10** 51 12N 22 38 E
Lubumbashi, *Zaïre* **33 G5** 11 40S 27 28 E
Lucknow, *India* **23 F8** 26 50N 81 0 E
Lüda = Dalian, *China* **21 C7** 38 50N 121 40 E
Lüderitz, *Namibia* **31 B2** 26 41S 15 8 E
Ludhiana, *India* **23 D5** 30 57N 75 56 E
Ludington, *U.S.A.* **42 D4** 43 58N 86 27W
Ludwigshafen, *Germany* **10 D3** 49 27N 8 27 E
Lugano, *Switz.* **10 F3** 46 0N 8 57 E
Lugansk, *Ukraine* **15 E6** 48 38N 39 15 E
Lugo, *Spain* **11 A2** 43 2N 7 35W
Lule →, *Sweden* **6 E12** 65 35N 22 10 E
Luleå, *Sweden* **6 E12** 65 35N 22 10 E
Lüneburg Heath, *Germany* **10 B4** 53 0N 10 0 E
Lunéville, *France* **8 C7** 48 36N 6 30 E
Luni →, *India* **23 G3** 24 41N 71 14 E
Luoyang, *China* **21 C6** 34 40N 112 26 E
Luray, *U.S.A.* **42 F8** 38 39N 78 26W
Lusaka, *Zambia* **33 H5** 15 28S 28 16 E
Luton, *U.K.* **7 G6** 51 53N 0 24W
Luxembourg, *Lux.* **8 C7** 49 37N 6 9 E
Luxembourg ■, *Europe* **8 C7** 49 45N 6 0 E
Luzern, *Switz.* **10 E3** 47 3N 8 18 E
Luzhou, *China* **20 D5** 28 52N 105 20 E
Luzon, *Phil.* **22 B4** 16 0N 121 0 E
Lvov, *Ukraine* **15 E3** 49 50N 24 0 E
Lyakhov Is., *Russia* **18 B16** 73 40N 141 0 E
Lydda, *Israel* **29 C13** 31 57N 34 54 E
Lydenburg, *S. Africa* **31 B5** 25 10S 30 29 E
Lynchburg, *U.S.A.* **42 G8** 37 23N 79 10W
Lynn Lake, *Canada* **38 C9** 56 51N 101 3W
Lyonnais, *France* **9 E6** 45 45N 4 15 E
Lyons, *France* **9 E6** 45 46N 4 50 E

M

Ma'an, *Jordan* **24 B2** 30 12N 35 44 E
Maastricht, *Neths.* **8 B6** 50 50N 5 40 E
Macapá, *Brazil* **46 B4** 0 5N 51 4W
Macau ■, *China* **21 D6** 22 16N 113 35 E
Macclesfield, *U.K.* **7 F5** 53 16N 2 9W
M'Clure Str., *Canada* **48 A11** 75 0N 119 0W
Macdonnell Ras., *Australia* **34 E5** 23 40S 133 0 E
Macedonia □, *Greece* **13 D10** 40 39N 22 0 E
Macedonia ■, *Macedonia, Yug.* **13 D9** 41 53N 21 40 E
Maceió, *Brazil* **46 C6** 9 40S 35 41W
Macgillycuddy's Reeks, *Ireland* **7 F2** 52 2N 9 45W
Mach, *Pakistan* **23 E1** 29 50N 67 20 E
Machakos, *Kenya* **32 E7** 1 30S 37 15 E
Machias, *U.S.A.* **43 C14** 44 40N 67 28W
Machilipatnam, *India* **25 D7** 16 12N 81 8 E
Mackay, *Australia* **34 E8** 21 8S 149 11 E
Mackay, L., *Australia* **34 E4** 22 30S 129 0 E
McKeesport, *U.S.A.* **42 E8** 40 21N 79 50W
Mackenzie →, *Canada* **38 B6** 69 10N 134 20W
Mackenzie Mts., *Canada* **38 B7** 64 0N 130 0W
Mackinaw City, *U.S.A.* **42 C5** 45 47N 84 44W
McKinley, Mt., *U.S.A.* **38 B4** 63 2N 151 0W
Maclear, *S. Africa* **31 C4** 31 2S 28 23 E
M'Clintock Chan., *Canada* **38 A9** 72 0N 102 0W
McMurdo Sd., *Antarctica* **48 C19** 77 0S 170 0 E
Mâcon, *France* **9 D6** 46 19N 4 50 E
Macon, *U.S.A.* **41 D10** 32 50N 83 37W
Macquarie Is., *Pac. Oc.* **36 N7** 54 36S 158 55 E
Madadeni, *S. Africa* **31 B5** 27 43S 30 3 E
Madagascar ■, *Africa* **33 J9** 20 0S 47 0 E
Madaripur, *Bangla.* **23 H13** 23 19N 90 15 E
Madeira, *Atl. Oc.* **28 C3** 32 50N 17 0W
Madeira →, *Brazil* **46 C4** 3 22S 58 45W
Madhya Pradesh □, *India* **23 H7** 21 50N 78 0 E
Madinat al Shaab, *Yemen* **29 G16** 12 50N 45 0 E
Madison, *Ind., U.S.A.* **42 F5** 38 42N 85 20W
Madison, *Wis., U.S.A.* **41 B9** 43 5N 89 25W
Madisonville, *U.S.A.* **42 G4** 37 20N 87 30W
Madiun, *Indonesia* **22 D3** 7 38S 111 32 E
Madras, *India* **25 D7** 13 8N 80 19 E
Madrid, *Spain* **11 B4** 40 25N 3 45W
Madurai, *India* **25 E6** 9 55N 78 10 E
Mafeking, *S. Africa* **31 B4** 25 50S 25 38 E
Mafeteng, *Lesotho* **31 B4** 29 51S 27 15 E
Magadan, *Russia* **18 D17** 59 38N 150 50 E
Magdalen Is., *Canada* **43 B17** 47 30N 61 40W
Magdalena →, *Colombia* **46 A2** 11 6N 74 51W
Magdeburg, *Germany* **10 B4** 52 8N 11 36 E
Magelang, *Indonesia* **22 D3** 7 29S 110 13 E
Magellan's Str., *Chile* **47 H2** 52 30S 75 0W
Maggiore, L., *Italy* **12 A3** 46 0N 8 35 E
Magnetic Pole (North), *Canada* **48 A4** 77 58N 102 8W
Magnetic Pole (South), *Antarctica* **48 C18** 64 8S 138 8 E
Magnitogorsk, *Russia* **14 D10** 53 27N 59 4 E
Magog, *Canada* **43 C11** 45 18N 72 9W
Mahakam →, *Indonesia* **22 D3** 0 35S 117 17 E
Mahalapye, *Botswana* **31 A4** 23 1S 26 51 E
Mahanadi →, *India* **23 J11** 20 20N 86 25 E
Maharashtra □, *India* **23 J5** 20 30N 75 30 E
Mahesana, *India* **23 H4** 23 39N 72 26 E
Maidstone, *U.K.* **7 G7** 51 16N 0 31 E
Maiduguri, *Nigeria* **30 B4** 12 0N 13 20 E
Maijdi, *Bangla.* **23 H13** 22 48N 91 10 E
Maikala Ra., *India* **23 J8** 22 0N 81 0 E
Maimana, *Afghan.* **24 B5** 35 53N 64 38 E
Main →, *Germany* **10 D3** 50 0N 8 18 E
Maine, *France* **8 D3** 47 55N 0 25W
Maine □, *U.S.A.* **43 C13** 45 20N 69 0W
Mainz, *Germany* **10 D3** 50 0N 8 17 E
Majorca = Mallorca, *Spain* **11 C7** 39 30N 3 0 E
Makasar, Str. of, *Indonesia* **22 D3** 1 0S 118 20 E
Makeyevka, *Ukraine* **15 E6** 48 0N 38 0 E
Makgadikgadi Salt Pans, *Botswana* **31 A4** 20 40S 25 45 E
Makhachkala, *Russia* **15 F8** 43 0N 47 30 E
Makkah = Mecca, *Si. Arabia* **24 C2** 21 30N 39 54 E
Makunda, *Botswana* **31 A3** 22 30S 20 7 E
Malabar Coast, *India* **25 D6** 11 0N 75 0 E
Malacca, Str. of, *Indonesia* **22 C2** 3 0N 101 0 E

114 INDEX TO WORLD MAPS

Málaga Mzimkulu

Málaga, *Spain* 11 D3 36 43N 4 23W
Malang, *Indonesia* 22 D3 7 59S 112 45 E
Malanje, *Angola* 32 F3 9 36S 16 17 E
Malar, L., *Sweden* 6 G11 59 30N 17 10 E
Malatya, *Turkey* 15 G6 38 25N 38 20 E
Malawi ■, *Africa* 33 G6 11 55S 34 0 E
Malay Pen., *Asia* 16 J14 7 25N 100 0 E
Malaysia ■, *Asia* 22 C3 5 0N 110 0 E
Maldives ■, *Ind. Oc.* 25 E6 5 0N 73 0 E
Malegaon, *India* 23 J5 20 30N 74 38 E
Mali ■, *Africa* 28 F6 17 0N 3 0W
Malin Hd., *Ireland* 7 E3 55 18N 7 24W
Mallorca, *Spain* 11 C7 39 30N 3 0 E
Malmö, *Sweden* 6 G10 55 36N 12 59 E
Malone, *U.S.A.* 43 C10 44 50N 74 19W
Malta ■, *Europe* 12 G6 35 50N 14 30 E
Malvinas, Is. = Falkland Is., *Atl. Oc.* 47 H4 51 30S 59 0W
Mamers, *France* 8 C4 48 21N 0 22 E
Man, I. of, *U.K.* 7 E4 54 15N 4 30W
Manado, *Indonesia* 22 C4 1 29N 124 51 E
Managua, *Nic.* 44 E7 12 6N 86 20W
Manama, *Bahrain* 24 C4 26 10N 50 30 E
Manaus, *Brazil* 46 C4 3 0S 60 0W
Mancelona, *U.S.A.* 42 C5 44 54N 85 5W
Manchester, *U.K.* 7 F5 53 30N 2 15W
Manchester, *U.S.A.* 43 D12 42 58N 71 29W
Manchuria, *China* 21 B7 42 0N 125 0 E
Mandal, *Norway* 6 G9 58 2N 7 25 E
Mandalay, *Burma* 25 C8 22 0N 96 4 E
Mandasaur, *India* 23 G5 24 3N 75 8 E
Mandi, *India* 23 D6 31 39N 76 58 E
Mandla, *India* 23 H8 22 39N 80 30 E
Mandvi, *India* 23 H2 22 51N 69 22 E
Mangalore, *India* 25 D6 12 55N 74 47 E
Manggar, *Indonesia* 22 D2 2 50S 108 10 E
Mangla Dam, *Pakistan* 23 C4 33 9N 73 44 E
Mangole, *Indonesia* 22 D4 1 50S 125 55 E
Manila, *Phil.* 22 B4 14 40N 121 3 E
Manila B., *Phil.* 22 B4 14 40N 120 35 E
Manipur □, *India* 25 C8 25 0N 94 0 E
Manistee, *U.S.A.* 42 C4 44 15N 86 20W
Manistee →, *U.S.A.* 42 C4 44 15N 86 21W
Manistique, *U.S.A.* 42 C4 45 59N 86 18W
Manitoba □, *Canada* 38 C10 55 30N 97 0W
Manitou Is., *U.S.A.* 42 C4 45 8N 86 0W
Manitoulin I., *Canada* 42 C6 45 40N 82 30W
Manitowoc, *U.S.A.* 42 C4 44 8N 87 40W
Manizales, *Colombia* 46 B2 5 5N 75 32W
Mannar, *Sri Lanka* 25 E6 9 1N 79 54 E
Mannheim, *Germany* 10 D3 49 28N 8 29 E
Manokwari, *Indonesia* 22 D5 0 54S 134 0 E
Manosque, *France* 9 F6 43 49N 5 47 E
Mansfield, *U.K.* 7 F6 53 8N 1 12W
Mansfield, *U.S.A.* 42 E6 40 45N 82 30W
Mantes-la-Jolie, *France* 8 C4 48 58N 1 41 E
Manton, *U.S.A.* 42 C5 44 23N 85 25W
Mantua, *Italy* 12 B4 45 20N 10 42 E
Manzai, *Pakistan* 23 C3 32 12N 70 15 E
Manzhouli, *China* 21 B6 49 35N 117 25 E
Manzini, *Swaziland* 31 B5 26 30S 31 25 E
Maoming, *China* 21 D6 21 50N 110 54 E
Mapam Yumco, *China* 23 D8 30 45N 81 28 E
Maputo, *Mozam.* 31 B5 25 58S 32 32 E
Mar del Plata, *Argentina* 47 F4 38 0S 57 30W
Marabá, *Brazil* 46 C5 5 20S 49 5W
Maracaibo, *Venezuela* 46 A2 10 40N 71 37W
Maracaibo, L., *Venezuela* 46 B2 9 40N 71 30W
Maracay, *Venezuela* 46 A3 10 15N 67 28W
Marajo I., *Brazil* 46 C5 1 0S 49 30W
Marañón →, *Peru* 46 C2 4 30S 73 35W
Marche, *France* 9 D4 46 5N 1 20 E
Mardan, *Pakistan* 23 B4 34 20N 72 0 E
Margate, *U.K.* 7 G7 51 23N 1 24 E
Mari Republic □, *Russia* 14 C8 56 30N 48 0 E
Maribor, *Slovenia* 12 A6 46 36N 15 40 E
Marico →, *Africa* 31 A4 23 35S 26 57 E
Maricourt, *Canada* 39 C12 56 34N 70 49W
Marie Byrd Land, *Antarctica* 48 C21 79 30S 125 0W
Marie-Galante, *Guadeloupe* 45 D12 15 56N 61 16W
Mariental, *Namibia* 31 A2 24 36S 18 0 E
Marietta, *U.S.A.* 42 F7 39 27N 81 27W
Marinette, *U.S.A.* 42 C4 45 4N 87 40W
Marion, *Ind., U.S.A.* 42 E5 40 35N 85 40W
Marion, *Ohio, U.S.A.* 42 E6 40 38N 83 8W
Maritime Alps, *Europe* 9 E7 44 10N 7 10 E
Mariupol, *Ukraine* 15 E6 47 5N 37 31 E
Markham, Mt., *Antarctica* 48 C19 83 0S 164 0 E
Marmande, *France* 9 E4 44 30N 0 10 E
Marmara, Sea of, *Turkey* 13 D13 40 45N 28 15 E
Marmora, *Canada* 42 C9 44 28N 77 41W
Marne →, *France* 8 C5 48 48N 2 24 E
Maroua, *Cameroon* 30 B4 10 40N 14 20 E
Marquesas Is., *Pac. Oc.* 37 H14 9 30S 140 0W
Marquette, *U.S.A.* 42 B4 46 30N 87 21W
Marrakech, *Morocco* 28 C5 31 9N 8 0W
Marseilles, *France* 9 F6 43 18N 5 23 E
Marshall Is., *Pac. Oc.* 36 G9 9 0N 171 0 E
Martaban, G. of, *Burma* 25 D8 16 5N 96 30 E
Martha's Vineyard, *U.S.A.* 43 E12 41 25N 70 35W
Martigues, *France* 9 F6 43 24N 5 4 E
Martinique ■, *W. Indies* 45 E12 14 40N 61 0W
Martinsburg, *U.S.A.* 42 F9 39 30N 77 57W
Martinsville, *U.S.A.* 42 F4 39 29N 86 23W
Marwar, *India* 23 G4 25 43N 73 45 E
Maryland □, *U.S.A.* 42 F9 39 10N 76 40W
Masan, *S. Korea* 21 C7 35 11N 128 32 E
Maseru, *Lesotho* 31 B4 29 18S 27 30 E
Mashhad, *Iran* 24 B4 36 20N 59 35 E
Mask, L., *Ireland* 7 F2 53 36N 9 24W
Massachusetts □, *U.S.A.* 43 D11 42 25N 72 0W
Massena, *U.S.A.* 43 C10 44 52N 74 55W
Massif Central, *France* 9 E5 44 55N 3 0 E
Massillon, *U.S.A.* 42 E7 40 47N 81 30W
Masvingo, *Zimbabwe* 33 J6 20 8S 30 49 E
Matadi, *Zaïre* 32 F2 5 52S 13 31 E
Matagami, *Canada* 42 A9 49 45N 77 34W
Matagami, L., *Canada* 42 A9 49 50N 77 40W
Matamoros, *Mexico* 44 B4 25 33N 103 15W
Matane, *Canada* 43 A14 48 50N 67 33W
Matatiele, *S. Africa* 31 C4 30 20S 28 49 E
Matera, *Italy* 12 D7 40 40N 16 37 E
Mathura, *India* 23 F6 27 30N 77 40 E
Mato Grosso □, *Brazil* 46 D4 14 0S 55 0W
Mato Grosso, Planalto do, *Brazil* 46 D4 15 0S 55 0W
Matsue, *Japan* 19 B3 35 25N 133 10 E
Matsuyama, *Japan* 19 C3 33 45N 132 45 E
Mattawa, *Canada* 42 B8 46 20N 78 45W
Mattawamkeag, *U.S.A.* 43 C13 45 30N 68 21W
Matterhorn, *Switz.* 10 F2 45 58N 7 39 E
Maubeuge, *France* 8 B5 50 17N 3 57 E
Maui, *U.S.A.* 40 H16 20 45N 156 20W
Maumee →, *U.S.A.* 42 E6 41 42N 83 28W
Maumere, *Indonesia* 22 D4 8 38S 122 13 E
Maun, *Botswana* 31 A3 20 0S 23 26 E
Mauna Loa, *U.S.A.* 40 J17 19 32N 155 28W
Maures, *France* 9 F7 43 15N 6 15 E
Mauriac, *France* 9 E5 45 13N 2 19 E
Mauritania ■, *Africa* 28 E5 20 50N 10 0W
Mauritius ■, *Ind. Oc.* 27 J9 20 0S 57 0 E
May Pen, *Jamaica* 44 K16 17 58N 77 15W
Mayenne, *France* 8 C3 48 20N 0 38W
Mayfield, *U.S.A.* 42 G3 36 45N 88 40W
Maysville, *U.S.A.* 42 F6 38 39N 83 46W
Mazar-i-Sharif, *Afghan.* 24 B5 36 41N 67 0 E
Mazatlán, *Mexico* 44 C3 23 10N 106 30W
Mazatlán, *Sinaloa, Mexico* 44 C3 23 13N 106 25W
Mbabane, *Swaziland* 31 B5 26 18S 31 6 E
Mbandaka, *Zaïre* 32 D3 0 1N 18 18 E
Mbanza Ngungu, *Zaïre* 32 F2 5 12S 14 53 E
Mbeya, *Tanzania* 32 F6 8 54S 33 29 E
Mbini □, *Eq. Guin.* 28 J9 1 30N 10 0 E
Mbuji-Mayi, *Zaïre* 32 F4 6 9S 23 40 E
Meadville, *U.S.A.* 42 E7 41 39N 80 9W
Meaford, *Canada* 42 C7 44 36N 80 35W
Meaux, *France* 8 C5 48 58N 2 50 E
Mecca, *Si. Arabia* 24 C2 21 30N 39 54 E
Mechelen, *Belgium* 8 B6 51 2N 4 29 E
Medan, *Indonesia* 22 C1 3 40N 98 38 E
Medellín, *Colombia* 46 B2 6 15N 75 35W
Medicine Hat, *Canada* 38 D8 50 0N 110 45W
Medina, *Si. Arabia* 24 C2 24 35N 39 52 E
Mediterranean Sea, *Europe* 26 C5 35 0N 15 0 E
Médoc, *France* 9 E3 45 10N 0 50W
Meekatharra, *Australia* 34 F2 26 32S 118 29 E
Meerut, *India* 23 E6 29 1N 77 42 E
Meghalaya □, *India* 23 G13 25 50N 91 0 E
Mei Xian, *China* 21 D6 24 16N 116 6 E
Mekhtar, *Pakistan* 23 D2 30 30N 69 15 E
Meknès, *Morocco* 28 C5 33 57N 5 33W
Mekong →, *Asia* 22 C2 9 30N 106 15 E
Melaka, *Malaysia* 22 C2 2 15N 102 15 E
Melanesia, *Pac. Oc.* 36 H7 4 0S 155 0 E
Melbourne, *Australia* 34 H8 37 50S 145 0 E
Melitopol, *Ukraine* 15 E6 46 50N 35 22 E
Melun, *France* 8 C5 48 32N 2 39 E
Melville I., *Australia* 34 C5 11 30S 131 0 E
Melville Pen., *Canada* 39 B11 68 0N 84 0W
Memphis, *U.S.A.* 41 C9 35 7N 90 0W
Menasha, *U.S.A.* 42 C3 44 13N 88 27W
Mende, *France* 9 E5 44 31N 3 30 E
Mendoza, *Argentina* 47 F3 32 50S 68 52W
Menominee, *U.S.A.* 42 C4 45 9N 87 39W
Menominee →, *U.S.A.* 42 C4 45 5N 87 36W
Mentawai Is., *Indonesia* 22 D1 2 0S 99 0 E
Mérida, *Mexico* 44 C7 20 58N 89 37W
Meriden, *U.S.A.* 43 E11 41 33N 72 47W
Mersey →, *U.K.* 7 F5 53 20N 2 56W
Mersin, *Turkey* 15 G5 36 51N 34 36 E
Merthyr Tydfil, *U.K.* 7 G5 51 45N 3 23W
Mesa, *U.S.A.* 40 D4 33 20N 111 56W
Mesopotamia, *Iraq* 24 C3 33 30N 44 0 E
Messina, *Italy* 12 E6 38 10N 15 32 E
Messina, *S. Africa* 31 A5 22 20S 30 5 E
Messina, Str. of, *Italy* 12 E6 38 5N 15 35 E
Metz, *France* 8 C7 49 8N 6 10 E
Meurthe →, *France* 8 C7 48 47N 6 9 E
Meuse →, *Europe* 8 B6 50 45N 5 41 E
Mexicali, *Mexico* 44 A1 32 40N 115 30W
México, *Mexico* 44 D5 19 20N 99 10W
Mexico ■, *Cent. Amer.* 44 C4 25 0N 105 0W
Mexico, G. of, *Cent. Amer.* 44 C7 25 0N 90 0W
Mhow, *India* 23 H5 22 33N 75 50 E
Miami, *U.S.A.* 41 E10 25 45N 80 15W
Mianwali, *Pakistan* 23 C3 32 38N 71 28 E
Michigan □, *U.S.A.* 41 B9 44 40N 85 40W
Michigan, L., *U.S.A.* 42 D4 44 0N 87 0W
Michipicoten I., *Canada* 42 B5 47 40N 85 40W
Micronesia, Federated States of ■, *Pac. Oc.* 36 G7 9 0N 150 0 E
Middelburg, *Neths.* 8 B5 51 30N 3 36 E
Middelburg, *C. Prov., S. Africa* 31 C3 31 30S 25 0 E
Middelburg, *Trans., S. Africa* 31 B4 25 49S 29 28 E
Middlesbrough, *U.K.* 7 E6 54 35N 1 14W
Middletown, *N.Y., U.S.A.* 43 E10 41 28N 74 28W
Middletown, *Ohio, U.S.A.* 42 F5 39 29N 84 25W
Midi, Canal du →, *France* 9 F4 43 45N 1 21 E
Midland, *Canada* 42 C8 44 45N 79 50W
Midland, *Mich., U.S.A.* 42 D5 43 37N 84 17W
Midland, *Tex., U.S.A.* 40 D6 32 0N 102 3W
Midway Is., *Pac. Oc.* 36 E10 28 13N 177 22W
Midwest, *U.S.A.* 41 B9 42 0N 90 0W
Mieres, *Spain* 11 A3 43 18N 5 48W
Milan, *Italy* 12 B3 45 28N 9 10 E
Mildura, *Australia* 34 G7 34 13S 142 9 E
Milford, *U.S.A.* 43 F10 38 52N 75 27W
Milford Haven, *U.K.* 7 G4 51 43N 5 2W
Milk →, *N. Amer.* 40 A5 48 5N 106 15W
Millau, *France* 9 E5 44 8N 3 4 E
Millinocket, *U.S.A.* 43 C13 45 45N 68 45W
Millville, *U.S.A.* 43 F10 39 22N 75 0W
Milton Keynes, *U.K.* 7 F6 52 3N 0 42W
Milwaukee, *U.S.A.* 42 D4 43 9N 87 58W
Minas Gerais □, *Brazil* 46 D5 18 50S 46 0W
Minatitlán, *Mexico* 44 D6 17 59N 94 31W
Mindanao, *Phil.* 22 C4 8 0N 125 0 E
Mindoro, *Phil.* 22 B4 13 0N 121 0 E
Mindoro Str., *Phil.* 22 B4 12 30N 120 30 E
Minneapolis, *U.S.A.* 41 B8 44 58N 93 20W
Minnesota □, *U.S.A.* 41 A8 46 40N 94 0W
Minorca, *Spain* 11 C8 40 0N 4 0 E
Minsk, *Belorussia* 14 D4 53 52N 27 30 E
Miramichi B., *Canada* 43 B15 47 15N 65 0W
Mirande, *France* 9 F4 43 31N 0 25 E
Mirpur Khas, *Pakistan* 23 G2 25 30N 69 0 E
Mirzapur, *India* 23 G9 25 10N 82 34 E
Mishawaka, *U.S.A.* 42 E4 41 40N 86 8W
Miskolc, *Hungary* 10 D9 48 7N 20 50 E
Misool, *Indonesia* 22 D5 1 52S 130 10 E
Mississippi □, *U.S.A.* 41 D9 33 0N 90 0W
Mississippi →, *U.S.A.* 41 E9 29 0N 89 15W
Mississippi, Delta of the, *U.S.A.* 41 E8 29 15N 90 30W
Missouri □, *U.S.A.* 41 C8 38 25N 92 30W
Missouri →, *U.S.A.* 41 C8 38 50N 90 8W
Misurata, *Libya* 28 C10 32 24N 15 3 E
Mitchell →, *Australia* 34 D7 15 12S 141 35 E
Mitumba Mts., *Zaïre* 32 F5 7 0S 27 30 E
Miyazaki, *Japan* 19 D2 31 56N 131 30 E
Mizoram □, *India* 25 C8 23 30N 92 40 E
Mjösa L., *Norway* 6 F10 60 48N 11 0 E
Mmabatho, *S. Africa* 31 B4 25 49S 25 30 E
Mobile, *U.S.A.* 41 D9 30 41N 88 3W
Mobutu Sese Seko, L., *Africa* 32 D6 1 30N 31 0 E
Mochudi, *Botswana* 31 A4 24 27S 26 7 E
Modena, *Italy* 12 B4 44 39N 10 55 E
Mogadishu, *Somali Rep.* 24 E3 2 2N 45 25 E
Mogalakwena →, *S. Africa* 31 A4 22 38S 28 40 E
Mogilev, *Belorussia* 14 D5 53 55N 30 18 E
Mojave Desert, *U.S.A.* 40 D3 35 0N 116 30W
Moldavia ■, *Europe* 15 E4 47 0N 28 0 E
Molde, *Norway* 6 F9 62 45N 7 9 E
Molepolole, *Botswana* 31 A4 24 28S 25 28 E
Mollendo, *Peru* 46 D2 17 0S 72 0W
Molokai, *U.S.A.* 40 H16 21 8N 157 0W
Molopo →, *Africa* 31 B3 27 30S 20 13 E
Molsheim, *France* 8 C7 48 33N 7 29 E
Molteno, *S. Africa* 31 C4 31 22S 26 22 E
Molucca Sea, *Indonesia* 22 D4 2 0S 124 0 E
Moluccas, *Indonesia* 22 D4 1 0S 127 0 E
Mombasa, *Kenya* 32 E7 4 2S 39 43 E
Mona Passage, *W. Indies* 45 D11 18 30N 67 45W
Monaco ■, *Europe* 9 F7 43 46N 7 23 E
Mönchengladbach = Munchen-Gladbach, *Germany* 10 C2 51 12N 6 23 E
Monclova, *Mexico* 44 B4 26 50N 101 30W
Moncton, *Canada* 43 B15 46 7N 64 51W
Monghyr, *India* 23 G11 25 23N 86 30 E
Mongolia ■, *Asia* 20 B5 47 0N 103 0 E
Mongu, *Zambia* 33 H4 15 16S 23 12 E
Monroe, *La., U.S.A.* 41 D8 32 32N 92 4W
Monroe, *Mich., U.S.A.* 42 E6 41 55N 83 26W
Monrovia, *Liberia* 28 H4 6 18N 10 47W
Mons, *Belgium* 8 B5 50 27N 3 58 E
Mont Cenis, Col du, *France* 9 E7 45 15N 6 55 E
Mont-de-Marsan, *France* 9 F3 43 54N 0 31W
Mont-Laurier, *Canada* 43 B10 46 35N 75 30W
Montagu, *S. Africa* 31 C3 33 45S 20 8 E
Montana □, *U.S.A.* 40 A5 47 0N 110 0W
Montargis, *France* 8 D5 47 59N 2 43 E
Montauban, *France* 9 E4 44 2N 1 21 E
Montbard, *France* 8 D6 47 38N 4 20 E
Montbéliard, *France* 8 D7 47 31N 6 48 E
Montbrison, *France* 9 E6 45 36N 4 3 E
Montceau-les-Mines, *France* 8 D6 46 40N 4 23 E
Montdidier, *France* 8 C5 49 38N 2 35 E
Monte-Carlo, *Monaco* 9 F7 43 46N 7 23 E
Montego Bay, *Jamaica* 44 J16 18 30N 78 0W
Montélimar, *France* 9 E6 44 33N 4 45 E
Montería, *Colombia* 46 B2 8 46N 75 53W
Monterrey, *Mexico* 44 B4 25 40N 100 30W
Montes Claros, *Brazil* 46 D5 16 30S 43 50W
Montevideo, *Uruguay* 47 F4 34 50S 56 11W
Montgomery, *U.S.A.* 41 D9 32 20N 86 20W
Monticello, *U.S.A.* 42 E4 40 40N 86 45W
Montluçon, *France* 9 D5 46 22N 2 36 E
Montmagny, *Canada* 43 B12 46 58N 70 34W
Montpelier, *U.S.A.* 43 C11 44 15N 72 38W
Montpellier, *France* 9 F5 43 37N 3 52 E
Montréal, *Canada* 43 C11 45 31N 73 34W
Montreux, *Switz.* 10 E2 46 26N 6 55 E
Montrose, *U.K.* 7 D5 56 43N 2 28W
Montserrat, *W. Indies* 44 L19 16 40N 62 10W
Mooi River, *S. Africa* 31 B4 29 13S 29 50 E
Moorreesburg, *S. Africa* 31 C2 33 6S 18 38 E
Moose Jaw, *Canada* 38 C9 50 24N 105 30W
Moosehead L., *U.S.A.* 43 C13 45 34N 69 40W
Mora, *Sweden* 6 F10 61 2N 14 38 E
Moradabad, *India* 23 E7 28 50N 78 50 E
Morava →, *Europe* 10 D7 48 10N 16 59 E
Moravian Hts., *Czech.* 10 D6 49 30N 15 40 E
Moray Firth, *U.K.* 7 D5 57 50N 3 30W
Mordovian Republic □, *Russia* 14 D7 54 20N 44 30 E
Morecambe B., *U.K.* 7 E5 54 7N 3 0W
Morehead, *U.S.A.* 42 F6 38 12N 83 22W
Morelia, *Mexico* 44 D4 19 42N 101 7W
Morena, Sierra, *Spain* 11 C3 38 20N 4 0W
Morgantown, *U.S.A.* 42 F8 39 39N 79 58W
Morlaix, *France* 8 C2 48 36N 3 52W
Moro G., *Phil.* 22 C4 6 30N 123 0 E
Morocco ■, *N. Afr.* 28 C5 32 0N 5 50W
Morogoro, *Tanzania* 32 F7 6 50S 37 40 E
Morotai, *Indonesia* 22 C4 2 10N 128 30 E
Morris, *U.S.A.* 42 E3 41 20N 88 20W
Moscow, *Russia* 14 C6 55 45N 37 35 E
Moselle →, *Europe* 8 B7 50 22N 7 36 E
Moshi, *Tanzania* 32 E7 3 22S 37 18 E
Mosselbaai, *S. Africa* 31 C3 34 11S 22 8 E
Most, *Czech.* 10 C5 50 31N 13 38 E
Mostar, *Bos.-H., Yug.* 13 C7 43 22N 17 50 E
Mosul, *Iraq* 24 B3 36 15N 43 5 E
Motherwell, *U.K.* 7 E5 55 48N 4 0W
Motihari, *India* 23 F10 26 30N 84 55 E
Moulins, *France* 9 D5 46 35N 3 19 E
Moulmein, *Burma* 25 D8 16 30N 97 40 E
Moundsville, *U.S.A.* 42 F7 39 53N 80 43W
Mount Carmel, *U.S.A.* 42 F4 38 20N 87 48W
Mount Desert I., *U.S.A.* 43 C13 44 15N 68 25W
Mount Gambier, *Australia* 34 H7 37 50S 140 46 E
Mount Isa, *Australia* 34 E6 20 42S 139 26 E
Mount Pleasant, *U.S.A.* 42 D5 43 35N 84 47W
Mount Sterling, *U.S.A.* 42 F6 38 3N 83 57W
Mount Vernon, *N.Y., U.S.A.* 43 E11 40 57N 73 49W
Mount Vernon, *Ohio, U.S.A.* 42 E6 40 20N 82 30W
Mourne Mts., *U.K.* 7 E4 54 10N 6 0W
Mozambique ■, *Africa* 33 H7 19 0S 35 0 E
Mozambique Chan., *Africa* 33 H8 17 30S 42 30 E
Mpumalanga, *S. Africa* 31 B5 29 50S 30 33 E
Muar, *Malaysia* 22 C2 2 3N 102 34 E
Mubarraz, *Si. Arabia* 24 C3 25 30N 49 40 E
Mudanjiang, *China* 21 B7 44 38N 129 30 E
Mufulira, *Zambia* 33 G5 12 32S 28 15 E
Muktsar, *India* 23 D5 30 30N 74 30 E
Mukur, *Afghan.* 23 C1 32 50N 67 42 E
Mulde →, *Germany* 10 C5 51 50N 12 15 E
Mulhacén, *Spain* 11 D4 37 4N 3 20W
Mulhouse, *France* 8 D7 47 40N 7 20 E
Mull, *U.K.* 7 D4 56 27N 6 0W
Muller Ra., *Indonesia* 22 C3 0 30N 113 30 E
Multan, *Pakistan* 23 D3 30 15N 71 36 E
Muna, *Indonesia* 22 D4 5 0S 122 30 E
Munchen-Gladbach, *Germany* 10 C2 51 12N 6 23 E
Muncie, *U.S.A.* 42 E5 40 10N 85 20W
Munich, *Germany* 10 D4 48 8N 11 33 E
Munising, *U.S.A.* 42 B4 46 25N 86 39W
Münster, *Germany* 10 C2 51 58N 7 37 E
Muqdisho = Mogadishu, *Somali Rep.* 24 E3 2 2N 45 25 E
Murchison →, *Australia* 34 F1 27 45S 114 0 E
Murcia, *Spain* 11 C5 38 5N 1 10W
Mureş →, *Romania* 10 E9 46 15N 20 13 E
Muret, *France* 9 F4 43 30N 1 20 E
Müritz, L., *Germany* 10 B5 53 25N 12 40 E
Murmansk, *Russia* 14 A5 68 57N 33 10 E
Murray, *U.S.A.* 42 G3 36 40N 88 20W
Murray →, *Australia* 34 H6 35 20S 139 22 E
Murwara, *India* 23 H8 23 46N 80 28 E
Muscat, *Oman* 24 C4 23 37N 58 36 E
Musgrave Ras., *Australia* 34 F5 26 0S 132 0 E
Musi →, *Indonesia* 22 D2 2 20S 104 56 E
Muskegon →, *U.S.A.* 42 D4 43 25N 86 25W
Muskegon Heights, *U.S.A.* 42 D4 43 12N 86 17W
Mustang, *Nepal* 23 E9 29 10N 83 55 E
Mutare, *Zimbabwe* 33 H6 18 58S 32 38 E
Muzaffarnagar, *India* 23 E6 29 26N 77 40 E
Muzaffarpur, *India* 23 F10 26 7N 85 23 E
Mwanza, *Tanzania* 32 E6 2 30S 32 58 E
Mweru, L., *Zambia* 32 F5 9 0S 28 40 E
Myanmar = Burma ■, *Asia* 25 C8 21 0N 96 30 E
Myingyan, *Burma* 25 C8 21 30N 95 20 E
Myitkyina, *Burma* 25 C8 25 24N 97 26 E
Mymensingh, *Bangla.* 23 G13 24 45N 90 24 E
Mysore, *India* 25 D6 12 17N 76 41 E
Mzimkulu →, *S. Africa* 31 C5 30 44S 30 28 E

115

Naab Ostrava

N

Naab →, Germany 10 D5 49 1N 12 2 E
Nābulus, Jordan 29 P21 32 14N 35 15 E
Nadiad, India 23 H4 22 41N 72 56 E
Nafud Desert, Si. Arabia 24 C3 28 15N 41 0 E
Nagaland □, India 25 C8 26 0N 94 30 E
Nagano, Japan 19 A6 36 40N 138 10 E
Nagaoka, Japan 19 G11 37 27N 138 51 E
Nagasaki, Japan 19 C1 32 47N 129 50 E
Nagaur, India 23 F4 27 15N 73 45 E
Nagercoil, India 25 E6 8 12N 77 26 E
Nagoya, Japan 19 B5 35 10N 136 50 E
Nagpur, India 23 J7 21 8N 79 10 E
Nairn, U.K. 7 D5 57 35N 3 54W
Nairobi, Kenya 32 E7 1 17S 36 48 E
Najibabad, India 23 E7 29 40N 78 20 E
Nakhichevan Republic □, Azerbaijan 15 G8 39 14N 45 30 E
Nakhon Ratchasima, Thailand 22 B2 14 59N 102 12 E
Nakhon Si Thammarat, Thailand 22 C2 8 29N 100 0 E
Nakina, Canada 42 A4 50 10N 86 40W
Nakuru, Kenya 32 E7 0 15S 36 4 E
Nalchik, Russia 15 F7 43 30N 43 33 E
Nam Co, China 20 C4 30 30N 90 45 E
Namaland, Namibia 31 A2 24 30S 17 0 E
Namaqualand, S. Africa 31 B2 30 0S 17 25 E
Namib Desert, Namibia 31 A1 22 30S 15 0 E
Namibe, Angola 33 H2 15 7S 12 11 E
Namibia ■, Africa 31 A2 22 0S 18 9 E
Namlea, Indonesia 22 D4 3 18S 127 5 E
Nampula, Mozam. 33 H7 15 6S 39 15 E
Namur, Belgium 8 B6 50 27N 4 52 E
Nan Shan, China 20 C4 38 30N 96 0 E
Nanaimo, Canada 38 D7 49 10N 124 0W
Nanchang, China 21 D6 28 42N 115 55 E
Nanchong, China 20 C5 30 43N 106 2 E
Nancy, France 8 C7 48 42N 6 12 E
Nanda Devi, India 23 D7 30 23N 79 59 E
Nanded, India 25 D6 19 10N 77 20 E
Nandurbar, India 23 J5 21 20N 74 15 E
Nanga Parbat, Pakistan 23 B5 35 10N 74 35 E
Nanking, China 21 C6 32 2N 118 47 E
Nanning, China 20 D5 22 48N 108 20 E
Nanp'ing, China 21 D6 26 38N 118 10 E
Nantes, France 8 D3 47 12N 1 33W
Nanticoke, U.S.A. 42 E9 41 12N 76 1W
Nantong, China 21 C7 32 1N 120 52 E
Nantua, France 9 D6 46 10N 5 35 E
Napier, N.Z. 35 H14 39 30S 176 56 E
Naples, Italy 12 D6 40 50N 14 17 E
Nara, Japan 19 B4 34 40N 135 49 E
Narayanganj, Bangla. 23 H13 23 40N 90 33 E
Narbonne, France 9 F5 43 11N 3 0 E
Narmada →, India 23 J4 21 38N 72 36 E
Narvik, Norway 6 E11 68 28N 17 26 E
Nashua, U.S.A. 43 D12 42 50N 71 25W
Nashville, U.S.A. 41 C9 36 12N 86 46W
Nasik, India 23 K4 19 58N 73 50 E
Nasirabad, India 23 F5 26 15N 74 45 E
Nassau, Bahamas 45 B9 25 5N 77 20W
Nasser, L., Egypt 29 E13 23 0N 32 30 E
Nata, Botswana 31 A4 20 12S 26 12 E
Natal, Brazil 46 C6 5 47S 35 13W
Natal □, S. Africa 31 B5 28 30S 30 30 E
Nathdwara, India 23 G4 24 55N 73 50 E
Natuna Is., Indonesia 22 C2 4 0N 108 15 E
Nauru ■, Pac. Oc. 36 H8 1 0S 166 0 E
Navarra □, Spain 11 A5 42 40N 1 40W
Navsari, India 23 J4 20 57N 72 59 E
Nawabshah, Pakistan 23 F2 26 15N 68 25 E
Náxos, Greece 13 F11 37 8N 25 25 E
Nazareth, Israel 29 N21 32 42N 35 17 E
Ndjamena, Chad 28 G9 12 10N 14 59 E
Ndola, Zambia 33 G5 13 0S 28 34 E
Neagh, L., U.K. 7 E3 54 35N 6 25W
Nebraska □, U.S.A. 40 B7 41 30N 100 0W
Neckar →, Germany 10 D3 49 31N 8 26 E
Neemuch, India 23 G5 24 30N 74 56 E
Neenah, U.S.A. 42 C3 44 10N 88 30W
Negaunee, U.S.A. 42 B4 46 30N 87 36W
Negrais, C., Burma 25 D8 16 0N 94 30 E
Negro →, Argentina 47 G3 41 2S 62 47W
Negro →, Brazil 46 C4 3 0S 60 0W
Negros, Phil. 22 C4 9 30N 122 40 E
Neijiang, China 20 D5 29 35N 104 55 E
Neiva, Colombia 46 B2 2 56N 75 18W
Nejd, Si. Arabia 24 C3 26 30N 42 0 E
Nellore, India 25 D6 14 27N 79 59 E
Nelson, N.Z. 35 J13 41 18S 173 16 E
Nelson →, Canada 38 C10 54 33N 98 2W
Nelspruit, S. Africa 31 B5 25 29S 30 59 E
Nemunas →, Lithuania 14 C3 55 25N 21 10 E
Nepal ■, Asia 23 F10 28 0N 84 30 E
Nérac, France 9 E4 44 8N 0 21 E
Ness, L., U.K. 7 D4 57 15N 4 30W
Netherlands ■, Europe 8 B6 52 0N 5 30 E
Netherlands Antilles ■, S. Amer. 45 E11 12 15N 69 0W
Neuchâtel, Switz. 10 E2 47 0N 6 55 E
Neuchâtel, L., Switz. 10 E2 46 53N 6 50 E
Neufchâteau, France 8 C6 48 21N 5 40 E
Neusiedl, L., Austria 10 E7 47 50N 16 47 E
Nevada □, U.S.A. 40 C3 39 20N 117 0W
Nevada, Sierra, Spain 11 D4 37 3N 3 15W
Nevada, Sierra, U.S.A. 40 C2 39 0N 120 30W
Nevers, France 8 D5 47 0N 3 9 E
New Albany, U.S.A. 42 F5 38 20N 85 50W
New Bedford, U.S.A. 43 E12 41 40N 70 52W
New Britain, Papua N. G. 34 B9 5 50S 150 20 E
New Britain, U.S.A. 43 E11 41 41N 72 47W
New Brunswick, U.S.A. 43 E10 40 30N 74 28W
New Brunswick □, Canada 43 B14 46 50N 66 30W
New Caledonia, Pac. Oc. 35 E12 21 0S 165 0 E
New Castle, Ind., U.S.A. 42 F5 39 55N 85 23W
New Castle, Pa., U.S.A. 42 E7 41 0N 80 20W
New Glasgow, Canada 43 C16 45 35N 62 36W
New Guinea, Oceania 36 H5 4 0S 136 0 E
New Hampshire □, U.S.A. 43 D12 43 40N 71 40W
New Haven, U.S.A. 43 E11 41 20N 72 54W
New Jersey □, U.S.A. 43 E10 40 30N 74 10W
New Lexington, U.S.A. 42 F6 39 40N 82 15W
New Liskeard, Canada 42 B8 47 31N 79 41W
New London, U.S.A. 43 E11 41 23N 72 8W
New Mexico □, U.S.A. 40 D5 34 30N 106 0W
New Orleans, U.S.A. 41 E9 30 0N 90 5W
New Philadelphia, U.S.A. 42 E7 40 29N 81 25W
New Plymouth, N.Z. 35 H13 39 4S 174 5 E
New Siberian Is., Russia 18 B15 75 10N 150 0 E
New South Wales □, Australia 34 G8 33 0S 146 0 E
New York □, U.S.A. 43 D9 42 40N 76 0W
New York City, U.S.A. 43 E11 40 45N 74 0W
New Zealand ■, Oceania 35 J13 40 0S 176 0 E
Newark, Del., U.S.A. 43 F10 39 42N 75 45W
Newark, N.J., U.S.A. 43 E10 40 41N 74 12W
Newark, N.Y., U.S.A. 42 D9 43 2N 77 10W
Newark, Ohio, U.S.A. 42 E6 40 5N 82 24W
Newaygo, U.S.A. 42 D5 43 25N 85 48W
Newberry, U.S.A. 42 B5 46 20N 85 32W
Newburgh, U.S.A. 43 E10 41 30N 74 1W
Newburyport, U.S.A. 43 D12 42 48N 70 50W
Newcastle, Australia 34 G9 33 0S 151 46 E
Newcastle, Canada 43 B15 47 1N 65 38W
Newcastle, S. Africa 31 B4 27 45S 29 58 E
Newcastle-upon-Tyne, U.K. 7 E6 54 59N 1 37W
Newfoundland □, Canada 39 C14 53 0N 58 0W
Newman, Australia 34 E2 23 18S 119 45 E
Newport, Gwent, U.K. 7 G5 51 35N 3 0W
Newport, I. of W., U.K. 7 G6 50 42N 1 18W
Newport, Ky., U.S.A. 42 F5 39 5N 84 23W
Newport, R.I., U.S.A. 43 E12 41 13N 71 19W
Newport, Vt., U.S.A. 43 C11 44 57N 72 17W
Newport News, U.S.A. 41 C11 37 2N 76 30W
Newry, U.K. 7 E3 54 10N 6 20W
Nganglong Kangri, China 23 C8 33 0N 81 0 E
Nha Trang, Vietnam 22 B2 12 16N 109 10 E
Niagara, U.S.A. 42 C3 45 45N 88 0W
Niagara Falls, Canada 42 D8 43 7N 79 5W
Niagara Falls, U.S.A. 42 D8 43 5N 79 0W
Niamey, Niger 30 B2 13 27N 2 6 E
Nias, Indonesia 22 C1 1 0N 97 30 E
Nicaragua ■, Cent. Amer. 44 E7 11 40N 85 30W
Nicaragua, L. of, Nic. 44 E7 12 0N 85 30W
Nice, France 9 F7 43 42N 7 14 E
Nicholasville, U.S.A. 42 G5 37 54N 84 31W
Nicobar Is., Ind. Oc. 25 E8 9 0N 93 0 E
Nicosia, Cyprus 24 B2 35 10N 33 25 E
Nicoya, Pen., Costa Rica 44 F7 9 45N 85 40W
Niger ■, W. Afr. 28 F9 17 30N 10 0 E
Niger →, W. Afr. 30 C3 5 33N 6 33 E
Nigeria ■, W. Afr. 30 C3 8 30N 8 0 E
Niigata, Japan 19 G11 37 58N 139 0 E
Niihau, U.S.A. 40 H14 21 55N 160 10W
Nijmegen, Neths. 8 B6 51 50N 5 52 E
Nikolayev, Ukraine 15 E5 46 58N 32 0 E
Nikolayevsk-na-Amur, Russia 18 D16 53 8N 140 44 E
Nile →, Africa 29 C13 30 10N 31 6 E
Nîmes, France 9 F6 43 50N 4 23 E
Ningbo, China 21 D7 29 51N 121 28 E
Ningxia Huizu Zizhiqu □, China 20 C5 38 0N 106 0 E
Niort, France 9 D3 46 19N 0 29W
Nipigon, Canada 42 A3 49 0N 88 17W
Nipigon, L., Canada 42 A3 49 50N 88 30W
Nipissing L., Canada 42 B8 46 20N 80 0W
Niš, Serbia, Yug. 13 C9 43 19N 21 58 E
Niterói, Brazil 47 E5 22 52S 43 0W
Nitra, Slovakia 10 D8 48 19N 18 4 E
Nitra →, Slovakia 10 E8 47 46N 18 10 E
Niue, Cook Is. 35 D17 19 2S 169 54W
Nivernais, France 8 D5 47 15N 3 30 E
Nizamabad, India 25 D6 18 45N 78 7 E
Nizhniy Novgorod, Russia 14 C7 56 20N 44 0 E
Nizhniy Tagil, Russia 14 C10 57 55N 59 57 E
Nkongsamba, Cameroon 30 D3 4 55N 9 55 E
Nobeoka, Japan 19 C2 32 36N 131 41 E
Noblesville, U.S.A. 42 E5 40 1N 85 59W
Nogales, Mexico 44 A2 31 20N 110 56W
Nogent-le-Rotrou, France 8 C4 48 20N 0 50 E
Noirmoutier, I. de, France 8 D2 46 58N 2 10W
Noranda, Canada 42 A8 48 20N 79 0W
Norfolk, U.S.A. 41 C11 36 40N 76 15W
Norfolk I., Pac. Oc. 35 F12 28 58S 168 3 E
Norilsk, Russia 18 C10 69 20N 88 6 E
Normandy, France 8 C4 48 45N 0 10 E
Norristown, U.S.A. 43 E10 40 9N 75 21W
Norrköping, Sweden 6 G11 58 37N 16 11 E
Norrland, Sweden 6 F11 62 15N 15 45 E
Norseman, Australia 34 G3 32 8S 121 43 E
North Battleford, Canada 38 C9 52 50N 108 17W
North Bay, Canada 42 B8 46 20N 79 30W
North C., Canada 43 B17 47 2N 60 20W
North Cape, Norway 6 D13 71 10N 25 44 E
North Carolina □, U.S.A. 41 C11 35 30N 80 0W
North Channel, Canada 42 B6 46 0N 83 0W
North Channel, U.K. 7 E4 55 0N 5 30W
North Dakota □, U.S.A. 40 A7 47 30N 100 0W
North Downs, U.K. 7 G7 51 17N 0 30 E
North European Plain, Europe 4 D11 55 0N 25 0 E
North I., N.Z. 35 H14 38 0S 175 0 E
North Ossetian Republic □, Russia 15 F7 43 30N 44 30 E
North Pt., Canada 43 B15 47 5N 64 0W
North Pole, Arctic 48 A1 90 0N 0 0 E
North Rhine Westphalia □, Germany 10 C2 51 45N 7 30 E
North Sea, Europe 4 D6 56 0N 4 0 E
North Vernon, U.S.A. 42 F5 39 0N 85 35W
North West Frontier □, Pakistan 23 C3 34 0N 71 0 E
North West Highlands, U.K. 7 D4 57 35N 5 2W
North West Territories □, Canada 38 B9 67 0N 110 0W
North York Moors, U.K. 7 E6 54 25N 0 50W
Northampton, U.K. 7 F6 52 14N 0 54W
Northampton, U.S.A. 43 D11 42 22N 72 31W
Northern Ireland □, U.K. 7 E3 54 45N 7 0W
Northern Marianas □, Pac. Oc. 36 F6 17 0N 145 0 E
Northern Territory □, Australia 34 E5 20 0S 133 0 E
Northumberland Str., Canada 43 B15 46 20N 64 0W
Norwalk, U.S.A. 42 E6 41 13N 82 38W
Norway ■, Europe 6 F10 63 0N 11 0 E
Norwegian Sea, Atl. Oc. 48 A7 66 0N 1 0 E
Norwich, U.K. 7 F7 52 38N 1 17 E
Norwich, U.S.A. 43 D10 42 32N 75 30W
Nossob →, S. Africa 31 B3 26 55S 20 45 E
Nottingham, U.K. 7 F6 52 57N 1 10W
Nouâdhibou, Mauritania 28 E3 20 54N 17 0W
Nouakchott, Mauritania 28 F3 18 9N 15 58W
Nouméa, N. Cal. 35 E12 22 17S 166 30 E
Noupoort, S. Africa 31 C3 31 10S 24 57 E
Nova Scotia □, Canada 43 C16 45 10N 63 0W
Novara, Italy 12 B3 45 27N 8 36 E
Novaya Zemlya, Russia 18 B7 75 0N 56 0 E
Novi Sad, Serbia, Yug. 13 B8 45 18N 19 52 E
Novocherkassk, Russia 15 E7 47 27N 40 15 E
Novokuznetsk, Russia 18 D10 53 45N 87 10 E
Novomoskovsk, Russia 14 D6 54 5N 38 15 E
Novorossiysk, Russia 15 F6 44 43N 37 46 E
Novoshakhtinsk, Russia 15 E6 47 46N 39 58 E
Novosibirsk, Russia 18 D10 55 0N 83 5 E
Nowy Sącz, Poland 10 D9 49 40N 20 41 E
Nubian Desert, Sudan 29 E13 21 30N 33 30 E
Nuevo Laredo, Mexico 44 B5 27 30N 99 30W
Nuku'alofa, Tonga 35 E16 21 10S 174 0W
Nullarbor Plain, Australia 34 G4 31 10S 129 0 E
Nuremburg, Germany 10 D4 49 26N 11 5 E
Nuuk = Godthåb, Greenland 48 A9 64 10N 51 35W
Nuweveldberge, S. Africa 31 C3 32 10S 21 45 E
Nyasa, L., Africa 33 G6 12 30S 34 30 E
Nyíregyháza, Hungary 10 E9 47 58N 21 47 E
Nylstroom, S. Africa 31 A4 24 42S 28 22 E
Nysa, Poland 10 C7 50 30N 17 22 E
Nysa →, Europe 10 B6 52 4N 14 46 E

O

Oahe L., U.S.A. 40 A6 45 30N 100 25W
Oahu, U.S.A. 40 H16 21 30N 158 0W
Oak Hill, U.S.A. 42 G7 38 0N 81 7W
Oakland, U.S.A. 40 C2 37 50N 122 18W
Oates Land, Antarctica 48 C19 69 0S 160 0 E
Oaxaca, Mexico 44 D5 17 2N 96 40W
Ob →, Russia 18 C8 66 45N 69 30 E
Ob, G. of, Russia 18 C9 69 0N 73 0 E
Oba, Canada 42 A5 49 4N 84 7W
Oban, U.K. 7 D4 56 25N 5 30W
Oberhausen, Germany 10 C2 51 28N 6 50 E
Obi Is., Indonesia 22 D4 1 23S 127 45 E
Ocean City, U.S.A. 43 F10 39 18N 74 34W
Oconto, U.S.A. 42 C4 44 52N 87 53W
October Revolution I., Russia 18 B11 79 30N 97 0 E
Odendaalsrus, S. Africa 31 B4 27 48S 26 45 E
Odense, Denmark 6 G10 55 22N 10 23 E
Odessa, Ukraine 15 E5 46 30N 30 45 E
Odessa, U.S.A. 40 D6 31 51N 102 23W
Odra →, Poland 10 B6 53 33N 14 38 E
Offa, Nigeria 30 C2 8 13N 4 42 E
Ogbomosho, Nigeria 30 C2 8 1N 4 11 E
Ogden, U.S.A. 40 B4 41 13N 112 1W
Ogdensburg, U.S.A. 43 C10 44 40N 75 27W
Ohio □, U.S.A. 42 E5 40 20N 84 10W
Ohio →, U.S.A. 41 C9 36 59N 89 8W
Ohre →, Czech. 10 C6 50 30N 14 10 E
Oil City, U.S.A. 42 E8 41 26N 79 40W
Oise →, France 8 C5 49 0N 2 4 E
Ōita, Japan 19 C2 33 14N 131 36 E
Ojos del Salado, Cerro, Argentina 47 E3 27 0S 68 40W
Okahandja, Namibia 31 A2 22 0S 16 59 E
Okaputa, Namibia 31 A2 20 5S 17 0 E
Okara, Pakistan 23 D4 30 50N 73 31 E
Okavango Swamps, Botswana 33 H4 18 45S 22 45 E
Okayama, Japan 19 B3 34 40N 133 54 E
Okazaki, Japan 19 B5 34 57N 137 10 E
Okha, Russia 18 D16 53 40N 143 0 E
Okhotsk, Russia 18 D16 59 20N 143 10 E
Okhotsk, Sea of, Asia 18 D16 55 0N 145 0 E
Oklahoma □, U.S.A. 40 C7 35 20N 97 30W
Oklahoma City, U.S.A. 40 C7 35 25N 97 30W
Okwa →, Botswana 31 A3 22 30S 23 0 E
Öland, Sweden 6 G11 56 45N 16 38 E
Old Town, U.S.A. 43 C13 45 0N 68 41W
Oldenburg, Germany 10 B3 53 10N 8 10 E
Oldham, U.K. 7 F5 53 33N 2 8W
Olean, U.S.A. 42 D8 42 8N 78 25W
Olekminsk, Russia 18 C14 60 25N 120 30 E
Olenek →, Russia 18 B14 73 0N 120 10 E
Oléron, I. d', France 9 E3 45 55N 1 15W
Olney, U.S.A. 42 F3 38 40N 88 5W
Olomouc, Czech. 10 D7 49 38N 17 12 E
Oloron-Ste.-Marie, France 9 F3 43 11N 0 38W
Olsztyn, Poland 10 B9 53 48N 20 29 E
Olt →, Romania 13 C11 43 43N 24 51 E
Olympia, Greece 13 F9 37 39N 21 39 E
Olympus, Mt., Greece 13 D10 40 6N 22 23 E
Omaha, U.S.A. 41 B7 41 15N 95 55W
Oman ■, Asia 17 G9 23 0N 58 0 E
Oman, G. of, Asia 24 C4 24 30N 58 30 E
Omaruru, Namibia 31 A2 21 26S 16 0 E
Ombai Str., Indonesia 22 D4 8 30S 124 50 E
Omdurman, Sudan 29 F13 15 40N 32 28 E
Ōmiya, Japan 19 B6 35 54N 139 38 E
Omsk, Russia 18 D9 55 0N 73 12 E
Ōmuta, Japan 19 C2 33 5N 130 26 E
Ondo, Nigeria 30 C2 7 4N 4 47 E
Onega →, Russia 4 C13 63 58N 37 55 E
Onega, G. of, Russia 14 B6 64 30N 37 0 E
Onega, L., Russia 14 B6 62 0N 35 30 E
Oneida, U.S.A. 43 D10 43 5N 75 40W
Oneida L., U.S.A. 42 D10 43 12N 76 0W
Oneonta, U.S.A. 43 D10 42 26N 75 5W
Onitsha, Nigeria 30 C3 6 6N 6 42 E
Ontario □, Canada 42 A2 48 0N 83 0W
Ontario, L., N. Amer. 42 D8 43 40N 78 0W
Ontonagon, U.S.A. 42 B3 46 52N 89 19W
Oostende = Ostend, Belgium 8 B5 51 15N 2 54 E
Opava, Czech. 10 D7 49 57N 17 58 E
Opole, Poland 10 C7 50 42N 17 58 E
Oporto, Portugal 11 B1 41 8N 8 40W
Oradea, Romania 10 E9 47 2N 21 58 E
Orai, India 23 G7 25 58N 79 30 E
Oran, Algeria 28 B6 35 45N 0 39W
Orange, Australia 34 G8 33 15S 149 7 E
Orange, France 9 E6 44 8N 4 47 E
Orange, U.S.A. 42 F8 38 17N 78 5W
Orange →, S. Africa 31 B2 28 41S 16 28 E
Orange Free State □, S. Africa 31 B4 28 30S 27 0 E
Orangeville, Canada 42 D7 43 55N 80 5W
Oranjemund, Namibia 31 B2 28 38S 16 29 E
Ordos, China 21 C5 39 0N 109 0 E
Örebro, Sweden 6 G11 59 20N 15 18 E
Oregon □, U.S.A. 40 B2 44 0N 121 0W
Orekhovo-Zuyevo, Russia 14 C6 55 50N 38 55 E
Orel, Russia 14 D6 52 57N 36 3 E
Orenburg, Russia 14 D10 51 45N 55 6 E
Orense, Spain 11 A2 42 19N 7 55W
Orinoco →, Venezuela 46 B3 9 15N 61 30W
Orissa □, India 23 J9 20 0N 84 0 E
Oristano, Italy 12 E3 39 54N 8 35 E
Orizaba, Mexico 44 D5 18 51N 97 6W
Orkney Is., U.K. 7 C5 59 0N 3 0W
Orlando, U.S.A. 41 E10 28 30N 81 25W
Orléanais, France 8 D4 48 0N 2 0 E
Orléans, France 8 D4 47 54N 1 52 E
Orléans, I. d', Canada 43 B12 46 54N 70 58W
Ormara, Pakistan 24 C5 25 16N 64 33 E
Ormoc, Phil. 22 B4 11 0N 124 37 E
Örnsköldsvik, Sweden 6 F11 63 17N 18 40 E
Orsk, Russia 14 D10 51 12N 58 34 E
Orumiyeh, Iran 24 B3 37 50N 45 30 E
Oruro, Bolivia 46 D3 18 0S 67 9W
Ōsaka, Japan 19 B4 34 40N 135 30 E
Oshawa, Canada 42 D8 43 50N 78 50W
Oshogbo, Nigeria 30 C2 7 48N 4 37 E
Osijek, Croatia 13 B8 45 34N 18 41 E
Osizweni, S. Africa 31 B5 27 49S 30 7 E
Oskarshamn, Sweden 6 G11 57 15N 16 27 E
Oslo, Norway 6 G10 59 55N 10 45 E
Oslo Fjord, Norway 6 G10 59 20N 10 35 E
Osnabrück, Germany 10 B3 52 16N 8 2 E
Osorno, Chile 47 G2 40 25S 73 0W
Ostend, Belgium 8 B5 51 15N 2 54 E
Östersund, Sweden 6 F10 63 10N 14 38 E
Ostrava, Czech. 10 D8 49 51N 18 18 E

117
Rainier, Mt. — Sault Ste. Marie

Rainier, Mt., *U.S.A.* **40 A2** 46 50N 121 50W
Raipur, *India* **23 J8** 21 17N 81 45 E
Raj Nandgaon, *India* **23 J8** 21 5N 81 5 E
Rajahmundry, *India* **25 D7** 17 1N 81 48 E
Rajasthan □, *India* **23 F4** 26 45N 73 30 E
Rajasthan Canal, *India* **23 F3** 28 0N 72 0 E
Rajkot, *India* **23 H3** 22 15N 70 56 E
Rajshahi, *Bangla.* **23 G12** 24 22N 88 39 E
Rajshahi □, *Bangla.* **23 G12** 25 0N 89 0 E
Rakaposhi, *Pakistan* **23 A5** 36 10N 74 25 E
Rakops, *Botswana* **31 A3** 21 1S 24 28 E
Raleigh, *U.S.A.* **41 C11** 35 47N 78 39W
Ramgarh, *India* **23 H10** 23 40N 85 35 E
Ramotswa, *Botswana* **31 A4** 24 50S 25 52 E
Rampur, *India* **23 E7** 28 50N 79 5 E
Rancagua, *Chile* **47 F2** 34 10S 70 50W
Ranchi, *India* **23 H10** 23 19N 85 27 E
Randers, *Denmark* **6 G10** 56 29N 10 1 E
Rangoon, *Burma* **25 D8** 16 45N 96 20 E
Rangpur, *Bangla.* **23 G12** 25 42N 89 22 E
Rantoul, *U.S.A.* **42 E3** 40 18N 88 10W
Rasht, *Iran* **24 B3** 37 20N 49 40 E
Ratangarh, *India* **23 E5** 28 5N 74 35 E
Ratlam, *India* **23 H5** 23 20N 75 0 E
Raurkela, *India* **23 H10** 22 14N 84 50 E
Ravenna, *Italy* **12 B5** 44 28N 12 15 E
Ravi →, *Pakistan* **23 D3** 30 35N 71 49 E
Rawalpindi, *Pakistan* **23 C4** 33 38N 73 8 E
Raz, Pte. du, *France* **8 C1** 48 2N 4 47W
Ré, I. de, *France* **9 D3** 46 12N 1 30W
Reading, *U.K.* **7 G6** 51 27N 0 57W
Reading, *U.S.A.* **43 E10** 40 20N 75 53W
Recife, *Brazil* **46 C6** 8 0S 35 0W
Red →, *U.S.A.* **41 D8** 31 0N 91 40W
Red Deer, *Canada* **38 C8** 52 20N 113 50W
Red Sea, *Asia* **29 E14** 25 0N 36 0 E
Redon, *France* **8 D2** 47 40N 2 6W
Ree, L., *Ireland* **7 F3** 53 35N 8 0W
Regensburg, *Germany* **10 D5** 49 1N 12 7 E
Reggio di Calabria, *Italy* **12 E6** 38 7N 15 38 E
Reggio nell' Emilia, *Italy* **12 B4** 44 42N 10 38 E
Regina, *Canada* **38 C9** 50 27N 104 35W
Rehoboth, *Namibia* **31 A2** 23 15S 17 4 E
Reichenbach, *Germany* **10 C5** 50 36N 12 19 E
Reigate, *U.K.* **7 G6** 51 14N 0 11W
Reims, *France* **8 C6** 49 15N 4 1 E
Reindeer L., *Canada* **38 C9** 57 15N 102 15W
Reitz, *S. Africa* **31 B4** 27 48S 28 29 E
Remscheid, *Germany* **10 C2** 51 11N 7 12 E
Renfrew, *Canada* **42 C9** 45 30N 76 40W
Rennes, *France* **8 C3** 48 7N 1 41W
Reno, *U.S.A.* **40 C3** 39 30N 119 50W
Resistencia, *Argentina* **47 E4** 27 30S 59 0W
Rethel, *France* **8 C6** 49 30N 4 20 E
Réthímnon, *Greece* **13 G11** 35 18N 24 30 E
Réunion ■, *Ind. Oc.* **27 J9** 21 0S 56 0 E
Revilla Gigedo, Is., *Pac. Oc.* **37 F16** 18 40N 112 0W
Rewa, *India* **23 G8** 24 33N 81 25 E
Rewari, *India* **23 E6** 28 15N 76 40 E
Reykjavík, *Iceland* **6 B3** 64 10N 21 57W
Reynosa, *Mexico* **44 B5** 26 5N 98 18W
Rhine →, *Europe* **8 B7** 51 52N 6 2 E
Rhineland-Palatinate □, *Germany* **10 D2** 50 0N 7 0 E
Rhode Island □, *U.S.A.* **43 E12** 41 38N 71 37W
Rhodes = Ródhos, *Greece* **13 F13** 36 15N 28 10 E
Rhodope Mts., *Bulgaria* **13 D11** 41 40N 24 20 E
Rhön, *Germany* **10 C3** 50 24N 9 58 E
Rhône →, *France* **9 F6** 43 28N 4 42 E
Rhyl, *U.K.* **7 F5** 53 19N 3 29W
Riau Arch., *Indonesia* **22 C2** 0 30N 104 20 E
Ribeirão Prêto, *Brazil* **46 E5** 21 10S 47 50W
Richards Bay, *S. Africa* **31 B5** 28 48S 32 6 E
Richlands, *U.S.A.* **42 G7** 37 7N 81 49W
Richmond, *Ind., U.S.A.* **42 F5** 39 50N 84 50W
Richmond, *Ky., U.S.A.* **42 G5** 37 40N 84 20W
Richmond, *Va., U.S.A.* **42 G9** 37 33N 77 27W
Ridder, *Kazakhstan* **18 D10** 50 20N 83 30 E
Ridgway, *U.S.A.* **42 E8** 41 25N 78 43W
Riet →, *S. Africa* **31 B3** 29 0S 23 54 E
Riga, *Latvia* **14 C3** 56 53N 24 8 E
Riga, G. of, *Latvia* **14 C3** 57 40N 23 45 E
Rijeka, *Croatia* **12 B6** 45 20N 14 21 E
Rimini, *Italy* **12 B5** 44 3N 12 33 E
Rîmnicu Vîlcea, *Romania* **13 B11** 45 9N 24 21 E
Rimouski, *Canada* **43 A13** 48 27N 68 30W
Rio de Janeiro, *Brazil* **47 E5** 23 0S 43 12W
Río Gallegos, *Argentina* **47 H3** 51 35S 69 15W
Rio Grande →, *U.S.A.* **41 E7** 25 57N 97 9W
Ripon, *U.S.A.* **42 D3** 43 51N 88 50W
Riverhead, *U.S.A.* **43 E11** 40 53N 72 40W
Riversdale, *S. Africa* **31 C3** 34 7S 21 15 E
Riverside, *U.S.A.* **40 D3** 33 58N 117 22W
Rivière-du-Loup, *Canada* **43 B13** 47 50N 69 30W
Riyadh, *Si. Arabia* **24 C3** 24 41N 46 42 E
Roanne, *France* **9 D6** 46 3N 4 4 E
Roanoke, *U.S.A.* **42 G8** 37 19N 79 55W
Roberval, *Canada* **43 A11** 48 32N 72 15W
Robson, Mt., *Canada* **38 C8** 53 10N 119 10W
Rochechouart, *France* **9 E4** 45 50N 0 49 E
Rochefort, *France* **9 E3** 45 56N 0 57W
Rochester, *Ind., U.S.A.* **42 E4** 41 5N 86 15W
Rochester, *Minn., U.S.A.* **41 B8** 44 1N 92 28W
Rochester, *N.H., U.S.A.* **43 D12** 43 19N 70 57W
Rochester, *N.Y., U.S.A.* **42 D9** 43 10N 77 40W
Rockall, *Atl. Oc.* **4 D3** 57 37N 13 42W
Rockford, *U.S.A.* **41 B9** 42 20N 89 7W
Rockhampton, *Australia* **34 E9** 23 22S 150 32 E
Rockland, *U.S.A.* **43 C13** 44 6N 69 6W
Rocky Mts., *N. Amer.* **38 C7** 55 0N 121 0W
Rodez, *France* **9 E5** 44 21N 2 33 E
Ródhos, *Greece* **13 F13** 36 15N 28 10 E
Roermond, *Neths.* **8 B6** 51 12N 6 0 E
Roeselare, *Belgium* **8 B5** 50 57N 3 7 E
Rogers City, *U.S.A.* **42 C6** 45 25N 83 49W
Rohtak, *India* **23 E6** 28 55N 76 43 E
Roma, *Australia* **34 F8** 26 32S 148 49 E
Romania ■, *Europe* **13 B11** 46 0N 25 0 E
Romans-sur-Isère, *France* **9 E6** 45 3N 5 3 E
Rome, *Italy* **12 D5** 41 54N 12 30 E
Rome, *U.S.A.* **43 D10** 43 14N 75 29W
Romney, *U.S.A.* **42 F8** 39 21N 78 45W
Romorantin-Lanthenay, *France* **8 D4** 47 21N 1 45 E
Rondônia □, *Brazil* **46 D3** 11 0S 63 0W
Ronne Ice Shelf, *Antarctica* **48 C23** 78 0S 60 0W
Roodepoort, *S. Africa* **31 B4** 26 11S 27 54 E
Roosevelt I., *Antarctica* **48 C20** 79 30S 162 0W
Roquefort, *France* **9 E3** 44 2N 0 20W
Roraima □, *Brazil* **46 B3** 2 0N 61 30W
Rosario, *Argentina* **47 F3** 33 0S 60 40W
Roscommon, *U.S.A.* **42 C5** 44 27N 84 35W
Roseau, *Domin.* **44 M20** 15 20N 61 24W
Rosenheim, *Germany* **10 E5** 47 51N 12 9 E
Ross Ice Shelf, *Antarctica* **48 C20** 80 0S 180 0 E
Ross Sea, *Antarctica* **48 C19** 74 0S 178 0 E
Rossignol, L., *Canada* **43 C15** 44 12N 65 10W
Rosslare, *Ireland* **7 F3** 52 17N 6 23W
Rostock, *Germany* **10 A5** 54 4N 12 9 E
Rostov, *Russia* **15 E6** 47 15N 39 45 E
Rothaar Gebirge, *Germany* **10 C3** 51 0N 8 5 E
Rotherham, *U.K.* **7 F6** 53 26N 1 21W
Rothesay, *U.K.* **7 E4** 55 50N 5 3W
Rotorua, *N.Z.* **35 H14** 38 9S 176 16 E
Rotterdam, *Neths.* **8 B6** 51 55N 4 30 E
Roubaix, *France* **8 B5** 50 40N 3 10 E
Rouen, *France* **8 C4** 49 27N 1 4 E
Roussillon, *France* **9 F5** 42 30N 2 35 E
Rouxville, *S. Africa* **31 C4** 30 25S 26 50 E
Rouyn, *Canada* **42 A8** 48 20N 79 0W
Rovaniemi, *Finland* **6 E13** 66 29N 25 41 E
Royal Leamington Spa, *U.K.* **7 F6** 52 18N 1 32W
Royan, *France* **9 E3** 45 37N 1 2W
Rub' al Khali, *Si. Arabia* **24 D3** 18 0N 48 0 E
Rugby, *U.K.* **7 F6** 52 23N 1 16W
Rügen, *Germany* **10 A5** 54 22N 13 25 E
Ruhr →, *Germany* **10 C2** 51 25N 6 44 E
Rumania = Romania ■, *Europe* **13 B11** 46 0N 25 0 E
Rumford, *U.S.A.* **43 C12** 44 30N 70 30W
Rupat, *Indonesia* **22 C2** 1 45N 101 40 E
Ruse, *Bulgaria* **13 C11** 43 48N 25 59 E
Rushville, *U.S.A.* **42 F5** 39 38N 85 22W
Russia ■, *Eurasia* **18 C12** 62 0N 105 0 E
Rustenburg, *S. Africa* **31 B4** 25 41S 27 14 E
Ruteng, *Indonesia* **22 D4** 8 35S 120 30 E
Ruwenzori, *Africa* **32 D5** 0 30N 29 55 E
Rwanda ■, *Africa* **32 E5** 2 0S 30 0 E
Ryazan, *Russia* **14 D6** 54 40N 39 40 E
Rybinsk, *Russia* **14 C6** 58 5N 38 50 E
Rybinsk Res., *Russia* **14 C6** 58 30N 38 25 E
Ryūkyū Is., *Japan* **21 D7** 26 0N 126 0 E
Rzeszów, *Poland* **10 C9** 50 5N 21 58 E

S

Saale →, *Germany* **10 C4** 51 57N 11 56 E
Saar →, *Europe* **10 D2** 49 41N 6 32 E
Saarbrücken, *Germany* **10 D2** 49 15N 6 58 E
Saaremaa, *Estonia* **14 C3** 58 30N 22 30 E
Saba, *W. Indies* **44 K18** 17 42N 63 26W
Sabadell, *Spain* **11 B7** 41 28N 2 7 E
Sabah □, *Malaysia* **22 C3** 6 0N 117 0 E
Sabhah, *Libya* **28 D9** 27 9N 14 29 E
Sabie, *S. Africa* **31 B5** 25 10S 30 48 E
Sable, C., *Canada* **43 D15** 43 29N 65 38W
Saco, *U.S.A.* **43 D12** 43 30N 70 27W
Sacramento, *U.S.A.* **40 C2** 38 33N 121 30W
Safi, *Morocco* **28 C5** 32 18N 9 20W
Saginaw, *U.S.A.* **42 D6** 43 26N 83 55W
Saginaw B., *U.S.A.* **42 D6** 43 50N 83 40W
Saguenay →, *Canada* **43 A12** 48 22N 71 0W
Sahara, *Africa* **26 D4** 23 0N 5 0 E
Saharanpur, *India* **23 E6** 29 58N 77 33 E
Sahiwal, *Pakistan* **23 D4** 30 45N 73 8 E
Saidabad, *Iran* **24 C4** 29 30N 55 45 E
Saidpur, *Bangla.* **23 G12** 25 48N 89 0 E
St. Albans, *U.K.* **7 G6** 51 44N 0 19W
St. Albans, *Vt., U.S.A.* **43 C11** 44 49N 73 7W
St. Albans, *W. Va., U.S.A.* **42 F7** 38 21N 81 50W
St.-Amand-Mont-Rond, *France* **9 D5** 46 43N 2 30 E
St. Andrews, *U.K.* **7 D5** 56 20N 2 48W
St. Boniface, *Canada* **38 D10** 49 53N 97 5W
St.-Brieuc, *France* **8 C2** 48 30N 2 46W
St. Catharines, *Canada* **42 D8** 43 10N 79 15W
St. Christopher-Nevis ■, *W. Indies* **44 K19** 17 20N 62 40W
St. Clair, L., *Canada* **42 D6** 42 30N 82 45W
St.-Claude, *France* **9 D6** 46 22N 5 52 E
St.-Dié, *France* **8 C7** 48 17N 6 56 E
St.-Dizier, *France* **8 C6** 48 38N 4 56 E
St.-Étienne, *France* **9 E6** 45 27N 4 22 E
St.-Félicien, *Canada* **43 A11** 48 40N 72 25W
St.-Flour, *France* **9 E5** 45 2N 3 6 E
St. Gallen, *Switz.* **10 E3** 47 26N 9 22 E
St.-Gaudens, *France* **9 F4** 43 6N 0 44 E
St-Georges, *Canada* **43 B12** 46 8N 70 40W
St. George's, *Grenada* **44 Q20** 12 5N 61 43W
St. George's Channel, *U.K.* **7 G4** 52 0N 6 0W
St.-Girons, *France* **9 F4** 42 59N 1 8 E
St. Gotthard P., *Switz.* **10 E3** 46 33N 8 33 E
St. Helena, *Atl. Oc.* **2 E9** 15 55S 5 44W
St. Helena B., *S. Africa* **33 L3** 32 40S 18 10 E
St. Helens, *U.K.* **7 F5** 53 28N 2 44W
St. Helier, *U.K.* **8 C2** 49 11N 2 6W
St-Hyacinthe, *Canada* **43 C11** 45 40N 72 58W
St. Ignace, *U.S.A.* **42 C5** 45 53N 84 43W
St.-Jean, *Canada* **43 C11** 45 20N 73 20W
St.-Jean, L., *Canada* **43 A11** 48 40N 72 0W
St.-Jean-d'Angély, *France* **9 E3** 45 57N 0 31W
St.-Jérôme, *Canada* **43 C11** 45 47N 74 0W
St. John, *Canada* **43 C14** 45 20N 66 8W
St. John's, *Antigua* **44 K20** 17 6N 61 51W
St. John's, *Canada* **39 D14** 47 35N 52 40W
St. Johns, *U.S.A.* **42 D5** 43 0N 84 31W
St. Johnsbury, *U.S.A.* **43 C11** 44 25N 72 1W
St. Joseph, *Mich., U.S.A.* **42 D4** 42 5N 86 30W
St. Joseph, *Mo., U.S.A.* **41 C8** 39 46N 94 50W
St. Lawrence →, *Canada* **43 A13** 49 30N 66 0W
St. Lawrence, Gulf of, *Canada* **43 A16** 48 25N 62 0W
St.-Lô, *France* **8 C3** 49 7N 1 5W
St-Louis, *Senegal* **28 F3** 16 8N 16 27W
St. Louis, *U.S.A.* **41 C8** 38 40N 90 12W
St. Lucia ■, *W. Indies* **44 P21** 14 0N 60 50W
St. Lucia, L., *S. Africa* **31 B5** 28 5S 32 30 E
St.-Malo, *France* **8 C2** 48 39N 2 1W
St.-Malo, G. de, *France* **8 C2** 48 50N 2 30W
St-Martin, *W. Indies* **44 K19** 18 0N 63 0W
St. Marys, *U.S.A.* **42 E8** 41 27N 78 33W
St.-Nazaire, *France* **8 D2** 47 17N 2 12W
St. Niklass, *Belgium* **8 B6** 51 10N 4 9 E
St.-Omer, *France* **8 B5** 50 45N 2 15 E
St. Paul, *U.S.A.* **41 B8** 44 54N 93 5W
St. Peter Port, *Chan. Is.* **8 C2** 49 27N 2 31W
St. Petersburg, *Russia* **14 C5** 59 55N 30 20 E
St. Petersburg, *U.S.A.* **41 E10** 27 45N 82 40W
St.-Pierre et Miquelon □, *St- P. & M.* **39 D14** 46 55N 56 10W
St.-Quentin, *France* **8 C5** 49 50N 3 16 E
St.-Raphaël, *France* **9 F7** 43 25N 6 46 E
St. Stephen, *Canada* **43 C14** 45 16N 67 17W
St. Thomas, *Canada* **42 D7** 42 45N 81 10W
St.-Tropez, *France* **9 F7** 43 17N 6 38 E
St. Vincent and the Grenadines ■, *W. Indies* **44 Q20** 13 0N 61 10W
Ste-Marie de la Madeleine, *Canada* **43 B12** 46 26N 71 0W
Ste.-Menehould, *France* **8 C6** 49 5N 4 54 E
Saintes, *France* **9 E3** 45 45N 0 37W
Saintonge, *France* **9 E3** 45 40N 0 50W
Sak →, *S. Africa* **31 C3** 30 52S 20 25 E
Sakai, *Japan* **19 B4** 34 30N 135 30 E
Sakhalin, *Russia* **18 D16** 51 0N 143 0 E
Sala, *Sweden* **6 G11** 59 58N 16 35 E
Salado →, *Argentina* **47 F3** 31 40S 60 41W
Salamanca, *Spain* **11 B3** 40 58N 5 39W
Salamanca, *U.S.A.* **42 D8** 42 10N 78 42W
Salayar, *Indonesia* **22 D4** 6 7S 120 30 E
Saldanha, *S. Africa* **31 C2** 33 0S 17 58 E
Salekhard, *Russia* **18 C8** 66 30N 66 35 E
Salem, *India* **25 D6** 11 40N 78 11 E
Salem, *Ind., U.S.A.* **42 F4** 38 38N 86 6W
Salem, *Mass., U.S.A.* **43 D12** 42 29N 70 53W
Salem, *Ohio, U.S.A.* **42 E7** 40 52N 80 50W
Salem, *Va., U.S.A.* **42 G7** 37 19N 80 8W
Salerno, *Italy* **12 D6** 40 40N 14 44 E
Salford, *U.K.* **7 F5** 53 30N 2 17W
Salisbury, *U.K.* **7 G6** 51 4N 1 48W
Salisbury, *U.S.A.* **43 F10** 38 20N 75 38W
Salisbury Plain, *U.K.* **7 G6** 51 13N 1 50W
Salon-de-Provence, *France* **9 F6** 43 39N 5 6 E
Salonica = Thessaloníki, *Greece* **13 D10** 40 38N 22 58 E
Salt Lake City, *U.S.A.* **40 B4** 40 45N 111 58W
Salta, *Argentina* **47 E3** 24 57S 65 25W
Saltcoats, *U.K.* **7 E4** 55 38N 4 47W
Saltillo, *Mexico* **44 B4** 25 30N 100 57W
Saltillo, *Coahuila, Mexico* **44 B4** 25 25N 101 0W
Salto, *Uruguay* **47 F4** 31 27S 57 50W
Salvador, *Brazil* **46 D6** 13 0S 38 30W
Salween →, *Burma* **25 D8** 16 31N 97 37 E
Salyersville, *U.S.A.* **42 G6** 37 45N 83 4W
Salzburg, *Austria* **10 E5** 47 48N 13 2 E
Salzgitter, *Germany* **10 B4** 52 13N 10 22 E
Samar, *Phil.* **22 B4** 12 0N 125 0 E
Samara, *Russia* **14 D9** 53 8N 50 6 E
Samarkand, *Uzbekistan* **18 F8** 39 40N 66 55 E
Sambalpur, *India* **23 J10** 21 28N 84 4 E
Sambhal, *India* **23 E7** 28 35N 78 37 E
Sambhar, *India* **23 F5** 26 52N 75 6 E
Sámos, *Greece* **13 F12** 37 45N 26 50 E
Samsun, *Turkey* **15 F6** 41 15N 36 22 E
San →, *Poland* **10 C9** 50 45N 21 51 E
San Agustin, C., *Phil.* **22 C4** 6 20N 126 13 E
San Angelo, *U.S.A.* **40 D6** 31 30N 100 30W
San Antonio, *U.S.A.* **40 E7** 29 30N 98 30W
San Bernardino, *U.S.A.* **40 D3** 34 7N 117 18W
San Bernardino Str., *Phil.* **22 B4** 13 0N 125 0 E
San Diego, *U.S.A.* **40 D3** 32 43N 117 10W
San Francisco, *U.S.A.* **40 C2** 37 47N 122 30W
San Jorge, G., *Argentina* **47 G3** 46 0S 66 0W
San José, *Costa Rica* **45 F8** 9 55N 84 2W
San Jose, *U.S.A.* **40 C2** 37 20N 121 53W
San Juan, *Argentina* **47 F3** 31 30S 68 30W
San Juan, *Puerto Rico* **45 D11** 18 28N 66 8W
San Lucas, C., *Mexico* **44 C3** 22 50N 110 0W
San Luis Potosí, *Mexico* **44 C4** 22 9N 100 59W
San Marino ■, *Europe* **12 C5** 43 56N 12 25 E
San Miguel de Tucumán, *Argentina* **47 E3** 26 50S 65 20W
San Pedro Sula, *Honduras* **44 D7** 15 30N 88 0W
San Salvador, *El Salv.* **44 E7** 13 40N 89 10W
San Salvador de Jujuy, *Argentina* **47 E3** 24 10S 64 48W
San Sebastián, *Spain* **11 A5** 43 17N 1 58W
Sana', *Yemen* **24 D3** 15 27N 44 12 E
Sancy, Puy de, *France* **9 E5** 45 32N 2 50 E
Sand →, *S. Africa* **31 A5** 22 25S 30 5 E
Sandakan, *Malaysia* **22 C3** 5 53N 118 4 E
Sandusky, *U.S.A.* **42 E6** 41 25N 82 40W
Sangli, *India* **25 D6** 16 55N 74 33 E
Santa Ana, *U.S.A.* **40 D3** 33 48N 117 55W
Santa Clara, *Cuba* **45 C9** 22 20N 80 0W
Santa Cruz, *Bolivia* **46 D3** 17 43S 63 10W
Santa Cruz de Tenerife, *Canary Is.* **28 D3** 28 28N 16 15W
Santa Fe, *Argentina* **47 F3** 31 35S 60 41W
Santa Fe, *U.S.A.* **40 C5** 35 40N 106 0W
Santa Maria, *Brazil* **47 E4** 29 40S 53 48W
Santa Marta, *Colombia* **46 A2** 11 15N 74 13W
Santander, *Spain* **11 A4** 43 27N 3 51W
Santarém, *Brazil* **46 C4** 2 25S 54 42W
Santarém, *Portugal* **11 C1** 39 12N 8 42W
Santiago, *Chile* **47 F2** 33 24S 70 40W
Santiago de Compostela, *Spain* **11 A1** 42 52N 8 37W
Santiago de Cuba, *Cuba* **45 D9** 20 0N 75 49W
Santiago de los Cabelleros, *Dom. Rep.* **45 D10** 19 30N 70 40W
Santo André, *Brazil* **47 E5** 23 39S 46 29W
Santo Domingo, *Dom. Rep.* **45 D11** 18 30N 69 59W
Santos, *Brazil* **47 E5** 24 0S 46 20W
São Francisco →, *Brazil* **46 D6** 10 30S 36 24W
São José do Rio Prêto, *Brazil* **46 E5** 20 50S 49 20W
São Luís, *Brazil* **46 C5** 2 39S 44 15W
São Paulo, *Brazil* **47 E5** 23 32S 46 37W
São Roque, C. de, *Brazil* **46 C6** 5 30S 35 16W
São Tomé & Principe ■, *Africa* **28 J8** 0 12N 6 39 E
Saône →, *France* **9 E6** 45 44N 4 50 E
Sapporo, *Japan* **19 F12** 43 0N 141 21 E
Saragossa = Zaragoza, *Spain* **11 B5** 41 39N 0 53W
Sarajevo, *Bos.-H., Yug.* **13 C8** 43 52N 18 26 E
Saranac Lakes, *U.S.A.* **43 C10** 44 20N 74 10W
Sarangani B., *Phil.* **22 C4** 6 0N 125 13 E
Saransk, *Russia* **14 D8** 54 10N 45 10 E
Saratoga Springs, *U.S.A.* **43 D11** 43 5N 73 47W
Saratov, *Russia* **14 D8** 51 30N 46 2 E
Sarawak □, *Malaysia* **22 C3** 2 0N 113 0 E
Sarda →, *India* **23 F8** 27 21N 81 23 E
Sardinia, *Italy* **12 E3** 39 57N 9 0 E
Sargodha, *Pakistan* **23 C4** 32 10N 72 40 E
Sarh, *Chad* **28 H10** 9 5N 18 23 E
Sarlat-la-Canéda, *France* **9 E4** 44 54N 1 13 E
Sarnia, *Canada* **42 D6** 42 58N 82 23W
Sarrebourg, *France* **8 C7** 48 43N 7 3 E
Sarreguemines, *France* **8 C7** 49 5N 7 4 E
Sartène, *France* **9 G8** 41 38N 8 58 E
Sarthe →, *France* **8 D3** 47 33N 0 31W
Sasebo, *Japan* **19 C1** 33 10N 129 43 E
Saser, *India* **23 B6** 34 50N 77 50 E
Saskatchewan □, *Canada* **38 C9** 54 40N 106 0W
Saskatchewan →, *Canada* **38 C9** 53 37N 100 40W
Saskatoon, *Canada* **38 C9** 52 10N 106 38W
Sasolburg, *S. Africa* **31 B4** 26 46S 27 49 E
Sassari, *Italy* **12 D3** 40 44N 8 33 E
Sassnitz, *Germany* **10 A5** 54 29N 13 39 E
Satmala Hills, *India* **23 J5** 20 15N 74 40 E
Satna, *India* **23 G8** 24 35N 80 50 E
Satpura Ra., *India* **23 J6** 21 25N 76 10 E
Satu Mare, *Romania* **10 E10** 47 46N 22 55 E
Sauðarkrókur, *Iceland* **6 B4** 65 45N 19 40W
Saudi Arabia ■, *Asia* **24 C3** 26 0N 44 0 E
Sault Ste. Marie, *Canada* **42 B5** 46 30N 84 20W
Sault Ste. Marie, *U.S.A.* **42 B5** 46 27N 84 22W

Saumur

T

Tabas, Iran . . . . **24 B4** 33 35N 56 55 E
Tablas, Phil. . . . . **22 B4** 12 25N 122 2 E
Table Mt., S. Africa . . **31 C2** 34 0S 18 22 E
Tabora, Tanzania . . . . **32 F6** 5 2S 32 50 E
Tabriz, Iran . . . . **24 B3** 38 7N 46 20 E
Tacloban, Phil. . . . . . . **22 B4** 11 15N 124 58 E
Tacna, Peru **46 D2** 18 0S 70 20W
Tacoma, U.S.A. **40 A2** 47 15N 122 30W
Tacuarembó, Uruguay . **47 F4** 31 45S 56 0W
Tadzhikistan =
　Tajikistan ■, Asia . . **18 F8** 38 30N 70 0 E
Taegu, S. Korea . . . . . **21 C7** 35 50N 128 37 E
Taejon, S. Korea . . . . **21 C7** 36 20N 127 28 E
Taganrog, Russia . . . . **15 E6** 47 12N 38 50 E
Tagus →, Europe **11 C1** 38 40N 9 24W
Tahiti, Pac. Oc. **37 J13** 17 37S 149 27W
Taichung, Taiwan . . . . **21 D7** 24 12N 120 35 E
Taimyr Peninsula,
　Russia . . . . **18 B11** 75 0N 100 0 E
Tainan, Taiwan . . . . . **21 D7** 23 17N 120 18 E
T'aipei, Taiwan . . . . . **21 D7** 25 2N 121 30 E
Taiping, Malaysia . . . . **22 C2** 4 51N 100 44 E
Taiwan ■, Asia . . . . . **21 D7** 23 30N 121 0 E
Taiyuan, China . . . . . **21 C6** 37 52N 112 33 E
Ta'izz, Yemen . . . . . . **24 D3** 13 35N 44 2 E
Tajikistan ■, Asia . . . **18 F8** 38 30N 70 0 E
Tak, Thailand . . . . **22 B1** 16 52N 99 8 E
Takamatsu, Japan . . . **19 B4** 34 20N 134 5 E
Takaoka, Japan . . . . . **19 A5** 36 47N 137 0 E
Takasaki, Japan . . . . . **19 A6** 36 20N 139 0 E
Takla Makan, China . . **16 F12** 38 0N 83 0 E
Talaud Is., Indonesia . **22 C4** 4 30N 126 50 E
Talca, Chile **47 F2** 35 28S 71 40W
Talcahuano, Chile . . . **47 F2** 36 40S 73 10W
Taliabu, Indonesia . . . **22 D4** 1 45S 124 55 E
Tallahassee, U.S.A. . . **41 D10** 30 25N 84 15W
Tallinn, Estonia . . . . . **14 C3** 59 22N 24 48 E
Tambov, Russia . . . . . **14 D7** 52 45N 41 28 E
Tamil Nadu □, India . . **25 D6** 11 0N 77 0 E
Tamo Abu Ra., Malaysia **22 C3** 3 10N 115 5 E
Tampa, U.S.A. **41 E10** 27 57N 82 38W
Tampere, Finland . . . . **6 F12** 61 30N 23 50 E
Tampico, Mexico **44 C5** 22 20N 97 50W
Tamworth, Australia . . **34 G9** 31 7S 150 58 E
Tana →, Norway . . . . **6 D13** 70 30N 28 23 E
Tana, L., Ethiopia . . . **29 G14** 13 5N 37 30 E
Tanami Desert, Australia **34 D5** 18 50S 132 0 E
Tananarive =
　Antananarivo, Madag. **33 H9** 18 55S 47 31 E
Tando Adam, Pakistan . **23 G2** 25 45N 68 40 E
Tanga, Tanzania . . . . . **32 F7** 5 5S 39 2 E
Tanganyika, L., Africa . **32 F6** 6 40S 30 0 E
Tangier, Morocco **28 B5** 35 50N 5 49W
Tangshan, China . . . . **21 C6** 39 38N 118 10 E
Tanimbar Is., Indonesia **22 D5** 7 30S 131 30 E
Tanjungbalai, Indonesia **22 C1** 2 55N 99 44 E
Tanzania ■, Africa . . . **32 F6** 6 0S 34 0 E
Tapajós →, Brazil . . . **46 C4** 2 24S 54 41W
Tapi →, India . . . . . . **23 J4** 21 8N 72 41 E
Tappahannock, U.S.A. . **42 G9** 37 56N 76 50W
Tarābulus = Tripoli,
　Lebanon . . . . **24 B2** 34 31N 35 50 E
Tarābulus = Tripoli,
　Libya . . . . **28 C9** 32 49N 13 7 E
Tarakan, Indonesia . . . **22 C3** 3 20N 117 35 E
Taranto, Italy . . . . **12 D7** 40 30N 17 11 E
Táranto, G. di, Italy . . **12 D7** 40 0N 17 15 E
Tarbagatai Ra.,
　Kazakhstan . . . . . . **18 E10** 48 0N 83 0 E
Tarbes, France . . . . . . **9 F4** 43 15N 0 3 E
Tarim Basin, China . . . **20 B3** 40 0N 84 0 E
Tarkastad, S. Africa . . **31 C4** 32 0S 26 16 E
Tarnów, Poland . . . . . **10 C9** 50 3N 21 0 E
Tarragona, Spain . . . . **11 B6** 41 5N 1 17 E
Tarrasa, Spain . . . . . . **11 B7** 41 34N 2 1 E
Tashkent, Uzbekistan . **18 E8** 41 20N 69 10 E
Tasman Sea, Pac. Oc. **36 L8** 36 0S 160 0 E
Tasmania □, Australia . **34 J8** 42 0S 146 30 E
Tatar Republic □,
　Russia . . . . **14 C9** 55 30N 51 30 E
Tatarsk, Russia . . . . . **18 D9** 55 14N 76 0 E
Tatta, Pakistan . . . . . . **23 G1** 24 42N 67 55 E
Tauern, Austria . . . . . **10 E5** 47 15N 12 40 E
Taung, S. Africa . . . . . **31 B3** 27 33S 24 47 E
Taunton, U.K. **7 G5** 51 1N 3 7W
Taunton, U.S.A. **43 E12** 41 54N 71 6W
Taunus, Germany . . . . **10 C3** 50 15N 8 20 E
Taurus Mts., Turkey . . **15 G5** 37 0N 32 30 E
Tawas City, U.S.A. . . . **42 C6** 44 16N 83 31W
Tawau, Malaysia . . . . **22 C3** 4 20N 117 55 E
Tay →, U.K. **7 D5** 56 37N 3 38W
Tay, Firth of, U.K. . . . **7 D5** 56 25N 3 8W
Tbilisi, Georgia . . . . . **15 F7** 41 43N 44 50 E
Tchad, L. = Chad, L.,
　Chad . . . . **28 G9** 13 30N 14 30 E
Tebingtinggi, Indonesia **22 C1** 3 20N 99 9 E
Tegal, Indonesia . . . . **22 D2** 6 52S 109 8 E
Tegucigalpa, Honduras **44 E7** 14 5N 87 14W
Tehran, Iran . . . . **24 B4** 35 44N 51 30 E
Tehuantepec, Gulf of,
　Mexico **44 D5** 15 50N 95 12W
Tehuantepec, Isthmus
　of, Mexico **44 D6** 17 0N 94 30W
Tel Aviv-Jaffa, Israel . . **29 P20** 32 4N 34 48 E
Telford, U.K. **7 F5** 52 42N 2 31W
Tell City, U.S.A. **42 G4** 37 55N 86 44W
Teluk Betung, Indonesia **22 C2** 4 13N 108 12 E

Tema, Ghana . . . . **30 C2** 5 41N 0 0 E
Temba, S. Africa . . . . **31 B4** 25 20S 28 17 E
Témiscaming, Canada . **42 B8** 46 44N 79 5W
Tenerife, Canary Is. . . **28 D3** 28 15N 16 35W
Tennessee □, U.S.A. . **41 C9** 36 0N 86 30W
Tennessee →, U.S.A. **41 C9** 37 4N 88 34W
Tepic, Mexico **44 C4** 21 30N 104 54W
Teramo, Italy . . . . **12 C5** 42 40N 13 40 E
Teresina, Brazil **46 C5** 5 9S 42 45W
Ternate, Indonesia . . . **22 C4** 0 45N 127 25 E
Terni, Italy . . . . **12 C5** 42 34N 12 38 E
Terre Haute, U.S.A. . . **42 F4** 39 28N 87 24W
Teruel, Spain **11 B5** 40 22N 1 8W
Tetouan, Morocco . . . **28 B5** 35 35N 5 21W
Tetovo,
　Macedonia, Yug. . . . **13 C9** 42 1N 21 2 E
Teutoburger Wald,
　Germany . . . . **10 B3** 52 5N 8 20 E
Texas □, U.S.A. **40 D7** 31 40N 98 30W
Texel, Neths. . . . . **8 A6** 53 5N 4 50 E
Tezpur, India . . . . **23 F14** 26 40N 92 45 E
Thabana Ntlenyana,
　Lesotho . . . . **31 B4** 29 30S 29 16 E
Thabazimbi, S. Africa . **31 A4** 24 40S 27 21 E
Thailand ■, Asia . . . . **22 B2** 16 0N 102 0 E
Thailand, G. of, Asia . . **22 B2** 11 30N 101 0 E
Thal, Pakistan . . . . . . **23 C3** 33 28N 70 33 E
Thal Desert, Pakistan . **23 D3** 31 10N 71 30 E
Thames →, Canada . . **42 D6** 42 20N 82 25W
Thames →, U.K. . . . . **7 G7** 51 30N 0 35 E
Thane, India . . . . **23 K4** 19 12N 72 59 E
Thar Desert, India . . . **23 E4** 28 0N 72 0 E
The Hague, Neths. . . . **8 A6** 52 7N 4 17 E
The Pas, Canada **38 C9** 53 45N 101 15W
Thessalon, Canada . . . **42 B6** 46 20N 83 30W
Thessaloníki, Greece . **13 D10** 40 38N 22 58 E
Thessaloníki, Gulf of,
　Greece . . . . **13 D10** 40 15N 22 45 E
Thessaly □, Greece . . **13 E9** 39 25N 21 50 E
Thetford Mines, Canada **43 B12** 46 8N 71 18W
Thiers, France . . . . . . **9 E5** 45 52N 3 33 E
Thies, Senegal **28 G3** 14 50N 16 51W
Thimphu, Bhutan . . . . **23 F12** 27 31N 89 45 E
Thionville, France . . . . **8 C7** 49 20N 6 10 E
Thonon-les-Bains,
　France . . . . **9 D7** 46 22N 6 29 E
Thrace □, Greece . . . **13 D11** 41 9N 25 30 E
Thule, Greenland **48 A10** 77 40N 69 0W
Thunder B., U.S.A. . . . **42 C6** 45 0N 83 20W
Thunder Bay, Canada . **42 A3** 48 20N 89 15W
Thuringian Forest,
　Germany . . . . **10 C4** 50 35N 11 0 E
Thurso, U.K. **7 C5** 58 34N 3 31W
Tianjin = Tientsin,
　China . . . . **21 C6** 39 8N 117 10 E
Tianshui, China . . . . . **20 C5** 34 32N 105 40 E
Tiber →, Italy . . . . . . **12 D5** 41 44N 12 14 E
Tiberias, Israel . . . . . . **N21** 32 47N 35 32 E
Tibesti, Chad . . . . **28 D9** 21 0N 17 30 E
Tibet = Xizang □, China **20 C3** 32 0N 88 0 E
Ticino →, Italy . . . . . . **12 B3** 45 9N 9 14 E
Ticonderoga, U.S.A. . . **43 D11** 43 50N 73 28W
Tien Shan, Asia . . . . . **16 E11** 42 0N 76 0 E
Tientsin, China . . . . . . **21 C6** 39 8N 117 10 E
Tierra del Fuego, I. Gr.
　de, Argentina **47 H3** 54 0S 69 0W
Tiffin, U.S.A. **42 E6** 41 8N 83 10W
Tignish, Canada **43 B15** 46 58N 64 2W
Tigris →, Asia . . . . . . **24 B3** 31 0N 47 25 E
Tijuana, Mexico **44 A1** 32 30N 117 10W
Tiksi, Russia . . . . **18 B14** 71 40N 128 45 E
Tilburg, Neths. . . . . . . **8 B6** 51 31N 5 6 E
Timaru, N.Z. . . . . **35 J13** 44 23S 171 14 E
Timbuktu =
　Tombouctou, Mali . . **30 A1** 16 50N 3 0W
Timișoara, Romania . . **13 B9** 45 43N 21 15 E
Timmins, Canada **42 A7** 48 28N 81 25W
Timor, Indonesia . . . . **22 D4** 9 0S 125 0 E
Tinaca Pt., Phil. . . . . . **22 C4** 5 30N 125 25 E
Tipperary, Ireland **7 F2** 52 28N 8 10W
Tiranë, Albania . . . . . . **13 D8** 41 18N 19 49 E
Tîrgovişte, Romania . . **13 B11** 44 55N 25 27 E
Tîrgu-Jiu, Romania . . . **13 B10** 45 5N 23 19 E
Tirich Mir, Pakistan . . . **23 A3** 36 15N 71 55 E
Tiruchchirappalli, India . **25 D6** 10 45N 78 45 E
Tirunelveli, India . . . . . **25 E6** 8 45N 77 45 E
Tisa →, Hungary . . . . **10 E9** 46 8N 20 2 E
Tisza →, Serbia, Yug. **10 F9** 45 15N 20 17 E
Titicaca, L., S. Amer. . **46 D3** 15 30S 69 30W
Titusville, U.S.A. **42 E8** 41 35N 79 39W
Tizi-Ouzou, Algeria . . . **28 B7** 36 42N 4 3 E
Toamasina, Madag. . . **33 H9** 18 10S 49 25 E
Toba Kakar Hills,
　Pakistan . . . . **23 D2** 31 30N 69 0 E
Tobago, W. Indies . . . **44 R21** 11 10N 60 30W
Tobermory, Canada . . **42 C7** 45 12N 81 40W
Tocantins →, Brazil . . **46 C5** 1 45S 49 10W
Toga, W. Afr. . . . . **30 C2** 8 30N 1 35 E
Tokelau Is., Pac. Oc. . **35 B16** 9 0S 171 45W
Tôkyô, Japan . . . . **19 B6** 35 45N 139 45 E
Tolbukhin, Bulgaria . . **13 C12** 43 37N 27 49 E
Toledo, Spain **11 C3** 39 50N 4 2W
Toledo, U.S.A. **42 E6** 41 37N 83 33W
Toliara, Madag. . . . . . **33 J8** 23 21S 43 40 E
Toluca, Mexico **44 D5** 19 20N 99 40W
Tomaszów Mazowiecki,
　Poland . . . . **10 C8** 51 30N 19 57 E
Tombouctou, Mali . . . **30 A1** 16 50N 3 0W
Tomini, G. of, Indonesia **22 D4** 0 10S 122 0 E
Tomsk, Russia . . . . . . **18 D10** 56 30N 85 5 E

Tonga ■, Pac. Oc. . . . **35 D16** 19 50S 174 30W
Tonga Trench, Pac. Oc. **35 E16** 18 0S 173 0W
Tongaat, S. Africa . . . **31 B5** 29 33S 31 9 E
Tongking, G. of, Asia . **20 E5** 20 0N 108 0 E
Tonk, India . . . . **23 F5** 26 6N 75 54 E
Tonlé Sap, Cambodia . **22 B2** 13 0N 104 0 E
Toowoomba, Australia . **34 F9** 27 32S 151 56 E
Topeka, U.S.A. **41 C7** 39 3N 95 40W
Torino = Turin, Italy . . **12 B2** 45 4N 7 40 E
Torne →, Sweden . . . **6 E12** 65 50N 24 12 E
Torne, L., Sweden . . . **6 E11** 68 24N 19 15 E
Tornio, Finland . . . . . . **6 E12** 65 50N 24 12 E
Toronto, Canada **42 D8** 43 39N 79 20W
Torquay, U.K. **7 G5** 50 27N 3 31W
Torreón, Mexico **44 B4** 25 33N 103 26W
Tortosa, Spain . . . . . . **11 B6** 40 49N 0 31 E
Toruń, Poland . . . . . . **10 B8** 53 2N 18 39 E
Toteng, Botswana . . . **31 A3** 20 22S 22 58 E
Toul, France . . . . **8 C6** 48 40N 5 53 E
Toulon, France . . . . . . **9 F6** 43 10N 5 55 E
Toulouse, France . . . . **9 F4** 43 37N 1 27 E
Touraine, France . . . . **8 D4** 47 20N 0 30 E
Tournai, Belgium . . . . **8 B5** 50 35N 3 25 E
Tournon, France . . . . . **9 E6** 45 4N 4 50 E
Tours, France . . . . **8 D4** 47 22N 0 40 E
Touwsrivier, S. Africa . **31 C3** 33 20S 20 2 E
Towanda, U.S.A. **42 E9** 41 46N 76 30W
Townsville, Australia . . **34 D8** 19 15S 146 45 E
Towson, U.S.A. **42 F9** 39 26N 76 34W
Toyama, Japan . . . . . . **19 A5** 36 40N 137 15 E
Toyohashi, Japan . . . . **19 B5** 34 45N 137 25 E
Trabzon, Turkey . . . . . **15 F6** 41 0N 39 45 E
Trafalgar, C., Spain . . **11 D2** 36 10N 6 2W
Trail, Canada **38 D8** 49 5N 117 40W
Tralee, Ireland **7 F2** 52 16N 9 42W
Trang, Thailand . . . . . **22 C1** 7 33N 99 38 E
Trangan, Indonesia . . . **22 D5** 6 40S 134 20 E
Transkei □, S. Africa . **31 C4** 32 15S 28 15 E
Transvaal □, S. Africa **31 A4** 25 0S 29 0 E
Transylvania, Romania . **13 B11** 45 19N 25 0 E
Transylvanian Alps,
　Romania . . . . **4 F10** 45 30N 25 0 E
Trapani, Italy . . . . **12 E5** 38 1N 12 30 E
Traverse City, U.S.A. . **42 C5** 44 45N 85 39W
Trent →, U.K. **7 F6** 53 33N 0 44W
Trentino-Alto Adige □,
　Italy . . . . **12 A4** 46 30N 11 0 E
Trento, Italy . . . . **12 A4** 46 5N 11 8 E
Trenton, Canada **42 C9** 44 10N 77 34W
Trenton, U.S.A. **43 E10** 40 15N 74 41W
Trier, Germany . . . . . . **10 D2** 49 45N 6 37 E
Trieste, Italy . . . . **12 B5** 45 39N 13 45 E
Trincomalee, Sri Lanka **25 E7** 8 38N 81 15 E
Trinidad & Tobago ■,
　W. Indies **44 S20** 10 30N 61 20W
Tripoli, Lebanon . . . . . **24 B2** 34 31N 35 50 E
Tripoli, Libya . . . . **28 C9** 32 49N 13 7 E
Tripura □, India . . . . . **23 H13** 24 0N 92 0 E
Tristan da Cunha,
　Atl. Oc. **2 F9** 37 6S 12 20W
Trivandrum, India . . . . **25 E6** 8 41N 77 0 E
Trnava, Slovakia . . . . **10 D7** 48 23N 17 35 E
Trois-Rivières, Canada **43 B11** 46 25N 72 34W
Trollhättan, Sweden . . **6 G10** 58 17N 12 20 E
Trondheim, Norway . . **6 F10** 63 36N 10 25 E
Trondheim Fjord,
　Norway . . . . **6 F10** 63 35N 10 30 E
Troy, N.Y., U.S.A. **43 D11** 42 45N 73 39W
Troy, Ohio, U.S.A. . . . **42 E5** 40 3N 84 10W
Troyes, France . . . . . . **8 C6** 48 19N 4 3 E
Trujillo, Peru **46 C2** 8 6S 79 0W
Truk, Pac. Oc. . . . . . . **36 G7** 7 25N 151 46 E
Truro, Canada **43 C16** 45 21N 63 14W
Truro, U.K. **7 G4** 50 17N 5 2W
Tsau, Botswana . . . . . **31 A3** 20 8S 22 22 E
Tselinograd, Kazakhstan **18 D9** 51 10N 71 30 E
Tshabong, Botswana . **31 B3** 26 2S 22 29 E
Tshane, Botswana . . . **31 A3** 24 5S 21 54 E
Tshwane, Botswana . . **31 A3** 22 24S 22 1 E
Tsimlyansk Res., Russia **15 E7** 48 0N 43 0 E
Tsu, Japan . . . . **19 B5** 34 45N 136 25 E
Tsumis, Namibia . . . . **31 A2** 23 39S 17 29 E
Tuamotu Arch., Pac. Oc. **37 J13** 17 0S 144 0W
Tubuai Is., Pac. Oc. . . **37 K12** 25 0S 150 0W
Tucson, U.S.A. **40 D4** 32 14N 110 59W
Tugela →, S. Africa . . **31 B5** 29 14S 31 30 E
Tula, Russia . . . . **14 D6** 54 13N 37 38 E
Tulcea, Romania . . . . **13 B13** 45 13N 28 46 E
Tulle, France . . . . **9 E4** 45 16N 1 46 E
Tulsa, U.S.A. **41 C7** 36 10N 96 0W
Tunis, Tunisia . . . . . . **28 B9** 36 50N 10 11 E
Tunisia ■, Africa . . . . **28 C8** 33 30N 9 10 E
Tunja, Colombia **46 B2** 5 33N 73 25W
Tura, India . . . . **23 G13** 25 30N 90 16 E
Turabah, Si. Arabia . . **24 C3** 28 20N 43 15 E
Turin, Italy . . . . **12 B2** 45 4N 7 40 E
Turkana, L., Africa . . . **32 D7** 3 30N 36 5 E
Turkey ■, Eurasia . . . **15 G6** 39 0N 36 0 E
Turkmenistan ■, Asia . **18 F7** 39 0N 59 0 E
Turks Is., W. Indies . . **45 C10** 21 20N 71 20W
Turku, Finland . . . . . . **6 F12** 60 30N 22 19 E
Tuticorin, India . . . . . . **25 E6** 8 50N 78 12 E
Tuvalu ■, Pac. Oc. . . **35 B14** 8 0S 178 0 E
Tuxtla Gutiérrez, Mexico **44 D6** 16 50N 93 10W
Tuz Gölü, Turkey . . . . **15 G5** 38 45N 33 30 E
Tuzla, Bos.-H., Yug. . . **13 B8** 44 34N 18 41 E
Two Rivers, U.S.A. . . . **42 C4** 44 10N 87 31W
Tychy, Poland . . . . . . **10 C8** 50 9N 18 59 E
Tynemouth, U.K. **7 E6** 55 1N 1 27W
Tyre = Sûr, Lebanon . **29 C14** 33 19N 35 16 E

Tyrol □, Austria . . . . . **10 E4** 47 3N 10 43 E
Tyrrhenian Sea, Europe **12 E5** 40 0N 12 30 E
Tyumen, Russia . . . . . **18 D8** 57 11N 65 29 E
Tzaneen, S. Africa . . . **31 A5** 23 47S 30 9 E

U

Ubangi = Oubangi →,
　Zaïre . . . . **32 E3** 0 30S 17 50 E
Ube, Japan . . . . **19 C2** 33 56N 131 15 E
Uberaba, Brazil **46 D5** 19 50S 47 55W
Uberlândia, Brazil **46 D5** 19 0S 48 20W
Ucayali →, Peru **46 C2** 4 30S 73 30W
Udaipur, India . . . . . . **23 G4** 24 36N 73 44 E
Udaipur Garhi, Nepal . **23 F11** 27 0N 86 35 E
Udine, Italy . . . . **12 A5** 46 5N 13 10 E
Udmurt Republic □,
　Russia . . . . **14 C9** 57 30N 52 30 E
Udon Thani, Thailand . **22 B2** 17 29N 102 46 E
Ufa, Russia . . . . **14 D10** 54 45N 55 55 E
Uganda ■, Africa . . . . **32 D6** 2 0N 32 0 E
Uitenhage, S. Africa . . **31 C4** 33 40S 25 28 E
Ujjain, India . . . . **23 H5** 23 9N 75 43 E
Ujpest, Hungary . . . . . **10 E8** 47 32N 19 6 E
Ujung Pandang,
　Indonesia . . . . **22 D3** 5 10S 119 20 E
Ukraine ■, Europe . . . **15 E5** 49 0N 32 0 E
Ulan Bator, Mongolia . **20 B5** 47 55N 106 53 E
Ulan Ude, Russia . . . . **18 D12** 51 45N 107 40 E
Ulhasnagar, India . . . . **23 K4** 19 15N 73 10 E
Ullapool, U.K. **7 D4** 57 54N 5 10W
Ulm, Germany . . . . . . **10 D4** 48 23N 10 0 E
Ulyasutay, Mongolia . . **20 B4** 47 56N 97 28 E
Umbria □, Italy . . . . . **12 C5** 42 53N 12 30 E
Ume →, Sweden . . . . **6 F12** 63 45N 20 20 E
Umeå, Sweden . . . . . **6 F12** 63 45N 20 20 E
Umtata, S. Africa . . . . **31 C4** 31 36S 28 49 E
Umzimvubu, S. Africa . **31 C4** 31 38S 29 33 E
Umzinto, S. Africa . . . **31 C5** 30 15S 30 45 E
Ungava B., Canada . . **39 C13** 59 30N 67 30W
Ungava Pen., Canada . **39 C12** 60 0N 74 0W
Uniontown, U.S.A. . . . **42 F8** 39 54N 79 45W
United Arab Emirates ■,
　Asia . . . . **24 C4** 23 50N 54 0 E
United Kingdom ■,
　Europe **7 F5** 53 0N 2 0W
United States of
　America ■, N. Amer. **40 C7** 37 0N 96 0W
Upington, S. Africa . . . **31 B3** 28 25S 21 15 E
Uppsala, Sweden . . . . **6 G11** 59 53N 17 38 E
Ural →, Kazakhstan . . **15 E9** 47 0N 51 48 E
Ural Mts., Russia . . . . **14 C10** 60 0N 59 0 E
Uralsk, Kazakhstan . . **14 D9** 51 20N 51 20 E
Uranium City, Canada . **38 C9** 59 34N 108 37W
Urbana, Ill., U.S.A. . . . **42 E3** 40 7N 88 12W
Urbana, Ohio, U.S.A. . **42 E6** 40 9N 83 44W
Uruguay ■, S. Amer. . **47 F4** 32 30S 56 30W
Uruguay →, S. Amer. . **47 F4** 34 12S 58 18W
Ürümqi, China . . . . . . **20 B3** 43 45N 87 45 E
Usakos, Namibia . . . . **31 A2** 21 54S 15 31 E
Ushant, France **8 C1** 48 28N 5 6W
Üsküdar, Turkey . . . . . **13 D13** 41 0N 29 5 E
Ussel, France . . . . **9 E5** 45 32N 2 18 E
Ust Urt Plateau,
　Kazakhstan . . . . . . **18 E7** 44 0N 55 0 E
Ústí nad Labem, Czech. **10 C6** 50 41N 14 3 E
Utah □, U.S.A. **40 C4** 39 30N 111 30W
Utica, U.S.A. **43 D10** 43 5N 75 18W
Utrecht, Neths. . . . . . **8 A6** 52 5N 5 8 E
Utsunomiya, Japan . . . **19 A6** 36 30N 139 50 E
Uttar Pradesh □, India **23 F8** 27 0N 80 0 E
Uttaradit, Thailand . . . **22 B2** 17 36N 100 5 E
Uusikaupunki, Finland . **6 F12** 60 47N 21 25 E
Uzbekistan ■, Asia . . **18 E8** 41 30N 65 0 E

V

Vaal →, S. Africa . . . . **31 B3** 29 4S 23 38 E
Vaal Dam, S. Africa . . **31 B4** 27 0S 28 14 E
Vaasa, Finland . . . . . . **6 F12** 63 6N 21 38 E
Vadodara, India . . . . . **23 H4** 22 20N 73 10 E
Vadsø, Norway . . . . . **6 D13** 70 3N 29 50 E
Váh →, Slovakia . . . . **10 E8** 47 43N 18 7 E
Val d'Or, Canada **42 A9** 48 7N 77 47W
Valdez, U.S.A. **38 B5** 61 14N 146 17W
Valdivia, Chile **47 F2** 39 50S 73 14W
Valence, France . . . . . **9 E6** 44 57N 4 54 E
Valencia, Spain **11 C5** 39 27N 0 23W
Valencia, Venezuela . . **46 A3** 10 11N 68 0W
Valenciennes, France . **8 B5** 50 20N 3 34 E
Valladolid, Spain **11 B3** 41 38N 4 43W
Valletta, Malta . . . . . . **12 G6** 35 54N 14 31 E
Valparaíso, Chile **47 F2** 33 2S 71 40W
Van, L., Turkey . . . . . **15 G7** 38 30N 43 0 E
Van Buren, U.S.A. . . . **43 B13** 47 10N 68 1W
Van Wert, U.S.A. **42 E5** 40 52N 84 31W
Vancouver, Canada . . **38 D7** 49 15N 123 10W
Vancouver I., Canada . **38 D7** 49 50N 126 0W
Vanderbijlpark, S. Africa **31 B4** 26 42S 27 54 E
Vaner, L., Sweden . . . **6 G10** 58 47N 13 30 E
Vännäs, Sweden . . . . **6 F11** 63 58N 19 48 E
Vannes, France **8 D2** 47 40N 2 47W
Vanrhynsdorp, S. Africa **31 C2** 31 36S 18 44 E
Vanua Levu, Fiji . . . . . **35 D14** 16 33S 179 15 E
Vanuatu ■, Pac. Oc. . **35 D12** 15 0S 168 0 E

T

Place	Ref	Lat	Long
Tabas, Iran	24 B4	33 35N	56 55 E
Tablas, Phil.	22 B4	12 25N	122 2 E
Table Mt., S. Africa	31 C2	34 0S	18 22 E
Tabora, Tanzania	32 F6	5 2S	32 50 E
Tabriz, Iran	24 B3	38 7N	46 20 E
Tacloban, Phil.	22 B4	11 15N	124 58 E
Tacna, Peru	46 D2	18 0S	70 20W
Tacoma, U.S.A.	40 A2	47 15N	122 30W
Tacuarembó, Uruguay	47 F4	31 45S	56 0W
Tadzhikistan = Tajikistan ■, Asia	18 F8	38 30N	70 0 E
Taegu, S. Korea	21 C7	35 50N	128 37 E
Taejon, S. Korea	21 C7	36 20N	127 28 E
Taganrog, Russia	15 E6	47 12N	38 50 E
Tagus →, Europe	11 C1	38 40N	9 24W
Tahiti, Pac. Oc.	37 J13	17 37S	149 27W
Taichung, Taiwan	21 D7	24 12N	120 35 E
Taimyr Peninsula, Russia	18 B11	75 0N	100 0 E
Tainan, Taiwan	21 D7	23 17N	120 18 E
T'aipei, Taiwan	21 D7	25 2N	121 30 E
Taiping, Malaysia	22 C2	4 51N	100 44 E
Taiwan ■, Asia	21 D7	23 30N	121 0 E
Taiyuan, China	21 C6	37 52N	112 33 E
Ta'izz, Yemen	24 D3	13 35N	44 2 E
Tajikistan ■, Asia	18 F8	38 30N	70 0 E
Tak, Thailand	22 B1	16 52N	99 8 E
Takamatsu, Japan	19 B4	34 20N	134 5 E
Takaoka, Japan	19 A5	36 47N	137 0 E
Takasaki, Japan	19 A6	36 20N	139 0 E
Takla Makan, China	16 F12	38 0N	83 0 E
Talaud Is., Indonesia	22 C4	4 30N	126 50 E
Talca, Chile	47 F2	35 28S	71 40W
Talcahuano, Chile	47 F2	36 40S	73 10W
Taliabu, Indonesia	22 D4	1 45S	124 55 E
Tallahassee, U.S.A.	41 D10	30 25N	84 15W
Tallinn, Estonia	14 C3	59 22N	24 48 E
Tamale, Ghana	30 C1	9 22N	0 50W
Tambov, Russia	14 D7	52 45N	41 28 E
Tamil Nadu □, India	25 D6	11 0N	77 0 E
Tamo Abu Ra., Malaysia	22 C3	3 10N	115 5 E
Tampa, U.S.A.	41 E10	27 57N	82 38W
Tampere, Finland	6 F12	61 30N	23 50 E
Tampico, Mexico	44 C5	22 20N	97 50W
Tamworth, Australia	34 G9	31 7S	150 58 E
Tana →, Norway	6 D13	70 30N	28 23 E
Tana, L., Ethiopia	29 G14	13 5N	37 30 E
Tanami Desert, Australia	34 D5	18 50S	132 0 E
Tananarive = Antananarivo, Madag.	33 H9	18 55S	47 31 E
Tando Adam, Pakistan	23 G2	25 45N	68 40 E
Tanga, Tanzania	32 F7	5 5S	39 2 E
Tanganyika, L., Africa	32 F6	6 40S	30 0 E
Tangier, Morocco	28 B5	35 50N	5 49W
Tangshan, China	21 C6	39 38N	118 10 E
Tanimbar Is., Indonesia	22 D5	7 30S	131 30 E
Tanjungbalai, Indonesia	22 C1	2 55N	99 44 E
Tanzania ■, Africa	32 F6	6 0S	34 0 E
Tapajós →, Brazil	46 C4	2 24S	54 41W
Tapi →, India	23 J4	21 8N	72 41 E
Tappahannock, U.S.A.	42 G9	37 56N	76 50W
Tarābulus = Tripoli, Lebanon	24 B2	34 31N	35 50 E
Tarābulus = Tripoli, Libya	28 C9	32 49N	13 7 E
Tarakan, Indonesia	22 C3	3 20N	117 35 E
Taranto, Italy	12 D7	40 30N	17 11 E
Táranto, G. di, Italy	12 D7	40 0N	17 15 E
Tarbagatai Ra., Kazakhstan	18 E10	48 0N	83 0 E
Tarbes, France	9 F4	43 15N	0 3 E
Tarim Basin, China	20 B3	40 0N	84 0 E
Tarkastad, S. Africa	31 C4	32 0S	26 16 E
Tarnów, Poland	10 C9	50 3N	21 0 E
Tarragona, Spain	11 B6	41 5N	1 17 E
Tarrasa, Spain	11 B7	41 34N	2 1 E
Tashkent, Uzbekistan	18 E8	41 20N	69 10 E
Tasman Sea, Pac. Oc.	36 L8	42 0S	160 0 E
Tasmania □, Australia	34 J8	42 0S	146 30 E
Tatar Republic □, Russia	14 C9	55 30N	51 30 E
Tatarsk, Russia	18 D9	55 14N	76 0 E
Tatta, Pakistan	23 G1	24 42N	67 55 E
Tauern, Austria	10 E5	47 15N	12 40 E
Taung, S. Africa	31 B3	27 33S	24 47 E
Taunton, U.K.	7 G5	51 1N	3 7W
Taunton, U.S.A.	43 E12	41 54N	71 6W
Taunus, Germany	10 C3	50 15N	8 20 E
Taupo, N.Z.	35 H6	38 41S	176 7 E
Taurus Mts., Turkey	15 G5	37 0N	32 30 E
Tawas City, U.S.A.	42 C6	44 16N	83 31W
Tawau, Malaysia	22 C3	4 20N	117 55 E
Tay →, U.K.	7 D5	56 37N	3 38W
Tay, Firth of, U.K.	7 D5	56 25N	3 8W
Tbilisi, Georgia	15 F7	41 43N	44 50 E
Tchad, L. = Chad, L., Chad	28 G9	13 30N	14 30 E
Tebingtinggi, Indonesia	22 C1	3 20N	99 9 E
Tegal, Indonesia	22 D2	6 52S	109 8 E
Tegucigalpa, Honduras	44 E7	14 5N	87 14W
Tehran, Iran	24 B4	35 44N	51 30 E
Tehuantepec, Gulf of, Mexico	44 D5	15 50N	95 12W
Tehuantepec, Isthmus of, Mexico	44 D6	17 0N	94 30W
Tel Aviv-Jaffa, Israel	29 P20	32 4N	34 48 E
Telford, U.K.	7 F5	52 42N	2 31W
Tell City, U.S.A.	42 G4	37 55N	86 44W
Teluk Betung, Indonesia	22 C2	5 29S	105 16 E
Tema, Ghana	30 C2	5 41N	0 0 E
Temba, S. Africa	31 B4	25 20S	28 17 E
Témiscaming, Canada	42 B8	46 44N	79 5W
Tenerife, Canary Is.	28 D3	28 15N	16 35W
Tennessee □, U.S.A.	41 C9	36 0N	86 30W
Tennessee →, U.S.A.	41 C9	37 4N	88 34W
Tepic, Mexico	44 C4	21 30N	104 54W
Teramo, Italy	12 C5	42 40N	13 40 E
Teresina, Brazil	46 C5	5 9S	42 45W
Ternate, Indonesia	22 C4	0 45N	127 25 E
Terni, Italy	12 C5	42 34N	12 38 E
Terre Haute, U.S.A.	42 F4	39 28N	87 24W
Teruel, Spain	11 B5	40 22N	1 8W
Tetouan, Morocco	28 B5	35 35N	5 21W
Tetovo, Macedonia, Yug.	13 C9	42 1N	21 2 E
Teutoburger Wald, Germany	10 B3	52 5N	8 20 E
Texas □, U.S.A.	40 D7	31 40N	98 30W
Texel, Neths.	8 A6	53 5N	4 50 E
Tezpur, India	23 F14	26 40N	92 45 E
Thabana Ntlenyana, Lesotho	31 B4	29 30S	29 16 E
Thabazimbi, S. Africa	31 A4	24 40S	27 21 E
Thailand ■, Asia	22 B2	16 0N	102 0 E
Thailand, G. of, Asia	22 B2	11 30N	101 0 E
Thal, Pakistan	23 C3	33 28N	70 33 E
Thal Desert, Pakistan	23 D3	31 10N	71 30 E
Thames →, Canada	42 D6	42 20N	82 25W
Thames →, U.K.	7 G7	51 30N	0 35 E
Thane, India	23 K4	19 12N	72 59 E
Thar Desert, India	23 E4	28 0N	72 0 E
The Hague, Neths.	8 A6	52 7N	4 17 E
The Pas, Canada	38 C9	53 45N	101 15W
Thessalon, Canada	42 B6	46 20N	83 30W
Thessaloníki, Greece	13 D10	40 38N	22 58 E
Thessaloniki, Gulf of, Greece	13 D10	40 15N	22 45 E
Thessaly □, Greece	13 E9	39 25N	21 50 E
Thetford Mines, Canada	43 B12	46 8N	71 18W
Thiers, France	9 E5	45 52N	3 33 E
Thies, Senegal	28 G3	14 50N	16 51W
Thimphu, Bhutan	23 F12	27 31N	89 45 E
Thionville, France	8 C7	49 20N	6 10 E
Thonon-les-Bains, France	9 D7	46 22N	6 29 E
Thrace □, Greece	13 D11	41 9N	25 30 E
Thule, Greenland	48 A10	77 40N	69 0W
Thunder B., U.S.A.	42 C6	45 0N	83 20W
Thunder Bay, Canada	42 A3	48 20N	89 15W
Thuringian Forest, Germany	10 C4	50 35N	11 0 E
Thurso, U.K.	7 C5	58 34N	3 31W
Tianjin = Tientsin, China	21 C6	39 8N	117 10 E
Tianshui, China	20 C5	34 32N	105 40 E
Tiber →, Italy	12 D5	41 44N	12 14 E
Tiberias, Israel	N21	32 47N	35 32 E
Tibesti, Chad	28 E10	21 0N	17 30 E
Tibet = Xizang □, China	20 C3	32 0N	88 0 E
Ticino →, Italy	12 B3	45 9N	9 14 E
Ticonderoga, U.S.A.	43 D11	43 50N	73 28W
Tien Shan, Asia	16 E11	42 0N	76 0 E
Tientsin, China	21 C6	39 8N	117 10 E
Tierra del Fuego, I. Gr. de, Argentina	47 H3	54 0S	69 0W
Tiffin, U.S.A.	42 E6	41 8N	83 10W
Tignish, Canada	43 B15	46 58N	64 2W
Tigris →, Asia	24 B3	31 0N	47 25 E
Tijuana, Mexico	44 A1	32 30N	117 10W
Tiksi, Russia	18 B14	71 40N	128 45 E
Tilburg, Neths.	8 B6	51 31N	5 6 E
Timaru, N.Z.	35 J13	44 23S	171 14 E
Timbuktu = Tombouctou, Mali	30 A1	16 50N	3 0W
Timişoara, Romania	13 B9	45 43N	21 15 E
Timmins, Canada	42 A7	48 28N	81 25W
Timor, Indonesia	22 D4	9 0S	125 0 E
Tinaca Pt., Phil.	22 C4	5 30N	125 25 E
Tipperary, Ireland	7 F2	52 28N	8 10W
Tiranë, Albania	13 D8	41 18N	19 49 E
Tîrgovişte, Romania	13 B11	44 55N	25 27 E
Tîrgu-Jiu, Romania	13 B10	45 5N	23 19 E
Tirich Mir, Pakistan	23 A3	36 15N	71 55 E
Tiruchchirappalli, India	25 D6	10 45N	78 45 E
Tirunelveli, India	25 E6	8 45N	77 45 E
Tisa →, Hungary	10 E9	46 8N	20 2 E
Tisza →, Serbia, Yug.	10 F9	45 15N	20 17 E
Titicaca, L., S. Amer.	46 D3	15 30S	69 30W
Titusville, U.S.A.	42 E8	41 35N	79 39W
Tizi-Ouzou, Algeria	28 B7	36 42N	4 3 E
Toamasina, Madag.	33 H9	18 10S	49 25 E
Toba Kakar Hills, Pakistan	23 D2	31 30N	69 0 E
Tobago, W. Indies	44 R21	11 10N	60 30W
Tobermory, Canada	42 C7	45 12N	81 40W
Tocantins →, Brazil	46 C5	1 45S	49 10W
Togliatti, Russia	14 D8	53 32N	49 24 E
Togo ■, W. Afr.	30 C2	8 30N	1 35 E
Tokelau Is., Pac. Oc.	35 B16	9 0S	171 45W
Tōkyō, Japan	19 B6	35 45N	139 45 E
Tolbukhin, Bulgaria	13 C12	43 37N	27 49 E
Toledo, Spain	11 C3	39 50N	4 2W
Toledo, U.S.A.	42 E6	41 37N	83 33W
Toliara, Madag.	33 J8	23 21S	43 40 E
Toluca, Mexico	44 D5	19 20N	99 40W
Tomaszów Mazowiecki, Poland	10 C8	51 30N	19 57 E
Tombouctou, Mali	30 A1	16 50N	3 0W
Tomini, G. of, Indonesia	22 D4	0 10S	121 0 E
Tomsk, Russia	18 D10	56 30N	85 5 E
Tonga ■, Pac. Oc.	35 D16	19 50S	174 30W
Tonga Trench, Pac. Oc.	35 E16	18 0S	173 0W
Tongaat, S. Africa	31 B5	29 33S	31 9 E
Tongking, G. of, Asia	20 E5	20 0N	108 0 E
Tonk, India	23 F5	26 6N	75 54 E
Tonlé Sap, Cambodia	22 B2	13 0N	104 0 E
Toowoomba, Australia	34 F9	27 32S	151 56 E
Topeka, U.S.A.	41 C7	39 3N	95 40W
Torino = Turin, Italy	12 B2	45 4N	7 40 E
Torne →, Sweden	6 E12	65 50N	24 12 E
Torne, L., Sweden	6 E11	68 24N	19 15 E
Tornio, Finland	6 E12	65 50N	24 12 E
Toronto, Canada	42 D8	43 39N	79 20W
Torquay, U.K.	7 G5	50 27N	3 31W
Torreón, Mexico	44 B4	25 33N	103 26W
Tortosa, Spain	11 B6	40 49N	0 31 E
Toruń, Poland	10 B8	53 2N	18 39 E
Toteng, Botswana	31 A3	20 22S	22 58 E
Toul, France	8 C6	48 40N	5 53 E
Toulon, France	9 F6	43 10N	5 55 E
Toulouse, France	9 F4	43 37N	1 27 E
Touraine, France	8 D4	47 20N	0 30 E
Tournai, Belgium	8 B5	50 35N	3 25 E
Tournon, France	9 E6	45 4N	4 50 E
Tours, France	8 D4	47 22N	0 40 E
Touwsrivier, S. Africa	31 C3	33 20S	20 2 E
Towanda, U.S.A.	42 E9	41 46N	76 30W
Townsville, Australia	34 D8	19 15S	146 45 E
Towson, U.S.A.	42 F9	39 26N	76 34W
Toyama, Japan	19 A5	36 40N	137 15 E
Toyohashi, Japan	19 B5	34 45N	137 25 E
Trabzon, Turkey	15 F6	41 0N	39 45 E
Trafalgar, C., Spain	11 D2	36 10N	6 2W
Trail, Canada	38 D8	49 5N	117 40W
Tralee, Ireland	7 F2	52 16N	9 42W
Trang, Thailand	22 C1	7 33N	99 38 E
Trangan, Indonesia	22 D5	6 40S	134 20 E
Transkei □, S. Africa	31 C4	32 15S	28 15 E
Transvaal □, S. Africa	31 A4	25 0S	29 0 E
Transylvania, Romania	13 B11	45 19N	25 0 E
Transylvanian Alps, Romania	4 F10	45 30N	25 0 E
Trapani, Italy	12 E5	38 1N	12 30 E
Traverse City, U.S.A.	42 C5	44 45N	85 39W
Trent →, U.K.	7 F6	53 33N	0 44W
Trentino-Alto Adige □, Italy	12 A4	46 30N	11 0 E
Trento, Italy	12 A4	46 5N	11 8 E
Trenton, Canada	42 C9	44 10N	77 34W
Trenton, U.S.A.	43 E10	40 15N	74 41W
Trier, Germany	10 D2	49 45N	6 37 E
Trieste, Italy	12 B5	45 39N	13 45 E
Trincomalee, Sri Lanka	25 E7	8 38N	81 15 E
Trinidad & Tobago ■, W. Indies	44 S20	10 30N	61 20W
Tripoli, Lebanon	24 B2	34 31N	35 50 E
Tripoli, Libya	28 C9	32 49N	13 7 E
Tripura □, India	23 H13	24 0N	92 0 E
Tristan da Cunha, Atl. Oc.	2 F9	37 6S	12 20W
Trivandrum, India	25 E6	8 41N	77 0 E
Trnava, Slovakia	10 D7	48 23N	17 35 E
Trois-Rivières, Canada	43 B11	46 25N	72 34W
Trollhättan, Sweden	6 G10	58 17N	12 20 E
Trondheim, Norway	6 F10	63 36N	10 25 E
Trondheim Fjord, Norway	6 F10	63 35N	10 30 E
Troy, N.Y., U.S.A.	43 D11	42 45N	73 39W
Troy, Ohio, U.S.A.	42 E5	40 3N	84 10W
Troyes, France	8 C6	48 19N	4 3 E
Trujillo, Peru	46 C2	8 6S	79 0W
Truk, Pac. Oc.	36 G7	7 25N	151 46 E
Truro, Canada	43 C16	45 21N	63 14W
Truro, U.K.	7 G4	50 17N	5 2W
Tsau, Botswana	31 A3	20 8S	22 22 E
Tselinograd, Kazakhstan	18 D9	51 10N	71 30 E
Tshabong, Botswana	31 B3	26 2S	22 29 E
Tshane, Botswana	31 A3	24 5S	21 54 E
Tshwane, Botswana	31 A3	22 24S	22 1 E
Tsimlyansk Res., Russia	15 E7	48 0N	43 0 E
Tsu, Japan	19 B5	34 45N	136 25 E
Tsumeb, Namibia	31 A2	19 9S	17 44 E
Tsumis, Namibia	31 A2	23 39S	17 29 E
Tuamotu Arch., Pac. Oc.	37 J13	17 0S	144 0W
Tubai Is., Pac. Oc.	37 K12	25 0S	150 0W
Tucson, U.S.A.	40 D4	32 14N	110 59W
Tugela →, S. Africa	31 B5	29 14S	31 30 E
Tula, Russia	14 D6	54 13N	37 38 E
Tulcea, Romania	13 B13	45 13N	28 46 E
Tulle, France	9 E4	45 16N	1 46 E
Tulsa, U.S.A.	41 C7	36 10N	96 0W
Tunis, Tunisia	28 B9	36 50N	10 11 E
Tunisia ■, Africa	28 C8	33 30N	9 10 E
Tunja, Colombia	46 B2	5 33N	73 25W
Tura, India	23 G13	25 30N	90 16 E
Turabah, Si. Arabia	24 C3	28 20N	43 15 E
Turin, Italy	12 B2	45 4N	7 40 E
Turkana, L., Africa	32 D7	3 30N	36 5 E
Turkey ■, Eurasia	15 G6	39 0N	36 0 E
Turkmenistan ■, Asia	18 F7	39 0N	59 0 E
Turks Is., W. Indies	45 C10	21 20N	71 20W
Turku, Finland	6 F12	60 30N	22 19 E
Tuticorin, India	25 E6	8 50N	78 12 E
Tuvalu ■, Pac. Oc.	35 B14	8 0S	178 0 E
Tuxtla Gutiérrez, Mexico	44 D6	16 50N	93 10W
Tuz Gölü, Turkey	15 G5	38 45N	33 30 E
Tuzla, Bos.-H., Yug.	13 B8	44 34N	18 41 E
Tver, Russia	14 C6	56 55N	35 55 E
Two Rivers, U.S.A.	42 C4	44 10N	87 31W
Tychy, Poland	10 C8	50 9N	18 59 E
Tynemouth, U.K.	7 E6	55 1N	1 27W
Tyre = Sûr, Lebanon	29 C14	33 19N	35 16 E
Tyrol □, Austria	10 E4	47 3N	10 43 E
Tyrrhenian Sea, Europe	12 E5	40 0N	12 30 E
Tyumen, Russia	18 D8	57 11N	65 29 E
Tzaneen, S. Africa	31 A5	23 47S	30 9 E

U

Place	Ref	Lat	Long
Ubangi = Oubangi →, Zaïre	32 E3	0 30S	17 50 E
Ube, Japan	19 C2	33 56N	131 15 E
Uberaba, Brazil	46 D5	19 50S	47 55W
Uberlândia, Brazil	46 D5	19 0S	48 20W
Ucayali →, Peru	46 C2	4 30S	73 30W
Udaipur, India	23 G4	24 36N	73 44 E
Udaipur Garhi, Nepal	23 F11	27 0N	86 35 E
Udine, Italy	12 A5	46 5N	13 10 E
Udmurt Republic □, Russia	14 C9	57 30N	52 30 E
Udon Thani, Thailand	22 B2	17 29N	102 46 E
Ufa, Russia	14 D10	54 45N	55 55 E
Uganda ■, Africa	32 D6	2 0N	32 0 E
Uitenhage, S. Africa	31 C4	33 40S	25 28 E
Ujjain, India	23 H5	23 9N	75 43 E
Újpest, Hungary	10 E8	47 32N	19 6 E
Ujung Pandang, Indonesia	22 D3	5 10S	119 20 E
Ukraine ■, Europe	15 E5	49 0N	32 0 E
Ulan Bator, Mongolia	20 B5	47 55N	106 53 E
Ulan Ude, Russia	18 D12	51 45N	107 40 E
Ulhasnagar, India	23 K4	19 15N	73 10 E
Ullapool, U.K.	7 D4	57 54N	5 10W
Ulm, Germany	10 D4	48 23N	10 0 E
Ulyasutay, Mongolia	20 B4	47 56N	97 28 E
Umbria □, Italy	12 C5	42 53N	12 30 E
Ume →, Sweden	6 F12	63 45N	20 20 E
Umeå, Sweden	6 F12	63 45N	20 20 E
Umtata, S. Africa	31 C4	31 36S	28 49 E
Umzimvubu, S. Africa	31 C4	31 38S	29 33 E
Umzinto, S. Africa	31 C5	30 15S	30 45 E
Ungava B., Canada	39 C13	59 30N	67 30W
Ungava Pen., Canada	39 C12	60 0N	74 0W
Uniontown, U.S.A.	42 F8	39 54N	79 45W
United Arab Emirates ■, Asia	24 C4	23 50N	54 0 E
United Kingdom ■, Europe	7 F5	53 0N	2 0W
United States of America ■, N. Amer.	40 C7	37 0N	96 0W
Upington, S. Africa	31 B3	28 25S	21 15 E
Uppsala, Sweden	6 G11	59 53N	17 38 E
Ural →, Kazakhstan	15 E9	47 0N	51 48 E
Ural Mts., Russia	14 C10	60 0N	59 0 E
Uralsk, Kazakhstan	14 D9	51 20N	51 20 E
Uranium City, Canada	38 C9	59 34N	108 37W
Urbana, Ill., U.S.A.	42 E3	40 7N	88 12W
Urbana, Ohio, U.S.A.	42 E6	40 9N	83 45W
Uruguay ■, S. Amer.	47 F4	32 30S	56 30W
Uruguay →, S. Amer.	47 F4	34 12S	58 18W
Ürümqi, China	20 B3	43 45N	87 45 E
Usakos, Namibia	31 A2	21 54S	15 31 E
Ushant, France	8 C1	48 28N	5 6W
Üsküdar, Turkey	13 D13	41 0N	29 5 E
Ussel, France	9 E5	45 32N	2 18 E
Ust Urt Plateau, Kazakhstan	18 E7	44 0N	55 0 E
Ústí nad Labem, Czech.	10 C6	50 41N	14 3 E
Utah □, U.S.A.	40 C4	39 30N	111 30W
Utica, U.S.A.	43 D10	43 5N	75 18W
Utrecht, Neths.	8 A6	52 5N	5 8 E
Utsunomiya, Japan	19 A6	36 30N	139 50 E
Uttar Pradesh □, India	23 F8	27 0N	80 0 E
Uttaradit, Thailand	22 B2	17 36N	100 5 E
Uusikaupunki, Finland	6 F12	60 47N	21 25 E
Uzbekistan ■, Asia	18 E8	41 30N	65 0 E

V

Place	Ref	Lat	Long
Vaal →, S. Africa	31 B3	29 4S	23 38 E
Vaal Dam, S. Africa	31 B4	27 0S	28 14 E
Vaasa, Finland	6 F12	63 6N	21 38 E
Vadodara, India	23 H4	22 20N	73 10 E
Vadsø, Norway	6 D13	70 3N	29 50 E
Váh →, Slovakia	10 E8	47 43N	18 7 E
Val d'Or, Canada	42 A9	48 7N	77 47W
Valdez, U.S.A.	38 B5	61 14N	146 17W
Valdivia, Chile	47 F2	39 50S	73 14W
Valence, France	9 E6	44 57N	4 54 E
Valencia, Spain	11 C5	39 27N	0 23W
Valencia, Venezuela	46 A3	10 11N	68 0W
Valenciennes, France	8 B5	50 20N	3 34 E
Valladolid, Spain	11 B3	41 38N	4 43W
Valletta, Malta	12 G6	35 54N	14 31 E
Valparaíso, Chile	47 F2	33 2S	71 40W
Van, L., Turkey	15 G7	38 30N	43 0 E
Van Buren, U.S.A.	43 B13	47 10N	68 1W
Van Wert, U.S.A.	42 E5	40 52N	84 35W
Vancouver, Canada	38 D7	49 15N	123 10W
Vancouver I., Canada	38 D7	49 50N	126 0W
Vanderbijlpark, S. Africa	31 B4	26 42S	27 54 E
Vaner, L., Sweden	6 G10	58 47N	13 30 E
Vännäs, Sweden	6 F11	63 58N	19 48 E
Vannes, France	8 D2	47 40N	2 47W
Vanrhynsdorp, S. Africa	31 C2	31 36S	18 44 E
Vanua Levu, Fiji	35 D14	16 33S	179 15 E
Vanuatu ■, Pac. Oc.	35 D12	15 0S	168 0 E

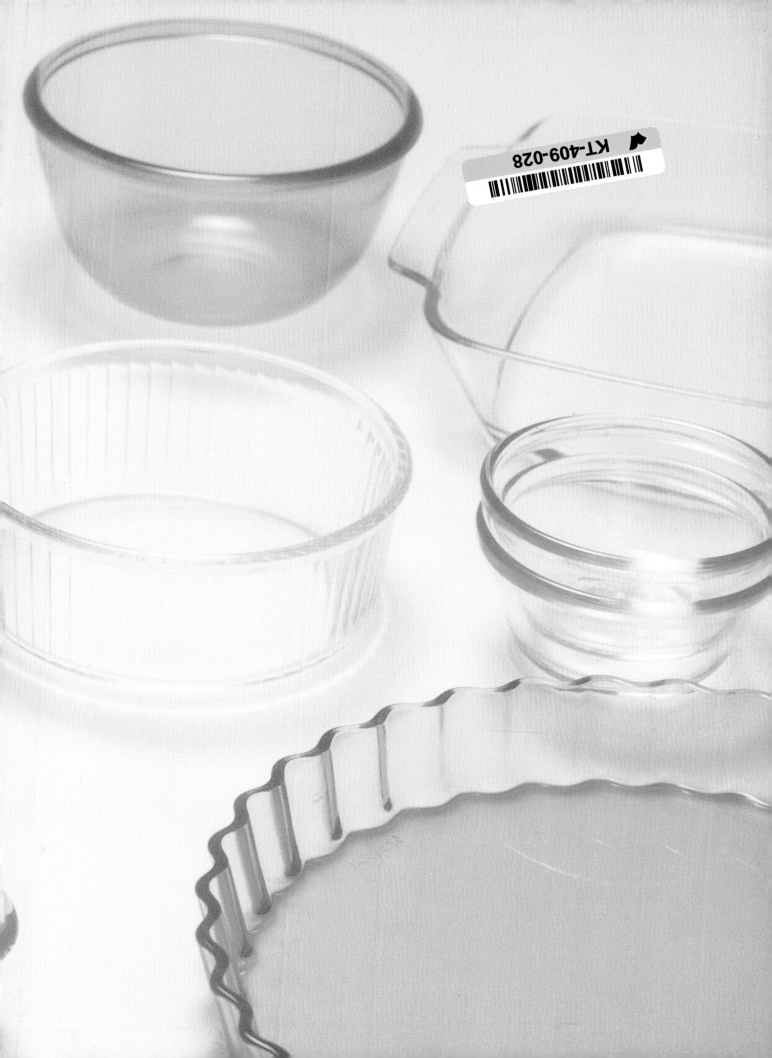

THE
MICROWAVE
COOK

THE
MICROWAVE
COOK

Shirley Guy and Marty Klinzman

NEWNES BOOKS

NEWNES BOOKS

First published 1984 as The South African
Microwave Cookbook by C. Struik (Pty) Ltd.

This adapted edition prepared 1985 by
Newnes Books Ltd, a division of
The Hamlyn Publishing Group Limited
84–88 The Centre, Feltham, Middlesex
and distributed by
Hamlyn Distribution Services Limited
Rushden, Northants, England.

© Text copyright Shirley Guy and Marty Klinzman
© Photographs copyright C. Struik (Pty) Ltd.

ISBN 0 600 33266 7

Printed in Hong Kong.

Acknowledgements

Photography by Peter Brooks.
Line drawings by Andrea Bagnall.
Adaptation for the Newnes edition by
Jenni Fleetwood.

The publishers would like to thank
THORN EMI for their help with both the
original and the Newnes edition.

Contents

Microwave energy— a new dimension

Microwave cooking is fast becoming part of our normal way of life, but many microwave owners do not realize the full potential of this electronic cooking wonder. And, even though it has been available in this country for well over a decade, the microwave is often still thought of only in terms of thawing frozen food, or warming yesterday's casserole. It is our hope that you will discover that microwave cooking is a very versatile and efficient way to prepare a wide spectrum of tasty foods, without mess or fuss. There is nothing difficult about cooking food in the microwave once you have mastered the basic techniques, all of which have been thoroughly dealt with in this book. However, like any other appliance it has certain limitations, as not all foods are suitable for microwaving. Accept these limitations, and use the microwave in conjunction with your conventional cooker. This way you will enjoy the benefits of both methods. Before attempting any recipes read 'How to use this book' on page 24.

Microwave energy

Microwave ovens have been in commercial use for several decades while models for home use have been manufactured for a number of years and are becoming increasingly popular. They are now accepted by many as indispensable items of kitchen equipment. Microwave cooking is, however, a completely new concept and before you begin to use your oven, it is important to have a good understanding of what microwave energy is, how it works, and how it can save time and effort in your kitchen.

What is microwave energy?

Microwaves work on the same principle as radio, television or light waves. They are simply a form of high-frequency electromagnetic energy that produces heat, depending on the substances it comes into contact with. Microwaves are not attracted to all substances; for example they cannot penetrate metal and so they are reflected by it. For this reason metal makes an ideal lining to microwave ovens as the waves bounce off the oven walls. Many other substances allow microwaves to pass straight through them without producing heat; for example, glass, pottery, china, paper, wood and some plastics. These make ideal containers as microwave energy passes through them directly into the food.

Microwaves are attracted by the moisture, sugar or fat content of foods and, depending on the size and density of the food, penetrate to 2 to 4 cm/ $3/4$–$1\frac{1}{2}$ inches. The microwave energy causes molecules to vibrate at very high speeds – over two thousand million times a second – producing heat through friction. This heat spreads rapidly throughout the food from the point of penetration, thus cooking the food by conduction. However, smaller pieces of food are penetrated completely by the microwaves and therefore cook more quickly than larger, more solid foods. It should also be remembered that larger quantities will take longer to microwave than smaller quantities because the microwave energy within the oven remains constant. Microwave ovens do not need preheating like conventional ovens, as microwave energy reacts with the food instantly.

What happens in the microwave oven?

When the microwave oven is plugged in, power flows to the magnetron which converts electrical energy to microwave energy. This energy passes through a wave-guide that directs it into the oven cavity. A wave-stirrer or fan distributes the microwaves in an even pattern around the oven. The metal lining reflects the microwaves which are then attracted by the food.

Are microwave ovens safe?

The microwave oven has no sharp edges or moving parts, and its form of heat generation helps prevent burns and scalding. As microwaves heat only the food, no energy is wasted heating the air inside, which remains cool, or the container. However, as the food is heated the container may become hot by conduction, so care should always be exercised when taking food out of the oven. Manufacturers have designed microwave ovens so that no microwaves escape. Special safety features are built into microwave ovens, making them one of the safest kitchen appliances. The see-through oven door incorporates a reflecting metal screen and the door frame is designed with special seals to keep microwaves safely within the oven. Cut-out devices ensure microwave energy is automatically switched off when the door is opened.

More about microwave energy

Although microwaves are similar to radio and television waves, they are of a much higher frequency. The number of cycles the wave completes in a second (the frequency) is measured in hertz (Hz) and megahertz (MHz).

1 Hz = 1 cycle per second

1 MHz = 1 million cycles per second

Radio waves have a frequency of	0,56 – 8 MHz
Television waves have a frequency of	30 – 300 MHz
Microwaves have a frequency of	2 450 MHz

It is this high frequency which causes molecules in the food to vibrate at such high speeds that they produce heat. Microwaves should not be confused with X-rays, ultra-violet or gamma rays, all of which are ionizing and cause irreversible, chemical and cellular changes with little or no temperature change. Microwave energy is a non-ionizing form of electromagnetic energy transmitted through space by microwaves, which are very short and travel in straight lines. Being non-ionizing, microwaves are not harmful, as they do not damage cells, nor do they accumulate in foodstuffs cooked in a microwave oven.

Microwaves have three important characteristics: they can be reflected by metals, attracted by foodstuffs and they can pass straight through certain materials, such as glass, plastics and paper, without affecting them.

Microwaves are reflected by the metal lining of the oven and attracted by the moisture in the food

Advantages of microwave cooking

There are many advantages to cooking in a microwave, as you will discover as you continue to use yours. The microwave oven is useful in busy households where family members can't always be together at meal times or when quick meals are needed, while anyone living alone will find it ideal for cooking small quantities. Here are some of the more obvious advantages:

Speed: This is one of the greatest advantages, as microwaving takes about one third to one quarter of conventional cooking time.

Economy: Not only do microwave ovens use less power than conventional ovens (650 watts as opposed to the 2 200 watts of one element in a conventional oven), but they are on for a shorter time. Moreover, there is no need to preheat the microwave, as heat is generated instantly in the food when the oven is switched on. It also switches off at the end of the set cooking time, so no power is wasted.

Mobility: Microwave ovens use a standard 13-amp plug and household current, so they can be used almost anywhere where there is a stable surface. Although they can be placed in any area of the kitchen, counter height is usually the most convenient. Some people find it handy to place the microwave on a sturdy trolley, so that it can be moved about.

Safe and easy to use: Microwave ovens are simple to operate and most dishes remain cool enough to handle easily. This means they can be used safely by the young, the elderly and the disabled, with little danger of burning.

Defrosting: There is no need to panic if you have forgotten to take a roast or casserole from the freezer. The microwave will defrost foods quickly and effectively without affecting the flavour or texture of the food.

Flavour and nutrition: Many foods cook in their own juices, or with the addition of very little liquid, thus retaining their natural flavour and most vitamins and nutrients. Many foods can be cooked in the microwave without the addition of oil or butter, making it useful for people on slimming diets or for those who are avoiding cholestrol.

Reheating: The microwave oven will reheat foods, such as casseroles, soups or individual plates of food, with no added moisture and no change in texture or flavour. Leftovers are just as appetizing as the first time they were served, and a plate of food saved for a latecomer will look and taste as fresh as newly cooked.

Cooler cooking: The microwave oven itself does not get hot, so even during long cooking periods, or when the temperature inside the oven is extremely high, the kitchen will stay cool. This is a great help with processes like preserving fruits and vegetables in the middle of summer.

Easy cleaning: The microwave oven is easier to clean than a conventional oven as foods do not often boil over and do not burn onto the oven surfaces. If spills occur, the metal or acrylic surfaces inside are easy to wipe clean.

Saves washing up: Food can often be cooked and served in the same container, so there is less washing up to do after cooking in the microwave oven.

Microwave features

You don't need great mechanical ability to use your microwave oven, but it is necessary to read and follow the manufacturer's operating instructions carefully. Be sure you understand all the features of the oven and how they work. Your oven will have some or all of the following features.

On/off control: This operates the fan and interior light, but usually does not control the microwave supply.

Cook or start control: This switch or button starts the microwave process but cannot be operated until the oven door is securely closed. When the door is opened, the microwave energy is automatically cut off.

Oven door: Most models have doors that open to the side. The door consists of a metal mesh panel and a glass panel fitted in a metal frame. You can watch food as it cooks, but the metal mesh stops microwaves from penetrating the glass door. Microwave ovens cannot be operated until the door is firmly shut.

Timer: Timing controls may be in the form of a dial, a sliding device or touch controls with a digital display. Timers that can be set for seconds as well as minutes give the most accurate cooking control. Some ovens can be timed for lengths of 25 to 30 minutes, while others have timing controls that can be set for longer periods. A bell or buzzer sounds when the cooking time is up.

Oven cavity: The metal lining is coated with acrylic and keeps the microwaves inside the oven. Food is cooked on the base of the oven or on specially designed glass or ceramic trays, shelves or turntables. The interior of each make of oven has been designed to allow microwaves to penetrate the food from all angles. Most ovens have an interior light that comes on when the oven door is opened and also operates during cooking.

Oven vent: All microwave ovens have a vent to allow moisture and air to escape during cooking. It is important that the vent be kept free whenever the oven is in operation. Built-in microwave ovens need space at the back or top for ventilation purposes.

Power control: This allows you to select the power level you want to use to cook food. Variable power offers flexibility in cooking so you can control the speed at which the food cooks. The number of power settings varies according to the model, so follow the manufacturer's instructions carefully. See page 24 for power levels used for recipes in the book.

Turntable: Most microwave ovens are likely to have hot and cold spots, so it is important that food be turned occasionally during defrosting, heating or cooking. Some microwave ovens have a turntable or rotating platform that automatically rotates the food during the cooking time, eliminating the need to turn or rotate containers and promoting even cooking. Follow the manufacturer's directions for using the turntable. In some models, the microwave oven should not be used without the turntable in position. Some of the latest models have no turntable at all. The manufacturers claim their new stirrer fans distribute the microwaves so efficiently that there is no need to rotate the food constantly.

Temperature probe: This takes the guesswork out of timing, and allows you to control the internal temperature of the food. The probe is especially useful for cooking roasts or whole poultry, for reheating foods

9

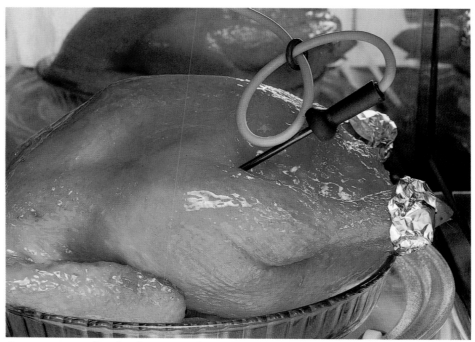

A temperature probe takes the guesswork out of timing

and, in some cases, for simmering and slow cooking. Follow directions for its use. The probe's flexible connection fits into a socket inside the oven and the point is inserted into the food being cooked. The placing of the probe is important, usually in the thickest part of the poultry or meat, or in the centre of a casserole or stew. Foods cook to a pre-set temperature, then the oven automatically turns off. However, food continues to cook even after the oven switches off, so you may wish to select a lower temperature. It is always easy to microwave the food for a few minutes more, but it is impossible to remedy overcooking.

Warning: Never use a conventional meat thermometer made of metal in your microwave.

Additional features

Defrost control: The defrost setting on the power control enables you to defrost large or small amounts of food easily and quickly. When the defrost setting is in use, the microwave energy inside the oven is turned on and off automatically, allowing rest periods between bursts of energy, so that foods are defrosted but not cooked.

Browning element: Manufacturers incorporate a browning element, similar to a grill unit, in some microwave ovens. It is used to brown food before or after it is cooked.

Touch controls: A few microwave models are operated by touching a control panel on the outside of the

oven. Many of these have a digital display to show power level, cooking time and any special instructions. They also incorporate a clock on the front panel.

Memory control: The use of the 'memory' on a microwave oven allows it to be programmed for two power settings and sometimes for special instructions such as 'hold'. The cooking will automatically be changed from one power level to another. With this feature, you do not have to wait for cooking time to finish at one level before physically resetting the oven.

Automatic start: Some ovens can be programmed to start at a pre-set time and continue cooking for a predetermined period.

Slow cook or simmer control: This is a setting or power level that reduces the energy used, therefore slowing down the cooking time. It is useful for recipes that require long slow cooking to develop flavour or tenderize ingredients.

Care and cleaning

As with any other appliance, it is important to read the manufacturer's instruction book on the cleaning and care of your oven. However, certain general guidelines can be followed:
- Wipe the inside surface of the oven with a damp cloth after each use. Also wipe moisture from the inside of the oven and door.

- For thorough cleaning, remove the base, glass shelf or turntable and wash with warm, soapy water if necessary.
- Harsh abrasives or oven cleaners may damage the inside surfaces of the oven and scratches may distort the microwave pattern within the oven.
- Since the interior walls of the oven remain relatively cool, splashing and spills should not burn on. Be sure to clean the oven interior if any spillage occurs, as the food particles left adhering to the oven surfaces will attract microwave energy and slow down cooking the next time you use the oven.
- Be sure to clean any grease or food particles from around the door seal. It is important that a good seal be maintained.
- To remove stubborn food particles from the inside surface, place a cup of water in the oven and let it boil for a few minutes. The moisture should loosen the pieces of food and they can then be wiped away.
- The outside of the oven can be wiped over with a damp cloth. Wipe exterior vents occasionally to remove any condensation, but do not splash water over them.

SAFETY

- Do not attempt to operate the oven with the door open. Do not tamper with the safety locking systems.
- Do not place any object between the oven door and the front of the oven. Make sure that sealing surfaces are clean.
- Do not operate the oven if it is damaged in any way. It is important that the oven door closes properly.
- Do not allow the oven to be adjusted or repaired by anyone other than qualified microwave service personnel.
- Do not remove the outer casing or oven door at any time.
- Never line the oven with foil, paper or any other material.
- Do not lean heavily on the oven door.
- Do not use the oven for storing utensils.
- Do not operate the oven when it is empty, as this may damage the magnetron. A cup of water left in the oven when it is not in use will attract the microwave energy if the oven is accidentally turned on.

Microwave techniques

Many of the techniques used in microwave cooking are similar to ones used in conventional cooking. Methods such as turning, rearranging or stirring foods are used to promote fast and even cooking. The application of these techniques is slightly different when microwaving, so for best results, be sure to follow recipe instructions when any of the following techniques are called for:

Standing time

Food continues to cook after it has been removed from the microwave, so it is important to let it 'stand' before serving. The length of standing time varies, but in general depends on the volume and density of the food. Meat dishes such as roasts or poultry will continue to cook for 10 to 20 minutes after the microwave energy has been turned off. Other foods, such as cakes or puddings, depend on standing time to finish cooking. Because of this it is important to take standing time into consideration when experimenting with foods or trying new recipes, so that foods will not be overcooked. It is always better to slightly undercook foods, as they can easily be heated again if they are not done. Follow recipe instructions for standing time.

Stirring

In conventional cooker-top cooking, food is stirred from the bottom up to ensure even heating. Since the outer edges of food normally cook first in microwave cooking, foods should be stirred from the outer edges inward to promote even cooking. Foods that normally need constant stirring, such as sauces or custards, need only occasional stirring in the microwave oven. However, these foods may need to be stirred a little more frequently in a microwave oven without a turntable.

Turning

Foods that cannot be stirred during cooking need to be repositioned to heat evenly or to brown each side.
- Large roasts, poultry, pieces of vegetables or meat, should be turned during the cooking time to ensure even heating.

Stir from the outside inwards

Turning ensures even cooking

Arrange equal-sized portions in a circle

- Foods microwaved in a browning pan, such as hamburgers, steaks or chops, will need turning to ensure even browning.
- In microwave ovens without a turntable it is advisable to rotate the container a quarter or half a turn during the cooking time if the food appears to be cooking unevenly.
- Foods defrost more evenly if turned during the defrosting time.

Arrangement

The arrangement of food in the microwave oven is another important factor for even cooking:
- Always place the thicker or larger portions of food towards the outside of the container because microwaves penetrate the outer edges of food first. For example, chicken legs or fish steaks should have the thinner part towards the centre of the dish.
- Arrange foods of equal size in a circular pattern. For example, potatoes to be baked or individual portions of custard or eggs can be placed in a ring pattern or circle in the microwave oven. If possible, do not place an entire portion in the centre. Foods such as meatballs will cook more evenly if arranged in a circular pattern in a round dish with the centre empty.
- For even cooking, food should be arranged to a uniform depth.
- Vegetables should be spread out rather than heaped in the middle.
- When reheating a meal on a plate, keep foods at an even depth, and arrange denser or thicker foods towards the outside of the plate.
- By rearranging food during cooking you help it cook more evenly. Moving foods from the centre to the outside, or from the outside towards the centre, gives more evenly cooked results, and can help shorten the cooking time.

1

2

3

6

7

Shielding

Sensitive areas of food should be shielded so that they do not overcook. Use small strips of aluminium foil (6) to shield thin parts of poultry, such as the tips of wings and legs or the breastbone, and bones on thin parts of joints of meat. Shielding can be useful in baking too. Use small pieces of foil (7) to shield the corners of square and rectangular dishes as these would overcook before the centre is done.

Browning

The attractive browning of foods during cooking is due to a chemical reaction between food sugars and amino acids which takes place slowly at low temperatures and more quickly at higher temperatures. During quick microwave cooking, the surface temperature of foods does not change enough to bring about natural browning, so foods do not have the same appearance as when cooked conventionally unless first brushed with a browning agent. Refer to chart on page 22. Foods such as large roasts and poultry will brown slightly if they are cooked longer than about

Covering and wrapping

In conventional cooking, many foods are covered to retain moisture and decrease cooking time. The same techniques are used in microwave cooking, but the application may be different. Follow the recipe instructions for covering food; if no mention is made microwave food uncovered.

Cling film: A tight cover of cling film (1) holds in steam as well as heat. Turn back one corner, or make two slashes in the film to prevent it from 'ballooning' during the cooking time. The lid of the dish (2) can be used instead of cling film when microwaving vegetables, casseroles and meats that require moisture.

Greaseproof paper: A loose cover of greaseproof paper (3) holds in heat without steaming the food. It is used to cover foods such as fruits and hamburgers, chicken, bacon or roasts where steam is not required to tenderize the food.

Cooking bags: Cooking bags (4) hold in steam and help to tenderize meat or poultry. Do not use a metal or foil strip to seal the bag. Fasten with string or an elastic band and make one or two slashes to prevent the bag from 'ballooning' during cooking.

Paper towel: A paper towel (5) allows steam to escape, promotes even heating and prevents spattering during cooking. It also absorbs excess moisture from foods. Use a paper towel to cover bacon during microwaving or to absorb moisture when drying herbs or freshening crisps, pretzels or savoury biscuits. Porous paper towels can be used to wrap such foods as hamburgers or hot dogs in rolls, bread rolls or pastries for heating. Use damp paper towels to steam fish fillets and scallops, or to soften crêpes in a few seconds.

4

5

8

9

25 minutes because the fats reach a high temperature, causing some change in colour.

Some microwave ovens have a special element to brown food either before or after microwave cooking. Browning dishes (see page 16) designed especially for microwave ovens sear and brown foods (8) the way a frying pan does, giving chops, steaks, sausages and hamburgers an appetizing appearance. Many recipes in this book make use of special toppings to improve the look of the food, and on page 22 there is a special section giving tips and hints on how to make microwaved foods look good.

Heating

Heating home-prepared meals, leftovers and 'fast foods' is one of the best features of microwave cooking. Many foods can be prepared ahead of time and reheated with no loss of flavour or texture. While heating, most foods should be covered with greaseproof paper (9) to hold in the heat and at the same time allow steam to escape. The plate or dish may need to be rotated if no turntable is used.

- Baked foods such as rolls and mince pies must be heated with care as they are easily overdone.
- Stews and casseroles may need to be stirred during heating.
- A plate of food that needs heating should have all the foods at the same temperature and arranged so that the one which takes longest to heat is on the outside.
- Canned foods need only be heated before serving.

Defrosting

Defrosting food in the microwave oven is not only quick and convenient, but most of the flavour or moisture is retained, and there is little risk of bacterial growth. When the defrost setting is used, the power is cycled on and off to produce a slow heating process. Defrosting charts for fish, poultry, meat, vegetables and baking are given in the relevant chapters.

- Defrost food slowly so that it does not begin to cook on the outside before it is completely thawed.
- Large roasts and poultry may need to stand after defrosting so that heat from the thawed outer layers will penetrate to the centre. The latest models incorporate this standing time automatically. For best results, be sure meat and poultry are completely defrosted before microwaving.
- It is often necessary to reposition or turn foods so they defrost evenly.
- Place frozen food in a container suitable for microwaving. Be sure the container is large enough to hold the food after thawing, and to allow for stirring if necessary.
- Foods frozen in foil trays or wrapped in foil should be removed from the container or wrapper and placed in a suitable dish.

Microwave equipment

Substances such as glass, pottery, porcelain and paper allow microwave energy to pass through them, so containers made of these materials are ideal for use in the microwave. Because metal reflects microwaves, containers of aluminium, copper, stainless steel or aluminium foil are not suitable and may cause arcing which will damage your appliance.

Equipment made of materials that meet the special requirements of microwave cooking is now available. However, there is no need to rush out and buy a complete new range of cookware. Although you will not be using metal pans or baking tins many utensils you already have are suitable for use in the microwave. These include such items as paper plates, paper towel, ovenproof casserole dishes and glass measuring jugs. It is often possible to cook and serve in the same container, saving not only time, but washing up too.

Testing containers for microwave safety

Measure 250 ml/8 fl oz water in a glass measuring jug. Place the container you wish to test in the microwave oven and stand the jug on it. Microwave on full power for about one minute. At the end of that time, the water should be warm and the container cool. If so, the container is ideal for microwave use. If both the water and container are warm, the container can be used, but the cooking time must be increased, as it has attracted some of the microwave energy. If the container is warm but the water is cool, the container has attracted much of the microwave energy and should not be used for microwave cooking.

Ideal containers for microwave cooking

Heat retention

Because microwaves pass through the container directly into the food, the dish stays relatively cool during the cooking process. However, as the food becomes hot some of the heat is absorbed by the container, so care should be taken when removing it from the microwave oven. Foods that are high in fat or sugar content or ones that have a long cooking time transfer heat more readily.

Materials suitable for microwaving

Paper: This is a good material for microwave use especially with foods that require low heat and short cooking times. Thawing, reheating and some cooking methods can make use of paper napkins, towels, cups and plates.
- Paper towel is useful for covering fatty foods such as bacon while cooking, as it absorbs excess fat and

prevents spattering. Paper towel can also be used to line cake pans. Just cut to fit, then spread the cake mixture over. The paper towel absorbs excess moisture and makes turning the cake out easy.
- Greaseproof paper can be used as light covering while foods cook because it holds in heat but allows steam to escape.
- Wax-coated paper plates and cups should be used only for heating foods for short periods, as high temperatures cause the wax to melt.
- Paper baking cups not only reduce washing up, but they absorb excess moisture when microwaving small cakes or muffins.
- White paper products are the best to use, as coloured ones may transfer their colours to the food.

Cling film, cooking bags and polythene bags: Cling film makes an excellent cover for microwaved foods as it keeps in both heat and moisture. To prevent

the film from 'ballooning' during cooking, make two slits in the surface or turn back one corner of the film.

Cooking bags are convenient for a variety of foods as they promote the browning of roasts and poultry while retaining moisture and heat. They also help cook vegetables or fruit with very little added moisture. As with cling film, it is important to make two slits near the top of the bag. Do not use the metal ties that come with the bags, but fasten them with string or an elastic band.

Do not use ordinary polythene bags in the microwave oven, as they will melt at high temperatures.

Plastic containers: 'Dishwasher safe' is a useful guideline when determining if a plastic container is safe for use in the microwave oven. Rigid plastic dishes made of thermoplastic material and usually marked 'dishwasher safe' or 'boilable' can be used for heating foods or microwaving for a short time. Special plastics have been developed for use in both microwave and conventional ovens, and may be safely used to cook any food item in the microwave.

Do not use:

- Freezer containers, as they absorb heat from the food during cooking and distort or melt.
- Plastic cream cartons or yoghurt cartons or any other lightweight plastic containers.
- Styrofoam trays for reheating or cooking, but they can be used for defrosting.
- Melamine as it absorbs microwave energy.

Glass: Ovenproof glass such as Pyrex and glass ceramic containers such as Corningware are ideal for both heating and cooking in the microwave. Such items are readily available in kitchen shops, ironmongers and some supermarkets. Clear glass containers allow you to see what is happening to the food. For anyone using a microwave oven for the first time, this is important, especially when checking bases of cakes or puddings to determine whether they are cooked. Ordinary glass without any lead content may be used for heating foods for a short time, but do not use ordinary glass for foods with high sugar or fat content, as the high temperatures reached by those ingredients may crack the glass.

When purchasing glassware for microwave use, remember that round shapes will give more even results than rectangular ones. A deep glass bowl

For more even cooking, choose ring pans and shallow round dishes rather than rectangular and deep ones

and two sizes of measuring jugs will be useful additions to your microwave cookware.

Pottery and china: Sturdy china and stoneware pottery containers without metal trim or content are usually suitable for microwave cooking and can be used in the same way as glassware. Foods can be cooked and served in the same dish, making cleaning up easy. Dark pottery or china slows the microwave cooking process slightly and may become fairly hot to the touch. Avoid containers with a shiny or metallic sheen. If you are unsure whether to use a stoneware or pottery container, test the container as described on opposite page.

Clay pots: Use a clay cooking pot or chicken brick for meat casseroles, poultry or joints of meat. Presoak the lid and base according to the manufacturer's instructions. The cooking time is somewhat longer than in an ordinary casserole dish because the moisture in the pot attracts some of the microwave energy. These pots become hot during cooking, so use oven gloves when handling them. Do not add cold liquid during the cooking period, as the sudden change in temperature may crack the pot.

Other materials

Natural shell: Scallop shells make attractive containers for individual servings of seafood and are safe to use in the microwave. Remember that the cooking time should be reduced for individual servings.

Wood: Items made of wood contain some moisture that evaporates during microwave cooking and eventually they may become so dry that they crack. Use wooden boards or platters for short-term heating rather than actual cooking. Small wooden utensils, such as wooden spoons, are ideal for use in the microwave.

Wicker and straw: Baskets made from wicker or straw can be used in the microwave oven for short periods, such as when bread rolls need to be thawed or heated for a few seconds. Long periods of heating may cause the wicker or straw to dry out and crack.

Aluminium foil: Many microwave oven manufacturers agree that small pieces of aluminium foil can be used to shield corners of a baking dish, or to prevent chicken legs or wings, or bone-ends of meat from overcooking.

Warning: Aluminium foil should not be used as a covering or wrapping as it may cause arcing and flashing which will damage your appliance.

Microwave cookware

Many new items on the market are marked 'safe for microwave use' by the manufacturer. Lugs and handles make containers easier to use as they generally stay cool even though the dish itself may become warm. A round container is more suitable for microwave use than an oval or rectangular one, and a dish with slightly rounded corners rather than square corners helps prevent food from overcooking at the edges. Small deep bowls are not as suitable as larger shallow ones, because food with a greater surface area cooks more evenly. It is important to have a few deep containers for making sauces, puddings, preserves and cream mixtures, as these may rise to almost double the volume during cooking. Avoid any ovenproof containers or plates that have metal trim, as the trim will reflect microwaves.

Due to the increasing popularity of microwave cooking, special microwave cookware has been developed. Designed of specially made plastics, many microwave containers can be used, within certain temperature ranges, in a conventional oven, and are safe to use in the dishwasher. It is now possible to purchase microwave containers such as ring moulds, roasting pans, cake dishes, muffin pans, bacon racks and loaf pans. Be sure to follow instructions for use and care.

Browning dishes

Because they cook quickly, many microwaved foods do not have the browned appearance associated with conventional cooking. With a special browning dish it is possible to brown such foods as hamburgers, steaks, chops and toasted sandwiches, and to fry eggs so that they have an appetizing appearance. Browning dishes are made of glass ceramic and have a special coating under the base. This coating absorbs microwave energy when the empty dish is preheated in the microwave oven, and the bottom of the dish becomes hot. Thus, the surface of food is seared and browned when placed in a preheated browning dish, while the rest of the food is cooked by microwave energy.

Foods such as steaks, toasted sandwiches or chops are normally turned during the cooking time to brown both sides. Preheating times will vary according to the size and shape of the dish, and the type of food to be cooked, so always follow the manufacturer's and recipe directions.

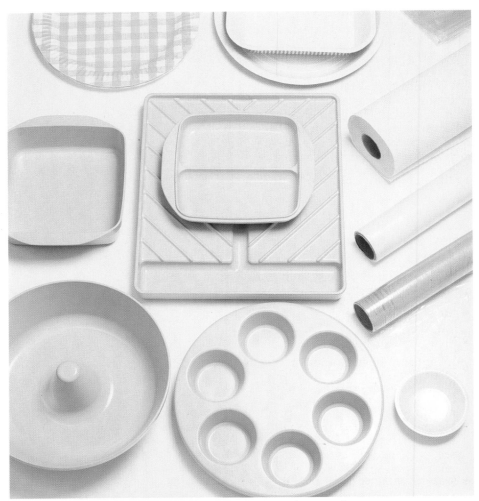

Special plastic cookware and ordinary paper products are a boon to microwave users

BROWNING DISH CHART

Always use full power when using the browning dish. Add butter or oil once the dish has been preheated. Do not use non-stick sprays or coatings as they scorch.

FOOD	PREHEAT TIME	BUTTER OR OIL	FIRST SIDE	SECOND SIDE
125 g/4 oz almonds	–	–	4-5 minutes, stir every 1 minute	
4 chicken pieces	5-6 minutes	1 tbsp	6 minutes	4-5 minutes
4 chops, lamb	5-6 minutes	1 tbsp	3 minutes	1-3 minutes
4 chops, pork	5-6 minutes	1 tbsp	4 minutes	5-7 minutes
2 eggs (yolks pricked)	2-3 minutes	1 tbsp butter	1½-1¾ minutes	
4 fish portions	4-5 minutes	1 tbsp	2-3 minutes	4-5 minutes
6 fish fingers (frozen)	5-6 minutes	brush food with melted butter or oil	2 minutes	1-2 minutes
2 toasted sandwiches or pieces of French toast	4-5 minutes	1 tbsp butter	30-40 seconds	15-25 seconds
4 hamburgers	4-5 minutes	–	2 minutes	1-2 minutes
250 g oven chips	4-5 minutes	–	2-3 minutes	2-3 minutes
4 sausages	5-6 minutes	1 tbsp	1½-2 minutes	1½-2 minutes
2 steaks	6-8 minutes	–	3 minutes	2-2½ minutes
2 veal escalopes (crumbed)	5-6 minutes	2 tbsp butter and 2 tbsp oil	45 seconds	1-1½ minutes

The browning dish does get hot, so wear oven gloves when handling it, and do not place the hot dish directly on the counter or work surface. The bottom of the dish cools as the food browns, so before browning a second batch of food, wipe the dish clean and reheat for about half the original time. Covering the dish with a lid or with greaseproof paper will reduce any spattering and splashing that may occur with fatty foods during cooking. Refer to the chart for specific cooking times.

EQUIPMENT THAT CANNOT BE USED IN THE MICROWAVE

The following equipment is unsuitable for microwave cooking:

- Metal or part-metal pans or baking tins.
- Metal thermometers, skewers or baking sheets.
- Foil baking dishes, trays, or foil-lined paper containers or boxes.
- Porcelain or ceramic dishes with metal trim.
- Melamine dinnerware and some oven-to-table ware. Check with the section on testing containers for microwave safety on page 14.
- Soft plastic containers or plastic yoghurt, margarine or cottage cheese containers.
- Metal or wire ties for cooking bags.

Equipment unsuitable for use in the microwave

Helpful microwave hints

- Read the manufacturer's instruction book carefully before using your microwave oven. Microwave ovens vary from model to model and it is important to know all the features of your oven.
- Do not switch on the oven when it is empty, as this could damage it. A cup of water left in the oven when not in use will attract microwaves if the oven is accidentally switched on.
- Be sure to remove any metal ties or twists before defrosting frozen foods in the microwave.
- Standing time is required for even distribution of heat throughout many foods in the microwave.
- Remember that containers absorb heat from the cooked food and may become warm to touch. Take care when removing them from the microwave.
- Best results are obtained if the food to be cooked is at an even temperature throughout. Make sure foods are completely defrosted

before cooking, unless otherwise indicated in the recipe.
- The microwave cannot improve the quality of food. Always start with good quality ingredients to ensure the best results.
- Cover food to keep it moist. Use pierced cling film or a non-metallic lid.
- Arrange food carefully for even cooking. As a general rule, place the thinnest part towards the centre, and place items such as potatoes or mushrooms in a circle rather than in rows.
- Cut food into even-sized pieces. Irregular sizes will cook unevenly, so some of the food may be overcooked while other pieces will be underdone.
- If your oven does not have a turntable, you may need to stir, rotate or rearrange food more frequently.
- When using boiling or roasting bags, always prick them to prevent them from bursting. Use string or elastic bands instead of metal ties or twists to close cooking bags.

When cooking whole vegetables or fruits, prick the skins to prevent them from bursting. Similarly, prick yolks before frying or poaching eggs in the microwave

- If a recipe has been doubled, allow one third to one half extra cooking time. When halving a recipe, use two thirds of the cooking time.
- Always check foods at the minimum suggested time. It is safer to undercook, as food can always be cooked for a few seconds more, but overcooking can spoil some dishes.
- Never attempt to deep-fry in a microwave oven.

Making the most of your microwave

Foods that microwave well

Some foods cooked in the microwave oven have such excellent flavour and texture that you may never want to cook them any other way. Foods that need constant stirring, such as puddings, sauces, custards or sweets, need only occasional stirring in the microwave. Many foods can be measured, mixed or cooked in the same dish, so cleaning up is easy. The following are foods that microwave exceptionally well:

Eggs scramble light and fluffy and with greater volume. Poached eggs can be microwaved in individual dishes for easy serving and omelettes are a treat to make. Refer to the chapter on breakfasts for how to cook eggs.

Bacon can be microwaved to just the desired crispness. It is quick and easy and there is no pan to scrub.

Snacks and appetizers can be heated in seconds, often on serving plates. It is easy to serve a variety of these foods, and there is little washing up to do later.

Fish is microwaved to perfection, retaining moisture and flavour. It can be steamed to just the right texture with little extra liquid.

Chicken pieces remain tender and juicy and are ready to serve quickly. A variety of coatings (see page 70) can be used to make the chicken look appetizing and to increase its flavour.

Casseroles can be reheated and served in the same dish and the flavour and texture will be just as good as when first cooked.

Meat loaf can be taken from the freezer, defrosted and cooked in the microwave in just over half an hour.

Leftovers can be reheated with no loss of texture or flavour. They stay moist and taste freshly cooked. Meat and rice can be reheated without overcooking.

Vegetables retain their bright colour and crisp, fresh texture when microwaved according to the chart on page 94.

Potatoes baked in the microwave for 4 to 5 minutes each, come out tender and moist.

Custards and puddings need only occasional stirring in the microwave. They cook smooth and creamy and can be made and chilled in the same dish.

Hot fruit desserts require less liquid to cook, so fruits retain their natural juices and flavours.

Chocolate can be melted in a glass measuring cup with very little danger of scorching or overcooking. Washing up is easy too.

Upside-down cake takes just minutes to bake in the microwave, and can be prepared just before serving.

Coffee cake is another quickly and easily baked cake that has excellent flavour and texture.

Sweets that used to take constant stirring are simple to make in the microwave oven and the flavour is the same.

Preserves retain the colour and flavour of the fruit when made in the microwave, and there is no sticking or burning.

Fish, vegetables and casseroles microwave exceptionally well

Foods that do not microwave well

There are some foods that should not be cooked in the microwave oven, either because the results are not good, or because conventional cooking is more efficient. For example, large food loads, such as a 10 kg/22 lb turkey or a dozen potatoes, will cook more efficiently in a conventional oven.

Eggs in shells should not be cooked in the microwave as they may burst. Do not attempt to heat hard-boiled eggs in their shells.

Deep-frying should not be attempted in the microwave oven, as it is difficult to control the temperature of the fat and food may burn.

Grilled toppings become bubbly, but will not become crusty and brown in the microwave.

Pasta and rice need time to absorb moisture and become tender and, as they take almost as long to cook in the microwave, it may be better to cook these conventionally.

Pastry does not crisp or brown well. Puff pastry, which needs dry heat to crisp, rises in the microwave but falls when removed. Meats, such as sausages, wrapped in pastry do not brown. The pastry or dough coating becomes soggy because it absorbs moisture from the meat.

Batter recipes such as pancakes, crêpes and Yorkshire puddings need conventional cooking to form a crust and become crisp.

Conventional meringues should be cooked by conventional methods. However, for meringues cooked in a microwave, see page 138.

Bottling requires a long period of high temperature and is better done conventionally.

Factors affecting cooking times

Several factors influence the timing and results of foods cooked in the microwave. Knowing what these factors are and how they affect the foods will help you make the most of your microwave.

Piece size: In microwave as in conventional cooking, small pieces of food cook faster than large ones. Microwaves penetrate the food to a depth of 2 to 4 cm/^{3}/$_4$–1^1/$_2$ inches and will cook small pieces quickly from all sides. When cooking a variety of foods together, such as in casseroles, pieces should be of similar size so that all the ingredients will be cooked at the same time.

Shape of food: When foods are uneven in shape, the thin portions will cook more quickly than the thick or wide parts. Arrange foods such as chicken portions, chops or courgettes and cauliflower so that the larger part of each piece is on the outside edge of the dish or pan where the microwaves penetrate first.

Density: Heavy foods, such as fruit cake or potatoes, take longer to microwave than light, airy ones like sponge cake, because microwaves do not penetrate as deeply into heavier foods. The centre of dense food is cooked by conduction of heat from the hot outer surfaces. For example, a solid piece of beef is denser than minced meat, so a meat loaf will cook more quickly than a roast. Dense foods hold the heat longer than porous foods, and standing time will allow such foods as a joint or baked potato to continue cooking after it has been taken out of the oven.

Quantity of food: Small amounts cook faster than large ones. The amount of time food should spend in the oven is directly related to the amount of food placed there. When doubling the amount of food, increase the cooking time by one third to one half, but always check whether it is ready after the shortest estimated time. When reducing the amount of food by half, reduce the cooking time by less than half. It is better to underestimate the cooking time as foods can be returned to the oven to finish cooking.

Starting temperature of food: Foods taken from the refrigerator take longer to cook than those kept at room temperature, and less time to cook than frozen foods. Even room temperature varies, and cooking times may need to be increased slightly on a cold winter's day.

Height of food in oven: In microwave as in conventional cooking, areas of food that are closest to the energy source cook faster. It is important to turn or shield foods which are higher than 10 to 12 cm/4 to 5 inches.

Same-sized pieces cook more evenly

Place thicker parts towards the outside where microwaves penetrate first

Composition of food: Foods such as cheese, eggs, cream, mushrooms, and others with a high ratio of water, fat or sugar can easily be overcooked in the microwave oven. These foods should always be cooked for the minimum amount of time and watched closely during cooking. They are often microwaved on low power levels in ovens with variable power. Foods such as slices of cheese cooked with other foods should be covered with other ingredients or sauce to prevent overcooking. Always add the minimum amount of liquid when microwaving vegetables, as the microwaves are attracted to the water rather than to the food and the more liquid there is, the slower the cooking time. Foods very low in moisture or fat content do not microwave well.

Shape of container: Since microwaves penetrate foods about 2 to 4 cm/^{3}/$_4$– 1^1/$_2$ inches from the top, bottom and sides, round containers or ring shapes allow the food to cook evenly. With square or rectangular shapes, the edges or corners may overcook. Ring shapes allow the centre of cakes or puddings to cook at the same rate as the outside edges. A straight-sided container is better than one with curved sides, as microwaves can penetrate more evenly. A large shallow dish is better than a small deep one, as the food layer is not so thick, and a greater surface area is offered for the microwaves to penetrate.

How to check whether food is ready

The major difference between conventional recipes and microwave recipes is the cooking time. The appearance of some foods cooked in the microwave differs from that of foods cooked conventionally, but many of the methods used for checking whether the food is done remain the same. Personal preference will decide the readiness of some foods, so cooking times will have to be adjusted accordingly. It is important to learn when to remove the food from the oven. Some foods must be removed while they look only partly cooked, as they will finish cooking during the standing time. Always undercook until you learn to judge accurately cooking times in your microwave, and become familiar with how the food should look.

Cakes and sponge puddings are done when a toothpick or skewer inserted in the centre comes out clean. Moist spots on the surface of the cake or pudding will dry during the standing time. Timing is very important with cakes and puddings, as overcooking will cause the outer edges to become hard and dry. Check whether cakes or puddings are done at the minimum suggested time.

Shortcrust pastries should be flaky, and the base should be dry and opaque. The pastry will not turn golden brown although a few brown spots may appear.

Custards and quiches should appear soft in the centre. A knife inserted halfway between the centre and the outer edge should come out clean. The centre will set during the standing time.

Reheated meals on plates are hot enough to serve when the base of the plate feels warm all over.

Vegetables should be fork-tender but not mushy because they continue to cook during the standing time.

A baked potato is heated through in 4 to 5 minutes, but if cut in half reveals an uncooked centre. The potato will finish cooking during standing time, and stay hot enough to serve for up to half an hour if wrapped in aluminium foil after cooking. This factor is a great help when planning menus.

Meat should be fork-tender when done. Less tender cuts should split at the fibres when tested with a fork. A temperature probe is one way of insuring meat is done as desired, but remember meat continues to cook during standing time. Only special microwave meat thermometers can be used in the microwave oven during cooking, but a conventional meat thermometer can be inserted to check the temperature after the joint has been removed from the oven.

Whole chicken feels soft when pinched and the leg moves easily at the joint. The juices should run clear with no trace of pink. During standing time, cover the chicken with a tent of aluminium foil, shiny side in, to keep in the heat.

Fish flakes easily with a fork when it is cooked. The centre of a piece of fish may be slightly translucent, but will finish cooking during standing time. Fish becomes tough and dry if overcooked.

Shellfish turn pink and opaque when cooked. To avoid toughening, undercook slightly and let stand.

Using a combination of microwave and conventional cooking

Many foods can be quickly and easily prepared by using a combination of microwave and conventional cooking. Use the microwave for its speed and conventional cooking for browning or baking. Remember to use a dish suitable for microwaving if you are cooking in both the conventional and the microwave oven.

- For toasted sandwiches, toast bread conventionally, then place the sandwiches in the microwave to heat fillings and melt cheese.
- Brown meats on a conventional stove top, then finish cooking in the microwave but reduce the cooking time by a quarter to a half.
- Make pancakes or crêpes conventionally, but heat fillings and toppings in the microwave.
- Partially cook chicken pieces or ribs in the microwave, and then finish cooking them on a barbecue.
- Bake double-crust pies conventionally, and reheat or defrost in the microwave oven.
- Prove yeast doughs in the microwave oven and bake conventionally for a crusty loaf.
- Bake a flan or quiche case conventionally, then add the filling and use the microwave to cook it quickly.

Combination ovens: In some microwave models it is possible to cook by microwave energy or by conventional power in the same oven although not, of course, at the same time. Conventional cooking for part of the period and microwave cooking for part of the time will give results that are similar to conventionally cooked dishes, but in a shorter time. The conventional oven in these models usually has a fan to distribute the heat and aid cooking.

Cauliflower cheese (p. 101) cooks to perfection in the microwave oven

Converting conventional recipes to microwave

Many of your favourite recipes can be adapted to microwave cooking with few changes other than shortening the cooking time. However, it is wise to understand microwave cooking thoroughly before attempting to convert conventional recipes. Study each recipe to determine whether it is suitable for microwave cooking. It is best to start with a familiar recipe because if you already know what the food should look and taste like, the conversion to microwave cooking will be easier. Look for cooking methods that are similar to both conventional cooking and microwaving, such as steaming and poaching. Also check the list of foods that microwave well (page 18) and those that should not be microwaved (page 19) before deciding to prepare a conventional recipe in the microwave oven. For example, if foods should have a crisp, fried crust, or a very dry surface, they are better prepared by conventional cooking.

You will want to experiment as you learn to use your microwave oven, adjusting cooking times, seasoning and methods to suit your tastes. It is important to select foods that microwave well and look for cooking methods that are successful in the microwave, such as:

Roasting meat or poultry is so easy in the microwave. Place the meat on a rack in the microwave, cover if moist heat is desired, and microwave on medium or full power until done.

Braising and stewing can be done in the microwave. Meat pieces are not browned first, and cooking liquid is reduced. The microwave dish should be covered and the power level set for the type of food to be cooked.

Poaching is a pleasure in the microwave, as foods cook with less liquid than in conventional cooking and retain good texture and flavour. Reduce the poaching liquid and cover the dish. The power level will depend on the type of food cooked.

Steaming may be done by placing foods in a tightly covered dish with very little water. If cling film is used as a cover, make two slashes in it with a sharp knife to prevent 'ballooning'.

Stir-frying can be done in a browning dish. Preheat the dish, add a little oil or fat, then the food and stir it every two minutes during cooking time.

Frying can be simulated by the use of a browning dish. Preheating the dish, then adding a small amount of fat or

SAMPLE RECIPE CONVERSION

Banana and passion fruit slice

Crust
100 g/3½ oz blanched almonds, chopped
65 g/2½ coconut
3 tbsp sugar
90 g/3 oz margarine

1. Toast in microwave (see page 23)

2. Combine, rub in margarine, pack half into loaf pan. Microwave on full power for 2 minutes. Cool.

Filling
2 tbsp water
1 tbsp gelatine
400 ml/14 fl oz plain yoghurt
3 tbsp honey
2 passion fruit
2 egg whites
2 bananas, sliced

3. Combine, stand for a few minutes, microwave on medium for 1 minute.

4. Combine and continue according to recipe instructions.

To make the crust, combine almonds, coconut and sugar, and rub in margarine. Press half the crust into a lined and greased 25 × 13 cm/10 × 5-inch loaf pan. Bake at 160°C/325°F, Gas Mark 3 for 15 minutes. Allow to cool. Place remaining crumb mixture onto a baking sheet, place in the oven for 8–10 minutes, until golden brown. Cool and reserve.

To make the filling, place water and gelatine in a heatproof jug, and allow to stand for a couple of minutes. Stand gelatine mixture in a pan with 2.5 cm/1 inch of boiling water, stir until dissolved. Combine yoghurt and honey, add passion fruit pulp. Beat egg whites until stiff. Stir dissolved gelatine into yoghurt, then fold in egg whites. Arrange bananas on the crust and pour yoghurt mixture over. Sprinkle with remaining crumb mixture. Chill for 4 hours. Turn out and cut into squares or slices.
Serves 8

oil, will give a nicely browned surface to many foods.

Sautéing can be done by heating a small amount of fat or oil, then adding food and cooking it for the required time. The food will not brown as in cooker-top cooking.

Baking many foods is successful in the microwave. See the chapter on baking for specific information. Some baked foods, such as angel or chiffon cakes and sheet cakes, puff or choux pastries, double-crust pies and some yeast breads are not suitable for microwave cooking.

The following guidelines will give you a good start on converting your own recipes to microwave cooking:

- In general, foods cook in about a quarter to a third of the time required for conventional cooking. Microwave ovens vary in speed and evenness of cooking, so always underestimate the cooking time and test whether foods are ready at the minimum time. Remember that foods continue to cook after removal from the microwave, so allow for standing time.
- Watch the cooking process closely and check the food often. If the food seems to be cooking unevenly, stir, rearrange or rotate it.
- Reduce the amount of herbs and spices used, especially strongly flavoured ones, as they keep their flavouring power in the microwave. For many casseroles and meat dishes the seasoning can be added near the end of the cooking time.
- Select containers that are larger than those used in conventional recipes and fill one third to one half full, as foods tend to rise higher and increase in volume in the microwave.
- As a general rule, use less liquid when cooking vegetables, stews and casseroles. Watch the dish and add a little more liquid if necessary during the cooking time.
- Converting recipes containing raw pasta or rice can be difficult. These ingredients need time to absorb moisture and become tender, so other ingredients may cook much more rapidly in the microwave, and you may find that when the meat or vegetables are cooked, the pasta or rice is still too raw to serve.
- Some changes may be needed in piece size of ingredients. Pieces of a uniform size cook evenly, and small pieces cook more rapidly than large ones.

Improving the appearance of microwaved foods

Food cooked in a microwave oven does not brown to the same degree as food cooked conventionally. Glazes, coatings, icings and garnishes help to improve the appearance of the food.

Cakes do not brown as they do in a conventional oven. Cakes and bars are usually iced before serving, so the difference in appearance is not noticeable. If no icing is used, there are several toppings that improve the appearance. A mixture of cinnamon and sugar, toasted coconut or chopped nuts, or a blend of soft brown sugar and nuts can be sprinkled on top of the cake or loaf before microwaving or after part of the cooking time. Sifted icing sugar on top of a baked cake also looks good.

Breads can be brushed with beaten egg or milk and sprinkled with seeds, bran or wheat germ before microwaving to give good colour to the finished product. Breads can also be browned under the grill for a few minutes, but be sure the container will withstand the heat. Many of the recipes in the chapter on baking include toppings which add both colour and flavour.

Meat cooked in small portions does not brown in the microwave oven because of the rapid cooking time, although larger roasts and whole poultry develop some natural colour when microwaved for longer than about 25 minutes. Soy sauce or Worcestershire sauce, dry onion soup, herbs, or beef stock powder brushed on before microwaving improve the appearance of beef, lamb and pork. Microwaved meats basted with a marinade during cooking or served with a sauce also have a better appearance and flavour.

Chicken can be brushed with melted butter and sprinkled with herbs, paprika, dry onion soup or chicken stock powder before microwaving, or small portions can be coated with egg and crumbs to develop a 'crust' during cooking. Soy sauce, Worcestershire sauce or barbecue sauce are useful coatings for poultry that needs extra colour.

Ham and poultry can be successfully glazed with fruit preserves or marmalade to add colour and flavour to the dish.

Casseroles can be topped with crushed potato crisps, buttered breadcrumbs, grated cheese or crumbled cooked bacon to give an attractive finish.

Clockwise from the bottom: plain microwaved cake, topped with toasted almonds (p. 23), streusel mixture (p. 122), cherry pie filling, icing sugar and chocolate icing

The following chart gives useful ideas for improving the appearance of many microwaved foods:

BROWNING AGENT CHART

AGENT	FOODS	METHOD
Soy sauce	Hamburgers, beef, lamb, pork, poultry and sausages	Brush onto meat or poultry, or add to marinades
Melted butter and paprika	Poultry and fish	Brush food with butter, sprinkle with paprika
Worcestershire sauce	Hamburgers, beef, lamb and pork	Brush on or add to marinade
Brown onion soup powder	Hamburgers, beef and lamb	Sprinkle on before microwaving
Barbecue sauce and steak sauce	Hamburgers, beef, lamb, poultry and sausages	Brush on or add to marinade
Bacon strips	Hamburgers, beef, lamb and poultry	Lay on food, which browns under bacon as it cooks
Streusel topping	Cakes and puddings	Sprinkle on before microwaving
Biscuit crumbs, cinnamon sugar or nuts	Cakes and puddings	Sprinkle on before microwaving
Wheat germ, oatmeal, crushed cereal, sesame or poppy seeds	Bread and rolls	Brush food with milk, then roll in topping
Breadcrumbs	Scones and casseroles	Brush scones with melted butter, sprinkle with crumbs. Combine crumbs with a little butter, sprinkle onto casseroles

Special uses for the microwave

- Individual meals can be heated on the serving plate. Family members who arrive late for a meal can still have appetizing food.
- Blanching vegetables for the freezer takes seconds in the microwave, and colour, texture and flavour are retained (see page 54).
- To eliminate a soggy top on an individual meat pie, cut a small piece of foil the same size as the pie and place it, shiny side up, on the bottom of the microwave oven. Cover with paper towel. Place pie upside down on the paper towel and microwave on full power for 3 to 4 minutes if frozen, or 1 to 2 minutes if thawed.
- To blanch almonds, microwave 250 ml/8 fl oz water for about 2½ minutes on full power, until it is boiling. Add the almonds and microwave for 30 seconds. Drain, then slip the skins off.
- To toast almonds, place the flaked or blanched nuts in a browning dish and microwave on full power for 4 to 5 minutes, stirring every minute.
- To soften jams and jellies to a spreading consistency, microwave on full power for 3 seconds per 250 ml/8 fl oz.
- Heat brandy for flambéing desserts or meats by microwaving on full power for about 15 seconds. Pour over the food and ignite.
- Place chocolate to be melted in an ovenproof glass bowl. To obtain a dipping consistency, microwave on defrost for about 2½ minutes per 30 g/1 oz. For general purposes, microwave on full power for 30 to 45 seconds per 30 g/1 oz.
- To shell pecans or walnuts, place the nuts in a glass bowl, add about 4 tbsp water, cover and microwave on full power for 1 to 2 minutes. Dry before shelling.
- Toast coconut by evenly spreading 125 g/4 oz desiccated coconut on a paper plate. Microwave on full power for 5 to 6 minutes, stirring every minute.
- For warm finger-towels, wet face cloths with water and lemon juice, wring out and roll up. Place in a wicker basket and microwave on full power for about 2 minutes.
- To plump raisins and dried fruit, heat 250 ml/8 fl oz water on full power for 2 to 3 minutes, then add dried fruit. Stand for a few minutes.

To improve their appearance, meats can be brushed with soy sauce or sprinkled with brown onion soup mix. Casseroles can be topped with crushed potato crisps and grated cheese

- To peel tomatoes, place them in a circle on paper towel in the microwave oven and microwave on full power for 10 to 15 seconds. Stand for about 5 minutes, then peel.
- To marinate meats quickly, microwave the marinade on high for 1 or 2 minutes, then pour it over the meat.

- To soften hard brown sugar, place 180 g/6 oz sugar in a glass dish. Add a slice of white bread or a wedge of apple, cover and microwave on full power for about 25 seconds. Stand for several minutes.
- To obtain all the juice from fresh citrus fruits, prick the skin lightly and warm in the microwave for a few seconds.

23

- For barbecued chicken, cook the chicken pieces in the microwave until partially done, then finish on the barbecue. Brush them with sauce or marinade during cooking.
- To reheat cold fruit pie, place a slice on a serving plate and cover with paper towel. Microwave on full power for a few seconds.
- To dry lemon or orange rind, place on a glass pie plate and microwave on full power until all moisture is gone. Crumble and store in an airtight container.
- Heat ice-cream toppings or sauces in a wide-mouthed glass jar without a lid on full power for 30 to 45 seconds.
- To separate bacon slices easily, microwave on full power for a few seconds. Do not microwave foil packets.
- To peel peaches, place a small amount of water in the bottom of a glass dish. Prick the peach skins, place the peaches in the bowl, cover and steam for 1 to 1½ minutes on high. Stand for 5 minutes, then peel.
- To make a quick glaze for ham or carrots, combine 150 g/5 oz brown sugar with 2 teasp dry mustard and 3 tbsp red wine in a glass measuring jug. Microwave on full power for 1½ to 2 minutes, then stir well.
- Dry a damp newspaper by microwaving on full power for about 15 to 20 seconds.
- To dry herbs, place 250 ml/8 fl oz fresh herbs between layers of paper towel on a paper plate. Microwave on full power for 4 to 6 minutes until dry and brittle, rearranging the herbs halfway through the cooking time. Cool between the layers of paper towel, then crush the leaves and store in an airtight container.
- To clarify sugared honey, remove the lid and microwave the jar on full power for 1 to 2 minutes. Stir well.
- To remove the last of the tomato sauce from the bottle, add a little orange juice, butter and wine. Microwave, without a lid, on full power for 2 minutes. Use for gravies or sauces.
- To warm a baby's bottle, invert the nipple, then microwave on full power for 1 minute. Make sure that no metal lids are used.
- To freshen soggy crisps, pretzels or savoury biscuits, microwave on full power for 10 to 30 seconds. Stand for 1 minute.

How to use this book

Power levels

All the recipes in this book have been tested using microwave ovens with variable power levels. Each level serves a definite purpose, and recommended power levels should be used if possible. If your oven does not have the recommended settings, you may not achieve the same results, although some foods may be microwaved at a higher power than recommended as long as additional attention is given to stirring, turning or rotating them. Foods that require slow simmering or delicate dishes should not be attempted at high power settings.

The following chart gives the percentage of power at the various levels used in the recipes in this book. Consult your instruction book for similar power levels for your microwave oven.

Power level	Percentage of power used
Full power	100%
High	70%
Medium	50%
Defrost	25-30%
Low	15-20%

Full power is used to cook foods at a high temperature in a short time. The full power setting is used in many of the recipes given.

High power setting is used for foods that require more attention than those cooked at full power.

Medium power is used for slower cooking, such as when microwaving some sauces and meats.

Defrost is used not only to defrost foods, but also to cook delicate foods or dishes that need long, slow simmering.

Low power is used for extremely gentle cooking and for keeping foods warm before serving.

Hold setting: Some microwave ovens have a hold setting for use with the temperature probe. It is used to

Measures
Quantities for all recipes are given in both metric and imperial measures. Follow one set of measurements only. Standard spoon measurements are used throughout – i.e. 15 ml tablespoon [tbsp] and 5 ml teaspoon [teasp]. All spoon measures must be level. For further information on Metric and Imperial measures and conversion tables see page 147.

Cooking times

The cooking times given for all recipes in this book are intended merely as a guide, since the amount of microwave energy required will differ according to the make of oven used, the size and type of container used, the food load, the temperature of the food before cooking, the depth of food in the container, and personal preferences where such foods as meats, poultry and casseroles are concerned.

Adapting recipe times

All the recipes in this book have been tested in microwave ovens with an output of 600 to 650 watts. Household current often varies from one part of the country to another and during periods of peak use such as early evening or in very cold weather. Always check food at the minimum cooking time to see whether it is done, then add more time if necessary.

If you are uncertain about the household current in your area, or if you wish to use the recipes in this book with microwave ovens of different wattage, you can check the timing and make adjustments to the recipe. To check that the timing is correct, pour 250 ml/8 fl oz iced water into a glass measuring jug. Place in the microwave oven and microwave on full power until the water reaches a good boil. Time the action carefully. If your oven takes 3¼ to 3¾ minutes, the recipes in this book should be correct for you. If your microwave oven takes considerably longer, add extra time to the cooking period, and if the water boils in less time, decrease the cooking time.

As a general rule, if you have a 500 watt microwave oven, add approximately 20 seconds to each minute of cooking time. If you have a 700 watt microwave, decrease the cooking time by about 15 seconds per minute.

Always check foods at the minimum suggested time

Breakfast

Traffic in your kitchen during the morning 'rush hour' can be kept to a minimum when the microwave is used to cook breakfasts. Eggs and egg dishes cook quickly with very little cleaning up for the cook. Hot beverages are almost instant and cooked cereals can be prepared either in one large dish or individually in serving bowls. Microwave cooking is ideal for weekend brunches too. The hostess can spend most of her time relaxing with her guests as she knows that each dish she plans to serve will be cooked or heated quickly and effortlessly. It is important to remember that because both egg and cheese dishes take a short time to microwave, care should be taken not to overcook them.

Microwaving eggs, cheese and cereals

Eggs are so versatile they can be prepared in a number of ways in the microwave oven. When frying, poaching or scrambling, it is important to remember that eggs are very delicate and will toughen when overcooked. Because the yolk of an egg contains more fat than the white, it will attract more microwave energy. If the egg is microwaved until the white is completely set, the yolk will then be overcooked. The times given in this chapter are to be used as a guideline only. Although personal preferences should be taken into consideration, always check eggs at the minimum cooking time. Remember that eggs continue to cook after being removed from the oven, so allow for standing time to complete the cooking process. When poaching or frying eggs in the microwave, always puncture the yolk membrane with a sharp skewer or toothpick to prevent it bursting during cooking. Do not try to cook an egg in its shell in the microwave as it expands during cooking and bursts the shell.

Cheese reacts to microwaving much as it does to conventional cooking, but faster because the high fat content attracts microwave energy and the cheese melts very quickly. When overcooked, cheese may become stringy and toughen, so check cheese dishes at the minimum suggested time. Processed cheese melts more smoothly than natural cheese, and very finely grated cheese added to casseroles or sauces takes only seconds to melt in the microwave. Some of the cheese dishes in this chapter also make good snacks, appetizers or even supper dishes.

Cereals and porridge are easily cooked in the microwave as it is not necessary to boil the water first, nor to stir constantly during cooking. Washing up is also easy as the cereals do not stick to the cooking dish. Personal preferences can always be accommodated as family members can microwave their favourite hot cereal in individual portions.

Microwaving breakfast cereals is a simple process. Mix the uncooked cereal with hot tap water in a container large enough to prevent the mixture boiling over. Microwave on full power, uncovered. Stir mixture halfway through the cooking time and, at the end of the time, let cereal stand a few minutes if desired.

Raisins, sultanas or currants can be stirred into the mixture before the last minute of cooking time. Other flavourings, such as fresh fruit, honey, butter, jam or marmalade, can be stirred into the mixture at the end of the cooking time, but before standing time.

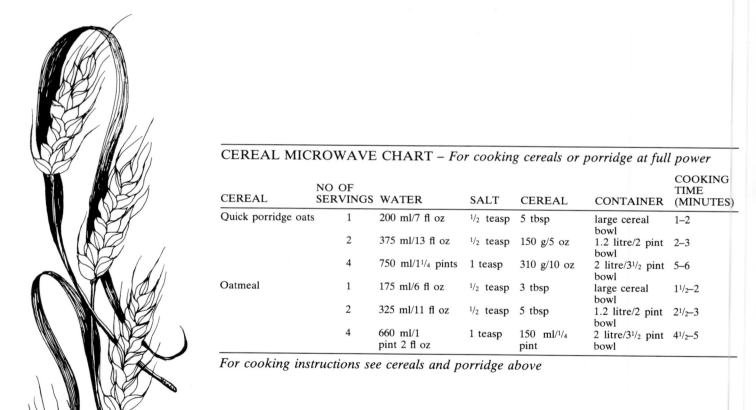

CEREAL MICROWAVE CHART – *For cooking cereals or porridge at full power*

CEREAL	NO OF SERVINGS	WATER	SALT	CEREAL	CONTAINER	COOKING TIME (MINUTES)
Quick porridge oats	1	200 ml/7 fl oz	½ teasp	5 tbsp	large cereal bowl	1–2
	2	375 ml/13 fl oz	½ teasp	150 g/5 oz	1.2 litre/2 pint bowl	2–3
	4	750 ml/1¼ pints	1 teasp	310 g/10 oz	2 litre/3½ pint bowl	5–6
Oatmeal	1	175 ml/6 fl oz	½ teasp	3 tbsp	large cereal bowl	1½–2
	2	325 ml/11 fl oz	½ teasp	5 tbsp	1.2 litre/2 pint bowl	2½–3
	4	660 ml/1 pint 2 fl oz	1 teasp	150 ml/¼ pint	2 litre/3½ pint bowl	4½–5

For cooking instructions see cereals and porridge above

Baked grapefruit and French toast (p. 34) with golden jelly marmalade (p. 142)

Breakfast fruit compote

Serve warm or cold

full power
5 minutes

1 (411-g/14½-oz) can apricot halves
4 tbsp water
4 whole cloves
1 cinnamon stick
2 oranges, peeled and segmented
250 g/8 oz strawberries, sliced
2 (2-cm/¾ inch) slices pineapple, cut into chunks

Drain apricots, reserving syrup. Combine syrup, water, cloves and cinnamon in a 1-litre/1¾-pint casserole dish, cover and microwave on full power for 3 minutes. Cut apricots in half and add to hot syrup. Microwave for 2 minutes more. Then let stand at room temperature until lukewarm. Add remaining fruit and chill if desired.

Serves 4 – 6

Baked grapefruit

full power
3 minutes

1 large grapefruit
2 tbsp apple juice
2 tbsp brown sugar
pinch cinnamon

Cut the grapefruit in half, remove pips and cut around each section to loosen. Place halves in individual bowls and spoon the apple juice over. Mix sugar and cinnamon together and sprinkle on top of the grapefruit halves. Microwave on full power for 2 – 3 minutes. Serve immediately. If necessary, rotate grapefruit halves a quarter turn after half the cooking time has elapsed.

Serves 2

VARIATION
For a delicious starter to a special brunch, replace apple juice with sherry or white rum.

Oatmeal with peachy sauce

Peachy sauce for porridge

full power
5 minutes

1 (425 g/15 oz) can peach slices
2 tbsp brown sugar
2 teasp cornflour
pinch of ground cinnamon
pinch of ground allspice
pinch of salt
120 ml/4 fl oz orange juice
6 glacé cherries, chopped

Drain peaches, reserving syrup, then chop coarsely and set
aside. Combine sugar, cornflour, ground cinnamon,
ground allspice and salt in a 1-litre/1³/₄-pint bowl. Stir in
orange juice and reserved syrup. Microwave, uncovered,
on full power for 2 minutes. Microwave for 3 minutes
longer, stirring after each minute. Add chopped peaches
and cherries. Spoon over hot oatmeal porridge.

Serves 4

Homemade yoghurt

full power
low
1¼ hours

600 ml/1 pint milk
1 tbsp plain yoghurt
2 tbsp dried full-cream milk powder

Pour the milk into a large bowl. Cover with cling film and
make two slits in the film to prevent 'ballooning' during
cooking. Microwave for 6 minutes on full power. Uncover
and cool over a bowl of cold water until warm to the
touch (about 46°C/115°F). Add the yoghurt and the milk
powder, and whisk to combine. Cover once more.
Microwave on low for 70 minutes. Cool and refrigerate.

Makes 600 ml/1 pint

Creamy yoghurt

low
1½ hours

90 g/3 oz skim milk powder
675 ml/1 pint 2½ fl oz warm water
175 ml/6 fl oz evaporated milk
2 teasp brown sugar
3 tbsp plain yoghurt

Combine skim milk powder and warm water in a large
bowl. Add remaining ingredients and mix well. Cover with
cling film, and make two holes in the film to prevent
'ballooning' during cooking. Microwave on low for 1¹/₂
hours. Cool, then refrigerate.

Makes approximately 900 ml/1¹/₂ pints

Shirred eggs

Use individual glass ramekins or soufflé dishes to make
perfect shirred eggs. Serve in the bowls in which they were
cooked or turn out onto hot toast

full power
medium
2½ minutes

2 teasp butter or margarine
2 eggs
salt and pepper to taste

Place 1 teasp butter in each small dish and place the dishes
on an ovenproof plate. Microwave on full power for about
30 seconds. Break 1 egg into each dish and gently pierce
yolk. Cover and cook on medium for 1½ – 2 minutes,
depending on how well done you like your eggs. Serve
shirred eggs in glass ramekins or invert onto hot toast or
toasted muffins.

Serves 2

Note: To increase the number of servings, increase the
cooking time by 45 – 60 seconds per egg. If no turntable is
used, rotate the plate half a turn halfway through the
cooking time.

Creamy yoghurt is easily made in the microwave

Poached eggs

It is easy to poach eggs in the microwave. Poach individual eggs in glass ramekins, or several eggs at a time in a casserole dish

full power
1½ minutes

For 1 or 2 eggs
4 tbsp hot water for each
½ teasp white vinegar for each

Pour water into individual ramekins and add vinegar. Microwave on full power for 1 minute or until boiling. Carefully break egg into boiling water and prick egg yolk twice with a skewer. Cover with greaseproof paper and microwave on full power for 30 seconds. Stand in liquid for about 2 minutes. For firmer eggs, stand longer.

full power
or medium
8 minutes

For 3 or 4 eggs

Proceed as above with individual ramekins. The timing for boiling the water will be 3½ – 4 minutes. The timing for cooking the eggs is about 30 seconds per egg.

To poach 3 or 4 eggs in a casserole dish heat 600 ml/ 1 pint water and 1 teasp white vinegar to boiling by microwaving on full power for 5–6 minutes. Break eggs, one at a time, into a small bowl. Pierce the membrane of the yolk with a skewer twice, then tip gently into the boiling water. Cover and microwave on medium for 45 seconds per egg. Stand in liquid to become firm.

Fried eggs

full power
4 minutes

These sunny-side-up eggs are microwaved in a browning dish

4 teasp butter or margarine
2 eggs
salt and pepper to taste
a little chopped parsley

Preheat a browning dish on full power for 2 – 3 minutes. Add butter to dish and allow to melt. Tilt dish to coat evenly with melted butter. Break eggs into dish and very gently pierce yolks with a needle or thin skewer. Season to taste. Cover and cook on full power for 30 – 60 seconds, depending on how well done you like your eggs. Serve sprinkled with a little chopped parsley.

Serves 2

Scrambled eggs

Eggs can be scrambled in a glass measuring jug or casserole dish

full power

For 1 – 3 eggs
1 teasp butter per egg
1 tbsp milk per egg
salt and pepper to taste

Melt the butter in the measuring jug on full power for 30 seconds or until melted. Add eggs and milk and beat well. Season to taste. Microwave on full power for about 45 seconds per egg, stirring after every minute (after 25 seconds if only one egg is being cooked). Eggs should be very moist when removed from the oven, as they will continue to cook when left to stand. Let eggs stand for 1 – 1½ minutes before serving.

For 4 – 8 eggs
Using a larger container, follow the above instructions, but increase cooking times as follows:

4 eggs on full power   2½ – 3¼ minutes
6 eggs on full power   3½ – 4¼ minutes
8 eggs on full power   4½ – 5¼ minutes

VARIATION
Creamy scrambled eggs. Add 4 tbsp soured cream and ½ teasp freshly chopped dill for every four eggs in the recipe for scrambled eggs.

Puffy omelette with mushroom filling

Puffy omelette

full power
medium
9 minutes

3 eggs, separated
3 tbsp mayonnaise
2 tbsp water
salt and pepper to taste
2 tbsp butter

Beat egg whites until soft peaks form. In a separate bowl, beat egg yolks, mayonnaise, water and seasonings. Gently pour yolk mixture over beaten whites and fold in. Place the butter in a 20-cm/8-inch glass pie dish and microwave on full power for 1 minute. Swirl melted butter to coat the dish. Gently pour in egg mixture and spread evenly in the dish. Microwave on medium for 6–8 minutes, rotating dish if necessary, until mixture is set but still glossy on top. Let set 30 seconds to 1 minute, then run a spatula around sides of dish. Fold half of the omelette over and gently slide onto a serving plate.

Serves 1 – 2

Chicken sauce for puffy omelette

full power
5 minutes

1 tbsp butter or margarine
1 tbsp plain flour
salt and pepper to taste
200 ml/7 fl oz single cream
210 g/7 oz cooked chicken
2 teasp chopped chives
1 teasp chopped dill
2 teasp chopped parsley
1 tbsp chopped green pepper
2 tbsp flaked almonds, toasted (see p. 23)

Microwave butter on full power in a glass measuring jug or bowl for 30 – 45 seconds. Stir in flour, salt and pepper. Add cream, mixing well. Microwave, uncovered, on full power for 2½ minutes, or until thickened and bubbly, stirring every minute. Add remaining ingredients and microwave on full power for about 2 minutes, or until heated through, stirring every minute. Spoon a little chicken sauce over half the cooked omelette, fold top over and slide gently onto a plate. Spoon more chicken sauce over, and serve immediately.

Serves 3 – 4

Cheese and chive omelette filling

full power
medium
30 seconds

60 g/2 oz Cheddar cheese, finely grated
2 teasp chopped chives

When omelette mixture is set, sprinkle with the cheese and microwave on medium for 30 seconds. Remove from oven, sprinkle with chives, fold omelette over and slide onto serving plate.

Serves 1 – 2

Mushroom omelette filling

full power
5 minutes

125 g/4 oz mushrooms, sliced
½ small onion, chopped
2 tbsp chopped parsley
3 tbsp chopped green pepper
1 tbsp oil
salt and pepper to taste

Combine all ingredients in a casserole dish, cover and microwave on full power for 3 – 5 minutes, or until vegetables are tender. Stir after half the time. Spoon filling over half the cooked omelette and fold omelette over. Slide gently onto serving plate.

Serves 2

Eggs benedict

Elegant and easy, both the eggs and the hollandaise sauce are cooked in the microwave

4 slices cooked ham
butter or margarine
4 muffins
175 ml/6 fl oz hollandaise sauce (see p. 51)
4 poached eggs (see p. 29)

Fry the cooked ham in a little butter or margarine until lightly browned on both sides. Split the muffins and toast. Spread with a little butter. Keep ham and muffins warm while making the hollandaise sauce. Keep sauce warm while cooking the eggs. To serve, place two muffin halves on each of four heated serving plates. Cover one muffin half with the cooked ham. Add one poached egg and spoon hollandaise sauce over. Serve immediately.

Serves 4

Cheese rarebit

A quick and delicious recipe to serve for brunch – or even supper

full power
medium
8 minutes

1 (180-g/6-oz) jar Cheddar cheese spread
1 tbsp butter
salt and pepper to taste
½ teasp dry mustard
½ teasp Worcestershire sauce
pinch of cayenne pepper
5 tbsp single cream
1 beaten egg yolk
hot toast
tomato wedges to garnish

Place cheese and butter in a casserole dish and microwave at full power for 2 – 3 minutes, stirring every minute until cheese has melted. Beat until smooth. Add salt and pepper, mustard, Worcestershire sauce and cayenne pepper and mix well. Stir in cream and egg yolk and microwave on medium for about 5 minutes, stirring every minute, until heated through. Serve over slices of toast and garnish with wedges of tomato.

Serves 2 – 3

VARIATIONS
Bacon rarebit: Stir in 3 tbsp cooked chopped bacon with the cream and egg yolk and continue as directed.
Chive rarebit. Stir in 2 tbsp chopped chives with the cream and egg yolk and continue as directed.
Egg rarebit: Stir in one chopped hard-boiled egg and 1 tbsp chopped parsley just before serving.

Mexican egg quiche

A crustless quiche to serve for a hearty breakfast or brunch

full power
16 minutes

2 tbsp butter
2 tbsp chopped green pepper
2 tbsp chopped onion
3 large button mushrooms, sliced
1 small tomato, peeled, seeded and chopped
5 eggs, lightly beaten
180 g/6 oz Cheddar cheese, grated
250 g/8 oz cottage cheese, well drained
4 tbsp plain flour
½ teasp baking powder
salt and pepper to taste

Melt butter on full power in a 23-cm/9-inch glass quiche dish for about 20 seconds. Add green pepper, onion, and mushrooms and microwave on full power for 20 seconds. Combine all other ingredients in a bowl, mixing well. Season to taste and add sautéed vegetables, mixing well. Turn the mixture into the quiche dish and microwave on high for 12 – 15 minutes, or until set. If necessary, rotate dish a quarter turn every 3 minutes.

Serves 4

Cheesy egg and vegetable ring

full power
11 minutes

150 g/5 oz cauliflower florets
150 g/5 oz broccoli pieces
3 tbsp chopped onion
2 tbsp butter or margarine
6 eggs
6 tbsp milk
1 tbsp grated Parmesan cheese
salt and pepper to taste
250 ml/8 fl oz cheese sauce (see p. 49)
parsley and tomatoes to garnish

Place vegetables and butter in a casserole dish, cover and microwave on full power for about 5 minutes, or until vegetables are just tender. Drain well and arrange vegetables in a greased ring mould. Combine eggs, milk, cheese, salt and pepper and beat well. Pour mixture over vegetables and microwave, uncovered, on full power for 4 – 6 minutes, or until almost set. Lift outer edges several times during the cooking to let uncooked mixture run under. Rotate if necessary. Let stand for 5–8 minutes.

To serve, turn out on a heated serving plate and pour half the cheese sauce over. Garnish with parsley and tomato wedges if desired, and serve with the remaining sauce.

Serves 4

Sausage and egg bake

full power
medium
18 minutes

250 g/8 oz pork or beef sausage meat, crumbled
1 bunch spring onions, diced
8 eggs
4 tbsp soured cream
4 tbsp milk
salt and pepper to taste
pinch of dry mustard
2 tbsp chopped parsley
100 g/3½ oz Swiss cheese, grated

Place crumbled sausage meat in a round baking dish and microwave, uncovered, on full power for 3 – 5 minutes, or until meat loses its pink colour. Stir once or twice during cooking. Drain meat well, set aside and keep warm. Place about 2 tbsp of the dripping in the baking dish. Add spring onions and microwave for 1 minute. Combine eggs, soured cream, milk, salt and pepper, mustard and chopped parsley in a bowl, mixing well. Pour over onion in the dish and microwave on full power for 5 – 7 minutes, or until eggs are almost set, stirring twice. Top the egg mixture with the sausage meat and sprinkle with grated cheese. Microwave on medium for 3 – 5 minutes just to melt cheese. Serve cut into wedges.

Serves 6

CHART FOR COOKING SAUSAGES

TYPE	QUANTITY	PREHEAT TIME FOR BROWNING DISH (Full power)	COOKING TIME (Full power)
Sausages	2	4–6 minutes	35–45 seconds on each side
	4	5–6 minutes	1–1½ minutes on each side
	8 (500 g/1 lb)	6–7 minutes	2 minutes on each side
Unlinked country sausage (boerewors)	1 piece 15 cm/6 inches long	4–5 minutes	35–45 seconds on each side
Country sausage links (Cumberland)	2	4–6 minutes	45–60 seconds on each side
	4	5–6 minutes	1½–2 minutes on each side

SAUSAGES AND BACON

Sausages microwaved in a browning dish look good and taste good. Let them stand for 2–3 minutes before serving.

Pork or beef sausages (500 g/1 lb)
Microwave a browning dish on full power for 5–6 minutes. Brush sausages lightly with soy or Worcestershire sauce, prick them and arrange on the dish, allowing a small space between each one. Cover with greaseproof paper or non-stick parchment to prevent spattering. Microwave for 2 minutes. Turn sausages over and microwave for a further 2 minutes.

Cumberland sausage and other country-style sausages (500 g/1 lb)
The method used to microwave country sausage is exactly the same as for pork sausage. Arrange country sausage in a circle in a browning dish. If cooking small pieces, arrange on the dish with a small space between each piece. Unless country sausage is extremely fatty, there is no necessity to prick it before microwaving.

Bacon
Bacon cooks very well in a microwave and there is less mess and shrinkage than if it is fried conventionally. A bacon rack is the ideal container for cooking bacon, as the fat drains off automatically. However, any flat, shallow dish will do. Drain bacon on paper towel before serving.

Place rashers of bacon, with or without rinds, on the rack. Cover with paper towel. Microwave on full power until cooked. Turn and rearrange bacon on rack to ensure even cooking.
To defrost bacon: Place a 250 g/8 oz packet of bacon on a plate. Microwave on defrost for 3–4 minutes. Turn packet over after half the cooking time. Stand for 5 minutes.
● Do not defrost bacon in foil-lined packets.

2 – 3 rashers	2 – 3 minutes
4 – 6 rashers	4 – 5 minutes
7 – 10 rashers	6 – 8 minutes

Cook slightly longer for very crisp bacon.

Farmer's breakfast

Farmer's breakfast

full power
24 minutes

4–6 rashers bacon, rind removed
salt and black pepper to taste
4 sheep's kidneys, cut in half
4 small pieces rump steak
4 large black mushrooms
2 tomatoes, sliced thickly
2 tbsp butter
4 eggs

Arrange rashers of bacon on a bacon rack. Microwave on full power for about 5 minutes, depending on size of rashers. Keep warm. Pour bacon fat into browning dish. Heat browning dish for 4 – 5 minutes. Season kidneys and steak lightly. Arrange steak and kidneys on dish, placing kidney on the inside. Microwave for 4 minutes, turning after 2 minutes. Microwave an extra 1 – 2 minutes if meat is preferred well done.

Brush mushrooms with a little of the dripping from the meat and season lightly. Season tomatoes, then arrange tomatoes and mushrooms on a plate. Microwave for 3 – 4 minutes. Keep warm.

Heat butter in a shallow casserole dish for 2 minutes. Carefully break eggs into dish. Pierce each yolk twice with the point of a skewer. Cover dish and microwave on full power for 2 minutes. Allow to stand for 1 minute. Microwave for approximately 1 minute more. The egg whites should be just set. Serve completed breakfast immediately.

Serves 4

Toasted cheese sandwich

Use a browning dish to 'toast' the bread

full power
7 minutes

2 slices wholewheat bread
a little French mustard
2 slices processed cheese
chopped spring onion or chives
1 slice cooked ham
butter or margarine

Spread one side of each slice of bread with a little mustard. Add 1 slice of cheese and sprinkle with a little chopped spring onion or chives. Add the ham and the remaining cheese. Top with remaining bread, mustard side down. Spread the outside of both slices with butter. Heat the browning dish on full power for 5 minutes. Place sandwich on browning dish. Flatten slightly and stand for about 25 seconds. Turn sandwich over and stand for 25 seconds. Microwave, uncovered, on full power for 30 – 45 seconds to melt the cheese. To make more than one sandwich at a time, increase time to 10 – 15 seconds per extra sandwich.

Serves 1

French toast

full power
6 minutes

2 eggs
3 tbsp milk
pinch of salt
few drops vanilla essence
90 g/3 oz butter
6 slices bread

Mix together eggs, milk, salt and vanilla. Preheat browning dish on full power for 4 minutes. Add a third of the butter and heat for 30 seconds. Dip two bread slices in egg mixture and microwave in browning dish on full power for 30 – 40 seconds. Turn slices and microwave for 15 – 25 seconds. Serve topped with golden syrup or jam and cream. Repeat process with remaining bread slices, adding more butter as needed.

Serves 6

Hot tomato cocktail

A tasty wake-me-up for a winter morning

full power
10 minutes

750 ml/1¼ pints tomato juice
1 (298-g/10½-oz) can beef consommé
½ teasp celery salt
1 thin slice onion
1 bay leaf
4 whole cloves
a few drops Tabasco sauce
thin lemon slices

In a 2-litre/3½-pint measuring jug, combine tomato juice, consommé, celery salt, onion, bay leaf, cloves and Tabasco. Cover and microwave on full power until the mixture boils, about 8 – 10 minutes. Stir twice. Strain and pour into four cups. Top each with a lemon slice.

Serves 4

Hot egg nog

Breakfast in a cup

full power
9 minutes

1 litre/1¾ pints milk
3 tbsp sugar
1 teasp vanilla essence
a few drops almond essence, if desired
pinch of salt
2 beaten eggs, plus 1 beaten egg yolk
1 egg white
2 tbsp icing sugar
ground cinnamon

In a 2-litre/3½-pint bowl, combine milk, sugar, vanilla, almond essence and salt. Microwave, uncovered, on full power until hot, but not boiling, 6–7 minutes. Stir. Combine eggs and egg yolk. Add 250 ml/8 fl oz of the hot milk mixture to the beaten eggs, stirring constantly. Gradually add the egg mixture to the hot milk, stirring constantly. Return mixture to oven and microwave,

uncovered, for 2 minutes more, stirring once. Whisk egg white to soft peaks, then beat in icing sugar until stiff peaks form. Pour egg nog into mugs, top with egg white and sprinkle with ground cinnamon.

Makes 8 small or 4 large servings

Tea in a minute

full power
1½ minutes

175 ml/6 fl oz water
1 teabag
sugar, milk or lemon as desired

Microwave water in a cup or mug on full power to boiling, about 1½ minutes. Add teabag and steep to desired strength. Add milk, sugar or lemon, as desired.

Serves 1

Café au lait

full power
1½ minutes

1-2 teasp instant coffee (or to taste)
175 ml/6 fl oz milk
sugar

Combine coffee and milk in a cup or mug and microwave on full power for about 1½ minutes. Add sugar to taste.

Serves 1

Easy instant coffee

Use coffee mugs for heating the coffee in an instant

full power

For each cup
1 teasp instant coffee
200 ml/7 fl oz water

Spoon instant coffee granules into each mug and add the water. Microwave on full power until hot.

1 cup	1¼ minutes
2 cups	2 minutes
4 cups	3½ minutes

Hot chocolate

full power
7 minutes

4 tbsp cocoa powder
4 tbsp sugar
750 ml/1¼ pints milk
1 teasp grated orange rind
few drops almond essence, if desired
4 marshmallows

In a 1 litre glass measuring jug, combine cocoa, sugar and half the milk. Mix until smooth, then stir in remaining milk. Add orange rind and essence and microwave on full power for 6 – 7 minutes, stirring twice. Pour into cups and top with a marshmallow if desired.

Serves 4

Appetizers sandwiches & snacks

A variety of tempting starters from dips and pâtés to artichokes hollandaise are easily prepared in the versatile microwave oven. What is more, there need be no last-minute fuss if starters are made in advance. All that need be done just before serving is to place individual portions in separate dishes, set the timer, and reheating will take only a moment. Prepared this way, the starters will stay hot while your guests settle down.

Snacks and sandwiches are prepared quickly and easily at any time of the day. Store leftovers in the refrigerator and use for a variety of delicious fillings for bread and rolls. You can even microwave interesting fare in a matter of minutes for unexpected guests.

Garlic bread

high
2 minutes

1 long French bread
250g/8 oz garlic butter (see p. 52)
60 g/2 oz Cheddar cheese, grated

Cut the French bread in half. Slice thickly at an angle, but do not cut completely through the slices. Spread bread thickly with garlic butter. To reshape, push slices together firmly. Spread a little of the butter along the top of the bread. Sprinkle cheese on top. Place each half of the bread in a cooking bag and tie ends with elastic bands or string. Microwave on high for 2 minutes. Serve immediately.

Makes 2 × 40-cm/16-inch loaves

Note: Garlic bread freezes well for up to a month. To serve, place frozen bread in the microwave on defrost for 4–5 minutes. Microwave on high for 2 minutes, or until piping hot.

Bacon sticks

A savoury snack to serve with drinks

full power
12 minutes

10 rashers streaky bacon, rinds removed
20 grissini (Italian bread sticks)

Cut bacon strips in half lengthwise. Wrap one strip in a spiral around each bread stick. Place two paper towels on each of three paper plates and divide bread sticks among plates. Cover with another paper towel. Microwave each plate on full power for 3–4 minutes, or until bacon is cooked.

Makes 20 bacon sticks

Shrimp and dill dip

medium
5 minutes

250 g/8 oz cottage cheese, sieved
2 (92-g/3¼-oz) cans shrimps, drained
1 tbsp tomato ketchup
1 tbsp finely chopped onion
1 teasp made English mustard
1 teasp Worcestershire sauce
pinch of garlic salt
2 teasp finely chopped dill or ½ teasp dried dill

Place cottage cheese in a 2-litre/3½-pint casserole dish and microwave on medium for 60 seconds. Stir in remaining ingredients and cover. Microwave for 3–3½ minutes, or until heated through. Stir before serving with savoury biscuits or toast.

Makes about 350 ml/12 fl oz

Hot cheese dip

full power
5 minutes

1 (180-g/6 oz) jar cheese spread
250 g/8 oz cottage cheese, sieved
4 tbsp dry white wine
2 tbsp milk
1 tbsp chopped chives
½ teasp dry mustard
few drops of Tabasco, if desired

In a covered 1.2-litre/2-pint casserole dish, heat cheese spread until bubbly, 2–3 minutes on full power. Stir in cottage cheese and remaining ingredients. Microwave to heat through, 1–2 minutes. Add a little more milk if mixture becomes too thick. Serve with potato crisps or biscuits. If mixture cools during serving, reheat for about 1 minute.

Makes 500 ml/17 fl oz

Tangy crab dip

medium
4½ minutes

250 g/8 oz cottage cheese, sieved
1 (177-g/6-oz) can crab meat, drained
1 tbsp milk
2 tbsp finely chopped onion
4 teasp lemon juice
4 teasp dry sherry
1½–2 teasp grated lemon rind
1 teasp prepared horseradish
salt and pepper to taste

Place cottage cheese in 1.2-litre/2-pint casserole and microwave on medium for 1 minute. Stir in remaining ingredients and microwave, covered, for 3–3½ minutes, or until heated through. Stir before serving with savoury biscuits or toast.

Makes about 350 ml/12 fl oz

Mexican bean spread

full power
medium
11 minutes

2–3 rashers bacon
1 (447-g/15¾-oz) can baked beans
2 teasp vinegar
2 teasp Worcestershire sauce
salt and cayenne pepper to taste
pinch of garlic salt
60 g/2 oz Cheddar cheese, grated

Place the rashers of bacon on a bacon rack. Microwave on full power for 4 minutes, or until crisp. Crumble and set aside. Combine all the remaining ingredients in a blender or processor and blend until smooth. Add bacon, turn into a bowl and cover. Microwave on medium for 7 minutes before serving. Serve as a dip with crisps or biscuits, or use as a spread over hot dogs. If the consistency is a little too thick, thin with a small quantity of milk.

Makes about 500 ml

Potted shrimp

Serve in one bowl as a spread, or in individual ramekins as a starter

full power
7 minutes

250 g/8 oz small shelled shrimps, thawed
230 g/7½ oz butter
2 teasp fresh dill or 1 teasp dried dill
pinch of pepper
lemon slices to garnish

Place shrimps in a small bowl. Cover and microwave on full power for 30 seconds. Stand for 1 minute, then microwave again for 1 minute. Put 150 g/5 oz of the butter in a glass measuring jug and microwave for about 3 minutes, or until melted. Process shrimps, melted butter, dill and pepper in a food processor or blender until the mixture is smooth. Spoon mixture into a serving dish or into six individual ramekins and press down well. Melt remaining butter in the microwave for about 2 minutes, then spoon over top of shrimp mixture. Chill, covered, for several hours or overnight. Serve garnished with lemon slices.

Serves 6

Chicken liver pâté

full power
high
7 minutes

100 g/3½ oz butter
1 clove garlic, crushed
250 g/8 oz chicken livers, cleaned and cut up
salt and black pepper to taste
pinch of thyme
1 slice white bread

2 tbsp water
2 teasp lemon juice
2 tbsp single cream
1 tbsp whisky
parsley, slice of gherkin and slices of lemon to garnish

Place butter in a shallow casserole dish. Microwave on full power for 3 minutes. Add garlic and chicken livers, toss in butter. Microwave, uncovered, on high for 4 minutes. Turn livers at least once during cooking time. Add seasonings and thyme. Soak the bread in water for a few minutes. Squeeze out excess water. Add moist bread to livers. Add remaining ingredients and blend until smooth. Taste for seasonings. Pour into a small prepared mould, an earthenware crock or small individual pottery containers. Refrigerate for 3 – 4 hours. Turn out mould onto a platter and garnish, or decorate individual servings with a small sprig of parsley and slices of gherkin and lemon. Serve with plenty of Melba toast.

Serves 4 – 6

Creamy chicken liver pâté

Cognac adds an elegant touch to this pâté

full power
8 minutes

2 tbsp butter
1 onion, chopped
1 small clove garlic, crushed
500 g/1 lb chicken livers, trimmed and cut up
pinch of ground allspice
pinch of nutmeg
salt and freshly ground black pepper to taste
4 tbsp cognac (or brandy)
250 g/8 oz cream cheese
2 tbsp chopped parsley
1 tbsp chopped chives

Melt butter in a large casserole dish on full power for 1 minute. Add onion, garlic and chicken livers. Microwave, covered, on full power for 5 – 6 minutes, stirring halfway through the cooking time. Add allspice, nutmeg, salt and pepper, and cognac. Cover and heat for 1½ minutes. Spoon half the mixture into work bowl of food processor, purée with half the cream cheese and set aside. Repeat with remaining liver mixture and cheese. Stir in parsley and chives and spoon into serving bowl. Chill for several hours or overnight before serving with bread or savoury biscuits.

Makes about 750 ml/1¼ pints

Clockwise: fish pâté (p. 38), creamy chicken liver pâté and potted shrimp

Fish pâté

full power
12 minutes

250 g/8 oz cod
125 g/4 oz haddock
1 small onion, sliced
bay leaf
a few peppercorns
7 tbsp milk
7 tbsp water
3 tbsp white wine
210 g/7 oz butter
3 tbsp lemon juice
1 teasp dried dill
3 tbsp single cream
salt and black pepper to taste
lettuce, slices of lemon and sprigs of
    parsley or fresh dill to garnish

Place the cod, haddock, onion, bay leaf, peppercorns,
milk, water and white wine in a shallow casserole dish.
Cover and microwave on full power for 6 minutes. Drain
fish, reserving onion and cooking liquid. Remove skin
and bones from fish, and flake. Place butter, lemon juice
and dill in a bowl. Microwave on full power for 4 minutes.
Add fish, then cover with cling film, making two slits to
prevent 'ballooning' during cooking. Microwave on full
power for 2 minutes. Stir in cream. In a food processor
or blender, purée the fish mixture with the onion and 3
tbsp of the cooking liquid. Season to taste. Pour into a
container or prepared mould and refrigerate for at least
6 hours. If using a mould, turn out onto a bed of lettuce.
Decorate with slices of lemon and chopped parsley or
sprigs of fresh dill. If not using a mould, place scoops of
paté on crisp lettuce leaves, then garnish with lemon and
parsley. Serve with hot toast, or Melba toast

Serves 6

Savoury mushrooms

A tasty appetizer to serve with drinks

full power
3 minutes

2 tbsp softened butter	1 teasp soy sauce
1 tbsp dry red wine	2 teasp chopped parsley
1 clove garlic, chopped	6 tbsp dry breadcrumbs
3 tbsp grated Cheddar cheese	12 mushrooms, about 2.5 cm/1 inch in diameter

Mix together butter, red wine, garlic, grated cheese, soy
sauce, parsley and breadcrumbs, blending well. Remove
stems from mushrooms and reserve for another use. Divide
breadcrumb mixture evenly among upturned mushroom
caps, mounding it up and pressing it lightly into shape.
Place a double layer of paper towel on a flat plate and
arrange stuffed mushrooms in a circle on the plate.
Microwave, uncovered, on full power for 2½ – 3 minutes,
rotating the plate twice during cooking if necessary. Let
mushrooms stand for about 3 minutes before serving.

Makes 12

Avocado Ritz

Avocado Ritz

full power
defrost
medium
13 minutes

24 prawns with shells	*For the sauce*
3 tbsp water	2 eggs
3 tbsp white wine	120 ml/4 fl oz oil
salt and black peppercorns	½ teasp dry mustard
2 teasp lemon juice	salt and cayenne pepper to taste
1 clove garlic, peeled	4 teasp tomato ketchup
3 avocados	3 tbsp double cream, beaten until
little lemon juice	thick
lettuce, shredded or whole leaves, chopped parsley and lemon twists to garnish	lemon juice to taste

Place prawns, water, wine, salt, peppercorns, lemon juice
and whole cloves of garlic in a shallow casserole dish.
Cover and microwave on full power for about 8 minutes.
Cooking time will vary considerably, depending on the size
of the prawns. Prawns are cooked when they start to turn
pink and become opaque. Do not overcook. Drain prawns,
and allow to cool slightly before removing shells.

Meanwhile, make the sauce. Place eggs in a bowl and
whisk lightly. Microwave on defrost for 1 minute. Whisk in
oil and seasoning. Microwave on medium for 4 minutes.
Whisk well after each minute of cooking time. Cool
slightly, then add tomato ketchup, cream and lemon juice
to taste. Set aside to cool further before adding to
prawns. Cut prawns into small pieces, saving six whole

prawns for decoration. Combine cooled sauce and prawns. Refrigerate for at least 30 minutes before serving.

To serve, cut avocados in half and brush with a little lemon juice. Place avocado half on lettuce and fill cavity with prawn mixture. Garnish with a whole prawn, chopped parsley and a twist of lemon.

Serves 6

Avocado Waldorf

full power
8 minutes

2 avocados	60 g/2 oz walnuts, chopped
few drops lemon juice	125 g/4 oz cream cheese
½ apple, peeled and chopped	1 tbsp mayonnaise
1 stick celery, chopped	1 tbsp dry vermouth
60 g/2 oz seedless green grapes, halved	salt to taste

Cut avocados in half and remove stones. Sprinkle each half with a little lemon juice and arrange in a microwave dish with the narrow end toward the centre. Mix together the remaining ingredients, season to taste with a little salt and set aside. Place avocados in oven and microwave, covered, on full power for 5 – 7 minutes, depending on size and ripeness of avocados. Uncover avocados and divide apple mixture among the four halves. Heat in microwave just to warm apple mixture, about 1 minute. Serve hot, garnished with a little parsley if desired.

Serves 4

Fresh asparagus with eggs and caviar

full power
7 minutes

500 g/1 lb fresh asparagus cooked (see p. 94)
3 tbsp butter
4 teasp chopped onion
6 eggs
1 teasp finely chopped fresh dill or ½ teasp dried dill
4 tbsp single cream
salt and pepper to taste
red lumpfish caviar and fresh parsley to garnish

Arrange cooked asparagus spears on a serving platter, cover and keep warm. Microwave butter in a glass jug for 45 – 60 seconds on full power. Add onion and microwave for 1½ minutes. In a mixing bowl, combine eggs, dill, cream, pepper and salt, mixing well. Add the butter and onion and microwave on full power for 4 – 5 minutes, stirring well after each minute. Eggs should still be slightly 'runny' in texture as they will continue to cook after having been taken from the oven. Stand for 1 – 2 minutes, then gently spoon over the asparagus. Garnish with parsley and caviar. Serve warm.

Serves 4 – 6

Fresh asparagus with eggs and caviar

Artichokes retain their full flavour when cooked in the microwave

Artichokes hollandaise

full power
high
25 minutes

4 medium globe artichokes
6 tbsp water
4 tbsp white wine
1/2 teasp salt
1 slice lemon
1 clove garlic, peeled
few black peppercorns
1 teasp oil
250 ml/8 fl oz hollandaise sauce (see p. 51)

Wash artichokes and trim off the stalk, lower leaves and tips. Place in a cooking bag or covered casserole. Combine all remaining ingredients except the hollandaise sauce, and pour over artichokes. Microwave on full power for 18 – 20 minutes. Rearrange artichokes halfway through cooking time. To test if artichokes are cooked, remove one of the lower leaves. The leaf should peel off easily. Drain upside down and cool. Carefully lift out the middle portion and set aside. Using the handle end of a teaspoon, scrape away the hairy choke. Replace leaves and level base so that artichoke can be served upright. To serve, arrange in a dish, cover and reheat on high for 4 – 5 minutes. Serve artichokes on individual plates with plenty of hollandaise.

Serves 4

Note: Artichokes may also be served cold with a French dressing (see p. 54) or a suitable sauce.

Pickled prawns with avocado

full power
7 minutes

375 g/12 oz prawns, shelled and deveined
2 avocados
1 tbsp chopped coriander leaves
few sprigs of fresh coriander to garnish

For the spiced vinegar
250 ml/8 fl oz white wine vinegar
1 onion, sliced
2 whole cloves
1 teasp black peppercorns
1/2 teasp salt
dash of cayenne pepper
1 tbsp sugar

In a large bowl, combine all the ingredients for spiced vinegar. Microwave on full power for 6 minutes. Add prawns, then microwave for 1 minute. Allow mixture to cool. Cover and chill for a few hours.
   Halve avocados lengthwise, remove stones and, using a melon baller, scoop out balls of avocado. Carefully stir into prawn mixture. Stir in chopped coriander. Using a slotted spoon, drain prawns and avocado and place in individual glasses. Garnish with sprigs of coriander.

Serves 6

Chicken salad sandwiches

These open sandwiches take only a minute to heat. Make up the mixture in advance and keep on hand for a really quick snack.

full power
2 minutes

250 g/8 oz cooked chicken, chopped
1 large dill pickle, finely chopped
8 stuffed olives, finely chopped
2 tbsp finely chopped onion
1 teasp made English mustard
4 tbsp mayonnaise, to moisten
90 g/3 oz Cheddar cheese, grated
salt and pepper to taste
4 slices rye bread or wholewheat bread

Mix all ingredients except bread, and season to taste. Refrigerate until needed. To heat, spread a quarter of the mixture on each slice of bread. Place two slices on a serving plate and heat on full power for about 1 minute, or until cheese is melted and mixture is hot. Repeat with remaining mixture and bread, and serve at once.

Serves 4

Ham salad sandwiches

Another open sandwich to make in minutes

full power
4 minutes

375 g/12 oz cooked ham, chopped
1 stick celery, finely chopped
1 gherkin, finely chopped
1 tbsp finely chopped onion
1 teasp made English mustard
4 tbsp mayonnaise, to moisten
100 g/3½ oz Cheddar cheese, grated
pepper to taste
6 – 8 slices rye bread or wholewheat bread

Mix all ingredients except bread and season with a little pepper. Refrigerate until needed. To heat, spread mixture on slices of bread and heat two at a time on full power for about 1 minute, or until mixture is hot and cheese has melted.

Serves 6 – 8

Tuna salad sandwiches

full power
2 minutes

1 (198-g/7-oz) can tuna, drained and flaked
2 hard-boiled egg yolks, chopped
1 tbsp chopped onion
2 tbsp chopped dill pickle or gherkin
salt and pepper to taste
1 teasp lemon juice
3–4 tbsp mayonnaise, to moisten
75 g/2½ oz Cheddar cheese, grated
4 slices rye bread or wholewheat bread

Mix all ingredients except bread, and refrigerate until needed. To heat, spread mixture on slices of bread and heat, two at a time, on full power for about 1 minute, or until cheese melts and mixture is hot.

Serves 4

Salmon rolls

full power
4 minutes

6–8 small crisp dinner rolls
1 (212-g/7½-oz) can red salmon, drained and flaked
2 tbsp finely chopped onion
20 stuffed olives, coarsely chopped
3–4 small mushrooms, chopped
few drops of Tabasco
pepper to taste
1 tbsp chopped parsley
100 g/3½ oz Cheddar cheese, grated
120 ml/4 fl oz single cream

Cut tops from rolls and remove soft centres, leaving hollow shells. Save centres for breadcrumbs. Place salmon in a mixing bowl, add onion, olives, mushrooms, Tabasco and pepper. Stir in parsley and about three quarters of the

cheese. Add enough cream to moisten well and spoon mixture into rolls. Sprinkle with remaining cheese and replace tops. Place in a circle on a flat plate and microwave at full power for 3 – 4 minutes, depending on number and size of rolls. Rotate halfway through cooking if necessary. Serve hot. Use tiny rolls for snacks or appetizers and larger ones for starters.

Serves 6 – 8 as a starter

Sloppy Joes

Make this mixture in advance and keep on hand for quick filled rolls or sandwiches

full power
6 minutes

500 g/1 lb minced beef
½ small onion, chopped
250 ml/8 fl oz tomato ketchup
2 tbsp made mild mustard
salt and pepper to taste
1 tbsp brown sugar
2 teasp vinegar
pinch of curry powder, if desired
60 g/2 oz Cheddar cheese, grated

Break up minced beef and place in a 1.2-litre/2-pint casserole dish. Add onion and microwave on full power for 4 minutes. Stir to break up meat, then microwave until meat is cooked. 1–2 minutes. Drain off excess moisture. Add tomato ketchup, mustard, salt and pepper, brown sugar, vinegar, curry powder and cheese. Mix well, then cover and refrigerate until needed. To serve, spoon about 5 tbsp of the mixture inside each roll or sandwich and microwave on full power, timing about 1 minute a roll.

Makes enough for 8 rolls or sandwiches

Sloppy Joe

Easy pizza served with salad

Easy pizza

full power
5 minutes

125 g/4 oz plain flour
½ teasp cream of tartar
pinch of bicarbonate of soda
pinch of oregano
2 tbsp margarine
6 tbsp milk

For the topping
350 ml/12 fl oz tomato topping
 (see p. 51)
100 g/3½ oz Cheddar cheese, grated
½ (56-g/2-oz) can flat anchovy fillets
few sliced stuffed olives

To make the base, sift the dry ingredients. Add the oregano and margarine, and rub in. Mix to a moist scone dough consistency with the milk. Grease a 20-cm/8-inch plate or pizza plate and press the dough to fit. Microwave on full power for 2 minutes. Spread tomato mixture over the dough. Sprinkle with cheese and arrange anchovy fillets in a lattice design. Place a slice of stuffed olive in each 'diamond'. Microwave on full power for 3 minutes. Stand for at least 2 minutes before serving.

Serves 4 – 6

Italian pizza

full power
defrost
25 minutes

120 ml/4 fl oz warm water
2 teasp fresh yeast
1 teasp sugar
250 g/8 oz plain flour
1 teasp salt
2 tbsp oil
750 ml/1¼ pints tomato topping (see p. 51)
375 g/12 oz Mozzarella cheese, thinly sliced
1 (56-g/2-oz) can anchovies, sliced lengthwise

Combine the water, yeast and sugar in a small bowl. Sprinkle 3 tbsp of measured flour onto the yeast mixture, but do not stir in. Cover with cling film. Microwave for 30 seconds on full power. Allow to stand until bubbly. Sift flour and salt into a mixing bowl. Add oil to yeast mixture, then add this liquid to the flour. Mix to a firm dough and knead until smooth. Shape into a ball and brush it with a little extra oil to prevent a skin from forming. Place in a large bowl and cover tightly with plastic wrap. Microwave on defrost for 15 seconds. Rest for 5 minutes. Repeat this 3 – 4 times, until the dough has doubled in size.

Divide risen dough into four portions and knead each lightly. Roll each portion into a 20-cm/8-inch round. Grease four plates and dust lightly with flour. Cover plates with dough. Microwave each round of dough on defrost for 15 seconds, then rest for 4 minutes. Repeat at least twice, or until dough has doubled in size.

Divide the tomato topping between the four pizzas, and spread over the dough. Cover with slices of cheese, and finally with slices of anchovy. Microwave pizzas, uncovered, one at a time on full power for 5 minutes. Stand for at least 3 minutes before serving.

Serves 4

VARIATIONS

Seafood pizza: 1 (198-g/7-oz) can shrimps, drained, 1 (250-g/8-oz) can mussels, drained, 1 tbsp chopped parsley. Arrange on top of cheese.

Mushroom pizza: 375 g/12 oz mushrooms, sliced, 2 tbsp oil, pinch of dried thyme. Combine all the ingredients. Add to pizza, on top of cheese.

Artichoke pizza: 2 (200-g/7-oz) cans artichokes, drained and sliced, 2 tbsp chopped parsley, 2 tbsp capers. Add to pizza, on top of cheese.

Salami pizza: 20 thin slices salami. Arrange salami around the edges of pizza, on top of cheese.

Ham pizza: 125 g/4 oz ham, diced, 2 tbsp chopped parsley, paprika. Combine ham and parsley, add to pizza on top of cheese and sprinkle with paprika.

Tuna pizza: 1 (198-g/7-oz) can tuna, drained and flaked, 2 teasp lemon juice, 2 sticks celery, chopped. Combine all the ingredients. Add to pizza, on top of cheese.

For a really special pizza use a combination of two or more of these variations.

Chicken curry crêpes

full power
medium
22 minutes

3 tbsp butter
1 small onion, chopped
2 sticks celery, chopped
1 clove garlic, crushed
2 tbsp plain flour
350 ml/12 fl oz chicken stock
2 tbsp tomato purée
1 teasp curry paste
310 g/10 oz cooked chicken, diced
6 tbsp chutney
1 apple, diced
4 tbsp raisins
salt and black pepper to taste
4 tbsp peanuts
approximately 12 crêpes (see p. 113)

Place the butter in a shallow casserole dish. Microwave on full power for 1 minute. Add onion, celery and garlic. Toss in butter. Microwave on full power for 4 minutes. Stir once during the cooking time. Stir in the flour. Pour in the chicken stock and stir well. Add tomato purée and curry paste. Cover and microwave on full power for 7 minutes. Stir three times during the cooking time. In a bowl, combine chicken, chutney, apple and raisins. Season well. Add a little of the sauce to bind the mixture. Place a little chicken mixture along one end of a crêpe and roll up. Arrange crêpes in a greased shallow ovenproof dish. Coat with the remaining sauce. Sprinkle with peanuts. Cover and microwave on medium for 8 – 10 minutes. Serve hot.

Serves 4 – 6

Asparagus lunch dish

full power
medium
23 minutes

5 slices white bread, crusts removed
butter
a little made English mustard
90 g/3 oz Cheddar cheese, grated
1 (340-g/12-oz) can asparagus cuts
250 ml/8 fl oz milk
3 eggs
1 tbsp chopped parsley
pinch of thyme
salt and black pepper to taste
1 tbsp oil
1 small onion, chopped
4 tbsp cornflakes, crushed

Butter bread, then spread on a little mustard. Cut each slice into three. Butter base of a shallow 1.2-litre/2-pint casserole dish. Arrange bread, butter side up, on the base and up the edges. Sprinkle half the cheese over the bread. Drain asparagus and reserve juice. Add asparagus to casserole dish. Combine milk, eggs, 6 tbsp reserved asparagus juice, parsley, thyme and seasoning.
   Place oil in a small bowl and microwave on full power for 1 minute. Add onion and toss well. Microwave for 2

minutes. Add to egg mixture. Stir to combine and pour over asparagus. Combine remaining cheese with cornflakes and sprinkle on top. Cover with cling film and make two slits in film to prevent 'ballooning' during cooking. Microwave on medium for about 20 minutes. The centre should still be lightly soft. Stand for 5 minutes before serving.

Serves 6

VARIATIONS

Add any one of the following to the basic recipe:

- 4 rashers bacon, cut up and sautéed for 2 minutes extra with the onion
- 100 g diced ham to the mixture
- 100 g/3½ oz diced ham to the mixture
- 100 g/3½ oz diced, cooked chicken to the mixture
- 2 medium, peeled and chopped tomatoes to the mixture

Cheese and onion quiche

full power
medium
17 minutes

1 (23-cm/9-inch) shortcrust pastry shell (see p. 129)
1 teasp Worcestershire sauce
1 egg yolk

For the filling
1 tbsp butter
1 onion, chopped
1 teasp dried mixed herbs
125 g/4 oz Cheddar cheese, grated
4 eggs
120 ml/4 fl oz single cream
120 ml/4 fl oz milk
dash of Tabasco
salt and pepper to taste
2 teasp chopped parsley to garnish

Brush pastry shell with mixture of Worcestershire sauce and egg yolk. Microwave on full power for 2 minutes, then cool. For the filling, microwave butter on full power for 30 seconds, add onion, toss to coat and microwave for 2 minutes. Add mixed herbs. Sprinkle three quarters of the cheese over bottom of the pastry and top with onion mixture. Combine eggs, cream, milk, Tabasco and salt and pepper to taste. Pour over onion and cheese and microwave on medium for 11 – 13 minutes, rotating dish if necessary. Sprinkle quiche with remaining cheese during last minute of cooking, then allow to stand for 5 minutes before serving. Garnish with parsley.

Serves 6 – 8

VARIATIONS

Italian quiche: Use Mozzarella cheese instead of Cheddar, and basil instead of mixed herbs. During last minute of cooking time, arrange sliced tomatoes on top.

Ham or bacon quiche: Add 125 g/4 oz cooked, chopped ham or 8 cooked, crumbled rashers of bacon to the quiche after adding the onion.

Soups, sauces & butters

Delicious hot or cold soups are simple to make in a microwave. Not only are cooking times considerably reduced, but the kitchen remains free of strong soup odours. Bones, seasonings, water and a few soup vegetables microwaved together make a perfect stock which can be used as a basis for many soups. Once prepared, these may be frozen in individual portions, offering each member of the family a soup of his choice. At first glance, it appears that making a sauce in the microwave takes almost as long as one made conventionally. However, microwave cooking offers a number of advantages as there are no scorched messy pans to wash up, and there is no need to stir the sauce continuously. Other ingredients may be added to the sauce once it has been made, and reheating takes only a few seconds.

Crab soup

full power
19 minutes

4 teasp butter
1 onion, chopped
400 ml/14 fl oz milk
200 ml/7 fl oz chicken stock
1 (64-g/2¼ oz) packet instant mashed potato
500 g/1 lb cooked crab meat, thickly sliced
150 ml/¼ pint white wine
1 teasp dried tarragon
salt and black pepper to taste
120 ml/4 fl oz single cream
2 teasp chopped parsley to garnish

Using a large bowl, microwave butter on full power for
1 minute. Add onion and toss in butter. Microwave for
5 minutes. Stir in milk, chicken stock and instant mashed
potato. Microwave on full power for 7 minutes, stirring
once during the cooking time. Now add crab, white wine,
tarragon and seasonings. Microwave for 4 minutes. Stir in
cream and microwave for 2 minutes. Sprinkle with parsley
and serve. This soup may also be served chilled.

Serves 6

Cold Senegalese soup

full power
7 minutes

2 tbsp butter
2 tbsp chopped onion
2 teasp curry powder
1 tbsp plain flour
1 litre/1¾ pints chicken stock
4 egg yolks
500 ml/17 fl oz single cream
90 g/3 oz cooked chicken, finely chopped

In a large casserole dish, microwave butter on full power
for 30 seconds. Add onion and microwave for 2 minutes.
Stir in curry powder and flour and microwave for 1 minute.
Stir until smooth, then gradually stir in chicken stock.
Microwave, covered, for 3 minutes, then remove from the
oven and stir. Beat egg yolks lightly, then add a little hot
soup and beat well. Return yolk mixture gradually to the
soup, stirring constantly. Microwave soup, covered, for
30 seconds, then stir very well. Pour soup through a sieve
into a serving bowl and chill well. Add cream and cooked
chicken just before serving. Serve very cold.

Serves 6

Curried apple soup

full power
medium
32 minutes

3 tbsp oil
5 sticks celery, chopped
2 onions, chopped
1 leek, chopped
3 tbsp butter
3 tbsp plain flour
1 teasp curry powder
1 litre/1¾ pints chicken stock
2 medium apples
black pepper to taste
120 ml/4 fl oz single cream
1 teasp lemon juice
2 teasp whisky
paprika and apple slices to garnish

Pour oil into a large casserole dish. Microwave on full
power for 1 minute. Add celery, onion and leek.
Microwave on full power for 5 minutes and set aside. Place
butter in a large jug. Microwave on full power for 1 minute.
Stir in flour and curry powder. Microwave for 30 seconds.
Stir in half the stock. Cover and microwave on full power
for 10 minutes, stirring every 2 minutes. Pour over sautéed
vegetables, and add remaining stock. Peel, core and dice
apples, and add to soup. Season with black pepper. Cover
and microwave on full power for 10 minutes. Stir in cream,
lemon juice and whisky. Microwave on medium for
5 minutes. Garnish with paprika and slices of apple. Serve
hot or cold.

Serves 6

French-style onion soup

full power
33 minutes

60 g/2 oz butter or margarine
3 large onions, peeled and sliced
1 teasp sugar
2 tbsp plain flour
1 litre/1¾ pints beef stock
salt and pepper to taste
4 tbsp sherry
6 slices French bread, toasted
90 g/3 oz Cheddar cheese, grated

Microwave butter in a large casserole dish on full power for
30 – 45 seconds, or until melted. Add onion and microwave
for 4 – 5 minutes. Stir in sugar and flour, and gradually stir
in beef stock. Season to taste with salt and pepper. Cover
and microwave for 22 – 25 minutes, or until onions are very
tender. Stir in the sherry. To serve, spoon soup into
individual serving dishes and top with toasted French
bread. Sprinkle with grated cheese and microwave for
about 2 minutes to melt cheese. The cheese can also be
melted under the grill. Serve hot.

Serves 6

Spiced carrot soup

Spiced carrot soup

full power
medium
32 minutes

1 tbsp oil
1 tbsp butter
6 medium carrots, sliced
2 onions, chopped
2 small turnips, sliced
pinch of curry powder
pinch of ground cloves
pinch of ground nutmeg
750 ml/1¼ pints chicken stock
3 tbsp long-grain rice, uncooked
salt and black pepper to taste
buttermilk
carrot curls to garnish

Microwave the oil and butter in a large casserole dish on full power for 1 minute. Add vegetables, toss in oil and cover. Microwave on full power for 6 minutes, stirring twice. Add curry powder, spices, stock, rice, salt and black pepper. Cover and microwave on full power for 15 minutes, stirring twice. Liquidize the soup in batches. Add buttermilk until soup has a pouring consistency. Reheat in microwave on medium for 10 minutes. Serve garnished with carrot curls. To make curls, use a vegetable peeler to shave off pieces of carrot lengthwise. Drop into iced water for a few minutes before using.

Serves 6 – 8

Cream of vegetable soup

Using one basic recipe, you can make a variety of delicious creamy soups

full power
16 minutes

For the basic soup
60 g/2 oz butter
1 large onion, chopped
1 large potato, peeled and chopped
750 ml/1¼ pints chicken stock
2 teasp cornflour
250 ml/8 fl oz milk
120 ml/4 fl oz single cream
salt and pepper to taste

Place butter in a 2-litre/3½-pint casserole dish and microwave on full power for 30–45 seconds to melt. Add onion and potato and microwave, covered, for 3 minutes. Add stock, cover and microwave for 10 minutes. Transfer mixture to a blender and purée. Mix cornflour with milk and gradually stir into the purée. Return to casserole dish and microwave, covered, for 2 minutes, stirring after 1 minute. Stir in cream and season to taste. Serve hot or chilled.

Serves 4 – 6

Cream of celery soup

cream of vegetable soup (above)
6 sticks celery, chopped
2 tbsp chopped parsley

Add chopped celery to basic soup mixture with the stock. Proceed as for basic soup, increasing cooking time by 1 or 2 minutes if necessary. Add chopped parsley with the cream and mix well. Serve hot.

Serves 6

Cream of mushroom soup

cream of vegetable soup (above)
310 g/10 oz fresh mushrooms, sliced

Add sliced mushrooms to basic soup mixture with the stock. Proceed as for basic soup. Serve hot.

Serves 4 – 6

Cream of cauliflower soup

cream of vegetable soup (above)
1 small cauliflower, broken into florets
2 teasp fresh dill or 1 teasp dried dill
120 ml/4 fl oz soured cream *instead of* 120 ml/4 fl oz fresh cream

Add cauliflower to basic soup mixture with the stock. Proceed as for basic soup, increasing cooking time by 1 or 2 minutes if necessary. Add the dill to the purée along with the cornflour and milk. When the soup is cooked, stir in soured cream instead of fresh cream. Serve hot.

Serves 6

Cream of leek soup

cream of vegetable soup (see p. 46)
2 tbsp butter
310 g/10 oz leeks, thinly sliced

Melt butter for basic soup, add an extra 2 tbsp butter, then the potato and onion from the basic recipe. Now add the leeks. Microwave for 4–4½ minutes on full power. Add stock and proceed as for basic soup. Serve hot or cold.

Serves 4 – 6

Cream of carrot soup

cream of vegetable soup (see p. 46)
430 g/14 oz carrots, peeled and sliced

Add the carrots to the basic soup mixture with the stock. Proceed as for basic soup, increasing cooking time by 1 or 2 minutes if necessary. Serve hot or cold.

Serves 6

Cream of broccoli soup

cream of vegetable soup (see p. 46)
430 g/14 oz fresh broccoli, or frozen and thawed

Add the broccoli to the basic soup mixture with the stock. Proceed as for basic soup, increasing cooking time by 1 or 2 minutes if necessary. Serve hot or cold.

Serves 6

Goulash soup

full power
medium
1¼ hours

4 tbsp oil
250 g/8 oz stewing beef, diced
4 tbsp plain flour
salt and black pepper to taste
1 onion, chopped
1 green pepper, seeded and chopped
1 clove garlic, crushed
2 large potatoes, diced
2 large tomatoes, peeled and chopped
4 tbsp tomato purée
1 teasp vinegar
1 litre/1¾ pints beef stock
2 tbsp paprika
1 teasp caraway seeds
1 small chilli, chopped (optional)

Pour half the oil into a browning dish. Microwave on full power for 4 minutes. Toss meat in flour and seasonings. Place in browning dish and microwave on full power for 4 minutes, stirring twice during the cooking time. Pour remaining oil into a large casserole dish and microwave on full power for 1 minute. Add onion, green pepper and garlic. Microwave on full power for 5 minutes. Now add meat, and all remaining ingredients. Cover and microwave on medium for 1 hour. Stir occasionally during cooking time. Serve with crusty bread.

Serves 6 – 8

Prawn bisque

full power
18 minutes

180 g/6 oz butter
1 onion, chopped
1 carrot, chopped
20 medium prawns, cleaned but not shelled
1 sprig thyme
1 small bay leaf
3 sprigs parsley
salt and pepper to taste
pinch of cayenne pepper
5 tbsp brandy
250 ml/8 fl oz white wine
1 litre/1¾ pints fish stock
3 tbsp flour, dissolved in a little cold fish stock

In a large casserole dish, microwave 3 tbsp butter on full
power for 30 seconds to melt. Add onion and carrot and
microwave for 3½–4 minutes. Add prawns, thyme, bay
leaf, parsley, salt and pepper, and cayenne. Cover and
microwave for 3–3½ minutes or until prawns are very
red. Add brandy and wine, then cover and microwave
for 2 minutes.

Remove prawns and shell, reserving the flesh. Process
prawn shells and heads in food processor with metal
blade until finely chopped. Add 90 g/3 oz butter and chop
again until well mixed.

Mix fish stock and dissolved flour into the vegetable
mixture in the casserole dish. Cover and microwave for
3 minutes, stirring after each minute. Add shell and butter
mixture to stock and microwave for 3 minutes, stirring after
each minute. Pass soup through a fine sieve, pressing
to extract all the juices. Add remaining butter and
microwave, covered, for 2 minutes. Strain soup again and
add reserved prawn flesh.

Serves 5 – 6

Hearty mussel soup

Creamy mussel soup

full power
18 minutes

2 tbsp butter
2 teasp chopped onion
4 sticks celery, chopped
2 (250-g/8-oz) cans mussels
350 ml/12 fl oz milk
salt and black pepper to taste
6 tbsp white wine
120 ml/4 fl oz single cream
2 teasp cornflour
2 tbsp chopped parsley

Using a large casserole dish, microwave butter on full
power for 1 minute. Add onion and celery, and toss in
butter. Microwave on full power for 4 minutes. Add
mussels and liquid, milk and seasonings. Cover and
microwave on full power for 5 minutes. Add white wine,
cover and microwave for a further 5 minutes. Combine
cream and cornflour. Stir into soup, cover and microwave
on full power for 2 – 3 minutes. Stir in parsley and serve
with crisp croûtons or Melba toast.

Serves 6

Hearty mussel soup

full power
36 minutes

2 tbsp oil
1–2 cloves garlic, crushed
1 onion, chopped
1 carrot, diced
2 sticks celery, chopped
1 litre/1¾ pints chicken stock
2 tbsp tomato purée
1 (425-g/15-oz) can whole peeled tomatoes, chopped
250 g/8 oz white fish trimmings
½ teasp sugar
salt and black pepper to taste
½ teasp dried basil
1 (793-g/1 lb 12-oz) can mussels with shells
125 g/4 oz frozen peas

Pour oil into a large bowl. Microwave on full power for
1 minute. Add garlic, onion, carrot and celery. Cover and
microwave on full power for 5 minutes. Stir in chicken
stock, tomatoe purée and peeled tomatoes. Microwave,
covered, on full power for 10 minutes. Add fish, sugar
seasonings and basil. Microwave, covered for 10 minutes.
Remove fish and discard, then add mussels and peas.
Cover and return to microwave for 10 minutes.

Serves 8

Basic white sauce

full power
4 minutes

2 tbsp butter or margarine
2 tbsp plain flour
salt and pepper to taste
250 ml/8 fl oz milk

Place butter in a 1.2-litre/2-pint glass jug and microwave on full power for about 30 seconds to melt. Stir in flour, salt and pepper. Microwave for 45 seconds. Stir, then slowly whisk in milk, blending well. Microwave for about 2 minutes, stirring twice. Remove from oven and stir well. Serve hot.

Makes about 250 ml/8 fl oz

VARIATIONS
Make up the basic sauce, then try one of the following:

Cheese sauce: Stir in 60–125 g/2–4 oz grated mature Cheddar cheese. Mix until cheese melts and sauce is smooth. If cheese has not completely melted, microwave on full power for about 30 seconds and stir again. Add ½ teasp made English mustard if a tangy cheese sauce is desired.

Dill sauce: Stir in 1 tbsp freshly chopped dill or 1 teasp dried dill, and 2 teasp lemon juice. Mix until smooth.

Mornay sauce: Add 60 g/2 oz grated Swiss or Parmesan cheese to the sauce, mixing until cheese has melted and sauce is smooth. Add a dash of cayenne pepper and mix in.

Curry sauce: Add ½–1 teasp curry powder or to taste, and 1 teasp lemon juice. Stir until smooth.

Horseradish sauce: Add 1–2 teasp prepared horseradish or to taste, and mix well.

Thick white sauce: Use 3 tbsp flour instead of 2 tbsp in the basic recipe.

Mild mustard sauce

This sauce is delicious with ham, beef or pastrami, and makes an excellent dip for cocktail sausages

defrost
medium
4 minutes

2 eggs
4 teasp made English mustard
2 tbsp castor sugar
salt and pepper to taste
pinch of dried dill
6 tbsp oil
3 tbsp white vinegar

Place eggs in a bowl and whisk lightly. Add mustard, sugar, seasonings and dill. Microwave, uncovered, on defrost for 1 minute. Slowly beat in oil. Microwave on medium for 3 minutes, whisking well after each minute of cooking time. Lastly, whisk in vinegar. Serve hot or cold.

Makes 175 ml/6 fl oz

Béchamel sauce

high
full power
10 minutes

300 ml/½ pint milk
1 thick slice onion
1 small carrot, cut up
1 sprig parsley
2 cloves
1 blade of mace
few black peppercorns
1 bay leaf
3 tbsp margarine
5 tbsp plain flour
salt

Place milk, onion, carrot, parsley, cloves, mace, peppercorns and bay leaf in a jug. Microwave, uncovered, on high for 3 minutes. Remove from oven, allow to stand for 15 minutes, then strain. Using a large jug or bowl, heat margarine on full power for 2 minutes. Stir in flour. Add half the infused milk and stir well. Stir in remaining milk. Microwave for about 5 minutes, stirring every minute during cooking time. Add a little salt and use as required.

Makes 300 ml/½ pint

Piquant sauce

A sweet and sour sauce for meat, poultry and hamburgers

full power
6 minutes

90 g/3 oz sugar
2 tbsp cornflour
4 tbsp water
1 (439-g/15½-oz) can crushed pineapple
½ green pepper, seeded and chopped
4 tbsp chopped pimiento (canned red pepper)
1 clove garlic, finely chopped
120 ml/4 fl oz white vinegar
2 tbsp soy sauce
salt to taste
few drops Tabasco

Place sugar, cornflour and water in a 2-litre/3½-pint casserole dish and mix well. Add pineapple, green pepper, pimiento, garlic, vinegar, soy sauce, salt and Tabasco. Microwave on full power for 5–6 minutes, stirring every 2 minutes. The sauce should be thickened and clear. Stand for 10 minutes before serving.

Makes about 450 ml/¾ pint

Clockwise: sherry mushroom sauce, dill sauce (p. 49), mild mustard sauce (p. 49) and barbecue sauce

Sherry mushroom sauce

full power
medium
10 minutes

60 g/2 oz butter
180 g/6 oz mushrooms, sliced
4 tbsp water
4 tbsp sherry
1 tbsp cornflour
salt and pepper to taste

Place butter in a 1.2-litre/2-pint casserole dish and microwave on full power for about 1 minute, until melted. Add mushrooms and microwave, covered, for 2¹/₂–3 minutes. Combine water, sherry and cornflour, mixing until smooth. Slowly stir into mushroom mixture. Cover and microwave on medium for 4–5 minutes until mixture thickens, stirring at least twice. Season to taste and microwave for 1 minute more. Serve with steaks or chops.

Makes about 375 ml/13 fl oz

Barbecue sauce

full power
8 minutes

1 tbsp butter
¹/₂ onion, chopped
1 tbsp finely chopped green pepper
2 cloves garlic, chopped
250 ml/8 fl oz seasoned canned tomato spaghetti sauce
2 tbsp brown sugar
2 tbsp lemon juice
1 teasp Worcestershire sauce
salt and freshly ground black pepper to taste
¹/₂ teasp paprika
¹/₂ teasp dry mustard
pinch of cayenne pepper
pinch of ground turmeric

Place butter in a 2-litre/3¹/₂-pint container and microwave on full power for about 30 seconds to melt. Add onion, green pepper and garlic. Microwave for 3 minutes, then stir in remaining ingredients. Cover and microwave for 4–5 minutes, until sauce is bubbly. Brush sauce over steaks, chops or ribs on the barbecue. The sauce can be kept in the refrigerator, but should be covered.

Makes about 300 ml/¹/₂ pint

Bearnaise sauce

full power
7 minutes

3 tbsp dry white wine
1 tbsp tarragon vinegar
2 spring onions, chopped
1/2 teasp dried tarragon
few black peppercorns
3 egg yolks
125 g/4 oz butter
salt to taste

Place white wine, tarragon vinegar, spring onion, dried tarragon and peppercorns in a flat dish. Microwave, uncovered, on full power for 4 minutes, until liquid has reduced to at least half. Strain and set aside. Using a food processor fitted with a metal blade, process egg yolks until light in colour. Microwave butter for 3 minutes (butter must be very hot). With machine running, pour hot butter onto yolks. Process for about 45 seconds. Add strained liquid and a little salt. Process to combine. Serve hot with beef, lamb, chicken or fish.

To reheat the sauce, microwave, covered, on defrost for 2 – 4 minutes, depending on how cold the sauce is. Whisk well and serve.

Makes about 175 ml/6 fl oz

VARIATIONS

Avocado bearnaise: Follow directions for making the bearnaise sauce, substituting white wine vinegar for tarragon vinegar. Finally, fold in 1 puréed avocado. Serve with beef, chicken or fish.

Pineapple bearnaise: Follow directions for making bearnaise sauce, substituting pineapple juice for dry white white wine. Finally, stir in 4 tbsp crushed pineapple. Serve with beef or chicken.

Tomato topping

full power
18 minutes

1 tbsp oil
1/2 onion, chopped
1 clove garlic, crushed
1 (425-g/15-oz) can whole peeled tomatoes, chopped
1 tbsp tomato purée
pinch of oregano
1 bay leaf
salt and black pepper to taste
1/2 teasp sugar

Use a deep bowl to prevent excess splashing in the oven. Pour oil into bowl and add onion and garlic. Microwave on full power for 4 minutes. Add remaining ingredients. Microwave, uncovered, on full power for 14 minutes, stirring every 3 minutes. The tomato mixture should be fairly thick. Remove bay leaf. Microwave for 1–2 minutes more if necessary.

Makes 350 ml/12 fl oz

Marmalade sauce

This tasty accompaniment to pork, ham or tongue can also be served as a dip for cocktail sausages

full power
10 minutes

1/2 teasp dry mustard
2 teasp brown sugar
pinch of ground ginger
salt to taste
pinch of ground cloves
175 ml/6 fl oz sweet red wine
4 tbsp raisins
2 tbsp apple jelly
1 1/2 teasp grated orange rind
1 tbsp cornflour
2 tbsp orange juice
1 tbsp lemon juice

Place all ingredients except cornflour and fruit juices in a bowl. Cover and microwave on full power for 6 minutes. Meanwhile, blend cornflour with orange and lemon juices. Add a little of the boiling liquid to the cornflour mixture, then return to the bowl. Stir well. Microwave, uncovered, for 4 minutes, stirring once during cooking time. Serve hot or cold.

Makes 250 ml/8 fl oz

Hollandaise sauce

full power
3 minutes

125 g/4 oz butter
2 egg yolks
1 tbsp lemon juice
1/2 teasp dry mustard
salt and white pepper to taste

Place butter in a glass measuring jug and microwave on full power for 2 1/2 – 3 1/2 minutes until hot and bubbly. Place remaining ingredients in a blender or food processor. When butter is ready, turn blender or processor to highest speed and slowly add hot butter, mixing until sauce is creamy and thickened.

Makes about 175 ml/6 fl oz

Easy spaghetti sauce

full power
20 minutes

2 tbsp oil
1 large onion, coarsely chopped
1 stick celery, thinly sliced
10 mushrooms, sliced
1/2 green pepper, seeded and coarsely chopped
2–3 cloves garlic, finely chopped
250 g/8 oz minced beef
1 (425-g/15-oz) can whole peeled tomatoes, chopped
1 tbsp tomato purée
2 tbsp chopped fresh parsley
1/2 teasp dried basil
2 teasp lemon juice
salt and black pepper to taste

Place oil in a 2-litre/3¹/₂-pint casserole dish. Add onion, celery, mushrooms, green pepper and garlic. Cover and microwave on full power for 5 minutes, stirring once. Break up minced beef and add to the vegetables. Microwave for 3 minutes, stirring after each minute. Blend Blend in chopped tomatoes and juice, tomato purée, parsley, basil and lemon juice. Season to taste. Cover and microwave on full power until the sauce is slightly thickened, about 12 minutes, stirring 3 or 4 times.

Makes about 900 ml/1¹/₂ pints

Lemon butter sauce

Serve with fish or vegetables such as asparagus and broccoli

full power
3 minutes

4 tbsp lemon juice
125 g/4 oz butter, cut into pieces
pinch of salt
2 teasp freshly chopped parsley

Place lemon juice in a glass measuring jug and microwave on full power until juice is bubbly, 30 – 45 seconds. Remove from oven and whisk in about a third of the butter. Return to oven for 30 – 45 seconds, then whisk in another third of the butter. Microwave for 30 – 45 seconds and finally whisk in remaining butter. Stir in salt and parsley. Heat again until bubbly, about 45 seconds. Serve hot.

Makes 150 ml/¹/₄ pint

Reduced cream

full power
medium
10 minutes

Place 250 ml/8 fl oz single cream in a deep 1.5-litre/2¹/₂-pint casserole dish or jug. Microwave on full power for 2 minutes. Stir, then microwave for a further 2 minutes. Stir again. Reduce power to medium, and microwave for 6 minutes more, stirring every 2 minutes. Various flavourings can be added to the reduced cream, such as wine, lemon juice, salt and pepper, grated cheese, savoury butter, mustard. This makes a rich, smooth sauce to serve with vegetables, meat or fish, depending on the flavouring.

Makes 200 ml/7 fl oz

Seasoned butter

low
45 seconds

Place 250 g/8 oz butter in a glass measuring jug and microwave on low for 30–45 seconds just to soften. Then flavour with ingredients of your choice, and beat with an electric mixer until light and fluffy. Transfer to a suitable container or shape into a roll. Keep refrigerated until needed and serve with roast meat, fish or vegetables.

VARIATIONS

Herbed butter: Add 2 teasp freshly chopped parsley, 2 teasp lemon juice, salt and pepper to taste and 1/2–1 teasp dried thyme, tarragon or rosemary, as desired.

Garlic butter: Add 2–3 crushed cloves of garlic, 2 teasp lemon juice and 1/2 teasp dry mustard. For parsley garlic, add 5 tbsp chopped parsley to the butter mixture.

Dill butter: Add 1 tbsp freshly chopped dill, salt and pepper to taste and the sieved yolk of 1 hard-boiled egg.

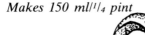

Salads & dressings

Whether a starter to a rich meal, an interesting accompaniment to a hot or cold spread, or even, a light main course, create a salad for every season and every occasion with freshly blanched, crisp vegetables. Moulded salads make an imposing centrepiece for a cold buffet – and are quick to prepare in the microwave. For the perfect salad toss an interesting selection of salad ingredients with just the right dressing.

To blanch vegetables

Place vegetables in a cooking bag or covered casserole dish with only a drop of water, microwave for a few minutes, then plunge into cold water. Blanching produces crisp, brightly coloured vegetables with maximum flavour. Remember, vegetables for salads should still be crunchy so take care not to overcook them.

French dressing

Although not made in a microwave, this classic dressing is used in many of the following recipes

6 tbsp oil
4 tbsp vinegar (white, wine or tarragon)
salt and black pepper to taste
pinch of cayenne pepper
½ teasp dry mustard
½ teasp sugar

Combine all ingredients well and use as required. French dressing may be kept in a cool place (not in the refrigerator) for a few days. The vinegar flavour will become stronger if it is stored for a longer period.

Makes about 150 ml/¼ pint

Boiled salad dressing

full power
low
4 minutes

2 teasp flour
1 tbsp sugar
pinch of salt
1 teasp made English mustard
5 tbsp white wine vinegar
4 tbsp water
1 tbsp margarine
1 egg, lightly beaten
little cream or milk

Combine the dry ingredients in a medium-sized bowl. Add the mustard, vinegar and water. Stir well to remove lumps. Microwave, uncovered, for 3 minutes on full power. Stir every minute. Remove from oven, add margarine and then pour onto the lightly beaten egg, mixing well. Return to oven and microwave on low for 1 minute. Beat well, then allow to cool. Dilute to desired consistency with cream or milk.

Makes 175 ml/6 fl oz

Beetroot salad

full power
33 minutes

6 medium beetroots
1 onion, sliced
3 tbsp water
1 tbsp sugar

300 ml/½ pint white wine vinegar
½ teasp salt
½ teasp black peppercorns
sprigs of parsley to garnish

Top and tail beetroot. Arrange in a circle in a shallow casserole dish. Add enough water to cover bottom of casserole, about 200 ml/7 fl oz. Cover and microwave on full power for 29–33 minutes, depending on the size of beetroot. Uncover and allow to cool. Peel and slice thinly. Place beetroot in a glass jar in layers, adding a little onion between each layer. Place water and sugar in a container and microwave for 30 seconds. Combine remaining ingredients and pour onto beetroot. Stand overnight before serving. To serve, drain beetroot, place in a serving bowl. Garnish with sprigs of parsley. This beetroot salad will keep for about 1 month in the refrigerator.

Serves 12

Marinated mushrooms

full power
3½ minutes

375 g/12 oz button mushrooms, wiped clean
250 ml/8 fl oz French dressing (opposite)
2 tbsp chopped chives
1 tbsp chopped parsley
2 tbsp white vinegar

Place cleaned mushrooms in a large glass bowl. Combine dressing, chives, parsley and vinegar in a casserole dish. Cover and microwave on full power for 3 – 3½ minutes. Pour over mushrooms, cover, and place in refrigerator for several hours or overnight. Drain dressing and serve mushrooms on lettuce leaves, if desired.

Serves 4 – 6

Potato salad

full power
28 minutes

6 potatoes
3 rashers bacon, rinds removed
150 g/5 oz mushrooms, sliced
1 small onion, chopped
2 tbsp chopped chives
2 tbsp chopped parsley
1 gherkin, chopped
mayonnaise
lettuce and parsley to garnish

For the dressing
6 tbsp white vinegar
1 teasp dry mustard
salt and black pepper to taste
cayenne pepper to taste
1 teasp sugar

Wash potatoes and wipe dry. Pierce each with a skewer or fork. Place in a circle on a plate and microwave on full power for 20 minutes. Test that they are ready and cook for 1 or 2 minutes longer if necessary. Allow to cool slightly. Peel and dice, then place in a bowl. Combine all the ingredients for the dressing in a jug. Microwave on full power for 1 minute. Pour over potato and allow to cool.

Microwave bacon on full power for 4 – 6 minutes. Remove bacon, reserving fat, then drain on paper towel. Chop bacon and add to potato. Toss mushrooms in the reserved bacon fat. Microwave on full power for 1 minute. Cool, then add to potato. Add onion, chives, parsley and gherkin. Carefully mix in enough mayonnaise to bind the potato mixture. Turn into a salad bowl. Garnish with a few lettuce leaves and parsley.

Serves 6 – 8

VARIATION

Use a mixture of mayonnaise and soured cream to bind salad, and add a few caraway seeds.

Chef's spinach salad

full power
3 minutes

4 leeks, white portion only
6 tbsp chicken stock
1 bunch spinach
1 small lettuce
180 g/6 oz chicken, diced
150 g/5 oz ham, diced
60 g/2 oz Feta or Gruyère cheese, diced
90 g/3 oz croûtons
2 tomatoes, sliced

For the dressing
150 ml/¼ pint oil
4 tbsp red wine vinegar
4 teasp French mustard
salt and black pepper to taste
pinch of cayenne pepper
1 teasp sugar

Place leeks in a small casserole dish, add chicken stock and cover. Microwave on full power for 3 minutes. Uncover and cool leeks in the stock. Drain and slice thickly. Wash, dry and break spinach and lettuce into bite-sized pieces. Place in a salad bowl. Add leeks, chicken, ham, cheese and croûtons. Toss well, and add tomato slices.

To make dressing, combine all ingredients and mix well. Pour dressing over salad, toss again and serve.

Serves 4 – 6

Minted sweetcorn and courgette salad

full power
9 minutes

6–8 courgettes
2 tbsp oil
1 onion, chopped
3 tbsp white wine vinegar
1 teasp fresh oregano, or ½ teasp dried oregano
1 tbsp finely chopped mint
2 (198-g/7-oz) cans sweetcorn kernels, drained
salt and black pepper to taste
fresh sprigs of mint to garnish

Cut ends off courgettes and slice thickly. In a shallow casserole dish, microwave oil on full power for 2 minutes. Add the courgettes and onion. Toss in the oil. Microwave, covered, for 5 minutes. Stir once during the cooking time. Add wine vinegar, oregano, mint, sweetcorn and seasoning. Cover and microwave for 2 minutes. Allow to cool, then chill. Serve garnished with sprigs of mint.

Serves 4 – 6

Minted sweetcorn and courgette salad

Salad Irma

Salad Irma

full power
7 minutes

250 g/8 oz prawns, heads removed
3 tbsp water
salt to taste
1 tbsp lemon juice
250 g/8 oz green beans
lettuce leaves
1 avocado, peeled and sliced
210 g/7 oz mushrooms, sliced
1 tbsp chopped parsley

For the dressing
3 tbsp oil
1 tbsp lemon juice
2 tbsp tarragon vinegar
1 teasp fresh tarragon, chopped
½ teasp sugar
salt and black pepper to taste

Place the prawns in a shallow dish. Add half the water, salt and 1 teasp lemon juice. Cover and microwave on full power for 3–4 minutes, depending on the size of the prawns. Cool slightly, shell prawns and cut into chunks. Reserve four for garnishing.

String the beans and cut in half. Place beans in a shallow dish. Add remaining water and a little salt. Cover and microwave on full power for 3 minutes. Drain and refresh in plenty of cold water. Allow to cool.

Line a shallow salad platter with lettuce leaves. Brush the avocado slices with a little lemon juice. Carefully arrange beans and avocado on the lettuce. Top with mushrooms and prawns. Combine all the ingredients for the dressing and pour over the salad. Sprinkle with chopped parsley.

Serves 4

Caesar salad

medium
4 minutes

1 lettuce
5 tbsp sunflower seed oil
1 egg
pinch of dry mustard
salt and black pepper to taste
5 anchovy fillets, mashed
½ teasp Worcestershire sauce
2 teasp lemon juice
2 tbsp wine vinegar
90 g/3 oz small croûtons, cooled
3 tbsp grated Parmesan cheese
few black olives

Wash and dry lettuce, break into bite-sized pieces and place in a salad bowl. In a jug, combine oil, egg, mustard, salt, black pepper, anchovy fillets, Worcestershire sauce, lemon juice and vinegar. Place in microwave, uncovered, and cook on medium for 4 minutes. Stir once during cooking time. Mix well and cool slightly. Add croûtons, cheese and olives to lettuce. Pour dressing over, toss and serve immediately.

Serves 4 – 6

Chunky vegetable salad

full power
22 minutes

6 small carrots, sliced
3 tbsp water
salt to taste
180 g/6 oz green beans, sliced
4 courgettes, sliced
3 tbsp water
2 tbsp oil
1 onion, chopped
1 green pepper, seeded and chopped
2 tbsp chopped almonds

For the dressing
120 ml/4 fl oz oil
120 ml/4 fl oz malt vinegar
3 tbsp sugar
1/2 teasp thyme
1 (397-g/10-oz) can concentrated tomato soup

Place the carrots, water and a little salt in a shallow casserole dish. Cover and microwave on full power for 7–8 minutes, stirring once or twice during cooking time. The carrots should still be crisp. Drain and refresh in cold water. Place the green beans and courgettes in the shallow casserole dish, add 3 tbsp water and a little salt. Cover and microwave on full power for 4 minutes. Drain and refresh in cold water.

Pour oil into a small dish, microwave on full power for 1 minute. Add onion and green pepper, and toss in oil. Microwave on full power for 4 minutes. Drain all the vegetables well, combine in a bowl and set aside.

In a glass jug, combine all ingredients for the dressing. Cover and microwave on full power for 5 minutes, stirring twice during cooking time. Pour hot dressing over the vegetables. Chill and serve very cold. Before serving, sprinkle with almonds.

Serves 8–10

Seasonal salad

full power
4 minutes

1/4 medium cauliflower or a few florets broccoli
4 courgettes, thickly sliced
2 tbsp water
1 medium lettuce
90 g/3 oz mushrooms, sliced
1 kohlrabi, thinly sliced
2–3 tomatoes, cut into wedges
1 small onion, sliced
2 tbsp chopped parsley
a few black olives
60 g/2 oz Feta cheese, cubed
1 avocado, cut up
6 tbsp French dressing (see p. 54)

Wash the cauliflower well and cut into small florets. Add the courgettes. Place in a shallow casserole dish. Add water and cover. Microwave on full power for 4 minutes. Drain and refresh in cold water. Cool completely. Wash and dry the lettuce. Break into bite-sized pieces and place in a salad bowl. Add all the vegetables, parsley, olives and Feta cheese. Cover and refrigerate until required. At the last minute add avocado. Pour the dressing over the salad, toss well and serve.

Serves 6–8

Hot potato salad

full power
24 minutes

4 large potatoes
6 rashers bacon, diced
2 tbsp plain flour
3 tbsp sugar
1 1/2-2 teasp salt
pepper to taste
250 ml/8 fl oz water
120 ml/4 fl oz wine vinegar
1 stick celery, finely chopped

Wash potatoes and wipe dry. Pierce with a skewer or fork. Microwave potatoes on full power for 10–12 minutes, turning them after 4 minutes. Remove from oven, cool slightly, then peel and cut into bite-sized pieces. Keep warm. Place diced bacon in a deep casserole dish and microwave on full power for 5–6 minutes, stirring after 2 minutes. Remove bacon with a slotted spoon and keep warm. Add flour, sugar, salt and pepper to bacon fat in the casserole dish, mixing well. Microwave for 1 minute, stir well, then microwave 1 minute more. Stir until smooth. Combine water and vinegar and gradually stir into flour mixture. Add chopped celery and microwave for 3 1/2–4 minutes, stirring after each minute. Remove from oven and stir well. Add potatoes and bacon, and mix well. Cover and stand for a few minutes before serving.

Serves 6

Pasta salad

full power
7 minutes

1/2 medium cauliflower
6 tbsp water
4 courgettes, thickly sliced
1/2 cucumber, cut into matchstick strips
250 g/8 oz ham or tongue, cut into matchstick strips
3 tomatoes, peeled and diced
1 bunch spring onions, chopped
2 tbsp chopped parsley
2 tbsp pine nuts or almonds, chopped
salt and black pepper to taste
6 tbsp French dressing (see p. 54)
1 tbsp tomato ketchup
150 ml/1/4 pint mayonnaise
250 g/8 oz noodles, cooked

Wash the cauliflower well and cut into small florets. Place in a casserole dish with 3 tbsp water, cover and microwave on full power for 4 minutes. Drain and refresh in plenty of cold water. Place the courgettes in the casserole dish and add the remaining water. Cover and microwave on full power for 3 minutes. Drain and refresh in cold water. Using a large bowl, combine all the ingredients. Toss well and chill before serving.

Serves 4 as a main course

Spicy three bean salad

full power
21 minutes

1 tbsp oil
2 rashers bacon, cut up
2 medium onions, chopped
1 green pepper, seeded and chopped
2 cloves garlic, crushed
2 teasp chopped fresh ginger
1 teasp curry paste
1 (793-g/1 lb 12-oz) can whole peeled tomatoes, chopped
salt and black pepper to taste
1/2 teasp sugar
1 bay leaf
1 (447-g/15¾-oz) can baked beans
1 (425-g/15-oz) can butter beans, drained
1 (432-g/15¼-oz) can red kidney beans
parsley to garnish

Use a large, deep casserole dish for this. Microwave oil on
full power for 1 minute. Add bacon, onion, green pepper,
garlic, ginger and curry paste. Toss in oil. Microwave on
full power for 5 minutes. Add tomatoes, seasonings, sugar
and bay leaf. Microwave, uncovered, on full power for
15 minutes. Stir from time to time. Remove the bay leaf.
Add all the beans. Decorate with sprigs of parsley. Serve
hot or cold.

Serves 12

Sweet and sour bean salad

full power
13 minutes

5 rashers bacon, diced
90 g/3 oz sugar
1 tbsp cornflour
salt and pepper to taste
150 ml/1/4 pint red wine vinegar
1 teasp made English mustard
1½ (284-g/10 oz) cans green beans, drained
1 (432-g/16⅓ oz) can red kidney beans, drained
1 (425-g/15 oz) can butter beans, drained
1 onion, sliced

Place bacon in a large, deep casserole dish. Microwave on
full power for about 4 minutes, or until bacon pieces are
crisp. Remove bacon with slotted spoon and drain on paper
towel. Add sugar, cornflour, salt and pepper, vinegar
and mustard to bacon fat in the casserole, mixing well.
Microwave for 3 minutes, stirring after each minute. The
mixture should be thick. Add all the drained beans and
the onion. Mix gently to coat all ingredients. Cover and
microwave for 6 minutes, stirring after 3 minutes. Stir at
the end of cooking time, then let salad stand, covered, for
about 10 minutes before serving. Sprinkle bacon over
beans and serve.

Serves 6

Spicy three bean salad

Bean and bacon salad

full power
6 minutes

3–4 rashers bacon, rinds removed
1 (432-g/15¼-oz) can red kidney beans, drained
1 small cucumber, diced
1 small onion, chopped
1 clove garlic, crushed
1 tbsp chopped chives
salt and black pepper to taste
few drops of Tabasco
4 tbsp French dressing (see p. 54)
1 hard-boiled egg, sliced

Place the bacon on a rack and microwave on full power for
4 – 6 minutes. Drain on paper towel. When cool, crumble.
In a bowl combine the beans, cucumber, onion, garlic,
chives, salt and pepper, and Tabasco. Pour the French
dressing over and toss lightly. Turn into a salad bowl. Top
with crumbled bacon and slices of egg.

Serves 4

Pepper, aubergine and tomato salad

full power
25 minutes

1 medium aubergine
salt to taste
oil
1 green pepper, seeded and cut into chunks
1 onion, sliced
2 tomatoes, sliced
2 tbsp lemon juice
1 clove garlic, crushed
black pepper, to taste
½ teasp dried basil
1 tbsp chopped parsley and black olives to garnish

Wash aubergine and slice into rings without peeling.
Sprinkle with a little salt, and set aside for 30 minutes.
Pat dry with paper towel, then brush with oil. Microwave
a browning dish on full power for 6 minutes. Add 1 tbsp
oil to the dish and microwave for 1 minute. Arrange
aubergine slices in browning dish, press down firmly for
30 seconds to sear, then microwave for 1 minute. Turn
and repeat. Drain on paper towel. Cut each slice into
four. Repeat with remaining aubergine by reheating
browning dish for 2 minutes before searing and
microwaving. Add more oil to browning dish if necessary.
    Heat browning dish for 3 minutes, add a little oil and the
green pepper. Microwave 1 minute on each side. Drain on
paper towel. Repeat with onion rings. Place tomato slices
on browning dish without reheating it. Microwave 1 minute
on each side and set aside.
    Add lemon juice, garlic, black pepper and basil to dish.
Stir to mix. Arrange cooked salad ingredients in a shallow
dish and pour lemon mixture over. Cover and chill well.
Before serving, sprinkle with chopped parsley and a few
black olives.

Serves 4 – 6

Hot tuna salad

Makes a good starter or a main course for supper

high
8 minutes

2 (198-g/7-oz) cans tuna in water, drained
5 sticks celery, chopped
180 g/6 oz croûtons
250 ml/8 fl oz mayonnaise
60 g/2 oz flaked almonds, toasted (see p. 23)
2 tbsp finely chopped onion
2 teasp capers, drained
1 tbsp lemon juice
salt and pepper to taste
60 g/2 oz Cheddar cheese, grated

In a 2-litre/3½-oz casserole dish, combine tuna, celery, half
the croûtons, mayonnaise, almonds, onion, capers and lemon
juice. Season to taste and mix well. Cover and microwave
on high for 7 minutes, stirring after 3 minutes. Sprinkle
remaining croûtons over casserole and top with grated
cheese. Microwave on high for 1½ minutes or until cheese
melts.

Serves 6 as a main course or serves 8 as a starter

Lettuce salad with a difference

full power
6 minutes

4 rashers streaky bacon, diced
4 tbsp white wine vinegar
2 teasp sugar
salt and pepper to taste
pinch of mixed herbs
1 stick celery, finely chopped
1 tbsp chopped chives
1 lettuce, broken into pieces
1 orange, peeled and segmented
60 g/2 oz walnuts, coarsely chopped

Microwave bacon in a deep casserole dish on full power for
3 minutes, or until crisp. Remove bacon with a slotted
spoon and drain on paper towel. Add vinegar, sugar, salt,
pepper and herbs to the casserole dish and mix well with
bacon fat. Microwave on full power for 2 – 2½ minutes.
Stir well, then mix in celery and chives. Microwave for
30 seconds. Add lettuce pieces, a few at a time, to the hot
dressing, tossing to coat pieces. When all have been added
and lettuce is slightly limp, gently stir in orange segments
and walnuts. Serve immediately.

Serves 8

Moulded apple salad with chive cream

full power
2 minutes

300 ml/½ pint water
1 (127-g/4½-oz) tablet lemon jelly
150 ml/¼ pint apple juice
3 sticks celery, chopped
1 apple, sliced
½ small cucumber, thinly sliced

For the chive cream
250 g/8 oz low fat cottage cheese
4 tbsp milk
3 tbsp chopped chives
60 g/2 oz chopped walnuts
cucumber slices (optional)

Microwave 150 ml/¼ pint water on full power for 1–1½ minutes, until boiling. Pour over lemon jelly cubes, stirring to dissolve. Return to microwave and heat for 20 seconds. Remove from oven and add remaining water and apple juice. Pour a third of the jelly into a ring mould and sprinkle with chopped celery. Chill until set. Pour in half the remaining jelly and let set slightly. Arrange apples slices around the ring. Chill until set, then add remaining jelly and place cucumber slices around, making sure all slices are submerged in the jelly. Chill until set.

To make the chive cream, beat cottage cheese with milk, stir in chives and nuts. Turn apple salad mould out onto serving plate, fill centre with chive cream and garnish with walnuts, chives or cucumber slices.

Serves 4 – 6

Fruity slaw

high
6 minutes

½ cabbage, shredded
water
4 tbsp seedless raisins
1 apple, cored and sliced
1 (298-g/10½-oz) can mandarin oranges, drained
90 g/3 oz seedless grapes, halved
4 tbsp chopped nuts
1 stick celery, sliced

For the dressing
5 tbsp honey
3 tbsp lemon juice
1 teasp sesame seeds
½ teasp dry mustard
pinch of paprika
½ teasp salt
120 ml/4 fl oz oil

Place cabbage in a large bowl, sprinkle with 6 tbsp water. Cover and microwave on high for 3 minutes. Refresh in cold water and drain well. Place raisins in a measuring jug, add enough water to just cover and microwave on high for 1½ minutes. Drain and cool. Place cabbage in a large bowl, add raisins, fruits, nuts and celery. Toss to mix.

To make the dressing, combine honey, lemon juice, sesame seeds, dry mustard, paprika and salt in a measuring jug. Microwave on high for 1 minute, stir, then microwave for 30 seconds more. Turn mixture into a blender or food processor and, with machine running, slowly add the oil. Blend until slightly thickened, then pour over cabbage mixture. Toss well. Chill for at least 2 hours, stirring occasionally.

Serves 6 – 8

Moulded green vegetable salad

Moulded green vegetable salad

full power
3 minutes

250 ml/8 fl oz water
1 (127-g/4½-oz) tablet lime jelly
3 sticks celery, chopped
1 small green pepper, seeded and chopped
1 tbsp chopped chives
125 g/4 oz chopped cucumber
250 g/8 oz cottage cheese
250 ml/8 fl oz mayonnaise

Microwave water on full power for 2 – 2½ minutes, until boiling. Pour over lime jelly and stir to dissolve. Return mixture to microwave and heat on full power for 30 seconds. Remove jelly from oven and cool until partially set. With an electric mixer, beat jelly, then add vegetables, cottage cheese and mayonnaise, mixing well. Spoon into a serving bowl or ring mould and chill until set, about 3 hours.

Serves 6 – 8

Fish

Fish does not enjoy the popularity it deserves, possibly because this delicate food is easily over-cooked. To make use of the wide variety of fish available in shops, whether fresh or frozen, cook it correctly in the microwave. Fish not only has an excellent flavour and texture, but it has a good appearance too. Little or no extra liquid is used when fish is cooked in the microwave, and this guarantees a delicious result. In addition, more vitamins and mineral salts are retained than when conventional cooking methods are used. Shellfish can also be cooked successfully in the microwave and the tender flesh remains moist and succulent.

When cooking fish

- Cover the fish tightly during cooking.
- Large whole fish should have 2 to 3 slits cut in the skin to prevent them from bursting.
- Defrost frozen fish before cooking in the microwave. Pieces should be separated during defrosting time.
- Do not deep-fry fish in the microwave oven.
- Arrange fish so that the thicker sections are towards the outside.
- Shield the narrow tail end of a large whole fish with a strip of aluminium foil.
- Always undercook rather than overcook fish. Check whether it is ready after the minimum cooking time.
- Brush the fish with melted butter to prevent it from drying out.
- Pierce the bag before microwaving 'boil in the bag' fish.

FISH DEFROSTING AND COOKING CHART

FISH	DEFROST TIME	COOKING TIME (Full power)
Fillets of white fish, plaice, cod, whiting etc., 500 g/1 lb	5-7 minutes, stand 5 minutes	5-6 minutes
Haddock, 500 g/1 lb	5 minutes, stand 5 minutes	4-5 minutes
Salmon steaks, 500 g/1 lb	5 minutes, stand 5 minutes	5-7 minutes
Trout. 2 medium	5-7 minutes, stand 5 minutes	5-6 minutes
Sole. 2 large	5-6 minutes, stand 5 minutes	4-5 minutes
Kipper fillets and 'boil in the bag' fish, 198 g/7 oz	3-4 minutes, stand 5 minutes	3-4 minutes
Prawns, 500 g/1 lb		
large, with shells and heads	7-8 minutes, stand 5 minutes	4-5 minutes
small, peeled and deveined	4-5 minutes, stand 5 minutes	2-4 minutes

Pickled fish

full power
21 minutes

500 g/1 lb firm white fish	1 tbsp sugar
4 tbsp plain flour	1 tbsp chutney
salt and black pepper to taste	1 tbsp apricot jam
4 tbsp oil	200 ml/7 fl oz white vinegar
2 onions, sliced	4 tbsp water
1 tbsp curry powder	2 bay leaves
1/2 teasp turmeric	slices of lemon and parsley
1 small green chilli, chopped	or celery leaves to garnish

Cut fish into small portions and pat dry. Sprinkle with flour, salt and black pepper. Heat 2 tbsp oil in browning dish for 4 minutes on full power. Microwave the fish for 5 minutes, turning once during cooking time. Drain on paper towel. Place the fish in an earthenware or glass dish.

In a shallow casserole dish, microwave remaining oil for 2 minutes. Add onion, curry powder, turmeric and green chilli. Toss the vegetables in hot oil and microwave for 3 minutes, stirring at least once during cooking time. Add sugar, chutney, jam, vinegar, water and bay leaves, cover and microwave for 3 minutes. Stir, then microwave,

uncovered, for 4 minutes. Pour hot sauce over fish. Cover and allow to stand for 2 days before serving. Serve cold. Garnish with slices of lemon and parsley or celery leaves.

Serves 4

Herbed bream

full power
10 minutes

1 bream, about 750 g/1½ lb
oil
salt and black pepper to taste
3 tbsp chopped chives
3 tbsp chopped parsley
2 teasp chopped fresh basil
1 clove garlic (optional)
3 tbsp butter
5 tbsp white wine

Wipe fish and pat dry. Oil a flat dish well. Brush fish with oil and season lightly. Combine chives, parsley and basil. Sprinkle a little on the base of the dish. Place fish on top and cover with remaining herb mixture. Combine garlic and butter, and dot on top of fish. Add white wine. Cover with cling film and make two slits in the film to prevent 'ballooning' during cooking. Microwave on full power for 8–10 minutes. Let stand for 4 minutes before serving. To serve, lift fish off bone in portions. Spoon a little of the cooking liquid onto each serving.

Serves 4

Note: Make sure the fish has been properly scaled before preparing this dish.

Baked salmon steaks

full power
8 minutes

4 (180-g/6-oz) salmon steaks, about 2 cm/¾ inch thick
2 tbsp butter
2 tbsp lemon juice
salt and freshly ground black pepper to taste
1 teasp chopped fresh dill or fennel
1 small onion, sliced
4 lettuce leaves, rinsed
lemon wedges to garnish

Arrange salmon steaks in a glass casserole dish with narrow ends toward the centre. Microwave butter in a glass measuring jug on full power for 30–45 seconds. Add lemon juice and pour mixture evenly over salmon. Sprinkle with salt and pepper to taste, and with dill or fennel. Top with onion slices. Arrange a damp lettuce leaf over each salmon steak. Microwave on full power for 5–7 minutes, rotating dish halfway through cooking time if necessary. Let stand for 5 minutes before serving. Serve with lemon wedges.

Serves 4

Salmon pie

full power
high
25 minutes

500 ml/17 fl oz water
1 (43-g/1½-oz) packet chicken noodle soup
2 tbsp margarine
2 tbsp plain flour
200 ml/7 fl oz milk
2 (212-g/7½-oz) cans pink salmon, drained and flaked
3 hard-boiled eggs, chopped
250 g/8 oz cooked rice
2 tbsp chopped parsley
black pepper to taste
120 ml/4 fl oz fruit chutney

Combine the water and soup in a bowl. Cover and
microwave on full power for 5 minutes. Stir, replace cover
and microwave on high for 4 minutes. Place the margarine
in a jug or bowl. Microwave on full power for 1 minute. Stir
in the flour. Add milk and stir well. Microwave on full
power for 3 minutes, stirring every minute. Add cooked
soup, microwave for 2 minutes more. The sauce should boil
for at least 1 minute. Stir once more. Add all the remaining
ingredients, except the chutney. Pour into a greased
casserole dish and dot spoonfuls of chutney on top. Cover
and microwave on high for 10 minutes. Serve hot.

Serves 6 – 8

Salmon steaks de luxe

full power
low
17 minutes

4 (180-g/6-oz) salmon steaks,
   about 2.5 cm/1 inch thick
6 tbsp water
6 tbsp white wine
1 tbsp lemon juice
1 bay leaf
1 slice onion
few peppercorns
1 small carrot, sliced
pinch of salt
1 blade of mace
60 g/2 oz butter
4 tbsp single cream
chopped parsley and slices
   of lemon to garnish

Wipe salmon steaks, pat dry and set aside. Place water,
wine, lemon juice, bay leaf, onion, peppercorns, carrot,
salt and mace in a large, shallow casserole dish. Cover and
microwave on full power for 3 minutes. Add salmon and
dot with butter. Replace cover and microwave for 6
minutes, or until the fish starts to turn opaque. Transfer
fish to a serving dish, cover and keep warm. Strain the
liquid and return to the casserole dish. Microwave,
uncovered, for 5 minutes. Whisk in the cream, then
microwave on low for 3 minutes. Pour over fish and serve
immediately, garnished with chopped parsley and slices of
lemon.

Serves 4

Salmon steaks ready for baking in the microwave

Marinated monkfish kebabs

Tuna-topped spaghetti Italiano

full power
9 minutes

230 g/7½ oz spaghetti
2 tbsp oil
1 clove garlic, chopped
1 (56-g/2-oz) can anchovy fillets, drained and chopped
4 tbsp tomato purée
1 (425-g/15-oz) can whole tomatoes
1 teasp sugar
½ teasp dried oregano
pinch of dried basil
salt and black pepper to taste
1 (198-g/7-oz) can tuna, drained and broken into chunks
20 ripe olives, stoned and halved
2 tbsp chopped parsley

Cook spaghetti and keep warm. Microwave oil in a large casserole dish on full power for 30 – 45 seconds. Add garlic and anchovy, and microwave for 1½ – 2 minutes. Stir in tomato purée, tomatoes with liquid, sugar, oregano and basil, and season with salt and pepper. Microwave for 3 – 4 minutes to blend flavours. Stir in tuna, olives and parsley and microwave on full power for 2 – 2½ minutes. Add half the tomato sauce to the spaghetti and toss gently to mix well. Turn spaghetti onto a large warmed platter and spoon remaining sauce over.

Serves 4

Savoury crêpes Newburg

full power
medium
10 minutes

230 g/7½ oz butter or margarine
1 tbsp chopped spring onion
4 tbsp Madeira
250 ml/8 fl oz single cream
3 egg yolks, beaten
460 g/15 oz cooked lobster
1 tbsp tomato purée
salt and pepper to taste
8 crêpes (see p. 113)
120 ml/4 fl oz double cream, lightly whipped
1 tbsp brandy

Microwave butter in a deep casserole dish on full power for 1 – 1½ minutes. Add onion and microwave, covered, for 1 minute. Add Madeira, replace cover and microwave for 1½ – 2 minutes. Add cream to butter mixture and mix well. Microwave, covered, for a further 1½ – 2 minutes. Gradually add some of the cream mixture to beaten egg yolks, stirring constantly. Now stir egg yolks into the cream mixture. Add lobster and tomato purée, and season to taste. Spoon a little lobster mixture into each crêpe, roll up and place in a casserole dish. Combine whipped cream and brandy and spoon over crêpes. Microwave, covered, on medium for 3 – 4 minutes, or until heated through.

Serves 4

Marinated monkfish kebabs

full power
8 minutes

850 g/1¾ lb monkfish, or any other firm white fish
2 teasp finely chopped fresh ginger
2 cloves garlic, crushed
150 ml/¼ pint plain yoghurt
90 ml/3 fl oz soured cream
2 teasp soy sauce
1 teasp curry powder
juice of ½ lemon
salt and black pepper to taste
1 tbsp chopped parsley

Remove skin from monkfish. Cut fish into 2-cm/¾-inch cubes and set aside. Combine all remaining ingredients, except parsley. Add fish to marinade and mix to coat all the cubes. Cover and refrigerate for 2 hours. Divide fish between six wooden kebab sticks and arrange on a plate. Microwave on full power for about 8 minutes. Spoon a little of the marinade over each kebab. Sprinkle with chopped parsley and serve immediately.

Serves 6

VARIATION

To add extra flavour, alternate cubes of fish with pieces of green pepper and a few blanched baby onions.

64

Baked stuffed sea bass

Baked stuffed sea bass

full power
high
26 minutes

1 kg/2 lb whole sea bass on the bone, or any other firm white fish
salt and pepper to taste
oil
2 leeks, including green portion

For the stuffing
60 g/2 oz butter
4 leeks
150 g/5 oz cooked brown rice
1 (250-g/8 oz) can mussels, drained
1 egg
1 tbsp chopped parsley
1 teasp lemon rind
salt and black pepper to taste
pinch of dried thyme

First make the stuffing. Microwave butter in a bowl for 1 minute on full power. Slice the white portion of leeks thinly, add to the butter and toss well. Microwave for 3 minutes. Add rice, mussels, egg, parsley, lemon rind, salt, black pepper and thyme, and stir to combine.

Wipe and pat dry the fish. Remove fins, but do not skin. Split fish along stomach to within 5 cm/2 inches of the tail. Starting at the thick end of the fish, remove backbone by slicing horizontally, just above and just below the bone. Cut bone away 5 cm/2 inches before the tail. Brush a sheet of non-stick parchment with oil. Season fish lightly, place on paper and open up. Place stuffing on bottom portion of fish and replace top portion. Brush top of fish with oil.

Wash two leeks well, but do not dry. Microwave on full power for 2 minutes, then refresh in cold water. Peel off each layer of leek. Starting at the large end of the fish, wrap leek leaves around fish and tuck the ends under. Brush with a little oil. Roll long edges of non-stick parchment together until the fish has been sealed inside, and tie ends with string or elastic bands. Place fish on a large plate and microwave on high for 18–20 minutes, depending on the thickness of the fish. Let stand for a few minutes before serving. Open parchment carefully and transfer the fish to a serving platter. Cut fish crosswise following the lines of the leek leaves.

Serves 4 – 6

Seafood bake

full power
high
16 minutes

60 g/2 oz butter or margarine
2 sticks celery, thinly sliced
1/2 onion, finely chopped
1 small green pepper, seeded and chopped
250 ml/8 fl oz white sauce (see p. 49)
1 tbsp Worcestershire sauce
250 g/8 oz cooked crab meat, chopped
250 g/8 oz cooked shrimps or small shelled prawns
250 ml/8 fl oz mayonnaise
1 tbsp lemon juice
1 tbsp chopped parsley
250 g/8 oz cooked rice
30 g/1 oz crushed potato crisps

In a shallow casserole dish, microwave butter on full power for 1 minute. Add celery, onion, green pepper and toss to coat. Cover and microwave for 3 minutes, stirring once. Add vegetables to white sauce, along with Worcestershire sauce, crab meat, shrimps, mayonnaise and lemon juice. Stir in chopped parsley. Press cooked rice gently into bottom of a buttered, 2-litre/3¹/₂-pint casserole dish. Top with seafood mixture, smooth over and sprinkle crushed crisps on top. Microwave on high for 10–12 minutes.

Serves 6 – 8

Fish bake with tomato salsa

This is a Spanish dish from the La Dorado restaurant, where succulent Mediterranean sea bass is served. The success of this dish, however, depends on the quality of the fish – it should be absolutely fresh.

high
18 minutes

1 kg/2 lb whole, firm white fish, sea bass, bream, grey mullet etc.
coarse salt

For tomato salsa
2 ripe tomatoes, chopped
2 half-green tomatoes, chopped
1 onion, chopped
1 small green chilli, chopped
2 teasp lemon juice

To make tomato salsa, combine all the ingredients and let stand for 1 hour before serving.

Wipe the cleaned fish and pat dry. Cover base of a shallow container with a 5 mm/1/4 inch layer of coarse salt, place fish on top and cover with another 5 mm/1/4 inch layer of salt. Cover container with cling film in which two slits have been cut to prevent 'ballooning' during cooking. Microwave on high for 15–18 minutes. Cooking time will depend on the thickness of the fish used. Remove cling film and lift fish onto a board. Carefully scrape away crust and skin from top of fish. Lift off flesh in portions. Turn fish over and repeat. Serve immediately with tomato salsa or hollandaise sauce.

Serves 4 – 6

Scallops with cream sauce

Scallops with cream sauce

Apple juice and a dash of whisky add interesting flavour to these scallops

full power
high
16 minutes

150 ml/¼ pint apple juice	salt and pepper to taste
2 tbsp whisky	2 tbsp butter
2 tbsp lemon juice	2 tbsp plain flour
1 small onion, chopped	4 tbsp single cream
1 kg/2 lb frozen scallops, thawed	60 g/2 oz Parmesan cheese, grated
2 teasp chopped fresh parsley	lemon and parsley to garnish

Combine apple juice, whisky, lemon juice and onion in a casserole dish. Microwave for 1½ – 2 minutes on full power. Add scallops, parsley, salt and pepper. Microwave on high for 5 – 7 minutes, or until scallops are opaque and feel firm when touched. Remove from the oven. With a slotted spoon, transfer scallops to a serving platter, cover and keep warm. Reserve cooking liquid.

In a large glass jug, microwave butter for 30 – 45 seconds on full power. Stir in flour and microwave for 30 seconds. Stir well, then gradually stir in cooking liquid from scallops. Microwave on full power for 2½ – 3½ minutes, stirring every 45 seconds, until the mixture is thick and bubbly. Stir in cream and microwave on high for 30 seconds to heat through. Pour sauce over scallops, sprinkle with cheese and microwave for 1½ – 2 minutes to melt cheese. Garnish with lemon and parsley and serve hot.

Serves 6

Poached trout with tarragon cream

full power
high
20 minutes

4 medium trout
salt and black pepper to taste
120 ml/4 fl oz white wine
2 tbsp water
1 slice onion
2 slices lemon
1 tbsp chopped tarragon
few sprigs parsley
6 tbsp single cream
3 tbsp plain yoghurt
4 lemon twists and sprigs of parsley to garnish

Rinse trout and pat dry with paper towel. Season well. Place in a rectangular shallow casserole dish. Add wine, water, onion, lemon slices, 1 teasp tarragon and a few sprigs parsley. Cover with cling film and make two slits in the film to prevent 'ballooning' during cooking. Microwave fish on full power for 8–10 minutes, depending on size. Drain fish and keep warm. Microwave cooking liquid for 6 minutes to reduce. Whisk in cream and yoghurt, then microwave on high for 4 minutes. Coat trout with a little sauce and sprinkle with remaining tarragon. Serve remaining sauce separately. Garnish with twists of lemon and sprigs of parsley.

Serves 4

French fish fillets

full power
6 minutes

500 g/1 lb fish fillets (cod or whiting)
5 tbsp French dressing (see p. 54)
90 g/3 oz dry breadcrumbs or cracker crumbs
paprika
salt to taste

Dip fillets in French dressing, then roll in crumbs. Arrange in a greased baking dish and sprinkle with paprika and salt. Cover with greaseproof paper and microwave for 5–6 minutes on full power, until fish flakes easily. Turn dish halfway through cooking time.

Serves 3 – 4

Prawns peri-peri

Peri-peri is a very hot pungent spice which is used in some Portuguese and Southern African dishes. If you are unable to obtain it, substitute ground red pepper or cayenne.

full power
22 minutes

1 kg/2 lb prawns in shells
250 g/8 oz butter
1 tbsp Worcestershire sauce
200 ml/7 fl oz tomato ketchup
2 tbsp lemon juice
salt to taste
peri-peri to taste (use sparingly)
oil
lemon roses and parsley or cress to garnish

Devein prawns and remove heads, if desired. Rinse and pat dry, then set aside. Place butter, Worcestershire sauce, tomato sauce, lemon juice, salt and peri-peri in a 3-litre/5½-pint casserole dish. Microwave on full power for 6 minutes. Add half the prawns and microwave, uncovered, for about 8 minutes. Stir twice during cooking time. The time will vary, depending on the size of the prawns. Prawns are cooked when they turn deep pink and become translucent. Using a slotted spoon, drain prawns well and set aside. Repeat with remaining prawns. Heat a little oil in a frying pan and fry prawns conventionally for 2–3 minutes, turning once during cooking time. Garnish with lemon roses and parsley and serve immediately with buttered rice.

Serves 4

Prawns peri-peri

Salmon quenelles served with dill sauce

Salmon quenelles with dill sauce

full power
medium
11 minutes

175 ml/6 fl oz dry white wine
1 tbsp water
2 tbsp butter
4 tbsp wholewheat flour
salt and pepper to taste
1 teasp chopped fresh dill
2 tbsp grated onion
1 egg
1 egg white
1 (212-g/7-oz) can red salmon, drained and flaked
375 ml/13 fl oz hot water
1 teasp salt

For the dill sauce
120 ml/4 fl oz plain yoghurt
2 tbsp cream cheese
2 teasp finely chopped fresh dill
fresh dill, radish slices, spring onions to garnish

Place 3 tbsp of the wine and the water in a 1.2-litre/2-pint glass bowl and microwave on full power for 45 seconds. Add butter and stir to melt. Add flour, salt and pepper and mix well to form a ball. Let cool for a few minutes, then add dill, onion paste and egg and beat well. Beat egg white to stiff peaks and fold into flour mixture. Fold in salmon and chill very well.

To cook, lightly grease a large deep casserole dish. Using two spoons, mould the fish mixture into eight ovals and place in casserole dish. Combine 375 ml/13 fl oz hot water, remaining wine and salt. Gently pour down side of dish. Cover and microwave on medium for 7–9 minutes until quenelles are set. Remove quenelles with a slotted spoon, draining well. Arrange two on each of four individual serving plates.

To make the sauce, place yoghurt, cream cheese and dill in a measuring jug and microwave on medium for 30–45 seconds. Stir well. Pour a little of the sauce over each quenelle and garnish with dill, radish slices and spring onions.

Serves 4

Poultry

The microwave oven can cook your favourite poultry dish in a third to half the time it would take to cook it in a conventional oven. Poultry needs little attention during cooking, and the white meat remains tender and juicy, while the dark meat retains more moisture than in conventional cooking. The only drawback to cooking chicken in the microwave is that the skin does not become golden brown and crisp. Chicken portions can be covered with a variety of coatings to improve their appearance, and add crispness and flavour; or they can be cooked in a sauce. Although whole birds will brown slightly during the longer cooking time, their appearance can be improved by using a browning agent (see page 22) or by basting with a glaze during cooking.

POULTRY DEFROSTING AND COOKING CHART

POULTRY	DEFROST TIME Per 500 g/1 lb (On defrost)	COOKING TIME Per 500 g/1 lb (Full power)	METHOD
Chicken (whole)	9-10 minutes, stand 30 minutes	10-12 minutes	Shield drumsticks for first half of cooking time. Use a cooking bag or covered casserole. Stand 10 minutes after cooking.
Chicken (portions)	6-8 minutes, stand 10 minutes	8-10 minutes	Separate during defrosting. Rearrange during cooking.
Duck	10-12 minutes, stand 30 minutes	10-12 minutes	Shield drumsticks for first half of cooking time. Place duck in microwave, breast side down, and turn over halfway through cooking time. Stand 10-15 minutes after cooking.
Turkey	10-12 minutes, stand 1 hour	11-13 minutes	Turn over 3-4 times during cooking. Shield drumstick and wings for first half of cooking time. Stand 15 minutes after cooking.

Note: When cooking poultry, the power used may be decreased to high, and the cooking time increased by approximately a third. Allow 5 – 8 minutes extra cooking time for stuffed chicken or duck. For stuffed turkey, allow 8 – 11 minutes additional cooking time.

When cooking poultry
- Improve browning by microwaving whole birds in a covered glass casserole dish or in a pierced cooking bag fastened with an elastic band.
- Completely defrost whole birds for quicker and more even cooking.
- To prevent overcooking, shield wing tips, bone-ends and even the breastbone with small strips of foil for half the cooking time.
- Whole birds should be well trussed with legs and wings pinned close to the body to promote even cooking.
- Cook poultry pieces skin side up and place the thicker parts towards the outer edge of the casserole dish. They may need to be turned or rearranged during microwaving.
- As a general rule, stuffed whole birds take a few minutes longer to cook.
- Standing time is important when cooking poultry. Cover the cooked bird loosely with aluminium foil, shiny side in, and stand for 10 to 15 minutes before serving.

Chicken liver stroganoff

high
full power
18 minutes

2 tbsp cornflour
500 ml/17 fl oz milk
1 chicken bouillon cube
1/2 teasp salt
pinch of pepper
pinch of nutmeg
2 tbsp butter or margarine
2 tbsp oil
2 onions, sliced
500 g/1 lb chicken livers, cleaned and halved
1 tbsp vinegar
120 ml/4 fl oz soured cream
paprika and parsley to garnish

Mix cornflour with 250 ml/8 fl oz milk and set aside. Add bouillon cube to remaining milk and microwave on high for 2–3 minutes, stirring occasionally. Add salt, pepper, nutmeg and butter and stir to melt butter. Stir into cornflour mixture, mixing well. Microwave on high for 3 – 4 minutes, stirring every minute, until the mixture thickens and bubbles. Stir well.

Place half the oil in a casserole dish, add the sliced onions, and microwave on full power for 5 minutes, stirring twice. Add onions to sauce and keep warm. Pour the remaining oil into the casserole dish and add chicken livers. Microwave on full power for 3 minutes, stirring after each minute. Add vinegar to the chicken livers, stir well and microwave for 3 minutes more. Remove from heat, pour sauce over livers, and toss to coat. Finally, stir in soured cream. Do not reheat. Serve over hot cooked noodles and garnish with paprika and parsley.

Serves 4 – 6

Tangy chicken casserole

full power
high
41 minutes

1 (1.5 kg/3¼-lb) chicken, jointed
4 tbsp plain flour
salt and black pepper to taste
2 tbsp oil
250 ml/8 fl oz mayonnaise
200 ml/7 fl oz orange juice
250 ml/8 fl oz fruit chutney
paprika

Toss the chicken joints in flour, salt and black pepper. Heat a browning dish for 4 minutes on full power. Add oil, heat for a further 2 minutes. Add joints, cook for 4 – 5 minutes, turning the chicken portions when they are golden brown. In a shallow casserole dish, combine mayonnaise, orange juice and chutney. Add chicken and cover. Microwave on high for 15 minutes. Remove the cover and turn the joints. Microwave, uncovered, for a further 15 minutes. Sprinkle with paprika before serving.

Serves 4 – 6

A variety of delicious crumbed chicken portions

Crumbed chicken portions

full power
medium
22 minutes

8 chicken drumsticks or mixed portions

For the coating
90 g/3 oz savoury biscuits, crushed
1/2 teasp paprika
salt and black pepper to taste

For the dip
1 egg, beaten
1 tbsp milk

Dry chicken pieces with paper towel. Mix ingredients for coating on a flat plate. Combine ingredients for dip in a shallow bowl. Dip chicken into liquid, then into coating. Press coating onto chicken pieces. Arrange chicken pieces on a bacon rack or a round plate, making sure the meatiest sections are towards the outside. Microwave, uncovered, on full power for 10 minutes. Turn chicken pieces to ensure each piece is evenly cooked. Microwave on medium for a further 8 – 12 minutes, depending on the thickness of the pieces.

Serves 4 – 6

VARIATIONS
Cornflake crumb treat: Combine 90 g/3 oz cornflake crumbs, 1/2 teasp mixed herbs, pinch of paprika and 1 tbsp chopped parsley. Dip chicken portions into a mixture of 1 tbsp lemon juice and 1 beaten egg, then into coating mixture. Microwave as above.
Crispy crumbled chicken: Combine 60 g/2 oz crushed barbecue-flavoured potato crisps and 1 tbsp poppy seeds. Dip chicken portions into 3 tbsp melted butter, then into coating mixture. Microwave as above.

Crusty crumbled chicken: Combine 60 g/2 oz crushed corn crisps with 2 tbsp instant mashed potato powder. Dip chicken portions into 4 tbsp evaporated milk seasoned with salt and black pepper, then into coating. Microwave as above.

Honey-glazed chicken

full power
28 minutes

1 (1.5-kg/3¼-lb) chicken
4 tbsp honey
2 tbsp soy sauce

For the marinade
120 ml/4 fl oz soy sauce
2 tbsp finely chopped onion
2 cloves garlic, chopped
1 tbsp oil
1/2 teasp freshly grated root ginger

To make the marinade, combine 120 ml/4 fl oz soy sauce, onion, garlic, oil and root ginger. Place chicken in a polythene bag and set in a bowl. Pour marinade over chicken and close bag. Chill for several hours, or overnight, turning chicken 2 or 3 times.

When ready to cook chicken, drain well, fold wings under and tie legs securely to the tail. Place chicken, breast side up, in a deep casserole dish. Microwave on full power for 24 – 28 minutes, rotating chicken every 6 minutes if necessary. (Chicken should cook for 10 – 12 minutes per 500 g/1 lb).

Meanwhile. combine honey and 2 tbsp soy sauce. Baste chicken frequently with this mixture during last 6 minutes of roasting time. Let chicken stand for 10 minutes, loosely covered, before carving.

Serves 6

Turkey duchesse

full power
high
15 minutes

250 g/8 oz minced turkey or chicken
250 g/8 oz sausage meat
1 onion, chopped
1 tbsp chopped parsley
1 (425-g/15-oz) can celery soup
salt and black pepper to taste
2 eggs, hard-boiled
4–6 potatoes, mashed (see p. 98)
2 tomatoes, sliced
sprigs of parsley to garnish

Line a 23 × 13-cm/ 9 × 5-inch loaf pan with greaseproof or non-stick parchment. In a large bowl, combine meats, onion, parsley, soup and seasonings. Pack half the mixture into the loaf pan. Place hard-boiled eggs down the length of the pan, then cover with remaining mixture. Pack down firmly. Cover with cling film and cut two slits in the plastic to prevent 'ballooning' during cooking. Microwave on full power for 5 minutes, then on high for another 8 minutes. Stand for 5 minutes. Uncover and turn out onto a platter. Cover top with piped stars of mashed potatoes. Press tomato slices onto the sides of the loaf. Microwave, uncovered, on full power for 2 minutes. Garnish with sprigs of parsley.

Serves 4

Turkey duchesse

Chicken breasts with apple

full power
high
29 minutes

4 small chicken breasts, boned
2 tbsp plain flour
salt and black pepper to taste
2 tbsp butter
1 onion, chopped
250 ml/8 fl oz apple juice
1 clove garlic, crushed
pinch of dried rosemary
1 tbsp French mustard
1 green apple
paprika

Place chicken breasts between two layers of foil or greaseproof paper and flatten slightly with a cleaver or mallet. Sprinkle chicken with flour and seasonings. Heat butter in browning dish on full power for 4 minutes. Microwave chicken for 2 minutes on each side. Place chicken in a shallow casserole dish. Add onion to browning dish and toss in butter. Microwave for 1 minute. Stir in any remaining flour. Now add apple juice, garlic, rosemary and mustard. Stir to combine. Pour over chicken and cover. Microwave on full power for 8 minutes, stir, then microwave on high for 10 minutes. Core, quarter and slice apple. Add to casserole dish and microwave on high for 2 minutes. Sprinkle with paprika before serving.

Serves 4

Chicken broccoli bake

full power
high
40 minutes

6–8 chicken portions	6 tbsp milk
4 tbsp plain flour	6 tbsp single cream
salt and black pepper to taste	500 g/1 lb fresh broccoli
3 tbsp oil	3 tbsp water
1 (425-g/15-oz) can cream of chicken soup	2 (198-g/7-oz) cans whole kernel sweetcorn, drained
2 teasp turmeric	125 g/4 oz grated Cheddar cheese
	1 tbsp chopped parsley

Toss the chicken joints in flour, salt and black pepper. Heat a browning dish for 5 minutes on full power. Add oil and chicken portions to the dish. Microwave chicken portions on full power for 2 minutes on each side. Place lightly browned portions in a shallow casserole dish. Add any remaining flour to chicken. Combine soup, turmeric, milk and cream. Pour over the chicken. Cover and microwave on high for 15 minutes.

Place the broccoli, water and a little salt in a dish and cover. Microwave on full power for 6 minutes (4 minutes if frozen broccoli is used). Drain, then arrange broccoli in a single layer in a casserole dish. Add corn and half the cheese to the chicken, and spoon over the broccoli. Sprinkle the remaining cheese on top. Cover and microwave on high for 10 minutes. Sprinkle with chopped parsley and serve.

Serves 4

Chicken and mushroom crêpes

Chicken chasseur

full power
33 minutes

1 (1.5-kg/3¼-lb) chicken, jointed
salt and black pepper to taste
½ teasp paprika
4 tbsp plain flour
1 tbsp oil
1 tbsp butter
8 chipolata sausages
1 onion, chopped
6 tbsp chopped celery
200 ml/7 fl oz chicken stock
5 tbsp white wine
1½ tbsp tomato purée
bouquet garni – few peppercorns, blade of mace, bay leaf, pinch
  of thyme
90 g/3 oz mushrooms, sliced

Toss chicken joints in salt, pepper, paprika and flour. Heat
a browning dish for 4 minutes on full power. Place the
oil and butter in the dish, add the chicken joints and
microwave on full power for 5 minutes. Turn the joints
over halfway through the cooking time. Remove the joints
and place in a casserole dish. Arrange the sausages in the
browning dish. Microwave on full power for 4 minutes,
turning when necessary. Remove the sausages and set
aside. Microwave the onion and celery in the browning dish
for 2 minutes. Add any remaining flour and stir well to
combine. Then add chicken stock, wine and tomato
purée, stirring well. Pour over the chicken and add the
bouquet garni. Cover and microwave on full power for 15
minutes. Add mushrooms and sausages, and stir well.
Microwave on full power for 3 minutes. Remove the
bouquet garni before serving.

Serves 4 – 6

Chicken and mushroom crêpes

full power
medium
19 minutes

60 g/2 oz butter or margarine
250 g/8 oz fresh mushrooms, cleaned and sliced
½ small onion, finely chopped
4 tbsp plain flour
500 ml/17 fl oz milk
2 chicken bouillon cubes
pepper to taste
½ teasp dried tarragon
120 ml/4 fl oz soured cream
3 tbsp dry sherry
210 g/7 oz cooked chicken, diced
2 tbsp finely chopped parsley
12 crêpes (see p. 113)

Microwave the butter in a deep casserole dish on full power
for 45 seconds. Add mushrooms and onion, stirring to coat
with butter and microwave, covered, for 2 – 2½ minutes.
Blend in flour, microwave for 30 seconds, stir, then
microwave for 45 seconds more. Stir well, then gradually
mix in milk. Add bouillon cubes, pepper and tarragon.
Cover and microwave on full power for 3 minutes,
stirring after each minute. Mix in soured cream and
sherry. Set aside 250 ml/8 fl oz of the sauce, and add
chicken and half the parsley to the remaining sauce,
mixing well.
    Spoon a little chicken mixture onto each crêpe. Roll
crêpes up and place in two shallow dishes. Spoon
remaining sauce over crêpes, cover and microwave each
dish on medium for 5 – 6 minutes, until heated through.
Sprinkle with remaining parsley before serving.

Serves 6

Tarragon chicken with apple brandy

high
full power
18 minutes

250 ml/8 fl oz chicken stock
250 ml/8 fl oz apple juice
1 tbsp chopped fresh tarragon or 1 teasp dried tarragon
6 large chicken breasts, skinned and boned
4 tbsp brandy
1 teasp cornflour
apple slices and parsley to garnish

Place chicken stock, apple juice and tarragon in a large
casserole dish. Microwave on high for about 3 minutes,
or until mixture boils. Add chicken breasts, cover and
microwave on high for 5 – 6 minutes, turning pieces once.
Remove chicken, cover and keep warm. Reduce liquid by
microwaving, uncovered, on full power for 8 minutes.
Mix brandy with cornflour and stir into remaining liquid.
Microwave for 1 – 1½ minutes, stirring every 30 seconds.
Arrange chicken on six warmed dinner plates and spoon a
little sauce over each. Serve garnished with apple slices and
parsley.

Serves 6

Chicken Kiev

full power
11 minutes

4 whole chicken breasts, boned and skinned
100 g/3½ oz butter
3 tbsp processed cheese spread
1 tbsp finely chopped onion
1 teasp salt
1 tbsp finely chopped green pepper
90 g/3 oz savoury biscuit crumbs
½ teasp pepper

Halve chicken breasts, place between two sheets of foil
and flatten with a mallet or the side of a meat cleaver.
Set aside. Mix together 40 g/1½ oz butter, cheese spread,
onion, salt and green pepper. Divide cheese mixture into
eight and freeze. Place a portion of cheese mixture on
each chicken breast and fold up securely. Microwave
60 g/2 oz butter on full power for 1 minute in a casserole
dish. Roll each stuffed chicken breast in melted butter,
then in a mixture of biscuit crumbs and pepper. Place
crumbed chicken breasts in the casserole dish and
microwave, covered, on full power for 9–10 minutes.
Serve immediately.

Serves 4

Glazed spring chickens

full power
22 minutes

2 (500-g/1-lb) young spring chickens

For the fruit stuffing	½-1 teasp fresh sage, chopped
4 slices bread, crumbed	2 tbsp butter, melted
60 g/2 oz pecan nuts, chopped	salt and pepper to taste
60 g/2 oz seedless raisins	
grated rind and juice of ½ orange	*For the glaze*
½-1 chicken bouillon cube	6 tbsp smooth apricot jam
3 tbsp chopped onion	2 tbsp orange juice or orange liqueur
1 tbsp Mandarin Napoleon liqueur	2 tbsp brown sugar

Clean the chickens and pat dry. Combine all ingredients for
the stuffing and season to taste with salt and pepper. Stuff
the chickens with this mixture. Fold wings under and tie
legs securely to tail with string. Shield wing tips and ends
of legs with foil and place chickens in a casserole dish. To
make the glaze, combine all the ingredients in a small bowl.
Microwave on full power for 1½ – 2 minutes, then mix
well.

Cover chickens and microwave on full power for about
8 minutes. Remove foil and brush with glaze. Microwave,
covered, for 8 minutes more, brushing frequently with
glaze. Coat evenly with the glaze and microwave, covered,
about 4 minutes more. Stand for 10 minutes before serving.
To serve, split chickens and serve with the stuffing.

Serves 4

Glazed spring chickens with fruit stuffing

Boned stuffed chicken

Boned stuffed chicken may be served hot or cold, arranged in neat, even slices and garnished attractively

full power
high
38 minutes

1 (1.5-kg/3¼-lb) chicken
salt and black pepper to taste

For the stuffing
2 tbsp oil
1 small onion, chopped
1 chicken liver, cleaned and chopped
250 g/8 oz sausage meat
60 g/2 oz fresh white breadcrumbs
2 tbsp chopped parsley
1 (411-g/14½-oz) can apricots, drained and chopped
4 tbsp raisins, chopped
salt and black pepper to taste
1 teasp mushroom ketchup

For the stock
1 litre/1¾ pints boiling water
1 onion, cut up
1 carrot, cut up
1 stick celery, cut up
salt to taste
1 chicken bouillon cube, crumbled
few black peppercorns
bay leaf
blade of mace

To debone chicken, turn the bird breast side down. Using a small sharp knife, split the skin along the backbone from the neck to the tail. Starting at the tail, gradually work the meat away from the bone. With a cleaver, chop the ends off the drumsticks and the wing bones. Work the flesh off the thigh bone and continue over onto the drumstick. Be sure to cut the sinews at this point. Now pull the drumstick bone through the flesh, which will be turned inside out. Continue along the wing joint, cutting the flesh close to the bone, then ease off the wing. Work carefully down towards the breast. Stop cutting once you have reached the top of the breastbone. Repeat the boning process for the other side of the bird. This time when you reach the breastbone, the bony carcass will fall away from the flesh. Set aside.

To make the stuffing, pour oil into a large bowl and microwave on full power for 2 minutes. Add the onion and chicken liver, and toss to coat. Microwave for 2 – 3 minutes. Add all remaining ingredients and mix well. Lay the boned chicken flat and season. Place stuffing down the centre, wrap the flesh around it and use the flaps of skin to neaten off the ends. Sew up with thick thread. Roll in a length of cheesecloth and tie the ends with string.

To make the stock, combine all the ingredients in a large, deep casserole. Microwave on full power for 5 minutes. Carefully add chicken roll and cover. Microwave on full power for 10 minutes. Reduce power to high and microwave for 15 – 18 minutes. Remove chicken roll from stock and allow to cool. Remove cheesecloth and slice the chicken thinly. Arrange the slices on a platter and garnish to taste.

Makes 18–20 slices

Hot boned stuffed chicken

full power
high
30 minutes

1 boned and stuffed chicken (see opposite), uncooked
2 teasp oil
2 teasp soy sauce

Bone and stuff chicken. Combine oil and soy sauce and brush chicken with the mixture. Place chicken in a cooking bag, remove as much air as possible and tie bag with string. Make two slits in the bag to prevent 'ballooning' during cooking. Microwave on full power for 10 minutes, reduce power to high, microwave for a further 15 – 20 minutes. Remove chicken from oven and let stand for 10 minutes before serving. Slice and serve with a sauce and a selection of vegetables.

Makes 12 – 14 slices

Chicken strata

high
22 minutes

8 slices bread
a little butter
250 g/8 oz cooked chicken, diced
1 small onion, finely chopped
1 stick celery, finely chopped
½ green pepper, seeded and chopped
200 ml/7 fl oz mayonnaise
salt and pepper to taste
½ teasp tarragon
½ teasp freshly grated root ginger
2 medium eggs, lightly beaten
375 ml/13 fl oz milk
1 (425-g/15-oz) can mushroom soup
125 g/4 oz mature Cheddar cheese, grated

Butter 3 slices of bread and cut into 1-cm/½-inch cubes. Set aside for the topping. Cut the remaining bread into cubes and place half in a deep 23-cm/9-inch casserole dish which has been lightly greased. Combine chicken, onion, celery, green pepper, mayonnaise, salt and pepper, tarragon and root ginger and spread over bread cubes. Top with the remaining unbuttered bread cubes. Beat eggs and milk and pour over bread. Cover and chill for at least 1 hour, or up to 12 hours. Spread soup on top and cover with buttered bread cubes. Microwave, covered, on high for 16–18 minutes. Uncover, sprinkle with cheese and microwave on high for about 3–4 minutes, or until cheese melts and bubbles. Let stand for about 8 minutes before serving.

Serves 6

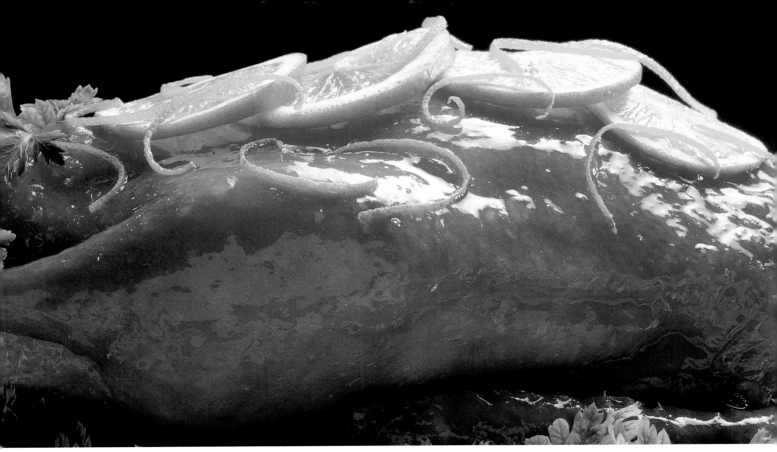

Caramelized duck

Caramelized duck

full power
high
58 minutes

1 (1.5-kg/3¼-lb) duck	*For the sauce*
salt and black pepper to taste	2 teasp cornflour
1 onion, peeled	2 teasp gravy powder
1 apple, quartered	150 ml/¼ pint giblet stock
1 tbsp butter	(see opposite)
½ teasp ginger	6 tbsp orange juice
3 tbsp honey	6 tbsp strained cooking liquid
3 tbsp brown sugar	1 tbsp Curaçao or van der Hum
3 tbsp Curaçao or van der Hum	
2 oranges	
2 tbsp butter	

Rinse duck and pat dry with paper towel. Scrape the skin very well with a knife to remove any feathers. Season inside and outside. Place onion and apple in the cavity. Tie duck into shape with string and shield wings with small strips of foil. Secure neck skin with a toothpick. Place duck, breast side down, on a roasting rack or in a cooking bag. To calculate the cooking time, allow 14–15 minutes per 500 g/1 lb. Microwave on full power for 10 minutes. Drain off excess fat. Combine 1 tbsp butter and ginger, and spread over breast and thighs. Return duck to rack, breast side down. Microwave for approximately half the remaining cooking time on high. Drain off excess fat and turn duck over. Microwave for 5 minutes.

Combine honey, brown sugar and liqueur. Spread this mixture over duck and microwave for the remaining time, basting with glaze once or twice. Remove string and toothpick and keep the duck warm. Let stand for 10 – 15 minutes.

Remove zest from oranges, peel them and slice thickly. Microwave 2 tbsp butter on full power in a shallow casserole dish for 1 minute. Add orange slices, turn slices over immediately, then microwave for 2–3 minutes. Keep warm. Place zest and 6 tbsp water in a bowl. Microwave on full power for 4 minutes, then drain.

To make the sauce, combine cornflour, gravy powder, giblet stock and orange juice in a bowl. Add cooking liquid, orange zest and liqueur, and stir to combine. Microwave on full power for 5 minutes, stirring every minute. Arrange orange slices along duck breast, and spoon a little sauce over. Serve remaining sauce separately. Garnish with cress, if desired.

Serves 3 – 4

Giblet stock

full power
medium
12 minutes

1 set giblets, duck or chicken, cleaned
1 thick slice onion
1 small carrot, cut up
1 sprig parsley
salt and black pepper to taste
1 bay leaf
200 ml/7 fl oz water

Combine all ingredients in a bowl. Cover and microwave on full power for 5 minutes. Reduce power to medium, microwave for a further 7 minutes. Strain and use as required.

Makes 200 ml/7 fl oz

Meat

It is often said that meat makes the meal, and the microwave cooks meat and meat dishes to perfection. Microwaved meats become tender and juicy in a third to half the time it takes to cook them conventionally. Many meats can be cooked on full power, but a lower power setting will cook tougher, more economical cuts until they are tender and full of flavour. Larger joints brown naturally during the cooking process, but small cuts cook too quickly to do so. The addition of a browning agent (see page 22) or basting with a marinade or glaze improves both the appearance and taste of these meats. Hints for cooking meats successfully as well as a defrosting and cooking guide have also been included.

MEAT DEFROSTING AND COOKING CHART

MEAT	DEFROST TIME Per 500 g/1 lb (On defrost)	COOKING TIME Per 500 g/1 lb (Full power)	METHOD
BEEF			
Steak	3-4 minutes, stand 5-10 minutes	3-5 minutes, stand 1 minute	Separate pieces as soon as possible. Microwave in browning dish.
Boned and rolled	8-12 minutes, stand 1 hour	*rare* 8-10 minutes *medium* 9-12 minutes *well done* 10-13 minutes	Defrost wrapped for half the time. Unwrap, shield warm sections, and lie meat on its side.
Large joints on the bone	10-14 minutes, stand 1 hour	*rare* 8-10 minutes *medium* 9-12 minutes *well done* 10-13 minutes, stand 10 minutes	Defrost wrapped for half the time, then shield bone. Turn meat over after half the defrosting time, then again after half the cooking time.
Minced beef, lamb or pork	9-12 minutes, stand 5 minutes	use as required	Break up during defrosting. Remove thawed pieces.
Stewing beef, lamb or pork	10-12 minutes, stand 15 minutes	use as required	Separate pieces during defrosting. Remove thawed sections.
LAMB OR VEAL			
Leg	8-10 minutes, stand 30 minutes	8-11 minutes, stand 15 minutes	Shield bone-end during defrosting and halfway through cooking.
Shoulder or loin	7-8 minutes, stand 30 minutes	8-11 minutes	Shield thin portion during defrosting and three quarters of the way through cooking time.
Chops	3-5 minutes, stand 5-10 minutes	8-10 minutes, stand 1 minute	Separate chops during defrosting. Microwave in browning dish, turn after 2½ minutes.
PORK			
Leg	8-9 minutes, stand 1-1½ hours	11-14 minutes, stand 20 minutes	Select a joint with a uniform shape. Tie into shape if necessary.
Loin	6-8 minutes, stand 30 minutes	8-11 minutes, stand 10 minutes	Shield bone-end during defrosting and halfway through cooking time.
Chops	3-5 minutes, stand 10-15 minutes	10-12 minutes, stand 2 minutes	Separate chops during defrosting. Microwave in browning dish. Turn after 3 minutes.
OFFAL			
Liver and kidney	8-10 minutes, stand 5 minutes	3-5 minutes, stand 1 minute	Separate pieces during defrosting. Use browning dish for cooking. Turn after 2 minutes.
SAUSAGES			
Sausages	6-8 minutes, stand 10 minutes	8-10 minutes, stand 3-4 minutes	Prick skins before cooking. Using browning dish if desired. For added colour, brush with a browning agent.

Note: When microwaving large pieces of meat, or less tender cuts, the power may be reduced so that the cooking period is longer. Meat should be microwaved on high for half the cooking time, then the power reduced to medium to complete the cooking process.

Example: 1.5 kg/3¼ lb rolled beef – rare

Full power method: Microwave for 24 – 30 minutes on full power. Stand for 10 minutes.

Alternative method: Microwave for 15 – 18 minutes on high. Microwave on medium for about 20 – 22 minutes. Stand for 10 minutes.

Cover all meat before placing it in the microwave. Joints of meat should be placed in a cooking bag, a microwave roasting dish, or a shallow dish before cooking. When using a browning dish, meat should be covered with paper towel to prevent spattering.

When cooking meat
- Defrost the meat completely for best results and even cooking.

- Joints of meat cook more evenly if they are symmetrical – that is, boned or rolled.
- Thin parts or bone-ends should be shielded with small strips of aluminium foil during the first half of the cooking time to prevent overcooking.
- Seasoning meats such as roast joints before cooking may dry them out and toughen the meat.
- When preparing casseroles or stews, cut the ingredients to uniform size to promote even cooking.
- Prevent spattering when cooking sausages, bacon or other fatty meats by covering with greaseproof paper or paper towel.
- To improve the natural browning of meat, microwave in a covered glass casserole dish or in a pierced roasting bag fastened with an elastic band or string.
- Reduce liquid in recipes such as casseroles as there is little evaporation during microwave cooking.
- Shape meat mixtures into individual loaves, ring shapes or flat round shapes rather than one large loaf so that the meat will cook quickly and evenly.
- Arrange such foods as meatballs in a circle to promote even cooking. Meats such as chops or steaks should have the narrow end towards the centre of the oven.

Ham mousse

A make-ahead dish for a cool summer lunch

medium
1 minute

150 ml/¼ pint unsweetened pineapple juice
1 tbsp gelatine
pinch of ground cloves
1 tbsp French mustard
20 g/¾ oz parsley leaves
250 g/8 oz cooked ham, finely chopped
1 egg white
120 ml/4 fl oz double cream

Combine pineapple juice and gelatine. Let stand for
5 minutes, then microwave on medium for 1 minute. Stir in
cloves and mustard, mixing well. Chop parsley finely with
blender or food processor, then set aside in refrigerator.
Stir ham into gelatine mixture. Beat egg white until stiff
and fold into ham mixture. Beat cream to soft peaks and
fold into ham mixture. Place mixture in a 750-ml/1¼-pint
mould and chill for at least 3 hours, or until set. To
serve, unmould and sprinkle with chopped parsley. Serve
with brown bread or savoury biscuits.

Serves 6 as a main course, 10 as an appetizer

Cannelloni

full power
high
55 minutes

2 tbsp oil
1 onion, chopped
1 clove garlic, crushed
½ green pepper, seeded and chopped
2 chicken livers, chopped
2 sticks celery, chopped
500 g/1 lb minced beef
½ (425-g/15-oz) can peeled tomatoes
150 ml/¼ pint tomato purée
1 teasp oregano
1 bay leaf
1 teasp Worcestershire sauce
1 teasp sugar
salt and black pepper to taste
1 bunch spinach
4 tbsp single cream
2 eggs
60 g/2 oz Parmesan cheese, grated
10–12 large lasagne noodles, cooked

For the sauce
60 g/2 oz margarine
60 g/2 oz plain flour
300 ml/½ pint milk
salt and black pepper to taste
½ teasp dry mustard
a little extra grated Parmesan cheese

Pour the oil into a large casserole dish. Microwave on full
power for 1 minute. Add onion, garlic, green pepper,
chicken livers and celery. Toss in oil. Microwave on full
power for 5 minutes. Add minced beef and microwave on

full power for 5 minutes, stirring once during the cooking
time. Add the tomatoes, tomato purée, oregano, bay
leaf. Worcestershire sauce, sugar and seasonings.
Microwave, uncovered, for 15 minutes on full power,
stirring every 5 minutes. Set aside.
　Wash spinach and remove stem ends. Place in a bowl
with only the water that clings to the leaves. Cover and
microwave on full power for 6 minutes. Drain and chop.
Combine spinach, cream, eggs and cheese. Season lightly.
　To make the sauce, place the margarine in a bowl.
Microwave on full power for 2 minutes. Stir in flour.
Add half the milk and stir well. Stir in remaining milk.
Microwave for 6 minutes, whisking well at the end of every
minute. Season to taste. Cover and set aside.
　To assemble cannelloni, cut the lasagne noodles into
7.5-cm/3-inch lengths, place a little of the spinach
mixture along one edge and roll up. Arrange in a greased
shallow dish. Repeat until the spinach mixture and the
noodles have been used up. Pour the sauce over the top,
followed by the meat mixture. Sprinkle liberally with
Parmesan cheese. Cover and microwave on high for 15
minutes. Serve hot.

Serves 6 – 8

Lasagne

full power
high
42 minutes

3 tbsp oil
1 onion, chopped
2 rashers bacon, chopped
1 small green pepper, seeded and chopped
1–2 cloves garlic, crushed
1 small carrot, grated
310 g/10 oz minced beef
1 (425-g/15-oz) can peeled tomatoes
1 tbsp tomato purée
salt and black pepper to taste
1 bay leaf
½ teasp dried oregano
5 tbsp red wine
150 g/5 oz ribbon noodles, cooked
400 ml/14 fl oz béchamel sauce (see p. 49)
90 g/3 oz Cheddar cheese, grated
little grated Parmesan cheese

Pour the oil into a large casserole dish. Microwave on full
power for 1 minute. Add the onion, bacon, green pepper,
garlic and carrot. Toss in oil. Microwave for 6 minutes on
full power, stirring twice during cooking time. Add the
meat, microwave for a further 5 minutes. Stir from time to
time. Add tomatoes, tomato purée, seasonings, bay leaf,
oregano and red wine. Microwave, uncovered, on full
power for 20 minutes, stirring from time to time. Remove
the bay leaf.
　Use a casserole dish deep enough to hold two layers of
lasagne. Pour half the meat mixture into the casserole,
cover with half the noodles and a little sauce. Sprinkle with
a little Cheddar cheese. Repeat the layers, ending with
sauce and cheese on the top. Dust with a little Parmesan.
Cover and microwave on high for 10 minutes.

Serves 6

Moussaka

full power
high
59 minutes

2 medium aubergines, sliced
salt
oil
1 onion, chopped
2 cloves garlic, crushed
500 g/1 lb minced beef
1 (425-g/15-oz) can peeled
   tomatoes
2 tbsp tomato purée

½ teasp oregano
½ teasp cinnamon
salt and black pepper to taste
3 potatoes
40 g/1½ oz Cheddar cheese,
   grated
2 eggs
300 ml/½ pint béchamel sauce
   (see p. 49)
1 tbsp grated Parmesan cheese

Sprinkle the aubergines with a little salt and set aside for
30 minutes. Drain and pat dry. Toss in a little oil.
Arrange the aubergine slices on the bottom of a large
shallow dish, overlapping them slightly if necessary.
Cover and microwave on full power for 6 minutes. The
aubergine should not be completely cooked. Drain on
paper towel.

Pour a little oil into a casserole dish and microwave on
full power for 1 minute. Add onion and garlic and toss in
oil. Microwave for 5 minutes. Add meat and microwave for
a further 5 minutes. Stir at least once during the cooking
time. Now add the tomatoes, tomato purée, oregano,
cinnamon and seasonings. Cook, uncovered, on full
power for 12 minutes, stirring from time to time.

Place washed potatoes on a plate. Microwave for
8 – 10 minutes. Potatoes should be only partially cooked.
Peel potatoes and slice thickly.

Moussaka served with seasonal salad (p. 57)

Fill a large greased casserole with layers of meat
mixture, aubergine and potato. Add half the Cheddar
cheese and the eggs to the sauce and mix well. Pour over
the top layer of potatoes. Sprinkle with the remaining
Cheddar and Parmesan cheese. Microwave, uncovered,
on high for 15–20 minutes. The mixture should be very
hot and the tomatoes bubbling round the sides of the
casserole. Traditionally, moussaka is served warm and
not piping hot.

Serves 6

Cheese-topped meat loaf

full power
12 minutes

375 g/12 oz lean minced beef
½ (43-g/1½-oz) packet mushroom soup mix
150 ml/¼ pint tomato ketchup
2 teasp made English mustard
1 egg
pepper to taste
5 tbsp dry wholewheat breadcrumbs
125 g/4 oz Cheddar cheese, grated

Mix beef with soup, 90 ml/3 fl oz tomato ketchup,
mustard, egg, pepper, wholewheat breadcrumbs and 90 g/
3 oz of grated cheese. Press into a lightly greased 20-cm/
8-inch deep glass baking dish and spread with the
remaining tomato ketchup. Sprinkle remaining cheese
on top and microwave on full power for 12 minutes. Stand
for 5 minutes, then microwave for 5 minutes more. Cut
in wedges or squares to serve.

Serves 6 – 8

Pork spareribs

medium
1¾ hours

1.5 kg/3¼ lb pork ribs
500 ml/17 fl oz hot water
1 onion, sliced
1 lemon, sliced
salt and pepper to taste

For the sauce
4 tbsp peach chutney
3 tbsp malt vinegar

3 tbsp brown sugar
2 tbsp lemon juice
1 tbsp made English mustard
4 tbsp tomato purée
1 tbsp Worcestershire sauce
½ teasp basil
½ teasp marjoram
2 tbsp finely chopped onion
300 ml/½ pint tomato juice

Place ribs, bone side up, in a large dish. Add the water,
cover and microwave on medium for 40 minutes. Turn ribs
over, cover with onion and lemon slices, and sprinkle with
salt and pepper. Cover and microwave on medium for
another 40 minutes. Drain ribs, discarding onion and
lemon, and keep warm.

To make the sauce, combine all ingredients, mixing well.
Cover and microwave on medium for 6 minutes, stirring
after 3 minutes. Pour over ribs, cover and refrigerate until
ready to serve. To reheat, microwave ribs and sauce,
loosely covered, on medium for 10 – 15 minutes. These ribs
are delicious heated on a barbecue.

Serves 3 – 4

From top to bottom: blue cheese burger, plain hamburger and cheese and wine burger

Blue cheese burgers

A double beefburger with a cheesy filling

full power
17 minutes

750 g/1½ lb minced beef
1 egg, lightly beaten
1 teasp salt
½ teasp freshly ground black pepper
4 hamburger buns, lightly toasted

For the filling
125 g/4 oz blue cheese, crumbled
1 teasp dry mustard
2 tbsp mayonnaise
1 tbsp Worcestershire sauce

Mix beef with beaten egg, salt and pepper. Shape into eight slim patties. Mix ingredients for the filling and top four of the beef patties with the mixture, leaving a 1-cm/½-inch margin around the edges for sealing. Cover filling with remaining patties and seal edges well.
   Preheat browning dish for 8 minutes on full power. Arrange burgers and microwave, covered, on full power for 5 minutes. Turn patties and microwave, covered, for another 3 – 4 minutes. Serve on toasted hamburger buns.

Serves 4

Cheese and wine burgers

Mix the cheese and wine with the beef, and top with extra cheese

full power
14 minutes

500 g/1 lb minced beef
3 tbsp tomato ketchup
4 tbsp dry red wine
90 g/3 oz cheese, such as Cheddar, grated
salt and black pepper to taste
2 tbsp chopped onion
4 slices processed cheese
4 hamburger buns, lightly toasted

Combine beef, tomato ketchup, wine, cheese, salt and pepper and chopped onion. Mix well and shape into four patties. Preheat browning dish on full power for 7–8 minutes. Place patties in dish, cover and microwave on full power for 2½ minutes. Turn patties, cover and microwave for 2½ minutes. more. Top each patty with a slice of cheese and microwave for 1 minute. Serve on toasted hamburger buns.

Serves 4

Hamburgers

This chart is for cooking lean minced beef patties in a browning dish. Each hamburger patty should weigh about 125 g/4 oz. Use full power and turn hamburgers after half the cooking time. Season the patties after turning.

Number of patties	Preheat browning dish	Cooking time
1	4 minutes	2-3 minutes
2	6 minutes	3-4 minutes
3	6 minutes	4-5 minutes
4	8 minutes	5-6 minutes

To cook hamburgers in a glass dish, increase the cooking time by about 20 seconds per patty. To add good colour to hamburgers not cooked in a browning dish, brush with barbecue sauce, soy sauce. Worcestershire sauce or sprinkle each side with a little brown onion soup powder. The length of cooking time depends on how well done you like your hamburgers.

Tasty meatballs

full power
low
40 minutes

1 tbsp oil
1 onion, chopped
1 green pepper, seeded and chopped
500 g/1 lb minced beef
1 teasp Tabasco
6 tbsp fresh white breadcrumbs
1 egg
1/2 teasp mixed dried herbs
salt and black pepper to taste
165 g/5 1/2 oz uncooked rice
1 (425-g/15-oz) can peeled tomatoes, chopped
350 ml/12 fl oz boiling water
2 beef bouillon cubes
2 teasp soy sauce

Pour the oil into a small casserole dish. Microwave on full power for 1 minute. Add onion and green pepper and toss in the oil. Microwave on full power for 4 minutes. In a large bowl, combine onion, green pepper, mince, Tabasco, breadcrumbs, egg, mixed herbs and seasonings. Form into small meatballs. Roll meatballs in rice and place in a deep casserole dish. Combine all the remaining ingredients and pour over the meatballs. Finally, add any remaining rice, cover and microwave on full power for 15 minutes, then on low for 20 minutes. Serve hot.

Serves 6

Easy beef stroganoff

full power
medium
19 minutes

500 g/1 lb sirloin steak, cut into thin strips
1 stick celery, thinly sliced
1/2 small onion, chopped
125 g/4 oz mushrooms, sliced
salt and pepper to taste
1/2 teasp mixed dried herbs
125 g/4 oz cream cheese
2 tbsp tomato ketchup
3 tbsp beef stock
6 tbsp single cream
2 teasp lemon juice
1/2 teasp paprika
90 g/3 oz Cheddar cheese, grated

Microwave browning dish for 4 minutes on full power. Place meat in dish with celery, onion and mushrooms. Season with salt and pepper and mixed herbs. Cover and microwave on full power for 5 – 6 minutes, stirring frequently. Drain. Meanwhile, mix together cream cheese, tomato ketchup, beef stock, cream, lemon juice and paprika. Stir in half the cheese. Microwave on full power for 45 seconds. Stir well and add to drained beef. Mix well, spoon into a casserole dish and cover. Microwave on medium for about 6 minutes. Uncover, sprinkle remaining cheese over meat and microwave for 1 1/2–2 minutes. Serve with hot buttered noodles or rice.

Serves 4 – 6

Monkeygland steak

full power
21 minutes

750 g/1 1/2 lb rump steak, cut into four pieces
1 tbsp oil
1 onion, chopped
2 cloves garlic, crushed
6 tbsp tomato ketchup
4 tbsp water
1 tbsp malt vinegar
3 tbsp fruit chutney
1 teasp dry mustard
2 teasp soy sauce
salt and black pepper to taste

Place steaks on a flat dish. Pour oil into a shallow casserole dish. Microwave on full power for 1 minute. Add onion and garlic. Toss in oil. Microwave, uncovered, for 2 minutes. Add all the ingredients, except salt and steak. Stir well. Microwave, uncovered, for 3 minutes. Cool. Pour over steaks. Allow to marinate for at least 1 hour.
Remove meat from sauce, drain well and pat dry with paper towel. Microwave browning dish for 6 minutes. Wipe dish with either a small piece of rump fat or a little oil. Microwave meat for 4 – 6 minutes, turning only once during cooking time. The cooking time will vary according to thickness of steaks, and how well done you wish to cook them. Remove steaks and keep warm on a serving dish. Microwave sauce for 3 minutes, stirring every minute during cooking time. Add salt to taste. Pour over steaks and serve immediately.

Serves 4

Hawaiian pork chops

full power
17 minutes

4 thick pork chops
90 g/3 oz drained crushed pineapple
1/2 small onion, chopped
4 tbsp brown sugar
3 tbsp cider vinegar
1 clove garlic, chopped
1 teasp salt
1/2 teasp grated orange rind
1 teasp freshly grated root ginger
pepper to taste
dash of Tabasco

Preheat a browning dish on full power for 5 minutes. Place chops in dish and microwave, covered, on full power for 5 minutes, turning chops halfway through cooking time. Drain off fat. Combine remaining ingredients in a blender and process until smooth. Pour mixture over chops and microwave, covered, for 6 – 7 minutes, rotating dish once. Let stand for 5 minutes before serving.

Serves 4

Sweet and sour pork chops

full power
22 minutes

1 kg/2 lb pork chops
1 tbsp oil
1 onion, sliced
1 green pepper, seeded and sliced
2 sticks celery, sliced
1 (439-g/15½-oz) can pineapple chunks, drained, juice reserved
black pepper to taste
1 tbsp cornflour
2 tbsp water

For the marinade
4 tbsp white wine vinegar
2 tbsp honey
1 tbsp soy sauce
1 clove garlic, crushed
2 tbsp brown sugar
150 ml/¼ pint pineapple juice

Place chops in a flat dish. Combine all ingredients for marinade. Pour over chops and stand for at least 1 hour. Drain chops, place in a shallow casserole dish and cover. Microwave on full power for 10 minutes. Keep warm. In another shallow dish, heat oil on full power for 1 minute. Add onion, green pepper and celery. Microwave on full power for 4 minutes, stirring once during cooking time. Add pineapple chunks and marinade. Season with black pepper. Cover and microwave on full power for 4 minutes. Combine cornflour and water. Add a little of the hot liquid to the cornflour and then return this mixture to the sauce. Stir, then cover and microwave for a further 3 minutes. Pour over meat and serve immediately.

Serves 4

Sweet and sour pork chops

Lamb curry

full power
high
medium
1 – 1¼ hours

750 g/1½ lb stewing lamb, cubed
2 tbsp plain flour
salt and black pepper to taste
4 tbsp oil
2 medium onions, chopped
1 green pepper, seeded and chopped
2 cloves garlic, crushed
1 tbsp curry powder
3 tomatoes, skinned and chopped
2 teasp apricot jam
250 ml/8 fl oz combined beef and chicken stock
½ teasp ground cumin
½ teasp ground coriander
½ teasp ground fennel seed
1 (5-cm/2-inch) stick cinnamon
1 tbsp curry leaves (optional)

Toss lamb in flour, salt and pepper. Microwave browning dish on full power for 5 – 6 minutes. Add half the oil and microwave for 2 minutes. Add lamb and stir to coat with oil. Microwave for 3 – 4 minutes, stirring twice during cooking time. Pour remaining oil into a 3-litre/5½-pint casserole dish and microwave on full power for 2 minutes. Add onions, green pepper, garlic and curry powder. Stir to combine. Microwave on full power for 4 minutes, stirring once during cooking time. Add browned meat, tomatoes, jam and stock, and stir to combine. Tie the spices and curry leaves in a small piece of muslin and add to curry. Cover, then microwave for 5 minutes on full power. Reduce power to high and microwave for 15 minutes. Stir. Uncover and reduce power to medium, then microwave for 30 minutes, stirring once or twice. Remove the spices and allow curry to stand for 10 – 15 minutes. Serve with rice and a selection of sambals.

Serves 4 – 6

Apricot-glazed ham

full power
medium
24 minutes

125 g/4 oz dried apricots
6 tbsp Curaçao or van der Hum
1½ tbsp water
1 (850-g/1 lb 8-oz) can cooked ham
200 ml/7 fl oz smooth apricot jam
pinch of ground ginger
2 tbsp orange juice
pecan nuts
few whole cloves

Soak apricots in liqueur and water for 30 minutes. Drain the ham well and pat dry with paper towel. Place on a meat rack. Combine apricot jam, ginger and orange juice. Brush thickly over ham. Microwave on full power for 6 minutes. Baste with apricot glaze. Place fruit and liquid in

Roast lamb with savoury topping, served with garlic mushrooms (p. 103), stuffed tomatoes (p. 100) and green beans almondine (p. 100)

a bowl. Cover and microwave for 3 minutes. Arrange rows of apricots on top of ham, leaving a space between each row large enough for a row of pecans. Fill the spaces with pecans and a few cloves. Brush the fruit and nuts with some of the apricot glaze. Microwave on medium for 15 minutes. Brush at least twice during the cooking time with glaze. Serve hot or cold.

Serves 6

Roast lamb with savoury topping

full power
33 minutes

1 (1.5-kg/3¼-lb) leg of lamb
2 slices brown bread, crumbed
1 tbsp brown sugar
2 teasp freshly chopped rosemary or ½ teasp dried rosemary
2–3 tbsp French mustard
salt and pepper to taste
3 tbsp chopped onion
2 tbsp brandy
1 tbsp melted butter

Dry leg of lamb with paper towel. Combine remaining ingredients and pat over surface and sides of lamb before roasting. Place in a cooking bag or covered casserole and microwave for 24–33 minutes (8–11 minutes per 500 g/ 1 lb), depending on how well done you like your meat. Shield bone-end with a strip of foil halfway through cooking. Stand for 15 minutes, before serving.

Serves 6

Marinated glazed lamb chops

full power
medium
19 minutes

6 lamb chops
250 ml/8 fl oz red wine
4 tbsp chopped spring onion
½ teasp dry mustard
salt and pepper to taste
1 teasp soy sauce

pinch of sugar
pinch of dried rosemary
pinch of dried basil
1 tbsp cornflour
a little red wine
fresh rosemary or parsley to garnish

Place chops in a glass microwave dish. Combine red wine, spring onion, dry mustard, salt and pepper, soy sauce, sugar, rosemary and basil. Mix well and pour over chops. Cover and marinate for at least 2 hours, turning chops at least once. Microwave chops in marinade on full power for 4 minutes. Reduce heat to medium and microwave for 5 – 6 minutes. Pour off marinade. Turn chops over and keep warm. Combine cornflour with a little red wine and stir into the marinade. Microwave on full power for 3 – 4 minutes, stirring every minute. Pour sauce over chops and microwave, covered, on medium for 4 – 5 minutes until chops are nicely glazed. Garnish with rosemary or parsley and serve with hot cooked rice.

Serves 6

French beef stew with wine

Pork delight

full power
high
medium
1 hour

2 tbsp oil
2 tbsp butter
750 g/1½ lb stewing pork, cubed
3 tbsp plain flour
salt and black pepper to taste
1 teasp dried sage
1 large onion, chopped
400 ml/14 fl oz chicken stock
4 tbsp tomato purée
4 tbsp sherry
1 tbsp soy sauce
2 bay leaves
310 g/10 oz button mushrooms
180 g/6 oz frozen peas
2 (200-g/7-oz) cans artichoke hearts, drained

Place oil and butter in a large casserole dish. Microwave on full power for 3 minutes. Toss cubes of pork in flour, salt, pepper and sage. Add to oil. Microwave for 5 minutes, stirring twice. Add onion, stir to combine, then microwave for 2 minutes. Stir in stock, purée, sherry, soy sauce and bay leaves. Cover and microwave on high for 15 minutes. Let stand for 10 minutes. Uncover, then microwave on medium for 30 minutes, stirring from time to time. Add whole mushrooms and peas, then stir. Microwave for 2 minutes. Cut artichokes into quarters and stir in. Microwave for 2 minutes. Let casserole stand for 5 minutes before serving.

Serves 4 – 6

Picnic loaf

Serve hot straight from the oven, or chill and take along on a picnic

high
26 minutes

1 round bread loaf, unsliced
6 tbsp milk
3 tbsp chopped parsley
1 small tomato, peeled and chopped
2 eggs
1½ teasp salt
pepper to taste
½ teasp dried oregano
½ teasp dried basil
500 g/1 lb lean minced beef
250 g/½ lb lean minced veal
3 tbsp grated cheese
2 tbsp finely chopped onion

Slice a small lid from the top of the bread. Pull enough soft bread out of the centre of the loaf to leave a 1-cm/½-inch shell. Crumb the bread and place 60 g/2 oz in a large mixing bowl. Stir in milk and chopped parsley. Add all remaining ingredients to the bread mixture and combine well. Pack the mixture into the bread loaf and replace the lid. Place loaf in a cooking bag and wrap tightly. Make 2 or 3 slits in the bag near the top. Place

French beef stew with wine

full power
low
1½ hours

6 rashers bacon, chopped
1 kg/2 lb stewing beef, cut into
   2.5 cm/1 inch pieces
4 carrots, peeled and sliced
180 g/6 oz shallots, peeled
1 clove garlic, peeled and chopped
3 tbsp tomato purée
250 ml/8 fl oz beef stock

250 ml/8 fl oz wine
250 g/8 oz mushrooms, cleaned
1 teasp mixed dried herbs
salt and pepper to taste
1 tbsp cornflour
a little extra wine
chopped parsley to garnish

Place bacon in a large casserole dish and microwave on full power for 3 minutes. Add beef, carrots, onions, garlic, tomato purée, beef stock and wine. Cover and microwave on full power for 5 – 8 minutes or until liquid boils. Reduce power to low and microwave, covered, for 30 minutes. Add mushrooms and mixed herbs, then microwave, covered, for 30 – 40 minutes more or until meat is tender and vegetables cooked. Season to taste. Combine cornflour with a little wine and stir into the cooked stew, mixing thoroughly. Microwave, covered, on full power for 3 – 4 minutes. Stir after 2 minutes and again before serving. Garnish with chopped parsley, and serve with hot noodles or rice.

Serves 6 – 8

loaf in a dish and microwave on high for 22–26 minutes. Internal temperature should be 57°C/135°F. Remove loaf from oven and stand for at least 10 minutes before serving. To serve, cut in wedges and serve with mustard or tomato ketchup. To serve cold, stand for 20 minutes to cool. Do not unwrap, just refrigerate until needed.

Serves 6 – 8

Pepper steak flambé

Use fillet or rump steaks

full power
high
12 minutes

4 (125-g/4-oz) beef steaks
Worcestershire sauce to taste
2 teasp freshly crushed black peppercorns
salt to taste

For the sauce
2 tbsp brandy
120 ml/4 fl oz single cream
1 tbsp lemon juice

Brush the steaks with Worcestershire sauce, and press crushed peppercorns into both sides of each steak. Preheat a browning dish for 7 minutes on full power. Sprinkle the dish with a light layer of salt and add steaks. Microwave on full power for 2 minutes. Turn steaks and microwave for another 2 minutes. Remove from oven and keep warm. In a small jug, microwave brandy on high for 30 seconds. Pour over steaks and ignite. When flame subsides, stir in cream and lemon juice and microwave on high for 30 – 60 seconds, until heated through. Serve immediately.

Serves 4

Note: The above timing will give a medium steak. Microwave 30 – 60 seconds less for rare or 30 – 60 seconds longer for well done.

Glazed stuffed roast pork

full power
46 minutes

1.5 kg/3¼ lb boned pork loin

For the stuffing
3 slices brown bread, broken into
   pieces
½ apple, cored and peeled
½ small onion
2 teasp fresh sage or ½ teasp dried sage
salt and pepper to taste
1 tbsp brown sugar
4 teasp brandy
2 tbsp butter

For the glaze
3 tbsp brown sugar
2 tbsp butter
1 tbsp brandy

Remove rind from pork, leaving a layer of fat. To make the stuffing, place bread, apple, onion, sage and salt and pepper in a food processor with a metal blade and process until bread is finely crumbed, and apple and onion are chopped. Add brown sugar, brandy and soft butter and mix well. Use mixture to stuff cavities of the pork, then reshape pork and tie securely. Place pork in a roasting dish.
   To make the glaze, combine brown sugar and butter in

Picnic loaf

add brandy and microwave for 30 seconds more. Brush meat with glaze. Cover with greaseproof paper and microwave on medium for 39–45 minutes (13–15 minutes per 500 g/1 lb). Internal temperature should be 56°C/133°F. Brush frequently with glaze. Stand for 10 minutes before serving.

Serves 6

Veal Milanese

full power
medium
26 minutes

6 veal escalopes
3 tbsp plain flour
salt and black pepper to taste
½ teasp paprika
1 tbsp oil
1 tbsp butter
1 onion, chopped
1 clove garlic, crushed
90 g/3 oz mushrooms, sliced
3 tbsp tomato purée

½ teasp oregano
60 g/2 oz ham, chopped
120 ml/4 fl oz chicken stock
250 ml/8 fl oz white sauce (see p. 49)
½ teasp made mild mustard
60 g/2 oz Cheddar cheese, grated
60 g/2 oz Swiss cheese, grated
1 tomato, sliced
sprigs of parsley to garnish

Toss meat in flour seasoned with salt, pepper and paprika. Microwave a browning dish on full power for 6 minutes. Add oil and butter, and microwave for 1 minute. Place 2–3 escalopes in the browning dish and press down firmly for 30 seconds to sear. Turn meat over, press down firmly again, then microwave for 1 minute. Remove meat from the dish. Reheat browning dish for 2 minutes. Cook remaining meat, 2 – 3 pieces at a time. Place meat in a shallow casserole dish.
   Add onion and garlic to the browning dish and stir to coat with oil. Stir in any remaining flour, the mushrooms, tomato purée, oregano, ham and stock. Pour over meat. Cover and microwave on full power for 4 minutes. To the white sauce, add mustard and half of each of the cheeses, then stir well. Pour over meat mixture. Sprinkle remaining cheese on top and cover with slices of tomato. Microwave on medium for 8 – 10 minutes. Garnish with parsley and serve immediately.

Serves 4 – 6

Casseroles pasta & rice

Casseroles are ideal to serve for any occasion – be it a family meal or a special celebration. Included in this chapter are many casseroles which can be made in moments, as well as some which require a longer cooking period. There are also those which can be made in advance and are ideal for reheating. Fish and canned foods have been used to provide a wide variety of recipes.

When making casseroles in the microwave, use slightly less liquid as there is very little evaporation. Cut meat and vegetables into similar-sized pieces to ensure even cooking. Remember that tougher, more economical cuts of meat will become more tender if the casserole is allowed to cool after cooking. Just reheat for a few minutes before serving.

Microwaving pasta and rice

The preparation of pasta and rice may be the most controversial issue of microwave cooking. Both foods must be re-hydrated during the cooking process, and the microwave oven does not speed up the re-hydration to any great extent. Those who cook pasta and rice in the microwave maintain the flavour is better and the texture is firmer or 'al dente'.

Pasta and rice can be reheated in the microwave with excellent results – a freshly cooked flavour and firm texture. To reheat pasta or rice just place in a suitable container, cover tightly and microwave for 1 to 3 minutes on full power, depending on quantity. A chart for cooking pasta and rice follows.

PASTA AND RICE COOKING CHART

PASTA/RICE	COOKING TIME (On full power)	PREPARATION
Egg noodles and, tagliatelle, 250 g/ 8 oz	7–9 minutes, stand 5 minutes	Add 600 ml/1 pint boiling water, ½ teasp salt, 2 teasp oil
Spaghetti, 250 g/ 8 oz	14–16 minutes, stand 5 minutes	Add 900 ml/1½ pints boiling water, ½ teasp salt, 2 teasp oil
Macaroni, 250 g/ 8 oz	10–12 minutes, stand 5 minutes	Add 600 ml/1 pint boiling water, ½ teasp salt, 2 teasp oil
Lasagne, 250 g/ 8 oz	14–16 minutes	Add 1 litre/1¾ pints boiling water, ½ teasp salt, 2 teasp oil
Pasta shells, 250 g/ 8 oz	18–20 minutes, stand 5 minutes	Add 1 litre/1¾ pints boiling water, ½ teasp salt, 2 teasp oil
Rice, 210 g/7 oz	12–15 minutes, stand 20 minutes	Add 500 ml/17 fl oz boiling water, ½ teasp salt, 1 teasp oil. Keep rice sealed during standing time
Brown rice, 210 g/ 7 oz	25–30 minutes, stand 20 minutes	Add 600 ml/1 pint boiling water, ½ teasp salt, 1 teasp oil. Keep rice sealed during standing time

Sausage and almond bake

full power
31 minutes

500 g/1 lb pork sausage meat
1 large onion, chopped
4 tbsp chopped green pepper
2 sticks celery, chopped
310 g/10 oz cooked brown rice

1 (425-g/15-oz) can cream of celery soup
120 ml/4 fl oz tomato ketchup
1 teasp mixed dried herbs
200 ml/7 fl oz water
210 g/7 oz flaked almonds, toasted (see p. 23)

Preheat browning dish on full power for 4 minutes. Break up sausage meat and place in dish with onion, green pepper and celery. Microwave, covered, for 5 – 6 minutes on full power, stirring frequently to break up meat. Remove from oven and drain off excess fat. Stir in rice, soup, tomato sauce, herbs, water and half the almonds. Place in a casserole dish and microwave, covered, on full power for 17 – 20 minutes, stirring twice and rotating dish if necessary. Uncover, sprinkle with remaining almonds and microwave 1 minute more. Let stand for 10 minutes. Serve.

Serves 6 – 8

Corned beef and asparagus casserole

full power
12 minutes

125 g/4 oz noodles
2 tbsp butter
½ small onion, finely chopped
2 tbsp chopped green pepper
1 (340-g/12-oz) can corned beef, chopped
125 g/4 oz Edam cheese, grated
1 (340-g/12-oz) can asparagus cuts, drained
1 (425-g/15-oz) can mushroom soup
120 ml/4 fl oz evaporated milk
salt and pepper to taste
4 tbsp crushed potato crisps

Cook noodles according to packet instructions and drain well. Microwave butter on full power for about 30 seconds to melt. Add onion and green pepper and microwave on full power for 2–2½ minutes. Place corned beef, grated cheese, asparagus cuts and noodles in a mixing bowl and add sautéed onion and green pepper. Mix together mushroom soup and evaporated milk, season with salt and pepper and stir gently into corned beef mixture. Place mixture in a lightly greased 1.5-litre/ 2½-pint casserole and top with crisps. Microwave, uncovered, on full power for 7–9 minutes to heat through.

Serves 4 – 6

Club chicken casserole

full power
19 minutes

60 g/2 oz butter
4 tbsp plain flour
300 ml/½ pint chicken stock
300 ml/½ pint evaporated milk
salt and pepper to taste
375 g/12 oz cooked rice
375 g/12 oz cooked chicken, diced
90 g/3 oz mushrooms, sliced
4 tbsp chopped pimiento (canned red pepper)
4 tbsp chopped green pepper
2 (198-g/7-oz) cans whole kernel sweetcorn, drained
60 g/2 oz flaked almonds, toasted (see p. 23)

Microwave butter in a 1-litre/2-pint bowl on full power for 45–60 seconds. Stir in flour, mixing well. Microwave for 30 seconds. Slowly beat in chicken stock and evaporated milk, blending well. Microwave for about 3 minutes, stirring every minute. Remove from oven and stir very well. Add salt and pepper, rice, chicken and vegetables. Pour into a greased baking dish, cover and microwave on full power for 12–14 minutes. Uncover, sprinkle with toasted almonds and microwave for 30 seconds. Let stand for 8–10 minutes before serving.

Serves 6 – 8

Macaroni cheese and ham bake

Macaroni cheese and ham bake

high
15 minutes

250 ml/8 fl oz cheese sauce (see p. 49)
210 g/7 oz Cheddar cheese, grated
4 eggs, beaten
2 tbsp plain flour
1 (425-g/15-oz) can cream of mushroom soup
210 g/7 oz cooked ham, chopped
60 g/2 oz mushrooms, sliced
2 tbsp chopped spring onion
2 tbsp chopped parsley
3 tbsp chopped stuffed olives
4 tbsp mayonnaise
375 g/12 oz macaroni, cooked

Combine cheese sauce with three quarters of the grated cheese. Mix in eggs, flour and mushroom soup, beating well. Add ham, mushrooms, spring onion, parsley and olives. Stir in mayonnaise, then fold in cooked macaroni. Turn into a 2-litre/3½-pint casserole. Microwave, covered, on high for 10–13 minutes, or until mixture is almost set. Uncover, sprinkle with remaining cheese and microwave on high for about 2 minutes to melt cheese. Let casserole stand for 8–10 minutes before serving.

Serves 6 – 8

Seafood Creole

full power
medium
22 minutes

2 tbsp oil
1 small aubergine, peeled and cut into cubes
2 small courgettes, sliced
6–8 mushrooms, sliced
½ small onion, chopped
½ small green pepper, seeded and sliced
1 stick celery, sliced
1 clove garlic, chopped
1 (425-g/15-oz) can whole tomatoes
120 ml/4 fl oz dry red wine
1 tbsp soy sauce
1 teasp dried oregano
½ teasp mixed dried herbs
½ teasp dried basil
pinch of dried sage
pepper to taste
2 (92-g/3¼-oz) cans shrimps, drained
4 tbsp sliced stuffed olives
2 tbsp capers
1 (198-g/7-oz) can tuna, drained

Pour oil into a deep casserole dish and microwave on full power for 45 seconds. Add aubergine, courgettes, mushrooms, onion, green pepper, celery and garlic. Toss lightly to coat, then microwave on full power for about 8 minutes, stirring occasionally. Add undrained tomatoes, wine, soy sauce, herbs and pepper. Microwave, covered, on high for 12 – 15 minutes. Add shrimps, olives and capers. Cover and microwave on high for 3 minutes. Stir in tuna, and microwave for a further 2 – 3 minutes to heat through. Serve in bowls with hot cooked rice.

Serves 4 – 6

Salmon lasagne

full power
13 minutes

2 tbsp butter
½ onion, chopped
½ green pepper, seeded and chopped
190 ml/6½ fl oz tomato purée
1 teasp cornflour
3 tbsp dry white wine
3 tbsp water
1 tbsp lemon juice
salt and pepper to taste
½ teasp dried basil
pinch of dried oregano
2 (212-g/7½-oz) cans salmon, drained and flaked
125 g/4 oz lasagne noodles, cooked
125 g/4 oz Mozzarella cheese, thinly sliced
60 g/2 oz Parmesan cheese, grated

Microwave butter in a casserole dish on full power for 45 – 60 seconds. Add onion and green pepper, and toss to coat. Microwave, covered, on full power for 3 minutes. Combine tomato purée, cornflour, wine, water and lemon juice, mixing well. Season with salt and pepper, basil and oregano. Add the salmon and mix in gently. Layer noodles, salmon mixture and the cheeses in a 23-cm/9-inch casserole, ending with a layer of cheese. Microwave on full power for 7–9 minutes. Let stand for 5–8 minutes before serving.

Serves 6

Crab and artichoke casserole

It's a bit expensive, but really delicious

full power
9 minutes

2 (200-g/7-oz) cans artichoke hearts
2 tbsp butter
250 g/8 oz cooked crab meat, chopped
1 (280-g/9-oz) can sliced mushrooms, drained
250 ml/8 fl oz white sauce (see p. 49)
1–1½ teasp Worcestershire sauce
4 tbsp dry sherry
1 egg yolk
salt and pepper to taste
3 tbsp grated Parmesan cheese
3 tbsp grated Cheddar cheese

Drain artichoke hearts and arrange in the bottom of a
greased 23-cm/9-inch baking dish. In a glass bowl,
microwave butter on full power for 30 seconds to melt.
Add crab meat and mushrooms and toss lightly. Spread
crab mixture over artichoke hearts. Mix together white
sauce. Worcestershire sauce, sherry and egg yolk and
season to taste with salt and pepper. Spoon over crab
mixture. Sprinkle with Parmesan and Cheddar cheeses
and microwave on full power for 7–9 minutes to
heat through.

Serves 4 – 6

Note: This recipe can be prepared in individual flan dishes.
Microwave two at a time on full power for 3 – 4 minutes.

Crab and artichoke casserole

Salmon and pasta bake

full power
medium
22 minutes

3 tbsp oil
2 onions, chopped
1 green pepper, seeded and chopped
210 g/7 oz mushrooms, sliced
2 (212-g/7½-oz) cans salmon, drained and flaked
2 (142-g/5-oz) cans tomato purée
2 teasp Worcestershire sauce
2 tbsp tomato ketchup
1 teasp dry mustard
salt and black pepper to taste
250 g/8 oz pasta shells, cooked
125 g/4 oz Cheddar sauce, grated
1 teasp butter

Pour the oil into a large casserole dish and microwave on
full power for 2 minutes. Add onions and green pepper and
toss well in oil. Microwave for 4 minutes. Stir in the sliced
mushrooms and microwave for 2 minutes. Add fish, tomato
purée, Worcestershire sauce, tomato sauce, mustard and
seasonings, and stir well. Microwave for 4 minutes. Stir in
pasta shells and half the cheese. Sprinkle remaining cheese
on top of the pasta mixture. Dot with butter, cover and
microwave on medium for 10 minutes. Serve hot.

Serves 6

Asparagus and tuna casserole

full power
medium
15 minutes

2 tbsp margarine
4 tbsp plain flour
120 ml/4 fl oz evaporated milk
4 tbsp mayonnaise
1 (340-g/12-oz) can asparagus cuts, drained and liquid reserved
salt and black pepper to taste
2 tbsp chopped chives
1 (198-g/7-oz) can tuna, drained and flaked
90 g/3 oz Cheddar cheese, grated
1 tbsp crushed cornflakes
1 (30-g/1-oz) packet plain crisps, crushed
sprigs of parsley to garnish

Place margarine in a bowl and microwave on full power for
1 minute. Stir in flour. Add evaporated milk, mayonnaise
and 120 ml/4 fl oz asparagus liquid and stir to remove
lumps. Microwave for 4 minutes, stirring every minute.
Season well. Add asparagus, chives, tuna and half the
cheese. Pour into a greased shallow casserole dish.
Combine remaining cheese, cornflake crumbs and crisps.
Sprinkle on top of casserole. Microwave, covered, on
medium for 10 minutes. Serve hot. Garnish with parsley.

Serves 4

Tuna and mushroom lasagne

full power
medium
22 minutes

75 g/2½ oz margarine
1 onion, chopped
3 sticks celery, chopped
1 small green pepper, seeded and chopped
210 g/7 oz mushrooms, sliced
5 tbsp plain flour
350 ml/12 fl oz milk
1 tbsp lemon juice
salt to taste
dash of Tabasco
4 tbsp single cream
2 (198-g/7-oz) cans tuna, drained and flaked
2 tbsp chopped parsley
125 g/4 oz Cheddar cheese, grated
1 teasp paprika
250 g/8 oz ribbon noodles, cooked

Place margarine in a large casserole dish and microwave, uncovered, on full power for 2 minutes. Add onion, celery and green pepper, and toss in margarine. Microwave for 3 minutes. Add the mushrooms and stir to combine ingredients. Microwave for 1 minute. Stir in flour. Now add milk and stir well. Microwave, uncovered, for 4 minutes, stirring every 30 seconds. Add lemon juice, seasonings, cream, tuna, parsley and half the cheese. Stir well. Combine remaining cheese with paprika and set aside. Arrange noodles in a shallow casserole dish, pour tuna sauce over and sprinkle cheese on top. Cover and microwave on medium for about 12 minutes until cheese has melted and the edges begin to bubble.

Serves 6 – 8

Seafood spaghetti

full power
high
23 minutes

2 tbsp oil
1 onion, chopped
1 green pepper, seeded and chopped
2 cloves garlic, crushed
2 tbsp plain flour
5 tbsp tomato purée
1 (425-g/15-oz) can whole peeled tomatoes
2 teasp fresh thyme
1 bay leaf
salt and black pepper to taste
5 tbsp white wine
150 g/5 oz prawns, peeled and deveined
1 (283-g/10-oz) can clams, undrained
1 (250-g/8-oz) can mussels, undrained
250 g/8 oz spaghetti, cooked
grated Parmesan cheese

Pour the oil into a deep casserole dish. Microwave on full power for 2 minutes. Add onion, green pepper and garlic, toss in oil and microwave on high for 5 minutes. Stir in flour, tomato purée, peeled tomatoes, thyme, bay leaf and seasonings. Microwave, uncovered, on full power for 10 minutes, stirring at least twice during the cooking time. Add wine and prawns. Cover and microwave on full power for 3 minutes. Stir in the clams and mussels. Cover and microwave on full power for 3 minutes. Serve with piping hot spaghetti and plenty of Parmesan cheese.

Serves 4 – 6

Tuna and mushroom lasagne

Sunday's rice

Sunday's rice

full power
16 minutes

4 tbsp oil
1 onion, chopped
1 green pepper, seeded and
    chopped
90 g/3 oz ham, diced
500 g/1 lb cooked rice
3 tbsp soy sauce

3 tomatoes, peeled and chopped
8 mushrooms, sliced
60 g/2 oz frozen peas
salt and pepper to taste
90 g/3 oz Cheddar cheese, grated
4–6 eggs

In a large shallow casserole dish, microwave the oil on full power for 2 minutes. Add onion and green pepper and toss in the oil. Microwave for 3 minutes. Stir in ham, rice and soy sauce. Microwave, uncovered, for 4 minutes, stirring after 2 minutes. Add tomatoes, mushrooms and peas and season well. Cover and microwave for 4 minutes, stirring once during the cooking time. Remove the lid and stir in the cheese. Make small hollows to hold the eggs. Carefully break the eggs into the hollows. Prick the yolks very carefully. Cover and microwave for 2 – 3 minutes. Allow to stand, covered, for 1 – 2 minutes before serving. The whites should be set. If not, microwave for a further 30 seconds. Serve immediately.

Serves 4 – 6

Farmhouse frankfurters

full power
medium
29 minutes

5–6 potatoes
2 medium onions, sliced
salt and black pepper to taste
150 ml/¼ pint milk
150 ml/¼ pint water
1 chicken bouillon cube
½ teasp mixed dried herbs
1 teasp grated orange rind
1 (375-g/12-oz) packet German frankfurters
1 tbsp oil
60 g/2 oz Cheddar cheese, grated
½ teasp paprika

Peel potatoes and slice thickly. Grease a shallow square or rectangular dish. Arrange potato and onion slices in layers. Sprinkle with salt and pepper. Mix milk, water, bouillon cube, herbs and orange rind and pour over potato and onion mixture. Cover with cling film and make two slits in the film to prevent 'ballooning' during cooking. Microwave on full power for 16–18 minutes.
　　Meanwhile, cut sausages into 1-cm/½-inch lengths. Microwave oil for 2 minutes. Add the sliced sausage and stir to coat. Microwave for 2 minutes. Sprinkle half the cheese over the potato mixture. Add sausages. Combine remaining cheese with paprika, and sprinkle on top of sausages. Microwave, uncovered, on medium for 5–7 minutes, or until cheese has melted. Serve immediately.

Serves 4 – 6

Chilli con carne

full power
medium
high
36 minutes

2 tbsp oil
1 onion, chopped
1 small green pepper, seeded and chopped
1 clove garlic, crushed
500 g/1 lb minced beef
1 (43-g/1½-oz) packet tomato vegetable soup
chilli powder to taste
salt and black pepper to taste
500 ml/17 fl oz boiling water
1 (447-g/15¾-oz) can baked beans in tomato sauce

Microwave oil in a shallow casserole dish on full power for 2 minutes. Add onion, green pepper and garlic. Toss in oil. Microwave, uncovered, for 3 minutes. Add meat and break up with a fork. Microwave for 4 minutes, stirring every minute. Add soup, chilli powder, salt and black pepper, and boiling water. Stir to combine. Microwave, covered, for 5 minutes. Stir again. Reduce power to medium and microwave, uncovered, for about 20 minutes or until soup is completely cooked. Stir at least twice during the cooking time. Finally, stir in baked beans and microwave on high for 2 minutes. Stir and serve hot.

Serves 4 – 6

Stuffed cabbage casserole

Stuffed cabbage casserole

full power
26 minutes

12 large cabbage leaves
4 tbsp water
375 g/12 oz minced beef
375 g/12 oz minced pork
100 g/3½ oz cooked rice
salt and pepper to taste
1 tbsp lemon juice
1 teasp mixed dried herbs
1 tbsp chopped parsley
2 tbsp finely chopped onion
1 clove garlic, finely chopped
1 (425-g/15-oz) can tomato soup
175 ml/6 fl oz tomato spaghetti sauce
4 tbsp water
2 tbsp dry sherry
1 teasp sugar
4 rashers bacon, chopped

Place cabbage leaves in a 3-litre/5½-pint casserole. Add water and microwave, covered, on full power for 5–6 minutes, until leaves are pliable. Drain and remove heavy core from each. Mix together beef, pork, rice, salt and pepper, lemon juice, herbs, parsley, onion and garlic, blending well. Divide mixture into twelve and place a portion on each cabbage leaf. Roll up each leaf, beginning at the wide end and folding sides in. Secure rolls with toothpicks and place seam side down in a lightly greased casserole dish. Mix together soup, tomato sauce, water, sherry and sugar and pour over rolls. Sprinkle bacon on top, then cover and microwave on full power for 17–20 minutes, turning dish if necessary during cooking. Let stand for 5–8 minutes before serving.

Serves 6

Spicy beef and cheese casserole

full power
medium
high
34 minutes

375 g/12 oz minced beef
1 onion, chopped
salt and pepper to taste
1 (300-g/10.6-oz) can tomato spaghetti sauce
1–1½ teasp chilli powder
125 g/4 oz cottage cheese
125 g/4 oz cream cheese
3 tbsp soured cream
3 tbsp chopped green pepper
3 tbsp chopped spring onion
180 g/6 oz noodles, cooked and drained
90 g/3 oz Cheddar cheese, grated
2 tbsp chopped parsley

Preheat browning dish for 5 minutes on full power. Add crumbled beef and onion. Microwave, covered, for 3 – 5 minutes, stirring once. Turn into a casserole dish. Add salt, pepper, tomato sauce and chilli powder. Microwave, covered, on medium for 6 – 8 minutes, stirring once. Meanwhile, combine cottage and cream cheeses, soured cream, green pepper and spring onion. Place half the cooked noodles in a large, greased casserole and top with cheese mixture, then remaining noodles. Pour meat mixture over top, cover and microwave on high for 10–12 minutes. Sprinkle with cheese and parsley and microwave, uncovered, on high for a further 3–4 minutes.

Serves 6

Quick and easy curry supper

full power
30 minutes

2 tbsp butter
1 onion, chopped
1 clove garlic, chopped
1 stick celery, thinly sliced
1 tbsp curry powder (or to taste)
350 ml/12 fl oz chicken stock
250 ml/8 fl oz apple sauce (see p. 115)
250 g/8 oz cooked chicken
1 (397-g/14-oz) can mixed vegetables, drained
4 tbsp chutney
3 tbsp chopped spring onions to garnish

Microwave butter in a casserole dish on full power for 45 seconds. Add onion, garlic, celery, and curry powder. Toss to coat vegetables evenly, cover, then microwave for 4 minutes, until onions are translucent. Add chicken stock and apple sauce. Microwave, uncovered, on full power for 18 – 20 minutes, stirring occasionally. Add chicken, mixed vegetables and chutney and microwave for 4 – 5 minutes to heat through. Garnish with chopped spring onion and serve with rice.

Serves 4 – 6

Vegetables

Vegetables cooked in the microwave retain their attractive colour, fresh flavour and natural texture, and since they are cooked in very little liquid, retain their minerals, and vitamins too. Some vegetables, such as spinach, are cooked with just the moisture clinging to the leaves, while other vegetables, such as whole potatoes or tomatoes, can be cooked with no added moisture at all.

FRESH VEGETABLE COOKING CHART

VEGETABLE	QUANTITY	WATER ADDED	COOKING TIME (On full power)	PREPARATION
Artichokes, globe	4	150 ml/¼ pint	15–20 minutes	Wash and trim lower leaves
Asparagus, green	250 g/8 oz	3 tbsp	6–8 minutes	Trim ends, leave whole
Asparagus, white	250 g/8 oz	3 tbsp	8–10 minutes	Trim ends, leave whole
Aubergines	2 medium	3 tbsp	8–10 minutes	Slice, sprinkle with salt. Stand 30 minutes, rinse and dry
Beans, broad	500 g/1 lb	3 tbsp	9–11 minutes	Remove from pods
Beans, green	500 g/1 lb	3 tbsp	8–10 minutes	String and slice, or cut
Beetroot	6 medium	150 ml/¼ pint	28–32 minutes	Trim tops, prick
Broccoli	500 g/1 lb	3 tbsp	8–12 minutes	Trim ends, cut into even-sized lengths
Brussels sprouts	500 g/1 lb	3 tbsp	12–15 minutes	Remove outer leaves, trim
Cabbage	500 g/1 lb	1 tbsp	7–9 minutes	Shred or chop
Carrots, whole new	500 g/1 lb	3 tbsp	7–9 minutes	Scrape
Carrots, sliced large	500 g/1 lb	3 tbsp	8–10 minutes	Peel, slice in rings or long strips
Cauliflower, whole	1 medium	3 tbsp	9–11 minutes	Trim outside leaves and stem
Cauliflower, in florets	1 medium	3 tbsp	7–9 minutes	Cut into medium-sized florets
Celery	500 g/1 lb	3 tbsp	10–12 minutes	Trim and slice
Corn on the cob	4 cobs		7–8 minutes	Rotate halfway through cooking time
Courgettes	500 g/1 lb	2 tbsp water or stock	6–8 minutes	Trim ends and slice
Leeks	4 medium	3 tbsp	7–11 minutes	Trim and slice or cook whole if small
Marrow, sliced	500 g/1 lb	1 teasp	8–10 minutes	Cut into slices and quarter
Marrow, young whole	1 medium	3 tbsp	12–15 minutes	Cut in half, remove membranes and seeds. Cook upside down. Turn halfway through cooking
Mushrooms	250 g/8 oz	2 tbsp water or stock or 2 tbsp butter	4–6 minutes	Wipe and slice or cook whole
Onions, whole	4–6	2 tbsp butter or oil	8–10 minutes	Peel
Onions, sliced	4–6	2 tbsp butter or oil	7–9 minutes	Peel and slice
Parsnips	500 g/1 lb	3 tbsp	9–11 minutes	Peel and slice
Peas, shelled	250 g/8 oz	2 tbsp	8–10 minutes	Add a sprig of mint
Potatoes, new	500 g/1 lb	2 tbsp	12–13 minutes	Scrub well and prick
Potatoes, baked	4 medium		12–16 minutes	Scrub well and prick
Potatoes, mashed	4 medium	3 tbsp	16–18 minutes	Peel and cut into cubes
Pumpkin	500 g/1 lb	3 tbsp	8–10 minutes	Peel and dice
Spinach	500 g/1 lb		6–9 minutes	Cook with water that clings to the leaves
Sweet potatoes	4 medium	3 tbsp	12–15 minutes	Peel and slice
Tomatoes, sliced	4 medium		4–5 minutes	Slice, dot with butter
Tomatoes, stewed	4 medium	1 tbsp	6–8 minutes	Peel and chop roughly
Turnips	3 medium	2 tbsp	10–12 minutes	Peel and dice

When cooking vegetables

- Cut vegetables into even-sized slices or pieces.
- If using a cooking liquid, add salt to the liquid. If not, add a little salt to the vegetable after it has been microwaved. Remember when vegetables are cooked in the microwave, far less salt is needed.
- Cooking time will vary depending on size, thickness and age of the vegetable. Always check vegetables after the minimum time stated on the chart.
- Allow 2 to 4 minutes standing time before serving vegetables as they continue to cook for some time after being removed from the microwave. Vegetables should still be firm or crisp when cooking time is up. If they are overcooked, they dehydrate.
- Arrange vegetables in a circle if they are being cooked whole, for example potatoes. Also arrange vegetables with woody stems, such as broccoli, with the stem end towards the outside. Vegetables which have an irregular shape, such as whole courgettes, should be arranged with the thin end towards the middle of the dish. Rearrange or stir vegetables halfway through cooking time to ensure even cooking.
- When possible, cook vegetables with their skins on. Simply pierce the skin to allow steam to escape.

- Cover vegetables before cooking. Use a lid or cling film, with two slits cut in the cling film to prevent 'ballooning' during cooking. When uncovering cooked vegetables, uncover from the edge farthest away from you because the escaping steam may cause a bad burn. Vegetables may also be cooked in a cooking bag or can be individually wrapped in cling film.
- All vegetables are microwaved on full power, unless otherwise stated.
- Microwave time increases with the amount of food cooked. If the quantity of vegetables given on the chart opposite is altered in a recipe, the cooking time must be adjusted accordingly. Allow one third to one half extra time if the amount is doubled.

To cook frozen vegetables

There is no need to thaw frozen vegetables before microwaving, nor to add any extra water. Just place them in a suitable container, even a boilable plastic container or a cooking bag. Before microwaving, frozen vegetables should always be covered and cooking bags or cling film must be pierced to prevent steam from building up. Microwave frozen vegetables for approximately two thirds

of the time required for fresh vegetables. Refer to the chart given opposite.

Dried vegetables

Pulses – dried peas, beans and lentils – require soaking before being cooked in the microwave. Soak, in plenty of cold water, for at least eight hours. If this is impossible, cover pulses with cold water. Microwave on full power until the water boils. Continue boiling for 3 to 4 minutes. Allow them to stand, covered, for 1 to 2 hours, then drain and rinse in plenty of cold water before using.

To cook pulses, select a large bowl or casserole dish, remembering that these vegetables absorb a great deal of liquid and will swell during the cooking process. Cover with boiling water, add salt and bring vegetables and water back to the boil in the microwave oven on full power. Continue cooking on high for approximately 1 hour, or until tender. Remember, it may be necessary to add extra water during the cooking time. Stir occasionally during the cooking time.

Smaller pulses, lentils and split peas (250 g/ 8 oz)	When boiling, microwave on high for 30-35 minutes
Larger pulses, haricot and sugar beans (250 g/8 oz)	When boiling, microwave on high for 60-70 minutes

Allow pulses to stand for 10 minutes before serving.

Stir-frying vegetables

Vegetables stir-fried in the microwave are not only bright in colour and look good, but they are also crisp in texture and have a far higher vitamin and mineral salt content than boiled or steamed vegetables. Create your own stir-fry combinations by using whatever vegetables are in season, and for interesting variations add thin slivers of meat or a few prawns.

Choose from the following selection of ingredients:

4–5 broccoli spears, cut into small florets
peas (use mange tout when available)
2–3 carrots, sliced
125 g/4 oz button mushrooms, whole
90 g/3 oz bean sprouts
3–4 courgettes, sliced
90 g/3 oz meat, sliced thinly (beef or pork)
  or 90 g/3 oz prawns, peeled and deveined
oil
salt and black pepper to taste

Prepare vegetables carefully. Slice long stems and roots at an angle to produce a long oval shape. Cut meat into paper-thin slices (semi-frozen meat cuts perfectly). Brush meat and vegetables lightly with oil. Toss to coat. Place mixture in a shallow casserole dish and microwave on full power for a few minutes. The time will depend on the quantity of vegetables being used. Stir vegetables every 2 – 3 minutes. Season lightly and serve.

Baked potatoes

Wash potatoes and pat dry, then pierce with a skewer or fork. Place potatoes on paper towel on the microwave shelf, making sure they are at least 2.5 cm/1 inch apart. If microwaving several potatoes, arrange them in a circle. Turn and rearrange potatoes after half the cooking time.

Quantity	Time	Power level
1	4-6 minutes	full power
2	6-8 minutes	full power
3	8-12 minutes	full power
4	12-16 minutes	full power
5	16-20 minutes	full power
6	20-25 minutes	full power

Potatoes may still feel firm when done, but will soften upon standing. Overcooking will toughen and dehydrate them.

Vegetables are cooked to perfection in the microwave

Left to right: seafood, anchovy, and cheesy vegetable potatoes

Cheesy vegetable potatoes

full power
6 minutes

6 large baked potatoes (see p. 95)
250 ml/8 fl oz white sauce (see p. 49)
salt and pepper to taste
90 g/3 oz cheese, grated
90 g/3 oz cooked peas
90 g/3 oz cooked carrots, chopped
3 tbsp chopped green pepper
3 tbsp chopped onion
60 g/2 oz butter

Cut potatoes in half and carefully scoop out flesh. Set aside shells and mash flesh. Season white sauce with salt and pepper and add half the cheese, the peas and carrots, and combine well. Add to potato flesh and mix well. Place green pepper and onion in a deep measuring jug and add butter. Microwave on full power for 3 minutes, stirring once. Add to potato mixture and mix well. Spoon mixture into empty potato shells and arrange in a casserole dish or on a plate. Top with remaining cheese and microwave on full power for about 3 minutes, or until hot.

Serves 6 – 12

Seafood potatoes

full power
10 minutes

6 large baked potatoes (see p. 95)
salt and pepper to taste
60 g/2 oz butter
1/2 small onion, finely chopped
120 ml/4 fl oz dry white wine
30 g/1 oz finely chopped mushroom
250 g/8 oz cooked crab or cooked lobster, flaked
6 tbsp soured cream
60 g/2 oz Cheddar

Cut tops from baked potatoes and carefully scoop out flesh. Salt and pepper the shells and set aside. In a casserole dish, microwave butter on full power for 1 minute to melt. Add onion and microwave for 2 minutes. Then add wine and microwave on full power for 3 – 5 minutes, until liquid has been reduced by half. Stir in mushrooms and cooked crab or lobster. Add to potato flesh and mix well. Stir in soured cream and a third of the cheese. Spoon mixture into potato shells and arrange in a casserole dish or on a plate. Sprinkle with remaining cheese. Microwave for about 2 minutes until hot.

Serves 6

Anchovy potatoes

full power
3 minutes

4 large baked potatoes (see p. 95)
2 egg yolks
90 g/3 oz Parmesan cheese, grated
6 anchovy fillets, mashed
60 g/2 oz butter
30 g/1 oz dry breadcrumbs

Cut tops from baked potatoes and carefully scoop out flesh. Set aside shells and mash flesh. Add beaten egg yolks, cheese and mashed anchovies. Microwave butter on full power for 1 minute to melt, then stir into potato mixture. Pile potato mixture into shells and arrange in a casserole dish or on a plate. Sprinkle with breadcrumbs. Microwave on full power for about 2 minutes until piping hot.

Serves 4

Potatoes Lyonnaise

full power
34 minutes

3 tbsp butter or margarine
500 g/1 lb onions, thinly sliced
2 cloves garlic, finely chopped
625 g/1¼ lb potatoes, peeled and thinly sliced
200 ml/7 fl oz chicken stock
1 teasp salt
pepper to taste
1 teasp chopped tarragon or dill (optional)
chopped parsley to garnish

In a 2-litre/3½-pint casserole dish, microwave butter on full power for 45 seconds to melt. Add onion and garlic and stir to coat. Microwave covered, for 12–15 minutes, until onion is very tender, stirring once. Add potatoes, stock, seasoning and herbs, mixing gently. Cover and microwave on full power for 10 minutes. Stir well, then microwave for a further 6–8 minutes until potatoes are tender. Sprinkle with chopped parsley.

Serves 6

Potatoes Parmesan

full power
19 minutes

90 g/3 oz butter
500 g/1 lb potatoes, peeled and cut into 2.5 cm/1 inch cubes
½ small clove garlic, finely chopped
60 g/2 oz Parmesan cheese, freshly grated
6 cream crackers, crumbed
pinch of paprika
salt and pepper to taste
2 tbsp chopped parsley
a little extra grated Parmesan cheese

Microwave butter in a large casserole dish. Add potatoes and garlic, stirring to coat, and microwave, covered, on full power for 17 minutes. Combine Parmesan cheese, cracker crumbs, paprika, salt, pepper and parsley and stir three quarters of the mixture into the potatoes. Microwave for 2–3 minutes until potatoes are tender. Sprinkle the remaining crumb and cheese mixture over, top with a little extra cheese and microwave for 1 minute.

Serves 4 – 6

Potatoes au gratin

full power
42 minutes

60 g/2 oz butter
750 g/1½ lb onions, peeled and thinly sliced
750 g/1½ lb potatoes, peeled and thinly sliced
1 teasp freshly grated nutmeg
salt and black pepper to taste
2 tbsp chopped parsley
210 g/7 oz Swiss cheese, grated
375 ml/13 fl oz milk

Microwave butter in a large casserole dish on full power for 1 minute. Add onion, stirring to coat evenly with butter. Cover dish and microwave for about 20 minutes, until onions are tender. Combine potatoes with nutmeg, salt, pepper and parsley, tossing to coat evenly. Place half the potatoes in a large casserole dish. Add half the onion, then half the grated cheese. Repeat layers. Microwave milk on full power for 1 minute, then pour over cheese. Microwave, covered, on full power for 18 – 20 minutes, until potatoes are tender.

Serves 6 – 8

Cheesy potatoes

full power
3 minutes

4 large baked potatoes (see p. 95)
90 g/3 oz butter
90 g/3 oz Gruyère cheese, grated
salt and pepper to taste
1 egg yolk
3 tbsp soured cream

Cut tops from baked potatoes and carefully scoop out flesh. Microwave butter on full power for 1 minute to melt. Add to potato flesh, mashing well. Stir in three quarters of the cheese, the salt, pepper, beaten egg yolk and soured cream. Pile potato mixture into potato shells and top with remaining cheese. Place in a casserole dish or on a plate and microwave on full power for about 2 minutes until piping hot.

Serves 4

Mashed potatoes

full power
high
20 minutes

4 medium potatoes
3 tbsp water
salt and pepper to taste
3 tbsp margarine
approximately 3 tbsp milk
pinch of baking powder

Peel and quarter potatoes. Place in a 1-litre/1³/₄-pint
bowl. Add water and a little salt and pepper. Cover and
microwave on full power for 16–18 minutes, or until
potatoes are soft. Drain off water, then stand for 2–3
minutes. Add margarine and milk to potatoes, then beat
until smooth. Add baking powder and taste for
seasoning. Beat once again until fluffy. Reheat for 2
minutes on high.

Serves 4

Spinach creams

full power
medium
22 minutes

1 large bunch spinach
1 egg
salt and black pepper to taste
pinch of nutmeg

For the cream sauce
150 ml/¹/₄ pint milk
1 slice onion
piece of carrot
pinch of mace
1 tbsp butter
2 tbsp plain flour

Wash spinach very well and remove coarse stems. Pat
leaves dry, then place in a large bowl and cover with
cling film. Cut two slits in the film to prevent 'ballooning'
during cooking. Microwave on full power for 6 minutes.
Drain well. Grease or spray six ramekins. Line bases and
sides of ramekins with spinach leaves. Place remaining
spinach in a food processor bowl or blender and purée.
Add egg, salt, black pepper and a pinch of nutmeg.

To make the sauce, place milk, vegetables and mace in
a large jug. Microwave for 2 minutes. Allow to stand for
5 minutes before straining the milk. Microwave butter in
the jug for 2 minutes. Add flour and stir well. Pour in
flavoured milk. Microwave for 2 minutes, stirring after
1 minute.

Add the sauce to the spinach purée. Process to combine.
Divide purée among cups. Cover purée with any long
pieces of spinach which remain over the edges of the cups.
Cover each cup with cling film and make a small slit in
each cover. Microwave on medium for 10 minutes. Allow
to stand for 3 minutes before turning spinach creams onto a
flat serving platter. Serve hot.

Serves 6

Baked layered potato

full power
high
18 minutes

4 large potatoes, peeled and sliced
2–3 leeks, sliced
6 tbsp milk
5 tbsp single cream
salt and black pepper to taste
¹/₂ teasp dry mustard
60 g/2 oz Emmenthaler cheese, grated
1 tbsp dry breadcrumbs
paprika

Arrange the potatoes and leeks in layers in a greased
shallow casserole dish. Combine the milk and cream. Pour
over the potatoes. Sprinkle with the seasonings. Cover and
microwave on full power for 15 minutes. Combine the
cheese and breadcrumbs, and sprinkle on top of potatoes.
Cover and microwave on high for 3 minutes. Dust with
paprika and serve immediately.

Serves 4 – 6

New potatoes with parsley butter

full power
16 minutes

500 g/1 lb new potatoes, unpeeled
4 tbsp water
2 tbsp butter
3 tbsp finely chopped parsley
¹/₂ small clove garlic, finely chopped (optional)
salt and pepper to taste

Wash potatoes and place in a 2-litre/3¹/₂-pint casserole.
Add water and microwave on full power for 12–14
minutes, or until tender. Drain well and keep warm.
Microwave butter, parsley and garlic in a glass measuring
jug for 2 minutes. Pour over potatoes and season with salt
and pepper.

Serves 4 – 6

Note: These potatoes can be cooked ahead of time, then
reheated with butter on medium for 3 – 4 minutes.

Stuffed marrow

Stuffed marrow

full power
24 minutes

2 medium yellow summer marrows
1 tbsp oil
1 onion, chopped
2 sticks celery, chopped
60 g/2 oz ham, chopped
salt and black pepper to taste
60 g/2 oz Cheddar cheese, grated
cayenne pepper
pinch of dried oregano
1 tbsp dry breadcrumbs

Cut marrows in half and remove seeds and membranes.
Place cut side down in a shallow dish. Cover and
microwave on full power for about 15 minutes. Turn over
halfway through cooking time. Microwave oil for 1 minute.
Add onion and celery, and microwave for 3 minutes.
Combine onion mixture and ham. Scoop marrow pulp out
of the skins. Combine pulp and onion mixture. Season to
taste. Use this mixture to fill shells, piling the filling high.
Combine remaining ingredients and sprinkle on top of
filling. Microwave, covered, for 4 – 5 minutes, until filling
is piping hot and the cheese bubbling.

Serves 4 – 6

Stuffed courgettes

full power
15 minutes

6 medium courgettes
2 tbsp margarine
1 small onion, chopped
2 rashers bacon, chopped
1 tomato, peeled and chopped
½ teasp dried thyme
salt and black pepper to taste
3 tbsp fresh breadcrumbs
pinch of paprika
1 tbsp chopped chives

Cut a wedge lengthways along the top of each courgette
to take the filling. Level off base, so that the courgette
does not roll over. Roughly chop the wedges of courgette.
In a small casserole dish, microwave margarine on full
power for 2 minutes. Add onion and bacon, and toss in
margarine. Microwave for 3 minutes. Add chopped
courgettes, tomato, thyme, salt and pepper. Microwave,
uncovered for 3–4 minutes. Fill courgette shells with this
mixture. Combine breadcrumbs, paprika and chives.
Sprinkle a little on top of each courgette. Arrange
courgettes on a plate in a radial design. Cover and
microwave for about 6 minutes. Cooking time will
depend on size of the marrows. Serve hot.

Serves 6

Stuffed tomatoes

full power
14 minutes

6 tomatoes
1 tbsp oil
1 small onion, chopped
2 sticks celery, chopped
90 g/3 oz frozen peas
40 g/1½ oz fresh white breadcrumbs
½ teasp mixed herbs
1 tbsp mushroom ketchup as seasoning
pinch of dry mustard powder
pinch of turmeric
salt and black pepper to taste
90 g/3 oz Cheddar cheese, grated
parsley to garnish

Cut tops off tomatoes and remove pulp. Place tomato shells in a circle on a plate. In a large casserole dish, microwave oil on full power for 1 minute. Add onion. Microwave for 2 minutes. Now add celery, peas and tomato pulp. Microwave, uncovered, for 6 minutes. Add breadcrumbs, herbs and seasonings. Stir to mix. Lastly stir in half the cheese. Fill shells with this mixture. Sprinkle remaining cheese on top. Cover and microwave for 4 – 5 minutes. Serve hot, garnished with a little parsley.

Serves 6

Cabbage casserole

full power
11 minutes

2 tbsp water
salt and a pinch of pepper to taste
1 small cabbage, shredded
2 tbsp butter
2 tbsp plain flour
½ teasp salt
pinch of pepper
250 ml/8 fl oz milk
pinch of caraway seeds
90 g/3 oz mature Cheddar cheese, grated
pinch of dry mustard powder
30 g/1 oz fresh wholewheat breadcrumbs

In a 2-litre/3½-pint casserole dish, combine water and seasoning. Add cabbage, cover and microwave on full power for 7–9 minutes for each 500 g/1 lb. Rotate dish halfway through cooking time if necessary. Stand for 5 minutes.

Microwave butter in a 600 ml/1 pint glass measuring jug on full power for 30 seconds. Stir in flour and seasoning and mix well. Gradually stir in milk. Microwave for 1 minute, stir, then microwave for 1½-2 minutes longer, stirring every 30 seconds until the mixture boils. Add caraway seeds, cheese and mustard, and mix thoroughly. Microwave for 1 minute, then mix well. Drain liquid from cabbage and stir in sauce. Top with breadcrumbs and microwave for 1 minute.

Serves 4 – 6

Mixed vegetable sauté

full power
8 minutes

3 tbsp butter
3 carrots, cut into matchstick strips
5 courgettes, cut into matchsticks strips
180 g/6 oz mushrooms, sliced
1 turnip, cut into matchstick strips
salt and black pepper to taste
2 tbsp lemon juice
1 tbsp chopped parsley
2 teasp chopped chives

Place butter in a shallow casserole dish. Microwave on full power for 1 minute. Add carrots and toss in butter. Cover and microwave for 3 minutes. Add courgettes, mushrooms and turnip. Season and toss lightly. Cover and microwave for 3 – 4 minutes. Vegetables should still be crisp. Add lemon juice, parsley and chives. Stir carefully to combine. Serve piping hot.

Serves 4 – 6

Green beans almondine

full power
12 minutes

2 tbsp butter
60 g/2 oz flaked almonds
310 g/10 oz frozen sliced green beans
4 tbsp water
salt and pepper to taste

Microwave butter in a glass measuring jug on full power for 1 minute. Add almonds, mixing well, and microwave for about 4 minutes until lightly browned, stirring after each minute. Set aside. Place green beans in a large casserole dish. Add water, cover and microwave on full power for 6 minutes. Drain beans, then return to casserole dish. Add nuts and butter, salt and pepper, tossing to coat evenly. Microwave on full power for 1 minute. Serve hot.

Serves 4

Casseroled onions

full power
high
12 minutes

10–12 small onions
2 tbsp water
4 tbsp honey

4 tbsp tomato ketchup
salt and black pepper to taste
1 tbsp margarine

Place onions and water in a shallow casserole dish. Cover and microwave on full power for 3 minutes. Drain. Combine honey and tomato ketchup, and season. Pour over onions. Dot with small pieces of margarine. Cover and microwave on high for 7–9 minutes. Serve hot.

Serves 6

Corn on the cob

Corn on the cob

full power

Remove husks and beards if necessary, and place the corn in a glass casserole dish. Cover and microwave on full power for the following times:

1 cob	2–3 minutes
2 cobs	4–6 minutes
3 cobs	6–7 minutes
4 cobs	7–8 minutes
6 cobs	8–9 minutes

Rotate corn halfway through the cooking time, and stand for 5 minutes before serving. Serve with melted butter, salt and pepper.

Cauliflower cheese

full power
9 minutes

1 medium cauliflower, trimmed
120 ml/4 fl oz mayonnaise
2 teasp made English mustard
salt and pepper to taste
90 g/3 oz mature Cheddar cheese, grated
pinch of paprika

Wash cauliflower and place in a 2-litre/3½-pint casserole dish. Cover and microwave on full power for 5–6 minutes per 500 g/1 lb. Let stand, covered, for 5 minutes, while making the sauce. Combine mayonnaise, mustard, and seasonings in a glass measuring jug and microwave for 1 minute. Stir to blend, then spoon sauce evenly over cauliflower. Sprinkle with grated cheese and microwave for 1½–2 minutes, until cheese melts. Sprinkle with paprika.

Serves 4 – 6

Ratatouille with cheese

full power
21 minutes

750 g/1½ lb aubergines
4 tbsp oil
2–3 cloves garlic, chopped
1 onion, thinly sliced
250 g/8 oz courgettes, thinly sliced
1 green pepper, seeded and sliced
2 sticks celery, thinly sliced
1 (425-g/15-oz) can whole tomatoes, chopped
120 ml/4 fl oz canned tomato purée
2 tbsp concentrated tomato purée
1½ teasp sugar
3 tbsp plain flour
1–1½ teasp salt
½ teasp pepper, or to taste
1 teasp mixed dried herbs
½ teasp dried oregano
pinch of dried thyme
210 g/7 oz Cheddar cheese, grated
fresh parsley to garnish

Pierce aubergines well with a fork and place on a microwave rack. Microwave on full power for 7 minutes, then set aside to cool. Place oil, garlic and onion in a large, deep casserole dish. Cover and microwave on full power for 5 minutes. Add courgettes, green pepper and celery, mixing well. Peel aubergines and cut into 2.5 cm/ 1 inch cubes. Add to vegetables. Cover and microwave on full power for 5 minutes.

Combine tomatoes and juice, tomato purée, concentrated tomato purée, sugar, flour, seasonings and herbs. Mix well, then spoon half the mixture over the vegetables. Add half the cheese. Top with remaining tomato mixture, then with remaining cheese. Cover and microwave on full power for 3–4 minutes, until mixture is hot and bubbly. Sprinkle with parsley just before serving.

Serves 6

Baked green pepper

Baked green peppers

full power
high
16 minutes

4 green peppers
1 tbsp oil
2 rashers bacon, chopped
1 onion, chopped
250 g/8 oz chicken livers, cleaned and chopped
salt and black pepper to taste
60 g/2 oz mushrooms, chopped
1 egg
90 g/3 oz cooked rice
1 tbsp chopped parsley
pinch of thyme
4 tbsp grated Cheddar cheese

Cut a slice off the top of each green pepper. Remove core
and seeds. Cover and microwave peppers on full power for
4 minutes, turning them over halfway through the cooking
time. In a shallow dish, microwave the oil for 1 minute.
Add bacon and onion and microwave for 3 minutes. Add
chicken livers. Microwave for a further 3 minutes. Season
well. Add mushrooms, egg, rice, parsley, thyme and three
quarters of the cheese. Use this mixture to stuff green
peppers. Top with remaining cheese. Stand peppers in a
shallow serving dish and cover. Microwave for 5 minutes on
high. Serve immediately.

Serves 4

Aubergines in cream sauce

full power
medium
15 minutes

3 medium aubergines
salt
3 tbsp butter
1 clove garlic, crushed
5 tbsp chicken stock
2 teasp plain flour
6 tbsp single cream
pinch of dried marjoram
1 tbsp chopped parsley

Wash and dice unpeeled aubergines. Sprinkle with a little
salt. Allow to stand for 30 minutes, then pat dry with
paper towel. Place butter in a shallow casserole dish.
Microwave on full power for 1 minute. Add aubergines
and garlic, and toss well in butter. Add chicken stock,
cover and microwave on full power for 8–10 minutes,
until tender. Stir in flour, cream and marjoram. Cover
and microwave on medium for 4 minutes. Dust with
parsley. Serve hot.

Serves 4

Stir-fried cabbage

full power
16 minutes

2 tbsp oil
1 onion chopped
2 cloves garlic, crushed
1/2 medium cabbage, shredded
2 tbsp soy sauce
black pepper to taste
1/2 teasp caraway seeds
2 teasp chopped parsley

In a shallow casserole dish, microwave oil on full power for
2 minutes. Add onion and garlic, and toss in oil. Return
to microwave for 3 minutes. Stir in cabbage. Cover and
microwave for 8 – 10 minutes, stirring every 2 minutes. Stir
in soy sauce, black pepper and caraway seeds. Microwave
for 1 minute. Dust with parsley.

Serves 4

Carrots Vichy

full power
11 minutes

6 carrots, cut in matchstick strips
2 tbsp orange juice
2 medium cucumbers, cut in matchstick strips
2 tbsp butter
salt and black pepper to taste
1 tbsp chopped parsley

Place carrots in a shallow casserole dish and add orange juice. Cover and microwave on full power for 7 minutes. Add cucumber, butter and seasonings. Cover and microwave for 4 minutes. Stir once during cooking time. Dust with parsley and serve.

Serves 6

Garlic mushrooms

full power
8 minutes

12–14 large black mushrooms, wiped
60 g/2 oz butter
1–2 cloves garlic, crushed
1 teasp fresh marjoram or 1/2 teasp dried marjoram
1 tbsp chopped parsley
salt and black pepper to taste
1 teasp lemon juice

Place mushrooms in a greased shallow casserole dish. Overlap mushrooms if necessary, as they shrink a great deal when cooked. Place butter in a small bowl. Microwave on full power for 2 minutes. Add remaining ingredients. Brush each mushroom with butter mixture. Pour leftover butter into the casserole dish. Cover with cling film and cut two slits in film to prevent 'ballooning' during cooking. Microwave for 5 – 6 minutes. Do not overcook, as the mushrooms continue to cook for some time after they have been removed from the oven.

Serves 6

Pâté-stuffed mushrooms

full power
6 minutes

10–12 large mushrooms
120 ml/4 fl oz creamy chicken liver pâté (see p. 37)
60 g/2 oz dry breadcrumbs
1 tbsp chopped parsley
6 tbsp grated Mozzarella cheese

Wipe mushrooms clean, remove stems and arrange on two microwave dishes. Divide pâté among the mushroom caps. Combine breadcrumbs, parsley and mozzarella cheese and sprinkle on top of pâté. Microwave each dish on full power for 3 minutes until stuffing is heated through. Serve hot.

Makes 10 – 12 mushrooms

Mushrooms with spinach and cheese

full power
6 minutes

10–12 large mushrooms
250 g/8 oz frozen chopped spinach, thawed
1 egg
2 tbsp thick white onion soup powder
60 g/2 oz cream cheese
pinch of nutmeg
salt and pepper to taste
1 tbsp dry breadcrumbs
4 tbsp grated Gouda cheese

Wipe mushrooms clean, remove stems and arrange on two microwave dishes. Drain spinach and mix with remaining ingredients, reserving 2 tbsp of the Gouda cheese. Place spoonfuls of the mixture on each mushroom and sprinkle remaining cheese on top. Microwave each dish on full power for 2½ – 3 minutes. Smaller mushrooms will be done more quickly.

Makes 10 – 12 mushrooms

Left to right: mushrooms with spinach and cheese, pâté-stuffed mushrooms and savoury mushrooms (p. 38)

Desserts

The variety of desserts which can be cooked in the microwave is never-ending. Recipes using gelatine are easily made, as are ice-cream toppings and hot desserts which can be cooked in advance and reheated before serving. Although traditional double-crust pies are unsuccessful because the fillings bubble over and the tops do not brown, crumbles are simply delicious in every form. Baked puddings should be removed from the microwave while still slightly moist, as cooking will continue during standing time. Fresh fruit cooked in a cooking bag or casserole dish with a little sugar (it is seldom necessary to add water) retains its full flavour and has a bright colour.
Check and stir or rearrange fruits often to prevent overcooking. Those cooked with their skins on, such as baked apples, should first be pricked to prevent them from bursting during the cooking process. Puréed fruits make a good sauce to pour over ice-cream, or to stir into yoghurt.

FRESH FRUIT COOKING CHART

FRUIT	QUANTITY	COOKING TIME (On full power)	PREPARATION
Apricots	500 g/1 lb	7–9 minutes	Cut in half and stone. Sprinkle with sugar to taste
Cooking apples puréed	500 g/1 lb	8–10 minutes	Peel, core and slice. Add sugar to taste
Cooking apples baked whole	4	7–8 minutes	Core and stuff, if desired
Gooseberries	500 g/1 lb	4–5 minutes	Sprinkle with 125 g/4 oz sugar
Peaches	4 medium	4–6 minutes	Peel, halve and stone. Cook halves or slices. Add sugar to taste
Pears	4 medium	7–9 minutes	Peel, halve and core. Sprinkle with a little lemon juice or cook in a syrup made of 60 g/2 oz sugar, 5 tbsp water, piece cinnamon stick
Plums and cherries	500 g/1 lb	4–5 minutes	Cut plums in half. Remove stones. Remove cherry stalks. Add a strip of lemon rind and sugar to taste
Rhubarb	500 g/1 lb	8–10 minutes	Wash and cut into 2.5-cm/1-inch lengths. Add 125 g/4 oz sugar and a strip of lemon rind
Soft Fruits			
Blackberries	500 g/1 lb	3–4 minutes	Add sugar to taste
Loganberrie-	500 g/1 lb	4–5 minutes	Add sugar to taste
Mulberries	500 g/1 lb	4–5 minutes	Remove stems and add sugar to taste
Raspberries	500 g/1 lb	4–5 minutes	Add sugar to taste
Strawberries	500 g/1 lb	4–5 minutes	Hull and add sugar to taste

To dissolve gelatine

Dissolving gelatine in any liquid is simply done in the microwave as less utensils are used and the amount of time taken is also reduced. Depending on the volume of liquid, the length of time the gelatine mixture is microwaved may vary slightly. Measure the liquid in a microwave-proof measuring jug, sprinkle gelatine onto liquid and stir to combine. Allow the mixture to stand for a few minutes, until it has thickened. Microwave, uncovered, on medium for about 1 minute, stir and use. Dissolved gelatine may also be kept warm on low or defrost for a few minutes before being used.

Basic custard

full power
7 minutes

500 ml/17 fl oz milk
2 tbsp custard powder
2 tbsp sugar

Pour milk into a large jug, saving a little to mix with the custard powder. Microwave milk, uncovered, on full power for 4 minutes. Combine remaining milk, custard powder and sugar. Pour a little of the hot milk onto custard mixture. Stir well. Pour custard mixture into the jug. Mix well. Microwave for a further 3 minutes, stirring at the end of each minute during the cooking time. The custard is ready to use.

To prevent a skin from forming, cover custard with a piece of greaseproof paper. Push paper onto custard so that there is no air trapped on the surface. When custard is required, lift paper off and remove excess custard from paper with the back of a knife. The thickness of the custard may be varied by using more or less custard powder.

Makes 500 ml/17 fl oz

Crème brûlée

full power
defrost
11 minutes

500 ml/17 fl oz single cream
2 tbsp sugar
6 egg yolks
2 teasp vanilla essence
6 tbsp white sugar
4 tbsp brown sugar
slices of kiwi fruit to garnish

Pour the cream into a jug and add 2 tbsp sugar. Microwave on full power for 3 minutes. Stir well to make sure the sugar has dissolved. Beat egg yolks until fluffy and light in colour. Add vanilla and cream. Beat to combine. Pour into six individual serving dishes. Cover and microwave on defrost for 7–8 minutes. Delicate food such as custard continues to cook for some time after being microwaved. To test that it is ready, shake the custard carefully. The inside should quiver like jelly. Cool, then chill well.

Combine the white and brown sugars. Divide between the six dishes and sprinkle evenly on top of each custard. Place custards on a baking sheet and grill conventionally for a few minutes, turning each custard as the top starts to caramelize. When deep golden brown, remove from the oven and chill once more. Serve with a few slices of kiwi fruit, or any other tart fruit.

Serves 6

Caramel coffee dessert

Fruit salad supreme

A heavenly fruit salad that is best served well chilled

high
4 minutes

2 eggs
100 g/3½ oz sugar
2 tbsp plain flour
juice of 1 lemon
1 (439-g/15½-oz) can pineapple pieces, drained and juice reserved
250 ml/8 fl oz double cream
6 tbsp curd cheese
1 (312-g/11-oz) can mandarin oranges, drained
60 g/2 oz miniature marshmallows (or large marshmallows, chopped)
60 g/2 oz desiccated coconut, toasted (see p. 23)
4 tbsp maraschino cherries, quartered
125 g/4 oz seedless green grapes, halved
60 g/2 oz flaked almonds, toasted (see p. 23)

In a large glass measuring jug, combine eggs, sugar, flour, lemon juice and 190 ml/6½ fl oz of the reserved juice from the pineapple. Microwave on high for 3–4 minutes, stirring well after each minute. The mixture should be thickened. Stir until smooth and let cool to room temperature. Whip cream lightly and fold into egg mixture, along with cheese. Fold in remaining ingredients, except almonds, cover and chill overnight. Just before serving, fold in almonds.

Serves 10 – 12

Caramel coffee dessert

medium
14 minutes

4 eggs
1 (397-g/14-oz) can condensed milk
250 ml/8 fl oz cold strong coffee
2 tbsp brandy

Beat eggs very lightly. Add remaining ingredients and beat to combine. Pour into a glass ring mould. Cover with cling film, and pierce to prevent 'ballooning' during cooking. Microwave for 14 minutes on medium. Cool and refrigerate for a few hours before turning out and serving.

Serves 6

Banana and passion fruit slice

full power
medium
3 minutes

For the crust	For the filling
100 g/3½ oz blanched almonds, toasted (see p. 23) and chopped	2 tbsp water
	1 tbsp gelatine
	400 ml/14 fl oz plain yoghurt
75 g/2½ oz coconut, toasted (see p. 23)	3 tbsp honey
	2 passion fruit
3 tbsp sugar	2 egg whites
60 g/2 oz margarine	2 bananas, sliced

To make the crust, combine almonds, coconut and sugar. Rub in margarine. Line a 23 × 13-cm/9 × 5-inch loaf pan with greaseproof or non-stick parchment. Grease well, so that the crust can be pressed in firmly. Line the pan with approximately half the crust, reserving the rest for the topping. Microwave on full power for 2 minutes. Cool.

To make the filling, combine water and gelatine in a jug, and allow to stand for a couple of minutes. Microwave on medium for 1 minute. Stir well before using. (Dissolved gelatine may be kept warm using the defrost cycle.) Combine yoghurt and honey, and add passion fruit pulp. Beat egg whites until stiff. Stir gelatine into yoghurt mixture, then fold in egg whites. Arrange banana slices on the base of the crust. Pour yoghurt mixture over this. Sprinkle with remaining crust mixture. Chill for 4 hours. Turn out and cut into squares or slices.

Serves 8

Apricot cream

full power
medium
8 minutes

8 apricots
4 tbsp water
sugar to taste
250 ml/8 fl oz milk
2 eggs, separated
5 tbsp cold water
5 teasp gelatine
190 ml/6½ fl oz double cream
a little whipped cream and sliced apricot to garnish

Wash apricots, cut in half and remove stones. Place in a shallow casserole dish and add 4 tbsp water and a little sugar. Cover and microwave on full power for 4 minutes. Purée apricots and sweeten to taste. Pour milk into a jug and microwave, uncovered, for 3 minutes. Beat egg yolks very well. Pour onto hot milk and beat again. Combine custard and apricot purée. Allow to cool.

Pour 5 tbsp water into a jug and add gelatine. Stand for a few minutes. Microwave, uncovered, on medium for 1 minute. Meanwhile beat the cream until thick. Stir gelatine into apricot custard. Chill over ice until mixture begins to thicken. Whisk egg whites until soft peaks form. Carefully fold cream, then egg whites into custard mixture. Pour into a rinsed mould and then refrigerate for at least 3 hours.

To turn out mould, dip into hot water for 3 seconds. Carefully draw a small area of the pudding away from the side of the mould – this will introduce an air bubble. Turn over onto a plate and wait for a few seconds before removing mould. Decorate with stars of whipped cream and a few slices of apricot.

Serves 6

VARIATIONS
Plum cream: Substitute 8 plums for the apricots, then continue as for apricot cream.

Raspberry cream: Substitute 150 ml/¼ pint raspberry purée for the apricots and the water. Microwave raspberry purée and sugar to taste for 4 minutes on full power, then continue as for apricot cream.

Chocolate mousse

Although this rich mousse makes a large quantity, half the mixture can be frozen if desired

medium
6 minutes

150 g/5 oz dark chocolate
60 g/2 oz milk chocolate
3 tbsp strong black coffee
6 eggs
3 egg yolks
180 g/6 oz sugar
3 tbsp light rum
2 teasp vanilla essence
1 tbsp gelatine
4 tbsp water
375 ml/13 fl oz double cream
whipped cream to garnish

Place chocolate and coffee in a deep measuring jug and microwave on medium for 5 minutes or until chocolate is melted, stirring frequently. Allow to cool.

Apricot cream

Beat eggs and yolks until very light and fluffy, about 10 minutes. Add sugar and beat until mixture is shiny, about 5 minutes. Add melted chocolate, rum and vanilla. Mix until thoroughly blended.

Sprinkle gelatine over water in a glass measuring jug. Let stand for 3 minutes, then microwave on medium for about 45 seconds to melt gelatine. With mixer running, slowly beat gelatine into chocolate mixture. Beat cream to soft peaks and fold into chocolate mixture. Pour into a large serving bowl (or two medium-sized bowls) and chill for at least 4 hours. Serve garnished with whipped cream.

To freeze, chill, then cover well and freeze for up to 3 weeks. Thaw in refrigerator.

Serves 16

Note: To change the flavour of the mousse, add orange liqueur, brandy or coffee liqueur instead of rum.

Chocolate fondue

A quick, easy dessert that is delightful to serve and fun to eat

full power
4 minutes

375 g/12 oz dark chocolate, broken up
120 ml/4 fl oz single cream
2 tbsp dark rum
banana slices, pineapple chunks, strawberries or
    squares of madeira cake to serve

Place chocolate, cream and rum in a deep serving dish and microwave on full power for 3½ – 4½ minutes to melt chocolate. Stir well until mixture is smooth, and serve immediately. To serve, give each person a skewer or fondue fork and a dish of fruit or cake pieces. Let each person dip pieces into the chocolate.

Serves 6

Pears Alicia

Pears Alicia

full power
19 minutes

250 ml/8 fl oz water	small piece cinnamon stick
75 g/2½ oz sugar	6 firm pears, peeled
120 ml/4 fl oz Madeira	4 teasp cornflour
3 tbsp Curaçao	2 tbsp brandy
2 strips orange rind	angelica and orange rind
1 tbsp apple jelly	strips to decorate

Pour water into a casserole dish. Add sugar and cover. Microwave on full power for 4 minutes. Add Madeira, Curaçao, orange rind, apple jelly and cinnamon, then stir to combine. Add pears and cover. Microwave for 7 – 10 minutes. The time will vary, depending on the type and ripeness of pears used. Remove pears and cinnamon.

Blend together cornflour and brandy. Add a little of the hot liquid to the cornflour, then pour the cornflour mixture into the sauce. Stir well. Microwave, covered, for 5 minutes, stirring twice during cooking time. The liquid should be of a pouring consistency, as it thickens when cold. Add pears and coat well with sauce. Cover and cool, then chill. Recoat pears with sauce from time to time. Decorate each pear with a 'leaf' of angelica and a strip of orange rind. Serve well chilled with plenty of whipped cream.

Serves 6

Champagne cream

full power
6 minutes

180 g/6 oz castor sugar
120 ml/4 fl oz water
2 oranges
2 lemons
500 ml/17 fl oz chilled champagne or sparkling wine
500 ml/17 fl oz double cream
4 tbsp brandy
6 boudoir biscuits, broken into pieces
a little brandy

Place sugar and water in a deep bowl and microwave on full power for 2 minutes. Stir until sugar dissolves, then

microwave for 4 minutes. Grate rind from one orange. Remove peel in thin strips from one lemon and set aside. Squeeze juice from oranges and lemons and strain. Add to sugar syrup along with orange rind. Let cool. Pour in champagne and turn mixture into freezer trays. Cover and freeze until frozen around edges.

Turn mixture into a large bowl and beat very well. Beat cream to stiff peaks, then fold into champagne mixture, mixing until well combined. Stir in 4 tbsp brandy, cover and freeze for about 4 hours, until frozen. About 30 minutes before serving, place biscuit pieces in six serving glasses and sprinkle with a little brandy. Leave to soak. To serve champagne cream, scoop into glasses and garnish with thin strips of lemon peel. Serve immediately.

Serves 6

Chocolate cream pie

full power
medium
6 minutes

For the crust
90 g/3 oz pecan nuts, chopped
8–10 digestive biscuits, crumbed
3 tbsp sugar
60 g/2 oz butter
3 tbsp single cream

For the filling
1 tbsp gelatine
4 tbsp cold water
150 g/5 oz dark chocolate, broken up
120 ml/4 fl oz boiling water
2 eggs
3 tbsp sugar
pinch of salt
1 teasp vanilla essence
60 g/2 oz pecan nuts, chopped
250 ml/8 fl oz double cream, whipped
whipped cream and grated chocolate to garnish

To make the crust, combine the nuts, biscuit crumbs and sugar. Microwave butter on full power for 1 minute to melt. Add to crumb mixture, mixing well. Add cream and combine well. Press mixture lightly into the bottom and sides of a 23-cm/9-inch glass flan dish and microwave for 2 minutes. Let cool.

For the filling, sprinkle gelatine over cold water in a glass measuring jug and stand for 5 minutes. Microwave on medium for 1 minute to dissolve the gelatine. Place the chocolate in a glass bowl and microwave on full power for 1½-2 minutes. Stir in the 120 ml/4 fl oz boiling water and gelatine and mix very well. Beat eggs, sugar, salt and vanilla essence until light and fluffy. Add nuts and chocolate mixture. Mix well, then gently fold in the whipped cream. Spoon mixture into the crust and chill until set. Decorate with whipped cream and chocolate. Cut into wedges to serve.

Serves 8 – 10

In a conventional oven: Bake the crust at 180°C/350°F, Gas Mark 4 for about 8–10 minutes.

Chocolate cheese triangle and banana and passion fruit slice (p. 106)

Chocolate cheese triangle

medium
high
4 minutes

5 teasp water	*For the coating*
2 teasp gelatine	3 tbsp sugar
75 g/2½ oz butter	3 tbsp water
75 g/2½ oz sugar	60 g/2 oz dark chocolate, chopped
125 g/4 oz cream cheese	2 tbsp cocoa
1 egg	2 tbsp butter
1 tbsp lemon juice	a few slivered almonds
½ teasp cinnamon	
75 g/2½ oz almonds, toasted (see p. 23) and chopped	
2 tbsp brandy	
2 tbsp milk	
24 Nice biscuits	

Combine water and gelatine. Stand for 1 minute, then microwave on medium for 1 minute. Stir well before using. Gelatine may be kept warm on low for a few minutes if necessary. Beat butter and sugar until light and fluffy. Add cream cheese and beat again. Add egg, lemon juice, cinnamon and nuts. Beat once more. Stir in gelatine.

Combine brandy and milk. Dip biscuits into milk mixture one at a time. Arrange on a piece of aluminium foil in a rectangle made up of 4 × 3 biscuits. Spread a thin layer of cheese mixture over biscuits. Repeat with remaining biscuits. Heap cheese mixture along centre row of biscuits, working cheese into a triangular form. Draw the outer edges of the foil up, so that the biscuits meet and form the apex of a triangle. Seal firmly and refrigerate. Care must be taken at this point that the biscuits meet perfectly, as the cheese mixture sets firmly and the biscuits cannot be moved at a later stage.

To make the coating, place sugar, water, chocolate and cocoa in a bowl and stir to combine. Microwave on high for 3 minutes, stirring at least twice during cooking time. Stir very well. Add butter and stir until melted. Allow coating to cool until it is thick enough to leave a trail. Unwrap cheese triangle. Stand on a cooling rack. Pour coating over the cake, taking care to coat the whole cake evenly. Arrange nuts along top immediately. Refrigerate until coating has set. Serve this rich dessert in small slices.

Serves 8 – 10

Banana crumble

medium
7 minutes

4 bananas, sliced	*For the topping*
1 tbsp lemon juice	90 g/3 oz plain flour
grated rind of ½ lemon	3 tbsp margarine
400 ml/14 fl oz basic custard (see p. 105)	1 tbsp castor sugar
	pinch of cinnamon
	2 tbsp finely chopped nuts
	2 tbsp brown sugar

Place bananas in a greased 23-cm/9-inch pie dish. Sprinkle with lemon juice. Add rind to custard and pour over bananas. To make the topping, sift flour, then rub in margarine. Add castor sugar and cinnamon. Sprinkle over custard. Combine nuts and brown sugar and sprinkle on top. Microwave on medium for 7 minutes. Serve hot or cold.

Serves 6 – 8

Boston cream cake

full power
medium
18 minutes

For the hot milk sponge	300 ml/½ pint milk
2 eggs	2 egg yolks, beaten
210 g/7 oz sugar	1 tbsp butter
125 g/4 oz plain flour	1 tbsp apricot liqueur or brandy
1 teasp baking powder	1 teasp vanilla essence
120 ml/4 fl oz milk	
2 tbsp butter	*For the chocolate glaze and white icing*
3 tbsp apricot jam	30 g/1 oz dark chocolate
	1 tbsp butter
For the custard filling	180 g/6 oz icing sugar
75 g/2½ oz sugar	1 teasp vanilla essence
2 tbsp plain flour	hot water
4 teasp cornflour	2 teasp milk
pinch of salt	

For the sponge, beat eggs at high speed for 4 minutes, then gradually add sugar, beating for 4 – 5 minutes or until sugar is nearly dissolved. Combine flour and baking powder and add to egg mixture, stirring until just blended. Place milk in a jug, add butter and microwave on full power for 20 – 30 seconds, just to melt butter. Add milk to cake mixture, stirring until smooth. Turn into a greased and lined 20-cm/8-inch round baking dish and microwave on medium for 7–8 minutes, rotating dish every 2 minutes if necessary. Then microwave on full power for 1½ minutes or until done. Cool on a wire rack for about 10 minutes, then turn out and cool completely.

To make the custard, combine sugar, flour, cornflour and salt in a 1-litre/2-pint bowl. Gradually stir in milk, mixing well. Microwave on full power for 4 minutes, stirring every minute. Microwave for 1 minute more. Gradually stir a small amount of milk mixture into beaten egg yolks, then return to bowl, mixing well. Microwave on full power for 45 seconds, stirring every 15 seconds. Add butter, liqueur and vanilla, and stir just until butter melts. Cover surface with greaseproof paper and cool without stirring. Chill well. Use to fill cake.

For the glaze, place chocolate and butter in a jug and microwave on full power for 1½ – 2 minutes or until the chocolate has melted. Stir in 100 g/3½ oz of the icing sugar and the vanilla, then 2 teasp hot water. Add a further 1–2 tbsp hot water a little at a time and blend well, until mixture is of pouring consistency. For the white icing, combine remaining icing sugar and 2 teasp milk to make a drizzling consistency.

To assemble, slice cake horizontally into two layers and spread bottom layer with apricot jam. Place on a serving plate. Top with custard filling, spreading to within 1 cm/½ inch of the edges. Place remaining cake half on top. Pour over chocolate glaze and spread evenly so that it runs over edges. Drizzle white icing in a spiral pattern on top of chocolate icing, then quickly draw a sharp knife from the centre to the edge of the cake several times. Let icing set, then chill the cake. Serve cut into wedges.

Serves 10 – 12

In a conventional oven: Bake sponge cake at 190°C/375°F, Gas Mark 5 for 25–30 minutes.

Hot fruit salad

high
4 minutes

juice of 2 lemons
juice of 3 oranges
1 (439-g/15½-oz) can pineapple pieces, drained and juice reserved
310 g/10 oz sugar
500 ml/17 fl oz water
3 tbsp plain flour
a little lemon juice
6 bananas, sliced
4 oranges, segmented
90 g/3 oz red pitted cherries
500 g/1 lb green seedless grapes

Combine lemon, orange and pineapple juices with sugar, water and flour in a deep casserole dish. Microwave on high for 3 – 4 minutes, stirring after each minute. Stir until smooth. Sprinkle lemon juice over sliced bananas and reserve. Add pineapple pieces, orange segments, cherries and grapes to the sauce mixture. Stir in bananas. Serve warm, topped with whipped cream.

Serves 10

Boston cream cake

110

Creamy cheesecake

full power
medium
high
23 minutes

For the crust
60 g/2 oz butter
125 g/4 oz digestive biscuit crumbs
3 tbsp brown sugar

For the filling
250 g/8 oz cream cheese
2 eggs
100 g/3½ oz sugar
pinch of salt
1 teasp vanilla essence
1 tbsp lemon juice
120 ml/4 fl oz soured cream

In a 23-cm/9-inch glass pie dish, microwave butter on full power for 1 minute. Stir in biscuit crumbs and sugar. Press mixture into bottom and sides of the dish and microwave on full power for 1½ minutes.

For the filling, beat together cream cheese, eggs, sugar, salt, vanilla and lemon juice. Stir in soured cream and microwave on medium for 10 – 12 minutes, stirring well every 2 minutes. Pour into baked crust and microwave on medium for 3 minutes. Carefully stir through the filling, rotating dish if necessary, and microwave on medium for 2 minutes. Stir through filling again, then microwave on high for about 3 minutes more, or until centre is just set. Chill. Serve sprinkled with cinnamon or with a fruit sauce.

Serves 6 – 8

Baked chocolate pudding

full power
10 minutes

230 g/7½ oz plain flour
210 g/7 oz sugar
5 tbsp cocoa
1 teasp bicarbonate of soda
1 teasp baking powder
1 (200-g/7-oz) jar mayonnaise (not salad cream)
1 egg
250 ml/8 fl oz water
1 teasp vanilla essence
cream or custard for serving

Stir together dry ingredients in a large mixing bowl. Combine mayonnaise, egg, water and vanilla essence and add to dry ingredients. Beat for 2 minutes, scraping bowl at least once. Pour mixture into a greased, deep 25-cm/10-inch baking dish. Microwave on full power for 8–10 minutes, rotating dish if necessary. Let stand for 10 minutes before serving. Spoon into individual pudding dishes and top with cream or custard.

Serves 12

In a conventional oven: Bake at 180°C/350°F, Gas Mark 4 for 35–40 minutes. Turn out and cool.

Sherry cream soufflé

Sherry cream soufflé

medium
1 minute

2 tbsp gelatine
120 ml/4 fl oz water
375 ml/13 fl oz medium sherry
6 eggs, separated
180 g/6 oz sugar
1 tbsp lemon juice
250 ml/8 fl oz double cream
whipped cream, chopped nuts and crystallized flowers to decorate

Sprinkle gelatine over water in a glass measuring jug and stand for 5 minutes. Microwave for 1 minute on medium to dissolve gelatine. Add sherry, mixing well, then let mixture cool until it is the consistency of unbeaten egg white.

Beat egg whites until frothy, then gradually beat in 125g/4 oz of the sugar. Add lemon juice and beat until stiff. Beat egg yolks until frothy. Add remaining sugar and beat until thick. Add slightly thickened sherry mixture to egg yolk mixture and beat well. Whip 250 ml/8 fl oz cream and fold into egg yolk mixture. Fold in a quarter of the egg white, then fold in remaining egg white. Spoon mixture into a 23-cm/9-inch soufflé dish with a deep greaseproof paper collar attached. Chill for 3–4 hours. To serve, pipe whipped cream stars around the top of the soufflé, remove collar and pat chopped nuts around the sides. Place a crystallized flower in the centre. Keep refrigerated until required.

Serves 10 – 12

Macadamia nut pie

Macadamia nut pie

full power
medium
20 minutes

1 × 23-cm/9-inch sweet shortcrust pastry pie shell (see p. 129)
250 ml/8 fl oz water
1 tbsp margarine
180 g/6 oz dates, chopped
3 eggs
90 g/3 oz white sugar
90 g/3 oz soft brown sugar
1 teasp vanilla essence
2 tbsp single cream
pinch of cinnamon
pinch of ginger
pinch of nutmeg
2 tbsp plain flour
90 g/3 oz macadamia nuts, chopped
whipped cream for serving

Place a piece of paper towel on the base of the pie shell. Add a few dried beans to weight it down. Microwave on full power for 2 minutes. Remove beans and paper towel. Microwave pie shell for 1 minute more. Cool slightly.

To make the filling, place water and margarine in a bowl. Microwave for 3 minutes. Add dates and allow to cool. Beat the eggs well. Add both sugars, vanilla and cream, and beat very well. Sift in the dry ingredients and beat to

combine. Stir in nuts, followed by date mixture. Pour into pie shell. Microwave on medium for 14 minutes. The centre should still be tacky. Allow to cool before serving. Serve slices with plenty of whipped cream.

Serves 8

In a conventional oven: Bake on the middle shelf at 160°C/325°F, Gas Mark 3 for 45 minutes.

Pecan meringue pie

high
medium
7 minutes

3 egg whites
pinch cream of tartar
210 g/7 oz castor sugar
1 teasp vanilla essence
20 Ritz crackers, crumbed
90 g/3 oz pecan nuts, coarsely chopped
cream for serving

Beat egg whites with cream of tartar until soft peaks form. Gradually beat in castor sugar until peaks become stiff. Fold in vanilla essence, biscuit crumbs and pecans. Spoon into a well-greased 20-cm/8-inch glass pie dish and microwave on high for 3 minutes, then reduce power to medium and microwave for 3½–4 minutes more. Cool on a wire rack for a few minutes before serving. Cut into wedges while still warm, and serve with cream.

Serves 8 – 10

In a conventional oven: Bake at 180°C/350°F, Gas Mark 4 for 25 minutes.

Mocha pie

high
defrost
4 minutes

1 × 25-cm/10-inch crumb crust (see p. 128)
3 tbsp double cream, whipped and chocolate leaves (see p. 136) to decorate

For the filling
150 ml/¼ pint milk
20 marshmallows
2 tbsp instant coffee powder
2 egg yolks
250 ml/8 fl oz double cream

To make the filling, pour milk into a jug or bowl and add marshmallows. Microwave on high for 2 minutes, then on defrost for 2 minutes. Stir in coffee. Stir from time to time to make sure that the marshmallows have melted completely. Beat egg yolks until fluffy and light. Pour in marshmallow mixture and beat well. Allow to cool, but do not chill. Beat cream until thick. Fold in marshmallow mixture. Pour into prepared crust and chill until firm. Decorate with swirls of cream and chocolate leaves.

Serves 6 – 8

Apple crumble

full power
9 minutes

1 (385-g/12-oz) apple pie filling
135 g/4½ oz brown sugar
3 tbsp raisins
1 teasp grated lemon rind
1 tbsp lemon juice
1 tbsp water
60 g/2 oz plain flour
60 g/2 oz butter
2 tbsp chopped nuts
30 ml chopped nuts
15 ml brown sugar

Place pie apples in the bottom of a 20-cm/8-inch baking dish and sprinkle with 75 g/2½ oz brown sugar. Scatter raisins and lemon rind on top and sprinkle with a mixture of lemon juice and water. Rub together flour, butter and 3 tbsp brown sugar until crumbly. Sprinkle evenly over fruit. Top with nuts and remaining brown sugar. Microwave on full power for 8–9 minutes, rotating dish a quarter turn every 3 minutes, if necessary. Stand for 5 minutes before serving with cream or ice-cream.

Serves 6

Date dessert

This dessert can be successfully reheated the day after it has been made

medium
high
12 minutes

90 g/3 oz plain flour
½ teasp bicarbonate of soda
pinch of salt
90 g/3 oz soft brown sugar
60 g/2 oz margarine, softened
2 eggs
½ teasp vanilla essence
120 ml/4 fl oz soured cream
125 g/4 oz dates, chopped
4 tbsp chopped pecan nuts

for the cream topping
120 ml/4 fl oz soured cream
3 tbsp fresh single cream
3 tbsp brown sugar

Sift flour, bicarbonate of soda and salt into a bowl. Add brown sugar, margarine, eggs, vanilla essence and soured cream. Mix well, then stir in dates and pecans. Pour into a greased deep. 25-cm/10-inch pie plate. Place pie plate on top of an inverted saucer. Microwave on medium for 6 minutes, then on high for approximately 5 minutes. Remove from oven and allow to cool for 10 minutes before pouring cream topping over. To make the topping, combine all ingredients in a bowl, then microwave on medium for 30 seconds. Serve dessert warm. To reheat, cover and microwave on medium for 2–3 minutes, depending on the size of the piece being reheated.

Serves 6–8

In a conventional oven: Bake at 180°C/350°F, Gas Mark 4 for 25–30 minutes.

Basic crêpe mixture

full power
30 seconds

125 g/4 oz plain flour
pinch of salt
2 eggs
150 ml/¼ pint milk
150 ml/¼ pint water
2 tbsp butter

To make batter, place all ingredients except butter, in a blender or processor. Blend for 30 seconds, scrape down sides of goblet, and process for a further 30 seconds. Place butter in microwave on full power for 30 seconds. Add to batter. Blend for a few seconds more to combine. Stand batter for 30 minutes. The batter should be the consistency of milk for paper-thin crêpes. Dilute the batter with a little more water if necessary. For thicker crêpes or pancakes, add less liquid to original mixture. Heat a crêpe pan until a slight haze forms. Wipe the pan with a little oil. Spoon sufficient of the mixture into the pan to coat the base thinly. Cook for a few seconds. Carefully loosen edges with a spatula, then turn crêpe over and cook for a few seconds more. Lift out of pan and place on a sheet of greaseproof paper.

Makes about 20 crêpes

Note: Crêpes and pancakes freeze very well. Make a large number, then stack ten, one on top of the other, on a piece of greaseproof paper. Add another layer of paper. Repeat until all the crêpes are packed, place in a plastic bag and freeze. To thaw, lift off a stack of ten crêpes, place on a plate and cover with cling film. Microwave on defrost for 4 minutes. The crêpes will peel off perfectly. Use as required.

Crêpes Marguerite

high
8 minutes

10–12 crêpes (above)

For the filling
1 (411-g/14½-oz) can apricots or plums
75 g/2½ oz butter
100 g/3½ oz icing sugar

For the topping
5 tbsp apricot or plum liqueur
extra apricot or plum halves
maraschino cherries

Drain apricots, reserving syrup, and chop. Cream butter and sugar. Add apricots and 2 tbsp of the syrup. Blend well. Place about 2 tbsp of the mixture on each crêpe and roll up. Place in a greased heatproof dish. Stir liqueur into any remaining filling and pour over crêpes. Decorate with extra fruit and cherries. Cover and microwave for about 8 minutes on high. Serve hot.

Serves 5–6

Apricot sorbet

full power
6 minutes

125 g/4 oz dried apricots
600 ml/1 pint water
100 g/3½ oz sugar
4 tbsp lemon juice
3 tbsp apricot liqueur
2 egg whites
2 tbsp icing sugar

Soak apricots for 1 hour in water. Place in a casserole dish and add sugar. Cover with cling film. Cut two slits in film to prevent 'ballooning' during cooking. Microwave on full power for 6 minutes. Cool slightly, then add lemon juice and liqueur. Using a blender, purée apricots. Place in an ice tray and freeze until firm. Beat egg whites until stiff, then slowly beat in icing sugar. Cut sorbet into blocks and, using a food processor, process in two batches until soft. Add half the egg white at a time and process to combine. Return to freezer. Freeze until firm. Serve in glasses, decorated with wafers.

Serves 6

VARIATION
Apricot ice-cream: Add 120 ml/4 fl oz single cream to sorbet when processing the frozen apricot mixture.

Caramel ice-cream and apricot sorbet

Caramel ice-cream

full power
high
8 minutes

1 (397-g/14-oz) can condensed milk
4 eggs, separated
1 teasp vanilla essence
500 ml/17 fl oz double cream
whipped cream and a few hazelnuts to decorate

Line the base of a 33 × 10-cm/13 × 4-inch loaf pan with foil. Pour condensed milk into a very deep bowl (if the bowl is too small, the boiling condensed milk will run over the sides). Microwave, uncovered, for 4 minutes on full power and 4 minutes on high. Allow to cool. Beat egg yolks, vanilla and caramelized condensed milk very well. Whip cream until thick, then fold into caramel mixture. Beat whites until stiff, but not dry. Fold into caramel mixture. Pour mixture into loaf pan and freeze overnight. Run a spatula around edges of pan. Turn ice-cream out onto a plate. Decorate immediately with stars of whipped cream and a few hazelnuts. Return ice-cream to freezer until ready to serve.

Serves 12

Hot fruit salad sauce

Jellied kir

Makes a light dessert or a refreshing jelly to serve between courses of a hot meal

medium
full power
1½ minutes

2 tbsp gelatine
120 ml/4 fl oz cold water
120 ml/4 fl oz hot water
75 g/2½ oz sugar
500 ml/17 fl oz dry white wine
2 tbsp Crème de cassis liqueur
lemon slices to garnish

Sprinkle gelatine over cold water in a glass measuring jug. Let stand for 5 minutes, then microwave on medium for 1 minute to dissolve gelatine. Add hot water and sugar, and stir well. Microwave on full power for 30 seconds. Stir until sugar dissolves. Add wine and crème de cassis and mix well. Pour into a 1-litre/2-pint mould, or six individual moulds, and chill until set. Unmould onto serving plates, garnish with lemon slices and serve.

Serves 6

Hot fruit salad sauce

full power
18 minutes

1 (411-g/14½-oz) can apricot halves
1 (425-g/15-oz) can peach slices
1 (439-g/15½-oz) can pineapple chunks
1 (425-g/15-oz) can stoned black cherries
small piece cinnamon stick
6 tbsp Cointreau or van der Hum liqueur
4 tbsp cornflour

Pour the undrained fruit into a large casserole dish. Add cinnamon. Cover and microwave on full power for 12 minutes. Remove cinnamon. Combine van der Hum and cornflour. Stir a little of the hot liquid into the cold mixture, then pour the cornflour mixture into the fruit. Stir well. Microwave, covered, on full power for 6 minutes. Stir the fruit mixture every 2 minutes. Serve hot over ice-cream.

Serves 10 – 12

Apple sauce

full power
8 minutes

500 g/1 lb cooking apples, peeled, cored and sliced
3 tbsp water
2 tbsp sugar, or to taste
pinch of salt

Place apples and water in a bowl and cover with a lid or cling film. Turn back corner of cling film or slit to prevent 'ballooning' during cooking. Microwave on full power for 8 minutes. Rotate dish a quarter turn every 2 minutes if necessary. Remove from oven and mash cooked apples. Stir in sugar and salt. Serve warm or cold.

Serves 4 – 6

Note: For added flavour, add 1 or 2 cloves to the apples while cooking, or add a dash of cinnamon with the sugar.

Butterscotch topping

full power
8 minutes

2 tbsp golden syrup
210 g/7 oz brown sugar
250 ml/8 fl oz milk and water mixed

3 tbsp butter
1 tbsp lemon juice
1 tbsp custard powder

Place syrup, brown sugar, milk and water, and butter in a large bowl. Microwave, uncovered, on full power for 4 minutes. Stir at least once during cooking time. Combine lemon juice and custard powder, adding a little extra water if necessary, to form a smooth paste. Add a little hot mixture to custard, then pour custard mixture into hot liquid. Stir well. Microwave for 3 – 4 minutes, stirring every minute during cooking time. Serve hot over ice-cream.

Makes 300 ml/½ pint

Caramel sauce

defrost
low
12 minutes

2 (68-g/2¼-oz) Mars bars, cut up
150 ml/¼ pint single cream
2 tbsp chopped hazelnuts

Using a deep jug, combine Mars bars and cream. Cover and microwave on defrost for 8 minutes. Stir every 2 minutes, then microwave, covered, on low for 4 minutes. Stir in nuts and serve hot over ice-cream.

Serves 6 – 8

Chocolate fudge sauce

Vary the flavour by using different liqueurs – orange, coffee or cherry, even brandy or rum

full power
3 minutes

2 tbsp honey   90 g/3 oz milk chocolate
120 ml/4 fl oz single cream 1 teasp vanilla essence
90 g/3 oz dark chocolate   1–2 tbsp liqueur

Place honey, cream and chocolate in a 1-litre/2-pint casserole dish or measuring jug and microwave on full power for 2½–3½ minutes. Stir until completely smooth. Add vanilla and liqueur and mix well. Serve warm.

Makes about 375 ml/13 fl oz

Hot chocolate sauce

full power
medium
6 minutes

4 tbsp water   4 tbsp golden syrup
2 tbsp butter   4 tbsp sugar
4 tbsp cocoa powder   1 teasp vanilla essence

Combine all ingredients in a large bowl. Microwave on full power for 3 minutes, stirring every minute during cooking time. Then microwave on medium for 3 minutes. Serve hot with ice-cream.

Makes 120 ml/4 fl oz

Orange sauce

full power
12 minutes

60 g/2 oz butter
60 g/2 oz sugar
1 (178-ml/6¼-fl oz) can frozen orange juice
6 tbsp water
2 tbsp cornflour
orange rind
2 tbsp Grand Marnier

Place butter in a bowl and microwave on full power for 2 minutes. Stir in sugar. Microwave, uncovered, for 2 minutes. Add orange juice and stir to combine. At this point lumps may form but they will disappear when the sauce is heated. Microwave, uncovered, for 3 minutes. Combine water and cornflour. Stir a little of the hot liquid into cornflour mixture, then pour all this liquid into hot orange juice. Stir well. Microwave, uncovered, for 5 minutes. Stir every minute during cooking time. Now add orange rind and Grand Marnier. Serve hot over ice-cream.

Makes 300 ml/½ pint

Maple nut sauce

full power
4 minutes

1 tbsp cornflour   pinch of salt
210 g/7 oz brown sugar   60 g/2 oz butter
120 ml/4 fl oz single cream 1 teasp vanilla essence
3 tbsp maple syrup   60 g/2 oz pecan nuts, chopped

Combine cornflour and brown sugar in a 2-litre/3½-pint casserole dish. Stir in cream, syrup and salt. Add butter. Cover and microwave on full power for 3–4 minutes, stirring after 2 minutes. The mixture should be thickened and sugar dissolved. Stir in vanilla and nuts. Serve warm or cool.

Makes about 375 ml/13 fl oz

Maple nut sauce served over ice-cream

Baking

Many cakes and breads can be baked in the microwave in less time than it takes to prepare them, so something delicious can always be served ovenfresh in next to no time.

The recipes in this chapter have been selected because they are particularly suitable for the microwave.

Follow the instructions carefully and your baking will be an instant success.

Quick breads

Many quick breads react well to microwave baking. Coffee cakes, fruit breads, muffins and yoghurt breads rise well and have a good appearance. Although scones can be baked in the microwave, they do not brown. However, the scone dough in recipes such as Caramel cherry ring or Golden nut ring, page 123, gives a finished product which looks appetizing and tastes delicious.

Cakes

Cakes bake quickly and rise to greater volume in the microwave, giving an airy, fluffy texture. They do not brown as they would conventionally, but with a sprinkling of icing sugar or a coating of icing, it is difficult to tell the difference (see page 22). Microwaving does not affect the flavour of cakes, so they taste just as great as if baked conventionally. Dark cakes, such as chocolate, ginger and carrot cakes, have a good appearance. Angel and chiffon cakes should not be baked in the microwave.

Biscuits and bars

Large batches of biscuits or cookies take longer to microwave than to bake conventionally, as only a few can be baked at a time. The texture and colour also differ because many biscuits need hot dry air to form the characteristic crisp crust. However, bars and squares, such as date bars and chocolate chip squares, microwave with excellent results. Their texture and appearance compare favourably with conventional baking, and they can be ready to serve in about 10 minutes.

Pastry and pies

Shortcrust pastry becomes tender and flaky when baked in the microwave oven but does not brown, so it will not have the golden appearance you are used to. Brushing with a little egg yolk, vanilla essence mixed with water, or adding a few drops of yellow food colouring to the dough will improve the colour. Most microwaved pies use a prebaked shell. If the pastry is not partially or fully baked before adding the filling, it absorbs moisture and becomes soggy.

Crumb crusts are perfect with many fillings. The butter for the crust can be microwaved in the pie dish, then crumbs and other ingredients added and mixed. Microwave the crumb crusts for a short time, and cool before using.

Pastries that need hot dry air to give the characteristic finish, such as puff pastry and choux pastry, are not suitable for microwave cooking.

Yeast breads

Dough for yeast breads can be proved in the microwave in half the normal time by using short bursts of microwave energy with resting periods of about 10 minutes. Follow the directions for mixing and proving yeast breads as accurately as possible. Once the dough has risen, it can be shaped and baked conventionally, as microwaved bread neither browns nor forms a crisp golden crust. However, the batter yeast bread recipes for microwave baking can be topped with cheese, seeds or crushed wheat to give colour and extra flavour to the crust.

To prove yeast doughs in the microwave oven

Mix and knead the dough according to recipe directions. Place in a large, greased bowl and cover. Microwave on full power for 15 seconds, then rest for 10 minutes. Repeat the process 2 or 3 times until the dough has doubled in bulk. It can then be punched down and shaped as desired. If you use a suitable container you may prove the dough a second time in the microwave before baking conventionally.

DEFROSTING OF BREADS AND CAKES

FOOD	QUANTITY	APPROXIMATE TIME (On defrost)	METHOD
Bread, whole or sliced	1 kg/2 lb	6-8 minutes	Unwrap. Place on paper towel. Turn over during defrosting. Stand 5 minutes.
Bread	30 × 13 cm/ 12 × 5 in	4-6 minutes	Unwrap. Place on paper towel. Turn over during defrosting. Stand 5 minutes.
Bread	1 slice	10-15 seconds	Unwrap. Place on paper towel. Stand 1-2 minutes. Time accurately.
Bread rolls	2	20-25 seconds	Unwrap. Place on paper towel. Stand 1-2 minutes. Time accurately.
	4	30-40 seconds	
Cupcakes or muffins	4	1-1½ minutes	Unwrap. Place on paper towel. Stand 5 minutes.
Sponge cake	23 cm/9 in	2-3 minutes	Unwrap. Place on paper towel. Turn over after 1 minute. Stand 5 minutes.
Doughnuts or sweet buns	4	1½-2 minutes	Unwrap. Place on paper towel. Turn over after 1 minute. Stand 5 minutes.
Loaf cakes or ring cakes	30 × 13 cm/ 12 × 5 in or 23–25 cm/ 9–10 in in diameter	5-7 minutes	Unwrap. Place on paper towel. Turn over after 3 minutes. Stand 10 minutes.
Bars		4-6 minutes	Unwrap. Place on paper towel. Stand 5-10 minutes.
Crumpets	20–23 cm/8–9 in square	25-30 seconds	Unwrap. Place on paper towel. Stand 3-4 minutes. Time accurately.
Pancakes or crêpes	10	3-4 minutes	Unwrap. Place on plate. Cover with cling film.
Pies or tarts	20–23 cm/8–9 in	4-6 minutes	Unwrap. Stand 10 minutes.
Pies, cooked (small individual, to thaw only)	1	25-30 seconds	Unwrap. Place upside down on paper towel. Stand 2 minutes.
	4	2-3 minutes	

When baking

- It is easy to overbake in the microwave oven, and baking times will vary with oven models, so most recipes give a range of times. Check the cake or loaf after the minimum time and cook for longer if necessary. Overcooking by even 1½ or 2 minutes will result in a cake with hard and dry outer edges.
- For even baking, turn pans frequently if the cake or loaf seems to be baking unevenly.
- Baked foods rise to a greater volume in the microwave than in a conventional oven, so be sure the container is large and deep enough to accommodate the mixture.
- Prepare pans and dishes for baking by spraying or greasing them generously. Line with greaseproof paper or paper towel for layer cakes. Sprinkle greased pans with finely chopped nuts or fine biscuit crumbs for ring cakes or breads, so that they will turn out of the pan easily.
- Sprinkling a greased baking pan with flour may result in a doughy coating on the outside of the food.
- A ring-shaped cake pan allows the centre of the cake to cook at the same rate as the outer edges. Although glass and microwave ring pans are available, it is easy to prepare one by placing an ordinary glass in the centre of a round glass baking dish.
- Fill cake pans a third to half full. If there is any batter left over, use it to make cupcakes.
- The tops of many baked items will still be slightly moist when cooked. Resist the temptation to turn cakes or loaves out of the pan immediately, as the top will dry during standing time.
- After microwaving, place the pan on a flat, heat-resistant surface so that the bottom will finish baking during standing time.
- In many microwave recipes the amount of liquid can be reduced, but with cakes the liquid is needed to make them moist, so use the amount of liquid stated.
- Let a cake mixture stand for 3 or 4 minutes before microwaving in order to start the reaction between the baking powder and the liquid.
- Try placing the cake pan on an inverted saucer in the microwave. The microwaves can penetrate the bottom of the pan more easily and cooking will be more even.
- To test when cakes, coffee cakes, quick breads or bars are done, insert a tooth pick in the centre and it should come out clean.
- When baking cakes or bars in a square dish, remember to shield the corners with foil to prevent overcooking or drying.

Fruit cake

full power
medium
27 minutes

150 g/5 oz sultanas	230 g/7½ oz plain flour
150 g/5 oz raisins	1 teasp baking powder
150 g/5 oz currants	½ teasp cinnamon
60 g/2 oz mixed peel	½ teasp ground ginger
150 g/5 oz butter	pinch of nutmeg
210 g/7 oz soft brown sugar	pinch of ground cloves
200 ml/7 fl oz water	2 teasp cocoa
1 teasp bicarbonate of soda	120 ml/4 fl oz sherry
100 g/3½ oz glacé cherries, chopped	75 g/2½ oz pecan nuts or almonds, chopped
125 g/4 oz dates, chopped	a few blanched almonds (optional)
1 teasp instant coffee powder	6 tbsp brandy
2 eggs, beaten	

Place sultanas, raisins, currants, peel, butter, sugar and water in a large bowl. Cover with cling film and cut two holes in film to prevent 'ballooning' during cooking. Microwave on full power for 7 minutes. Stir at least twice during cooking time. Add bicarbonate of soda, cherries, dates and instant coffee. Allow to cool completely.

Stir in eggs. Sift all dry ingredients and add, alternately with sherry, to the fruit mixture until all ingredients have been combined. Stir in pecans. Pour into a lined 18-cm/7-inch cake pan. If the cake is not going to be iced, arrange a few almonds attractively on top of the cake before baking. Cover top of cake with greaseproof paper. Microwave on medium for 18–20 minutes. Allow cake to cool before turning out of pan. When cool, slowly pour brandy over cake. Wrap in aluminium foil and store until required.

Makes 1 cake

In a conventional oven: Bake at 140°C/275°F, Gas Mark 1 for 2 hours.

Sponge cake

full power
4 minutes

3 eggs
100 g/3½ oz sugar
½ teasp vanilla essence
100 g/3½ oz plain flour
pinch of salt
½ teasp baking powder

Beat eggs, sugar and vanilla essence together until very light and fluffy. Sift together flour, salt and baking powder, and fold into egg mixture. Pour into a 25-cm/10-inch greased and lined round glass baking dish and microwave on full power for 4–4½ minutes. Let stand in the dish for 5 minutes, then turn out and cool. Alternatively, pour mixture into two 18-cm/7-inch greased and lined baking dishes and microwave on full power, one at a time, for 2½–3 minutes.

Makes 1 large or 2 smaller sponges

In a conventional oven: Bake at 190°C/375°F, Gas Mark 5 for 15–18 minutes for the large cake, 10–12 minutes for the smaller ones.

Banana cake

medium
full power
14 minutes

125 g/4 oz butter, softened
280 g/9 oz sugar
2 eggs
2 large bananas, mashed
½ teasp almond essence
280 g/9 oz plain cake flour
½ teasp baking powder
½ teasp bicarbonate of soda
pinch of salt
4 tbsp yoghurt
banana fudge icing (see p. 129) to decorate

Grease a 25-cm/10-inch ring pan. Cream butter and sugar until light and fluffy. Beat in eggs, one at a time. Add banana and almond essence. Sift dry ingredients together. Add about a third of the dry ingredients to banana mixture. Beat to combine. Add a third of the yoghurt and beat. Continue until all ingredients have been combined. Pour mixture into ring pan. Microwave on medium for 12 minutes. Increase to full power and microwave for a further 1–2 minutes. Allow cake to stand in pan for about 15 minutes before turning out onto a rack. Cool completely before icing with banana fudge icing.

Makes 1 ring cake

In a conventional oven: Add ½ teasp extra baking powder. Bake in two layer pans at 180°C/350°F, Gas Mark 4 for 30 minutes, or in a bundt pan for 35–40 minutes.

Chocolate liqueur cake

full power
4½ minutes

125 g/4 oz soft margarine
125 g/4 oz castor sugar
125 g/4 oz self-raising flour
2 tbsp cocoa
2 eggs
3 tbsp Crème de Cacao

For the icing
90 g/3 oz softened butter
180 g/6 oz icing sugar
2 tbsp orange juice
drained mandarin orange segments and slivered almonds to decorate

Line a 16-cm/6½-inch cake pan with greaseproof paper. Place all ingredients for cake in a mixing bowl. Beat for 3–4 minutes, using an electric mixer. Pour into prepared pan and microwave on full power for 4½ minutes. Allow cake to stand for 15 minutes before turning out onto a cooling rack.

To make the icing, combine all the ingredients in a bowl. Beat until smooth. Cut the cooled cake in half and sandwich together with one-third of the icing. Use the remaining icing to coat the sides and top of the cake. Decorate with swirls of icing and mandarin orange segments. Press slivered almonds onto the sides of the cake as in the illustration on page 117.

Makes 1 layer cake

In a conventional oven: Bake at 180°C/350°F, Gas Mark 4 for 35–40 minutes. Cool before icing.

Jam cake

medium
full power
14 minutes

180 g/6 oz plain flour
½ teasp bicarbonate of soda
salt to taste
½ teasp cinnamon
½ teasp mixed spice
150 g/5 oz sugar
150 g/5 oz margarine, softened
120 ml/4 fl oz gooseberry jam
4 eggs
6 tbsp milk
1 teasp grated lemon rind
60 g/2 oz hazelnuts, chopped
lemon glaze (see p. 129) to decorate

Sift dry ingredients into a mixing bowl. Add remaining ingredients, except icing. Beat very well until light and smooth. Pour into a well-greased 25-cm/10-inch ring pan and microwave on medium for 12 minutes. Increase to full power and microwave for 2 minutes. Allow cake to become almost cool before turning out. Drizzle with lemon icing.

Makes 1 ring cake

In a conventional oven: Bake at 180°C/350°F, Gas Mark 4 for 40–45 minutes.

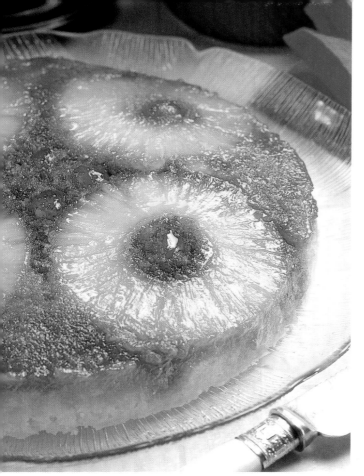
Upside-down cakes bake perfectly in the microwave

Upside-down cake

full power
12 minutes

150 g/5 oz plain flour
150 g/5 oz sugar
2 teasp baking powder
1/2 teasp salt
1 egg
60 g/2 oz butter, softened
pineapple liquid and milk to
    make 120 ml/4 fl oz
1 teasp vanilla essence

For the topping
60 g/2 oz butter
75 g/2 1/2 oz brown sugar
1 (439-g/15 1/2-oz) can pineapple slices
6 maraschino cherries, halved

To make the topping, place butter in a 20-cm/8-inch round glass baking dish and microwave on full power for 1 minute. Tilt dish to coat bottom evenly. Sprinkle brown sugar evenly over the bottom. Arrange pineapple slices and cherries in the dish.

Place all ingredients for the cake in a bowl and beat on low speed until mixture is smooth, about 3 minutes. Spread mixture evenly over pineapple. Place dish on inverted saucer and microwave on full power for 9 – 11 minutes, or until a toothpick inserted near the centre comes out clean. Invert cake onto serving plate and let dish stand over cake for a few minutes. Serve warm or cool.

Makes 1 cake

In a conventional oven: Bake at 180°C/350°F, Gas Mark 4 for 25 minutes, or until skewer inserted in centre comes out clean.

VARIATION
Peach upside-down cake. Use 1 (425-g/15-oz) can peach slices instead of pineapple and add a few drops almond essence to the cake mixture.

Pineapple cake

full power
8 minutes

250 g/8 oz self-raising flour
125 g/4 oz brown sugar
125 g/4 oz soft butter or margarine
2 eggs
1 (227-g/8-oz) can pineapple slices, drained and juice reserved
125 g/4 oz raisins or sultanas
honey to glaze

In a large mixing bowl, combine flour, sugar, butter and eggs. Add 6 tbsp reserved pineapple juice, mixing thoroughly. Beat for 2 minutes until mixture is smooth and glossy. Chop four slices pineapple and add, with raisins, to the mixture. Spread evenly in a greased 25-cm/10-inch microwave ring pan. Place pan on an inverted saucer and microwave on full power for 7–8 minutes. Remove cake from oven and brush top with warmed honey. Stand on a rack until cool, then remove cake from pan. Store wrapped in foil in a covered container.

Makes 1 ring cake

In a conventional oven: Add 2 teasp baking powder to the dry ingredients. Follow mixing method, then spread mixture evenly in a greased and floured loaf pan or cake pan. Bake at 160°C/325°F, Gas Mark 3 for 1 1/2–1 3/4 hours. Brush cake with warmed honey and leave to cool in pan.

Butter cake

full power
16 minutes

340 g/11 oz plain flour
375 g/12 oz sugar
2 teasp baking powder
1/2 teasp salt

210 g/7 oz butter, softened
250 ml/8 fl oz milk
1 1/2 teasp vanilla essence
1 egg

Combine flour, sugar, baking powder and salt in a large mixing bowl. Add butter, milk, vanilla and egg and beat on low speed for 30 seconds. Scrape down bowl and beat on low for 2 minutes. Line two 20-cm/8-inch round glass baking dishes with single layers of paper towel cut to fit the bottom. Turn cake mixture into dishes and spread evenly. Microwave one cake at a time on an inverted saucer on full power for 7–8 minutes, rotating dish half a turn after 4 minutes if necessary. Remove from oven and stand on a wooden board for 15 minutes before turning out. Sandwich together and ice as desired.

Makes two 20-cm/8-inch layers

In a conventional oven: Bake at 180°C/350°F, Gas Mark 4 for 25 minutes, or until a skewer inserted in the centre comes out clean. Turn out and cool on a wire rack.

Strawberry coffee cake

Streusel coffee cake

full power
8 minutes

150 g/5 oz sugar
60 g/2 oz butter or margarine
½ teasp vanilla essence
1 egg
120 ml/4 fl oz milk
180 g/6 oz plain flour
2 teasp baking powder
½ teasp salt

For the streusel topping
90 g/3 oz brown sugar
2 tbsp plain flour
2 teasp cinnamon
2 tbsp butter
60 g/2 oz nuts (hazel or pecan), chopped

Beat sugar, butter, vanilla essence and egg until light and
fluffy. Stir in milk. Sift dry ingredients together and add
to mixture. Stir until smooth. Make streusel mixture by
combining all ingredients thoroughly. Spread half the
batter in a greased 23-cm/9-inch baking dish and sprinkle
with half the streusel mixture. Cover with the remaining
batter and top with the remaining streusel mixture.
Microwave on full power for 7–8 minutes, rotating dish
a quarter turn every 3 minutes if necessary. Remove from
oven and stand for 10 minutes before serving.

Serves 9 – 12

In a conventional oven: Bake at 180°C/350°F, Gas Mark
4 for 25 minutes.

VARIATIONS
Apple coffee cake: Spread half the contents of 1 (385-g/
12-oz) can of apple pie filling over the first layer of cake
mixture. Sprinkle with half the streusel mixture, then
repeat the cake, apple and streusel layers.

Jam coffee cake: In a measuring jug, microwave 6 tbsp
fruit jam or marmalade on full power for 45–60 seconds to
soften. Drizzle half the warmed jam over the first layer of
cake mixture, sprinkle with half the streusel mixture, then
repeat the cake, jam and streusel layers.

Southern peach coffee cake: Drain 1 (425-g/15-oz) can of
peach slices well, then soak the peach slices in 2 tbsp
brandy. Drain. Arrange the peach slices on the first layer
of cake mixture, sprinkle with half the streusel mixture,
then repeat the cake, peach and streusel layers.

Strawberry coffee cake: Slice 210 g/7 oz fresh strawberries
and sprinkle with 2 tbsp castor sugar and 2 tbsp Kirsch lique
Stand for 10 minutes, then drain. Arrange the strawberry
slices on the first layer of cake mixture, sprinkle with
streusel mixture, then repeat the cake, strawberry and
streusel layers.

Carrot cake

full power
11 minutes

180 g/6 oz plain flour
2 teasp cinnamon
1½ teasp bicarbonate of soda
1 teasp nutmeg
½ teasp salt

500 g/1 lb grated carrot
280 g/9 oz sugar
250 ml/8 fl oz oil
90 g/3 oz walnuts, chopped
3 eggs, beaten

For the icing
250 g/8 oz cream cheese
125 g/4 oz butter, at room temperature
60 g/2 oz walnuts, chopped
1 teasp vanilla essence
about 400 g/13 oz icing sugar, sifted

Sift together flour, cinnamon, bicarbonate of soda, nutmeg
and salt. Set aside. Combine grated carrot, sugar, oil,
walnuts and eggs, mixing well. Add dry ingredients and mix
well. Turn mixture into a deep, greased 25-cm/10-inch
microwave ring pan. Place pan on an inverted saucer
and microwave on full power for 10–11 minutes. The cake
should shrink away slightly from edges of pan. Turn pan
during baking if the cake looks as if it is cooking unevenly.
Cool slightly before inverting onto a serving plate.
    To make the icing, beat cheese until smooth. Add butter
and beat well. Add nuts and vanilla and mix thoroughly.
Gradually add icing sugar, beating well to the desired
consistency. Spread over cake.   *Makes 1 ring cake*

In a conventional oven: Bake at 180°C/350°, Gas Mark 4
for 35–40 minutes.

Lemon and yoghurt loaf

full power
medium
13 minutes

150 ml/¼ pint plain yoghurt
6 tbsp oil
150 g/5 oz sugar
250 g/8 oz self-raising flour
2 eggs
pinch of salt
1 teasp grated lemon rind
2 tbsp lemon juice
lemon glaze (see p. 129)

Beat yoghurt, oil and sugar together until well combined. Sift in flour. Beat to combine. Add remaining ingredients, mixing well. Pour into a greased or sprayed 25 × 10 cm/ 10 × 4 inch microwave loaf pan and microwave on full power for 3 minutes. Reduce power to medium. Microwave for a further 8–10 minutes. Allow cake to cool in dish on a rack. Turn out after 20 minutes. When cold, drizzle lemon glaze over top. Allow glaze to set before serving cake. *Makes 1 loaf*

In a conventional oven: Add 1 teasp baking powder to ingredients and bake at 160°C/325°F, Gas Mark 3 for 45–55 minutes.

Basic scone mix

500 g/1 lb plain flour
2 tbsp baking powder
1 teasp salt
2 tbsp sugar
180 g/6 oz butter

Sift together flour, baking powder, salt and sugar. Rub in butter until mixture resembles fine crumbs. Keep refrigerated in a tightly covered container and use as directed in recipes such as Golden nut ring or Caramel cherry ring, or in other recipes calling for basic scone dough. To make up scone dough, add enough milk mixed with egg to make a soft but not sticky dough, and use as desired.

Makes 700 g/1 lb 7 oz

Caramel cherry ring

full power
high
10 minutes

60 g/2 oz butter
100 g/3½ oz brown sugar
½ teasp cinnamon
3 tbsp golden syrup
60 g/2 oz pecan nuts, halved
3 tbsp marraschino cherries, quartered
250 g/8 oz basic scone mix (above)
1 egg
200 ml/7 fl oz milk

Place butter in a microwave ring pan and microwave on full power for about 45 seconds to melt. Tilt pan so that butter coats evenly. Sprinkle with brown sugar and cinnamon. Microwave for 1 minute, then stir well and spread evenly in pan. Drizzle with golden syrup. Arrange halved pecans evenly around pan and sprinkle with cherries. Place scone mix in a mixing bowl. Combine egg and milk, and add enough liquid to dry ingredients to form a soft, but not sticky, dough. Form dough into ten balls. Place balls of dough on top of cherries in ring pan. Let rest for 5 minutes. Place pan on an inverted saucer and microwave on high for 6 – 8 minutes, rotating pan during cooking if necessary. Let rolls stand in pan for about 3 minutes, then invert onto a serving plate and let pan stand over rolls a few minutes. Serve warm. *Makes 1 ring of 10 pieces*

In a conventional oven: Bake at 200°C/400°F, Gas Mark 5 for 20–25 minutes until well risen and golden brown. Invert onto serving plate and serve warm.

Golden nut ring

full power
medium
9 minutes

4 teasp butter
60 g/2 oz walnuts, chopped
3 tbsp brown sugar
1 tbsp sugar
1 teasp cinnamon
4 tbsp golden syrup
250 g/8 oz basic scone mix (see left)
1 egg
200 ml/7 fl oz milk

Place butter in a microwave ring pan and microwave on full power for 20 – 30 seconds. Tilt pan so that butter coats evenly. Mix together nuts, brown sugar, sugar and cinnamon. Place golden syrup in a small glass measuring jug and microwave on full power for 15 seconds to warm.

Place scone mix in a mixing bowl. Combine egg and milk and add enough liquid to dry ingredients to make a soft, but not sticky, dough. Knead lightly, then roll out on a lightly floured board and cut into ten 5-cm/2-inch rounds. Brush each round with warmed syrup, then dip in nut mixture, coating well. Place rounds in ring pan with edges overlapping. Microwave on medium for 6 – 8 minutes, rotating pan half a turn after 3 minutes. Let cool in pan for 5 minutes. Invert onto a serving plate and sprinkle with any remaining nut mixture. Serve warm.

Makes 1 ring of 10 pieces

In a conventional oven: Bake at 200°C/400°F, Gas Mark 6 for 20 minutes. Turn out onto a wire rack and let cool slightly before serving.

Soured cream apple bake

full power
12 minutes

1 egg, beaten
2 tbsp plain flour
120 ml/4 fl oz golden syrup
120 ml/4 fl oz soured cream
½ teasp caramel flavouring
3 large apples, peeled, cored and sliced

For the topping
230 g/7½ oz butter
210 g/7 oz brown sugar
1 egg
180 g/6 oz plain flour
1 teasp bicarbonate of soda
½ teasp salt
250 ml/8 fl oz soured cream
½ teasp caramel flavouring

Combine egg, flour, syrup, sour cream and caramel flavouring, beating well. Mix in apple slices and turn into a deep 23-cm/9-inch baking dish.

For the topping, cream butter and sugar well. Add egg and beat until light and fluffy. Sift dry ingredients and add to the creamed mixture along with soured cream and caramel flavouring. Mix until smooth, then pour over apple mixture. Microwave on full power for 10–12 minutes. Serve from the dish, with cream or custard.

Serves 10 – 12

In a conventional oven: Bake at 180°C/350°F, Gas Mark 4 for 45 minutes.

Wholewheat batter bread and cinnamon sticky buns

Cinnamon sticky buns

full power
8 minutes

500 g/1 lb basic scone mix (see p. 123)
1 egg
120 ml/4 fl oz milk

For the filling and topping
125 g/4 oz butter
60 g/2 oz pecan nuts, chopped
100 g/3½ oz brown sugar
1½ teasp cinnamon
60 g/2 oz raisins

Place scone mix in a mixing bowl. Mix egg with milk and add enough of this liquid to dry ingredients to make a soft dough. Knead gently several times, then roll out into a large rectangle on a lightly floured surface.

For the filling and topping, microwave butter on full power for about 2 minutes to melt. Brush dough generously with melted butter, then pour remaining butter into a deep, 23-cm/9-inch glass baking dish. Mix together pecans, brown sugar, cinnamon and raisins. Sprinkle two thirds of the filling mixture over the dough and sprinkle remainder in the baking dish. Roll up dough, swiss roll fashion, and cut into 2.5 cm/1 inch thick slices. Arrange slices close together in the prepared baking dish. Microwave on full power for 5–6 minutes. Stand in the dish for 3–4 minutes, then turn out onto a plate and serve warm.

Makes about 12 buns

In a conventional oven: Bake at 190°C/375°F, Gas Mark 5 for 20–25 minutes, until lightly golden brown and well risen. Turn out at once.

Basic batter bread

This recipe can be adapted to make a variety of tasty yeast breads

full power
10 minutes

1 tbsp active dry yeast
300 ml/½ pint warm water
2 tbsp honey
2 tbsp butter
1 teasp salt
375 g/12 oz plain cake flour

Dissolve yeast in warm water in a large glass bowl. Stir in the honey, mixing well. Microwave the butter on full power for 10 seconds to soften, then add to the yeast mixture along with salt and 250 g/8 oz of the flour. Beat on high speed for 1 minute, scrape down bowl and beat for 1 minute more. Stir in remaining flour, mixing well. Cover bowl and microwave for 15 seconds on full power, then rest in microwave oven for 10–12 minutes. Repeat heating and resting at least twice more, or until dough has doubled in bulk.

Stir down with a wooden spoon and turn into a well-greased 20-cm/8-inch round casserole dish with straight sides. Cover with greased greaseproof paper and microwave on full power for 15 seconds, then rest in the microwave oven for 10–12 minutes. Repeat heating and resting at least twice more, or until dough has risen to level with the top of the casserole dish. Remove cover and microwave on full power for 8–9 minutes. Let bread stand in dish for 3–4 minutes, then turn out and cool. Store tightly covered.

Makes 1 loaf

In a conventional oven: Microwave as directed to prove dough, then bake at 190°C/375°F, Gas Mark 5 for 30–35 minutes. Turn out on a wire rack to cool.

VARIATIONS

Bacon and pepper bread: Stir in 1/2 teasp freshly ground black pepper and 180 g/6 oz bacon, cooked and diced, when stirring down dough. Increase microwave time when baking by 30 seconds to 1 minute.

Cheddar cheese bread: Reduce butter to 1 tbsp and add 90 g/3 oz grated Cheddar cheese and a pinch of dry mustard to the remaining flour. Increase microwave time when baking by 30 seconds to 1 minute.

Raisin batter bread: Add 2 teasp cinnamon with remaining flour. Add 90 g/3 oz raisins after stirring the batter down.

Wholewheat batter bread

An easy-to-make health loaf with a number of variations

full power
11 minutes

1 tbsp active dry yeast
300 ml/1/2 pint warm water
2 tbsp honey
2 tbsp butter or margarine
1 teasp salt
180 g/6 oz plain flour
180 g/6 oz wholewheat flour

In a large mixing bowl, dissolve yeast in warm water. Stir in honey. Microwave butter on full power for 15 – 20 seconds, 60 g/2 oz of the wholewheat flour. Beat for 1 minute, scrape down bowl and beat for 1 minute more. Stir in remaining flour, mixing well. Cover and microwave on full power for 15 seconds, then rest for 10–12 minutes. Microwave again on full power for 15 seconds and rest. Repeat at least once more, or until the dough has doubled in bulk.

Stir down dough, then turn into a well-greased 20-cm/ 8-inch round casserole dish with straight sides. Cover

with greased greaseproof paper and microwave for 15 seconds on full power, then rest in microwave for 10–12 minutes. Repeat heating and resting at least twice more, or until dough has risen to level with top of casserole dish. Remove cover and microwave on full power for 8–9 minutes. Let bread stand in casserole for 3–4 minutes, then turn out and cool. Store tightly covered.

Makes 1 loaf

In a conventional oven: Microwave as directed above to prove dough, then bake at 190°C/375°F, Gas Mark 5 for 30–35 minutes. Turn out onto a wire rack and cool.

VARIATIONS

Bran and wheat bread: Reduce wholewheat flour to 60 g/ 2 oz and increase plain flour to 250 g/8 oz. Add 1 egg with the salt, butter and all the cake flour. Then add 4 tbsp wheat germ and 4 tbsp natural bran with the remaining wholewheat flour.

Sunflower yoghurt bread: Reduce warm water to 200 ml/ 7 fl oz and add 120 ml/4 fl oz plain yoghurt and 4 tbsp sunflower seeds with remaining flour.

Wholewheat onion bread: Finely chop 1/2 onion and add with the remaining flour.

Brown yoghurt bread

full power
6 minutes

60 g/2 oz plain flour	1 egg
60 g/2 oz cornmeal	200 ml/8 fl oz yoghurt
75 g/2½ oz wholewheat flour	5 tbsp molasses
1 teasp bicarbonate of soda	1 tbsp oil
½ teasp salt	2 tbsp wheat germ

Combine dry ingredients in a large mixing bowl. Mix together egg, yoghurt, molasses and oil and add to dry ingredients, mixing well to moisten. Grease a small microwave ring pan or a small loaf pan well and sprinkle with half the wheat germ. Spoon in bread mixture, smoothing evenly. Sprinkle remaining wheat germ on top. Microwave on full power, uncovered, for 4 minutes, then rotate pan a quarter turn. Microwave for 1½ – 2½ minutes longer, until a skewer inserted in the centre comes out clean. Let stand for 10 minutes in pan, then invert bread onto wire rack and cool.

Makes 1 loaf

In a conventional oven: Bake in a greased loaf pan at 180°C/350°F, Gas Mark 4 for 45 minutes, until a skewer inserted in the centre comes out clean.

VARIATIONS

Savoury onion bread: Mix 3 tbsp dry onion soup mix with dry ingredients and increase oil by 1 teasp.

Seed loaf: Add 2 tbsp sesame seeds and 3 tbsp sunflower seeds to dry ingredients. Increase oil by 1 teasp. Omit wheat germ and sprinkle greased pan with 1 tbsp sesame seeds.

Clockwise: spicy apple muffins, apple nut bread, apple coffee cake (p. 122)

Basic microwave muffins

For best results, use a microwave muffin pan

high

250 g/8 oz plain flour
100 g/3½ oz sugar
1 tbsp baking powder
½ teasp salt
2 eggs, beaten
120 ml/4 fl oz oil
120 ml/4 fl oz milk

Sift together dry ingredients. Beat together eggs, oil and milk, and add to dry ingredients. Mix until just moistened. Fill paper muffin cups half full of batter and place in a microwave muffin pan. Microwave on high according to chart below. The muffins are done when a toothpick inserted in the centre comes out clean.

Makes 10 – 12 muffins

Number of muffins	Time (on high power)	Method
3	1½-2 minutes	Rotate the pan half a turn after half the cooking time. Batters with other ingredients (see variations) may take slightly longer than the time stated.
4	2-3 minutes	
5	2½-3½ minutes	
6	3-5 minutes	

In a conventional oven: Spoon mixture into greased muffin cups, filling two thirds full. Bake at 190°C/375°F, Gas Mark 5 for 20 minutes, until well risen and golden brown.

VARIATIONS

Spicy apple muffins: Add ½ teasp cinnamon to dry ingredients and add 1 peeled and chopped apple with liquid. Top with cinnamon sugar topping.

Herby cheese muffins: Add ½ teasp mixed herbs, 1 teasp chopped parsley and pinch of dry mustard to dry ingredients. Stir in 60 g/2 oz grated cheese with liquid. Top with extra grated cheese.

Lemon coconut muffins: Add 1 teasp grated lemon rind and 4 tbsp toasted coconut, (see p. 23) to dry ingredients. Add 1 tbsp lemon juice to liquid and top with more toasted coconut.

Orange nut muffins: Add 1 teasp grated orange rind and 60 g/2 oz chopped pecan nuts to dry ingredients. Replace 2 tbsp of the milk with orange juice in the liquid. Top with streusel topping.

MUFFIN TOPPINGS

Streusel topping: Combine 90 g/3 oz brown sugar, 2 tbsp plain flour, 2 teasp cinnamon, 2 tbsp butter and 60 g/2 oz chopped nuts.

Nut crunch topping: Combine 5 tbsp plain flour, 2 tbsp brown sugar, 2 tbsp butter, 3 tbsp chopped nuts, 2 tbsp cornflake crumbs.

Cinnamon sugar topping: Combine 3 tbsp brown sugar with ½–1 teasp cinnamon.

Banana molasses bread

high
14 minutes

3 ripe bananas
1 egg
75 g/2½ oz sugar
75 g/2½ oz brown sugar
2 tbsp molasses
2 tbsp butter, melted
1 tbsp oil
250 g/8 oz plain flour
1 teasp bicarbonate of soda
½ teasp salt
90 g/3 oz walnuts, chopped

Mash bananas until no lumps remain. Add egg and beat well. Beat in sugars, molasses, melted butter and oil. Sift together dry ingredients and stir into banana mixture. Fold in three quarters of the nuts. Grease a microwave ring pan well and dust with remaining chopped nuts. Spoon in banana mixture and microwave on high for 11 – 14 minutes, until a toothpick inserted in the centre comes out clean. Rotate pan a quarter turn every 4 minutes of cooking time. Let stand in pan for 5 minutes, then turn out and cool.

Makes 1 ring loaf

In a conventional oven: Bake in ring mould or loaf pan at 160°C/325°F, Gas Mark 3 for about 1 hour, until a skewer inserted in the centre comes out clean.

Gingerbread ring

high
15 minutes

280 g/9 oz flour
2 teasp freshly grated root ginger
1½ teasp bicarbonate of soda
1 teasp cinnamon
½ teasp salt
pinch of ground cloves
125 g/4 oz butter, at room temperature
90 g/3 oz brown sugar
100 g/3½ oz sugar
2 eggs
250 ml/8 fl oz buttermilk
250 ml/8 fl oz molasses
1 tbsp grated orange rind
1 tbsp grated lemon rind
a little extra cinnamon

Mix together flour, ginger, bicarbonate of soda, cinnamon, salt and cloves. Cream butter and sugars and add to flour mixture. Beat in eggs, buttermilk, molasses and rinds, mixing thoroughly. Grease a large microwave ring pan and sprinkle with a little cinnamon, shaking out excess. Turn gingerbread mixture into pan and microwave on high for 13 – 15 minutes, turning the pan if the mixture seems to be baking unevenly. Stand in the pan for about 20 minutes before turning out to cool.

Makes 1 large ring

In a conventional oven: Bake at 160°C/325°F, Gas Mark 3 for 1–1¼ hours, or until a skewer comes out clean.

Apple nut bread

high
12 minutes

125 g/4 oz butter
210 g/7 oz sugar
2 eggs, beaten
2 tbsp soured milk or buttermilk
1 small apple, peeled and grated
60 g/2 oz sultanas
60 g/2 oz nuts (hazel or pecan), chopped
250 g/8 oz plain flour
1 teasp bicarbonate of soda
pinch of salt

Beat butter and sugar until creamy. Add eggs and beat until fluffy. Add sour milk, apple, sultanas and half the nuts, mixing well. Stir in sifted dry ingredients. Grease fluted microwave ring pan and dust with remaining chopped nuts. Spread batter in pan and microwave on high for 10 – 12 minutes, rotating ring pan a quarter turn every 4 minutes. A toothpick inserted in the centre should come out clean when the loaf is done. Let loaf stand in pan for 5 minutes, then turn out onto cooling rack. Serve warm or cool.

Makes 1 ring loaf

In a conventional oven: Bake in a ring mould or greased loaf pan at 180°C/350°F, Gas Mark 4 for 45–55 minutes. Turn out to cool.

Date bars

full power
high
18 minutes

For the filling
250 g/8 oz dates chopped
300 ml/½ pint water
5 teasp lemon juice

For the crumble topping
90 g/3 oz plain flour
½ teasp bicarbonate of soda
60 g/2 oz oats
pinch of cinnamon
125 g/4 oz soft brown sugar
3 tbsp chopped pecan nuts
125 g/4 oz margarine

Place dates, water and lemon juice in a bowl. Cover with cling film and then cut two slits in the film to prevent 'ballooning' during cooking. Microwave on full power for 5 minutes. Uncover and cool slightly.

To make crumble, sift flour and bicarbonate of soda. Stir in oats, cinnamon, sugar and pecans. Microwave margarine on high for 3 – 4 minutes, until completely melted. Pour into dry ingredients and mix well. Press half the crumble into a greased 23-cm/9-inch square glass dish. Cover with date mixture and top with crumble. Press down well. Shield corners of dish with foil. Microwave on full power for 9 minutes. Cool, then cut into squares.

Makes 20 squares

In a conventional oven: Bake at 180°C/350°F, Gas Mark 4 for 20–25 minutes.

Date bars (p. 127) and chocolate chip squares

Chocolate chip squares

full power
6 minutes

125 g/4 oz butter, softened
150 g/5 oz brown sugar
1 egg
1 tbsp milk
1 teasp vanilla essence
150 g/5 oz plain flour
½ teasp baking powder
pinch of ground cinnamon
pinch of salt
1 (99-g/3½-oz) package chocolate polka dots
60 g/2 oz nuts, chopped (optional)

Cream butter and sugar until light and fluffy. Add egg and beat well. Stir in milk and vanilla. Combine flour, baking powder, cinnamon and salt and add to the butter mixture. Mix well, then stir in chocolate dots and nuts. Turn the mixture into a greased 20-cm/8-inch baking dish and shield corners of dish with small pieces of foil. Microwave on full power for 5–6½ minutes, rotating dish a quarter turn every 2 minutes if necessary. Cool in the pan before cutting into squares.

Makes 16 large or 24 small squares

In a conventional oven: Bake at 180°C/350°F, Gas Mark 4 for 25–30 minutes, until a skewer inserted in the centre comes out clean.

Muesli pie crust

full power
4 minutes

125 g/4 oz biscuit crumbs (about 8 digestive biscuits)
45 g/1½ oz muesli
1 teasp ground cinnamon
2 tbsp ground almonds
90 g/3 oz butter
3 tbsp single cream

Mix biscuit crumbs, muesli, cinnamon and almonds together. Microwave butter on full power for 1½–2 minutes to melt. Add to dry ingredients, mixing well. Add cream and mix in. Press into bottom and sides of a 23-cm/9-inch pie dish and microwave on full power for 2 minutes. Let cool before using.

Makes one 23-cm/9-inch pie crust

In a conventional oven: Bake at 190°C/375°F, Gas Mark 5 for 5–8 minutes.

Basic crumb crust

full power
2½ minutes

4 tbsp butter
125 g/4 oz digestive biscuit crumbs (about 8 biscuits)
2 tbsp brown sugar

Microwave butter in a 23-cm/9-inch pie dish on full power for 45–60 seconds. Add crumbs and brown sugar and mix well. Gently press the mixture into bottom and sides of the dish and microwave on full power for 1–1½ minutes. Cool before using.

Makes one 23-cm/9-inch crust

VARIATIONS
Nutty crust: Proceed as for basic crust, adding 60 g/2 oz chopped nuts and 2 tbsp single cream to the crumbs.

Spicy crust: Use 125 g/4 oz ginger biscuit crumbs (about 14 biscuits). Add ½ teasp cinnamon and 2 tbsp single cream. Proceed as for basic recipe.

Malted crust: Use 125 g/4 oz malt biscuit crumbs (about 14 biscuits) and proceed as for basic recipe.

Chocolate crumb crust

full power
2½ minutes

10–12 chocolate cream biscuits, broken
4 tbsp butter
2 tbsp single cream

Place biscuits in a food processor with a metal blade and process to fine crumbs. Microwave butter in a 23-cm/9-inch pie dish on full power for 45–60 seconds. Add crumbs and cream, mixing well. Press into bottom and sides of the dish and microwave crust on full power for 1–1½ minutes. Cool before using.

Makes one 23-cm/9-inch crust

Shortcrust pastry

full power
6 minutes

125 g/4 oz plain flour	4 tbsp butter
½ teasp salt	1 egg yolk
1 teasp sugar	3 tbsp cold water

Combine flour, salt and sugar. Rub in butter until mixture resembles fine crumbs. Combine egg yolk and water and add enough to the dry ingredients to form a dough. Turn pastry onto a lightly floured surface and knead gently, then roll out and use as desired.

To microwave pastry shells, line pie dish with pastry. Cut a long foil strip about 2.5 cm/1 inch wide and line the edge of the pastry shell. Place a double layer of paper towel in the base of the pastry shell, pressing gently into the edges. Microwave on full power for 3½–4 minutes, rotating dish after 2 minutes if necessary. Remove foil and paper towel and microwave for 1½–2 minutes more. Use cooked pastry shells for pies and tarts with cold or uncooked fillings.

Makes a 20–23-cm/8–9-inch single crust

VARIATIONS

Herbed pastry: Leave out sugar and add 1 teasp mixed dried herbs, or herb of your choice.

Cheese pastry: Omit sugar, add 1 pinch of dry mustard to the dry ingredients and stir in 3 tbsp grated cheese after rubbing in the butter.

Sweet pastry: Increase the sugar to 3 tbsp, add ½ teasp vanilla essence, and proceed as for shortcrust pastry.

Lemon glaze

full power
3 minutes

250 g/8 oz icing sugar, sifted	1 tbsp water
1 tbsp lemon juice	½ teasp finely grated lemon rind

Place all ingredients in a bowl. Microwave on full power for 2–3 minutes. Stir well. Cool 5 minutes. Use as required.

Ices 1 cake

Coconut crunch topping

Spread on top of a butter cake or chocolate layer cake for a quick and delicious 'icing'

full power
2 minutes

210 g/7 oz brown sugar	2 tbsp butter
1 tbsp cornflour	40 g/1½ oz desiccated coconut
2–3 tbsp milk	60 g/2 oz nuts, chopped

Combine brown sugar, cornflour, 2 tbsp milk and the butter. Microwave on full power for 1 minute. Stir thoroughly, then microwave for 1 minute more. Stir well, then add coconut and nuts. Mix well, adding a little more milk if mixture is very stiff. Spread on cake while the mixture is still warm.

Makes enough topping for two 20-cm/8-inch layers

Butter cream icing

high
2 minutes

500 g/1 lb icing sugar, sifted
2 tbsp milk
pinch of salt
1 teasp vanilla essence
125 g/4 oz butter

Combine sugar, milk, salt and vanilla in a bowl and mix to blend. The mixture will be very stiff. Cut butter into pieces and place on top. Microwave on high for 1–2 minutes, until mixture can be beaten smoothly. If icing is too hot, it may run off the cake. Cool the icing in the bowl, stirring occasionally before using.

Makes enough for icing two 20-cm/8-inch layers

Banana fudge icing

medium
high
8 minutes

2 tbsp butter
180 g/6 oz soft brown sugar
3 tbsp milk
140 g/4½ oz icing sugar, sifted
1 tbsp single cream
1 banana, sliced
a little lemon juice

Place butter, brown sugar and milk in a bowl. Microwave on medium for 5 minutes. Stir well. Microwave on high for 3 minutes. Pour into a cold bowl and cool slightly. Beat icing sugar and cream into icing. The mixture should be of a 'drizzling' consistency. Use this icing to sandwich two cake layers together, then drizzle on top of cake, or drizzle all over a ring cake. Whilst still soft, decorate icing with banana slices dipped in a little lemon juice.

Ices 1 cake

Banana cake (p. 120) covered with banana fudge icing

Beverages

Microwaving speeds up and simplifies the making of beverages. Try these hot drinks for cold nights – you can make them quickly after a late show, or as an impromptu treat after dinner. Exotic chilled drinks are easily made in advance and there are recipes for homemade liqueurs too. When making single quantities, heat the liquid in a cup or heatproof glass, but take care not to use those with a metal trim. If heating more than 2 cups or glasses at a time, arrange them in a ring with a space between each one. Stir liquids before microwaving, and do not overfill cups as the liquid will spill over as it expands. Milk-based drinks should be watched carefully and as soon as they start to boil, the door should be opened. The microwave can also be used to reheat that forgotten cup of tea or coffee without it losing any flavour.

Strawberry party punch

Popular treat for a children's party

full power
2 minutes

1 (142-g/5-oz) tablet strawberry jelly
250 ml/8 fl oz water
1 (178-ml/6¼-fl oz) can frozen lemon concentrate, thawed
1 litre/1¾ pints pineapple juice
1 litre/1¾ pints ginger ale, chilled
ice cubes
sliced strawberries to garnish

Place strawberry jelly cubes in a large bowl and set aside. Microwave water on full power for 2 minutes, then stir into the jelly, mixing well to dissolve. Add lemon concentrate and stir well. Pour in pineapple juice and chill well. Just before serving, add the ginger ale and ice cubes. Garnish with sliced strawberries.

Serves about 20

Plantation frost

full power
3 minutes

600 ml/1 pint water
1 tbsp instant coffee powder
3 tbsp sugar
3 bananas
120 ml/4 fl oz single cream

Place water and instant coffee powder in a large jug and microwave on full power for 2 – 3 minutes. Chill the coffee. Place chilled coffee, sugar and sliced bananas in a blender and blend until smooth. Stir in cream and serve in chilled glasses.

Serves 6

Danish coffee punch

full power
3 minutes

750 ml/1¼ pints water
2 tbsp instant coffee powder
6 eggs
grated rind of 1 lemon
100 g/3½ oz sugar
120 ml/4 fl oz brandy

Place 600 ml/1 pint of the water and the coffee powder in a large jug and microwave on full power for 2–3 minutes. Add the remaining 150 ml/¼ pint water, then chill the coffee. With an electric mixer, beat the eggs with grated lemon rind until frothy. Gradually add the sugar, beating until mixture is thick. At low speed, stir in the cold coffee and the brandy. Serve in punch cups.

Serves 10 – 12

Hot apple wine

full power
medium
low
47 minutes

750 ml/1¼ pints apple cider (or apple juice)
4 tbsp sugar
3 cinnamon sticks
6 whole cloves
rind of 1 small lemon, cut into strips
1 litre/1¾ pints dry white wine
juice of 1 lemon
5 tbsp brandy

Combine apple cider, sugar, cinnamon, cloves and lemon rind in a 3-litre/6-pint casserole dish. Microwave on full power for 4 minutes, stirring after 2 minutes and again at the end of the cooking time. Reduce power to medium and microwave, uncovered, for 10 minutes. Strain the mixture to remove spices. Return apple cider to the casserole, then add the wine and lemon juice. Microwave on full power for 3 minutes, then reduce power and microwave, covered, on low for about 30 minutes. Stir in brandy and serve warm.

Serves 12 – 16

Hot spicy tea

full power
2 minutes

1.5 litres/2½ pints boiling water	juice of 1 orange
3 cloves	2 teasp lemon juice
small piece cinnamon stick	60 g/2 oz sugar
1 tbsp tea leaves	orange and lemon slices to garnish

Pour the boiling water over the cloves, cinnamon and tea. Allow to infuse for 4 minutes. Strain. Meanwhile, place the fruit juices and sugar in a small jug and stir. Microwave on full power for 2 minutes, stirring after 1 minute. Strain into tea mixture. Serve hot with slices of orange and lemon as a garnish. (Illustrated left)

Makes 1.5 litres/2½ pints

VARIATION

For an alcoholic tea, soak 60 g/2 oz raisins or sultanas in a little rum or brandy for a few hours. Add a few to each glass of steaming tea.

Hot spiced wine

full power
medium
25 minutes

250 ml/8 fl oz orange juice
3 tbsp sugar
3 tbsp brown sugar
1 (750-ml/1¼-pint) bottle red wine
1 cinnamon stick
4 whole cloves
3 whole allspice
1 small piece whole nutmeg
1 little orange and lemon rind, cut into strips
orange slices to garnish

Combine orange juice and sugars in a large bowl, then microwave on full power for 5 minutes, stirring every few minutes. Add all the remaining ingredients. Microwave on medium for 20 minutes. Strain and serve hot. Garnish with orange slices.

Makes 1 litre/1¾ pints

Mocha chocolate

full power
9 minutes

120 ml/4 fl oz milk
250 ml/8 fl oz water
60 g/2 oz dark chocolate, chopped
60 g/2 oz sugar
1 teasp vanilla essence
250 ml/8 fl oz freshly made coffee
120 ml/4 fl oz single cream
a little cinnamon to garnish

Combine the milk and water in a large jug. Microwave on full power for 4 minutes. Add chocolate to the hot milk mixture, then stir in the sugar and vanilla. Microwave on full power for 2 minutes. Now stir in the coffee and cream and microwave for 3 minutes. Pour into four small, heatproof glasses and sprinkle with a little cinnamon. Serve immediately.

Serves 4

Quick cappuccino

full power
7 minutes

750 ml/1¼ pints freshly made coffee
120 ml/4 fl oz single cream
little cocoa to decorate

Pour the coffee into a large jug. Microwave on full power for 6 minutes. Stir in the cream. Microwave on full power for 1 minute. Pour half the coffee mixture into a blender and blend for 30 seconds or until very foamy. Pour into two cups. Repeat the process with the remaining coffee. Sprinkle a little cocoa on top of each.

Serves 4

Clockwise: mocha chocolate, hot spiced wine, quick cappuccino

Irish coffee

full power
1 minute

150 ml/¼ pint Irish whiskey
3 tbsp brown sugar, or to taste
900 ml/1½ pints freshly made strong black coffee
150 ml/¼ pint whipped cream

Divide whiskey and sugar between four Irish coffee glasses. Arrange glasses in a circle in the microwave oven. Microwave on full power for 1 minute. Place a long-handled metal spoon in each glass and pour in hot coffee until glasses are three quarters full. Stir to dissolve sugar. Carefully pour whipped cream over the back of a spoon so that it floats and does not sink into the coffee mixture. Serve immediately.

Serves 4

VARIATIONS
Leave out whiskey and make the following coffees:

Mexican coffee: Add 150 ml/¼ pint Kahlua and sprinkle a little grated chocolate on top.

French coffee: Add 150 ml/¼ pint Mandarin Napoleon liqueur.

Jamaican coffee: Add 150 ml/¼ pint Coco Rico and top with a little grated chocolate.

Irish coffee: Add 150 mℓ Irish whiskey.

Mediterranean coffee

full power
low
56 minutes

1 litre/1¾ pints water
3 tbsp instant coffee powder
4 tbsp chocolate syrup
75 g/2½ oz sugar
4 cinnamon sticks
1 teasp whole cloves
½ teasp anise flavouring
120 ml/4 fl oz orange liqueur
rind of 1 orange, cut into strips
rind of 1 lemon, cut into strips
whipped cream to garnish

Place 450 ml/¾ pint of the water and the instant coffee in a deep jug. Microwave on full power for 3 minutes. Add chocolate syrup, sugar, cinnamon, cloves, anise and orange liqueur. Place remaining water in a deep 3-litre/6-pint casserole dish and add coffee mixture. Microwave on full power for 8 minutes, stir well, then reduce power and microwave on low for 30–45 minutes, stirring occasionally. Add orange and lemon rind during last 15 minutes. Strain and serve in coffee cups, topped with whipped cream.

Serves 10 – 12

Hot brandied chocolate

full power
1½ minutes

1 tbsp drinking chocolate powder
1 teasp instant coffee powder
1 tbsp brandy
175 ml/6 fl oz milk
whipped cream to garnish

Place chocolate, coffee powder, brandy and milk in a large mug. Stir to mix, then microwave on full power for 1 – 1½ minutes. Serve topped with whipped cream.

Serves 1

Iced lemon coffee

full power
3 minutes

500 ml/17 fl oz water
1 tbsp instant coffee powder
500 ml/17 fl oz lemon sorbet or lemon-flavoured ice-cream
2 tbsp grenadine syrup

Place water and instant coffee powder in a large jug. Microwave on full power for 2 – 3 minutes, then chill the coffee. Place coffee, sherbet or ice-cream and grenadine syrup in a blender and blend until smooth. Serve in tall glasses.

Serves 4

Hot spiced rum

full power
6 minutes

1 tbsp brown sugar
4 strips lemon rind
pinch of cinnamon
600 ml/1 pint water
2 teasp butter
120 ml/4 fl oz rum

Divide the sugar, lemon rind, cinnamon, water and butter between four heatproof glasses. Microwave on full power for 6 minutes. Remove the lemon rind and stir well. Stir in the rum and serve piping hot. If desired, add a twist of fresh lemon to each glass.

Serves 4

Homemade coffee liqueur

full power
5 minutes

250 ml/8 fl oz water
310 g/10 oz sugar
4 tbsp pure instant coffee
1 teasp vanilla essence
275 ml/9 fl oz vodka

Combine water, sugar and coffee in a bowl. Microwave, uncovered, on full power for 5 minutes. Stir at least twice during cooking time. Add vanilla and cool. Stir in vodka. Pour into a bottle and cover. Label and store in a cool, dark place. Shake bottle from time to time. Allow liqueur to mature for about 6 months before using.

Makes about 750 ml/1¼ pints

Coffee liqueur

Berry liqueur

full power
3 minutes

250 g/8 oz fresh loganberries or youngberries
180 g/6 oz sugar
750 ml/1¼ pints gin

Wash loganberries and drain. Place sugar and 120 ml/4 fl oz of the gin in a measuring jug and microwave on full power for 2 minutes. Stir and microwave for 1 minute. Pour sugar mixture over berries in a bowl, stir gently, then cool to room temperature. When cool, place mixture in a large jar with a tight-fitting lid. Add remaining gin. Close tightly and keep in a cool place. Turn jar every few days. The liqueur is ready to drink after about 3 weeks, but it is better if left for about 2 months before using.

Makes about 750 ml/1¼ pints

Youngberry liqueur

Hot spiced sherry

medium
low
1¼ hours

2 (184-g/6½-oz) cans frozen orange juice, thawed
1 (750 ml/1¼ pint) bottle dry or medium sherry
600 ml/1 pint water
12 cloves
60 g/2 oz sugar
2 cinnamon sticks
½ teasp mixed spice
2 tbsp butter

Mix orange juice with sherry. Add water and remaining ingredients except butter. Place mixture in a 3-litre/6-pint deep casserole dish and microwave, covered, on medium for 10 minutes. Reduce power to low and microwave, still covered, for about 1 hour, letting flavours blend. Add butter and stir to dissolve. Serve warm.

Serves 12 – 16

Rio chocolate

full power
7 minutes

60 g/2 oz dark chocolate, chopped
750 ml/1¾ pints milk
250 ml/8 fl oz water
1 tbsp instant coffee powder
pinch of ground nutmeg
½ teasp cinnamon
4 tbsp sugar
5 tbsp brandy
whipped cream, grated chocolate and cinnamon sticks to garnish

Combine the chocolate, milk, water, instant coffee, spices and sugar in a large jug or bowl. Microwave, uncovered, on full power for 6 – 7 minutes, stirring every 2 minutes. Add the brandy. Whisk very well, until foamy. Pour into cups or heatproof glasses. Top generously with whipped cream and sprinkle with grated chocolate. Stand a piece of cinnamon stick in the cream and use to stir.

Makes just over 1 litre/1¾ pints

Cocoa

full power
7 minutes

4 tbsp cocoa powder	2 teasp grated orange rind
3 tbsp sugar	a few drops almond essence (optional)
750 ml/1¼ pints milk	4 marshmallows

Combine cocoa and sugar in a 1-litre/2-pint glass measuring jug. Add a little of the milk and mix to a smooth paste. Stir in remaining milk and add orange rind and almond essence, if used. Microwave on full power for 6–7 minutes. Pour cocoa into four mugs and top each with a marshmallow.

Serves 4

Sweets & nuts

For those with a sweet tooth, the microwave works wonders, producing delectable dainties with no mess and no fuss. This section is packed with recipes for a wide selection of sweet treats, homemade chocolates and crunchy nuts that are ideal for children's parties or to give that final touch to a special dinner. Hints on how to work successfully with melted chocolate have also been included.

Working with chocolate

Chocolate responds very well to being microwaved. However, as it is particularly sensitive to heat, care must be taken.

- When making chocolate leaves, or moulded or dipped chocolates, a grey film sometimes appears on the surface of the chocolate one or two days after the chocolates have been made. This is due to overheating, so it is best to microwave chocolate on defrost.
- When working with chocolate, the consistency often becomes too thick. Simply place chocolate in the microwave for a few seconds to soften.
- Chocolate is sometimes poured into piping bags and used to decorate chocolates or cakes. If the chocolate hardens, place the piping bag in the microwave for a few seconds – this saves a great deal of time and chocolate.
- Always chop or break up chocolate before microwaving.

Chocolate leaves

defrost
2 minutes

60 g/2 oz dark chocolate, preferably cooking chocolate
fresh rose leaves or ivy leaves

Chop chocolate and place in a container. Microwave, uncovered, on defrost for 1 – 2 minutes. Wash and dry leaves well. If using rose leaves, spread chocolate on the underside of the leaf. Do not spread too thinly. Place on a piece of foil. Refrigerate for a few minutes. Carefully peel leaf away from chocolate. Store until needed in a sealed container. Refrigerate if weather is very hot. If using ivy leaves, spread chocolate on top of the leaf.

Makes about 30 leaves

White chocolate and almond fudge

full power
6 minutes

100 g/3½ oz white chocolate
100 g/3½ oz butter
500 g/1 lb icing sugar, sifted
4 tbsp milk
2 teasp vanilla essence
¼ teasp almond essence
4 tbsp flaked almonds

Break up chocolate and place in a large bowl with butter. Microwave on full power for 1 minute. Add icing sugar, milk and essences and mix to combine. Microwave, uncovered, on full power for 5 minutes. Remove from oven and stir well. Stir in nuts. Pour into a greased 30 × 23-cm/12 × 9-inch pan and refrigerate for 30 minutes. Cut into squares, then refrigerate for a further 30 minutes. Pack into an airtight container.

Makes about 40 squares

VARIATION
Chocolate fudge: Leave out white chocolate and flaked almonds, and add 60 g/2 oz cocoa. Microwave all ingredients together on full power for 5 minutes.

Chocolate cherry fudge

Chocolate cherry fudge

full power
2½ minutes

375 g/12 oz milk chocolate, broken into pieces
4 tbsp evaporated milk
pinch of salt
½ teasp vanilla essence
10 maraschino cherries, chopped
90 g/3 oz walnuts, chopped

Lightly grease a 20-cm/8-inch square baking dish and set aside. Place chocolate, evaporated milk and salt in a 1-litre/2-pint bowl and microwave on full power for 2–2½ minutes to melt chocolate. Stir in vanilla essence, mixing until smooth. Mix in cherries and nuts and pour into prepared pan. Cool until firm, then cut into squares.

Makes about 500 g/1 lb

Chocolate glaze

This glaze has a beautiful, glossy appearance and is ideal for pouring over chocolate eclairs or Devonshire cream cake. Frozen bananas may also be dipped into this glaze. Freeze again for a few minutes before serving.

defrost
8 minutes

250 g/8 oz chocolate, broken up
3 tbsp oil

Place chocolate in a bowl and microwave, uncovered, on

defrost for 6 – 8 minutes. Stir chocolate every 2 minutes. Add oil and mix well. The chocolate should be completely smooth before it is ready to use. Pour chocolate over a layer cake or loaf cake and allow to set.

Makes 200 ml/7 fl oz

Piped chocolate creams

defrost
10 minutes

250 g/8 oz chocolate, preferably cooking chocolate
6 tbsp single cream
100 g/3½ oz butter
6 tbsp icing sugar, sifted
liqueur to taste, or flavouring oil (available from speciality shops)

Break chocolate into small pieces and place in a bowl. Add cream. Microwave on defrost for 6 – 8 minutes, stirring every 2 minutes during cooking time. Chocolate should be completely combined with cream when cooking time is completed. Cool, but do not chill. Place butter in a bowl and microwave on defrost for 2 minutes to soften slightly. Beat in icing sugar and flavouring. Carefully beat in the chocolate cream. It is important not to melt the butter as the cream is added. Beat well. Pipe into small paper cases. Allow to become firm at room temperature. If the weather is particularly hot, refrigerate for a short while. Stand chocolate at room temperature for a few minutes before serving.

Makes about 40

Rum truffles

defrost
6 minutes

90 g/3 oz dark chocolate, chopped
2 tbsp butter
2 tbsp icing sugar
6 tbsp fresh cake crumbs
2 egg yolks
2 teasp rum
chocolate vermicelli

Place chocolate in a shallow dish. Microwave, uncovered, on defrost for 3 minutes. Add butter, icing sugar and cake crumbs. Mix well. Microwave on defrost for 3 minutes. Add egg yolks and rum, and mix well. Refrigerate for 1 hour, or until firm enough to roll into small balls. Shape and roll in chocolate vermicelli. Place in paper cups.

Makes about 30

Raisin cups

defrost
3 minutes

60 g/2 oz raisins, chopped
2 tbsp brandy, rum or liqueur
125 g/4 oz chocolate, broken up
preserved ginger, thinly sliced

Chocolate selection

Soak raisins in brandy for a few hours. Place chocolate in a shallow dish and microwave, uncovered, on defrost for about 3 minutes. Brush the inside of paper cases with chocolate and allow to set in the refrigerator. Brush once again with chocolate. Allow to set. Spoon a little of the raisin mixture into the cases. Do not overfill, as the chocolates will leak when the top is added. Cover with melted chocolate and decorate with slivers of ginger whilst chocolate is still soft. Allow to set for at least 30 minutes in the refrigerator. Peel off paper cases and place the chocolates in fresh cases. If chocolate hardens whilst using, place in the microwave and heat on defrost for 1 minute or until the chocolate reaches desired consistency.

Makes about 30

Marshmallow treat

full power
15 seconds

2 chocolate-coated digestive biscuits
½ large marshmallow

Place 1 biscuit, chocolate side up, on a small plate and place the half marshmallow on top. Microwave on full power for 15 seconds, or until marshmallow puffs up. Immediately place 2nd biscuit, chocolate side down, on the marshmallow. This makes a delicious sweet treat. To microwave more than one treat at a time, increase time by a few seconds, but watch carefully and stop as soon as the marshmallow puffs up.

Makes 1

Nut clusters

defrost
3 minutes

90 g/3 oz chocolate, broken up
90 g/3 oz hazel or pecan nuts, chopped
1 teasp grated orange rind
a few drops orange oil (available from speciality shops)

Place broken pieces of chocolate in a shallow dish.
Microwave on defrost for about 3 minutes. Add the nuts,
rind and oil. Mix well and allow to cool slightly. Using two
teaspoons, drop small quantities of the mixture in cluster
shapes on greaseproof paper. Allow to set before removing
from the paper. Place in small paper cases.

Makes about 30

Coconut and chocolate bars

full power
6 minutes

75 g/2½ oz butter
125 g/4 oz digestive biscuit crumbs (about 8 biscuits)
90 g/3 oz chocolate, grated
60 g/2 oz desiccated coconut
90 g/3 oz nuts (walnuts or pecans), chopped
150 ml/¼ pint sweetened condensed milk

Microwave butter on full power for 1 minute in a 20-cm/
8-inch square glass baking dish. Stir in crumbs and press
evenly to cover bottom of dish. Microwave for 1–1½
minutes. Sprinkle with grated chocolate, then coconut
and chopped nuts. Pour condensed milk evenly over
surface. Microwave on full power for 3–4 minutes until
mixture is bubbly all over the surface. Cool, then cut into
bars.
Makes 60

Coconut and chocolate bars

Microwave meringues

full power
1½ minutes

1 egg white
½ teasp flavouring, such as vanilla, rum or almond essence
pinch of salt
250 g/8 oz icing sugar

Combine all ingredients and beat well until mixture forms a
ball. Roll mixture into small balls about the size of walnuts
and place in paper baking cups or in wafer cake cups.
Arrange seven at a time on a plate, leaving a space
between each as they puff up. Microwave on full power for
1½ minutes. Remove from oven and cool.

Makes about 30

VARIATION
For colourful meringues, add a few drops of food colouring
with the flavouring, and continue as for microwave
meringues. These meringues are very popular at children's
parties.

Crunchy toffee

full power
6 minutes

90 g/3 oz nuts, chopped
210 g/7 oz brown sugar
60 g/2 oz butter
3 tbsps water
90 g/3 oz dark or milk chocolate, grated

Sprinkle nuts over the bottom of a well-greased 20-cm/8-
inch square dish. Combine sugar, butter and water in a
deep bowl and microwave on full power for 5–6 minutes,
stirring every 2 minutes. Mix well, then immediately spread
over nuts. Sprinkle grated chocolate over hot toffee, cover
dish and stand for 5 minutes until chocolate has melted.
Carefully spread chocolate over the top. Chill until set,
then turn out and break into pieces.

Makes about 500 g/1 lb

Sugar caramel

full power
12 minutes

210 g/7 oz sugar
175 ml/6 fl oz water

Mix sugar and water together in a medium-sized bowl.
Microwave on full power for 2 minutes. Stir. Microwave for
a further 8 – 10 minutes, depending on how dark the
caramel is required. Do not allow caramel to become too
brown, as cooking continues for some time. Use as a base
for cream caramel, dipping fruit and nut friandise, as part
of a dessert, or for making spun sugar.

Makes about 300 ml/½ pint

Friandise

300 ml/½ pint sugar caramel (see opposite)
fruits such as tangerine segments, grapes, strawberries and cherries
a few dates
a selection of nuts

Remove pith from tangerine segments. Leave stems on grapes, strawberries and cherries. Wash and dry thoroughly.

Make caramel, removing from microwave when light golden in colour. Have two oiled forks ready and a well-oiled baking sheet. Dip fruit sections, one at a time, into caramel, remove and allow excess caramel to drip off. Place on baking sheet. Continue in this way until all the fruit has been used up. Should the caramel become too thick to work with, microwave for 1 minute on high. Continue as before. When caramelized fruits are hard, lift off baking sheet, trim off any excess caramel and serve in tiny paper cups.

Makes 50 friandises

Popcorn balls

high
5 minutes

3–3.5 litres/5½–6¼ pints popped popcorn
210 g/7 oz sugar
1 (142-g/5-oz) tablet raspberry jelly
250 ml/8 fl oz golden syrup

Place popcorn in a large bowl and set aside. Combine sugar and jelly cubes in a deep bowl. Add syrup and stir until ingredients are well mixed. Microwave on high until all the ingredients have dissolved and mixture boils, about 3½ – 4 minutes, stirring after every minute. Microwave for 1 minute more. Pour syrup over the popcorn and mix well. Wait until the mixture is cool enough to handle, then shape into balls with buttered hands. Do not press corn tightly together.

Makes about 12 balls

Nut and date balls

defrost
8 minutes

90 g/3 oz pecan nuts, chopped
75 g/2½ oz dates, coarsely chopped
125 g/4 oz crunchy peanut butter
3 tbsp icing sugar
1 tbsp lemon juice
½ teasp grated lemon rind
1 tbsp butter, at room temperature
½ teasp vanilla essence
pinch of ground cinnamon
280 g/9 oz dark chocolate or cooking chocolate
90 g/3 oz milk chocolate

Combine all ingredients except chocolate and mix well. Chill for 1 hour, then shape mixture into small balls and

Fruit and nut friandises

place on a baking sheet lined with greaseproof paper. Chill for 2 hours. Break chocolate into small pieces and place in a deep glass bowl. Microwave on defrost for 7–8 minutes, stirring after every minute. Let chocolate cool slightly, then dip balls one at a time. Return to baking sheet or to a wire rack to cool.

Makes about 30

Preserves

The microwave oven is ideal for making jams, chutneys, marmalades and preserves. Not only does your kitchen remain cool and steam-free but there are no messy saucepans to scour, and very little chance of burning utensils and fingers. The preserves themselves retain the bright, clear colours and rich flavours of the fruit. Even small quantities of jams and chutneys can be made without the ingredients scorching or sticking to the saucepan. Preparation is so quick you can make a batch of marmalade before breakfast! The greatest difference between jams made the traditional way and those made in the microwave is that the preserve will cook on its own, with only an occasional stir, and will not burn. As microwaves are particularly attracted to sugar molecules, there is the possibility of the preserve boiling over. With this in mind, choose very large or deep bowls. Remember the bowls become very hot, so always use oven gloves when handling them. For the best results when making preserves, use very fresh slightly under-ripe fruits. Those high in pectin, such as citrus fruits and apples. preserve well.

When preserving fruits

- Select good quality, barely ripe fruit. Soft or bruised fruit will result in an inferior product. Wash, wipe and peel the selected fruit according to the type.
- Wash jars well. Sterilize according to instructions below.
- Using a brush dipped in water, remove any sugar crystals which may have adhered to the sides of the bowl.
- To test whether jam or marmalade is ready:
  - Stand a sugar thermometer in the preserve but do not leave the thermometer in the microwave when it is switched on, unless it is specifically designed for microwave use. For a good set when making jam, the temperature should reach 105°C/221°F.
  - Spoon a little jam onto a saucer and when it is cool push the surface gently with your finger. If the jam wrinkles, it is set.
  - When you think the jam is ready, stir well with a wooden spoon. Lift a spoonful of jam out of the bowl, cool slightly then allow the jam to drop off the spoon. It should drop off in 'flakes'.
- Allow the jam to cool only slightly before pouring it into hot, sterile jars. Fill them right to the top and when the jam is cool, top up the jars once more and cover with brandy papers or waxed papers. To make brandy papers, cut circles of greaseproof or non-stick parchment the size of the top of the jars. Dip into brandy and place on cooled jam. To make waxed papers, dip the circles of paper into melted candle wax. Allow to set before placing on top of the jam.
- To prevent air bubbles from forming, do not allow the jam to cool for too long before pouring it into jars. If the jam is poured into jars whilst still too hot, the fruit may rise in the jars.

To sterilize jars for preserving

Pour a little water into the jars. Place no more than three jars in the microwave oven. Microwave on full power for up to 5 minutes, depending on the size of the jars and on the thickness of the glass. Pour out the water and stand the jars upside down to drain. Plastic lids, each containing a little water, may be sterilized in the microwave but do not sterilize metal lids this way.

Apricot jam

full power
35 minutes

1 kg/2 lb half-ripe apricots
1 kg/2 lb sugar
juice of 1 lemon

Wash the fruit well. Cut in half and remove stones. Combine the apricots and sugar in a large bowl. Allow to stand overnight. Add lemon juice and stir well. Cover with cling film and cut two slits in the film to prevent it from 'ballooning' during cooking. Microwave on full power for 10 minutes, stirring every 2 minutes. Uncover and microwave for 25 minutes, stirring every 5 minutes. The jam should now be at setting point. Remove from the microwave. Allow jam to cool for at least half an hour to prevent the fruit from rising in the jar when it has cooled. Pour the warm jam into warm, dry bottles. When cool, top up with a little more jam. Cover the top of the jam with a disc of brandy paper or waxed paper. Cover, label and store.

Fills 3 × 400-ml/14-fl oz bottles

Kumquat preserve

full power
44 minutes

750 g/1½ lb kumquats	400 g/13 oz sugar
750 ml/1¼ pints boiling water	175 ml/6 fl oz water
4 teasp bicarbonate of soda	2 tbsp lemon juice

Wash the kumquats and place in a large bowl. Pour the boiling water over fruit and add the bicarbonate of soda. Cover with cling film and make two slits in the film to prevent 'ballooning' during cooking. Microwave on full power for 5 minutes. Allow to cool. Drain off water and rinse well in cold water. Using a small, sharp, pointed knife, make incisions right through the sides of fruit. Place fruit once again in a large bowl, cover with boiling water, and cling film. Microwave on full power for 10 minutes. Allow to cool slightly, then squeeze out the pips.

Place sugar and water in a large bowl. Microwave, uncovered, on full power for 10 minutes, stirring every few minutes. Strain the syrup through a sieve lined with cotton wool. Return to bowl, then microwave for 3 – 4 minutes until syrup is boiling once more. Add kumquats and lemon juice. Microwave, uncovered, on full power for 15 minutes. The syrup should have thickened, and the fruit should be translucent. Pour into sterilized bottles. Cover loosely and allow to cool. Once cool, top up with syrup. Cover tightly, label and store.

Fills 2 × 400-ml/14-fl oz bottles

Passion fruit curd

full power
high
medium
7 minutes

125 g/4 oz butter
3 eggs
125 g/4 oz castor sugar
8 passion fruits
1 teasp grated lemon rind
juice from 3 lemons
1 teasp cornflour

Microwave butter on full power for 2 minutes. Meanwhile, beat together eggs and castor sugar until light and fluffy. Add the fruit pulp, lemon rind and most of the lemon juice. Mix remaining lemon juice and cornflour to a smooth paste and stir into egg mixture, along with the melted butter. Microwave, uncovered, on full power for 2 minutes. Stir well. Microwave on high for 2 minutes more, stirring at the end of each minute. Change setting to medium and microwave for 1 minute. Stir very well. The mixture should be thick enough to coat the back of a wooden spoon. Cool slightly. Pour into two medium-sized jars and top with brandy papers or waxed papers. Cover when cold. Label and store in the refrigerator.

Fills 2 × 400-ml/14-fl oz jars

Fig preserve served with streusel muffins (p. 126)

Fig preserve

full power
57 minutes

500 g/1 lb small green figs	*For the syrup*
1 litre/1¾ pints water	625 g/1¼ lb sugar
1 teasp slaked lime	750 ml/1¼ pints boiling water
750 ml/1¼ pints boiling water	2 teasp lemon juice

Wash the figs well and remove stems. Cut a small cross in the rounded end. Place figs in a bowl. Combine the water and slaked lime. Pour over figs and stand for 12 hours. Rinse figs very well, then stand in fresh cold water for about 15 minutes. Drain and add 750 ml/1¼ pints boiling water to figs. Cover with cling film and make two holes in the film to prevent 'ballooning' during cooking. Microwave on full power for 7 minutes. Drain well.

To make the syrup, combine sugar, water and lemon juice in a large bowl. Cover and microwave for 10 minutes, stirring twice during the cooking time. Add fruit to boiling syrup. Then microwave, uncovered, for 30 minutes, stirring from time to time during cooking. Drain the figs from the syrup. Pack into warm, dry bottles. Microwave the syrup, uncovered, for 10 minutes. Pour over figs, and cover loosely with lid. When cool, tighten lid and store.

Fills 2 × 400-ml/14-fl oz bottles

Bottled yellow peaches

full power
40 minutes

750 ml/1¼ pints water
310 g/10 oz sugar
1 small piece cinnamon stick
1 small piece lemon rind
1 kg/2 lb yellow cling peaches

Combine water and sugar in a large bowl. Microwave on full power for 10 minutes, then stir well to dissolve the sugar. Add cinnamon and lemon rind, and microwave for another 10 minutes. Peel the peaches, cut into halves or quarters and remove the stones. Add peaches to the syrup. Microwave for 8 – 10 minutes, stirring once or twice during cooking time. Remove cinnamon and lemon rind. Pack peaches into warm, dry, sterilized bottles. Microwave the syrup for a further 10 minutes. Fill jars with syrup, cover tightly and store.

Fills 2 × 750-ml/1¼-pint jars

Ginger marmalade

full power
40 minutes

3 oranges
1 litre/1¾ pints water
500 g/1 lb green apples
1.5 kg/3¼ lb sugar
1 piece fresh root ginger, grated
2 tbsp chopped preserved ginger
½ teasp ground ginger

Wash the oranges well. Squeeze the juice. Remove the membranes and pips, then mince or chop the peel finely. In a large bowl, combine orange juice, minced peel and water. Tie the membranes and pips in a piece of muslin and add to bowl. Cover bowl with cling film and make two slits in the film to prevent 'ballooning' during cooking. Microwave on full power for 20 minutes. Remove the muslin bag. Peel, core and dice apples finely. Add all the remaining ingredients to the bowl. Microwave, uncovered, on full power for 15 – 20 minutes, stirring every 5 minutes. Check for setting point, allowing extra time if necessary. Pour into warm, sterilized jars. Cover loosely. When cold, top up bottles and cover tightly. Label and store.

Fills 3 × 400-ml/14-fl oz bottles

Golden jelly marmalade

full power
1¾ hours

1 kg/2 lb oranges
2 lemons
2 litres/3½ pints water
1.25 kg/2½ lb sugar

Using a zester, remove the zest from the oranges and lemons or peel thinly and cut rind into fine shreds. Cover zest with boiling water, stand for 10 minutes, then drain. Peel the oranges and the lemons. Chop the pulp, place in a

Four fruit marmalade

large bowl and add 1 litre/1³/₄ pints water. Cover with cling film and cut two slits in the film to prevent 'ballooning' during cooking. Microwave on full power for 20 minutes. Strain pulp through a jelly cloth and reserve liquid. Meanwhile, cover the zest with 500 ml/17 fl oz water and microwave on full power for 10 minutes. Drain and add this liquid to the pulp. Return pulp to bowl, add 500 ml/17 fl oz water and re-cover. Microwave on full power for 15 minutes. Strain pulp again through jelly cloth. Reserve liquid and discard pulp.
Microwave, uncovered, for 50 – 55 minutes on full power, stirring every 5 minutes. Skim from time to time, if necessary. To prevent the marmalade from rising in the jar, allow to cool slightly before pouring into warm, sterilized jars. Cool completely, top up with a little more marmalade, then cover tightly. Label and store.

Fills approximately 3 × 400-ml/14-fl oz bottles

Four fruit marmalade

full power
55 minutes

2 oranges	900 ml/1¹/₂ pints boiling water
2 grapefruit	2 kg/4¹/₂ lb sugar
2 lemons	1 tbsp molasses or dark treacle
2 tangerines	4 tbsp whisky

Wash and dry fruit. Squeeze juice and set aside. Remove pips and pith, and tie in a piece of muslin. Slice peel according to taste – thin, medium or coarse. Place juice, sliced peel and muslin bag in a large mixing bowl. Add half the boiling water, stand for 1 hour, then add remaining boiling water. Cover with cling film and make two slits in the film to prevent 'ballooning' during cooking.

Microwave on full power for about 25 minutes (depending on the thickness of the peel). Uncover, remove muslin bag and stir in sugar and molasses. Microwave, uncovered, for 25 – 30 minutes until setting point is reached, stirring every 5 minutes. If any scum forms on top, scoop it off. Allow marmalade to cool. Stir in the whisky, then pour into sterilized bottles. Cover, label and store.

Fills 3 × 400-ml/14-fl oz bottles

Cherries in brandy

full power
7 minutes

500 g/1 lb cherries, stems removed
1 cinnamon stick
230 g/7¹/₂ oz sugar
120 ml/4 fl oz water
1 tbsp lemon juice
150 ml/¹/₄ pint brandy

Wash and dry cherries. Pack into a warm, sterilized glass jar together with a cinnamon stick. Combine sugar, water and lemon juice in a bowl. Microwave on full power for 3 minutes, stirring every minute during cooking time. Now microwave without stirring for 4 minutes. Allow to cool slightly, and add brandy. Pour over cherries, seal, label and store in a dark place. Keep for at least one month before using. Serve the cherries on top of ice-cream. The liquid can also be strained, and drunk as a liqueur.
   To make a cherry sauce, mix a little cornflour with the cold cherry liquid and microwave on full power for 1 – 2 minutes, stirring every 30 seconds. Add a few chopped cherries to the thickened sauce. Serve hot over ice-cream.

Fills 1 × 750-ml/1¹/₄-pint jar

Cherries preserved in brandy

Banana chutney

full power
20 minutes

10 ripe bananas, sliced
400 ml/14 fl oz white vinegar
75 g/2½ oz seedless raisins
1 onion, finely chopped
150 g/5 oz brown sugar
1 green pepper, seeded and chopped
½ teasp salt
½ teasp ground ginger
pinch of cayenne pepper
2 cloves garlic, crushed
2 teasp dry mustard

Combine all ingredients in a large bowl. Cover with cling film and cut two slits in the film to prevent 'ballooning' during cooking. Microwave on full power for 20 minutes. Stir twice during cooking time. Pour into clean, dry jars and cool before sealing. Store in a cool, dry place.

Fills approximately 2 × 400-ml/14-fl oz jars

Spicy cucumber pickle

This is excellent served with cheese, salads, or as a snack

full power
11 minutes

3 medium cucumbers
375 ml/13 fl oz water
200 ml/7 fl oz vinegar
1 tbsp salt
2 teasp peppercorns
2 bay leaves
2 cloves garlic, chopped

Wash the cucumbers. Using a fork, score the cucumbers down the length. Slice thickly. Combine the remaining ingredients in a large bowl. Cover and microwave on full power for 7 minutes. Add cucumber slices and microwave, covered, on full power for 4 minutes. Pour into a large bottle whilst still hot. Cool, cover and refrigerate. This pickle will keep in the refrigerator for some weeks.

Fills approximately 1 × 750-ml/1¼-pint bottle

Cucumber pickle

This pickle is delicious served sliced or chopped in salads, on sandwiches or with cheese

full power
16 minutes

2 very large cucumbers
2 tbsp salt
300 ml/½ pint white wine vinegar
1 teasp dill
1 teasp mustard seed
75 g/2½ oz sugar
1 large onion, sliced

Peel cucumbers. Slice thickly down length of cucumber and discard fleshy centre portion. Place cucumber strips in a flat, non-metallic basin and sprinkle with salt. Stand for 8 hours. Drain off liquid and pat dry with paper towel.

Place vinegar, dill, mustard seed and sugar in a large bowl. Cover with cling film and make two slits in the film to prevent 'ballooning' during cooking. Microwave on full power for 7 minutes. Divide cucumber strips into three batches. Microwave each batch, uncovered, for 3 minutes on full power. Add a little onion to each batch once it is cooked, then place cucumbers in a clean, dry jar. Cover with pickling liquid. Cover jar and refrigerate. Keep for a few days before using. This pickle lasts for up to 6 months.

Fills 1 × 750-ml/1¼-pint jar

Pickled onions

full power
10 minutes

1 kg/2 lb pickling onions
2 tbsp salt
300 ml/½ pint white vinegar
4 tbsp sugar
2 teasp mustard seed
2 teasp pickling spice
2–3 blades mace
2 red chillies

Carefully remove tops and roots from onions. Place in a large bowl and cover with boiling water. Stand for 30 seconds, drain and cover with cold water. Peel onions under cold water. Place onions in a bowl, layering them with salt. Stand overnight. Using a colander, rinse well.

Combine all remaining ingredients in a large bowl. Microwave on full power for 5 minutes. Add onions, then microwave again on full power for 5 minutes. Pack onions into clean, dry jars. Pour over the hot, strained vinegar. Cover loosely while still hot. Tighten lid when cool and stand for at least 3 weeks before serving. To make pickled onions with an extra bite, add 1 or 2 additional chillies to bottled onions.

Fills 3 × 400-ml/14-fl oz bottles

Mixed vegetable pickle

full power
8 minutes

Use a selection of the following vegetables:

½ small cauliflower	*For the pickling liquid*
1 small cucumber	300 ml/½ pint white vinegar
2–3 carrots	1 bay leaf
a few small onions	1 small piece fresh ginger
green beans	1 green chilli
courgettes	1 small piece of mace
salt	6 whole allspice

First prepare vegetables. Cut cauliflower into small florets. Slice unpeeled cucumber thickly and cut into quarters. Peel carrots, then slice thickly. Peel and quarter onions. Slice beans into short lengths. Cut the unpeeled courgettes thickly. Layer vegetables in a bowl with salt. Cover and stand overnight. Drain, then rinse well in a colander and allow to dry.

Combine all remaining ingredients in a large bowl. Cover

with cling film and make two slits in the film to prevent 'ballooning' during cooking. Microwave on full power for 4 minutes. Add vegetables, cover and microwave on full power for another 4 minutes. Using a slotted spoon, pack vegetables into clean, dry jars. Strain pickling liquid and cool. Cover vegetables with the liquid. Cover jars, label and store.

Fills about 2 × 400-ml/14-fl oz jars

Piccalilli

full power
21 minutes

1 cucumber
250 g/8 oz small onions, peeled
1 piece vegetable marrow, 10–15 cm/4–6 inches long, peeled
1 cauliflower
4 courgettes
125 g/4 oz green beans
4 teasp salt

For the sauce
600 ml/1 pint white wine vinegar
1 tbsp pickling spice
180 g/6 oz brown sugar
4 tbsp plain flour
2 teasp turmeric
2 teasp dry mustard
1½ teasp ground ginger

Cut the vegetables into small, even-sized pieces. Place in a bowl, sprinkle with salt and stand for 12 hours. Rinse and drain. To make the sauce, pour the vinegar into a large jug and add the pickling spice. Microwave on full power for 5 minutes. Strain. Meanwhile, combine all the remaining ingredients in a large bowl. Pour on the hot vinegar and stir well. Microwave on full power for 8 minutes, stirring every 2 minutes. Add vegetables. Microwave on full power for a further 8 minutes, stirring from time to time. Cool, pack into clean dry bottles, cover and store. This pickle may be eaten immediately.

Fills 4 × 400-ml/14-fl oz bottles

Chilli vinegar

full power
1½ minutes

60 g/2 oz fresh green or red chillies
1 litre/1¾ pints cider vinegar

Place chillies in a glass bowl and just cover with water. Microwave, covered, on full power for 1 – 1½ minutes. Drain and rinse in cold water. Place chillies in a sterilized bottle or jar and add vinegar. Seal and stand in a cool dark place for about 10 days before using.

Makes 1 litre/1¾ pints

Flavoured oils and vinegars

Lemon vinegar

medium
2 minutes

1 litre/1¾ pints red or white wine vinegar
1 long spiral lemon peel
3–4 sprigs fresh mint
2 cloves garlic, split

Place vinegar in a glass jug and microwave on medium for about 2 minutes, or until warm. Place the remaining ingredients in a jar or bottle and pour vinegar over. Seal and stand in a sunny place for several days before using. Use for fish or chicken, or in a dressing for fish salads.

Makes 1 litre/1¾ pints

VARIATION
Herb vinegar: Use 1 sprig rosemary, 2 sprigs fresh dill, 1 sprig thyme and 1 bay leaf instead of lemon peel, mint and garlic. Proceed as for Lemon vinegar.

Pickle vinegar

medium
4 minutes

2 litres/3½ pints white vinegar
40 g/1½ oz black mustard seed
1 tbsp fresh root ginger, peeled and chopped
2 teasp whole allspice
2 teasp cloves
1 tbsp black peppercorns
1½ teasp celery seeds
180 g/6 oz brown sugar
2 teasp grated horseradish
1 clove garlic, peeled
½ lemon, sliced

Place vinegar in a large casserole dish and microwave on medium for 4 – 4½ minutes, or until warm, but not boiling. Divide remaining ingredients evenly between two sterilized jars or bottles. Pour warm vinegar over, seal and place in a sunny spot for several days. After the sun has extracted oils from the spices, strain the vinegar and use for pickling fruits or vegetables.

Makes 2 litres/3½ pints

Spiced French vinegar

Combined with oil, this vinegar makes an exciting French dressing

high
4 minutes

1 litre/1¾ pints cider vinegar
75 g/2½ oz sugar
2 teasp whole cloves
1 teasp whole allspice
3 blades of mace
2 teasp celery seeds
2 teasp mustard seed
2 teasp whole black peppercorns
2 teasp turmeric
2 teasp sliced root ginger
1 clove garlic, peeled

Combine all ingredients, except garlic, in a large glass bowl. Microwave on high for 3 – 4 minutes, until the mixture is hot. Place mixture in a sterilized bottle or jar, add garlic and seal. Let stand in a cool place for 3 weeks before using.

Makes 1 litre/1¾ pints

Spiced oil

medium
1½ minutes

10 coriander seeds, lightly crushed
2 cloves garlic, cut in half
2 pieces cinnamon stick
5 whole allspice
5 whole cloves
1–2 hot chillies
1 small piece fresh root ginger
750 ml/1¼ pints oil

Place all ingredients, except oil, in a glass bowl and microwave on medium for 1 – 1½ minutes, stirring every 30 seconds. Place warm ingredients in a sterilized bottle or jar and add oil to almost fill. Seal and store in a cool place for about 10 days before using. Use oil to fry or marinate vegetables, or combine with vinegar for salad dressings.

Makes 750 ml/1¼ pints

VARIATIONS
Double olive oil: Place 8 whole olives with their liquid in a glass jug and microwave on medium for 1 – 1½ minutes. Drain and place in a sterilized bottle and add olive oil to almost fill. Proceed as for Spiced oil.

Garlic oil: Place 15 – 20 unpeeled cloves garlic in a glass jug and just cover with water. Microwave on medium for 3 minutes to soften. Drain and thread garlic on a strong cord. Place garlic in a sterilized bottle, securing cord at the top and add oil to almost fill. Proceed as for Spiced oil.

Conversion tables

Metrication is part of our daily lives. Once you are accustomed to this simple way of measuring, cooking becomes easier and definitely more accurate. Remember, accuracy means success.

Small measurements:

METRIC	APPROXIMATE IMPERIAL
1 ml	1/4 teasp
2 ml	1/2 teasp
5 ml	1 teasp
15 ml	1 tbsp
45 ml	3 tbsp
75 ml	5 tbsp

Mass:
This is an approximate conversion. 500 g is slightly heavier than 1 lb.

METRIC	APPROXIMATE IMPERIAL
30 g	1 oz
60 g	2 oz
100 g	3 1/2 oz
125 g	4 oz
250 g	8 oz
500 g	1 lb

Volumes:

METRIC	APPROXIMATE IMPERIAL
60 ml	1/4 cup
80 ml	1/3 cup
120 ml	4 fl oz (1/2 cup)
175 ml	6 fl oz (3/4 cup)
250 ml	8 fl oz (1 cup)
500 ml	17 fl oz (2 cups)
600 ml	1 pint
1.2 litres	2 pints

Approximate mass in grams per 250 ml:

INGREDIENTS	MASS
Butter or margarine	250 g/8 oz
Cheese, grated	125 g/4 oz
Cocoa powder	125 g/4 oz
Coconut, desiccated	90 g/3 oz
Cornflour	140 g/4 1/2 oz
Dried fruit: raisins, etc	180 g/6 oz
Flour: bread or cake flour	125 g/4 oz
self-raising flour	125 g/4 oz
wholemeal flour	125 g/4 oz
Nuts, chopped	150 g/5 oz
whole	125 g/4 oz
Oats, uncooked	90 g/3 oz
Rice, uncooked	210 g/7 oz
Sugar: granulated	250 g/8 oz
castor sugar	250 g/8 oz
icing sugar	140 g/4 1/2 oz

Menu planning

Once you have learned to cook simple foods in the microwave oven, you will want to use it to combine foods to cook a complete meal. Different foods cook in different ways and require different cooking times, so careful planning is needed to prepare foods in sequence.

As with any meal, microwave menus should be balanced for nutrition, colour, flavour, texture and appetite appeal. Plan meals so that not all the foods will need last-minute cooking or heating and take advantage of standing time and holding time to present foods at their best. Last-minute preparation should be reserved for foods that heat and cool quickly.

Starters can be prepared early in the day and refrigerated if necessary, and then reheated if they are to be served hot. Bread rolls should be warmed for a few seconds in the microwave just before serving.

Meats and main dishes usually require not only the longest cooking time of any part of the meal, but also the longest standing time, and other parts of the meal can be microwaved while the roast, chicken or casserole is standing. Cooking in advance foods that can easily be reheated simplifies the meal preparation and may improve the flavour of such foods as casseroles.

Vegetables and other foods that retain heat well can be cooked before those that require very short cooking, or ones that do not retain heat for a long period. For example, while the main dish is standing before serving, potatoes can be microwaved. They hold heat well so they can stand, wrapped in aluminium foil, while quick-cooking vegetables such as peas are microwaved.

Desserts can be made ahead of time and refrigerated until needed. Baked apples, crumbles and desserts to be served hot can be prepared in advance and microwaved while the main course is being eaten.

Planning tips

- Allow plenty of time to plan your first microwave meals. Try to serve at least one cold course or one dish that can be made ahead, leaving the microwave oven free for the main course and last-minute cooking.
- Soups, sauces, gravies and some vegetables can be cooked in advance, placed in serving dishes and microwaved to reheat when required.
- Fish, seafood, egg and cheese dishes cook very quickly, but do not retain heat well. It is difficult to reheat these dishes without overcooking, so they should be microwaved just before serving.
- It makes sense to cook foods that do not microwave well in a conventional oven, leaving the microwave oven free for other courses.
- Plan the menu so that while one course is being eaten, the next can be cooking or heating.
- Use aluminium foil to wrap cooked items, such as baked potatoes or chicken, to help retain heat. If large amounts of food need to be kept warm, use a warming oven or hot tray.
- Rice and pasta reheat quickly and well in the microwave oven, but they require the same cooking time as when boiled on the cooker top. Cook those items conventionally, leaving the microwave free for other foods.
- Microwave as many foods as possible in the serving dish. This helps to retain heat during standing or holding time, and cuts down on the washing up.
- Any single serving placed on a plate can be reheated quickly for a latecomer with no change in texture or flavour.

Use the following sample menus as a guide to planning microwave meals.

Breakfast

Creamy yoghurt* served with fresh fruit
Farmer's breakfast*
Coffee, filter or instant*
Hot fresh toast and warm croissants
Four fruit marmalade*

- Make yoghurt the day before required.
- 20 minutes before serving, make the Farmer's breakfast.
- Place the Farmer's breakfast, toast and croissants in the microwave on low to keep warm whilst eating the first course.
- Whilst eating breakfast, keep filter coffee warm in the microwave, or boil water for instant coffee.

*Recipes included in this book.

147

Light lunch –
ideal when not much time is available

Chef's spinach salad*
Brown bread rolls
Ice-cream with
Hot fruit salad*

- Make the Chef's spinach salad in advance, either early in the day, or cook the leeks and chicken the day before.
- Combine all ingredients for the Hot fruit salad in advance, and 30 minutes before serving lunch, cook it in the microwave.
- 1 to 2 minutes before serving lunch, warm the brown bread rolls.
- Keep the Hot fruit salad warm in the microwave whilst eating the Chef's salad.

Summer lunch –
an interesting lunch and quick to serve, as everything is prepared in advance

Cream of carrot soup*
Club chicken casserole*
Fruity slaw* or Seasonal salad*
Chocolate mousse*
Coffee*

- Make Cream of carrot soup the day before required and serve chilled or piping hot – to reheat, microwave for 8 to 10 minutes after heating the Club chicken casserole, as covered casseroles retain heat for a long time.
- Make the Club chicken casserole the day before and 25 minutes before serving microwave, covered, on medium for 15 minutes. Keep warm in the microwave whilst eating soup.
- Make the Fruity slaw the day before, cover and refrigerate.
- Vegetables for the Seasonal salad may also be blanched in advance; merely combine a short while before serving.
- Make the Chocolate mousse the day before.
- Keep freshly filtered coffee warm in the microwave whilst eating the main course, or boil water for instant coffee.

Informal dinner

Caesar salad*
Pepper steak flambé*
Potatoes Lyonnaise*
Stuffed courgettes*
Carrots Vichy*
Caramel ice-cream*
Irish coffee*
Nut clusters*

- Make the Caesar salad 2 to 3 hours in advance and chill.
- Cook the Pepper steak flambé 12 to 15 minutes before serving.
- Microwave the Potatoes Lyonnaise 1¼ hours before serving.

- Prepare the Stuffed courgettes 2 to 3 hours in advance, and microwave with the Carrots Vichy 30 minutes before serving. Cover and keep warm.
- Make the Caramel ice-cream the day before.
- Microwave the South African coffee for 1 minute after dinner.
- Make the Nut clusters in advance.

Celebration dinner

Potted shrimp*
Glazed stuffed roast pork*
Roast potatoes
Green beans almondine*
Garlic mushrooms*
Pears Alicia*
Quick cappuccino*
Rum truffles*

- Make the Potted shrimp the day before.
- Microwave the prepared Glazed stuffed roast pork 1¼ hours before serving. Cover and keep warm.
- Cook the Green beans almondine 12 to 15 minutes before serving.
- Microwave the Garlic mushrooms for 8 minutes whilst eating the first course.
- Prepare the Pears Alicia the day before.
- Make the Rum truffles in advance.
- Microwave the Irish coffee for 1 minute after dinner

*Recipes included in this book.

Convenience foods

Using convenience foods is a quick way to serve snacks or meals, and they take only minutes to prepare in the microwave oven. The following chart gives a guide for defrosting, heating or cooking many frozen and canned foods. There are also instructions for baking cake and pudding mixes in the microwave, as well as packet or canned soups. More and more convenience or instant foods are finding their way onto supermarket shelves and into freezers, and they cannot all be included here. Recipes making use of many convenience foods are found throughout this book, but the hints that follow will help you convert most instant foods to quick and tasty meals.

When microwaving convenience foods

- Be sure foods are really heated through before serving. Steam or bubbling around the edges may not mean the food is completely heated. When the food is hot enough, the centre of the bottom of the dish will be warm to the touch.
- Most foods are covered when heating or reheating. Cover starters cooked with a sauce or main dishes with greaseproof paper or cling film. Be sure to slash the cling film. Sandwiches that are defrosted, then warmed, can be covered with paper towel or a napkin. Soups may be covered with greaseproof paper to prevent
- spattering. thawing or warming as they may become soggy.
- Remove casseroles, 'frozen dinners' or baked foods from foil trays before microwaving. Place those foods in a casserole dish or on a plate.
- Some foods, such as sausage rolls or double crust pastries, can be defrosted in the microwave, but give much better results if heated in a conventional oven.

Mixes

Hot sponge pudding mix

1 (191-g/6½-oz) packet

Follow packet instructions for mixing then microwave on full power for 5 minutes. Let stand 5 minutes. Serve warm.

Cooked pudding mixes

1 (99 g/3½ oz) packet

Use 600 ml/1 pint milk and follow packet instructions for mixing. Place in a deep bowl and microwave for 2–2½ minutes, beating well every 45 seconds.

Cake mixes
Mix as directed on the packet, using 2 eggs. Grease a deep microwave ring pan and sprinkle with digestive biscuit crumbs if desired. Pour batter into prepared pan and place on an inverted saucer in the microwave oven. Microwave on defrost for 6 minutes. Rotate the pan a quarter turn and microwave on full power for 5–6 minutes or until surface is almost dry, rotating dish a quarter turn every 3 minutes. Alternatively, microwave on full power for 4 minutes, rotate dish a quarter turn and microwave for

3–5 minutes or until surface is almost dry. When cooking is complete, stand the pan on a heatproof surface for 10 minutes, then turn cake out onto a wire rack to cool.

Cupcakes

Spoon prepared cake mix batter into paper cases in a microwave muffin pan or custard cups. Fill cases a third to half full. Arrange in a circle in the oven and microwave as follows:

Number	Time	Power
2	1 minute	full power
4	1¼ -1½ minutes	full power
6	2½ -3 minutes	full power

Soups

Packet Soups

Reconstitute according to packet instructions, reducing the liquid by about a fifth. For example, instead of 750 ml/1¼ pints water use 600 ml/1 pint.

vegetable, microwave on full power for 6 – 7 minutes, stirring several times.
- For soups with liquid and solids, such as beef vegetable, microwave on high for 10 – 12 minutes, stirring occasionally.

Canned Soups

Add liquid according to directions and place soup in a deep bowl.
- For soups with water added, microwave on full power for 5 – 6 minutes.
- For soups with milk added, microwave on high for 8 – 10 minutes, stirring occasionally.

For extra flavour add a generous splash of sherry or white wine to vegetable soups, or brandy to meat soups. For a rich, creamy soup, stir in 4–6 tbsp single cream or soured cream just before serving. For soups such as tomato or mushroom, add grated cheese after heating.

MICROWAVE CHART FOR CONVENIENCE FOODS

	QUANTITY	PREPARATION	DEFROST TIME	COOKING TIME	POWER LEVEL	METHOD
CANNED FOODS						
Soup	425 g/15 oz	Place in bowl, add liquid as directed	–	5-6 minutes	full	Cover, stir frequently
Pasta in sauce	447 g/15¾ oz	Place in dish	–	3-4 minutes	full	Cover, stir at least once
Baked beans	447 g/15¾ oz	Place in dish	–	3-4 minutes	full	Cover, stir at least once
Peas or other small vegetables	227 g/8 oz	Place in dish	–	2-3 minutes	full	Cover, stir gently once
Asparagus spears or other large vegetables	340 g/12 oz	Place in dish	–	4-5 minutes	full	Cover, stir once
Meat in sauce	418 g/14¾ oz	Place in dish	–	5-6 minutes	full	Cover, stir once
Sauces or gravy	376 g/13¼ oz	Place in bowl	–	3-4 minutes	full	Cover, stir occasionally
Custard or pudding	approx 400 g/13 oz	Place in bowl	–	3-4 minutes	full	Cover, stir once
Fruits, such as fruit cocktail or sliced peaches	411 g/14½ oz	Place in bowl	–	4-5 minutes	full	Cover, stir once
FROZEN FOODS						
Individual meat pies	3	Remove foil	1½-2 minutes	3-3½ minutes	full	Place on paper towel, carefully turn over halfway through heating
Sausage rolls or pastry snacks	6-8	Place on paper towel	2 minutes, stand 3 minutes	2-3 minutes	full	Pastry may become soggy so defrost in microwave and heat conventionally for best results
Quiche	20-23 cm/8-9 inches	Remove from foil, place on plate	5 minutes, stand 5 minutes	6-8 minutes	full	Cover with greaseproof paper
Pizza	approx 230 g/7½ oz	Place on paper plate or towel	–	4-5 minutes	full	Cover with greaseproof paper to prevent spattering
Meat casserole	approx 500 g/1 lb	Remove from foil, place in dish	4 minutes, stand 3 minutes, defrost 3 minutes more	10-12 minutes	full	Cover with greaseproof paper, stir if possible
'Boil in bag' fish	approx 198 g/7 oz	Slit top of bag, place in bowl	–	6 minutes	full	Shake contents of bag before serving

For frozen baked goods, see chart page 118
For frozen vegetables, see page 95

Index

150